Hugo Grotius, the Portuguese and Free Trade in the East Indies

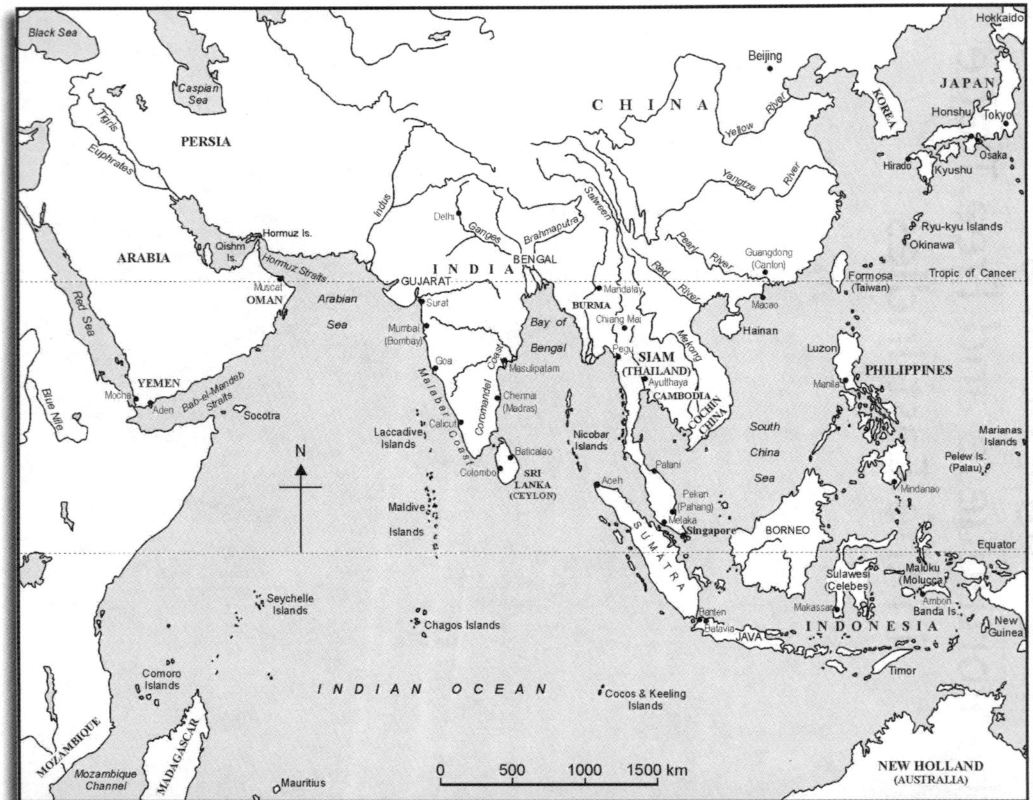

Illus. 1 Map of Asia featuring modern settlements and historic trading emporia of the 16th and 17th centuries.

Hugo Grotius, the Portuguese and Free Trade in the East Indies

Peter Borschberg

NUS PRESS
SINGAPORE

Published by:

NUS Press
National University of Singapore
AS3-01-02, 3 Arts Link
Singapore 117569

Fax: (65) 6774-0652
E-mail: nusbooks@nus.edu.sg
Website: http://www.nus.edu.sg/nuspress

ISBN 978-9971-69-467-8 (Paper)

National Library Board, Singapore Cataloguing-in-Publication Data
A catalogue record for the book is available from the National Library, Singapore

Cover Image: Hand-coloured depiction of a Dutch ship with four inserts depicting views of the trading cities (clockwise, top left) of Antwerp, Amsterdam, Middelburg and Enkhuisen. Taken from the first edition of Jan Huyghen van Linschoten's *Itinerario*, 1596. The Hague, Koninklijke Bibliotheek, 1702 B 4.

Printed Insert: Portrait of Hugo Grotius, c. 1614–5, at the height of his political career in the Dutch Republic. The Hague, Rijksbureau voor Kunsthistorische Dokumentatie.

Back Cover: Portrait of Hugo Grotius around 1613. Replica by Jan van Ravensteijn based on the original in the Collection Rothschild in Paris. Leiden University Library, Icones 66.

Typeset by: International Typesetters Pte Ltd
Printed by: Vetak Services

Contents

List of Illustrations

towels are distributed and displayed in [illegible] quite [illegible] caught a comic response

36 Letter of [illegible] signed 15 October 1613 212
The [illegible] the [illegible] of
[illegible] English and [illegible] East India Company

37 Dutch reply of 29 April 1615, presented at the Anglo-Dutch 222
[illegible] conferences in The Hague in 1615. The document
[illegible]

List of Abbreviations

AJSS — Asian Journal of Social Science

BHR — Bibliothèque d'Humanisme et Renaissance

BKI — Bijdragen van het Koninklijk Instituut voor Land-, Taal-, en Volkenkunde

BMH — Bijdragen en Mededelingen van het Historisch Genootschap

BV — Isaac Commelin, *Begin ende Voortgang Vande Vereenigde Neerlandsche Geoctroyeerde Oost-Indische Compagnie*, 4 vols. (Amsterdam: no publisher, 1646).

BW — *Briefwisseling van Hugo Grotius*, ed. P.C. Molhuysen *et al.* (The Hague: Martinus Nijhoff and Instituut voor Nederlandse Geschiedenis, 1928–2001).

CC — G.N. Clark and W.J.M. van Eysinga, "The Colonial Conferences between England and the Netherlands in 1613 and 1615", part I, *Bibliotheca Visseriana* 15 (1940): 1–270.

CE — G.N. Clark and W.J.M. van Eysinga, "The Colonial Conferences between England and the Netherlands", part II, *Bibliotheca Visseriana* 17 (1951): 1–155.

CIPC — Hugo Grotius, *De Iure Praedae Commentarius. Commentary on the Law of Prize and Booty. A Translation of the Original Manuscript of 1604*, tr. Gwladys L. Williams and Walter H. Zeydel, the Classics of International Law, ed. James Brown Scott (Oxford: Clarendon Press, 1950).

CiT	Hugo Grotius, *Commentarius in Theses XI: An Early Treatise on Sovereignty, the Just War and the Legitimacy of the Dutch Revolt*, ed. and intr. P. Borschberg, tr. Philip Burton (Bern: Lang, 1994).
CML	*Mare Liberum, The Freedom of the Seas, or, The Right which Belongs to the Dutch to Take Part in the East Indian Trade*, tr. Ralph van Deman Magoffin, ed. and intr. J.B. Scott (New York: Oxford University Press, 1916).
CUP	Cambridge University Press
Dig.	Digest of Justinian. The Latin text edition used forms part of the *Corpus Juris Civilis,* 3 vols., ed. Theodor Mommsen and Paul Krüger (Berlin: Apud Weidmannos, 1928–9).
EIC	The (English) East India Company
GA	Germanistische Abteilung
GNS	Grotiana, New Series
HML	*The Free Sea*, ed. and intr. David Armitage, tr. Richard Hakluyt (Indianapolis: Liberty Fund, 2004).
IBP	Hugo Grotius, *De Iure Belli ac Pacis Libri Tres* (*Three Books on the Law of War and Peace*). The different editions of this work, including translations from the original Latin text, are specified by placing the year of publication after the abbreviation, for example, IBP (2005). The Latin text used is the edition prepared by B.J.A. de Kanter-van Hettinga Tromp with notes by R. Feenstra and C.E. Persenaire (Aalen: Scientia Verlag, 1993).
Inst.	Institutes or Enactments of Justinian. The Latin text edition used forms part of the *Corpus Juris Civilis,* 3 vols., ed. Theodor Mommsen and Paul Krüger (Berlin: Apud Weidmannos, 1928–9).
IPC	Hugo Grotius, *Commentary on the Law of Prize and Booty,* edited and introduced by Martine J. van Ittersum, Natural Law and Enlightenment Classics, ed. gen. Knud Haakonssen (Indianapolis: Liberty Fund, 2006).

JMBRAS	Journal of the Malaysian Branch of the Royal Asiatic Society
JSBRAS	Journal of the Straits Branch of the Royal Asiatic Society
JSEAH	Journal of Southeast Asian History
JSEAS	Journal of Southeast Asian Studies
JSS	Journal of the Siam Society
KA	Kanonistische Abteilung
LML	Hugo Grotius, *Mare Liberum, sive de iure quod Batavis competit in rebus Indicanis* (Leiden: L. Elsevier, 1609).
MKNAW	Mededelingen van de Koninklijke Nederlandse Akademie van Wetenschappen
NR	Nieuwe Reeks
OUP	Oxford University Press
RA	Romanistische Abteilung
RC	Revista de Cultura
RH	J.G. Frederiks, "Cornelis Cornelisz Matelieff de Jonge en zijn geslagt", *Rotterdamsche Historiebladen,* J.H. Scheffer and Fr. D.O. Obreen, ed., 3 afd., 1.1 (1871): 204–357.
TGS	Transactions of the Grotius Society
TMD	Jacob ter Meulen and P. J.J. Diedermanse, *Bibliographie des écrits imprimés de Hugo Grotius* (The Hague: Martinus Nijhoff, 1950).
VOC	Vereenigde Oost-Indische Compagnie, United East India Company; commonly known as the Dutch East India Company
WHGU	Werken Uitgegeven door het Historisch Genootschap te Utrecht
ZRG	Zeitschrift der Savigny-Stiftung für Rechtsgeschichte

Preface

This is a study in the history of ideas in context. It focuses on a 17th-century thinker — Hugo Grotius — who is widely acknowledged as a key figure in the history of political and legal thought in the West. I am concerned to show how the Southeast Asian political, diplomatic and commercial context framed his visions of law and international relations and how his ideas and theories, in turn, came to impact Southeast Asia. This shall be done by focusing on the interaction of historical context and agency. Particular attention will be paid to identifying the written sources that Grotius worked with, reconstructing how he worked with them and showing how his thinking crystallised in the context of developments within the Dutch East India Company (VOC) on the ground in Southeast Asia c.1602–20. Although the impact of his ideas is often discussed in general terms with reference to the Western historical and geographic theatre, this study seeks to demonstrate the relationship between Grotius and the emergence of a new international order and maritime trading regime in Southeast Asia.

Preface

Acknowledgements

The revised and updated studies contained in the present volume have been prepared over a course of two decades. I am especially thankful to my former colleagues at the History Department of the National University of Singapore (NUS), Paul H. Kratoska and Ng Chin Keong, without whom I would have probably never ventured into the Southeast Asian colonial history and specifically early modern Johor. Their unwavering enthusiasm, encouragement and steady guidance over the years changed the course of my academic research and, indeed, my career.

Earlier versions of the chapters in this book have been published in leading journals and as chapters in books. I am especially grateful to the *Journal of Southeast Asian Studies*, *Itinerario*, the Institute for International Law and Justice at New York University (NYU) and Brill Academic Publishers for kindly consenting to the publication of substantially revised and enhanced versions of these earlier articles.

Over the past one decade, a number of specialists across a range of disciplines have commented on various versions and drafts at different stages of their composition. I think here especially of David Armitage (Harvard); Andreas Aure (Humboldt-Universität Berlin); Hans Blom (Erasmus University, Rotterdam, EUR); Robert Batchelor (Georgia Southern University); Leonard Blussé (Leiden); Cheah Boon Kheng (Universiti Sains Malaysia and NUS); Alexander Drost (Greifswald); Jurrien van Goor (Utrecht); Martine van Ittersum (Dundee); Benedict Kingsbury (New York University, NYU); Kwa Chong Guan (Rajaratnam School of International Studies [RSIS] and NUS); Bruce Lockhart (NUS); Anthony Milner (ANU and Melbourne); Terry Nardin (NUS); Henk Nellen (Constantijn Huygens Instituut, the Hague); Roderich Ptak (Ludwig-Maximilians-Universität, München); Merle Ricklefs (NUS);

Roopanjali Roy (Lisbon and New Delhi); Sebastian Song (National Library of Singapore); Benjamin Straumann (NYU); M. Sornarajah (NUS); Syed Ad'ha Aljunied (RSIS); Richard Tuck (Cambridge and Harvard); Corinna Vermeulen (Leiden); Jan Waszink (Utrecht); and Laurens Winkel (EUR).

My research could have never been completed without the excellent facilities and library holdings in key institutions in Europe, North America, Asia and Australia. I would like to specially thank the curators of the Special Collections Department at Leiden University, André Bouwman and Anton van der Lem, for granting access to their rare prints and Grotius manuscripts, particularly the original manuscript of *De Iure Praedae* and the bundle B.P.L. 922 which I consulted extensively between 1988 and 2007. Leiden University Library has been and remains, my favourite library and an intellectual home for the past 23 years. Tim Yap Fuan and all the staff at the Rare Prints and Singapore-Malaysia Collection (SMC) of NUS Central Library deserve a special note of appreciation. Thanks must also be extended to the staff and curators in the special collections departments of the Koninklijke Bibliotheek in the Hague, the Nationaal Archief van Nederland in the Hague and the Bibliotheca Thysiana in Leiden.

I gratefully acknowledge the access and assistance I have received from many libraries and archives over the past two decades, especially Amsterdam University Library, the Archivo Nacional / Torre do Tombo in Lisbon, the Bayerische Staatsbibliothek in München, the Biblioteca Apostolica Vaticana (Vatican Library), the Biblioteca Nacional de Portugal in Lisbon, the Biblioteca Nacional de España in Madrid, the British Library in London, Cambridge University Library, the Filmoteca Ultramarina Portuguesa in Lisbon, the Folger Library in Washington D.C., the Gemeentearchief Rotterdam, Gemeentebibliothek Rotterdam, the Instituut Kern in Leiden, the Institut für Europäische Geschichte in Mainz, Leiden University Law Library, Lund University Library, the National Library of Australia in Canberra, the Netherlands Institute for Advanced Studies in Wassenaar, the Library of the Peace Palace in the Hague, the Public Record Office (PRO) in London, the library of the monastery San Esteban in Salamanca, the Sächsische Landesbibliothek in Dresden, the Staatsbibliothek-Preussischer Kulturbesitz in Berlin, Stanford University Library, the Stadtbibliothek Mainz, the Universitätsbibliothek Greifswald and last but certainly not least the NUS Central and Law Libraries.

Institutional support has been most forthcoming over the past two decades. I would like to extend my sincere gratitude to the History Department and the Faculty of Arts and Social Sciences at NUS for generously funding my research activities over many years; for a three-month research leave in 2001 at the Department of Asian Studies (Sinological Section) of the Ludwig-Maximilians-Universität München; a sabbatical spent in 2005 as a member of the Grotius Research Group and a fellowship-in-residence at the Netherlands Institute for Advanced Studies (NIAS) of the Royal Netherlands Academy of Arts and Social Sciences (KNAW) in Wassenaar, the Institut für Europäische Geschichte in Mainz, and the Folger Library in Washington, D.C.

Singapore, 10 November 2010

General Introduction

Four hundred years ago, in the spring of 1609, an anonymous booklet titled *Mare Liberum* (The Free Sea) was released for sale in the Dutch city of Leiden.[1] This booklet, which was originally published in Latin, staked out arguments asserting the right of the Dutch to sail to the East Indies, and participate in the lucrative trade with this region against concerted efforts by Portugal and Spain to shut out all European competitors. The timing of its release was most certainly no coincidence. *Mare Liberum* had been hastily sent through the press before the signing of a landmark treaty between representatives of the United Provinces (that is, the Dutch Republic) and the Spanish Empire on 10 April 1609. This established the beginning of what is known as the Twelve Years Truce and marked the outcome of protracted negotiations that endorsed a truce in Europe and also granted Dutch traders free access to ports and emporia where the Iberian powers, Spain and Portugal, had no settlements or colonies proper. If the Dutch Republic had brought its struggle against the expansive empires of Spain and Portugal to the far corners of the world, the Twelve Years Truce became one of the first — if not *the* first — European treaty proper to globally impact diplomacy, alliance-making and trade.

Though controversial already in its day, *Mare Liberum* has come to be regarded as something of a visionary treatise acknowledging the need for a global trading regime with the free exchange of goods and persons both in times of war and especially also in peace. It does so by upholding the right of free trade as something so basic, so fundamental to humankind, that it cannot be rightfully denied, curtailed or impeded. *Mare Liberum* treats the high seas as vast pelagic spaces that remain in their natural state and cannot be appropriated by a sovereign, let alone by an individual.

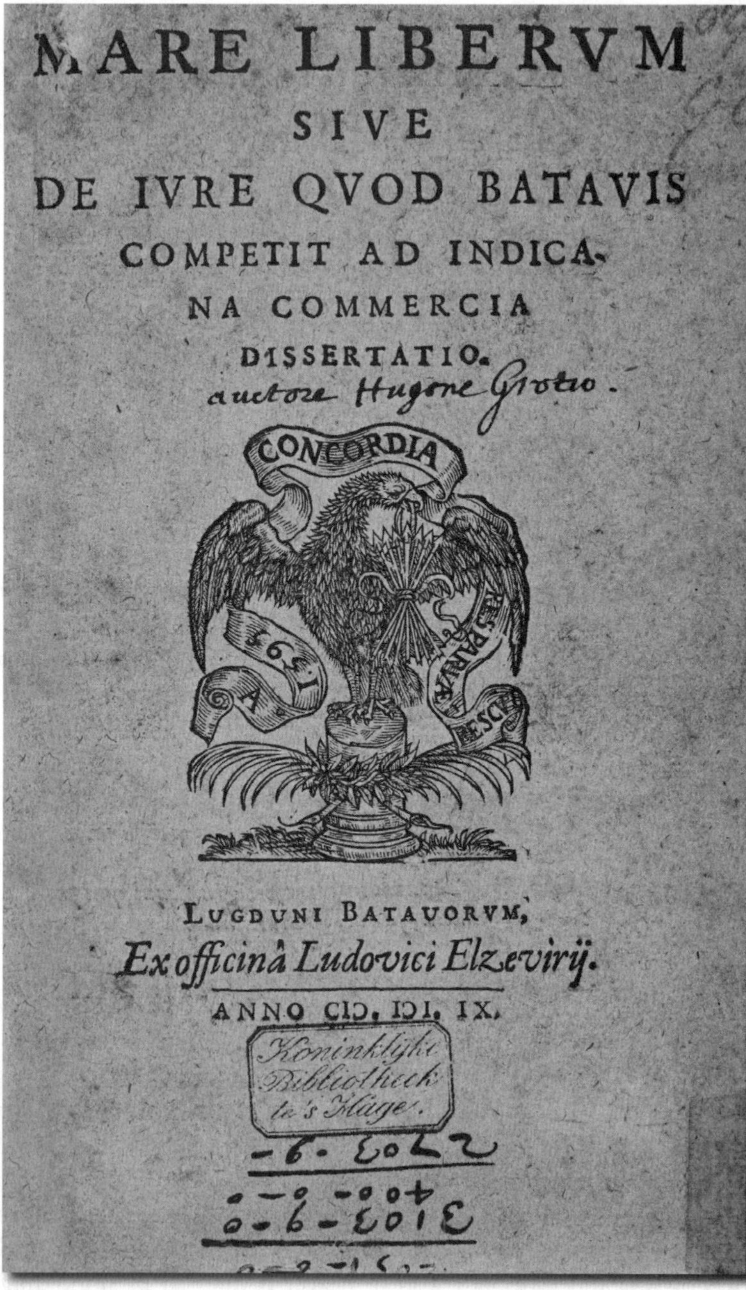

MARE LIBERVM
SIVE
DE IVRE QVOD BATAVIS
COMPETIT AD INDICA-
NA COMMERCIA
DISSERTATIO.
auctore Hugone Grotio.

LVGDVNI BATAVORVM,
Ex officinâ Ludovici Elzevirij.
ANNO CIↃ. IↃI. IX.

Illus. 2 Title page of the first edition of *Mare Liberum,* bearing the imprint of Ludovicus Elsevier of Leiden, 1609. It was published anonymously, and Grotius' name as author was added in this copy by hand. (The Hague, Koninklijke Bibliotheek, 893 G 6)

The vast seas and their maritime highways, thus, do not always separate or divide, but serve as a maritime highway to facilitate interaction between peoples from around the globe as nature and the Creator had foreseen. The key word here is "access", which in the context of *Mare Liberum* has two fundamental meanings: access to the seas and access across the unappropriated seas to marketplaces in the far corners of the world.

After its first publication in 1609, but especially following the retrieval of the autograph manuscript around the middle of the 19th century, the scholarly community has learnt much about the authorship, genesis, context and underlying purpose of this work. Since the 1614 Dutch translation prepared by the Leiden academic Pieter Bertius and printed by Jan Huybertsz of Leiden, *Mare Liberum* bears the name of its author, namely, Huig de Groot (1583–1645), who is better known in contemporary academic circles by his Latinised name, Hugo Grotius.[2] Already during his lifetime, this polymath and native of Delft was widely celebrated as a great and innovative thinker. He remains a widely respected authority in the fields of law, political science and international relations. Students and researchers today best remember Grotius for his classic work on the law of nations *De Iure Belli ac Pacis Libri Tres* (Three Books on the Law of War and Peace), which was first published in Paris in 1625. Over approximately two decades, subsequent editions featured an enhanced text and a critical footnote apparatus.[3]

In 1864 a chest of manuscripts was found among the belongings of Hugo de Groot, a direct blood descendant of the 17th-century luminary. This chest contained a series of documents pertaining to the history of the family, but importantly, it also contained a series of then still unknown manuscripts that traced their authorship to Grotius. These came into the possession of the late Hugo's Rotterdam-based tobacconist, Chris Snelleman, and were sold in November that year at a public auction organised by Martinus Nijhoff in the Hague.[4] The excitement generated by the sale of the celebrated lawyer's manuscripts and working papers can be well imagined. Among the successful bidders at the sale were members of the Netherlands' commercial and political élite, the diplomatic community, as well as representatives from public institutions, archives and libraries. In preparing the papers for sale, the auctioneers at Martinus Nijhoff and academic advisors — among them Pieter Anton Tiele of Leiden University — discovered an expansive autograph manuscript that was initially thought to represent an early draft of *De Iure Belli ac Pacis* but was subsequently recognised as a separate work in its own right.

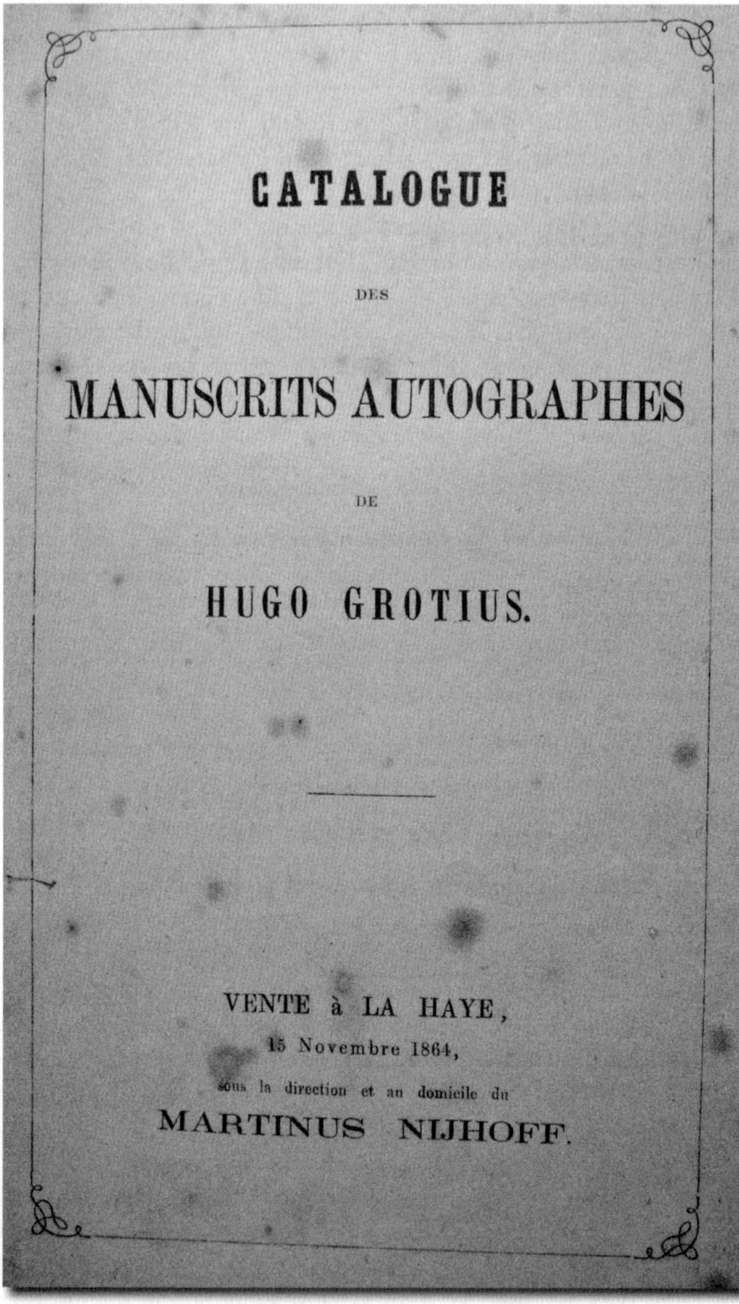

Illus. 3 Cover of the auction catalogue of Grotius' papers held in The Hague in 1864. (The Hague, Nationaal Archief, *Collectie Hugo de Groot, Supplement I* [1.10.35.02, no. 40])

The manuscript, which was sold in two separate lots, was acquired by Grotius' *alma mater*, Leiden University, and today is generally known as *De Iure Praedae Commentarius* (Commentary on the Law of Prize and Booty).[5] In evaluating the manuscripts for sale, the auctioneers and their academic advisors made an unexpected discovery: the treatise *Mare Liberum* had not been written as a self-standing treatise, but originally formed a single chapter in a more expansive manuscript written in Latin. It features substantially as chapter 12 of *De Iure Praedae*, which Grotius began to draft around October 1604, and some years later reworked for publication. As has been argued by the Dundee historian Martine van Ittersum, Grotius hastily revised chapter 12 of *De Iure Praedae* between the closing months of 1608 and the beginning of 1609 and published it as *Mare Liberum*.[6] Van Ittersum's scholarly inquiries supplement an older but still authoritative contribution on the genesis and contextual background of *De Iure Praedae* prepared by the Leiden historian Robert Fruin, which the latter published in conjunction with the first full Latin edition prepared by H.G. Hamaker.[7] Fruin's article has established itself as a critical historical introduction that is most unfortunately lacking in the first Latin edition.[8] Drawing on drafts, notes and letters, Fruin reconstructed how Grotius became engaged by, and acted over years as a spokesman for, the United Netherlands East India Company, better known by its historic initials from the Dutch name, VOC. It had been formed in 1602 through a merger of six regionally based trading firms known as the *voorcompagniën*, or fore-companies.[9] Specifically, Fruin identified the seizure of the *Santa Catarina* as the single incident that served as the immediate historical backdrop of *De Iure Praedae.*

Luminaries of law and jurisprudence of the early 20th century, such as Cornelis van Vollenhoven and Willem J.M. van Eysinga, took a great interest in how the legal and philosophical principles developed in *De Iure Praedae*, and implicitly also *Mare Liberum* were later incorporated into *De Iure Belli ac Pacis Libri Tres* (Three Books on the Law of War and Peace). This was, and remains, a key aspect of enquiry, as can be evidenced by the study of the Geneva academic Peter Haggenmacher titled *Grotius et la doctrine de la guerre juste* (Grotius and the Doctrine of the Just War), published in 1983.[10]

In the context of this study, two works deserve special mention, not least because they have been frequently used and quoted. They include, first, George Norman Clark and Willem J.M. van Eysinga's two volumes (published in 1940 and 1951 respectively) on the Anglo-Dutch maritime

Illus. 4 Map of the southern portion of the Malay Peninsula, the Singapore and Melaka Straits and the Johor River's historic upstream towns.

and colonial conferences of the early 17th century.[11] As is now widely known, Grotius played a role as one of the leading members of the Dutch delegation both at the conference in London in 1613 as well as during the follow-up discussions in the Hague in 1615. Clark and van Eysinga's two volumes have become important milestones for Grotius research, as they attempt to shed light on the broader diplomatic and commercial wrangling between the English and the Dutch at the dawn of the 17th century. The documents reproduced from archival holdings in England and the Netherlands also cast a very different light on Grotius — in this instance not as the brilliant legal thinker or talented linguist but as nothing less than a shrewd, uncompromisingly tough and to many of the English delegates a most awkward, irritating and hair-splitting pedant. It is implicit from the documents transcribed and reproduced by Clark and van Eysinga that Grotius should not only be ranked among the early thinkers of a recognisably modern international order, but also as one of the hitherto unacknowledged champions of early European commercial and colonial expansion.[12]

The second work deserving special mention here is the lengthy article published in 1965 by W.Ph. Coolhaas titled *Een bron voor het historische gedeelte van Hugo de Groots de jure praedae* (A source for the historical section of Hugo Grotius' *De Iure Praedae*).[13] In the Nationaal Archief van Nederland (formerly the Algemeen Rijksarchief) Coolhaas discovered a collection of 15 notarised statements (or affidavits) by mariners who had participated in the early Dutch voyages to the East Indies. The article by Coolhaas has proven its worth to researchers, as it brought new evidence to the fore and also raised a series of important questions relating to what Grotius knew about the early Dutch voyages and specifically also the *Estado da Índia* and the Luso-Asian trading regime in the East Indies. Coolhaas forms one of the pillars in the argument of van Ittersum's book *Profit and Principle: Hugo Grotius, Natural Rights Theories and the Rise of Dutch Power in the East Indies.*[14] This latter study meticulously reconstructs the genesis of *De Iure Praedae* against the historical backdrop of enhanced VOC commercial penetration into the East Indies as well as in the more immediate European context of shifting relations between the Dutch, French and English, together with the Dutch and the Iberian powers at the dawn of the 17th century.

As mentioned earlier, Leiden University participated in the bidding at the 1864 auction and successfully acquired several lots that included the autograph manuscript of *De Iure Praedae* together with a series of smaller treatises, reading notes, outlines and textual fragments that now bear the shelfmark B.P.L. 918–922. In 1987 my attention was drawn to these Leiden papers. In the following two decades, up to the year 2006, I prepared a series of studies on the unpublished manuscripts contained in B.P.L. 922. After initial investigations on almost all of the manuscripts shelved as B.P.L. 922, I have concluded that many, if not most, of them should be classified as "early Grotius", which means complete books, treatises, drafts or notes penned before August 1618. Of special interest are themes, issues and sources encountered in both B.P.L. 922 and B.P.L. 917, the latter being the manuscript of *De Iure Praedae Commentarius.*[15] These parallels are especially interesting in the case of *De Societate Publica cum Infidelibus* (On Public Society with Non-Christians), as they bear in parts a strong resemblance to ideas, patterns of quotations, wording, and even watermarks contained in the historical chapters 11 through 15 of *De Iure Praedae.* My study of B.P.L. 922 for well over two decades has led me to radically reassess many of my earlier findings on the historical context, authorial intentions and sources of Grotius' early works. Consequently I also question an array of common assumptions. My discoveries and conclusions are presented in chapters 2 through 4 of this book. Although the chapters draw on my earlier materials, they also feature revised and enhanced arguments that have been updated in the light of recent research findings.

Setting the wider stage for the reader, it is useful to explore the academic training, career and works of Grotius. Placing his reading notes, treatises, books and fragments generated over a course of almost five decades into a proper chronological sequence is crucial for appreciating the historical contexts and purpose for which they were written. Although covering all of Grotius' life, the present study is chiefly concerned with the early phase of his career. This spans his study of classics at the States College in Leiden (now Leiden University) during the 1590s, his service as "official chronicler of [the province of] Holland", as well as his tenure in various official capacities, including *advocaat fiscaal* (public prosecutor). In the period under review he also served as Pensionary of Rotterdam, member of the States of Holland, the Dutch States General, as well as a spokesman for the VOC. Grotius' arrest and incarceration in August 1618 and the subsequent charge of *lèse majésté* mark a major rupture both in terms of his career as well as his further personal development. Importantly, the biographical chapter takes into account recently published studies on his life, career and works. Many hitherto unknown or sparsely known facets of his life, career and working habits are placed into a biographical synopsis that is written in a language accessible to the present-day reader. This is the programme staked out in the biographical chapter 1, titled "Grotius, the 'Oracle of Delft': The Man, VOC Lobbyist, Politician and Diplomat".

This book focuses on *De Iure Praedae Commentarius* and its 17th-century spin-off publication *Mare Liberum*, as well as a series of texts and fragments contained in ms. B.P.L. 922. The latter manuscript bundle includes the full-length treatise *Commentarius in Theses XI* (Commentary to Eleven Theses), as well as the fragments or skeletal outlines titled *De Societate Publica cum Infidelibus* (On Public Society with Unbelievers), *De Pace* (Of Peace), *De Bello ob Libertatem Eligendo* (On Choosing War for Freedom) and *Theses LVI* (Fifty-Six Theses).[16] Adducing also many letters, unpublished reading notes and working papers that derive from the possession of the Dutch humanist, I am particularly interested in answering a set of basic questions that link the remaining three chapters of this book together. The overarching questions I ask are these: What did Grotius actually know about the dynamics of Dutch commercial and political penetration into the East Indies, specifically within the Southeast Asian cultural setting? Did he ever conduct research on Asian works, or explore specific problems from an Asian perspective? Is there any evidence that he concerned himself with Asian maritime law and customs? How familiar was Grotius with the activities, policies and commercial practices of Dutch competitors, such as specifically the Portuguese, the English, as well as Southeast Asian princes and rulers? Charles H. Alexandrowicz and also more recent authors have asked whether the law of nations (*ius gentium*) and international law are uniquely or even substantially European in origin. Alexandrowicz's now classic work *An Introduction to the Law of Nations in the East Indies*, published in 1967, plotted the historical origins of international law and the law of the sea with a focus on Asia,[17] Alexandrowicz recognised in Grotius an agent who could successfully weave together different strands of thinking, both European as well as Asian. He explored pertinent issues about the possible Asian contributions to international law, especially in the context of maritime navigation and diplomacy, but some of his conclusions about Grotius amounted to little more than guesswork or speculation.[18]

One of the unique facets of historically and theoretically justifying the seizure of the Portuguese carrack *Santa Catarina* is the supposed alliance entered into by Dutch Admiral Jacob van Heemskerk with King 'Ala'uddin

Ri'ayat Shah III of Johor and his younger sibling, Raja Bongsu. The latter acted as co-ruler and also dominated relations with foreign powers. Against this backdrop of his engagement with VOC interests during the period 1604–15, Grotius took an active interest in specific problems associated with early Dutch advances into the East Indies. These included not only issues pertaining to the idea of a "just war", but also the obstacles facing the Dutch when forging trade agreements and military alliances with non-Christian powers. Questions he addressed include these: Could the Dutch, as Christians, ally with a non-Christian power such as Johor, ostensibly to wage war against another European people, the Portuguese? How could this be justified against the background of Portuguese efforts to impede the Dutch from accessing emporia across Asia? In answering these questions, Grotius helped prepare the theoretical ground for the VOC's evolving forward policy that accepted Asian rulers as equal members of the international community who enjoyed full rights of sovereignty. When he entered the negotiation chambers at the colonial conferences in London (1613) and the Hague (1615), he argued that the liberty of Asian rulers was capable of being limited or curtailed as a result of (voluntarily) signing exclusive and perpetual treaties with the Dutch. In assuming this position, Grotius helped pave the theoretical and legal grounds for Dutch colonial rule in Asia. These considerations, together with the justification of the *Santa Catarina*'s seizure by Heemskerk, Portuguese obstruction, and the sovereignty of the Asian princes assume centre stage in chapter 2, titled "Grotius, Johor and Trade in the East Indies".

As noted, the only portion of Grotius' *De Iure Praedae* to be published during his lifetime was a single chapter which he reworked and first released anonymously as *Mare Liberum.* Prepared at the behest of the Zeeland chamber of the VOC with the objective of influencing the negotiations for a truce with the Spanish Empire, *Mare Liberum* came to serve numerous commercial and political causes that sought to uphold the freedom of commerce and unrestricted maritime navigation. The English quoted from the work at the maritime colonial conferences in the 17th century to underscore their right to free navigation; in the early 18th century the Ostend Company, formed in 1717 in the Austrian Netherlands (now Belgium and Luxemburg) to compete in the Indies trade, cited from *Mare Liberum* in its charter in order to assert the right of navigation against an entrenched Dutch monopoly in Asia; and in 1916, toward the height of World War I, an English translation was published in a then still neutral United States of America to ostensibly defend the interests of their merchant marine against submarine attacks by the German Reich.[19] Thus, over the centuries, *Mare Liberum* — like many other important texts in the history of law and political thought — has been used or cited frequently, sometimes beyond recognition and certainly beyond authorial intentions. For this reason, I find it of considerable importance to return to the historical context in which it was drafted to ask: What is this treatise really all about? Is it really about championing the cause of the freedom of navigation? How did Grotius justify his case against Portuguese efforts to obstruct access to ports and emporia in the East Indies, and was he even consistent in explaining or expounding his ideas?

The methodology applied in this book has been influenced by key facets of the Cambridge School of political thought, as well as the writings of Michael Oakshott and John G.A. Pocock.[20] I am interested to explore and reconstruct, as far as possible, the evolution or refinement of ideas based on a close reading of original sources, fragments, letters and other surviving materials, including reading notes, skeletal drafts, as well as marginalia in neat copies and books. In keeping with the rigour of historical enquiry and the historical discipline, I focus on the interaction of developments on the ground and the (re)formulation of various aspects of political and economic thought. Specifically, I highlight how (documented) developments on the ground impacted Grotian thought, and how Grotius ideas, in turn, fed into evolving Dutch policies for the East Indies and elsewhere. The conclusions drawn from such a close, source-focused reading of *Mare Liberum, De Iure Praedae Commentarius* and other early works and fragments contained in B.P.L. 922 are surprising: Grotius evidently regarded the idea of free access to emporia and marketplaces in Asia as far more important than the freedom of navigation on the high seas. His core tenet, that the high seas must remain unappropriated, and therefore also freely navigable, may have been based on his (selective) reading of Roman law and the Spanish Late Scholastics, but the principles he elicited from these sources were hardly palatable to his contemporaries. His adversaries, including the Scottish professor of law William Welwood and especially the Iberian theologian and jurisconsult Seraphim de Freitas, charged him with misquotation, misunderstanding and misrepresentation. Some of these accusations are explored in greater detail to reveal that, in the haste of revising the text, Grotius targeted the Portuguese and remained silent on similar positions taken by strategic allies of the Dutch Republic, mishandled or selectively read his sources and took quotations from the publications of other authors. This close reading of *Mare Liberum* stands at the centre in chapter 3, titled "Free Trade and Unimpeded Access to Emporia in the East Indies: Rereading Mare Liberum (1609)".

The critical examination of *Mare Liberum* undertaken in chapter 3 raises a number of issues regarding Grotius' access to, and handling of, source materials. The questions raised are these: What did he actually know about Asia, and specifically also about the practices, institutions and policies of the Portuguese in Asia? What sources did he consult directly and which did he (likely) quote second hand? This line of questioning is admittedly not uncontroversial to contemporary researchers, as a range of assumptions have become deeply entrenched about the depth and breadth of Grotius' original research. In this vein two statements by leading academics concerning the quality of his research stand at the centre of attention. Robert Fruin exalted *De Iure Praedae* as "clean research" of "enduring value" and speculated that its author must have conducted independent research in the archives of the VOC as well as the holdings of its *voorcompagniën*. Almost one century later, Alexandrowicz surmised that Grotius had familiarised himself with Asian maritime law and customs. Is there any proof to support such claims? A close reading of Grotius' correspondence and the documents which he verifiably had at his disposal while drafting *De Iure Praedae* indicates that he had access to far fewer sources than has been believed until now. He resorted to the classics as well as a range of sources supplied to him among others by the VOC directors in Amsterdam. As shall be shown, there was no independent research in the VOC archives, and there is not a shred of evidence to suggest that Grotius ever studied Asian maritime law or custom. Still, Grotius was placed in a position to extract crucial information and insights from a series of epistolary memorials written, for example, by Admiral Cornelis Matelieff de Jonge, who served as a director on the board of the VOC's Rotterdam chamber. While important, Matelieff's letters and memoranda proved to be of limited value to Grotius while he was preparing *Mare Liberum* for the press, because the insights divulged by the admiral were almost certainly considered sensitive or classified. Explorations into the source materials that Grotius perused or had at his disposal, as well as his knowledge and familiarity with the affairs of the East Indies in the period 1604–9, stand at the heart of chapter 4, titled, "How Grotius Acquired a Working Knowledge of the East Indies".

What did Grotius know about Dutch penetration into the East Indies as well as *Asia Portuguesa* in general? The documentary appendices reproduced in their original together with translations into English provide not only an important cross section of sources that Grotius either wrote or had at his fingertips between 1604 and 1618, they additionally yield crucial insights into the various options weighed by the nascent VOC officials across the Indian Ocean and Asia. These documents should enlighten readers on the history of early modern European commerce, diplomacy and colonial presence around the Malay Peninsula and across the Indonesian Archipelago. All the appendices have a significant bearing on issues, themes and questions raised in this book.

According to Adriaen ten Haeff's post-script of 17 November 1607, Grotius received a packet of letters that were collectively titled "letters by the King of Spain" (for images, see pp. 128, 132).[21] While the royal letters of instruction originally contained in this packet may no longer be available, the date and summary of the letters provided in the post-script have made it possible to track down some copies of the Portuguese language originals. Two letters to the Portuguese viceroy in Goa, Dom Martim Affonso de Castro, have been transcribed and published in Raymundo de Bulhão Pato's first volume of the *Livros das Monçoes* (commonly known in English as the Letters of the Monsoon).[22] A third source is a letter by King Philip III/II to the King of Cananor dated 23 December 1606. An excerpt from ten Haeff's post-script is transcribed and translated into English as appendix 1, and the three royal letters of instruction in their Portuguese original with translation are found in appendices 2, 3 and 4 respectively.

At the end of the first edition of *Mare Liberum*, Grotius appended a letter in Latin by King Philip III/II to Martim Affonso de Castro dated 27 January 1607. A comparison of Grotius' Latin translation with the full text transcribed and translated in appendix 4, however, clearly evidences that the passage in question could not have been taken from the original. It remains unclear whether the Latin translation is a forgery, or whether it was possibly taken from another letter altogether. The unverifiable Latin excerpt reproduced in *Mare Liberum* together with its English translation are featured in appendix 5.

The 1864 auction catalogue of Grotius' working papers lists a partial Dutch translation from a letter by the Bishop of Melaka, Dom João de Ribeiro Gaio, to Philip III/II.[23] Grotius translated this letter fragment into

Latin and reproduced it as an annex to the first edition of *Mare Liberum*. Although the original translation sold in 1864 appears to be lost and is certainly not available in any public collection, its buyer, Frederik Muller of Amsterdam, prepared a full transcript for the Leiden historian, Robert Fruin. This transcript survives and can be found among the professor's working papers owned by Leiden University Library.[24] The letter was first reproduced in Dutch in the 1950 Carnegie edition of *De Iure Praedae* and has since been translated into English by Martine van Ittersum and added to her revised edition of that work in 2006.[25] Appendix 7 provides a transcript of the Dutch text from the copy owned by Leiden University together with a new English translation.

As part of a package of documents forwarded by the Amsterdam directors of the VOC, Grotius received a series of letters and affidavits which have been bound together in a volume that bears the Dutch title *Boeck Tracterende vande Wreede, Verradische ende Hostile Proceduren der Portugesen In Oost-Indien* (Book Concerning the Cruel, Treacherous and Hostile Proceedings of the Portuguese in the East Indies, see the image on p. 113).[26] This volume was identified, transcribed and exhaustively discussed by Coolhaas in 1965.[27] Some of the documents contained in this bound volume, however, were published before the revision of *Mare Liberum* for the press in 1608–9. In the foreword to their German language edition of the *Achter Theil der Orientalischen Indien* (liberally translated: Eighth Voyage [of the Dutch] to the East Indies), published in Frankfurt in 1606, Theodor de Bry and M. Gotthard Arthus reproduced a series of short letters touching on Admiral Jacob van Heemskerk's seizure of the carrack *Santa Catarina* off the coast of Singapore in February 1603 as well as the events that followed. This book transcribes both the Dutch and the German texts of four letters exchanged between Admiral van Heemskerk and Portuguese Melaka's governor, Fernão d'Albuquerque, the *câmara* (city council) of Melaka, and the captain of the ill-fated *Santa Catarina,* Sebastião Serrão, all dating from March 1603. These four letters are also translated into English and are arranged in chronological order as appendices 7 through 10 (see the images on pp. 183, 197).

As is known, the *Santa Catarina* incident paved the way for the opening of long-term ties and strategic alliances between the Dutch and the kingdom of Johor which feature so prominently in *De Iure Praedae* as well as in some of the materials exchanged later between the Dutch and English delegates at the maritime and colonial conferences in London (1613) and the Hague (1615). Grotius' early impression of this kingdom, its ruler 'Ala'uddin Ri'ayat Shah and two of his brothers, known from most period documents as Raja Bongsu and Raja Siak, was shaped by materials forwarded to him by the directors of the Amsterdam chamber of the VOC around or after October 1606. Several aspects have been transcribed and discussed by Coolhaas and also van Ittersum in more recent times. Grotius' views based on these and related materials were later refined based on materials received from Cornelis Matelieff de Jonge. In 1605, the admiral set sail for the Malay Peninsula carrying aboard his flagship the surviving members of Johor's first diplomatic mission to the Dutch Republic.[28] He forged a landmark treaty with Johor in May 1606, laid siege to Melaka, and engaged the Portuguese *armada* in the Melaka Strait near Cape Rachado.[29] It is certain that Grotius had perused these materials touching on the voyage of Matelieff to the East Indies. His reading notes (of admittedly uncertain dating) survive in the Nationaal Archief van Nederland in the Hague (see image on p. 205). Appendices 11 through 15 are testimonies translated from 17th-century Dutch and relate chiefly to Matelieff's dealings with, and descriptions of, Johor in the year 1606. Appendix 15 transcribes an epistolary memorial of Matelieff written on his return from the East Indies in 1608 and which is addressed to Grotius (see image on p. 46). This memorial, a copy of which was subsequently passed to the *landsadvocaat*, Johan van Oldenbarnevelt, provided a sweeping political and economic synopsis of the East Indies, and also recommended the establishment of a permanent rendezvous in the Southeast Asian region. Among the possible sites for this proposed Dutch base the admiral singled out Johor, Aceh, Palembang, Banten and Jayakerta. Matelieff's memorial counts as one of the most important sources consulted by Grotius that touches on commerce and trading opportunities in Asia. The question remains to what extent it served as a source for *Mare Liberum*, as the information presented in this epistolary memorial was almost certainly deemed sensitive.

Johann Verken was a member of Admiral Pieter Willemsz. Verhoeff's crew. He arrived with the Dutch fleet in the waters off Johor Lama in January 1609 (see the map on p. 6). While the admiral proceeded upstream to the Johorese capital, Batu Sawar, Verken remained on the ships at anchor in the lower reaches of the Johor River. Verken was a careful observer and in a short passage described the appearance of Raja Bongsu of Johor. The passage reproduced in appendix 16, has been taken from the *Neundter Theil der Orientalischen Indien,* or liberally translated, the "Ninth

Voyage [of the Dutch] to the East Indies", published in Frankfurt am Main in 1612.

The apex of Grotius' engagement as a spokesman for the VOC and its nascent strategic, political and commercial interests in the East Indies is without doubt his participation in the two maritime and colonial conferences held in London and the Hague. Although much ground has already been covered in the two volumes published by Clark and Eysinga in 1940 and 1951 respectively, many of the documentary appendices were reproduced in their original Latin, French and Dutch without translation. As a result, this document collection is of limited value to those researchers not proficient in these European languages. Appendices 17 and 18 transcribe Grotius' opening address in Latin presented before King James I/VI in London on 6 April, together with his farewell address of 21 May 1613. These two documents have been translated into English for the first time and furnish readers with a valuable historical overview of Anglo-Dutch tensions over the East Indies in the early 17th century.

On his arrest and incarceration in August 1618, and faced with charges of *lèse majesté,* Grotius consistently affirmed his past support for the VOC as well as his unwavering hostility towards the Spanish and Portuguese. On hindsight, he claimed that he was not party to the truce negotiations with Spain between 1606 and 1609, not least because he was, as he later claimed, "too young" or "junior" at the time. In any case he was not in favour of the truce, as a range of documents and memoranda prepared in those years can testify. Appendix 19 transcribes an excerpt from Grotius' political memoirs of 1619 in which he spoke about his support for the VOC, his unyielding hostility towards the Spanish and Portuguese empires under the personal union of Philip III/II, concerns about the Twelve Years Truce, as well as problems surrounding the formation of the then still unfounded Dutch West India Company (WIC).[30] Importantly, Grotius also staked out some of his differences with his former political patron van Oldenbarnevelt. It should be always remembered that these political memoirs were self-serving. When they were written, van Oldenbarnevelt had already been found guilty of treason and executed, while Grotius had just started to serve his lifetime prison sentence in the fortress of Loevesteyn.

The materials used in this study have been collected over a period of approximately two decades and include both published and unpublished sources from across a spectrum of European languages, including Latin, Dutch, German, French, Italian, Spanish and Portuguese. The transcription of early modern ligands, personal names and toponyms has followed a limited number of basic rules. Ligands such as the German umlaut have been retained, while others, such as the single "tz" and even the "ß", have been transcribed as "tz" and "ss" respectively.

Readers need to bear in mind that in the early 17th century, the Gregorian calendar was already being used on continental Europe, including the Dutch Republic. In England, the Julian calendar continued to be used, and at the time the discrepancy between the two calendar systems amounted to ten days. As a rule, dates have been taken over from the actual documents (including materials from the Public Record Office in London) or as featured in transcribed and published sources, such as Grotius' *Briefwisseling* (Correspondence) as well as Clark and van Eysinga's *The Colonial Conferences between England and the Netherlands in 1613 and 1615.* References such as "Old Style" for dates in the Julian calendar, or "New Style" for the Gregorian calendar, have been omitted. Readers will need to make their own calendar adjustments. As a rule of thumb, and unless otherwise specified, dates from England need to be moved ahead by ten days. For example, a letter written in London on 5 April 1613 according to the Julian calendar bears the adjusted date 15 April 1613 in the Gregorian calendar.

Huig de Groot is always referred to by his Latinised name, Hugo Grotius, but his brother and other descendants of his family are referred to by their proper Dutch surname, de Groot. Personal names were left in the spelling as they are encountered in the original early modern documents, though admittedly, the same person may not always spell his name exactly in the same way. In this case, the "majority" rule applies. In order to forestall any confusion among contemporary readers, toponyms have been adapted as far as possible to current spelling, hence the name Malacca becomes Melaka, or the variant spellings Ior, Jhor, Gior, Djohor are given as Johor throughout. Humanist renderings of Ptolemaic toponyms have also been adapted to present-day usage. Taprobana, for example, can be taken as a reference to the island of Ceylon or Sumatra, depending on the 16th- or early 17th-century map or chart consulted. Apart from employing some very seriously garbled toponyms, early modern European sources, especially Dutch and Portuguese language materials, show a strong propensity to corrupt Asian titles, functions, legal concepts and even cultural conventions. It is not that the European observers on the ground were always unfamiliar with local titles, functions or cultural conventions, but in preparing documents for the home market, titles or concepts were generally translated or transposed into terms familiar to European readers. This poses some genuine challenges to the present-day historian, as translated titles, functions, legal concepts or cultural conventions implied something quite specific in a European context. Take, for example, the title "king" or "emperor". These titles are variously applied to the sultans, rajas and rulers across South, Southeast and East Asia. The Sultan of Johor is consistently called the "King of Johor" (see, for example, the image of Grotius' draft letter on p. 155). So when a European reader sees the phrase "King of Johor", this is likely to conjure up the idea of a ruler administering a territorially defined polity called Johor. There are many more examples like this. The forefather of the present-day Sultan of Brunei is consistently called the "Emperor of Borneo". Other rulers are variously labeled "vassal", "prince", "monarch" or "petty king". These Europeanised titles have been retained from the original as far as possible, as each of these titles entails an implicit set of rights and obligations in a European context. Some kings exercised the full range of sovereign rights, or more frequently disposed over a limited number of them, depending on the constitution or nature of a given polity. Vassals are not considered sovereign overlords proper, even if they do exercise certain rights associated with sovereignty, such as pronouncing supreme judgment, promulgating laws, minting coins, waging war and concluding peace.[31] In such instances, vassals are understood to exercise these on the basis of delegated authority. Thus, when Grotius employed terminology such as the "King of Johor", he was already endowing this officeholder in the minds of his European readers with a distinct and in Europe widely accepted set of rights. The noteworthy exception to this general pattern appears to be Raja Bongsu of Johor. Despite variant spellings of the title "raja" he is known across Portuguese and Dutch sources by his Malay title Raja Bongsu (the younger raja), Raja Seberang (the raja from the other side [of the river]) or Raja di Ilir (the raja from downstream).[32]

It is hoped that the forensic analysis of *De Iure Praedae, Mare Liberum* as well as the notes and fragments contained in the bundle of early manuscripts known as B.P.L. 922 evokes further reflection on the part of the reader to question and reassess Grotius' ideas on a range of core topics. It is clear that his knowledge of Asian societies and of the *Estado da Índia* was limited at the time he drafted *De Iure Praedae* and even some years later when he revised its chapter 12 for publication as *Mare Liberum.* It is also evident that his ideas on early Dutch expansion into insular and peninsular Southeast Asia underwent a significant evolution between October 1604 and the Anglo-Dutch maritime and colonial conference at The Hague in 1615. The studies contained in this book elucidate Grotius' working habits, including also his lapses, omissions and weaknesses. The specifically Southeast Asian context provides a new theoretical base for exploring his originality, his impact in Southeast Asia and in Europe as well as on the theories of war, peace, alliance-making, sovereignty and the freedom of trade.

CHAPTER 1

Hugo Grotius, the "Oracle of Delft": The Man, VOC Lobbyist, Politician and Diplomat

Huig de Groot, who is today better known by his Latinised name Hugo Grotius, has entered the annals of history as one of the most important authorities of natural rights and the law of nations. His interests, activities and writings, however, span a wide array of academic disciplines — from literature, poetry and philology to history, politics and law. Today scholars and researchers regard him as a polymath or a "Renaissance man", but he was still very much a man of his day and age. He was a humanist and something of a *wunderkind*, or miracle child. King Henry IV of France called him "the Miracle of Holland". On the basis of this title and in their quest for great national figures or *erflaters* (great ancestors) some Dutch historians have — rightly or not — compared Grotius to the composer Wolfgang Amadeus Mozart.[1] For sure, any parallels between these two restless and indefatigable child prodigies are tenuous. While in the late 19th and early 20th centuries it might have been fashionable to speak of Grotius as the "Father of Modern International Law", scholars and researchers today no longer celebrate him as *the* father proper, but at least as one of the *many* pathbreakers of the modern international system.[2]

Illus. 5 Portrait of King Henry IV who on the occasion of the Dutch diplomatic mission to France in 1598 called Grotius the "Miracle of Holland". (Taken from the 1652 edition of Emmanuel van Meteren's *Commentariën ofte Memoriën van den Nederlantsen Staet, Handel, Oorloghen ende Gheschiedenissen van onsen tyden* [Commentaries or Memoirs concerning the Dutch State, Trade and War and the History of our Times]. Private collection, Peter Borschberg)

Hugo was born on 10 April 1583, to a patrician family in the thriving commercial centre of Delft. The family de Groot belonged to the regents of the nascent Dutch Republic. It is therefore hardly surprising that the young Hugo was nothing less than predestined by birth to become a regent and to embark on what appeared to be an assured career in law and politics. Hugo matriculated at the States College in Leiden (later known as Leiden University) which at the time was a young academic institution. In 1597 he graduated from the States' College at the age of 11 after studying the Greek and Roman classics, rhetorics as well as philosophy.[3] A letter to the French nobleman Benjamin Aubéry du Maurier of 13 May 1615 reflects his academic grounding in philosophy, the classics and politics and also mirrors his own humanist intellectual development.[4] However, to the best of my knowledge there is not a shred of evidence to prove that young Hugo ever attended any of the lectures at Leiden on the subjects of law and jurisprudence, an observation, incidentally, that is also made in the early 20th century by W.S.M. Knight.[5] Many academics today surmise that he did — or must have — and readily point towards such Leiden luminaries of jurisprudence such as Everard Bronckhorst or even, his predecessor Hugo Doneau (Latinised: Donellus).[6] They also point to a testimony dating from a later period, namely a letter by Hugo to his younger brother Willem, dated 18 May 1615, in which he furnishes his younger sibling an outline for the preparation and defence of Willem's legal theses — an outline that includes the principles of natural law. Willem is thought to have defended his theses at Leiden University the following year 1616.[7]

What Grotius most certainly did enjoy during his studies in Leiden was personal and academic exposure to some of Europe's most formidable scholars and humanists of his era. The three years of study in Leiden do not appear to have prepared him for, and did not necessarily expose him to, law and jurisprudence. In truth, this makes it ever the more intriguing that he was awarded at the age of 15 a doctoral degree *utriusque iuris* — that is, in ecclesiastical and civil law — from the University of Orléans in France. If he did indeed "study" at Orléans it was only very briefly. Some historians surmise that he used family or political connections to purchase the doctorate, receive it *honoris causa* (honorary), or probably both.[8]

Grotius was conferred his doctorate *utriusque iuris* in the very same year he undertook a visit to the court of King Henry IV of France. He joined a diplomatic delegation headed by a senior Dutch politician whose

Illus. 6 A portrait of Hugo Grotius, aged 15, shortly after returning from his diplomatic mission to France in 1598. He is flaunting a gold medallion gifted to him by King Henry IV. (From Caspar Brandt and Adriaen van Cattenburgh, *Historie van het leven des Heeren Huig de Groot* [History of the Life of Mr. Huig de Groot], vol. I, Amsterdam and Dordrecht, 1727. Private collection, Peter Borschberg)

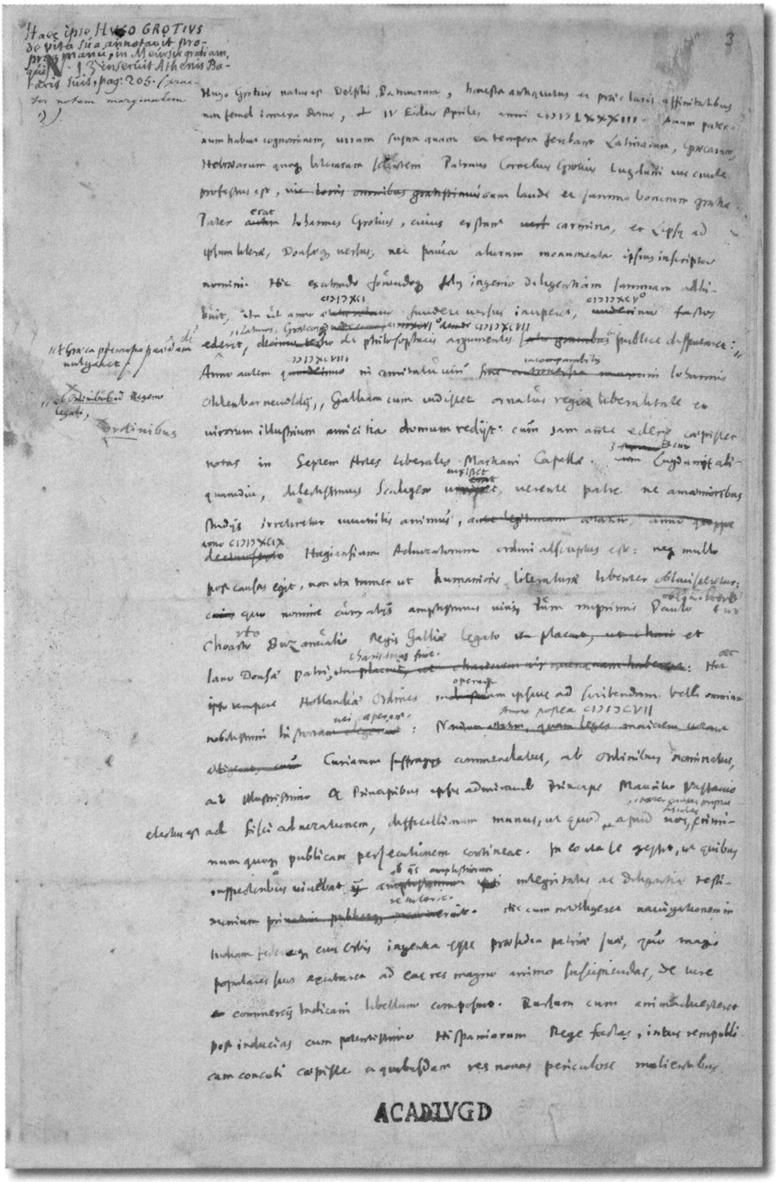

Illus. 7 First page of Hugo Grotius' *curriculum vitae,* written in his own hand and dating from around 1612–3. (Leiden University Library, Papenbroeckii 13A, fol. 3 recto). A shortened version was published in Johannes Meursius' *Illustris Academia Lugd-Batava* (1613) and later in his *Athenae Batavae* (1625), being a collection of illustrious persons closely associated with the city of Leiden and its university.

political fate and fortune would become inseparably intertwined with his own, namely, the *landsadvocaat* (Advocate of the Land) Johan van Oldenbarnevelt.[9]

Though he registered as a barrister in the Hague upon his return from France in 1598[10] — as Grotius himself states in his short *curriculum vitae* dating from about 1613 — he left his mark in Dutch republican society in a range of other appointments and capacities. In 1601 he was appointed to the position of official historiographer or chronicler of Holland. One need immediately add considerable caution to this title, for "history" as an academic discipline proper is a development of the 19th century. Historians from the age of Renaissance and Humanism were little more than appointed apologists, or what in modern terminology might be cynically known as "propagandists" or "spin doctors".[11] Certainly, Grotius may have been selective with the truth and occasionally massaged the evidence — an art, one might contend, he mastered through his legal practice and also from his study of classics at Leiden — but one thing is certain: he was a powerful and effective writer, mastering the Latin language to the envy of many of his contemporaries. This was a talent, one should immediately adjoin, that was duly acknowledged by his 17th-century contemporaries and most significantly by his patron van Oldenbarnevelt.

In his capacity as official chronicler of Holland — or at least closely around this official function — Grotius is thought to have written a series of works amongst which we find his *De Antiquitate Reipublicae Batavicae* (Of the Antiquity of the Batavian Republic) as well as his *Annales et Historiae de Rebus Belgicis* (Annals and Histories of the Low Countries). The former was first published in 1610, and the *Annales et Historiae* were completed in 1612 but only posthumously brought to print by his son Pieter in 1657.[12]

Two other works that stem from this early period of writing and may be directly or indirectly connected with his appointment as official chronicler of Holland are his treatises *De Republica Emendanda* (On the Emendation of the [Dutch] Republic) and *Parallelon Rerumpublicarum* (Parallels between Republics).[13]

It was Grotius' acknowledged and respected abilities as a linguist, writer and "historian", as well as his practice of law, that induced the directors of the then recently founded Dutch East India Company (VOC) to seek his assistance in 1604 in defending the seizure in Februrary 1603 by Admiral Jacob van Heemskerk of a Portuguese carrack off the coast of Singapore.[14] The intellectual fruit from his engagement in defending

Illus. 8 Johan van Oldenbarnevelt, the political patron of Hugo Grotius since the late 1590s, served as the *landsadvocaat* or Land's Advocate of Holland. He was arrested on 18 August 1618 together with Hugo Grotius, Rombout Hogerbeets, Jacob Dircksz. de Graeff and Gilles van Ledenberg. He was subsequently found guilty by a special court and executed on 13 May 1619. (The Hague, Rijksbureau voor Kunsthistorische Dokumentatie)

this incident is first a comprehensive histo-theoretical treatise that has been known since its publication in 1868 as *De Iure Praedae Commentarius* (Commentary on the Law of Prize and Booty).[15] The Dutch historian Robert Fruin deserves credit for having written a substantial article, later translated into English, in which he sought to place the genesis of this important work within its proper historical setting both in Europe as well as in Southeast Asia.[16] Coolhaas, almost a century later, transcribed and critically edited some of the immediate sources that Grotius received from the VOC that were evidently used for the writing of portions of *De Iure Praedae*.[17] But only very recently was an in-depth examination of the developments and circumstances leading to the composition of *De Iure Praedae* undertaken by van Ittersum.[18]

As is widely known since Fruin first published his long article on *De Iure Praedae*, the work is divided into two distinct sections, a theoretical and a historical part. While the latter presents the historic evidence to corroborate the position that the seizure of the Portuguese carrack *Santa Catarina* was justifiable, beneficial and honourable, the theoretical portion represents Grotius' attempt to mentally distill and formulate his primordial insights on the laws of war and on the laws of nations generally speaking. Fruin dated the genesis of this work to the years 1604–6,[19] but on the basis of research conducted on the surviving autograph manuscript preserved at Leiden University,[20] it is becoming increasingly evident that Grotius probably revised the text — especially the theoretical chapters 1 through 10 — as late as 1607 or even 1608.[21] This coincides with a period when he held the appointment of *advocaat fiscaal* (a public prosecutor)[22] and also took an active interest in the on-going truce negotiations between the Dutch Republic and the Spanish Empire.[23] In 1608 he also married the Maria van Reigersberch, the daughter of the burgomaster of Veere in Zeeland,[24] and the couple had five offspring who survived to adulthood.

In view of chronological sequence and also thematic discourse, it is apt at this juncture to introduce a series of fragments and short pieces, some of which remain unpublished and consequently are not readily accessible to many contemporary researchers. These consist of a brief published by Willem J. van Eysinga in 1955 that pertains directly to the truce negotiations with Spain, the treatise *Commentarius in Theses XI* (Commentary to Eleven Theses),[25] the fragments *De Pace* (Of Peace) and *De Bello ob Libertatem Eligendo* (On Choosing War for Freedom), as well as the skeletal outlines titled *De Societate Publica cum Infidelibus* (Of Public Society with Non-Christians) and *Theses*

Illus. 9 Maria van Reigersberch, daughter of the burgomaster of Veere, married Grotius in 1608. She bore five children who lived into adulthood. In this portrait she is in her early 50s. (From Caspar Brandt and Adriaen van Cattenburgh, *Historie van het leven des Heeren Huig de Groot* [History of the Life of Mr. Huig de Groot], vol. I, Amsterdam and Dordrecht, 1727. Private collection, Peter Borschberg)

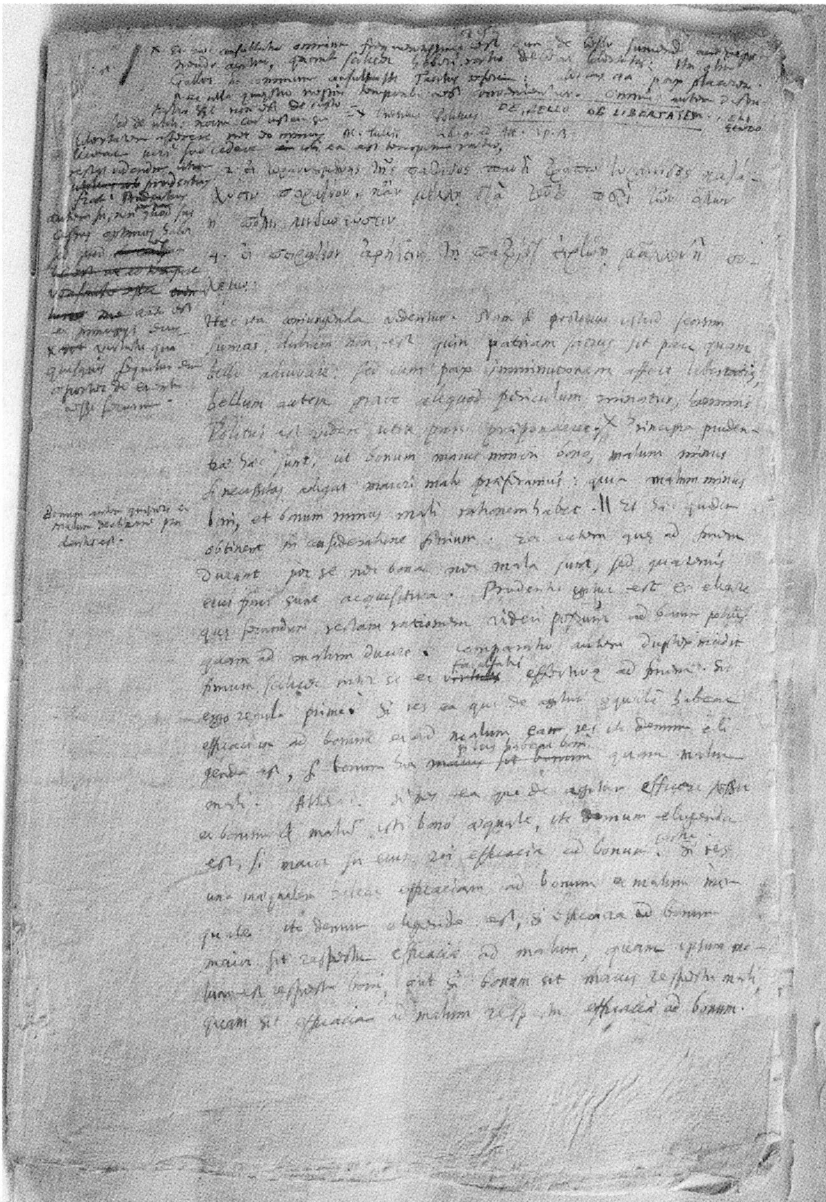

Illus. 10 First page of Grotius' fragment titled *De Bello ob Libertatem Eligendo ex Thesibus Politicis M. Tullii Lib. 9 ad Attic. 4.* (On Choosing War for Freedom, from the Political Theses of Marcus Tullius [Cicero], Letters to Atticus, book 9, [number] 4). (Leiden University Library, B.P.L. 922, fol. 293 recto)

LVI (Fifty-Six Theses).[26] Additional images of these manuscripts can be viewed on pp. 29, 57, 63, 148, 149, 158, 160. Many of these texts, drafts and concepts also feature separate sheets with reading notes that were evidently jotted down by Grotius in great haste. Despite verging on the illegible in parts, these notes yield priceless insights into how the man worked, which authors he consulted for writing these shorter works and fragments, and generally how he handled his sources. As will be shown in greater detail below, these shorter treatises, fragments and skeletal outlines probably date from the years 1607–9, but possibly as late as 1612–3. It was also during this period of the truce negotiations that Grotius, with the assistance and cooperation of Jan ten Grootenhuys, singled out and prepared for publication one chapter of his manuscript *De Iure Praedae*. This was published anonymously in 1609 under the title *Mare Liberum, sive de iure quod Batavis competit ad Indicana commercia dissertatio* (The Free Sea, or a Dissertation on the Right that Belongs to the Dutch to Engage in the Indies Trade).[27] Grotius' intention to influence the final stages of the acrimonious and protracted Hispano-Dutch truce negotiations remained unfulfilled for a variety of reasons.[28] Two factors merit specific mentioning in this context: Opposition to the treatise from Grotius' patron van Oldenbarnevelt and delays in the physical production of *Mare Liberum*.[29]

But Grotius and his anonymous publication on the free sea were both still to have their day, not in the dealings with the Spaniards, but notably in the Dutch Republic's negotiations with the English some four years later. The origins of the Anglo-Dutch tensions over fishing and trade in the East Indies during the second decade of the 17th century have been the subject of several excellent studies, including Clark and van Eysinga's source publication and commentary as well as John Grayson's unpublished doctoral dissertation completed at the University of London in 1978.[30] Grotius was deputised to the 1613 London conference to help tackle several issues on the agenda, including Dutch herring fishing off the coast of Scotland, as well as Anglo-Dutch rivalry in the East Indies trade at large.[31] One of the more curious points of discussion was the proposal put forth already in 1612 by the Dutch ambassador in London, Noël Caron, that the two East India Companies, the Dutch and the English, merge into a single entity in order to forestall competitive erosion of profits from trade. But the English merchants — rightly — distrusted this Dutch scheme and were wary of Grotius' unwavering insistence that the cost of maintaining a physical presence in the East Indies — including military infrastructure — was an expensive enterprise that ate considerably into trading gains. The proposal was more than just about a merger; it was about sharing heavy long-term financial commitments and about the need for the English to inject additional capital into the merged entity. In the opening address held before King James I/VI, Grotius' insistence that there could be "no peace among nations without armies, no armies without pay and no pay without tributes" (see appendix 17) encapsulates the tone of the exchanged documents between the negotiators in London (1613) and later also the Hague (1615).[32] An agreement was eventually struck in 1619 — primarily because of pressure exerted by King James I/VI on his negotiators — but the "cooperation agreement" between the English and the Dutch East India Companies was not to bear the desired fruit. It was practically (but not nominally) null and void by the time the so-called "Amboina Massacre" took place in 1623.[33]

Let us briefly return to the London conference of 1613. A translation of *Mare Liberum* was completed by no less an authority than Richard Hakluyt for the benefit of the members of the English delegation and the East India Company in London.[34] Grotius found himself at the conference fending off citations excerpted from his own anonymous work and hurled against him by the English negotiators.

But that was not all. At the 1613 conference Grotius had another — one might say secret — mission to fulfill. This was to win the ear and sympathy of James I/VI as well as of leading English theologians for the stance assumed by the States of Holland in settling religious disputes that were not only quickly getting out of hand, but had deeply divided the republic.[35] The controversy between the Arminians and Gomarists, or Remonstrants and Counter-Remonstrants, has been extensively documented and does not warrant further discussion here.[36] It is known that Grotius took a keen and active interest in these disputes, which had erupted in seriousness after 1610. In close consultation with the Zeeland theologian Antonius Walaeus,[37] he wrote a treatise titled *Meletius sive de iis quae inter Christianis conveniunt epistola* (Meletius, or a Letter on the Points of Consensus between Christians).[38] In this, the Dutch humanist contended that disputing parties set aside their differences for the time being and, instead, work towards their long-term resolution through a General Council, preferably in cooperation with other reformed churches of the Christian world. But as the prodigy from Delft and his political patron van Oldenbarnevelt came to know all

Illus. 11 Portrait of Prince Maurice of Orange. (From the 1647 edition of Emmanuel van Meteren's *Commentariën ofte Memoriën van den Nederlantsen Staet, Handel, Oorloghen ende Gheschiedenissen van onsen Tyden* [Commentaries or Memoirs Concerning the Dutch State, Trade and War and the History of our Times]. The Hague, Koninklijke Bibliotheek, 1790 A 122)

too well, the divisions and religiously inspired fault lines were becoming increasingly polarised and progressively politicised. Tough action was planned by van Oldenbarnevelt and the States of Holland; and understanding, if not open support, from the court of James I/VI and his leading theologians was deemed essential in 1613. Grotius returned to the Netherlands from his London missions in the belief that he had scored successes, especially on the religious front.[39] This may well have encouraged him to seize the defence of the States of Holland, among other domestic political developments,[40] in his work *Ordinum Hollandiae ac Westfrisiae Pietas* (The Piety of the States of Holland and Western Frisia) published in 1613.[41] In this treatise, he upheld the rights of the estates to settle religious disputes, including by recourse to the force of law. Similar politico-religious writings followed, significant among which was his work *De Imperio Summarum Potestatum circa Sacra* (The Rights of the Sovereign in Ecclesiastical Affairs).[42] As a member of the *Gecommitteerde Raden* (Committee of Council of the States of Holland) after 31 May 1617,[43] Grotius was also seen to have been responsible for drafting and pushing through the Erastian ecclesiology he developed earlier in his politico-religious works.[44] Among these is his *Decretum pro Pace Ecclesiae* (Decree for Ecclesiastical Peace), promulgated in January 1614.[45] Grotius also wrote a defence of this controversial decree, but this was never published in his lifetime.[46]

Enforcement of ecclesiastical peace became a serious problem, and for this reason van Oldenbarnevelt and Grotius pushed through the *Scherpe Resolutie* (Sharp Resolution, 4 August 1617) and arranged for the hiring of *waardgelders* (town watches) conscripted in the province of Holland and elsewhere. Their function was reportedly justified on the basis of article 13 of the Union of Utrecht (1579), the Dutch Republic's de-facto constitution, which was interpreted in such a way as to attribute full sovereignty to each of the seven provincial estates.[47] The issue of the *waardgelders* erupted into a full-blown constitutional crisis, with the Stadholder, Prince Maurice of Orange, calling for their dissolution. He contended that their existence and oath of allegiance violated his prerogatives as supreme commander of the armed forces.[48] Van Oldenbarnevelt and Grotius, by contrast, defended the sovereignty of the individual provinces and implicitly their authority to regulate religious affairs independently and without requiring the consent of the other provinces of the union.[49] With the evident consent of King James I/VI, who benignly looked away in August 1618, Prince Maurice staged a *coup d'état*, as a result of which van Oldenbarnevelt, Grotius (the Pensionary of Rotterdam), Rombout Hogerbeets (Pensionary of Leiden), Jacob Dircksz. de Graeff (Burgomaster of Amsterdam) and Gilles van Ledenberg (Pensionary of Utrecht) were arrested on 28 August 1618.[50] After months of questioning and detention in custody in an almost completely boarded-up room, Grotius was sentenced to life imprisonment on the grounds of *lèse majésté*[51] while his patron van Oldenbarnevelt was charged by the Dutch States General, found guilty and sentenced to death.

Grotius was to serve his life sentence in the fortress of Loevesteyn at a cost of 24 *stuiver* per day.[52] Through his wife Maria and his network of learned friends, he gained access to books that were delivered to him in his prison "cell";[53] and despite his reported illness, he used his time in prison to research and write. During this captivity he wrote and completed his political memoirs[54] as well as a formal defence or apology of his actions known as *Verantwoordingh van de Wettelijcke Regieringh van Hollandt en West-Vrieslandt* (Defence of the Lawful Government of Holland and Western Frisia),[55] which was published in 1622 after his escape from Loevesteyn. Grotius started a number of works, including *Inleidinghe tot de Hollandsche Rechtsgeleerdheid* (Introduction to the Jurisprudence of Holland)[56] as well as his comprehensive commentary on the Sermon on the Mount that later grew into a full Biblical commentary that is still considered by many Biblical scholars today among the best of its time.[57] During his captivity in Loevesteyn he also prepared a Dutch-language apology of the Christian religion, which was published in 1622 as *Bewys van den Waeren Godsdienst* (Proof of the Christian Religion).[58] This text was later reworked into a Latin treatise better known as *De Veritate Religionis Christianae* (On the Truth of the Christian Religion) and published in 1627. To this day, the latter remains one of Grotius' best-known and most frequently published works.[59]

After escaping lifetime imprisonment in 1621 by hiding in a book chest, Grotius fled the Netherlands and headed for Paris.[60] His contacts at the court of King Louis XIII of France helped him receive an annual stipend of 3,600 guilders,[61] but this amount was insufficient and payments were reportedly irregular and usually tardy.[62] Here he prepared within the relatively short period of 18 months his historically seminal *De Iure Belli ac Pacis Libri Tres* (Three Books on the Law of War and Peace), that work for which Grotius is best remembered by scholars and researchers in present times. The first Latin edition was published in Paris in 1625, with revised and enhanced editions prepared by the author over a course of almost two decades.

The publication of *De Iure Belli* also marks the year that Frederick Henry succeeded Maurice as stadholder of Holland and Zeeland, and Grotius held out serious hopes for a restoration of his good name under the new leadership. Negotiations were evidently under way, but they appear to have failed — not because of an unwillingness to readmit Grotius to the Dutch Republic, but because the fugitive former official was convinced of his complete innocence and demanded nothing less than a full apology, a demand that was not and most certainly could not be fulfilled. Grotius briefly returned to the Netherlands in 1631, but with no apology forthcoming and rehabilitation denied, he decided to flee the country for a second time after a bounty was put on his head. Between 1632 and 1634 he lived in the Hanseatic port city of Hamburg, where he forged critical contacts with the Swedish chancellor and statesman Axel Oxenstierna.[63] This contact proved important for the course of the Dutch luminary's subsequent career. After the death of her king, Gustavus Adolphus at the battle of Lützen (1632), Sweden's position as a leading military power in the German lands quickly began to wane. Clearly weakened by the course of developments, Oxenstierna now sided with France opening a new and conclusive phase of the Thirty Years War. Grotius appeared to be the man of the moment. In 1635, in the Rheinish city of Mainz or Worms, he was appointed Swedish ambassador to France after earlier foreswearing his Dutch citizenship.[64] He returned to Paris, this time not to seek asylum from persecution in the Netherlands, but as a diplomat and ambassador of Sweden's Oxenstierna and the young Queen Christina, daughter of the late Gustavus Adolphus. Grotius' career as a diplomat in this crucial period of Franco-Swedish cooperation was problematic and should not be considered his finest hour. Some controversy accompanied his appointment to this important position, and he soon found himself progressively isolated and ignored by politicians in France and beyond. A sense of embitterment is reflected in his correspondence written during his second period in Paris. Intellectually, he engrossed himself with plans already announced in his religious treatise *Meletius* of 1611, namely, the physical reunification of Western Christendom. He also completed and published in the early 1640s his *Annotationes in Novum et Veterum Testamentum* (Annotations to the New and Old Testament) and indulged in a written "debate" with Johannes de Laet of the Dutch West India Company between 1642–3 — the 150th anniversary of Christopher Columbus' "discovery" of the New World — over the origin of the Amerindians.[65] These and related publications did not necessarily place Grotius in good standing with his superiors in Stockholm, but he did exercise self-restraint so as not to threaten or compromise the wider geo-strategic, political and economic interests of Sweden. This self-restraint is evidenced by the attentiveness with which he monitored the reception of John Selden's treatise *Mare Clausum* (The Closed Sea, the "Un-Free" Sea) in the Hanseatic towns as well as in Denmark after its first publication in 1635.[66] He certainly passed on a unique opportunity to pen a reply to Selden's learned exposé and may have forfeited this opportunity for fear that he may compromise Sweden's own claims to *dominium* of the Baltic Sea.[67] He made his position clear in a letter to Paul du May, the Sieur of Saint-Aubin and on 10 August 1635: "Respondeant Batavi. Ego nunc Suedica curo" (Let the Dutch reply! I am now concerned with Swedish affairs).[68] In any case, Grotius correctly foresaw a deterioration in Anglo-Dutch relations and (wrongly, as it turned out) surmised in his correspondence that Pieter Cunaeus, a friend and professor at Leiden University, would receive a formal commission by the Dutch States General to pen a reply to Selden. As it turned out, it was Dirk Graswinckel and not Cunaeus, who would receive that commission.[69]

Once exalted as a miracle child who — as is widely assumed — from an early age unshakably knew what he stood for, the mature Grotius was more self-critical and distanced himself from some of his early writings, including specifically *Mare Liberum* and *De Antiquitate Reipublicae Batavicae*, pieces he had written in the services of the Dutch Republic that later had forsaken him. He also distanced himself from the impassioned poetry of his youth and was incensed when a Leiden-based publisher reprinted a collection of his poems without his permission.

Grotius' efforts at reconciling the Christian churches may have been manifestations of deeper religious struggles experienced at an intimately private level. In his earlier years he might have verbally lashed out at the second generation of church Reformers, but he now began to criticise the first Reformers for simply having gone too far, and for having shattered both the spiritual and physical unity of the Western Church. The argument was advanced some decades ago that in the later years of his life Grotius leaned heavily towards Roman Catholicism.[70] It cannot be ascertained with any certainty whether he was really about to make a formal "conversion", but it is clear that, like so many intellectuals of his day, he seriously contemplated denominational reorientation on more than one occasion. The single most important testimony to this effect is found in a letter

Illus. 12 Printed portrait of the mature Hugo Grotius. (Taken from the 1659 edition of Grotius' *Annales et Historiae de Rebus Belgicis* [Annals and Histories of the Low Countries] printed by Johannes Blaeu in Amsterdam in 1659. Private collection, Peter Borschberg)

addressed to his brother, Willem de Groot, dated 26 July 1642, in which he raised the issue of his possible reunion with Rome alongside additional personal afterthoughts of similar "religious reunions" by other scholars and intellectuals. But in the postscript he readily confessed to his younger brother Willem: "Still, I'm not in a hurry."[71]

By 1645 Sweden's finances were being stretched to the limit by the war effort in, and occupation of, lands in the Holy Roman Empire. Word also had it that the crown of Sweden wished to save on the high costs of maintaining a permanent ambassador to France.[72] It is said that Grotius hoped to take on work for the French side, but in order to smoothen the transition between government employers and before assuming any new formal appointment, he wished to discuss matters with Chancellor Oxenstierna in person.[73] A Swedish subject now aged 62, Grotius made his way to the capital city Stockholm via Rotterdam, Amsterdam, Hamburg, Lübeck, Wismar and Kalmar. In his letters he reported that city officials and magistrates received him cordially and often with great honours. In Stockholm, Grotius conferred with Oxenstierna and was also granted by Queen Christina a lump sum pension amounting to 10,000 riksdaler as well as a gold chain inset with precious stones appraised at another 4,000 ducats.[74] He declined an offer to become a royal councilor in Stockholm as he may have already hedged plans to proceed first to the great Hanseatic port of Lübeck and later perhaps also assist Henri d'Orléans, the Duc de Longueville, in Münster in negotiating for peace in Europe. As is known, these latter efforts resulted, within three years, in the landmark Treaties of Osnabrück and Münster that together form the backbone of the so-called "Peace of Westphalia" or "Westphalian Settlement".[75]

Grotius left Stockholm on 11 August 1645 on a sloop that carried him southwards to the nearby port of Dalarö, and the island Öland was sighted two days later. The vessel on which Grotius travelled was caught in a terrible storm in the night of 15 to 16 August and suffered serious damage. The midmast broke and the sails had been ripped to shreds. The passengers and crew were rescued and taken to shore in eastern Pomerania, about 80 kilometres from the Baltic port of Gdańsk (Danzig).[76] Grotius and his servants headed westward by cart, but by the time they reached the outskirts of Szczecin (Stettin), Grotius had already fallen seriously ill. He continued his onward journey through Pasewalk and Anklam and Greifswald, bypassing Stralsund, and reached the Baltic port of Rostock on Saturday, 26 August 1645. There he passed away in the night to Monday, 28 August 1645.[77] There are several stories surrounding his final hours in his chamber at the Grosse Wasserstrasse 17 in Rostock. In his recently published and meticulously researched biography, Henk Nellen recounts three stories surrounding the death of the Dutch luminary, but leaves it to his readers which one they prefer to believe.[78] Whether his death can be associated with shunning an intellectual engagement with the local Lutheran pastor Johannes Quistorp on questions of theological interest, or whether Grotius passed away at the stroke of midnight — peacefully or otherwise — is frankly of little relevance in the present context. His heart and intestines were buried *in situ* in Rostock, and his embalmed corpse was brought back to his native Holland. Grotius' mortal remains rest in the *Nieuwe Kerk* (New Church) in Delft.

This biography has provided a synopsis of the different contexts, landmarks, twists and turns in Grotius' personal and intellectual development. While attempting to provide as complete a picture as possible, emphasis has been placed on his early career and development, that coincides with his steep political career in the Dutch Republic leading up to his arrest and incarceration in August 1618. In the following chapter I turn to examine more closely the period between 1605 and 1615 bearing these questions in mind: How did Grotius become involved with the issues of VOC trade in the East Indies? Taking into consideration his early treatises, drafts and a plethora of reading notes surviving in public collections in the Netherlands — and beyond — what were the issues he contended with intellectually, and thus stand out as being especially important? Bearing these questions in mind, I now turn to answer them in the following chapter.

CHAPTER 2

Grotius, Johor and Trade in the East Indies

This chapter is divided into three sections and draws attention to a series of documents and papers that trace their authorship or original possession to Grotius. Some of them remain little known or, indeed, unpublished.[1]

The first section provides a historical account of how the celebrated humanist became involved in the issues concerning Dutch commercial and political expansion into Southeast Asia. To this end I shall adduce both little-known as well as some key documents, unpublished drafts, fragments reading notes which are primarily written in Latin and Dutch.

The second section is specifically dedicated to Grotius' defence of the *Santa Catarina* incident and places a special focus on its relevance to Dutch-Johor cooperation in the early 17th century. On the basis of published and unpublished materials, a case will be made that the VOC's negotiations with the king of Johor were crucial in stimulating Grotius to formulate his ideas on the issues of sovereignty, trade, just war and alliance-making. In this context a link will be established between the published treatise *De Iure Praedae Commentarius* (Commentary on the

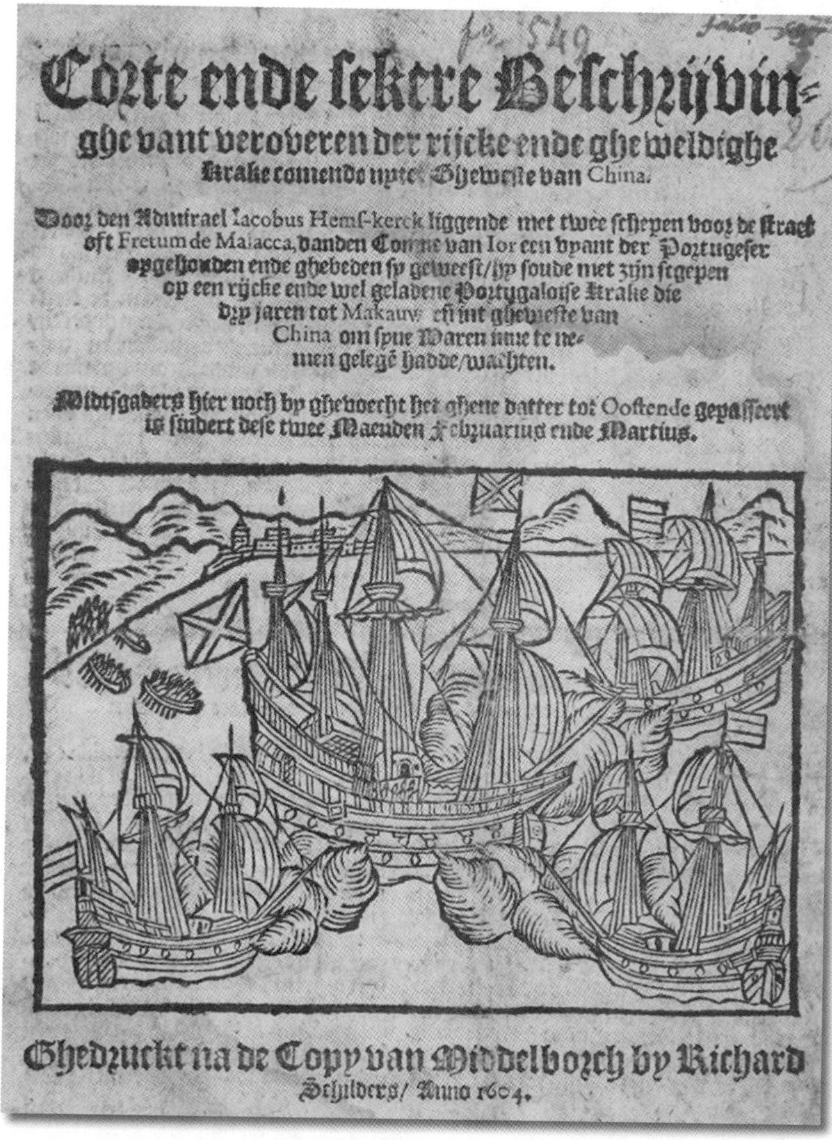

Corte ende sekere Beschrijvinghe vant veroveren der rijcke ende gheweldighe Krake comende uyte Ghewesten van China.

Door den Admirael Iacobus Hemſ-kerck liggende met twee schepen voor de Straet oft Fretum de Malacca, vanden Coninc van Ior een vyant der Portugeser opgehouden ende ghebeden sy geweest/hy soude niet zijn scepen op een rijcke ende wel geladene Portugaloise Krake die by jaren tot Makauw, en int ghewesten van China om syne Waren inne te nemen gelegē hadde/wachten.

Midtsgaders hier noch by ghevoecht het ghene datter tot Oostende gepasseert is sindert dese twee Maenden Februarius ende Martius.

Ghedruckt na de Copy van Middelborch by Richard Schilders/ Anno 1604.

Illus. 13 Title page of the rare pamphlet *Corte en sekere Beschrijvinghe vant veroveren der rijcke ende gheweledighe Kracke comende uyte Ghewesten van China* (Short and Accurate Description of the Seizure of the Rich and Mighty Carrack Coming from the Region of China) printed by Richard Schilders in Middelburg in 1604. The picture shows the Portuguese carrack *Santa Catarina* under attack by the three smaller ships of Jacob van Heemskerk on 25 February 1603, off the coast of Singapore. Troops of the Johor monarch are watching the event from the shore as well as from three rowed galleys. The landscape in the background is pure imagination, but the question remains whether the city at the top left is meant to be *Singapura.* (Amsterdam University Library, OTM pfl. K 26)

Law of Prize and Booty) and the hitherto unpublished fragment *De Societate Publica cum Infidelibus* (On Public Society with Non-Christians).[2] At the same time, the exploration of various issues surrounding trade and alliance-making will serve as an original contribution to the history of Dutch-Johor relations before the ratification of the first formal alliance in 1606.

The third and final section of the chapter examines how the concepts originally developed in the context of the *Santa Catarina* incident in general and specifically in his justification of Dutch-Johor cooperation, were subsequently reformulated and refined at the Anglo-Dutch maritime and colonial conferences of 1613 and 1615. These set Anglo-Dutch relations in the East Indies on conflicting paths and help explain the tension that subsequently arose between the two nascent colonial powers, as well as the different policies that they pursued in conducting trade and colonisation.

Grotius, the Seizure of the *Santa Catarina* and East India Trade

On 25 February 1603, a large Portuguese-flagged vessel, the *Santa Catarina*, was attacked by the Dutch captain (later Admiral) Jacob van Heemskerk. The incident took place in the Johor River estuary between the eastern coast of Singapore and the Johor mainland near present-day Pengerang. This area is known from early modern Dutch materials as the *Hoek van Barbukit* (Hook of Berbukit [see map on p. 6]).[3] The Portuguese carrack is described as a vessel of about 1,400 tons.[4] The attack by the Dutch continued for most of the day. As evening fell, the *Santa Catarina* was seriously damaged and had sprung several leaks. The crew agreed to surrender under the condition that they be set free. Heemskerk brought all safely to shore, an act for which he was subsequently thanked by the *câmara* (city council) of Melaka as well as the Portuguese colony's governor Fernão d'Albuquerque (see appendices 7, 10).[5]

The seizure of the *Santa Catarina* became a controversial incident, irritating the Iberian powers over European competition and their geo-strategic vulnerability in the Indies,[6] causing some tension in the Dutch alliance with England and upsetting certain circles of stakeholders over the recourse to (unnecessary) violence.[7] It was perhaps only symptomatic of the blurred divide between permissible commercial practices and outright piracy. In a decision cast on 9 September 1604, Amsterdam's Admiralty Court recalled the harrowing experiences of the van Heemskerk expedition, the atrocities previously inflicted on the Dutch by the Portuguese, as well as the crimes and injustices committed against the peoples of the East Indies.[8] In view of the evidence adduced in support of the incident, the Admiralty Court resolved that the vessel had been lawfully seized and its cargo confiscated in an act of war.[9] Van Heemskerk escaped what — theoretically at least — could have amounted to a charge of piracy.

It was about this time (September 1604) that the young and talented lawyer Hugo Grotius was asked to write an official account — or should one rather say official justification — of van Heemskerk's actions. The fruit of his labours is an expansive treatise in Latin, now known as *De Iure Praedae Commentarius* (Commentary on the Law of Prize and Booty) the original of which was retrieved and published only in the second half of the 19th century. This treatise initiates Grotius' prolonged engagement with the commercial and political affairs of the East Indies up to his arrest and incarceration in August 1618.

While not published at the time, the manuscript proved useful during the tense truce negotiations with Spain just a few years later (1608–9). It is well known that Spain sought, as one of the conditions of the truce, to impose the complete withdrawal of Dutch merchants from the East Indies.[10] It was precisely over the issues of religion and the Indies trade that talks between the Dutch and Spanish broke down (albeit temporarily) in August 1608. The continued state of war outside of Europe, the disappointingly low profits from the East India trade as well as the increased competition, notably from the English, brought Grotius to his next engagement with East Indian affairs, namely, the two colonial and maritime conferences of 1613 and 1615.[11]

Grotius was deputised to the London conference of 1613 at short notice,[12] and historians have long speculated about the ulterior agenda behind his embassy.[13] Perhaps no one but the English ambassador to the Hague, Ralph Winwood, immediately realised that the Hollander's deputation to the London negotiations spelt serious trouble.[14] This is evidenced by the tone and wording of his despatch to King James I/VI of 6 April 1613.[15] It was against this backdrop that Grotius was seen even by foreign diplomats in London as the leading member of the Dutch delegation.[16]

Illus. 14 Portrait of James I/VI. From the 1647 edition of Emmanuel van Meteren's *Commentariën ofte Memoriën van den Nederlantsen Staet, Handel, Oorloghen ende Gheschiedenissen van onsen Tyden* (Commentaries or Memoirs concerning the Dutch State, Trade and War and the History of our Times). (The Hague, Koninklijke Bibliotheek, 1790 A 122)

Yet his reputation as an effective diplomat left something to be desired,[17] even if other researchers have recently declared his performances at the colonial conferences of 1613 and 1615 "the high tide of Grotius' political career" that showcase "the best example of his diplomatic talents".[18] The tone for the whole conference was set at the opening of the negotiations with the presentation of credentials and a speech held before the king on 6 April 1613 (see appendix 17 for the full Latin text with English translation). The whole process, according to the Dutch envoy in London, Noël Caron, "lasted a bit too long", referring here especially to Grotius' opening address.[19] His pedantic attitude displayed during the negotiations in London was certainly remembered years later with considerable acrimony.[20]

The underlying objective of the 1613 conference was to settle ongoing disputes between the Dutch and the English over the colonial enterprise in Asia.[21] English merchants complained about ill treatment by the Dutch in the Indies and accused the VOC of excluding them from participating in the East Indian trade. Their objective in London was not so much to seek reparation for damages suffered arising from this exclusion, but rather to obtain guarantees from the Dutch that they would be able to conduct trade freely and without hindrance.[22]

A plan to "merge" or "unite" the Dutch and English East India Companies — a concrete scheme for which had been devised in 1612 — was one of the more intriguing points on the agenda. The purpose of this merger, which never materialised but was supplanted by a cooperation agreement,[23] was to persuade the English to contribute towards the cost of maintaining an armed presence in the East Indies.[24] It is difficult to ascertain how seriously the English considered this proposal, as it was clearly conceived by the Dutch to inject fresh capital into the VOC which struggled to achieve long-term profitability.[25] Irrespective of these considerations, the merger issue was variously considered over a period of approximately six years and represents a curious chapter in the history of the two companies that could have doubtlessly changed the course of world history. Had the merger been approved, resulting in a united Anglo-Dutch East India Company, the political nature of the English and Dutch colonial enterprise in Asia, the Americas and Africa would most certainly have been very different.

As history would have it, the English could not be persuaded of the merits of such a merger. They certainly could not identify with the sense of frustration expressed by members of the Dutch delegation, who

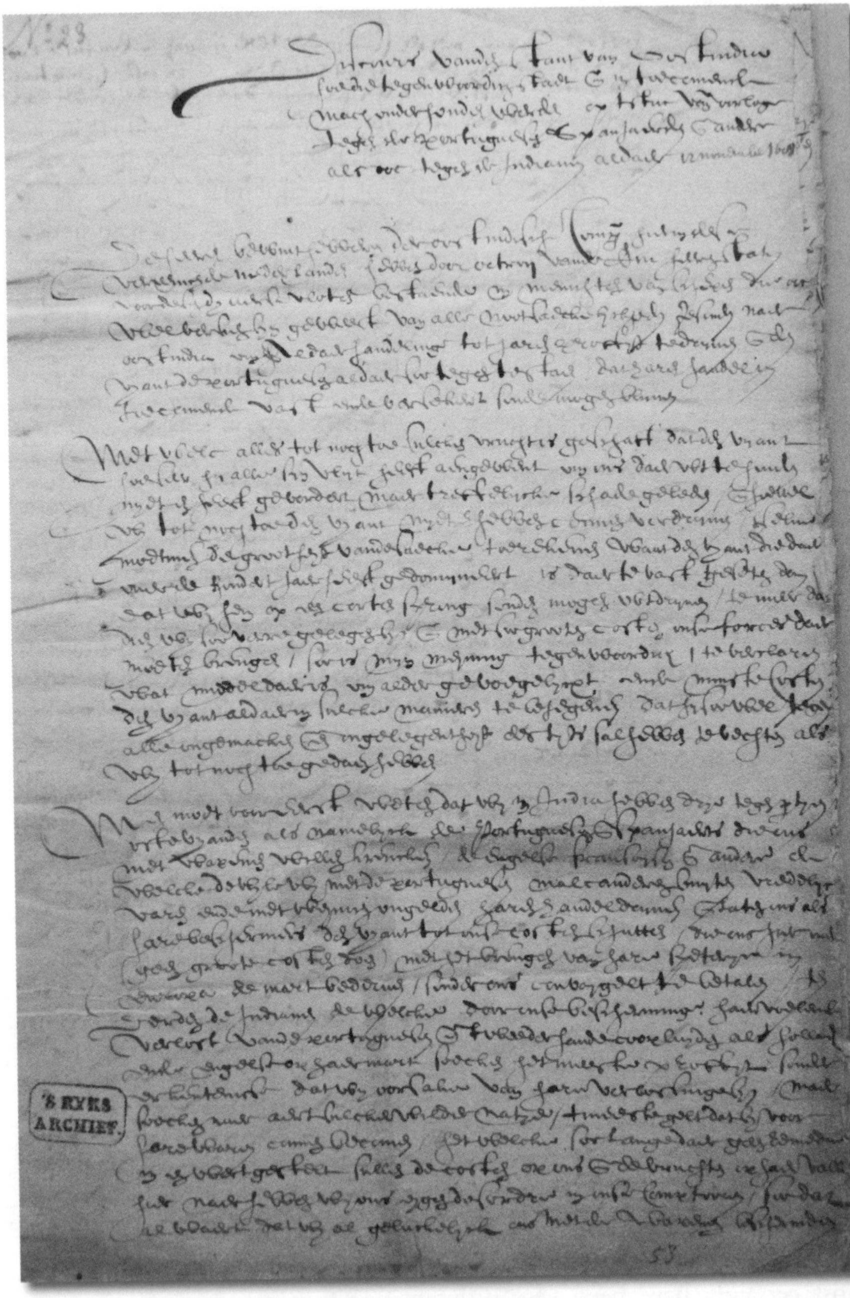

Illus. 15 First page of Admiral Cornelis Matelieff de Jonge's epistolary memorial *Discours van den stant van Oost Indiën* (Discourse on the State of the East Indies) written on his return to the Netherlands in 1608. (The Hague, Nationaal Archief, Archief Oldenbarnevelt, no. 3104, fol. 53 recto)

repeatedly reminded their English counterparts of the high costs incurred by maintaining an armed presence in the East[26] as well as "defending the natives" against Spanish and Portuguese advances.[27] Grotius' memorable line from his opening speech of 1613 — that there could be "no peace among nations without armies, no armies without pay, and no pay without tributes" (see appendix 17) — summarises the Dutch position at this first meeting in London.

The colonial and maritime conference of 1615 was convened in the Hague and revived problems that had been left unresolved. It also addressed the Greenland fishery dispute.[28] Access of the English merchants to marketplaces in the East Indies remained one of the core issues, as did the possible merger of the two East India Companies.

Grotius' engagement with the *Santa Catarina* incident, as well as his high-level participation at the two conferences of 1613 and 1615, gave him a hands-on working experience with the political and commercial dynamics of early 17th-century Southeast Asia. His knowledge, however, was largely second-hand, and he owed much to the personal experience of seasoned VOC officers such as Admiral Matelieff and almost certainly also Jacob Boreel of Middelburg. Matelieff made an appearance together with Grotius when extending a warm welcome to the English delegates on alighting in Rotterdam for the 1615 conference. Matelieff accompanied the English delegates as far as Delft.[29] As will be argued in chapter 4, it is highly improbable that Grotius ever immersed himself with Asian legal systems, and his working knowledge of commercial practices prevalent in the Southeast Asian theatre derived from the epistolary memorials of Matelieff.[30] These may have served as a blueprint for the early VOC, and judging by the surviving correspondence between the two men, Matelieff appears to have used Grotius to receive an *entrée* to, and gain the attention of, senior statesman Johan van Oldenbarnevelt.[31] The conclusion of several treaties and alliances of war with Asian rulers during the first two decades of the 17th century may be traced, in one way or other, to aspects of the theoretical and legal ground assumed and advocated by the Dutch humanist.[32] This should not surprise, for one finds various draft treaties among Grotius' East India papers that are addressed to, or at least intended for, individual Southeast Asian monarchs, including importantly also the King of Johor. (See the image of a draft letter to the King of Johor on p. 155.)

The VOC, the *Santa Catarina* and the King of Johor

The second part of this chapter will bring the *Santa Catarina* incident and the manuscript written by Grotius, known today as *De Iure Praedae Commentarius*, into closer association with several related documents, some of which remain unpublished or sparsely known. A closer examination of these will provide a deeper understanding of the implications arising from the policy that the Hollander developed and advocated. Focus shall be placed on the VOC's negotiations and commercial relations with Johor before Matelieff concluded two treaties with Raja Bongsu and King 'Ala'uddin in 1606 (see appendix 14). These not only assume a special role within the conceptual parameters staked out by Grotius in *De Iure Praedae*, but also can be brought into closer association with the hitherto unpublished fragment *De Societate Publica cum Infidelibus*.[33] In the latter manuscript dating almost certainly from the first decade of the 17th century, Grotius set out to explore a series of issues that bear a direct relationship to the early commercial and political expansion of the VOC into Asia.

Grotius' Account of Dutch-Johor Relations Before the Treaty of 1606 as Described in *De Iure Praedae*

Grotius' account of Dutch-Johor relations up to the ratification of their alliance in 1606 should be understood against the backdrop of two broader themes that represent the core of his *De Iure Praedae*: first, the theories of the just war and the rightful seizure of booty in chapters 1–10; and second, in chapters 11–15, the history of specific attempts on the part of the Portuguese to establish and preserve (by force) a trading monopoly in the Eastern hemisphere. This monopoly the Portuguese asserted, was premised on the basis of discovery, first occupation (*terra nullius*), worldly and spiritual donation, as well as the law of war. Dutch incursions into the exclusive trading zones claimed by the Portuguese, the seizure of the *Santa Catarina* and the theoretical justification of this incident should be seen as an effort to undermine Portuguese claims to dominion over vast pelagic spaces in the Atlantic and Indian Oceans.

Chapter 14 of *De Iure Praedae*, describes how the VOC and the King of Johor entered into an alliance of war against their common enemy, the Portuguese.[34] When Jacob van Heemskerk and the three vessels under his command were about to return to Europe, he was approached by Raja

Bongsu (alias Raja Seberang or Raja di Ilir), who acted as emissary of his brother, King 'Ala'uddin Ri'ayat Shah III of Johor.[35] The monarch let van Heemskerk be informed that his territory was open to the Dutch for trade and could offer any produce that they might be looking for.[36]

When the Portuguese learned of the friendly diplomatic relations between the Dutch and Johor, Portuguese Melaka hastily dispatched an emissary to the King of Johor. His mission was very clear: he was to incite friction with the Dutch; and should this fail, threaten Johor with war. According to sources perused by Grotius,[37] the king saw through this deception and informed the emissary that he had not experienced the Dutch in the ways described to him by the Portuguese.[38] Should they have any old scores to settle with the Dutch, the monarch opined, this was of no real concern to him and was certainly not his problem.[39] Shortly after the emissary returned to Melaka, the Portuguese equipped three warships and four or five foists that ravaged the settlements along the coasts of Johor, massacred civilians and laid siege to the capital city.[40] According to other accounts, this city was Batu Sawar, Johor's royal residence and administrative centre located in the upper reaches of the Johor River (see map on p. 6).[41]

The Johorese sought the assistance of van Heemskerk, who had moved on to the island of Tioman. The Dutch helped repel the Portuguese forces.[42] These developments led to the seizure of the *Santa Catarina* on 25 February 1603.[43] As is known, the carrack was captured after a fierce battle that lasted for most of the hours of daylight.[44] Yet there is one aspect of this seizure that is curious and served as a key argument in underscoring the legality of what on hindsight was an incredibly rich prize. Grotius claimed that the King of Johor himself was present throughout the battle that took place at sea between the Dutch vessels and the *Santa Catarina*.[45] On the basis of this claim, he concluded that it was seized directly under the king's auspices. Van Heemskerk's letter to the directors of the United Amsterdam Company of 27 August 1603, mentioned nothing about the presence of any of the Johor "royals" aboard the Dutch ships while engaging the *Santa Catarina*.[46] But there is additional evidence cited by van Ittersum indicating the presence of King 'Ala'uddin, Raja Bongsu and many *orang kaya* aboard the Dutch flagship *Witte Leeuw* (White Lion) during the exchange of fire with the Portuguese carrack.[47] According to yet another source — François Valentijn's *Nieuw en Oud Oost-Indië* (New and Old East Indies) that generally paraphrases from collections of early Dutch voyages to Asia — it was not the king, but his younger brother, Raja Bongsu, who was present aboard van Heemskerk's flagship during the attack.[48]

The Principles of Grotius' Forward Policy Based on this Case Study of Johor

As mentioned earlier, two broader guidelines for the VOC's forward policy were formulated for the Asian theatre. First, Grotius not only denied the Portuguese a commercial monopoly, but in view of the authority they claimed for themselves, he shared the vision of the company's directors, the Heren XVII, to stifle further expansion of Iberian political and mercantile interests.[49] Second, in order to contain Portuguese and Spanish commercial and political influence in Asia, it was necessary to acknowledge the full sovereign capacity of the indigenous rulers. Unlike the Portuguese, who — against the principles of the law of nations — allegedly sought to assert their monopoly on the legal foundation of first discovery and occupation or even papal donation, the Dutch would secure their trading privileges by establishing a system of exclusive trade and mutual assistance.[50]

De Iure Praedae's defence of van Heemskerk's actions as a whole, and specifically its account of Dutch-Johor relations during the period 1602–3, provides a rewarding case study on the genesis and implementation of these twin policies.

The first and most basic assertion advanced in *De Iure Praedae* is that the King of Johor was a truly independent overlord in whom all the rights of sovereignty are vested:[51]

> There is in [the East] Indi[ies] a kingdom called Johor, which has long been considered a sovereign principality, so that its ruler clearly possessed the authority necessary to conduct a public war.

The second concerns the unjust impediments imposed by the Portuguese on the Johor monarch. In *De Iure Praedae*, as in his later works, Grotius established his case that the Portuguese violated the sovereign authority of this particular Southeast Asian overlord and also broke accepted conventions (and even the law of nature) by blocking the use of sea routes to and from Asia.

The third point concerns the right to seize booty of war. In the case of the *Santa Catarina*, this right belonged not so much to the Dutch, as to the King of Johor:[52]

> ... [I]t is certain that the cause of the King of Johor was exceedingly just. For what could be more inequitable than a prohibition imposed by a mercantile people [the Portuguese] upon a free king [the ruler of Johor] to prevent him from carrying on trade with another people [the Dutch]?

As will be discussed in greater detail in chapter 3, the denial of free communication and consequently also of free trade, as Francisco de Vitoria contended, provided in itself a sufficient legal foundation upon which to initiate and wage a just public war.[53] Yet the prohibition in question not only assumed the form of a verbal admonition, but also involved the application of force, which Grotius considered, in line with established rules,[54] as a sufficient cause by its own merit upon which to wage a just public war:[55]

> The King of Johor and the [East Indian] nations elsewhere mentioned by us, are being ravaged by the Portuguese with slaughter and rapine under no other pretext than this, that the said ruler and nations granted admittance to the Dutch [to conduct trade]. ... Therefore, since the injury in question was inflicted upon the King of Johor with official authorization [of the Portuguese], and since he was also formally threatened with war as the penalty for his failure to comply with their order, and since war was forthwith begun against him, he rightly regarded the Portuguese — collectively and individually — as enemies; for no one will deny that those who have decreed war against us are indeed our enemies.[56]

Fourth, the king is said to have acted upon "excellent motives" to "uphold his sovereign rights" and "protect his subjects".[57] At this juncture, the question emerges as to how the seizure of the richly laden *Santa Catarina* could be deemed legally permissible, especially since the captain and his crew were Dutch and the legal right to seize booty of war clearly belonged to the King of Johor.

The king's brothers Raja Bongsu and Raja Siak approached van Heemskerk, first in Patani and later in Tioman.[58] Grotius deemed it significant to highlight that it was not the Dutch who, driven by revenge, resolved to lend assistance to the Johor ruler. Van Heemskerk and the

Dutch were asked (and thus invited) to participate as allies in the Johor monarch's just public war against Portugal.[59]

Grotius was fully aware that, while his line of argument here was not unacceptable, it was to most European ears certainly unconventional. During that age, Christian powers that allied with Islamic sovereigns still could raise the eyebrows of court lawyers in Europe, although in the East Indies the Portuguese — unlike the Spaniards — had informally dropped their anti-Islamic attitude for the sake of maximising profits.[60] The French King Francis I entered into an alliance of war with Ottoman Sultan Süleyman the Magnificent in 1535 and justified this alliance to Pope Paul III on the grounds of a shared humanity with the Turks.[61] This treaty is historically significant insofar as it marks a turning point in relations of European powers with the Ottoman Empire and helped pave the way for future treaty-making with Islamic overlords.[62] Grotius (perhaps conveniently and deliberately) failed to mention this controversial pact in this context. Rather, he supported his claims by reference to a multitude of sources.[63] It is against this uneasy background of Christians allying with non-Christians for the purpose of war,[64] and particularly with Islamic rulers, that the following elaboration on the Dutch-Johor alliance should be understood:[65]

> Or do we perhaps believe that we have nothing in common with persons who have not accepted the Christian faith? Such a belief would be very far removed from the pious doctrine of Augustine, who declares (in his interpretation of the precept of Jesus whereby we are bidden to love our neighbours) that the term "neighbours" obviously includes *every human being*. Moreover, the famous parable of the good Samaritan which is contained in the Gospels, teaches us that the obligations of humane conduct are not dispelled on the grounds of religion.[66] Accordingly, not only is it universally admitted that the protection of infidels from injury (even from injury by other Christians) is never unjust, but it is furthermore maintained, by authorities who have examined this particular point, that alliances and treaties with infidels may in many cases be justly contracted for the purpose of defending one's own rights, too. Such a course of action was adopted (so we are told) by Abraham, Isaac, David, Salomon and the Maccabees.[67]

The passage represents an effort to defuse possible objections to the Dutch-Johor alliance on the grounds of religious and cultural incompatibility.[68] It is with regard to such considerations of mutual fitness that he was able to advance the following important proposition:[69] "[T]he entrance of the Dutch into the war as allies of the King of Johore was permissible."

As allies in war, the Dutch and the Johorese initiated joint efforts to repel the Portuguese invaders. The attack launched on the *Santa Catarina* enabled the king to recover the losses inflicted on him by the Portuguese, to which he was arguably entitled as a result of his waging a just public war. The seizure was also intended to disrupt the conduct of trade between Macao and Melaka by targeting maritime traffic between the two Portuguese-held port cities.

As indicated, Grotius emphasised the presence of the king's brother, Raja Bongsu, aboard van Heemskerk's flagship *Witte Leeuw*. It is this supervisory presence in the joint operations against the *Santa Catarina* that legitimised the seizure of the vessel as a prize in the king's just public war against Portugal. Not only did the plunder of the Lusitanian vessel take place under the direct auspices of the Johor monarch (or his officially designated representatives such as Raja Bongsu), but the action was conducted in his name:[70]

> … [F]rom every standpoint the war was just both for the King of Johore, as well as for the Dutch as defender of that King. Therefore, the seizure of prize was also just.

In his step-by-step account of events there remained one last but nevertheless crucial aspect to be clarified. By right, the prize of the joint operation belonged to the King of Johor; yet it was van Heemskerk who set off with the booty to Europe. Grotius remained — deliberately perhaps — vague on what further sequence of events might have led to these intriguing circumstances. In *De Iure Praedae*, he gave the impression of dodging potentially sensitive counter-arguments by contesting that:[71]

> … [B]y the natural law the right to that prize [that is the *Santa Catarina*] was vested in the ruler of Johore himself; but it *was also capable of becoming* a Dutch right, through a grant on his part.[72]

The lawyer Grotius was fully aware that there was no agreement that would have validated the cession of this highly valuable war booty to van

Heemskerk and the company directors. Also, the documents that were forwarded to him may not have mentioned such an arrangement, although it is clear from the reconstructions of van Ittersum that some division of the spoils took place. Grotius may not have been cognizant of this facet of the *Santa Catarina* incident. Still, it was in light of these historical circumstances that he hoped to convince his readers of the merits of the case he defended by assuming the following stance:[73]

> … [S]ince war was waged on his behalf by means of ships belonging to the East India Company, at the company's expense and at its peril, … as well as by the exertions of the company's servants, *without any formal agreement as to compensation*, the commonly accepted usages of war, confirmed by natural equity, quite clearly indicate that the prize in question was acquired *ipso iure* for the said Company.[74]

Whatever the circumstances might have been, the benefits of co-operating with this Southeast Asian monarch were very clear. Not only was Johor opened to conclude agreements of commerce and trade, Grotius confidently reasoned:[75]

> When I think of this monarch, I sincerely feel as if we are gazing upon the supreme and true reward of our voyages to the East Indies.…

Treaty- and Alliance-Making: Beyond the Case of Johor

The alliance between van Heemskerk and the King of Johor was simply one of many cases during the first decades of the 17th century. The cooperation initiated between the Dutch and the Johorese would prove formative for the history of the VOC and Dutch colonial rule in insular and mainland Southeast Asia. It would also, in the long term, tip the regional balance of power in favour of Johor. In the words of Leonard Andaya:[76] "A decisive factor in Johor's resurgence as a power in the area was its long and friendly relations with the Dutch, dating back to 1602."

On the basis of working papers, including Matelieff's memorial of August 1608,[77] it becomes clear that Grotius and the Heren XVII saw an exceptional opportunity in dealing with this Southeast Asian ruler: the Dutch — and indeed most of the early European colonial powers around 1600 — recognised the strategic and commercial significance of the southern Malay Peninsula well before the British acknowledged it with the founding of modern Singapore in 1819.[78] In fact, the VOC at one time in the early 17th century considered establishing its main Asian base, or rendezvous, in Johor.[79] Significantly, the Dutch were also aware that the Johor ruler staked a claim to the legacy of the fallen Melaka sultanate and actively supported him in his aspirations.[80] Both considerations fitted in well with the company's efforts to stem Portuguese commercial and political expansion in Southeast Asia and to cooperate more closely with Portugal's sworn enemies in the region.

As will be argued in greater depth in chapter 4, at the time Grotius drafted the text of *De Iure Praedae*, his knowledge of the political dynamics of Southeast Asia, and specifically also of Portugal's role within the Southeast Asian trading world, was limited. While it is true that the Portuguese did have a long history of on-again, off-again relations with Johor, Grotius made no reference to Luso-Johor cooperation in fending off attacks by the Acehnese.[81] He also appears to have been unfamiliar (at least at this point in time around 1604–6) with the grave problems faced by the Johor monarchs with regard to other powers in the region.[82] Apart from the Acehnese, who were recognised by the Dutch — and indeed, by other Europeans — as the mightiest regional power and sporadic marauders of Johorese possessions, the Patanese also often proved hostile in this period. One might claim that when Raja Bongsu approached van Heemskerk and later other Dutch commanders, the Johorese were not merely scouting for armed assistance in their ongoing hostilities with Portuguese Melaka, but also searching for long-term allies to help them jockey for political supremacy and moral leadership across the Malay world.[83]

As established above, the forging of the informal Dutch-Johor alliance in the years 1602 and 1603 featured four facets that are characteristic of the VOC's broader treaty system that evolved during the first two decades of the 17th century: first, recognising the full sovereignty of the Asian rulers paved the way for concluding treaties of international standing;[84] second, Portugal's curbs on Asian rulers and other European traders were deemed unacceptable; third, Portugal's efforts to undermine free trade and the sovereignty of the Asian rulers were understood to be tantamount to an act of war; and fourth, affected parties had a right to form alliances of mutual interest and self-defence to stave off unwarranted interference by the Portuguese or any other offending nation, to wage a just public war and thus rightfully seize booty or disrupt trade by recourse to violence.

The conclusion of commercial treaties and alliances of war with Johor and other rulers in insular and mainland Southeast Asia evoked further reflection by Grotius. His expanded ideas on treaty- and alliance-making between the Christian Dutch and the non-Christian peoples in Asia were brought to paper in an unpublished Latin outline, *De Societate Publica cum Infidelibus*, which appears to have been written in the first decade of the 17th century.[85] Its argument provides a link between the principles of commercial interaction, treaty- and alliance-making raised in *De Iure Praedae* and the more systematic exposition of these questions in *De Iure Belli ac Pacis Libri Tres* (Three Books on the Law of War and Peace) published in 1625.

The fragment *De Societate Publica cum Infidelibus* (Of Public Society with Non-Christians) features a general examination of the interaction between Christians and non-Christians, both at the level of individuals as well as at the level of peoples and states.[86] These inferences and parallels drawn by Grotius are characteristic of his method of discussion and analysis. The same holds true for his tendency to establish general principles and work towards more specific problems and questions.[87]

De Societate Publica cum Infidelibus draws widely on the Greek and Roman classics, the Bible, Patristic sources, as well as a series of authors from the Middle Ages to the 16th century. Arguably, his single most important source are the *Relectiones Theologicae XII* (Twelve Theological Relections) of the Spanish theologian Francisco de Vitoria.[88]

As announced in the opening lines of *De Societate Publica cum Infidelibus*, the skeletal exposé aims to "shed new light on an old problem" by examining a host of issues in a general, theoretical manner, dissociated from their original historical context.[89] There are thus no specific references to the treaties signed with, or alliances entered into, any specific ruler during this period of early Dutch overseas expansion. The case study of Johor has broadly familiarised the reader with Grotius' assumptions and concerns, as well as with his sources and framework of reference. The following underscores a direct link between the questions expounded in the case study of Johor in *De Iure Praedae* and some of the core themes addressed in *De Societate Publica cum Infidelibus*. The parallels will serve to deepen appreciation for the VOC's nascent treaty system and some of its more pressing problems.

One of the most interesting points worth exploring concerns the right of free trade. In *De Iure Praedae* Grotius explained the origins of trade

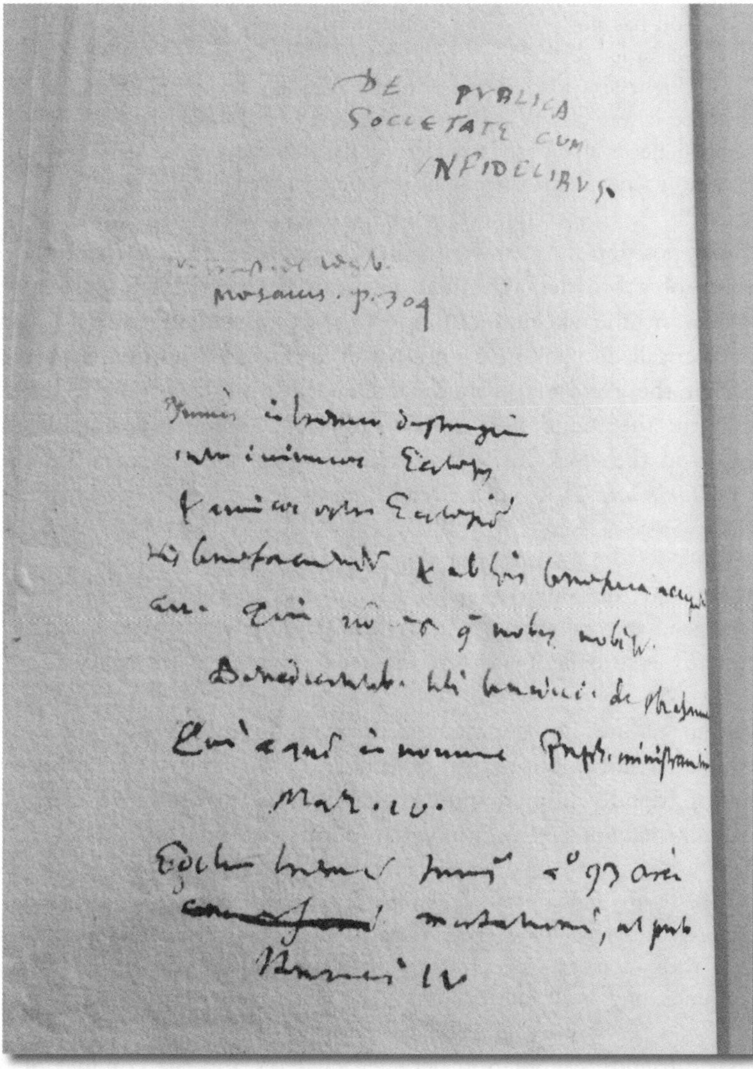

Illus. 16 Notes belonging to Grotius' draft titled here *De Publica Societate cum Infidelibus* (Of Public Society with Non-Christians). (Leiden University Library, B.P.L. 922, fol. 317 verso)

in terms of the Divine will, a necessity of life as well as Stoic premises relating to the natural sociability of mankind:[90]

> For God has not willed that nature shall supply every region with all the necessities of life; and furthermore, He has granted pre-eminence in different arts to different nations. Why are these things so, if not because it was His Will that human friendships should be fostered by mutual needs and resources, lest individuals, in deeming themselves self-sufficient, might thereby be rendered unsociable?

This position is abandoned in *De Societate Publica cum Infidelibus* in favour of a broader argument that can be reconstructed from tenets laid down in the skeletal outline. The view that all things originally belonged to all humans in common (*res communis*) is ultimately based on book 2 of the *Institutes* promulgated in the time of Emperor Justinian. These form the foundation for Grotius here and in his other writings, as well as in the works of the so-called School of Salamanca.[91] The idea of a *res communis* is confirmed and expanded upon in a reflection on Matthew, 5:45:

> The Lord Almighty makes his sun rise and set and lets it rain over the good and the wicked: whereby in using the terms sun and rain he wanted us to understand all of the goods of nature.[92]

What nature has spontaneously given to man is common to all. That includes not only physical objects, but also some of the fundamental aspects of friendly human interaction. Grotius explained his position in *De Societate Publica cum Infidelibus* as follows:[93]

> Good deeds and offices of commerce, charity, civility and utility are rightly cultivated between Christians and non-Christians or heretics. For these, too, are the products of nature and are consequently the common property of all mankind.

Basic friendly interaction between civilians and the conduct of trade are thus viewed as fundamental and natural to all human societies. There is already here a subtle but nevertheless recognisable indication that these rights may not be alienated by any other human party and that includes — without mentioning them here by name — the Portuguese and the Spaniards. Moreover, the theoretical groundwork established here fully complies with the arguments in favour of free trade and free navigation of the high seas expounded in *Mare Liberum*.

The idea of a common thing (*res communis*) also serves Grotius in the context of *De Societate Publica* for defending the sovereignty of non-Christian rulers, one of the key assumptions underpinning the web of treaties concluded by the VOC across Asia. The claims advanced are neither novel nor unfamiliar and are largely derived from the writings of Thomas Aquinas and his commentators in the 16th century, especially by the authors of the so-called School of Salamanca. Many of the problems encountered and the questions raised by the Dutch élite in these first years of overseas enterprise and expansion had already been debated and re-debated in Spain's New World dominions. The picture presented in Portugal's Estado da Índia was a very different one, and as will be argued in chapter 4, Grotius was initially unfamiliar with its legal foundations, structure and administration due to the lack of certain Portuguese sources. By default, therefore, Grotius plucked ideas and references from the works of the Thomists of the School of Salamanca who wrote specifically with an eye cast on the Spanish conquest and missionisation of the Americas.[94]

Nature, as seen, has been given to all mankind equally. What natural law has given to all mankind, Grotius argued with specific reference to the *Secunda Secundae* of Thomas Aquinas, is not affected in any way by "errors of faith".[95]

Since the Middle Ages and especially in view of the Crusades against Islam, a school of thought emerged whereby *dominium* — both public and private — was essentially denied to non-Christians on account of their "infidelity" or because they lived in a "state of sin" and were thus removed from the grace of God. This found its advocates in a series of well-established authorities, including Henry of Segusio, John Wycliff and of course Pope Clement VI. After the Reformation, even a number of Protestant thinkers could be counted among the ranks of those who held this view, especially if they relied on Wycliff, who "did not refer to infidels directly, but only indirectly by denying the exercise of sovereign power to any ruler (temporal or spiritual) not being in a state of grace".[96] Thus, when the early Spanish *conquistadores* landed in the New World and annexed lands in the name of the crown of Castile, they claimed these on the basis of discovery or first occupation (*terra nullius*) and the deep-seated belief that non-Christians had no title to public or private *dominium*.[97]

Illus. 17 Portrait of Pope Clement VI (Pierre Roger). Clement VI denied that unbelievers could possess public or private *dominium,* a passage that was also taken into the *Corpus Juris Canonicus* (Corpus of Canon Law). His statement was (ab)used, among other reasons to justify the early phase of colonial expansion that stripped native rulers of their sovereignty and property. (Private collection, Peter Borschberg)

In denying the link between infidelity and *dominium*, Grotius sided specifically with the Salmantinos and generally with the 16th-century Thomists.[98] These authors maintained that lands, possessions or public power may not be taken away from any people or ruler simply on the basis of "infidelity", that is on the grounds that they were not Christians. The reasons for this will be discussed in chapter 4. What the Iberian doctors fought out intellectually among themselves in the context of the native peoples in the Americas was then broadly projected by Grotius to the rulers of the East Indies.[99] In doing so, however, Grotius must have realised the comparison could not be fully justified.[100] In the Americas the Spaniards were dealing with peoples and religions that were believed to have been isolated from contact with other, non-American societies and thus were ignorant of the Christian religion — or, in fact, of Islam (where Jesus is acknowledged as a prophet) — prior to the arrival of missionaries from Europe. In the East, however, the Europeans were dealing with rulers who had for centuries entered into contract with Europeans and other Westerners and also had already espoused Islam, including of course the Johor monarch. The presence of Islam in the East Indies itself implied that Christianity could not have been completely unknown to exist as a religion, since references to it are made in the Qur'an. Grotius, however, chose to ignore these very different religious circumstances in this particular context.

In view of these conditions, the equality and sovereignty of the Asian rulers was thus incontestable to Grotius and was to be duly respected by the European traders and enterprises.[101] As sovereigns responsible to no higher worldly authority, the rulers also had the power and the legal capacity to conclude treaties of trade and forge alliances with the Europeans, as the King of Johor evidently did with van Heemskerk in late 1602 or early 1603.

Respecting the sovereignty of a ruler is one thing; entering into treaties of commerce and alliances of war is a different matter altogether. Recognising this, Grotius developed a set of specific arguments to this effect in *De Societate Publica cum Infidelibus*.

As has been seen, the first cornerstone in Grotius' theoretical edifice is the aforementioned idea of the *res communis* and the implications that arise therefrom. A second cornerstone is provided through the right of self-defence and the additional deliberations the Dutch humanist spin around this.[102] It is now an established view that the right of self-defence (or self-preservation) is taken by some early modern thinkers as a right of such fundamental significance that it was taken as the core natural right of man.[103] In the case of Thomas Hobbes, a contemporary of Grotius, it assumed such a central significance that it may be regarded as one of the axiomatic foundations in his doctrine of the social contract and in the theoretical edifice of his civil society as a whole.[104] In view of this primordial significance of self-defence for the humanists in the 16th and 17th centuries, Grotius advanced in *De Societate Publica* the following line of reasoning that is ultimately based on the ancient Roman jurisconsult Ulpian:[105] "The law of nature prescribes that no one should inflict evil on another, and Christ inculcates [this message] a thousand times." From this follows the first conclusion: "That it is permitted to private persons as well as to public entities to enter into pacts with non-Christians or heretics not to harm one another." This statement is subsequently elaborated upon with the following afterthought:[106] "Not only is it permitted to do good to non-Christians or heretics, in some circumstances it is often necessary." Grotius also highlighted that, while one is morally obliged and even encouraged by the Apostle Paul, to show civility and perform good works for non-Christians,[107] members of the Christian community should not be forgotten and enjoy a greater degree of charity, friendship and familiarity than non-Christians. In any case, the fundamental rule that derives from Matthew 6:33 still remains intact: "Strive first for the Kingdom of Heaven!" Any influence that might negatively affect the individual's Christian faith should be treated with great caution or, in case of doubt, perhaps simply avoided.[108]

Grotius was fully aware that his position sharply contrasted with the precepts contained in parts of the Old Testament. The Hebrews were not encouraged to mingle with any individual who was not of their faith.[109] As in the case of Thomas Aquinas and his commentators of the 16th century, casual interaction for Christians with non-Christians was seen as a matter of individual conscience and one's good judgment.[110]

It is in light of such precepts that the Christian individual and the Christian people were not only forbidden from inflicting harm, but were encouraged to do good to their non-Christian neighbours. This is understood to be a precept not of Divine Voluntarism, but of natural law and in some instances also a matter of sheer necessity. In view of these considerations Grotius justified the conduct of trade and the conclusion of alliances of war by reference to pre-Mosaic Biblical history[111] and based his case on two powerful ideas derived from Vitoria's *First Relection on the Indies*, part III, arts. 15 and 17.[112]

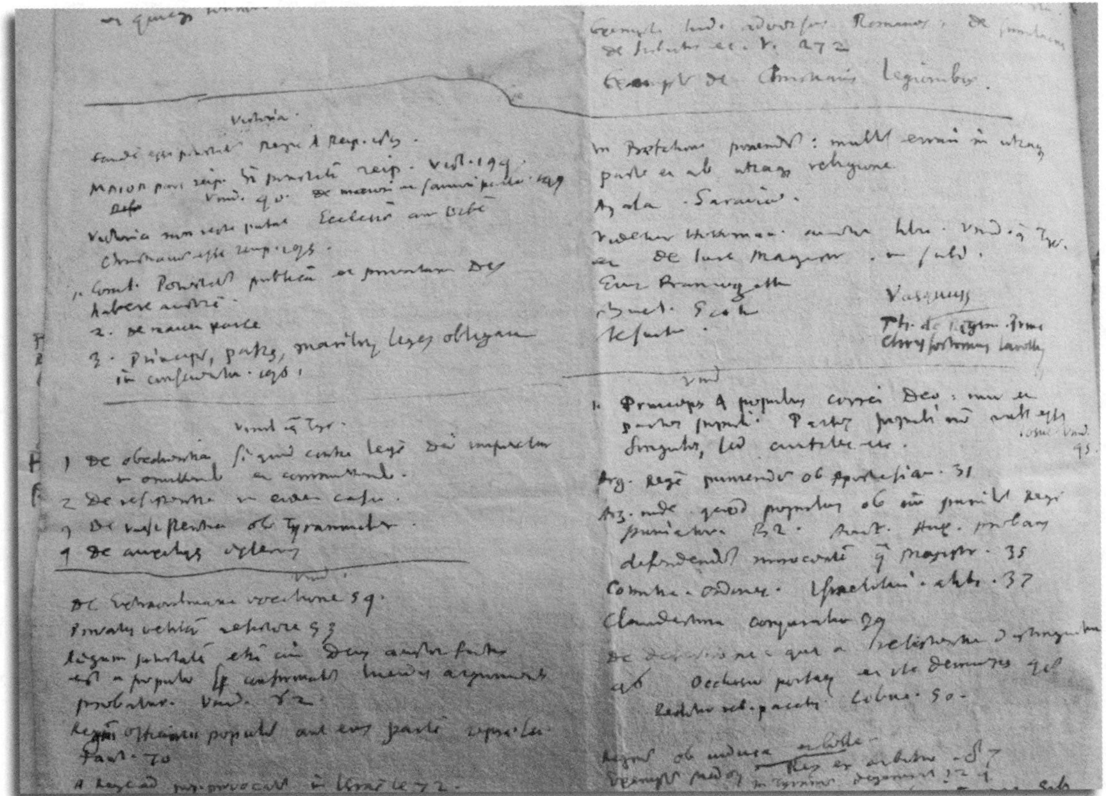

Illus. 18 Reading notes in the hand of Grotius taken from the Francisco de Vitoria's *Relectiones Theologicae XII* (Twelve Theological Relections) published in Lyon in 1557. The *relectio*, literally re-reading, was equivalent to the course roundup held at the end of an academic year at the University of Salamanca. Vitoria's original manuscripts are lost, and the texts reproduced in this collection of 12 relections are what contemporary terminology would dub student notes. (Leiden University Library, B.P.L. 922, fol. 285 verso)

In explaining how the Native Americans could have legitimately come under the *dominium* of Spain, Vitoria elaborated in section 15 on the defence of the innocent against tyranny.[113] The concept is multifaceted for Vitoria, and pertain to the defence of the innocent. Vitoria underscored his insights with the comment that all humans, Christians and non-Christians alike, have a right to protection and are to be regarded as "brothers" or "neighbours" by the Christian community. They also have a right to request the active support of the Christians against oppression from any party, including oppression from other Christians.

Adding to this, Vitoria stipulated in section 17 that there exists a right to assist one's friends and allies in emergencies, just as any sovereign has the right to call on his allies to help him fend off enemies. Vitoria relied, among others, on the authority of Cajetanus to advance his case that one may wage a just public war in the name of an ally, or rely on foreign powers to punish one's own public enemies.[114] The Biblical example of Abraham is adduced from Genesis chapter 14 to support this claim.[115]

These considerations lead us back to the justification of the Dutch-Johor alliance. There are astonishing parallels between *De Iure Praedae* and *De Societate Publica cum Infidelibus* with reference to the problem of alliance-making and religious incompatibility. It is not just the broader line of argument that rings familiar; the express reference to Vitoria's *First Relection* as well as the Biblical examples adduced in support of his reasonings, are almost identical and include the pact (*foedus*) mentioned in Genesis (21.27; 26:29) between Abraham and later Isaac with Abimelech, the pact between Jacob and his father-in-law Laban (Gen., 31:49), as well as the treaties between David and Salomon with Hiram, the King of Tyre (2. Sam., 5:11; 1. Kng. 5:12).[116]

As a result of comparing the more detailed arguments and acknowledged sources used by Grotius in *De Iure Praedae* and *De Societate Publica cum Infidelibus*, it is possible to bridge the two treatises and explain their significance against the backdrop of the VOC's early policies of trade in general, and specifically also *De Iure Praedae*'s justification of the Dutch-Johor alliance. There can be little doubt that Grotius' opinions carried a degree of authority in Dutch circles before his political downfall in 1618. Their abstraction and subsequent incorporation into book 2, chapter 15 of his monumental *De Iure Belli ac Pacis* ensured their lasting place in European and world history.

The Colonial and Maritime Conferences of 1613 and 1615 and Their Impact on Grotius' Ideas on Trade and Treaty-Making

When Grotius conceived his defence of van Heemskerk's seizure of the *Santa Catarina*, little did he realise what long-term implications his contention with the issues of war, booty, trade and alliance-making would have, not only for the history of the VOC and Dutch colonial politics in Southeast Asia, but also with regard to his own writings on interstate relations. In his later works, the luminary incorporated and subsequently refined many of the insights he had developed earlier through his exposure to the wider issues of trade, commerce and alliance-making. The insights gained in this context were developed into a more systematic theory of interstate relations that is universally applicable and is dissociated from any specific historical context. The parallels between *De Iure Praedae* and *De Iure Belli ac Pacis* are long known: the broader issues of war and peace, sovereignty and alliance-making broadly characterise both works. In *De Iure Belli ac Pacis*, however, arguments were expanded and enhanced, which can be expected from a book that reflects a mental incubation period of more than two decades. The historical influence of this mature discourse on the questions of war and peace needs no further elaboration in the context of this chapter. It is the subject of many learned contributions and has earned Grotius a prominent place among the forbearers of modern international law. Less widely known are the various stages that induced him to refine his ideas; including among other significant events, the Anglo-Dutch maritime and colonial conferences of 1613 and 1615.

When Grotius wrote his defence of van Heemskerk, the VOC was a recently founded company engaged in the East Indies trade. By pooling financial resources and capital, the VOC hoped to establish a viable basis from which to launch a better coordinated trade with the East by simultaneously forging a profitable monopoly in select commodities, as well as by thwarting the further spread of Iberian commercial and political authority in Asia. Grotius' defence of the *Santa Catarina* incident was almost certainly written with this broader underlying agenda in mind. He also shared with the VOC directors the vision of tapping into this commercial bonanza by arguing for free and unimpeded access of the company and its agents to marketplaces in the East Indies. The 21-year-old Hollander often displays an optimism

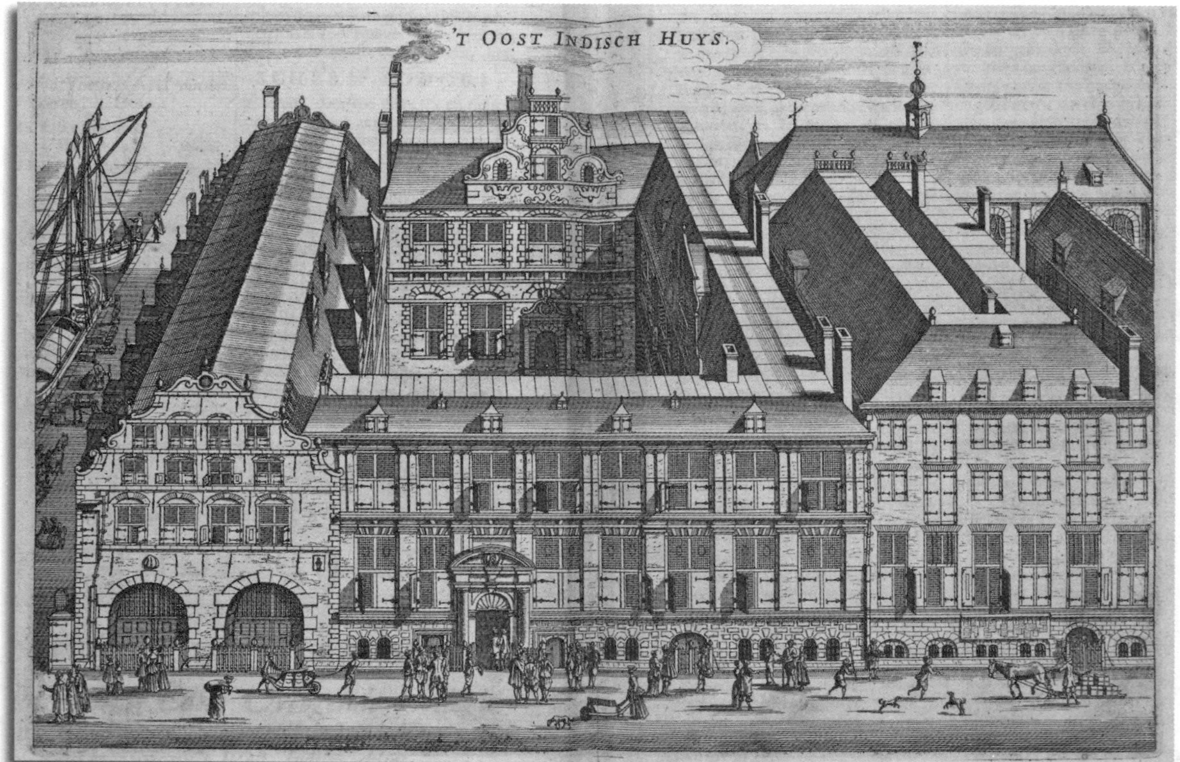

Illus. 19 The premises of the VOC in Amsterdam in the early 17th century. (From J.I. Pontanus, *Rerum et Urbis Amstelodamensium Historia* (History of City of Amsterdam) 1611. The Hague, Koninklijke Bibliotheek, 136 B 20, after p. 448)

in his defence of free trade and military alliance with Asian rulers, whose validity and reliability seemed less sure to the more mature scholar and diplomat.

What is also clear is that many of the principles Grotius advocated and the problems he addressed, specifically within the ramifications of the early Dutch-Johor cooperation, were predigested by the authors of the School of Salamanca whom he cites frequently and with a visible degree of preference.[117] What the Salmantinos debated and re-debated in their influential writings was evidently shaped by Spain's contentious colonisation of the New World. The principles developed for the setting in the (Spanish) Americas were generally applied to the East Indies, as is notably also apparent from his justification of Dutch-Johor cooperation after 1602.

The case study of Dutch-Johor cooperation has revealed four general principles that underpin support for VOC activities in the East Indies: first, the full sovereignty of the Asian rulers; second, the unjust restrictions imposed on the conduct of trade by the Portuguese and the Spaniards; third, the right of the Johor monarch to wage a just war in protection of his sovereign rights as well as commercial interests; and fourth, Johor's just war against Portugal. The Luso-Johor conflict was to be regarded as a just public war that helped legitimise the despoliation of the Portuguese carrack. In this instance the Dutch set cultural and religious differences aside and formed an alliance by which they assisted the Johor monarch in fending off Portuguese commercial encroachment.

In a nutshell, the justification of Dutch-Johor cooperation adumbrates the position Grotius would assume in his later writings such as his *Mare Liberum*, but more significantly during the Anglo-Dutch conferences of 1613 and 1615. Throughout the official documents that he drafted, the Dutch position can be captured via three broader themes: first, that the VOC's military activities were defensive in protecting their commercial operations and political alliances with Asian sovereigns; second, the issue of free trade must be seen as inherently linked to the support of Asian rulers through armed defence; and third, the company's commercial pursuits and wars in the region should be deemed beneficial to all non-Iberian nations keen on containing Portuguese and Spanish influence in the East Indies. These three core aspects now merit further exploration, whereby specific attention shall be paid to the position defended by Grotius at the Anglo-Dutch maritime and colonial conferences in London (1613) and the Hague (1615).

Sovereignty of the Asian Rulers as the Cornerstone of the Treaty System

Recognising the full sovereignty of the individual Asian monarchs laid the cornerstone of Grotius' theoretical-political edifice at the Indies conferences. It was on the basis of this sovereignty that he was placed in a position to counter the English with the objective of containing Portuguese and Spanish influence and expansion in Asia. He argued that these Iberian powers were infringing the Asian rulers' sovereign rights and engaged in dubious maneuvers to exclude other (European) parties from trading in the region. The Dutch, operating through the VOC, acted as guarantors of the Asian rulers' liberties through exclusive procurement contracts and standing alliances of mutual defence.[118] Grotius was fully aware that not all monarchs required armed protection from (alleged) Portuguese and Spanish military aggression, nor could the Dutch prevent so-called "petty princes" from accepting generous offers from the Iberian powers in return for shunning trade with the VOC.[119] The Dutch delegation ranked Johor among the noteworthy but vulnerable locations, among which are also the cities of Aceh and Banten, the island of Ambon, and the Bandas.[120] The same need for diplomatic and especially armed defence most certainly did not arise for all kings and princes, as was specifically highlighted.[121] From the latter one can conclude that the European powers recognised at the turn of the 17th century the power of the larger, land-based kingdoms to be sufficiently strong and often comparable with their own.

Thus, in upholding the unfettered sovereignty of the Asian rulers and by treating them as members of the greater family of monarchs, Grotius, and the VOC at large, established a moral and legal justification against a Spanish and Portuguese commercial monopoly and their efforts to politically dominate the region.

Of Trade by Force of Arms, Corporate Mergers and Monopolies

As has been seen, the VOC used the sovereignty of the Asian rulers to serve its ulterior motive of securing for itself what could be seen as a contractual monopoly that was directed not so much against Spain and Portugal as against other European traders. This contractual monopoly was aimed initially at the English,[122] but later also at the

Danes and the French. With this point I have arrived at the centre of the dispute between the English and the Dutch at the maritime and colonial conferences of 1613 and 1615.[123] Both factions perceived the ideal flow of trade in sharply contrasting terms. The English pressed for free trade and free access to all ports against Spanish, Portuguese and Dutch policies of exclusion and appealed for unimpeded access to emporia in the East Indies on the basis of the law of nations (*ius gentium*).[124] The Dutch inseparably linked free trade to the need to defend the "petty princes" by recourse to violence.[125] Arms were the ultimate guarantors of free trade; in addition, they were argued to uphold the sovereignty of the Asian rulers upon whose sustained existence the Dutch case for free trade ultimately rested.[126]

In asserting a contract or treaty-based monopoly at the two conferences, it was hoped to render "trade supported by force of arms" (*coophandel met force*) a profitable enterprise.[127] Yet it was clear that maintaining an extensive armed presence in the East Indies was an expensive affair that diminished the company's profits.[128] Competition from other European nations, including the English, the French and the Danes was eroding profits that were intended to help pay for the armed support of Southeast Asia's "petty princes".[129]

The VOC's notorious commercial practices known from later decades were thus already well in the making. While in the first years after the VOC's formation the armed hostilities were directed against the Iberian powers, Spain and Portugal, acts of violence were by this stage already being directed at other real and potential competitors, both Asian as well as European. It is in this context that the Dutch sought to establish their expansionist policy in the East Indies. English dissatisfaction with the Dutch was exploited and used by the Dutch to lure the English company into joining the VOC's cause.

The Dutch delegation contended that a host of developments in the European diplomatic scenario, notably the Anglo-Spanish peace of 1604 and France's peace with Spain concluded in 1598, had enabled the already mighty Spanish empire to strengthen its status and influence in the East Indies. The VOC directors feared that the Iberian monarch would divert funds to crush the trade of other European powers in Asia and to alienate the Asian rulers from their Dutch allies by force.[130] Concerns were also openly voiced that Spain could rush a fleet across the Pacific from Mexico to strengthen its presence in Asian waters.[131] On the English side of the negotiating table, however, Spain's policy towards other European traders in the East Indies was held to be one of obstruction rather than outright expulsion and destruction in distinction to the Portuguese one.[132]

In order to prevent the Spanish and Portuguese from consolidating their authority in Asia to the exclusion of other European trading nations, priority was placed on enticing the English to share the financial burden of the armed effort. This could be done by joining the cause of the VOC in the East Indies.[133] English negotiators noted that Grotius did not desist from demanding that they join the Dutch in a "vigorous and prevent[ive] war".[134] The English were evidently perturbed that their participation in such an armed engagement would be tantamount to joining the Dutch in their protracted war against Spain. Such concerns are reflected in several despatches from the Hague by the English delegates and especially in their final report of 7 April 1615:[135]

> Having considered of this writing and finding that their[136] scope and end was to draw us into a warr against the Spannyard in the Indies, wee prest them further by conference to declare them selves cleerely therein.[137] And thereuppon, after they had withdrawne them selves a while, they kowld alter from what was contayned in that writing, that nothing could bee undertaken by us for th'advancement of the common utillytie in those parts but by joyning with them in a vigorous [and] preventing warr against the Spannyard. To which purpose there was dellivered us from Mons.r Barnavile[138] a coppye of an Artykle made after the truce[139] was concluded, together with an explanacon of the [fourth][140] Artikle of the treaty,[141] by both which His Majesty was ingadged (as they sayd) to warrant them a free trade in the Indies, and to protect such Indian Kinges and people as were in any way mollested by the Spannyard[142] for trading with the Hollanders, and thereuppon finding them firmly to insist uppon suche poyntes as were directly against the purport of our instruccons, we brake of the treatie, and parted farely one from the other.

The English delegates were quick to recognise that, over time, defensive and offensive action against the Spanish could not be cleanly separated and this, as King James I/VI also realised, would almost certainly lead to an open breach of England's peace with Spain concluded in 1604.[143] An alternative was to synergise entrepreneurial efforts by forming a "union" of the English and Dutch East India Companies.[144] This "union" in its most extreme form was to be an outright merger of the two corporate

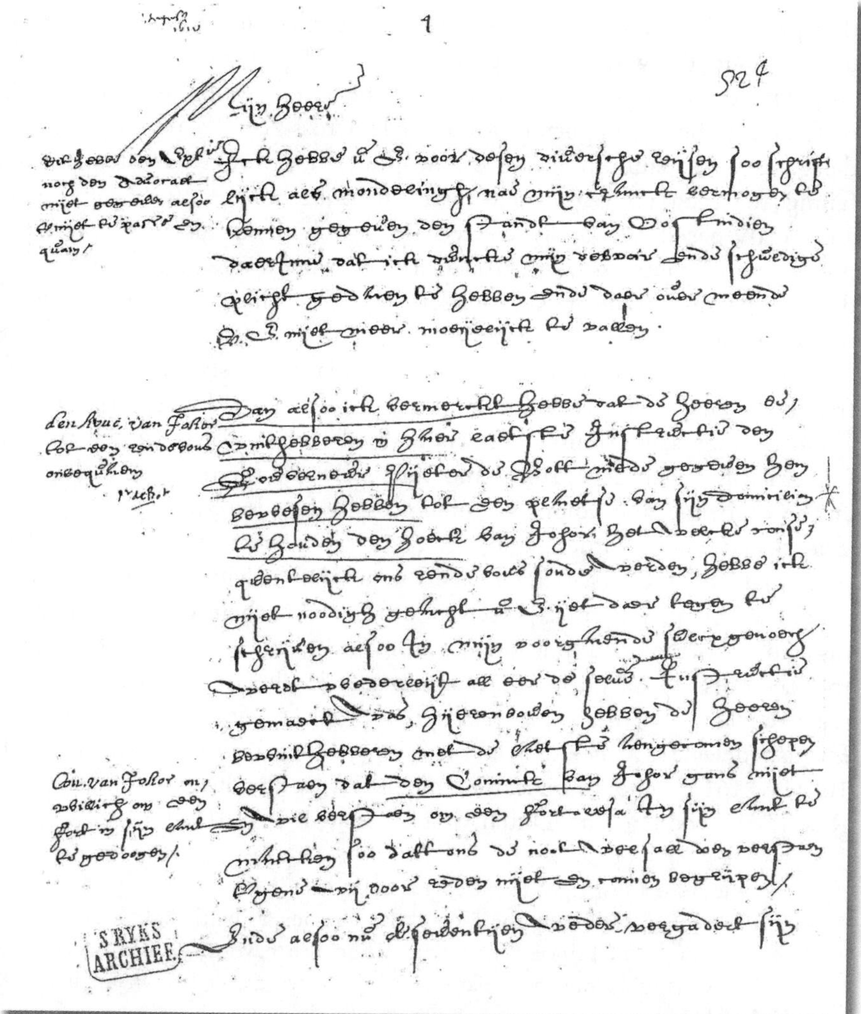

Illus. 20 First page of Admiral Cornelis Matelieff de Jonge's epistolary memorial dated 31 August 1610, addressed to Hugo Grotius. The marginal note states that the "Hook of Johor is not suitable for a rendezvous — Pieter de Both". The Hague, Nationaal Archief, *Collective Hugo de Groot, Supplement I* (1.10.35.02, no 40, fol. 524 verso).

entities, whereby the English were to inject capital into the new united company in proportion to the costs incurred by the VOC for maintaining their armed presence in the Indies.[145] The English delegation found this proposal unacceptable[146] and were concerned about how close this union would be, what role the English would play in this new united corporate entity and what implications the union would have in terms of foreign policy or opportunities of trade across Asia.[147] Yet the English delegates were painfully aware of the price they would have to pay for failing to reach any agreement with the Dutch. The VOC's contract and treaty-based monopoly created by a web of exclusive supply and procurement contracts with Asian rulers would effectively close the door to English trade in key ports of the East Indies.[148] That too was unacceptable.

Against this background one should place the staunch defence of free trade and free access to emporia in the East Indies put up by English ambassador Ralph Winwood in his letter to the Dutch States General of 1 February 1612, and later also by the English delegates at the maritime and colonial conferences in London and the Hague.[149] They listed, among other examples, Francis Drake's treaty with the ruler of Ternate of 1580 (see the image on p. 73).[150] Evidently the English sought to break out of a perceived deadlock in their negotiations and insisted — as they had indeed right from the onset — on their own right to free access to all ports and marketplaces in the Indies in accordance with the law of nations (*ius gentium*) as well as natural liberty. As the English delegates concluded in their report to the Privy Council dated 10 May 1613, echoing an earlier memorial by the English ambassador Ralph Winwood to the Dutch States General of 1612:[151]

> … [w]e have a just right to a free Trade into the East Indies and every part thereof, as well as by the Law of the Nations, as by the admittance of the Kings and Princes there, with whom we have made Contracts and Covenants before those parts in question were ever known to the Hollanders.

This demand for free access was not limited to European powers engaged in the Asian enterprise but was further extended to Asian peoples, such as the Ming Chinese Empire, which, as is known, resisted opening its markets to European and indeed other foreign traders.[152] Perhaps cynically, *Mare Liberum* was cited to underscore English claims that free trade was conceded by nature and the unanimous consensus of nations and could

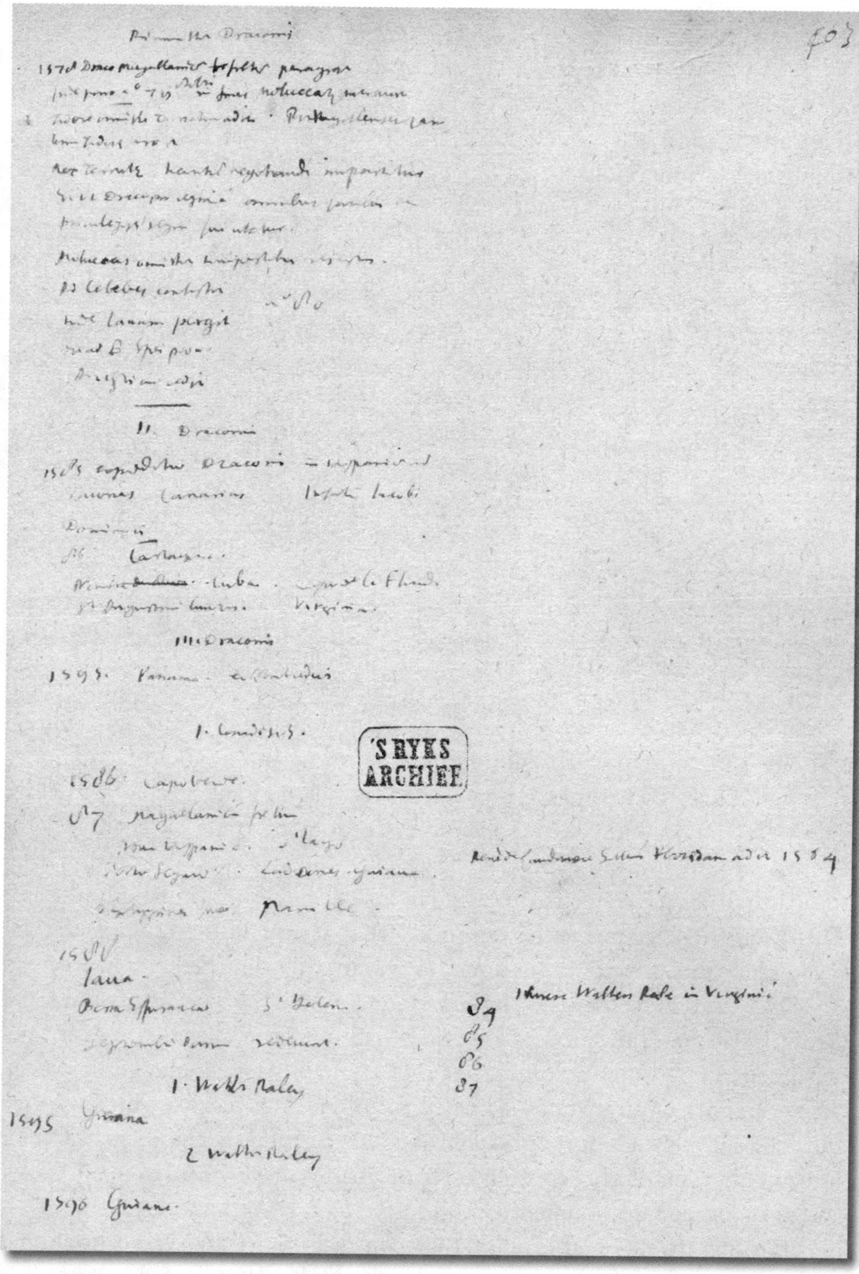

Illus. 21 Reading notes in the hand of Grotius relating to the voyages of Francis Drake and Thomas Cavendish between 1578 and 1596. They probably date from the time of the Anglo-Dutch colonial conferences in London (1613) when English delegates insisted that Drake had signed treaties with Southeast Asian rulers that predated Dutch contracts. (The Hague: Nationaal Archief, *Collectie Hugo de Groot, Supplement I* (1.10.35.02, no. 40, fol. 403 recto)

not be limited by claims of discovery, donation, custom or even treaty.[153] The latter point was directed specifically against Dutch claims to have established a monopoly based on a web of exclusive contracts of trade secured with Southeast Asian rulers.

The English delegates resorted to two additional considerations in support of their open-market strategy. First, they claimed for themselves contractual rights of trade in the Indies that predated the agreements signed between the Asian rulers and the VOC.[154] Second, the English also sought to undermine the validity of the Dutch monopoly by challenging the grounds upon which individual contracts had been procured.[155] Many a treaty of exclusive trade, the English highlighted, had been exacted through the application of force against the Asian peoples and were consequently of questionable validity. This accusation was intended to liken Dutch practices and the VOC's contractually secured monopoly to Spanish and Portuguese exclusion policies in the Indies.[156]

Grotius begged to differ and explained at length that the Dutch did not claim or impose a monopoly in the manner that the Portuguese and Spaniards did — that is, on the basis of discovery, first occupation or papal donation. Instead, they secured their monopoly legally through mutual consent and limited such monopolies to ports and marketplaces under contract. These contracts were governed by bilateral and exclusive treaties and were not intended to abolish the freedom of trade as such.[157] This counter-argument was evidently directed at the English contention that the natural liberty conceded by the law of nations could not be limited.[158] The English delegates were reminded that it was common practice for sovereigns and sovereign nations to voluntarily limit their liberty via contracts and agreements. The freedom granted by the law of nature, Grotius clarified, prevailed as long as it had not been curtailed by contract or agreement.[159] Once a contract or a treaty had been concluded, however, the sovereign's natural state of liberty is limited as a result of his own free will, and all contracting parties are obliged to abide by the terms of their agreement, even if the contractual concessions have been exacted under duress or other questionable conditions.

Grotius dwelt on the point that contracts must always be honoured (*pacta sunt servanda*).[160] He contended that the VOC's policy was not tantamount to a denial of free trade, as was the case with Portugal, but was strictly limited to certain places where the VOC had established its forts and factories; and compared to what the Spanish and Portuguese claimed for themselves, this territory was tiny.[161] Exclusion was further limited to specific commodities, such as cloves. This exclusion, however, did not entitle the VOC to engage in profiteering (an accusation Grotius brought against the Portuguese in his *Mare Liberum*), and the English were reminded that commodities such as cloves were sold to them at a fair price.[162] The English delegates certainly begged to differ on the latter. One comment added to the English translation of Grotius' final paper presented earlier at the 1613 conference in London bluntly states:[163]

> The contrary whereof we find by experience, that our cloves being sold they [the Dutch] raise the price of theirs to an unreasonable rate, (although both wet and rotten) ...

Evidence of a Shift in Thinking?

Finally, there appears to be shift in attitudes towards the Asian rulers, merchants and societies. When the European traders first came to Asia, they arrived with a degree of open-mindedness that generally helped them form a favourable impression of Asian societies, even to the extent of openly evoking reciprocal admiration. Grotius, it appears, was inspired by favourable reports, and he shared his sense of enthusiasm with his readers when, in *De Iure Praedae*, he described Asians in such favourable terms as *solertes* (clever, intelligent) or *ingeniosi* (talented, inventive, dexterous, astute).[164]

By the time Grotius was deputised to the maritime conferences in London and the Hague one decade after writing *De Iure Praedae*, a significant shift in his views on Asia and Asian societies had already set in. Perhaps one of the most visible aspects concerns the defence of the VOC's contractually secured monopoly. Asian rulers and their subjects were reluctant to fulfill their trade contracts with the Dutch. To Grotius this did not mean that the contracts were invalid (as the English delegates argued) but simply that the Asians were perfidious.[165] It was thus legitimate for the Dutch to compel the Asians to honour their contracts and to prevent them from trading with the English or any other party, Asian or European. This appears to be an extraordinary reversal for a man who, just six years earlier, had published a treatise on the freedom of navigation and the concept of free trade.

The English delegates probably saw this as simply another one of Grotius' hair-splitting legal contortions. The language does, nevertheless, reflect a shift in tone that can be partially explained by the sense of frustration that filled the chamber of the Dutch negotiators. However, there is also evidence to suggest that hostility was now increasingly directed against Asian princes and merchants. Grotius was already aware in *De Iure Praedae* of the strong competition and formidable commercial skills of Asian traders, especially the Arabs and the Chinese. For the contractually secured monopoly of the VOC to be effective, these traders would have to be singled out for exclusion. In the undated Dutch memorial spelling out the benefits and disadvantages deriving from a future merger or union of the two East India companies, the following case is made unambiguously clear:[166]

> This union would impede the commerce of the Chinese, Malays, Javanese and others who trade in the Malukus.... To the contrary, when the two companies remain separate, the Malays, Chinese, Javanese and others will gradually take over all of the trade in the Indies, especially that along the Coromandel Coast, in the Malukus, and elsewhere.

Did Grotius change his mind? It would appear that in the course of more than a decade between the writing of *De Iure Praedae* and the two maritime conferences of 1613 and 1615, Grotius, through his exposure to the vernacular world of politics, had become less classically idealistic in his outlook. While his position at the conferences did not necessarily reflect a fundamental change of heart, or even a moderation in his opposition to Spanish and Portuguese commercial authority in the East Indies, it is clear that he had become more responsive, and perhaps even accommodating, to political realities. This responsiveness is visible in his defence of the VOC's treaty system and also from his *De Iure Belli* of 1625, for which he is best remembered in modern times.

Afterword

It is astonishing what long-term impact a casual seizure of a Portuguese-flagged vessel off the coast of Johor in 1603 could have had on the career path of a young lawyer and ambitious politician like Grotius, as well as on the early development and politico-commercial strategies of the Dutch company.[167] The incident, its legal justification and the policy guidelines were to prove seminal for the VOC, as well as for the pattern of political and colonial expansion by the Dutch in insular and to a far lesser extent on mainland Southeast Asia. Moreover, as Leonard Blussé has contended, the seizure of the *Santa Catarina* had a formative impact on how the Chinese authorities came to view the Dutch and the VOC in the opening decades of the 17th century.[168]

Grotius' intentions were probably as genuine and sincere as one could expect from an intellectual placed in his cultural circumstances and of his acknowledged calibre. As time would eventually show, the policy of protecting and allying with Asian rulers, such as the King of Johor, led these princes in Southeast Asia into a state of political symbiosis with the VOC, whose presence, like that of other European powers, shifted the fragile balance of power at the court and across the region.[169] One might go as far as to claim that, as a result of his efforts to safeguard the independence of Asian rulers from encroachments by Spain and Portugal, Grotius (perhaps inadvertently) lent his support in preparing the moral, legal and commercial ground for almost three and a half centuries of Dutch colonial rule in Southeast Asia.[170]

CHAPTER 3

"Free Trade" and Unimpeded Access to Emporia in the East Indies: Rereading *Mare Liberum* (1609)

The setting was 25 February 1603. At dawn, the three ships under the command of Jacob van Heemskerk spotted a Portuguese carrack anchor off the eastern shores of Singapore island. She was richly laden with wares from China and Japan. The battle for the carrack lasted for most of the hours of daylight, and as night was about to fall, the Portuguese captain, crew, soldiers and passengers surrendered. They forfeited ship and cargo to have their lives spared.[1]

This was the seizure of the *Santa Catarina*, one of the best-known acts of privateering committed by the Dutch. As has been seen in chapter 2, the incident became famous — if not infamous — because its cargo, brought back to Europe, reaped proceeds that amounted to double the paid-in capital of the VOC.[2] But the seizure of the *Santa Catarina* was not without controversy erupting over the European market value of the cargo and also the international attention that the public sale of her lading attracted.[3]

Encouraged by the profitable show of force such as demonstrated in the *Santa Catarina* incident, the VOC stepped up its privateering

Illus. 22 Portrait of Jacob van Heemskerk taken from the 1647 edition of Emmanuel van Meteren's *Commentariën ofte Memoriën van den Nederlantsen Staet, Handel, Oorloghen ende Gheschiedenissen van onsen tyden* (Commentaries or Memoirs concerning the Dutch State, Trade and War and the History of our Times). (The Hague, Koninklijke Bibliotheek, 1790 A 122)

activities and attacked Iberian targets on every possible occasion.[4] The Straits of Singapore, where richly laden westbound vessels quickly emerged as soft targets, became a favourite site for such attacks.[5] The year 1605 was particularly notorious, for no fewer than four Portuguese merchant vessels were seized by the Dutch in and around the Singapore Straits.[6] The response from the Iberian Peninsula was swift and firm. In 1606 and 1607 the King of Spain and Portugal instructed his Viceroy of India, Dom Martim Affonso de Castro, and his governor of Melaka, André Furtado de Mendonça, to expel European foreigners from the possessions of the Portuguese Estado da Índia; to beef up security in Melaka; to build forts at critical points around the Straits of Singapore, in Kundur (Sabam) as well as in Aceh; and to reinforce positions in the commercially important colony of Macao (see appendix 1 and the images on pp. 128, 132). Simultaneously, the Estado da Índia was to invoke existing agreements with local rulers to prevent the Dutch from accessing emporia across Asia.

The seizure of the Portuguese carrack *Santa Catarina* marks the cornerstone in the politico-historical apology *De Iure Praedae* commenced around October 1604 and completed in 1606 or probably even later.[7] The more precise circumstances that led to the writing of this exposé, as well as the reasons for publishing but a single chapter from this larger work as *Mare Liberum*, have been reconstructed with great diligence by van Ittersum in her monograph *Profit and Principle* as well as in her learned articles *Mare Liberum in the West Indies* and *Preparing Mare Liberum for Press*.[8] Suffice it in the present context to observe that Grotius revised chapter 12 of his manuscript *De Iure Praedae* and published it under considerable time pressure. The finished product was ready for the press in by the opening weeks of 1609. *Mare Liberum* underscores that direct trade with the Indies was natural, necessary and beneficial for the prosperity of the Dutch Republic.

In his now classic *Introduction to the History of the Law of Nations in the East Indies*, Charles H. Alexandrowicz wrote:[9]

> ... Grotius defended the rights of the Dutch and opposed the validity of Portuguese legal titles in the East Indies *inter alia* by putting emphasis on the status of independent East Indian communities in the law of nations. This enables historians to gain more insight into the views of Grotius on the growth of the family of nations. It also throws light on the legal nature of relations of Christian powers in Europe with the sovereign powers of Asia with whom they had to deal

if the much desired trade with the East was to flourish. The second problem with which Grotius concerned himself was the freedom of the seas....

The present chapter will identify two central topics and five core principles that form the backbone of *Mare Liberum*'s argument.[10] It shall be noted that while Alexandrowicz's two aforementioned insights shall not be rejected outright, a rather different significance will be attributed to them within the broader historical, economic and political parameters staked out by the treatise.

Mare Liberum was published anonymously — and probably for good reason. Many of the points raised in the course of this treatise were not so much unorthodox as they were hardly accepted by learned contemporaries. The evidence presented is selective. The second part of this chapter will thus dwell upon select aspects pertaining to the more immediate reception of *Mare Liberum*'s arguments. William Welwood's reply, as well as Grotius' response to Welwood through the *Defence of Chapter Five of the Mare Liberum* (see image on p. 82) are easily accessible to contemporary researchers.[11] Far less familiar in the English-speaking world is the substantial reply drafted by Seraphim de Freitas, published in 1625 after some official delay by the Spanish Inquisition and the crown of Castile.[12] It also seems prudent in this context to explore some of Grotius' acknowledged sources, including specifically the Spanish jurisconsult and senator Ferdinando Vázquez de Menchaca.[13]

Navigation, Trade and Access to Marketplaces

After these introductory observations, a basic but very important question must be asked: What is the treatise *Mare Liberum* actually about? Where better to start than with the full title from the original Latin, which can be translated as: "The Free Sea, or a Dissertation on the Right Which Belongs to the Dutch to Participate in the Indies Trade."[14] Addressed in the full title are two central themes wrought together in this treatise. The second part of the title takes on the problem of free trade and access to marketplaces and emporia. This lays, in my opinion, the theoretical cornerstone in Grotius' politico-historical edifice proper.[15]

From this core of free trade flow other entitlements that are argued to be anchored in nature.[16] The second core upon which *Mare Liberum*

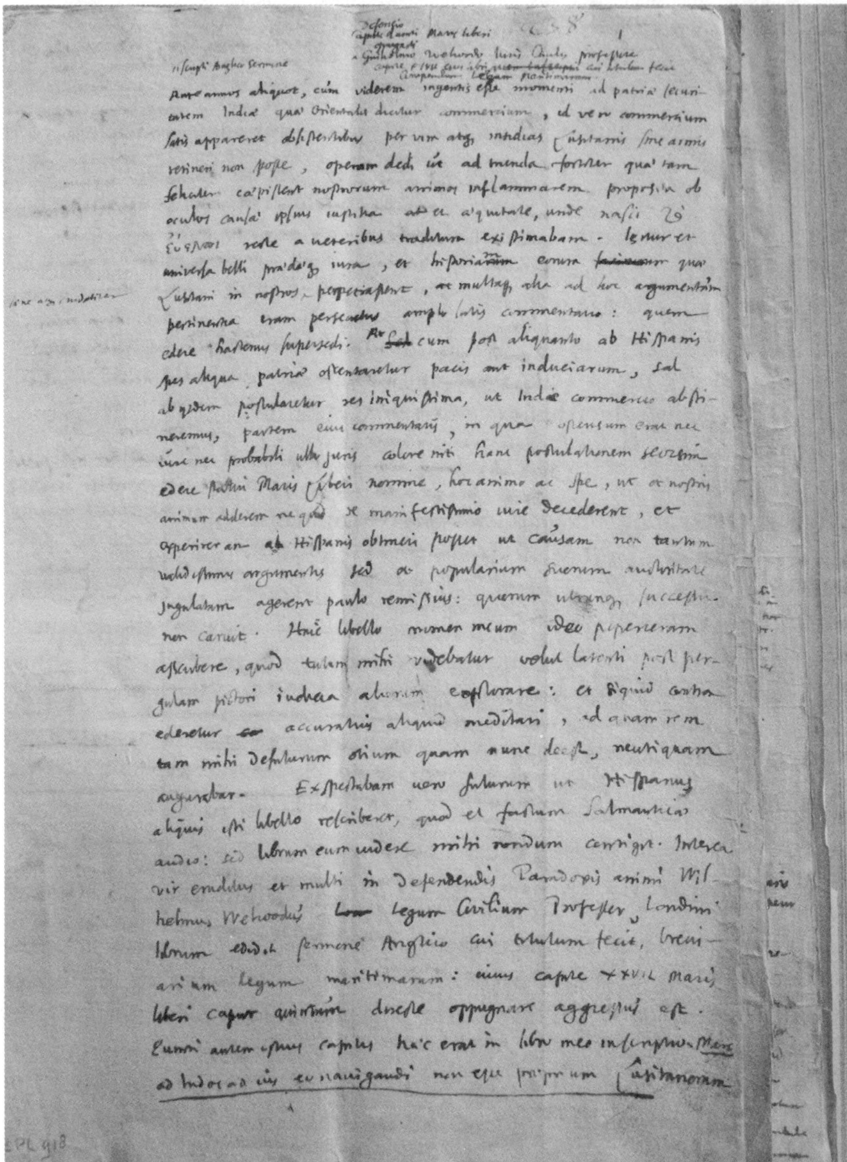

Illus. 23 First page of Grotius' treatise *Defensio capitis quinti maris liberi* (Defence of Chapter Five of Mare Liberum) which he drafted against William Welwood. The treatise remained unpublished until the 19th century. (Leiden University Library, B.P.L. 918, fol. 238 recto)

constructs its arguments pertain to the historically challenging problem of rightful (or at least legally permissible) market access. By this term I understand unimpeded access (via the high seas or maritime highways) to emporia outside the European continent.[17] It is important to bear in mind that Grotius was only advocating free access for the procurement of goods, mainly spices, for transhipment to, and resale in, the Dutch Republic and beyond. He did not (yet) advocate the penetration of local Asian markets for the resale of goods by the Dutch to Asian consumers.[18] Grotius did not seriously concern himself in *Mare Liberum* with the problem of accessing Asian markets or consumers, at least not until *after* its publication in 1609.[19]

Unimpeded access to emporia and marketplaces assumes an important position in *Mare Liberum*'s line of thought.[20] In order to freely access these in the East Indies (and by extension also other marketplaces around the globe), the Dutch sail the high seas.[21] Grotius attacked the aspirations of Portugal and Spain to assert, with the help of diplomacy, law and the force of arms, a maritime-based trading preserve. He contended that concrete measures to establish such a trading preserve represented an open violation of nature or the natural order. The Dutch humanist understood unimpeded and peaceful maritime navigation as an extension of the *ius communicationis* (right of [free and unimpeded] communication) that, as has been seen in chapter 2, he adopted from Francisco de Vitoria.[22]

From the theoretical cornerstones of free or unimpeded access to marketplaces via innocent and peaceful passage across pelagic spaces, I am now placed in a position to elaborate on a series of core arguments gleaned from a close reading of *Mare Liberum*. To contemporary researchers, these are not new and are encountered here in *Mare Liberum* and also in some of Grotius' other treatises and working drafts, including *De Iure Praedae Commentarius* (Commentary on the Law of Prize and Booty), *De Societate Publica cum Infidelibus* (Of Public Society with Non-Christians),[23] *De Pace* (Of Peace),[24] *Commentarius in Theses XI* (Commentary to Eleven Theses),[25] *Defensio Capitis Quinti Maris Liberi* (Defence of Chapter Five of the Mare Liberum)[26] and, of course, *De Iure Belli ac Pacis Libri Tres* (Three Books on the Law of War and Peace).[27] From the theoretical foundations of trade and unimpeded access via innocent and peaceful passage across pelagic waters, it is now possible to discuss five underlying principles that can be extracted from *Mare Liberum*. These foreshadow some of the basic positions assumed by Grotius at the Anglo-Dutch colonial conferences in London and the Hague discussed more extensively in chapter 2. In brief, the five principles are these:

(1) Nature foresees engagement in peaceful societal interaction (*ius communicationis* — right of [free and unimpeded] communication), with the corresponding prohibition that no one (and this would implicitly include any sovereign, as outlined in the subsequent sections) may impede others in pursuing such interaction.[28]
(2) Nature wills that certain sites remain common to all, with the corresponding prohibition that certain sites and spaces may never or cannot be appropriated.
(3) Nature wills that all men share in the riches of the earth and Creation,[29] with a corresponding prohibition that no one may engage in acts of profiteering and permit waste of nature's bounty.[30]
(4) Nature has spontaneously given the fruits of its bounty to all mankind.[31] Correspondingly, no one may alienate or destroy what nature has spontaneously given. Nature's spontaneous gifts include tangibles as well as intangibles.[32]
(5) In the absence of just, viable or effective arbitration, any person (or sovereign) may ensure that these basic principles are not violated. If they are, recourse to violence is permissible, with certain limitations imposed on the proportionality of retaliation and acts of revenge.[33]

The first principle is that trade is perfectly natural and is bestowed upon mankind through Creation. This is evidenced *inter alia* by the winds and currents of the sea.[34] The latter observation was taken on from the writings of the Roman philosopher Seneca, albeit second-hand from Alberico Gentili and arguably out of context, as W.S.M. Knight and Jonathan Ziskind have observed.[35] Trade is thus seen as part of an interactive human process willed by the Creator. The following excerpt from *Mare Liberum* weaves together strands of thought that broadly characterise Grotius' early political treatises — the centrality of Divine Voluntarism, perceptions of man's innate desire to cultivate friendly relations with fellow men, and also the *oikeosis* (innate sociability of man), the latter which is widely associated with the Stoics of antiquity:[36]

> Every nation is free to travel to every other nation, and to trade with it. God Himself says this speaking through the voice of nature;

> and inasmuch as it is not His will to have Nature supply every place with all the necessaries of life,[37] He ordains that some nations excel in one art and others in another.[38] Why is this His will, except it be that He wished human friendships to be engendered by mutual needs and resources,[39] lest individuals deeming themselves entirely sufficient unto themselves should for that very reason be rendered unsociable?

The second principle is that — in line with the premises outlined in Roman law, notably the *Institutes/Enactments of Justinian* — private property is not instituted by Divine will or nature but is a creation of man for his own convenience and for the satisfaction of his bodily needs.[40] According to the testimonies of the ancient writers and poets, certain places, sites or objects remain unappropriated or common to all. These include specifically places of public worship, air and running water.[41] Taking these tenets of Roman public law as a foundation, *Mare Liberum* postulated that certain spaces remained unappropriated and could not be made the property of individuals or sovereign states. Common utilisation was, therefore, to remain intact, and each individual or sovereign could enjoy such spaces. Among these unappropriated areas, *Mare Liberum* includes pelagic spaces.[42]

The third principle is that private property, which is an institution created by man, may not be enjoyed by individuals without observing certain conditions that are anchored in nature or Creation. Nature wills that there be no wastage of its bounty and also that people should not appropriate more than they can use for themselves.[43] Grotius explained that the Portuguese monopolised trade to the exclusion of others, deliberately drove up prices and consequently also engaged in profiteering.[44] Such behaviour was directed against the very design of nature and Divine Providence. The Creator foresaw through nature a free flow and exchange of goods to all parts of the world. A facet of this principle is that people may not acquire common things if such appropriation injures others. People can suffer harm not just through the infliction of physical pain or injury, but also through the denial of their rightful benefits and their entitlement to share in nature's bounty. Thus, profiteering and the denial of common benefits, not only violate the order and design of Creation, but also the very principles of Christian charity.

The fourth principle: What nature has bestowed unto all cannot be alienated through the actions of man.[45] This is a very important point developed in considerable detail by the commentators of Thomas Aquinas in 16th-century Spain.[46] Grotius conceded in *Mare Liberum* as well as in his other works that there are some noteworthy exceptions. These include avenging one's enemies and the waging of a just (public) war.[47] Booty of war and punitive prizetaking encompass tangibles as well as intangibles[48] and include also nature's gifts to man, unhindered access to marketplaces and political authority. Grotius' scholastic predecessors established (in line with the tenets of Christian charity) that the value of goods alienated in the course of a just war, together with acts of retaliation and punishment must be commensurate with, and directly proportional to, the injury suffered.[49]

The fifth principle is that every person may defend himself and his interests.[50] In the absence of (effective or unbiased) arbitration, recourse to violence (by individuals and implicitly also states) is permissible. The violated party may take action to avenge injury and to restore what has been unduly denied or impeded.[51]

The right to punish has received considerable attention in recent decades, especially since the publication in 1983 of Peter Haggenmacher's expansive study *Grotius et la doctrine de la guerre juste* (Grotius and the doctrine of the just war). Although Haggenmacher's work has been rightly praised for being comprehensive, exhaustive and very learned, it has also been criticised for over-interpreting Grotius, especially with reference to his early works such as *De Iure Praedae* and implicitly also *Mare Liberum.* Haggenmacher has the propensity to treat references as the fruits of direct engagement with the sources Grotius acknowledged or cited, either in the footnotes or in the margins. More recent scholarship, however, advises caution.[52] A reassessment of Grotius' theory of rights has crystallised on the basis of new manuscript materials that have surfaced since 1983, including Ms. B.P.L. 922, and several focused studies touching on the Dutch luminary's theory of natural and subjective rights.[53] With particular reference to the right to punish, I refer to the shorter contributions of Benjamin Straumann and Guus van Nifterik, and from the vantage point of the historian also to the various publications of Martine van Ittersum.[54] When all the materials, the familiar, published works, as well as the early manuscript fragments in Ms. B.P.L. 922 are taken into account, it becomes clear that Grotius deeply struggled with ideas concerning the right to punish. How is it possible to argue in favour of a sovereign's right to punish if, as the Spanish Late Scholastics already conceded, such a right be treated as a facet of civil law?[55] The Spanish and the Portuguese theorists regarded the vast open pelagic spaces as falling under their *dominium,* their "jurisdictional space", but *Mare Liberum* treated the high seas as spaces that cannot be appropriated and must consequently remain in their original state of nature.[56] For Grotius the right to punish must, therefore, derive from a source other than civil law. He saw this right anchored in the law of nature. He wrote in his later work *De Iure Belli ac Pacis:* "*Huius quoque iuris puniendi potestas naturaliter penes unamquemque est*" (Also, the power of this right to punish naturally rests with everyone).[57] The individual's right to punish must therefore derive from the law of nature and also the natural right of self-defence. The sovereign acquires this right, in theory at least, through the social contract, whereby in creating civil society and the state, the individual transfers his natural rights conditionally or unconditionally to a central authority. Explained via the social contract, the package of rights vested in the sovereign must therefore be identical and — in any case — can never exceed what the individual is believed to possess in a state of nature. It also implies that where there is no supreme jurisdiction at hand, such as on the unappropriated high seas, the sovereign must still possess and be endowed with a right to punish.[58]

So much for the right to punish belonging to individuals and sovereigns with reference to the high seas. Grotius declared that the cause of the Dutch against the Portuguese and their (Spanish) king was an honourable one. He rhetorically underscored the goodwill and preparedness of his Dutch people to be judged and submit to a majority opinion.[59] He appealed to his readers (whom he invokes as "[Y]e Princes, your good faith, ye Peoples, whoever and wherever ye may be")[60] to judge the Dutch case. Grotius emphasised the goodwill and willingness of the Dutch Republic ("a state, not ... illegally founded, but ... a government based upon law")[61] to submit to a majority opinion.[62] This verdict of the majority, he firmly believed, would not conform to the ambitions, pursuits and policies of the Iberian monarch.[63]

The core message of *Mare Liberum* may thus be summarised as follows: trade is natural, good and beneficial. The Dutch could travel to the emporia of the Indies and do so by maritime navigation. Unfortunately, they have suffered grave injury in pursuit of their natural right on two important counts: first, because the Portuguese claimed for themselves spaces that may not be appropriated (i.e., the oceans or open pelagic spaces); and second, because they monopolised trade to the disadvantage of others in Europe and Asia. This was reflected in the exorbitant prices of goods the Portuguese charged for Asian products and commodities in Europe. Seeing unimpeded participation in international trade as a natural right, rather than the privilege of any one nation, Grotius opined that unilateral and arbitrary restrictions of the Portuguese had compelled Holland-based merchants to take up armed defence.[64] For the Dutch, such a defence legitimised acts of retaliation against crimes committed by the Portuguese on the high seas or in the colonies.[65] Grotius does not list the individual crimes and injuries against the right of free trade in the hastily reworked treatise *Mare Liberum*, but he does so in chapter 11 of *De Iure Praedae*.

How does this square with the ostensible agenda staked out by the full title of *Mare Liberum*? Grotius underscored access to marketplaces and the freedom of navigation on the high seas as an efficient means of undermining Iberian policies of obstruction and commercial exclusion.[66] His pleas for unimpeded access to emporia and freedom of navigation were subsequently incorporated into a set of arguments that were used to morally distinguish the competitive political and economic nature of contrasting colonial systems.

Sources, Historic Reception and Criticism of *Mare Liberum*

This insight leads to part 2 of this chapter, which explores select points of criticism of *Mare Liberum* raised almost immediately after its publication in 1609. Three points of interest merit further exploration here.

First, criticism can be directed specifically at the arguments derived from the writings of the Spanish Late Scholastics. This included Vitoria's historically influential *Two Relections on the Indies*.[67] Considerations developed by the Salamanca theologian in the context of the American conquest were broadly projected onto and into the Asian scenario. On the one hand, Grotius was careful to distance himself from Vitoria's deference to the authority of the pope, perceptions of the non-European societies, as well as justifications of Spanish atrocities committed against the "infidels".[68] On the other hand, it is not entirely certain whether Grotius was simply adding flesh and perhaps even a bit of sensationalism to his discourse on unimpeded access to marketplaces. As he conceded at the end of chapter 2 of *Mare Liberum*, there was consensus, particularly in Spain, that the views Vitoria had attacked were indeed unjust and unholy.[69] So why revive this argument other than for rhetorical purposes? Why did Grotius find it necessary to flog a proverbial dead horse?

This material falls into a category which can be conveniently described as ballast arguments: Grotius simply reiterated what was already broadly accepted among the intelligentsia of the Iberian Peninsula. Far more interesting, perhaps, are the arguments he *did not* appropriate from the *Relectiones* of Vitoria and indeed from other Spanish authors he is known to have consulted, such as Diego de Covarruvias y Leyva. One such topic (conveniently) shunned by the Dutch humanist — and later expressly condemned as sheer folly in *De Iure Belli ac Pacis* — is the universal authority of the Holy Roman Emperor.[70] It is not sufficiently clear why Grotius deftly avoided this topic altogether, but it may have had to do with the fact that, at least nominally, the Dutch Republic remained an integral part of the Holy Roman Empire until the Peace of Westphalia in 1648. Of considerable interest to the present discussion is the not uncommon view among 16th- and even some 17th-century writers that the universal authority of the Holy Roman Emperor also extended across pelagic spaces. This is evidenced, for example, by the treatise of Julius Pacius à Beriga published in 1619.[71]

It should not escape attention that *Mare Liberum* specifically invoked the *ius communicationis*, or right of [free and unimpeded] communication, mentioned by Vitoria.[72] As has already been shown in chapter 2, a denial of this right, the good professor from Salamanca argued, offered sufficient grounds for commencing a just (public) war, although with some important limitations.[73] Vitoria's position was firmly anchored in a discourse that explored the right to evangelise and enter into contact with the indigenous peoples of the New World.[74] Grotius' contribution (if this is even the appropriate expression) was to amplify the underlying intentions and programmes of Vitoria by heightening the emphasis on free trade and market access.

Indeed, Vitoria's *ius communicationis* is a concept that is not easily grasped by contemporary scholars. Domingo de Soto did not espouse the validity of such a (natural) right, not even in the original but limited context raised by Vitoria, namely, the preaching of the Gospel.[75] In his *Relection* of 1534 (which actually predates Vitoria's own discourse on the subject of the Indies), de Soto argued that if the Amerindians refused to listen to the Word of God, they could not be compelled to do so under any circumstances.[76] De Soto did not advocate a *ius communicationis* along the parameters set by his contemporary and colleague Vitoria.

Given that there are only two references to de Soto's *De Iustitia et Iure* (On Justice and Right) in Grotius' *De Iure Praedae*, one of which is

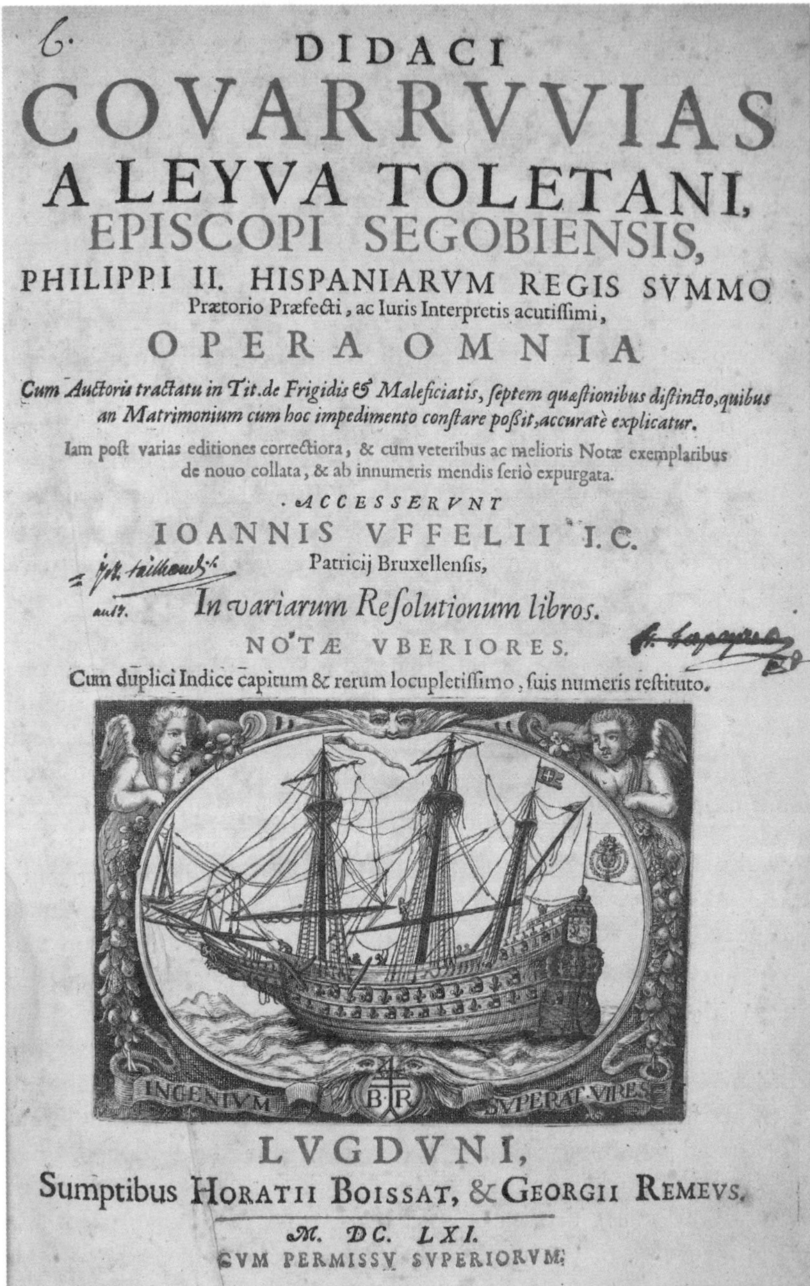

DIDACI
COVARRVVIAS
A LEYVA TOLETANI,
EPISCOPI SEGOBIENSIS,
PHILIPPI II. HISPANIARVM REGIS SVMMO
Prætorio Præfecti, ac Iuris Interpretis acutissimi,
OPERA OMNIA
Cum Auctoris tractatu in Tit. de Frigidis & Maleficiatis, septem quæstionibus distincto, quibus an Matrimonium cum hoc impedimento constare posit, accuratè explicatur.
Iam post varias editiones correctiora, & cum veteribus ac melioris Notæ exemplaribus de nouo collata, & ab innumeris mendis seriò expurgata.
ACCESSERVNT
IOANNIS VFFELII I.C.
Patricij Bruxellensis,
In variarum Resolutionum libros.
NOTÆ VBERIORES.
Cum duplici Indice capitum & rerum locupletissimo, suis numeris restituto.

LVGDVNI,
Sumptibus HORATII BOISSAT, & GEORGII REMEVS.
M. DC. LXI.
CVM PERMISSV SVPERIORVM.

Illus. 24 Title page of Diego de Covarruvias y Leyva's *Opera Omnia* (Collected Works) printed in Lyon, France, in 1661. (Leiden University Library, Meyers, II B 5) featured as a marginal insertion to the manuscript,[77] it is unlikely that Grotius was familiar with the different positions among the Salmantino doctors at that point in his life. It is against the broader canvass of this observation together with evidence extracted from Vázquez de Menchaca, Covarruvias y Leyva,[78] and Rodrigo Juárez (Rodericus Zuaresius),[79] that one should understand the Dutch humanist's boastful claim to have "invoke[d] the very laws of Spain itself".[80] Grotius may have invoked the "laws of Spain", but the sources he consulted when drafting *De Iure Praedae* (and implicitly also *Mare Liberum*) were few and those he carefully studied fewer still.

As anyone who has studied the learned work of Seraphim de Freitas will be able to testify,[81] the issues surrounding the concept of the just war and the denial of free trade most certainly do not end here. The Iberian professor was well aware that outside the European cultural sphere, the idea of market access was wanting. He pointed specifically to the example of China as a country that does not abide by this principle. Although de Freitas hastily criticised the punishments meted out by the Chinese authorities, even to those who had been shipwrecked along the coast, it is clear that he did not condemn the principle of barring access to peaceful trading, even if he readily acknowledged that both trade and navigation were conceded by the law of nations (*ius gentium*).[82] But according to *De Iure Praedae*, the freedom of interaction for the exchange of goods or ideas was a right so fundamental and natural that neither the Portuguese, nor any other sovereign people, could prevent others from exercising it. Following the reasoning of Vitoria, any attempt to impede such an exchange is a cause for a just war.[83] In resorting to the right of self-defence, the Dutch (and also some Asian rulers, such as the King of Johor) were deemed to wage a just war on the Portuguese, and even forged alliances with other similarly injured parties. In this context, *De Iure Praedae* asserted that the Dutch and the Johorese were justified in entering into such a pact of trade, mutual assistance and cooperation.[84] But were Christians permitted to ally themselves with non-Christians to wage a war against another Christian party (and perhaps even Christian heretics), if the latter was clearly in violation of natural rights or Divine Revelation?[85] At this juncture de Freitas assumed a conservative stance and denied that under such circumstances.[86] This was the position not only of Roman Catholic scholars of the time, but also of many Protestant thinkers.[87] As have argued in chapter 2, Grotius did recognise this as a serious problem and addressed it in some of his other writings, including the full manuscript of *De Iure Praedae*, the skeletal outline *De Societate Publica cum Infidelibus* and also *De Iure Belli ac Pacis*.

The second point that merits further exploration is that Grotius was not always loyal to the sources he quoted from. He is known to have quoted selectively, quoted out of context, extracted clusters of quotations from other printed sources,[88] and even (dishonestly) changed the wording of the text to suit his case. Any reader who studies de Freitas' diligently researched counter-arguments will soon learn of several such shameful contortions found in *Mare Liberum*.[89] One particular passage is the young Dutchman's reference to the jurisconsult Hugo Doneau (Donellus), who, as de Freitas underscored, was quoted in a sense contrary to the original.[90] In another instance Grotius changed the original word "canal" to "particular sea".[91] The two terms can hardly be considered synonyms.

Selectively quoting from acknowledged sources poses a different set of problems. For example, Grotius deferred to the authority of Vázquez de Menchaca on several counts, such as in chapter 7 of *Mare Liberum*. Here the Spanish jurisconsult was used to argue that "public places and spaces common to all by the law of nations cannot become objects of prescription" (that is the acquisition of something over a long period of time),[92] Grotius cited this passage while discussing the claim "Neither the Sea nor the right of navigation thereon belongs to the Portuguese by title of prescription or custom." Perhaps deliberately, perhaps inadvertently, the Hollander lets his readers conclude that Vázquez' argued against the appropriation of the sea, in support of the freedom of navigation. But the quotation is not actually representative of the Spaniard's thinking. Anyone who simply thumbs through Vázquez' *Controversiae* may be surprised to discover that the Castilian (whom Grotius exalted as the "Pride of Spain", "one of the most learned Spaniards" and "that Glory of Spain")[93] was not at all consistent in his views on navigation.[94] On the contrary, Vázquez' frequently cited collection of legal cases, memorials and advisories contains several lengthy sections that assert exactly the opposite of the "free seas".[95] Vázquez invoked the authority of the Roman jurists and the ancients, including poets, to drive home his point that navigation across the high seas was tantamount to suicide and therefore something undesirable, unnatural and most certainly against Providence and Revelation. It was in view of such unacceptable risks that Grotius, in contrast to Vázquez, extolled the inherent and undeniable perils associated with overseas trade as a great human achievement and a courageous enterprise. He invoked the authority of Aristotle (hardly a source of Divine Revelation)[96] to assert that the "most honourable of all [forms of trade] is the wholesale overseas trade, because it makes so many people sharers of so many things".[97] What could be more natural than that?

Is trade something that is bestowed unto man by the "spontaneous hand of nature" — to borrow a famous phrase from John Locke's *Second Treatise on Government* — or is it, as the Iberian authorities Vázquez and de Freitas contended, something unnatural, that is, a sign of (Platonic) decadence and a form of human interaction not foreseen by God who created the Garden of Eden without need or want? The question of whether trade is part of nature's perfect design is of central significance — precisely because of its implications on the right of maritime navigation — but it is also a question that found sparse consensus among the luminaries of the 16th and 17th centuries. It should not surprise that Grotius and Vázquez did not share the same outlook, and de Freitas broadly sided with his Spanish counterpart. Indeed, de Freitas made it clear — and this marks a sharp contrast to Grotius — that he did not hold Vázquez in high esteem but tended to regard him more as a politician than a scholar of jurisprudence.

The third important point is that *Mare Liberum* treats the sea as space that, by the law of nature, cannot be appropriated by any person, any people or, implicitly, any sovereign.[98] The tenets underpinning this stance can be retrieved in chapter 5 of the treatise, the section that specifically evoked a refutation by William Welwood.

To begin with, it shall be shown how this position fits into the broader framework staked out by *Mare Liberum*. Grotius stipulated that the Dutch, in exercising their right of free trade and interaction, must implicitly also possess a right to access ports and marketplaces in the Indies via pelagic spaces. This is because he deemed the oceans as spaces that cannot be appropriated, remaining in their original, primordial state bestowed unto man by nature. He contended that the seas must be freely navigable to all peoples, Christians and non-Christians alike, for what nature has given to all mankind cannot be alienated by the acts of some men or even their rulers. This argument was directed at Spanish and Portuguese claims to have appropriated exclusive control of pelagic spaces in the Atlantic, Pacific and Indian Oceans. The legal grounds upon which the Iberian powers based their claims are well known; they include, of course, the rights of ownership by first discovery (*res nullius*), papal donation,[99] prescription as well as custom and continuous use.[100] Foreign parties could ply "their" maritime routes or cross the high seas claimed by the Iberian powers only if they were in possession of a *cartaz* (safe-conduct pass). The navigational arrangements based on letters of safe passage, such as the *cartazes,* were admittedly not a new creation of the Portuguese — even if their European critics argued otherwise — and similar documents were issued by the Ottoman Turks and also the Ming Chinese. This licence to navigate was issued only after payment of an upfront fee and was designed to divert trade to Portuguese-controlled ports around the Indian Ocean.[101] It also bears some resemblance to the passes issued later in the 17th century by the VOC. Depending on political circumstances and the financial state of the crown, the issuance of *cartazes* in the Estado da Índia was restricted to the "natural subjects" of Portugal, which means to Portuguese subjects born in Portugal.[102]

Citing passages from Roman law and the ancients, Grotius argued that by nature the high seas remained open and common to all. By definition, the sea extends to the level of the highest tide,[103] for which reason the beach was also rendered a common space. Such spaces cannot be appropriated by any individual, people or sovereign. This also holds true for maritime routes across the high seas. A sign of ownership, *Mare Liberum* argued, was when the claimant can occupy and physically defend his claim to proprietorship. Grotius questioned: Even if it were permissible to appropriate the vast open ocean, how could any person, let alone a sovereign, defend it? It is on such grounds that *Mare Liberum* rejected all Iberian claims to dominion and ownership of the seas as simply unfeasible and unreasonable.[104]

In advancing his case for access to marketplaces in the East via oceanic waters, Grotius defended free access and free trade for his compatriots. But he was treading on proverbial thin ice, and the Dutch humanist appears to have been well aware of this. Chapter 5 of *Mare Liberum* was one of the boldest and most controversial political discourses of its generation. There is no doubt that he was highly conscious that his arguments ran contrary to actual state practices in Europe at the time and would not be readily accepted.[105]

This can be evidenced by the treatise *Dominio del Mar Adriatico* which has been attributed on occasion to the famed Venetian cleric and state chronicler Paolo Sarpi.[106] On the basis of apostolic concession (many issued in the context of the Crusades), imperial edicts and popular festivities, including a special discussion on the law of war and its effects, the author of *Dominio del Mar Adriatico* constructed his case for Venice based on custom and prescription.[107] He was not particularly interested in delving into the subject of natural rights, but extrapolated that over the centuries the despatch of navies against pirates had given the Venetian Republic real and effective control over the Adriatic.[108] Cardinal Gasparo Contarini and the treatise *Dominio del Mar Adriatico* saw Venetian republican liberty and the control of the Adriatic as intrinsically inseparable. In his treatise *Relationi del Mare* (Pavia, 1598), Giovanni Botero assumed another line. Arguing for Christian unity against the Ottoman threat, he "territorialised" the sea by distinguishing the open oceans from relatively enclosed maritime spaces, such as the Mediterranean, and implicitly the Baltic, Persian Gulf and arguably also the Singapore and Melaka Straits.[109] Another treatise, published by Pacius in 1619, differentiated among three types of maritime *dominium*: property, use and jurisdiction. In terms of property, the sea belonged to no one; in terms of its use, the sea was technically open to everyone; and as far as jurisdiction over pelagic spaces was concerned, this belonged to the prince.[110] Still, Pacius underscored that Venice was in a position to claim *dominium* of the Adriatic on a number of important practical counts: long-established custom, effective occupation, keeping the waters clear of pirates, pursuing and punishing delinquents, issuing regulations pertaining to maritime navigation and imposing tolls on ships plying Venetian waters.[111] In modern terminology, one could say that the Venetians were simply exercising sovereign control over the Adriatic and parts of the eastern Mediterranean.

But what did the Adriatic represent in the eyes of 17th-century politicians, lawyers and merchants? Was it just a bay? Or was it a sea? Did the issues surrounding *dominium* of the Adriatic by Venice pose a completely different set of practical problems, demanding different answers or solutions? Or was it just a matter of political and commercial expediency? As a European power favourably disposed towards the Dutch Republic, did Venice not find itself addressed, or even threatened by, the very argument of *Mare Liberum*?

The author of *Dominio del Mar Adriatico* regarded the Adriatic as the noteworthy exception rather than the norm.[112] Besides, closer scrutiny of *Mare Liberum* reveals a starkly different vocabulary employed when discussing the Portuguese on the one hand and the Venetians and Genoese on the other. It is clear that when Grotius wrote of those vast pelagic spaces, he had the Portuguese and Spanish maritime policies of exclusion in mind, but he became significantly more accommodating when mentioning bays and gulfs. When writing about the latter, Grotius argued far more deftly and diplomatically. The following excerpt from *Mare Liberum* illustrates how the maritime interests of Genoa and also Venice[113] were not the target of his scornful pen:[114]

> [Those authors …] are talking about the Mediterranean, we are talking about the Ocean; they speak of a gulf, we of the boundless sea; and from the point of view of occupation these are wholly different things. And too, those peoples, to whom the authorities just mentioned concede prescription, the Venetians and Genoese for example, possess a continuous shore line on the sea, but it is clear that not even that kind of possession can be claimed for the Portuguese.

This excerpt shows how Venetian *dominium* of the Adriatic and Genoese control of the Ligurian Sea were not seen as points of serious controversy.[115] Admittedly, the Dutch humanist was far more willing to accommodate the control of confined maritime spaces (bays and gulfs) later in *De Iure Belli ac Pacis* than he was in *Mare Liberum*.[116] From this vantage point, it appears that Grotius saw eye to eye with the author of *Dominio del Mar Adriatico*, even if superficially their thinking may appear divergent. This insight may also serve to explain why *Mare Liberum* was ignored in *Dominio del Mar Adriatico.*

The publication of *Mare Liberum* seriously ruffled the feathers of court and university lawyers. That is clear from printed reactions, and one only need point to the now classic exposés of Welwood,[117] de Freitas or John Selden to underscore this point.[118] The concrete objections historically brought forward against the treatise *Mare Liberum* are well known. Welwood upheld the principle of territorial waters, citing the security needs of coastal commerce and shipping, as well as the protection of marine fishing stock. For this purpose he proposed, as had some mediaeval Italian jurisconsults, that a notional boundary of 100 leagues from the coastline apply for establishing territorial waters (other than bays, straits, etc.). But in his *Defence of Chapter Five of the Mare Liberum*, Grotius rejected outright Welwood's demands for territorial waters as being arbitrary and ultimately meaningless. "And what reason operates, if the sea can be occupied up to one hundred miles, to prevent it being occupied up to 150, thence to 200 and so on?"[119]

While Welwood — not unlike Botero — was prepared to keep the seas open for international commerce by distinguishing the "open ocean" from "enclosed regions of the sea", de Freitas was not. In an argument that, on hindsight, rings very modern indeed, de Freitas elaborated that no part of the world should be placed outside the authority of the sovereign and therefore beyond jurisdiction. If it was not possible to appropriate the high seas, then it was imperative that quasi-possession apply. This was not least because it was both desirable and necessary to preserve order along the main maritime trading routes and to keep pirates at bay.

Evidence gleaned by Grotius from Roman law was meant to highlight that "air and water" generally speaking — and with this of course implicitly also the sea or maritime spaces — were common to all by nature.[120] In their replies, Welwood and de Freitas retorted that references to the communality of water referred only to fresh running water. If the seas were indeed free and open to "all" in ancient Rome, de Freitas explained, this was not because they were "common to all by the law of nature", but because they were common to all Roman citizens (as the patrimony of the Roman people), an arrangement effected by public policy.[121] The Roman jurisconsults employed the expression "no one" in the sense of "no one individual",[122] but this was clearly not valid for a prince or sovereign who represented the interests of the people and body politic at large.

In his *Defence of Chapter Five of the Mare Liberum*, Grotius rebuffed the two-pronged argument concerning "fresh running water" and "patrimony". Not only did he render passages that identified "running water and the sea" as two distinct but identifiable cases of natural common property,[123] he equally dismissed the view that the freedom of navigation traced its origins in Roman public policy. Freedom of navigation and free access to marketplaces from across the sea is clearly a *natural* right,[124] and Grotius underscored that all[125] "those who, borne from abroad, navigate on the sea, do not do this on another's property by the right of servitude, but on something that is common to all by the right of liberty". He later also explained:[126]

> [Celsus said] that the use of the sea is common "to all men",[127] which phraseology manifestly excludes every exception. For it is one thing to say "all men" and another to say "all citizens". Neratius likewise stated no less absolutely that the shores have come into the dominion "of no one".[128] He did not say "of no private citizen", but simply "of no one", therefore neither the people nor the prince.

Critics such as de Freitas singled out inconsistencies in *Mare Liberum* in treating the sea as a possession or even a quasi-possession. On the one hand, Grotius advocated that the freedom of the seas extended to the shores at the level of the highest tide; from this he deduced that no sovereign authority may lawfully impede his citizens from engaging in something as "natural" as trade. But these were bold, categorical statements on which the Dutch humanist also imposed certain limitations to accommodate commercial and political realities. Grotius openly conceded

Illus. 25 The Amsterdam Bourse in the early 17th century. (From J.I. Pontanus, *Rerum et Urbis Amstelodamensium Historia* [History of the City of Amsterdam], Amsterdam 1611. The Hague, Koninklijke Bibliotheek, 136 B 20, after p. 452)

that his argument was not about "Goa or Melaka", ports, in other words, that were held as colonies proper by the Estado da Índia.[129] For Grotius the issue was the open sea,[130] not the coastal waters, bays, gulfs, ports or estuaries.[131] Why concede one but not the other? The answer depends on a nation's military ability to physically defend these waters and effectively exercise control over them. The Venetians patrolled the waters of the Adriatic, but the Portuguese could not possibly control the whole of the South Atlantic and the Indian Oceans. These seas are so vast, even sizeable Portuguese armadas would have inevitably failed in their efforts to monitor and exercise effective control over such expansive pelagic spaces.

In criticising British maritime hegemony during the late 19th century, the German historian Heinrich von Treitschke cited Friedrich Schiller's *Die Braut von Messina oder die Feindlichen Brüder* (The Bride of Messina, or the Hostile Brothers):[132] "Auf den Wellen is alles Welle, Auf dem Meer ist kein Eigenthum" (On the sea everything is in flux, on the sea there is no property).[133] This latter image is not far removed from Grotius' own ideas on the freedom of the high seas, albeit a freedom that effectively translates into a fiercely competitive, sometimes necessarily brutal, but most certainly not a lawless regime governed by an indivisible trinity of commerce, war and plunder.[134] The Dutch humanist was not alone in arguing that the high seas remain vast zones common to all, governed by a basic set of natural laws, including self-defence and the right to act as judge and executor in one's own cause. The oceans represent open zones where fundamentals of human intercourse — including the *ius communicationis* — necessarily apply, and where in any case believers were bound by Revelation and also the principles of Christian charity. Such views were readily espoused by political superiors in the Dutch Republic and, of course, by a powerful faction among Dutch merchants. The unfolding of VOC history after its formation in 1602 lends ample evidence to this.

Did Grotius Change His Mind?

The present section examines some individual points of contention. The central question here is this: Did Grotius change his mind over the years?

Not only are there internal problems with the argument of *Mare Liberum*, it also appears that Grotius adapted his ground of defence with the evolution of VOC policies, the shifting circumstances in the East Indies' trade, especially against the backdrop of the Twelve Years' Truce. This is evidenced by the documents drafted or perused by the Dutch humanist in the course of the Indies Conferences of 1613 and 1615, and later in his *De Iure Belli ac Pacis*.

Let me first turn to the issue of prohibiting what nature had supposedly given to all mankind, namely, *ius communicationis* or the "right of [free and unimpeded] communication".[135] *Mare Liberum* advanced the position that the "Portuguese, even if they were sovereigns in those parts to which the Dutch make voyages, would nevertheless be doing them an injury if they should forbid access to those places and to prevent them from trading there."[136] In other words, the Portuguese did not have the capacity to deny access to emporia or the pursuit of free trade in ports under their direct sovereignty, let alone those that did not fall under their control. This was later elevated to a general principle in *Mare Liberum*: "Besides, what are we to say of the fact that not even temporal lords in their own dominions are competent to prohibit the freedom of trade."[137] This statement on the unconditionality of free trade is placed in perspective in chapter 11 of *Mare Liberum*. While it is possible to curtail free trade, a sovereign may not be arbitrary or even selective in barring access to ports or emporia under his control. Any prohibition of access must be categorical, across the board. In the words of Grotius: "It is not sufficient that some be coerced, but it is indispensable that all be coerced."[138] The situation envisaged is simply all or nothing; either everyone is granted access to trade, or one becomes a completely isolationist nation, hermetically sealed off from the rest of the world.[139] In theory the latter is possible, but in reality it is not a viable option.

The English delegates at the Anglo-Dutch maritime and colonial conferences opined that, ultimately, Dutch practices of exclusion differed insubstantially from Portuguese policies, a verdict that Grotius swiftly rebuffed. Was the Dutch humanist first advocating unhindered access to the East Indies by the Dutch when they were hoping to establish themselves there? And after the Dutch had consolidated outposts, factories and forts, did he not seek to exclude real and potential competitors from trading in Asia's great emporia? Did the prodigy from Delft change his mind about "free trade"?

The answer is negative. Grotius legitimised Dutch exclusion policies by invoking the only condition upon which exclusion may be legitimate: by excluding everyone, including Asian traders. As has been discussed in chapter 2, treaties signed between the Dutch and the Asian princes were valid but *exclusive* contracts. The Portuguese, by contrast, were (supposedly) selective in their exclusion policies, and Asian traders continued to engage in commerce as they had done before the arrival of the European colonial powers. Portuguese contracts with Asian sovereigns were, according to the Dutch luminary, not exclusive in nature. This is not quite accurate, for the Portuguese did sign treaties that, after about 1600, began to contain clauses specifically singling out the Dutch, the English or the French for exclusion.[140] But this too corroborates Grotius' earlier position, for one excludes either all or nobody. The VOC, of course, excluded all real and potential competitors and bound princes in Asia to abide by their contracts with the Dutch — no matter how dubious the conditions might have been under which the contractual concessions were conceded.[141] Grotius was painfully aware of the grave implications such treaties, exacted by arm-twisting and force, would invariably bear on the liberty of princes and peoples. His citation from Isocrates, loosely rendered in *Mare Liberum*, should have served many potential and future Asian allies of the VOC as a classic warning:[142]

> Demosthenes in his speech on the liberty of the Rhodians says that it was necessary for those who wished to be free to keep away from treaties which were imposed on them, because such treaties were almost the same as slavery.

Surely, one might retort, this all or nothing option is tantamount to creating a monopoly, and we have already familiarised ourselves with *Mare Liberum*'s stance on monopolies.[143] It criticised the Portuguese on the grounds that they drove up prices, engaged in profiteering and failed to share with the other European nations the bounty of the East Indies. It shall be recalled that for Grotius, monopolies were legitimate and justified in one single instance: if the party claiming the monopoly did not engage in hoarding and profiteering. At the Anglo-Dutch Conferences, he drove home two points: Dutch prices were justified because of the high costs incurred in protecting Asian princes from Iberian encroachment;[144] but ultimately the cost of lending armed protection to trade should not be excessive or disproportionate.

This position, in turn, led to two scenarios: one, the Dutch had to sustain the independence of the rulers on whose continued (but legally compromised) sovereignty Dutch presence in the East Indies ultimately rested. The price for such political involvement with Asian rulers was paid by

European consumers, who paid a hefty surcharge on commodities imported from the East Indies. This position was as unbelievable then as it appears to the contemporary reader.

Two, Grotius distinguished the Iberian exclusionary policy from the Dutch case on the additional grounds that his countrymen did not claim for themselves and occupy vast tracts of land, but only specific locations. As has been seen in the preceding chapter, exclusion was thus limited to certain ports and places under contract. With this argument Grotius almost certainly sought to thwart the accusation that other parties were unjustly excluded from sharing in the bounty and wealth. Given how much of the discussion with the English over the Indies addressed the spice trade, surely Grotius and the delegates present at the conferences in London and the Hague were painfully aware that the key spices — nutmeg, mace and cloves — grew in only a few places and not everywhere in Asia. This would have left the "other European parties" engaged in the spice trade, such as the English, with little more than dealings in pepper. But commerce in this crop was not where the fat profits were reaped.

Afterword

It would appear that *Mare Liberum* has been widely misunderstood in its intention and rhetorical objective. It addresses navigation on the high seas, not in coastal waters, gulfs, bays or estuaries. It focuses on Spanish and Portuguese policies of obstruction, not on Genoese and Venetian claims to maritime *dominium* or *imperium*. It targets the crimes committed by the Portuguese against nature and Creation. The Portuguese seriously offended in that they sought to impede commerce and communication at large between the Dutch traders and the Asian princes and their peoples; they committed a serious crime by unjustly claiming the oceans to be their exclusive preserve; and they committed a serious offence by abusing their monopoly, by hoarding and by letting nature's bounty simply go to waste.

Mare Liberum makes a plea for the right of Dutch traders to freely access marketplaces and emporia in Asia by unimpeded and undisturbed navigation on the high seas. The freedom of navigation forms a subset to the overarching arguments on the freedom of access and trade. This reading of Grotius' treatise stands in sharp contrast to past interpretations, insofar as these have placed the freedom of navigation on the seas — and not the issues of unimpeded access and free trade — at the forefront of scholarly attention. From this vantage point, Grotius was surprisingly consistent in his thinking on the wider issues of maritime trade and navigation, including the two colonial conferences of 1613 and 1615 and even beyond.

To the Dutch, free trade and free access to marketplaces and emporia that had to be defended by peace, by treaty or by war became enshrined in a series of contracts signed between the VOC (as a representative of the Dutch States General) and individual rulers across Southeast Asia. Most of these agreements concluded between sovereign parties (and therefore carrying the weight of an international treaty) feature clauses that were either specifically directed against Portugal and Spain, or in other ways curtailed the freedom of the contracting Asian prince and his people to sell commodities to outside parties. In the early years of the VOC's corporate lifespan, Grotius is known to have influenced the drafting of such provisions. From a historical perspective, the outcome is clear: the treaties effectively curtailed the scope of action for the Asian princes and their peoples, and also divided their sovereignty. Any breach of these provisions was interpreted by the VOC as an invitation to attack and punish the defaulting party, chiefly citing the principle of *pacta sunt servanda* (contracts must be honoured). Grotius insisted on this principle throughout the colonial conferences of 1613 and 1615. He also sanctioned the idea of a divisible sovereignty.[145] The various marks of sovereignty could be distributed among different officeholders both inside and outside a given body politic. This position was advanced by Grotius in his treatise *Commentarius in Theses XI* and later in his *De Iure Belli ac Pacis* of 1625. The divisibility of sovereignty in Grotius' writings has captured the imagination of several contemporary researchers and is recognised by a growing number of scholars, including myself, to have significantly strengthened the legal foundations for European colonial rule in Asia, Africa and the Americas.[146] All peoples are originally free; they are even free to irreversibly sign away their liberty of choice at the stroke of a pen.[147]

For much of the 1900s Grotius was celebrated as a prince of peace, champion of reconciliation or early advocate of the freedom of maritime navigation. Twentieth-century scholars have also ascribed to the famed humanist certain intellectual faculties that could only be described as superhuman.[148] These, together with the beaming sense of enthusiasm expressed by Dutch luminaries of jurisprudence, especially Cornelis van

Illus. 26 Early 18th-century engraving depicting the "Apotheosis of Grotius" on the title page of the Brandt-Cattenburgh biography. Exaggerated accounts of his almost superhuman abilities were already well established by the late 17th and early 18th centuries. (Title page from Caspar Brandt and Adriaen van Cattenburgh, *Historie van het leven des Heeren Huig de Groot* [History of the Life of Mr. Huig de Groot], vol. I, Amsterdam and Dordrecht, 1727. Private collection, Peter Borschberg)

Vollenhoven and Willem J. M. van Eysinga, have served to distort almost beyond recognition Grotius' standing among the architects of early modern colonial rule. This skewed perspective of Grotius as the champion of the free seas is captured, in a nutshell, by the following testimony of Christian Meurer in 1919 and verbally enriched by Anand in 1981:[149]

> "The freedom of the seas slumbered the sleep of a Sleeping Beauty" … until this gallant knight from the Netherlands appeared "whose kiss awakened her once more."

While that much enthused-about awakening did not occur until several hundred years later, that kiss from Grotius' forked silver tongue could only serve to engender troubled rest. In European nations — including the Dutch Republic — and their respective colonial possessions, the principle of *mare clausum* (the closed or un-free sea) prevailed and in most recent times is experiencing something of a revival.

In today's age of globalisation, the issues of free trade and navigation are as important as they were in the 16th and 17th centuries. With the ratification of the new law of the sea, it is very clear that the problems already addressed by Grotius and his opponents, such as Welwood and de Freitas, remain core issues that plague nations today.[150] The ongoing disputes cover the reach of territorial waters and economic zones, the protection of fishing stocks in coastal waters,[151] the need to combat piracy, the rights and obligations of neutral shipping as well as the development of marine resources, including the exploitation of the deep-sea bed.[152] With the benefit of historical hindsight, it is apparent that on some issues of maritime law and policy Grotius was less "modern" in his thinking than some of his opponents, such as de Freitas. For all his flaws, though, the Portuguese scholar actually foresaw the need for sovereign bodies to possess, or at least exercise control over the seabed and spaces filled by (deep) pelagic waters.[153] With the advancement of technology, it is now possible to extract minerals from the seabed. Oil has been extracted offshore for decades.[154] Contemporary environmental problems underscore the recognition that the high seas are subject to different aspects of legal order.

What about the freedom of trade and commerce? One thing becomes very clear from a close reading of Grotius' *Mare Liberum*: Free trade has never really been cleanly separated from politics. Issues of trade and commerce have been, and may always remain, inseparably coupled with the tenets of political expediency.

CHAPTER 4

How Grotius Acquired a Working Knowledge of the East Indies

As has been seen in the preceding chapters, it is now an academic commonplace to treat Grotius' early work on the law of nations, *De Iure Praedae Commentarius* (Commentary on the Law of Prize and Booty) as a commissioned response to the seizure of the Portuguese-flagged carrack *Santa Catarina* in 1603. Sadly, however, many researchers begin to seriously disagree after this very basic insight. They part company over who actually commissioned the work. Some believe it was the *landsadvocaat* (the land's advocate), Johan van Oldenbarnevelt, while a far larger group point a finger at the directors of the VOC in Amsterdam.[1] There is also substantial disagreement over authorial intention: exactly what kind of a "response" is this treatise? Is it a legal brief? Is it a court petition (*pleidooi voor het groote proces*) or a *gelegenheidsgeschrift* (treatise of occasion) as Fruin had called it?[2] Should *De Iure Praedae* be classified under the general category of patriotic literature along with his other pieces written in the first decade of the 17th century, such as the *Annales et Historiae de Rebus Belgicis* (Annals and Histories of the Low Countries) and

De Antiquitate Reipublicae Batavorum (On the Antiquity of the Batavian Republic)?[3] Or should *De Iure Praedae* be deemed an early piece of what in present-day language could be dubbed "politico-commercial propaganda"?[4]

Consensus is also absent with regard to the work's proper title. *De Iure Praedae Commentarius* was not the name given to the work by its 21-year-old author, Grotius. The name was given by the auctioneers at Martinus Nijhoff, by the 19th-century librarians (especially Pieter Anton Tiele)[5] at Leiden University Library and also by H.G. Hamaker, the first editor of the Latin text.[6] In his correspondence, Grotius referred to *De Iure Praedae* in a vague and descriptive manner, calling it *De Rebus Indicanis* (On the Affairs of the Indies) on at least two occasions.[7] Some academics, such as the political theorist Richard Tuck, think that such authentic references, including *De Indis* (his preferred title), are probably the closest contemporary scholarship can get to an original or authentic title for the work, especially because it was employed by Grotius himself.[8] But admittedly, Tuck's views are not widely accepted, and a distinct majority of researchers — rightly or wrongly — continue to employ the 19th-century title. For the sake of simplicity and as a means of forestalling any confusion among my readers, I am abiding by accepted convention and referring to this work as *De Iure Praedae Commentarius*, or in English as *Commentary on the Law of Prize and Booty*.[9] In the context of the present chapter I will also accept its established dates of composition, namely October 1604 to the autumn of 1606, with some revisions made and marginal source references added to parts of the text in later years, especially 1608 and early 1609.[10] Such amendments were made to chapter 12 — among others — which was separately published as *Mare Liberum* (The Free Sea) in 1609.[11]

Grotius, Archival Research and Asian Maritime Customs

In the present chapter I do not wish to engage in the debate over the supposed nature or authorial intention of Grotius' early oeuvre as a whole, especially since I have already addressed several of these issues in the preceding chapters. The question I place at the centre of attention in the present context concerns the sources used by Grotius for drafting and completing the second part of the manuscript, commonly known as the *pars historica*, or historical section of *De Iure Praedae*. This spans chapters 11 through 15.[12] For the record, the historical section also includes substantially the text of the aforementioned publication *Mare Liberum*.

Most of what is known about the background and historical context of *De Iure Praedae* was brought to print in a lengthy exposé by the Leiden professor of national history Robert Fruin. In 1868 he published in the Dutch periodical *De Gids* an article titled *Een onuitgegeven werk van Hugo de Groot*, which was translated into English and brought into print as *An Unpublished Work of Hugo Grotius*.[13] Fruin's lengthy article has long established itself as something of a critical introduction to the text, which is lacking in the first Latin edition prepared by Hamaker. But Fruin's research — conducted almost one and a half centuries ago — is not without questionable assumptions and false conclusions. Some of these have been identified and corrected in the study of van Ittersum's titled *Profit and Principle: Hugo Grotius, Natural Rights Theories and the Rise of Dutch Power in the East Indies, 1595–1615*. I refer to this work for further information on the importance and historic reception of Fruin's article.

Though a seminal study, Fruin's publication proves problematic in several instances. Unfortunately, some of his false or baseless assumptions have been accepted by the scholarly community as commonplace or — worse still — as unassailable truths. *De Iure Praedae*, taken as a whole, explores the theoretical and historical grounds for the attack and seizure of the Portuguese carrack *Santa Catarina* on 25 February 1603.[14] Following in the footsteps of Grotius, Fruin misidentified the location of this act of hostility as the Strait of Melaka,[15] whereas in fact it was between the Hook of Berbukit (see map on p. 6) and Singapore island's eastern seaboard near the present-day international airport at Changi. This clearly places the event not in the Melaka, but the Singapore Strait, specifically in the waters around the Johor River estuary.[16]

Fruin also erred when he singled out as a central concern of *De Iure Praedae* the supposed need to mollify the pacifist concerns of the Dutch East India Company's (VOC's) Mennonite stakeholders. The early VOC did have its Mennonite stakeholders, and concerns were voiced about the recourse to violence, either in offensive prizetaking against Iberian shipping or even in self-defence.[17] But disgruntled and disappointed Mennonites could hardly have been the targeted audience of *De Iure Praedae*. Fruin's claim would hardly seem problematic to contemporary scholarship had it not been repeated and even amplified in a number of publications of more recent decades.[18] Van Ittersum has convincingly rebuffed the centrality of the "Mennonite shareholder" thesis with evidence dredged in the Nationaal Archief in the Hague.[19] Yet there is one additional aspect of Fruin's article that requires explicit rebuttal here and that concerns his assumptions about the sources to which Grotius had access at the time of writing *De Iure Praedae*:[20]

> Hugo de Groot took on himself the writing of such a treatise. I cannot assure that he had been incited to this by the [VOC] directors; I've not been able to find any proof of this. In a letter to his brother [Willem] dating from a later period, he admits to have stood in close relationship with the Company. And there can be no doubt that he made use of the archives of the United Company and of its predecessors[21] when writing his piece.

Fruin's assumption about Grotius' supposed archival research activities would probably seem innocuous if it had not been taken on and developed further by Charles Alexandrowicz in his *Introduction to the History of the Law of Nations in the East Indies*, published in 1967. The following two excerpts from Alexandrowicz are classic examples of how unproven or assumed positions can — and indeed have — become accepted as almost incontestable truths: [22]

> When Grotius studied the facts of the case of the *Santa Catharina*, which led to the writing of the treatise *De Iure Praedae*, he acquired from the relevant documents and sources first-hand knowledge of the problems of the East Indies and the habits and laws of its peoples and Rulers. ... It is therefore possible to assume that Grotius in formulating his doctrine of the freedom of the sea found himself encouraged by what he learned from the study of Asian maritime custom. In fact it would be difficult to believe that he could have ignored the outstanding precedent for maritime freedom offered by the régime in the Indian Ocean in contrast to maritime practice in Europe. A brief analysis of various passages of Grotius's *Mare Liberum* may confirm the correctness of the above assumption.

Not only was it assumed that Grotius had gained access to, or even studied in, the VOC archives (that presumably included the holdings of its various corporate predecessors known as the voorcompagniën), he was now seen to have also examined the habits and laws of Asian rulers, nay, even delved into Asian maritime custom. Is that true? Is there any evidence to support this claim? Is it sufficient to simply defer to the published text of *Mare Liberum* as a pool of evidence for the "correctness of the above assumption"? The reader may already surmise that my answer to the latter is negative. In the present context I shall pose a basic but important question: What did Grotius actually know at the time of writing *De Iure Praedae*? Specifically, I am interested to explore what Grotius could have known about Asian customs, polities and the intra-Asian maritime trading regime at large. I will focus attention on the role of the Estado da Índia within the Asian maritime trading regime.

Early Materials from Jan ten Grootenhuys (1604)

Which source materials — published or unpublished — did Grotius actually have at his fingertips while drafting *De Iure Praedae*? Where better to search for answers than in Grotius' expansive and learned correspondence. As is widely accepted, the young humanist was asked to write a piece justifying the seizure of the *Santa Catarina*. It is unlikely that the treatise was meant to influence the decision of the court, as the Amsterdam Admiralty Court had adjudicated the *Santa Catarina* and its cargo legal prize on 9 September 1604. First evidence of Grotius working on the manuscript of *De Iure Praedae* dates from a later period, namely, mid-October that year.[23] In other words, Grotius had begun drafting his treatise around the time, or certainly after, the verdict on the *Santa Catarina* incident was cast by the Admiralty Court. Of special interest to my investigations are personal letters that underscore two aspects of his toiling on the manuscript: The piece was most probably commissioned by the directors of the VOC in Amsterdam, and the directors arranged to furnish Grotius with materials to complete his task.

Attention is now drawn to two letters written by Jan ten Grootenhuys[24] dating from the second half of October 1604. These can be found in their original Latin in the first volume of Grotius' *Briefwisseling* (Correspondence), as well as in the 2006 English-language edition of *De Iure Praedae*.[25] In the first letter, dated 15 October 1604, ten Grootenhuys wrote:[26]

> At last, oh most learned of men, we send you the Indian Reports which you have been expecting for a long time. These reports were taken from the captains of the ships themselves, who had to confirm them under oath as well. You will clearly understand from them what the Portuguese have attempted against each of the voyages for the purpose

> of destroying our men. In addition, you will derive from them countless proofs of perfidy, tyranny and hostility suitable to your apology. We trust that your apology, begun so felicitously, will be completed in a short while thanks to your attentiveness. The letters of Petrus Plancius, the privateering commissions and other documents if necessary will be delivered to you at the first opportunity, as will those that your affection should subsequently demand from us, you to whom we offer every service with the greatest pleasure.

On the reverse side of this letter, Grotius noted as received:[27]

> privateering commissions[28]
> the verdict of the Admiralty court[29]
> the edict of the Estates of Holland[30]
> obtain from Plancius the titles of such books on Portuguese trade in the East Indies as may be purchased here.

This first surviving letter by ten Grootenhuys reveals a number of important aspects about the commissioned nature and the working habits of the young scholar. Broadly staked out, one can say that by mid-October Grotius had already started writing on his treatise. Ten Grootenhuys' letter served as a reminder that there was some urgency about completing the project, and also that Grotius would be given access to more documentation if he so desired. Importantly, the letter also served to reinforce the parameters staked out by the VOC directors: The commissioned work was to highlight the perfidy, tyranny and hostility of the Portuguese in the East Indies and underscore their countless misdeeds against Dutch traders. Ten Grootenhuys may have called the work in progress an *apologia* (apology, written defence), but the anti-Iberian tone and thrust desired of the work is little more than what in contemporary circles might be considered propaganda.

Given the nature of the materials either forwarded or promised, it is tempting to conclude that in October 1604 Grotius was toiling on the historical section of *De Iure Praedae* (chapters 11–16).[31] It is uncertain how long ten Grootenhuys had kept Grotius waiting for the "Indian reports" — the wording may very well be just a pose of courtesy.

Of special interest to the present chapter are the affidavits mentioned by ten Grootenhuys. These documents, bound together in a single volume as the "Book Concerning the Cruel, Treacherous and Hostile Proceedings of the Portuguese in the East Indies", presently belong to the Nationaal

Archief in the Hague.[32] They were identified, transcribed, discussed and published by the Dutch historian Coolhaas in 1965 as *Een bron van het historische gedeelte van Hugo de Groots 'De Iure Praedae'* (A Source of the Historical Part of Hugo Grotius' 'De Iure Praedae').[33] As the study of Coolhaas is academically outstanding as well as exhaustive, suffice it to observe here that this "Book ... of the Portuguese in the East Indies" can be deemed little more than the embittered and vindictive carping of interviewees who earlier suffered at the hands of the Estado da Índia's officials. This collection of affidavits supplied Grotius with some concrete historical examples and evidently also the anti-Lusitanian tone that contributed meaningfully to the shape and rhetorical objective of the *pars historica*, especially chapter 11.[34]

Ten Grootenhuys promised more documents, and judging from the notes jotted down by Grotius on the original letter of 15 October as well as from the contents of a second letter dated 20 October 1604, these were indeed received. In the latter we read: [35]

> We hope that you have received those documents pertaining to the Indies trade that I recently sent to you. For the present we enclose the edict of the Estates of Holland, and the sworn statement of Mr. Apius,[36] along with the verdict of the Amsterdam Admiralty Court.[37] The day after tomorrow, God willing, we will send you the rest, wherein I will write to you at length.

On the back of the letter, Grotius recorded as received: [38]

> the placard of the Estates General
> edict
> the instructions mentioned by them
> ...
> of Amsterdam
> ...
> map of the East Indies
> the location of the carrack's capture and a description of its seizure
> placards and extracts from the instructions with regard to the prize
> Plancius' memorial
> map of the East Indies[39]

From the two letters by ten Grootenhuys and the notes recorded by Grotius on their reverse side, it is evident that the materials supplied

Illus. 27 Cover with title of the bound volume *Boeck Tracterende vande Wreede, Verradische ende Hostile proceduren der Portugesen In Oost-Indien* (Book Concerning the Cruel, Treacherous and Hostile Proceedings of the Portuguese in the East Indies) which was forwarded to Grotius by the VOC directors in Amsterdam around October 1604. He used the booklet at the time of drafting the historical chapters of his *De Iure Praedae Commentarius* (Commentary on the Law of Prize and Booty). (The Hague, Nationaal Archief, Collectie Baron H. van Zuylen van Nyevelt, suppl. 2, no. 13 [2.21.179.01 no. 13])

were of a dual nature: first, affidavits outlining the personal and harrowing experiences of officers and ships' mates who had sailed and returned from the Indies; second, official documentation pertaining specifically to the *Santa Catarina* incident as well as to Dutch privateering activities in general. The latter fundamentally confirmed the seizure of the *Santa Catarina* as a lawful act of prize taking and also endorsed attacks on Spanish and Portuguese targets as legitimate acts of war. These official documents include the following: the edict of the Dutch States General; the decree of the States of Holland of 1 September 1604;[40] and the verdict of the Amsterdam admiralty court of 9 September 1604 adjudicating the *Santa Catarina* case as good prize.[41] Suffice it to observe here that the intricate theory behind the concept of the just war and the taking of prize as a lawful act within the context of a just war, was worked out by Grotius in the *pars dogmatica*, or theoretical section, of *De Iure Praedae* (chapters 1–10).

Of special interest to the present exposé are the affidavit of Martin Apius, the letters and the memorial of Plancius, the map(s) of the East Indies and a question reserved for the Dutch cleric Plancius.

Apius was one of the members of Admiral van Neck's crew taken prisoner by the Portuguese in Macao. Seventeen of his mates were executed in the Luso-Chinese enclave, but Apius was brought to Goa, where he was cross-examined by officers of the Estado da Índia and later set free. His affidavit was filed on his return to the Netherlands. As is known, the execution of 17 mates of van Neck's crew triggered the decision on the part of van Heemskerk and his *breede raad* (officers' council) to attack Portuguese mercantile shipping off the coast of the Malay Peninsula,[42] and the name of Martin Apius is also found in the main text of *De Iure Praedae*.[43] This first package of documents dispatched to Grotius in mid-October 1604 also finds a strong echo in the *pars historica* (historical section).

The entry "location of the carrack's capture and a description of its seizure" probably refers to a document, or several documents, such as the *Discours ende* advertisement as well as a notarised testimony of Jacob van Heemskerk dated 27 August 1603. Copies of the earlier manuscript formed part of the 1864 auction of Grotius' working papers and are presently preserved in the Nationaal Archief van Nederland in the Hague.[44] They yield important information about the supposed Portuguese harassment of Johor at the beginning of the 17th century, the events leading up to the seizure of the *Santa Catarina* and the course of events off the Hook of Berbukit near the Johor River estuary.[45]

A Question for Plancius

Evidence gleaned from the two letters of Jan ten Grootenhuys from October 1604 points at the existence of letters as well as a memorial by Plancius. As observed by Philipp Christiaan Molhuysen, editor of the first volume of Grotius' *Briefwisseling* (Correspondence), Plancius was "bekend door zijn studiën over the zeevaart" (known for his studies on navigation).[46] But he is today also celebrated for his work on astronomy and especially also geography.[47] Acknowledged as one of the founding fathers of cartography in the Dutch Republic, Plancius was an avid collector of travelogues of Spanish and Portuguese voyages and incorporated information mined from these into his cartographic creations. Plancius played a role in the board of the *Compagnie van Verre* (Long-Distance Company) and served with Arendt ten Grootenhuys on the board of directors of the *Oude Compagnie* (Old Company) of Amsterdam, one of the voorcompagniën that was subsequently merged into the VOC in 1602.[48] Described by the VOC historian Femme Gaastra as a disciple of the famed cartographer Gerard Mercator,[49] Plancius drew an estimated 100 maritime charts, many of which were used during the early voyages of the Dutch to Asia. He was, in other words, a pioneer and an acknowledged expert on the geography of, and maritime navigation to, the East Indies.[50] This expertise provides the immediate context for understanding the question jotted down by Grotius — evidently intended as a reminder for himself — "Te vraghen aen Plancius om de namen derghene dye in den Portugese handel in Oostindie hebben geschreven om hyer te becomen" (to ask Plancius about titles of such books on Portuguese trade in the East Indies to be obtained here). We will return to that request in just a short while, after engaging with some thoughts on the map(s) of the East Indies passed on to Grotius to assist him in fulfilling his commission.

What remains shrouded in mystery is the map, or possibly two maps, forwarded by ten Grootenhuys in October 1604. Discussing possible specimens is really nothing more than speculation. It is certain that Plancius prepared scores of maps for the VOC and fundamentally based his charts on Cornelis Claesz. Another source of cartographical information might have been Pieter Bertius, a friend and correspondent of Grotius during

Illus. 28 Map of the East Indies titled *Insulae Moluccae* (the Maluku Islands) by the Dutch theologian and cartographer Pieter Plancius, c.1592. A copy of this specimen, or probably a similar one, was sent to Grotius during the closing weeks of 1604 as part of a package of documents from the VOC directors. (Amsterdam University Library, OK 131)

this period. He is known to have published maps depicting the Malay Peninsula, then commonly referred to in Dutch circles as "Malakka" after the great emporium situated on its western coast. Judging from a number of internal arguments of *De Iure Praedae*, such as the author's misplacement of the *Santa Catarina* incident, and also in view of Grotius' occasional penchant for Ptolemaic geographic nomenclature (which doubtless stemmed from his familiarity with Greek and Roman classical sources), it seems plausible that he was working with specimens such as Claesz, Plancius or even Bertius.[51] But, as stated, this is just speculation. The former two maps were widely available at the time, and a copy of Claesz was adjoined to Jan Huyghen van Linschoten's widely consulted and readily available *Reysgeschrift*. There is no firm evidence in *De Iure Praedae* that Grotius actually consulted the *Reysgeschrift* and *Itinerario*, published in 1595–6. Admittedly, a copy of the latter was confiscated from Grotius' private library in 1618,[52] but it is not certain when he consulted this work, let alone purchased his personal copy.

With these deliberations I am placed in a position to answer the question concerning the books available in the Netherlands on Portuguese India. There is no surviving record to confirm that such a request was ever lodged, and even if Grotius did, it appears to have remained unfulfilled or negative. This is because there is not a single Portuguese source cited or even mentioned throughout the complete manuscript of *De Iure Praedae* that even as much as alludes to the Estado da Índia or its maritime intra-Asian trading regime. Portuguese materials touching on the East Indies were difficult to obtain, partially because of Portugal's policies of secrecy, but also because there were genuinely few printed sources that could have been successfully mined for writing *De Iure Praedae*.

Among Grotius' surviving reading notes[53] is a double-sided folio sized page numbered 429 and features points in Latin that are written in what appears now as rust-brown ink. The colour of this ink is strongly reminiscent of the autograph manuscript of *De Iure Praedae* at Leiden University. With this observation I do not necessarily wish to make a connection between the two, but simply place it among the realm of possibilities. The top half of folio 429 recto, incip. *Ṛegnum Guzarat* (kingdom of Gujarat), features notes about piracy, commerce, and commodities traded. There are also brief notes for *Canam Regnum* (probably a reference to the kingdom of Cananor) and *Cambaia* (Cambay). The source of these notes is not known. One entry of just over a line mentions the work of Thomas Lopes (or Lopez).[54] The bottom half

ITINERARIO,

Voyage ofte Schipvaert / van Jan Huygen van Linschoten naer Oost ofte Portugaels Indien inhoudende een corte beschryvinghe der selver Landen ende Zee-custen / met aenwysinge van alle de voornaemde principale Havens / Revieren / hoecken ende plaetsen / tot noch toe vande Portugesen ontdeckt ende bekent: Waer by ghevoecht zijn / niet alleen die Conterfeytsels vande habyten / drachten ende wesen / so vande Portugesen aldaer residerende / als vande ingeboornen Indianen / ende huere Tempels / Afgoden / Huysinge / met die voornaemste Boomen / Vruchten / Kruyden / Speceryen / ende diergelijcke materialen / als ooc die manieren des selfden Volckes / so in hunnen Godts-diensten / als in Politie en Huijs-houdinghe: maer ooc een corte verhalinge van de Coophandelingen / hoe en waer die ghedreven en ghevonden worden / met die ghedenckweerdichste geschiedenissen / voorghevallen den tyt zijnder residentie aldaer.

Alles beschreven ende by een vergadert, door den selfden, seer nut, oorbaer, ende oock vermakelijcken voor alle curieuse ende Liefhebbers van vreemdigheden,

t'AMSTELREDAM.

By Cornelis Claesz. op't VVater, in't Schrijf-boeck, by de oude Brugghe.

Anno CIↃ. IↃ. XCVI.

Illus. 29 Title page of Jan Huyghen van Linschoten's first edition of his *Itinerario* published in 1596. (The Hague, Koninklijke Bibliotheek, 1702 B 4) of folio 429 recto features notes that have been taken from "Eduardus Barbosa" or the travel account of Duarte Barbosa (see the image on p. 120).[55] The information collated here relates mainly to issues of commerce and trade on the Indian Subcontinent.

The verso of folio 429 contains reading notes under the heading "Malabar Pauli Veneti" (Malabar of Paul the Venetian, see the image on p. 121). Venetus, who is better known for his works on Aristotle, lived at the turn of the 14th and 15th centuries which also makes him a contemporary of the Italian merchant and adventurer Niccolò Conti. The date indicated by Grotius slightly further to the right, namely the year 1250, can almost certainly be taken as a reference to Venetus' edition of Marco Polo. Again the geographic focus is on subcontinental India, specifically the Malabar Coast. Most of the notes relate to matters of commerce and commodities of trade. There are also some loose references to the Brahmins and other points pertaining to the ruler. No insights that would show a connection with *De Iure Praedae* or *Mare Liberum* are recorded here. It is not certain which edition(s) Grotius was working with in compiling his notes on this page, or whether he used a single or multiple sources. Judging by the writing and the ink, however, it seems that he likely compiled these in a single session. In turn, this could be taken as an indication that he probably used a compilation of travel literatures such as notably the series prepared by Ramusio titled *Delle Navigazioni e Viaggi*. Its first volume was published in Venice in 1550 and reprinted several times thereafter.[56]

The annotated edition of the 1864 auction published by L.J. Noordhoff lists under "part I" a single sheet of notes taken in the French language and excerpted from Bartolomé Leonardo de Argensola's *Conquista de las Islas Malucas* (Conquest of the Maluku Islands). As this book was first published in 1609, it is certain that these notes were not prepared at the time of writing *De Iure Praedae* or even revising *Mare Liberum* for the press. Given the themes covered in these notes, it appears that they were probably compiled around the time of the Anglo-Dutch maritime and colonial conferences. They reveal their author's specific interest in English activities against the Dutch on islands of Ambon and Tidor in the Malukus.[57]

The sources most readily available in the Dutch Republic at the time would have been Linschoten's *Itinerario* and *Reysgeschrift*, which incorporate and reproduce many translated materials of Portuguese origin. An easily accessible source would have been the first volume of *Delle Navigazioni*

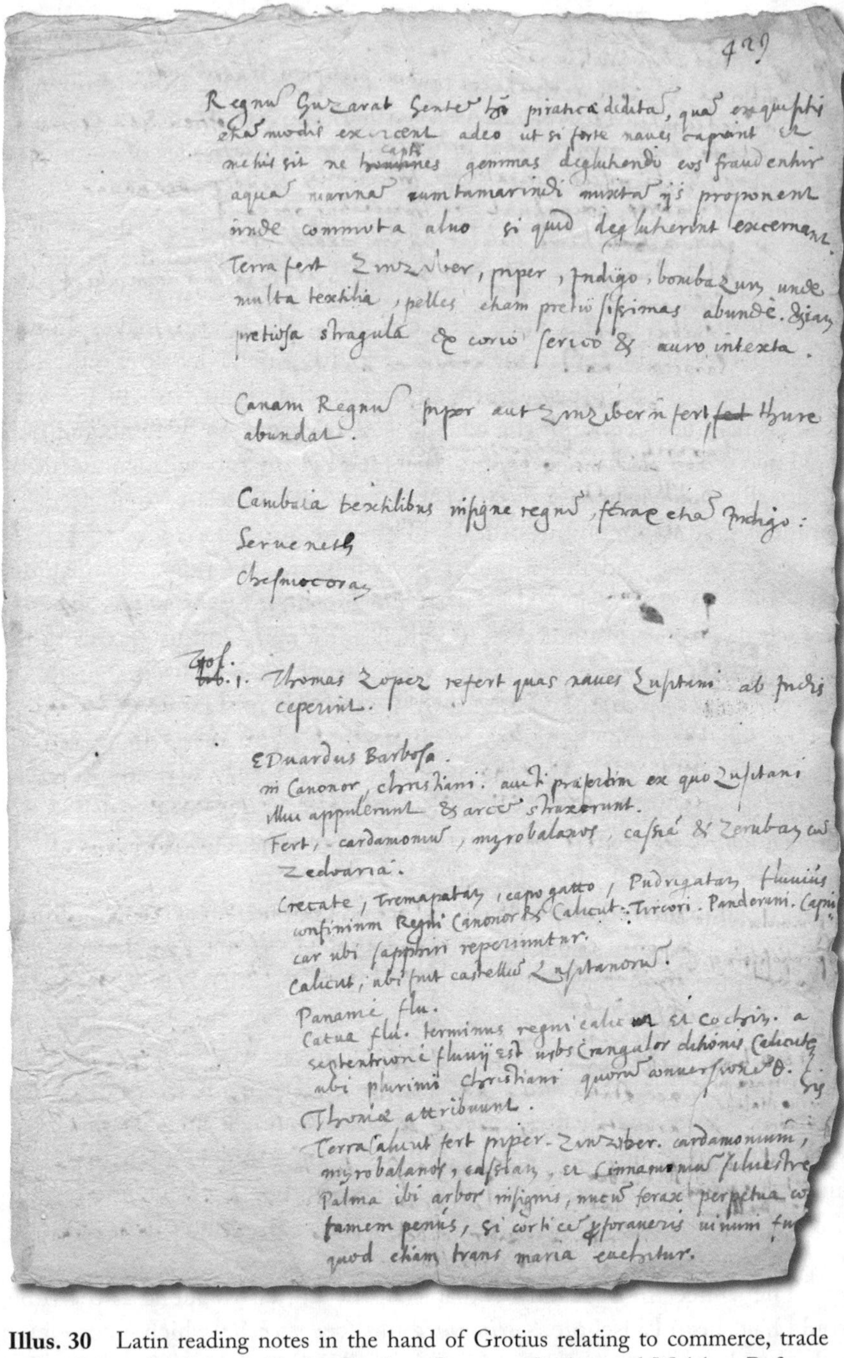

Illus. 30 Latin reading notes in the hand of Grotius relating to commerce, trade and politics of India, specifically Cambay, Cananor, Cochin and Malabar. References are also found to the authors "Thomaz Lopes" and "Eduardus Barbosa". (The Hague: Nationaal Archief, *Collectie Hugo de Groot, Supplement I* [1.10.35.02, no. 40])

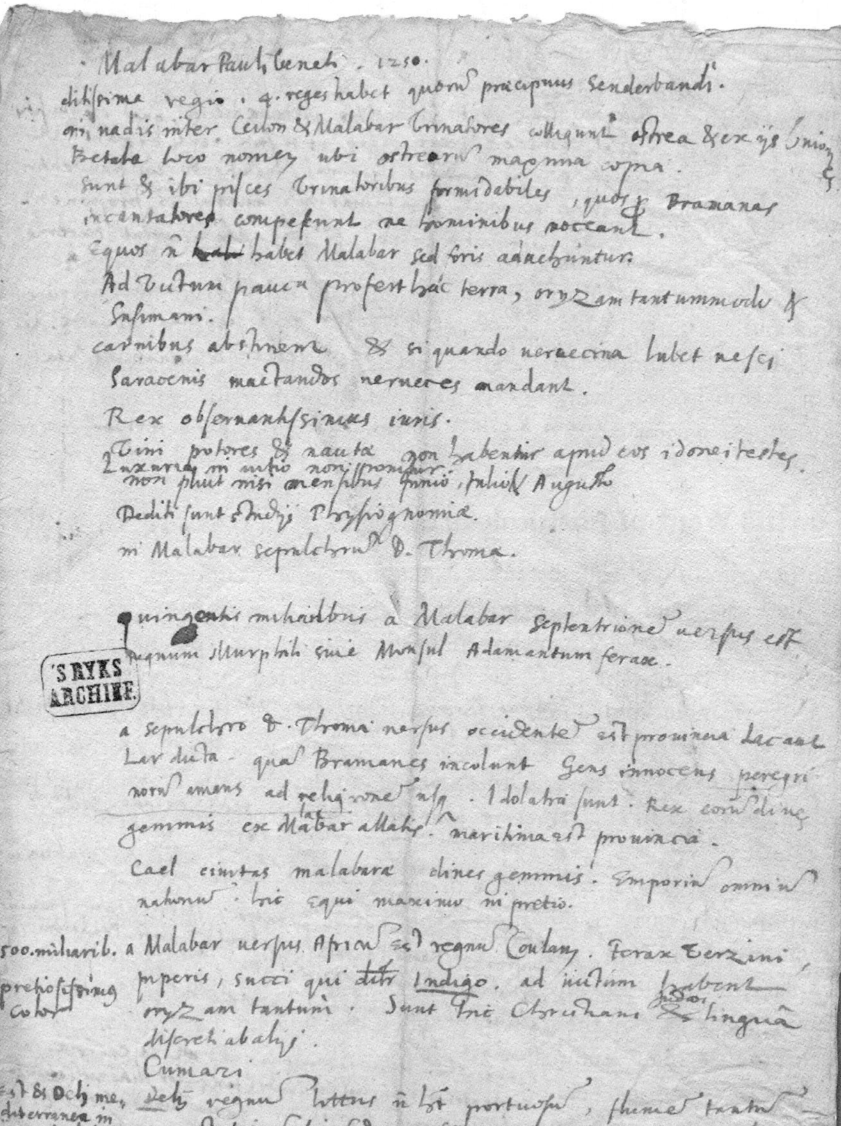

Malabar Pauli Veneti . 1250.
ditissima regio . quae reges habet quorum praecipuus Senderbandi.
in vadis inter Ceilon & Malabar Urinatores colliguntur ostrea & ex iis Uniones
Betala loco nomen ubi ostrearum magna copia.
Sunt & ibi pisces Urinatoribus formidabiles, quos Bramanas
incantatores compescunt ne hominibus noceant.
Equos non habet Malabar sed foris advehuntur.
Ad victum pauca profert haec terra, oryzam tantummodo &
Sesamum.
carnibus abstinent & si quando vaccina habet [illegible]
Saracenis mactandos [illegible] mandant.
Rex observantissimus iuris.
Vini potores & nautae non habentur apud eos idonei testes.
Luxuria in vitio non ponitur.
non pluit nisi mensibus Junio, Julio, Augusto
Dediti sunt Indi Physiognomiae.
in Malabar sepulchrum D. Thomae.

Quingentis miliaribus a Malabar Septentrionem versus est
regnum Murphili sive Monsul Adamantum ferax.

a sepulchro D. Thomae versus occidentem est provincia Lacaal
Lar dicta quam Bramanes incolunt Gens innocens peregrinorum amans ad religionem [illegible] . Idolatrae sunt . Rex eorum dives
gemmis ex Malabar allatis . maritima est provincia .
Cael civitas malabarica dives gemmis . Emporium omnium
nationum . hic equi maximo in pretio.
500. miliarib. a Malabar versus Africum est regnum Coulam . Ferax Verzini
piperis, succi qui dicitur Indigo . ad victum habent
oryzam tantum . Sunt hic Christiani & Judaei lingua
differentes ab aliis.
preciosissimus color
Cumari
Deli regnum littus non habet portuosum, flumen tantum
nec statio satis fida . nascitur piper zinziber & alia
aromata . gens fallax, & mercatoribus infida . Sequitur
est & Cochim mediterranea in regno Malabar maiore.
Malabar regnum proprie sic dictum . Rex non agnoscens
superiorem . Gens [illegible] bello valida, [illegible]
fert piper, zinziber, cubebe, nuces indicas . aes ibi in pretio,
quod advehunt pro saburra.
vide fol. 7. b. ubi [illegible] in ea [illegible] Delli.
132

Illus. 31 See Illustration 30 for the caption.

e Viaggi. Among the more interesting accounts included in the *Viaggi* is the *Suma Oriental* of the early 16th-century Portuguese apothecary and diplomat Tomé Pires. This was published by Ramusio without providing the name of the author and in a text version so abridged that it is difficult to recognise the treatise for what it really is. The full text of Pires was published in an English translation by the Hakluyt Society in London in 1944.[58] Still, a closer comparison of the full text with Ramusio's version reveals that the best information about the nature of pre-colonial Southeast Asia and the early Luso-Asian trading regime around the Strait of Melaka and across the Indonesian Archipelago is missing.[59] It has been surmised that Ramusio was working with a transcript heavily censored by the Portuguese authorities.[60]

For the Want of Portuguese Sources

Without useful published sources explaining Asian customs or mechanisms of the Luso-Asian trading regime at his fingertips, Grotius resorted instead to materials on the Spanish conquest of the Americas. The *Brevísima Relación* of Bartolomé las Casas had been translated into several European languages, including Dutch, before and shortly after the turn of the 17th century.[61] The treatise was given a title — and was richly adorned with engraved images — that sought to visually underscore the tyrannical nature of Spanish rule in the Americas and implicitly also in the (Spanish) Low Countries.[62]

Concerns about the advent of the Spaniards in the New World and the impact of early colonisation on its native peoples were openly vented by a group of 16th-century Spanish Dominicans whom contemporary scholars have collectively dubbed the School of Salamanca. Grotius was certainly inspired by their writings when drafting his *De Iure Praedae* and incorporated many references to their works both in the theoretical as well as the historical sections.[63] This is especially true of the works of two Spanish clerics, Covarruvias y Leyva and Vitoria.[64] It further transpires that Grotius had received from the VOC directors a copy of Vitoria's *Relectiones XII* published in Lyon in 1557.[65] Supporting this claim are testimonies from Grotius' *Briefwisseling* dating to the early 1640s. In May 1643, while rummaging through his study,[66] he retrieved the copy of Vitoria's *Relectiones* that he claimed Grootenhuys had passed on to him a long time ago. Grotius expressed his intention to return this copy to its rightful owner.[67] Based on such epistolary testimony, two conclusions are warranted in the present context: First, the impact of the School of Salamanca on Grotius' early thought on war, peace and trade can be partially explained by the fact that ten Grootenhuys forwarded a copy of Vitoria at a relatively early stage of the drafting of *De Iure Praedae*; second, in the evident absence of Portuguese sources on the Luso-Asian trading regime, Grotius appears to have based his argument on Spanish authors such as Vitoria and transposed the principles from the Americas to the Asian scenario.[68] Such parallels were not always warranted, not least because the early European colonial powers — these include the Dutch as much as the Portuguese — treated Asian rulers as full members of the international community and family of rulers, as sovereigns co-equal to their counterparts in Europe.[69] Period treaties can be taken as evidence of this fundamental acceptance. Grotius himself drafted a letter on behalf of the VOC to the ruler of Tidor in 1606 or early 1607, beseeching him to unite with the company against the Iberian enemy and other possible (European) competitors in the East Indies trade.[70] Other draft treaties found among the working papers presently preserved at the Nationaal Archief van Nederland in the Hague include letters or treaties addressed to the "King of Johor" (see the image on p. 155), the "Emperor of Borneo" (that is, the Sultan of Brunei, who for much of the early modern period controlled most of Borneo island), the Kings (Rajas) of Siau and Ternate, and the "seigneurie" (probably a translation of the term *negrij* or *negeri*) of Ambon and Banda.[71] *De Iure Praedae* speaks of the King of Johor as a legitimate sovereign lord and therefore implicitly as an equal to any sovereign counterpart in Europe.[72] Grotius was aware of the serious problems raised by his transposition of principles from the New World to Southeast Asia, as is wonderfully evidenced from a short deleted comment found in chapter 2 of *De Iure Praedae*'s manuscript. The Dutchman wrote: "Alia enim India, alia Americana ratio est." (The case of the East Indies and the Americas is different.)[73] This was true — they were very different indeed — especially with regard to the principles historically associated with the idea of discovery, the treatment of (and treaties with) native rulers, and the conduct of trade and missionisation.[74] But Grotius saw the same principles of free access to emporia across the high seas as applicable to both the Americas as well as Asia.[75]

Although *De Iure Praedae* echoes many arguments from Vitoria, there are also noteworthy deviations. Two such instances merit further exploration in the present context. The first concerns the pattern of arguments extracted from Vitoria. Grotius follows the Salmantino professor in examining possible scenarios for Spain's just and unjust conquest of the New World.

Illus. 32 Portrait of Pope Nicholas V (Tommaso Parentucelli). In the bull *Romanus Pontifex* issued in 1455, this pope praised Portuguese achievements in early colonisation, expansion and the wars against the Muslims in northern Africa. The bull extended apostolic concessions to the Portuguese which in turn set the stage for the circumnavigation of Africa and the acquisition of colonies in the East Indies. (Private collection, Peter Borschberg)

Illus. 33 Portrait of Pope Alexander VI (Roderic Llançol, later Roderic de Borja i Borja). Alexander VI famously issued the bull *Inter Caetera* in 1493, drawing a line from the north to the south Pole and thus dividing the Atlantic into a Spanish and a Portuguese sphere. (Private collection, Peter Borschberg)

He took on the arguments about the humanity and equality of the native Americans, the influence exerted by the pope over the faithful, providing they had accepted him as the vicar of Christ on earth, and of course the issue of papal donations or apostolic concessions.[76] The point not taken on from Vitoria is the argument dismissing the universal authority of the Holy Roman Emperor. Given that the Dutch Republic remained formally a part of the Holy Roman Empire until the Peace of Westphalia in 1648, this issue may have been deemed sensitive.

The second deviation from Vitoria concerns the infidelity of the native peoples of the New World and its impact on their exercise of *dominium*. As seen in chapter 2, this is an important argument that, when transposed to the East Indies, served Grotius to underscore the independence and sovereignty of the rulers of Southeast Asia. As a subset to this argument, he shared with Vitoria the idea of a *ius communicationis* (right of [free and unimpeded] communication). As has been mentioned previously, Grotius modified the *ius communicationis* into a far more comprehensive entitlement that also entailed the right to conduct trade and access emporia via the high seas. While assuming a prominent place within the context of his argument, especially in chapter 12 (*Mare Liberum*), Grotius betrayed his minimal knowledge of the Estado da Índia and the Luso-Asian trading regime at large. His reliance on Vitoria, and the projection of principles from the New World to the Asian scenario, are especially evidenced by his exclusive reliance on the bulls of Pope Alexander VI.[77]

The Alexandrine bulls issued in 1493 on the return of Christopher Columbus to Europe formed an important pillar in Spain's legal claims to the Americas. As such, they do not stake out Portugal's possessions — real as well as assumed — in the East, but rather draw a notional boundary between Spanish and Portuguese claims in the Atlantic and define the Eastern perimeter of Spain's new claims to the Americas. By contrast, the Lusitanian crown based its claims of apostolic concession on a series of bulls issued after the conquest of Ceuta in 1415, as the Portuguese began to progressively explore the Western coastline of the African continent (and in the process also sanctioned the reintroduction of the slave trade). In this context, bulls promulgated by Popes Martin V, Eugene IV and Nicholas V are of noteworthy historical significance.[78] The Alexandrine bulls of 1493 marked not the beginning, but rather the beginning of the end, of such apostolic concessions. In any case, for Portugal the Alexandrine bulls only really defined its "western boundary" with Spain in the Atlantic.[79] The Lusitanian crown's claims in Africa and

Asia — and indeed to the vast open high seas surrounding these great continents — were broadly staked out in earlier donations. Additional bulls followed in the early 16th century after the conquest of Melaka and the Spice Islands (Maluku and Banda island groups).[80] It is in the light of these important colonial acquisitions that historians should also place the papal donations in favour of Portugal made by Medici Pope Leo X in November 1514.[81]

Grotius ignored all earlier apostolic concessions made in favour of Portugal. In *De Iure Praedae* (and implicitly *Mare Liberum*) he also failed to drop but a single reference to the treaties signed at Tordesillas (1494) and Saragossa (1529), which privately settled competing claims for *dominium* between Spain and Portugal in the eastern hemisphere.[82] Vitoria had no need to mention them, as they were only very marginal to his argument. In his *De Indiis Recenter Inventis* (Relection on the Indies Recently Discovered), the question is not focused on "who can claim what" by discovery, apostolic concession or conquest. The Salmantino theologian Vitoria was primarily concerned with moral and religious issues, questions surrounding Christian charity as well as select problems associated with the missionisation of the Amerindians in the New World.

As for deference to other authors of the School of Salamanca, marginal references in the manuscript of *De Iure Praedae* should be evaluated with the greatest possible caution. With an eye cast specifically on chapter 12, not all references are the fruit of Grotius' own labour, as he was known to have copied entire clusters from other sources, notably Vitoria and Covarruvias y Leyva. This raises a number of questions as to how deeply familiar he really was with the works of the Salmantino theologians. As late as 1617 the Dutch humanist privately conceded in a letter: "Dominicanorum vix legi quemquam" (I have hardly read any of the Dominicans), a clear confession that, apart from Vitoria and Covarruvias y Leyva, he had hardly perused any of the writings of the Spanish Late Scholastics.[83]

It is clear that in the early stages of drafting *De Iure Praedae* Grotius was being furnished with materials pertaining to the *Santa Catarina* incident, the Estado da Índia's activities and the maritime Luso-Asian trading regime at large. Of special interest to Grotius' knowledge of the Estado da Índia and intra-Asian commerce are a series of documents listed at the end of the manuscript of *De Iure Praedae* owned by Leiden University Library. He noted: "A copy of each of the following documents will be appended."[84] This list includes items already familiar to us from

Illus. 34 Portrait of Pope Eugene IV (Gabriele Condulmer). (Private collection, Peter Borschberg)

Illus. 35 Portrait of Pope Leo X (Giovanni di Lorenzo de Medici). (Private collection, Peter Borschberg)

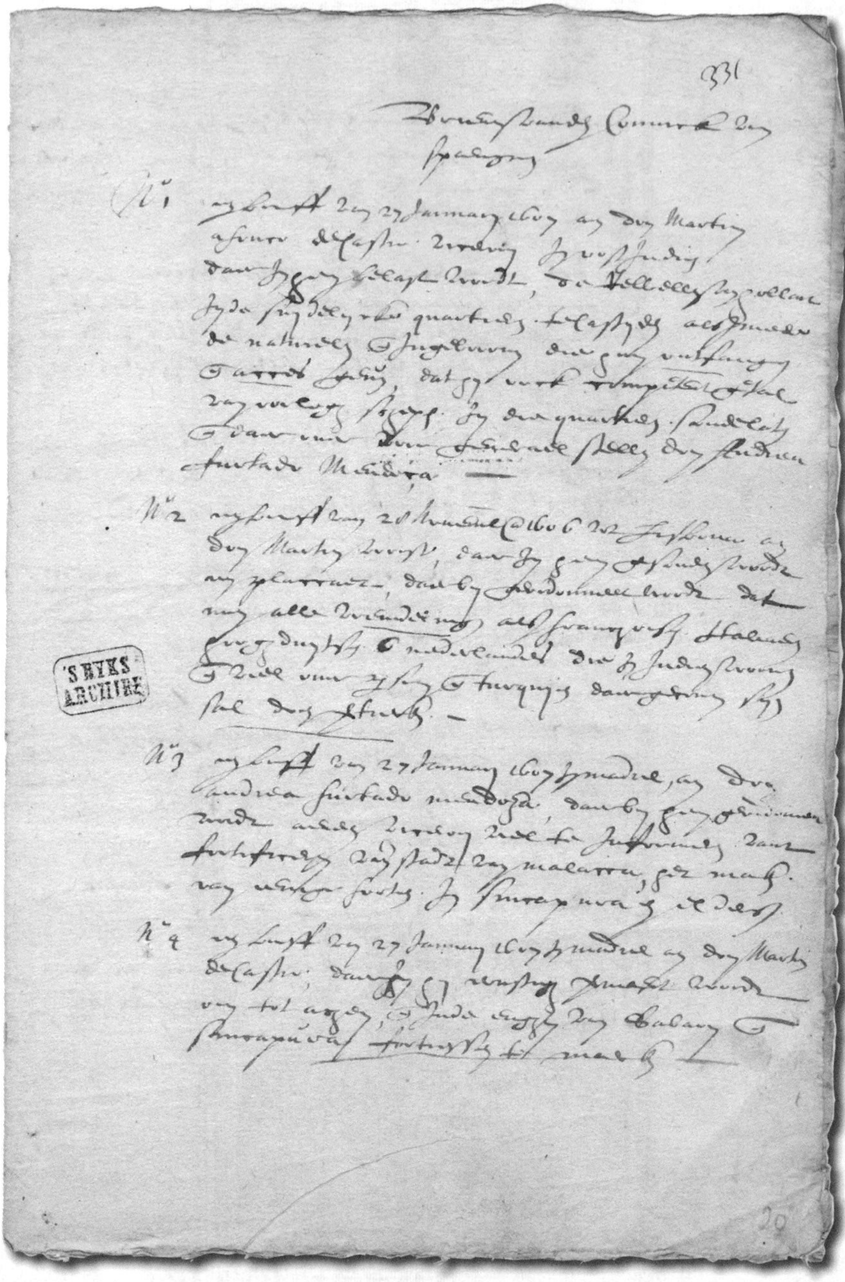

331

Brieven vande Coninck van Spaengien

N° 1

N° 2

N° 3

N° 4

Illus. 36 *Brieven van den Coninck van Spaengien* (Letters by the King of Spain) written in the hand of Adriaen ten Haeff. This list was sent to Grotius on 17 November 1607, together with translations of the individual letters. A partial transcript and translation of this list is found in appendix 1. (The Hague, Nationaal Archief, *Collectie Hugo de Groot, Supplement I* [1.10.35.02, no. 40, fol. 331 recto-verso]) the two letters of ten Grootenhuys: The edict of the Dutch States General of 1599, the verdict of the Admiralty Court of 1604 and the Decree of the States of Holland of September 1604.[85] Certain documents have until now not been mentioned, such as the "excerpt from a letter of the Bishop of Melaka to the King" (see appendix 6), the letter by the "Senate of Melaka" (see appendix 7), two letters addressed to van Heemskerk by Fernão d'Albuquerque (see appendices 8 and 10) and a letter of the "Commander of the captured vessel to Heemskerk" (see appendix 9).[86] With the exception of the bishop's letter, all of the documents concerned deal with specifics of the *Santa Catarina* incident. The Portuguese governor of Melaka, Fernão d'Albuquerque, conceded to van Heemskerk the carrack as "valid prize of war" and thanked the Dutch admiral for keeping his word and bringing all survivors of the captured carrack safely to the Portuguese enclave. A message with a similar content of gratitude stemmed from Melaka's *câmara,* or "senate", as it is called in the Latin translation. There was a separate request from Albuquerque to intervene with the King of Johor to free some Christian hostages.[87] And finally the mentally and financially broken captain Sebastião Serrão, a *casado* of Goa, humbly beseeched van Heemskerk for a piece of cloth from which to sew new clothes. These latter four situational letters have very little to offer on the Estado da Índia or the intra-Asian trading regime. In any case, the four short letters from Melaka and of Serrão were readily available in the accounts of the early Dutch voyages to the East Indies published in German in 1606 and also in Dutch translation in the *Boek tracterende vande Wreede, Verrradische ende Hostile procedure der Portugesen In Oost-Indien* (Book Concerning the Cruel, Treacherous and Hostile Proceedings of the Portuguese in the East Indies).[88]

Of some interest to the present chapter, is the letter by Dom João Ribeiro Gaio, the Bishop of Melaka, addressed to King Philip III/II dated 30 April 1600 (see appendix 6). The original Portuguese transcript together with a translation into Dutch were found among the personal papers of Grotius but now are lost. However, French language excerpts in the hand of Grotius survive and probably date from the time of the Anglo-Dutch conference in London.[89] A copy of the notarised Dutch translation of October 1604, which may have been one of the first items Grotius received from ten Grootenhuys, was sold to Frederik Muller at the Martinus Nijhoff auction in 1864. A copy of the letter prepared by Muller is preserved at Leiden University Library among the papers of Robert Fruin, who used it in the late 1860s for writing his landmark article on the genesis of *De Iure Praedae*.[90] This Dutch translation of Bishop Ribeiro Gaio's letter features as an appendix to the English edition of *De Iure Praedae* prepared by Williams and Zeydel for the Classics of International Law Series.[91]

To the present-day reader, the extant text portion of Ribeiro Gaio's letter is as interesting as it must have been to a Dutch audience in the early 17th century. It provides a snapshot of the dissatisfactions experienced by the Portuguese on the arrival of their first competitors from northern Europe. The epistolary report is intrinsically designed as a wake-up call for King Philip III/II, explaining that the setbacks experienced against the Dutch and some Asian allies occur "because these southern regions have been neglected" by the Estado da Índia. The bishop petitioned his monarch to "take action promptly, if this is possible, for the benefit of these southern regions, which are the key [possessions] of the entire *Estado [da Índia]* and of Portugal. Your Majesty should keep a close eye on these, for they are very excellent and rich lands."[92] Bishop Ribeiro Gaio's main grudge against the Dutch is not so much that they represented a "locust plague of heretics", "faithless scoundrels", "pirates" or "rebels", as period sources of Spanish and Portuguese origin often labeled them, but that they were simply spoiling the market for the Portuguese and Luso-Asian traders. As proverbial "greenhorns" in the Southeast Asian world of trade, the Dutch were entirely ignorant of local prices, business practices and market conditions. The bishop patiently lectured his monarch not only on the deals struck by the newcomers, but importantly also on their likely long-term consequences:[93]

> Of the ten ships, that arrived in the [Strait of] Sunda, four immediately received a cargo of pepper and spices, and these ships departed for their homeland in January 1599. They had not inflicted any evil on the locals,[94] let alone on the Portuguese, nor had they caused problems or difficulties with any other nation. They purchased this pepper at 30 pardaos per bahar, and the mace at between 80 and 90 pardaos. They also purchased nutmeg and cloves together with other goods of these lands, not realising at the time the price at which they made their purchases. But they bought these at the highest price and they paid very well. They were well respected and desired [clients] among the peoples of these lands, for they made honest purchases, without resorting to evil disturbances or force. They also brought with them many goods, merchandise and wares from their lands, and they sold what was useful to the locals. The Dutch also brought there many weapons

of all kinds and sold these or bartered them against ryals-of-eight, and in turn sold these ryals to the locals of Sunda and also to the Fujian traders. They also forged great friendship and an alliance with the king and regents of Sunda, and they roused great hope to continue these dealings on a yearly basis. God forbid that this may happen.

Ten Haeff and Six Letters by the Iberian Monarch (1606–8)

Based on the observations made so far, it is evident that Grotius' knowledge of the Estado da Índia and the Luso-Asian trading regime was insubstantial at the time of writing *De Iure Praedae*. Additional evidence in support of this conclusion derives from Eelco Nicdaas van Kleffens in the early 1960s and the *Briefwisseling Supplement* of 2001.[95] As a matter of special interest I point to a letter dated 17 November 1607, written by the Middelburg magistrate Adriaen Hendricksz ten Haeff, who acted as the personal contact on behalf of the VOC directors.[96] This epistolary testimony evidences that Grotius was being supplied with more information, this time by the company's Zeeland Chamber. The immediate context is provided by the ongoing truce negotiations between the Dutch Republic and Spain with an eye specifically cast on overseas trade. As ten Haeff himself confessed, the materials were intended as "poincten van consiterasiën … in de sake van den Oostindischen handel" (points of consideration … in the matter concerning trade in the East Indies). These materials were thus intrinsically meant "tot voltrecken u.E. begonste werck" (for the completion of the work that Your Honour has begun). Ten Haeff invited Grotius to cite from these letters wherever he found them useful.[97]

Within the scope of the present study are the letters that are summarised in Dutch and listed under the heading "Brieven van den Coninck van Spaengien" (letters by the king of Spain).[98] It shall be recalled that during the period under review Spain and Portugal were ruled by the same monarch under the Union of the Two Crowns (1580–1640). The majority of the letters highlight reactions of the Estado da Índia to the arrival of the Dutch in the waters and marketplaces of the East Indies. Some of the enclosed letters either beseech Asian allies not to admit the Dutch for trade in their ports, or exhort Asian princes to expel the Dutch where they are already present. Other letters issue instructions to heighten security in Portuguese-held forts and ports or around waters plied by Lusitanian-

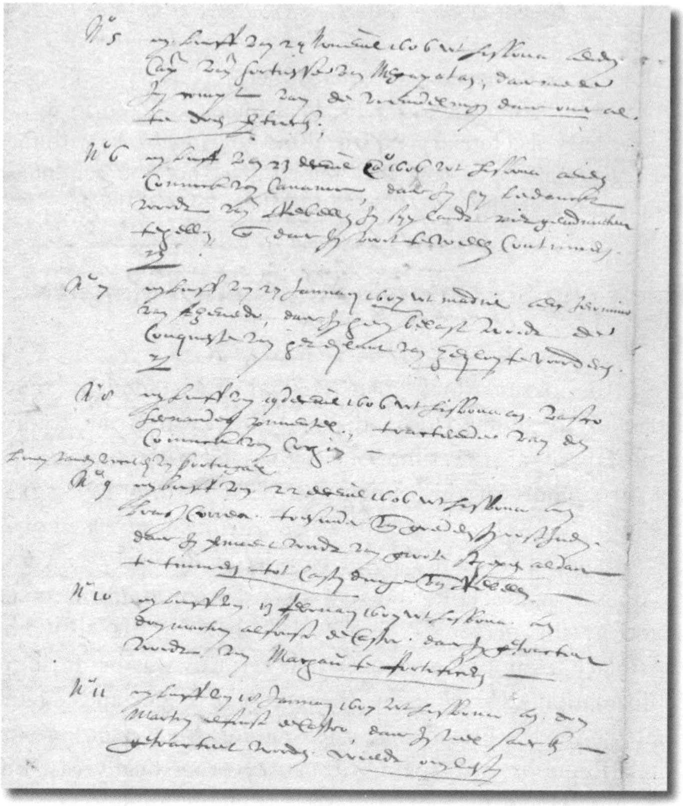

Illus. 37 See Illustration 36 on p. 128, this is the second page of the letter.

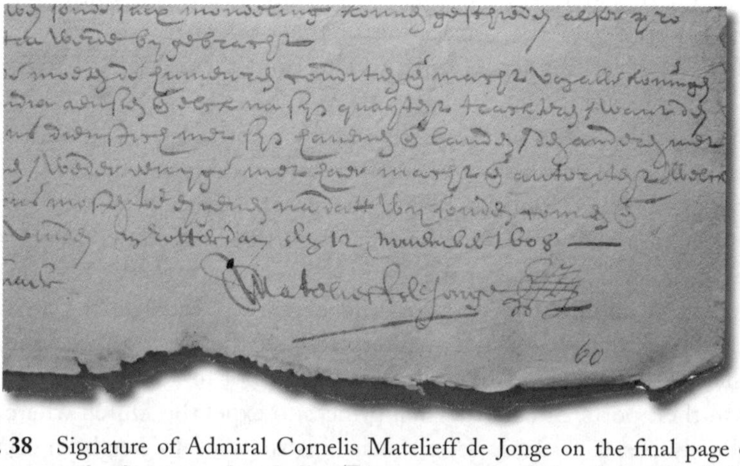

Illus. 38 Signature of Admiral Cornelis Matelieff de Jonge on the final page of his *Discours van den Stant van Oost Indiën* (Discourse on the State of the East Indies) written on his return to the Netherlands in 1608. (The Hague, Nationaal Archief, Archief Oldenbarnevelt, no. 3104, fol. 60 recto)

flagged commercial vessels. With reference to the latter, enclosure number 3 merits further explanation. This is the letter written in Madrid on 27 January 1607 instructing the governor of Melaka and admiral of the "Armada of the Southern Seas", André Furtado de Mendonça, to increase security in the Portuguese-held emporium of Melaka and to construct "eenige forten in Sincapura en elders" (some fortresses around Singapore and elsewhere).[99]

A second letter, enclosure number 4, bearing the same date, was dispatched to the Portuguese viceroy of India, Dom Martim de Castro. In this he is earnestly admonished to construct fortresses "om tot Achem" (around Aceh) near the northern tip of Sumatra, as well as "in de enghten van Sabaon ende Sincapura" (around the Straits of Sabam [or Kundur] and Singapore).[100] The latter represented a crucial point in Portuguese intra-Asian trade; and as the VOC would quickly learn, anyone who commanded the Strait of Sabam also controlled traffic between the Melaka Strait and onward ports in Java, Makassar, Timor and the Malukus. Anyone who controlled the Singapore Straits could also disrupt maritime trade between ports in subcontinental India and Melaka, with destinations around the Gulf of Siam, Champa, Cambodia, Borneo, Makassar, Macao and Japan.[101]

Unfortunately, the actual letters forwarded to Grotius can no longer be retrieved, but some of them survive in copy and have been added in the appendices in their original Portuguese with an English translation. From the *Livros das Monções* (Books or Letters of the Monsoon), as the official Portuguese correspondence between Europe and the Estado da Índia is known, it transpires that security for commercial shipping in the Singapore and Melaka Straits became of paramount concern to Portuguese officials.[102] This was especially the case after the 1603 seizure of the *Santa Catarina*, the capture of the carrack *Santo António* in the port of Patani in 1605,[103] as well as Matelieff's unsuccessful seaborne siege of Melaka in 1606.[104]

Judging by the Dutch summary of the royal letters, it is clear that these epistolary testimonies represented the most credible and probably the most comprehensive first-hand pieces of information that Grotius received about the Estado da Índia and the nature of Portuguese maritime intra-Asian trade. According to Henk Nellen, the editor of the *Briefwisseling Supplement*, as well as van Ittersum, the transcripts or translations mentioned ten in Haeff's letter no longer survive.[105] Nellen observed:

> In his letter he refers to the enclosed documents that could be of use to Grotius in his defence of Company interests; as a result of the negotiations with Spain for peace or a truce, these interests had come under pressure. Grotius could have incorporated the documents of ten Haeff in a memorial which he was preparing at the time and which is preserved in various drafts among his [personal] papers.[106]

So the "work that you have begun", as ten Haeff wrote, does not likely refer to *De Iure Praedae*, but almost certainly to a memorial being prepared for the VOC at the time.

The Epistolary Memorials of VOC Admiral Matelieff de Jonge

Another valuable source of information for Grotius about commerce, politics and trade in Southeast Asia dating from this period is an epistolary memorial of Admiral Cornelis Matelieff de Jonge dated 12 November 1608.[107] Matelieff's fleet left Europe in 1605 and arrived in the waters of the Melaka Strait in 1606. He unsuccessfully besieged the Portuguese stronghold at Melaka, engaged the Portuguese armada in the Melaka Strait in August and October 1606,[108] and concluded an important treaty with the kingdom of Johor. With the benefit of hindsight, this evolved into one of the most enduring alliances forged by the VOC with the rulers of the Malay Archipelago and the Peninsula. Matelieff's memorial of 1608 evidences how the Dutch had quickly learnt about the dynamics of power in the East Indies. Significantly also, the Heren XVII had instructed Matelieff to forge commercial relations with China through Siamese territory (see also appendix 15).[109] He returned to the Netherlands in 1608 accompanied by envoys of the King of Siam.[110]

In his memorial titled "Discours van den Stant van Oost Indiën" (Discourse concerning the State of the East Indies; for the full text and English translation see appendix 15), Matelieff explored various means by which the war effort could be successfully waged against the Spanish, Portuguese and other competitors, both European and Asian.[111] The admiral devised in this a blueprint for the VOC's economic and political ascendancy in Southeast Asia and articulated several priorities for the company.[112] Matelieff comprehensively analysed the logistical and organisational problems facing the early Dutch company arising from the long lines of communication between Asia and Europe as well as the lack of

Illus. 39 Pieter Both, a native of Amersfoort, became the first Governor-General of the VOC in 1609. (The Hague, Rijksbureau voor Kunsthistorische Dokumentatie)

a permanent Asian base (which is referred to as the rendezvous). Matelieff advised to step up security around towns and fortresses including Ambon, the Bandas and Batu Sawar (Johor). The memorial recommended the seizure of Portuguese ships in the Strait of Melaka, around Ceylon and in the Bay of Bengal, underscoring that the most damage the VOC could inflict on the Portuguese would be to attack and capture ships outbound from Macao en route to Melaka. Matelieff also alluded to the substantial maritime trade taking place between coastal cities of southern China and Manila.

One could claim that Matelieff's *Discours* represented the flip side of the situation addressed in the aforementioned packet of letters forwarded by ten Haeff and collectively titled "Brieven van den Koning van Spaingien" (Letters by the King of Spain). In this sense, the memorial of 1608 spelt out priorities for the VOC across the East Indies, yielded a synopsis of the security situation in East and Southeast Asia and identified vulnerabilities in the intra-Asian trading networks of the Estado da Índia. The *Discours* and the aforementioned royal letters of instruction taken together probably form the most comprehensive, first-hand information on Portuguese Asia and the intra-Asian maritime trading regime that are known to have passed through Grotius' hands before 1609.

The question arises as to what impact, if any, Matelieff's 1608 memorial and the packet of letters by ten Haeff might have had *De Iure Praedae* and especially the revisions applied to chapter 12 of the manuscript during late 1608 and early 1609. It is extremely difficult to provide a reliable assessment, especially of the royal letters, some of which have not been retrieved. Impact of the royal letters was almost certainly cosmetic and superficial, even if (supposed) fragments were appended to the 1609 edition of *Mare Liberum* (see appendices 1, 2, 4, 5, and the illustration on p. 166).

As for Matelieff's epistolary memorial of 1608, there is no tangible evidence that his *Discours* meaningfully influenced the revision of chapter 12 as *Mare Liberum*. Unlike the letters from the enemy, which Grotius was given a free hand to peruse and liberally cite from, Matelieff's memorial was deemed sensitive information at the time, not least because it staked out priorities for the Dutch company's future operations in Asia.

So much for the supplementary information passed on to Grotius approximately at the time of preparing *Mare Liberum* for the press. The question now arises as to what he learnt from the memorials and epistolary reports of Matelieff in the period leading up to the maritime and colonial conferences held in London and later in the Hague. As a director of the VOC's Rotterdam chamber and as one of the few early directors of the Dutch company to have actually sailed to the East Indies and back, Matelieff not only imparted valuable personal, first-hand experience, but he also remained abreast of developments taking place, both in the boardrooms in Europe as well as on the ground in Southeast Asia. The seasoned admiral's willingness to share his thoughts, concerns and experience with Grotius over a period of well over a half a decade proved invaluable in the years leading to the Anglo-Dutch conferences. The letters also vent Matelieff's personal frustration with the VOC and the Dutch Republic and their reluctance — or even outright unwillingness — to honour him as they had promised on his return from the East Indies in late 1608. The parties concerned, Matelieff lamented in March 1616, appear to have completely forgotten about their earlier promises.[113]

Apart from the 1608 *Discours*, there are at least two additional letters by Matelieff that warrant express mentioning in the present context. The first is dated 31 August 1610 and has been reproduced in the *Briefwisseling Supplement*.[114] The second bears the date 27 April 1615 and has been published in first volume of the *Briefwisseling*.[115] Both memorials provide important updates on a range of issues already identified in the *Discours*.

The single most important issue that runs through all three documents is the urgent need to establish a rendezvous, or permanent base, in Asia.[116] Although the key criterion remained constant (namely, any rendezvous need be easily accessible all year round and ships should never have to face unfavourable winds) the shortlist of possible locations had been whittled down. Even the locational shortcomings of Melaka had been clearly recognised, diminishing the urgency to pluck this emporium from the Portuguese in a future military campaign:[117]

> The city of Melaka, apart from the difficulty we would have to take it, is rather ill-situated: it is difficult to reach regardless of the season, especially if one has large and heavy ships which are filthy and have damaged sails from the long voyage. We need a place where we can call coming from the Cape of Good Hope without being subjected to the monsoon.

The Heren XVII would need to urgently look into the matter and come to a final decision, lest the serious problems besetting the company (and obviously the costs of not tackling them promptly) should escalate.[118] Palembang's shortcomings were now well known, and the Sumatran polity was no longer mentioned as a possible location; the region around the tip of Johor (that is around Changi, the Johor River estuary and Pengerang) was deemed "inconvenient" by the new Governor-General Pieter Both, at least that is what Grotius jotted down in a marginal note for himself.[119] Most unfortunately, the nature of this inconvenience was not explained, but considerable space was dedicated in the letter of 1610 to the political problems facing Johor. In his *Discours* of 1608, Matelieff expressed a preference for a rendezvous near the Sunda Strait. He reasoned at the time:[120]

> The city of Banten, albeit well-situated, is not only very unwholesome, but also has a very young king — fourteen or fifteen years old — who is impossible to negotiate with; moreover, his council is so divided by factionalism that one cannot accomplish anything.... We need a place where we can call coming from the Cape of Good Hope without being subjected to the monsoon.... But then we can expect some inconveniences here from the people of Banten, for as soon as they learn that we want to establish our residence at Jacatra, they may well make common cause with the Portuguese and become our and Jacatra's enemies. We therefore have to proceed with caution here, so that we do not make the barbarians any wiser until they cannot inflict harm any more. For insofar as I have noticed in my dealings with them, they would not consider it bad if we set up our quarters at Jacatra.... In any case, we would have to keep our quarters and factory at Banten at first, so that we do not estrange them in any way, and negotiate with Jacatra in the meantime.... We should forge a secure contract with this king [of Jacatra], for he should profit from such a contract as much as we will, and without that it should not be submitted to him. This would be best done in his presence, and then one thing given more weight and another less, depending on how one would find the king to be inclined. In my opinion such a contract would be necessary, rather similar to the one the Portuguese have with Cochin. If we choose Jacatra, they should give us a suitable location, be it big or small, close to Jacatra's river, where we could build our fortified quarters to protect ourselves from Portuguese attacks. For we cannot flee inland if the Portuguese come and take our belongings with us as the blacks[121] do, as our goods are more cumbersome. Therefore we have to be strong, placing our trust not in flight but in defence. This location should be large enough that all the Dutch we could bring to the Indies over time could easily live

Illus. 40 Photograph of Robert Fruin, professor of national history at Leiden University. His long article on the genesis of *De Iure Praedae Commentarius* was first published in 1868. (Leiden University Library)

> there. There should be as much land, both inland and around the city, as they can cultivate or use as pasture. Those who wish to be under Dutch rule should be allowed this, but this point needs to be negotiated with discretion.

In 1610, Matelieff reiterated his preference for a location along the northwestern coast of Java, furnishing updates on the latest developments in both Banten and Jayakerta (Jacatra).[122] As already reported in August 1608, Banten was problematic and remained so for years to come. In a communication dated 14 December 1613, the admiral lamented that the authorities of Banten had imposed building restrictions on the construction of any future Dutch lodge.[123]

As reported by Matelieff in his epistolary memorial of August 1610, the VOC faced hostility as well as a crisis of confidence among treaty partners. The situation was particularly precarious along what could be considered the frontlines in the war effort against the Iberian powers: the Bandas, the Malukus and especially also Johor.[124] Developments in the Bandas after 1609 had cast a particularly negative image of the Dutch on the Southeast Asian rulers and peoples.[125] Dutch brutality and acts of aggression committed on those islands made the Portuguese look comparatively good, or at least less evil. The admiral sounded the alarm and commented on the VOC's image problems as well as English agitation against the Dutch. A note in the left hand margin of the letter reads: "The conquest of Banda arouses hate against us" and in the margin a few paragraphs below "as time passes, the Netherlands are more and more hated in the Indies".[126] Intervention in the Bandas did not bring the desired results or revenues, the costs of protecting them remained high, and Matelieff candidly admitted to the "inexperience of our nation in governing Muslims".[127] In expanding and consolidating its trade in the East Indies spice market, the Admiral saw the VOC faced with a terrible dilemma, the blame for which he squarely placed at the feet of the Portuguese and the English, a point that Grotius promptly noted for himself in the margin. Against the backdrop of the Twelve Years Truce concluded in 1609 and the silence of arms (theoretically still) expected from the VOC outside the European theatre, the Dutch were increasingly disliked among their Asian allies and trading partners, and their "friendship" either deemed utterly useless or simply held in low esteem. For this reason: "If we proceed in the Portuguese manner, as had initially done, by conquering lands and cities, we engender hatred; and if we proceed in the English manner [which is to focus on trade and commerce], we are held in low esteem."[128] In order to salvage the situation as far as possible, the Admiral recommended additional security measures for Ambon, the Bandas and the Malukus.

The political situation in Johor was also deteriorating rapidly. Matelieff's letter of August 1610 dedicates a good deal of space to the problems in Johor, though admittedly not in a cohesive manner. Grotius, who had written about Johor and Raja Bongsu in *De Iure Praedae,* confirmed his continued interest in the Malay kingdom with a series of notes or points scribbled in the left-hand margin. Problems in Johor had arisen over the interpretation of the two treaties signed between Raja Bongsu and Admiral Matelieff in 1606, as well as the implementation of the Twelve Years Truce in the Asian theatre.[129] Following the failed siege of Melaka in the months of May and September 1606, a second treaty signed between the VOC and Raja Bongsu dated 23 September 1606 promised the Dutch a location where they would be able to set up shop, and build warehouses and residences for company servants (see appendix 14). During his visit to the Batu Sawar court in early 1609, Admiral Pieter Willemsz. Verhoeff sought to revise the terms of the 1606 treaties with Johor and gain concessions from Raja Bongsu to construct a fortress.[130] The raja rejected this proposal and was sufficiently angered by Verhoeff — and Dutch haggling over the twin 1606 treaties in general — that he wrote a letter of complaint addressed to the stadholder, Prince Maurice of Orange, and the Dutch States General.[131]

Verhoeff's wrangling with Raja Bongsu at Batu Sawar is also echoed in Matelieff's letter of August 1610. Raja Bongsu's rejection of the fortification is specially noted in the left-hand margin by Grotius: "King of Johor [is] unwilling to consent to a fortification in his lands."[132] Subsequent paragraphs yield additional information. In letters of complaint written to the Heren XVII, as well as Prince Maurice, Raja Bongsu expressed his profound unhappiness that fewer VOC ships were calling at Johor to trade.[133] In the light of such dissatisfaction Matelieff conceded with evident consternation:[134]

> Johor, who is our friend, is reduced to misery on account of our friendship; indeed what is more, the pepper that is harvested in its lands is brought to Patani and purchased by us there for a higher price than in Johor. As a result, we deprive Johor of the trade which by contrast we owe her. We drive the business to Patani, which has nothing of its own, and reaps as much tax from us as it wants.

Raja Bongsu's grievances had become known among the commercial and political elites in the Dutch Republic.[135] This is evidenced by a passage found toward the end of Matelieff's letter of August 1610. The admiral — who had signed two treaties with Johor in 1606 and met Raja Bongsu on several occasions — evidently believed that the problems in Johor could have been averted, if the VOC did not despatch "new commanders every year". This was a point he already raised in the *Discours* of 1608, but in a different context and citing different negative side effects.[136] VOC policy and Verhoeff's actions — especially the latter's inexperience in negotiating with Asian rulers — were squarely to blame for the VOC's growing problems with Johor:[137]

> It is also a great mistake of the gentlemen directors that they have sent every year new commanders to the East Indies, for the new man always wants to fault or improve on the work that has already been done. But because of his inexperience he often does not properly understand what his predecessor had done, who had more extensive experiences and was familiar with the mindset of the Indians.[138] This happened in the case of the king of Johor with whom Admiral Pieter Willemsz. [Verhoeff] wanted to forge a treaty different from the one that I had concluded with him. The king was very unhappy about this and said that he did not want to conclude a new treaty every day, and that whoever should come after him, that is Pieter Willemsz., would want to conclude yet another treaty. What is needed is a solid foundation that can be expanded upon, and not every day something new.

As the unfolding of events evidences, this particular concern was addressed and rectified by the Dutch company — much to its long-term success.

Emmanuel van Meteren's *Memoriën*

Finally I turn to a source that is not specifically mentioned in the *Briefwisseling* but certainly influenced the argument in the *pars historica* of *De Iure Praedae*. This concerns the work of the Dutch historian Emmanuel van Meteren. The library of Lund University in Sweden is in possession of Grotius' personal copy of this work. It was printed in Delft in 1599 and features several underlinings, marginalia and notes by its former proprietor.[139] With reference to the Estado da Índia, one section stands out. This is found on folio 406 verso, where van Meteren discusses the early voyages of the Dutch to the East Indies. What caught Grotius' eye were three distinct snippets of information that he also underlined in the book: The ships had been *gevordert* (sponsored) by the States of Holland; they were armed with artillery; and the voyages were intended to forge regular trade with Asian partners in areas where the Portuguese had no *ghebiet* or loosely translated "sovereignty" or "command", that is, where they had no factories or colonies.[140] The latter echoes not only a specific passage found in chapter 12 of *De Iure Praedae* (and also in *Mare Liberum*) but more importantly also in the instructions of the VOC issued to its Asian-based servants in April 1608.[141] Arguably, the inspiration Grotius gained from reading van Meteren's *Memoriën* nuanced his argument for the freedom of navigation. The underlying issue at hand was not whether the Portuguese legitimately possessed sovereignty over colonies such as Melaka or Goa, but whether their policy of preventing others from calling at emporia over which they did not exercise any degree of authority was justifiable.

Refuting Fruin and Alexandrowicz

At the end of this chapter, I return to the two claims of Fruin and Alexandrowicz that provided my point of departure (see p. 109). As has been seen, Fruin claimed that the author of *De Iure Praedae* had conducted research in VOC archival holdings while Alexandrowicz expanded on this theme to assert that Grotius had conducted extensive first-hand research on documents pertaining to Asia's maritime Custom 6 law at large.

Evidence drawn from Grotius' correspondence and unpublished reading notes refutes these or related assertions. The epistolary testimonies illustrate that the VOC's hired author did not seize the initiative to conduct in-depth research in the company's archival holdings, but instead relied on materials that were forwarded to him from its directors in Amsterdam and later also Middelburg. It is difficult not to share the verdict of van Ittersum:

> The 'book treating of the cruel, treasonous and hostile procedures of the Portuguese in the East Indies' is conclusive proof that Grotius had never done any independent investigations of his own and simply used the materials put at his disposal by the VOC directors.[142]

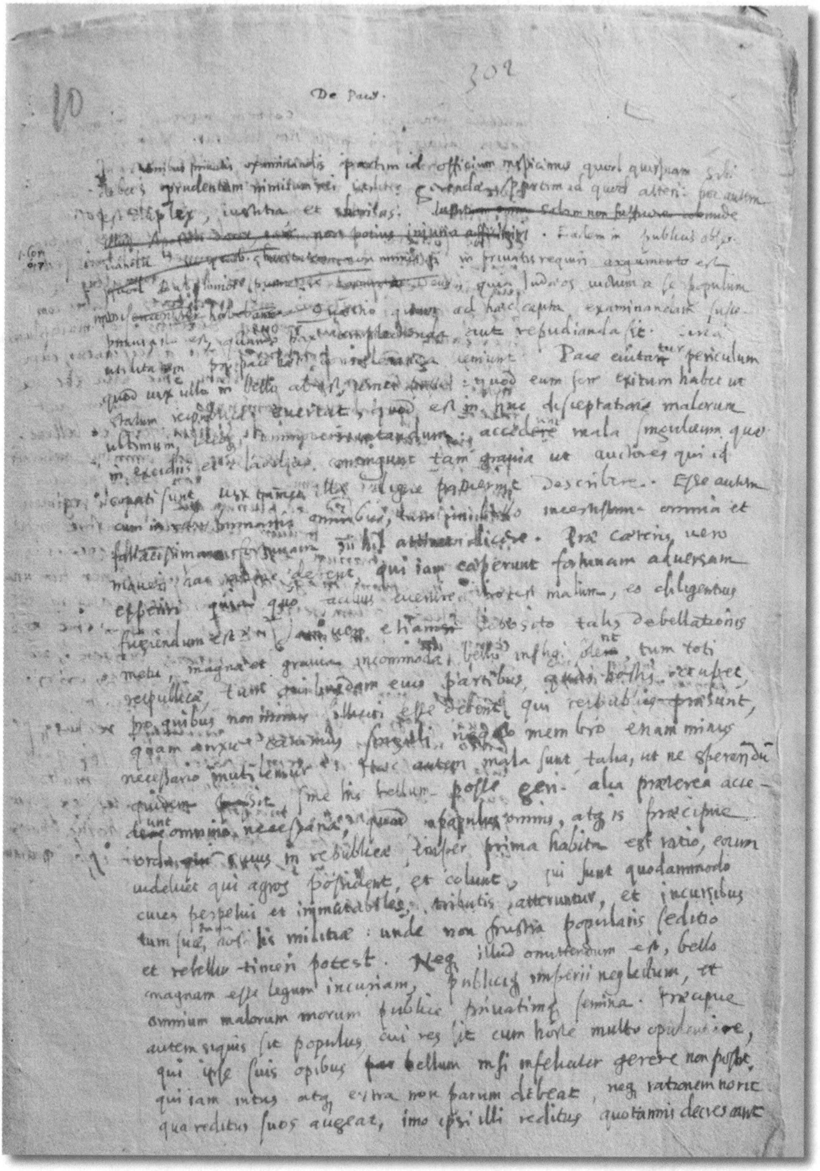

Illus. 41 First page of the fragment *De Pace* (On Peace) written in the hand of Grotius. (Leiden University Library, B.P.L. 922, fol. 302 recto)

As can be seen by the evidence and deliberations presented in this chapter, the lack of "independent research" extends well beyond the affidavits identified and published by Coolhaas in 1965.

Based on the sources Grotius consulted, his knowledge of the Estado da Índia, Asian customs and the maritime trading regime of the East Indies was minimal at the time he was drafting *De Iure Praedae* in 1604–6. In the absence of ready available works pertaining to the Estado da Índia, he relied on a collection of affidavits extolling the harrowing experiences of ships' mates at the hands of the Portuguese. The dearth of reliable information on the legal and commercial foundations of the Estado da Índia was made up for by gleaning general principles and tenets from the works of the Spanish Late Scholastics, notably Vitoria and to a lesser extent Covarruvias y Leyva. These principles were subsequently modified and projected from the Spanish Americas into the Luso-Asian theatre. It is almost inevitable that Grotius' reliance on superficial geographical accounts, affidavits of disgruntled mariners and the transposition of principles from the Americas to Asia would provide a opaque view of the Estado da Índia and Luso-Asian trade. Added to this, his strong reliance on Vitoria underlines his ignorance of the very legal foundations upon which Portuguese India was established as well as the mechanisms of colonial administration and trade that sustained it.[143] He did read van Meteren's *Historiën*, but there is no evidence in either *De Iure Praedae* or any of his surviving reading notes dating from 1609 or before to suggest that he had consulted available travel literature, including Ramusio's *Viaggi* or Linschoten's *Reysgeschrift* and *Itinerario*. He was evidently also not familiar with the text of papal bulls and treaties between Spain and Portugal that formed the legal foundations for Portugal's claims to Africa, Asia and the open seas. Grotius' knowledge of East and Southeast Asian geography was sketchy at best. He sometimes preferred topographical expressions of classical antiquity and Ptolemaic geography to some Asian toponyms that was already well established in European cartography by the beginning of the 17th century.[144]

Finally, there is not a shred of evidence to indicate that he had ever studied Asian customs or legal codes, let alone any accounts that touched upon Portuguese intra-Asian trade. Fruin's confident statement that *De Iure Praedae* represents "clean research" commanding "lasting [academic] value" now seems highly problematic.[145] The "Alexandrowicz thesis" extolling Grotius' supposed familiarity with Asian commercial and maritime practices cannot be sustained by any stretch of the imagination.[146] There is also no evidence that Holland's humanist prodigy was being supplied such information by or on behalf of the VOC directors. In addition, no evidence is available to suggest that such information might have even been important within the ramifications of *De Iure Praedae*'s commission. Certainly, Grotius' own boastful assertion to have written something on "the universal law of war and booty" must be understood within its strictly Eurocentric context and nothing more.

It is almost inevitable that at first glance, researchers will feel greatly disappointed by such findings. But they will soon find relief when they ponder their fuller consequences. From an aerial perspective, it is clear that the evidence presented here open new dimensions to research on Grotius. Much remains to be done on the unpublished notes and fragments found scattered in archives in the Netherlands, Europe and beyond. Rather than just synthesising or rationalising existing commercial trade practices prevalent in the Asian theatre, Grotius arrived at his insights based on far less diverse material than anyone has hitherto ventured to surmise. After all, his commission from the Amsterdam directors was to defend the seizure of the *Santa Catarina* as an act of war against the broader canvass of Iberian exclusion in the East Indies. Therefore, far from knocking the great Dutchman off his humanist pedestal, these insights should nudge contemporary researchers to seriously rethink the originality of early Grotian thought.

Evidence from the *Briefwisseling* touching the genesis of *De Iure Praedae* also raises a number of important questions about the work as a whole: When were the different parts of the treatise actually drafted?[147] Which parts were written first? How important is the *pars historica* (historical section, chapters 11–15) for understanding the *pars dogmatica* (theoretical section, chapters 1–10)? How familiar was Grotius with the diverse sources that he supposedly cited from? These are questions that cannot be explored in a short article, chapter or even book. They pose a challenge that can — and will — crystallise over the coming decades.

General Conclusion

During the first two decades of the 17th century, Hugo Grotius embarked on a career in the Netherlands in which he rapidly rose to prominence, filling capacities such as the official chronicler of Holland, *advocaat fiscaal* (public prosecutor), pensionary of Rotterdam, member of the States of Holland as well as delegate to the Dutch States General. As he reminded his descendants and readers of his political memoirs written in 1619, Grotius consistently assumed a staunch anti-Spanish stance, and defended over many years the political, commercial and strategic penetration of the VOC into Asia. In his early historical works and political treatises, he upheld the legitimacy of the Dutch Revolt and supported in both word and deed the oligarchic constitution of the nascent Dutch Republic. He may have considered himself as a cautious defender of liberty against Iberian "tyranny", or even as a vociferous critic of Portuguese obstructions of maritime navigation on the high seas. But he never saw himself as championing the cause of free trade and free commerce for all peoples and most certainly not in its contemporary sense of a deliberate global trading regime.

The present book has dissected and critiqued Grotius' work that is known today as *De Iure Praedae Commentarius* (Commentary to the Law of Prize and Booty), together with its spin-off publication *Mare Liberum* (The Free Sea). The close reading of these works against the backdrop of the Dutch luminary's crystallising ideas on war, plunder, sovereignty, alliance-making and long-distance maritime trade was greatly facilitated by consulting a range of his working papers, notes, excerpts, letters and fragments that survive in archives in the Netherlands, England, Sweden and elsewhere. Of special consideration have been

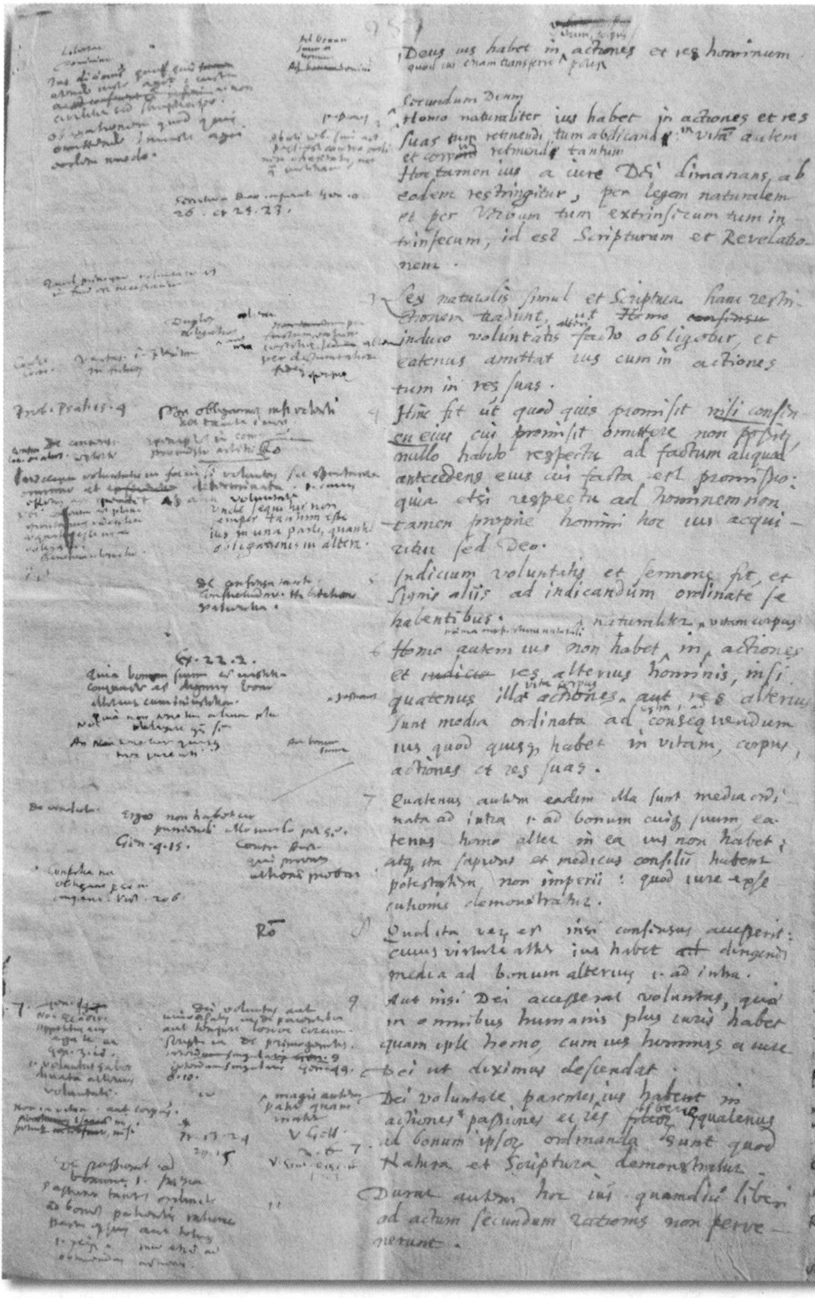

Illus. 42 First page of the skeletal treatise *Theses LVI* (Fifty-Six Theses) written in the hand of Grotius. (Leiden University Library, B.P.L. 922, fol. 287 recto)

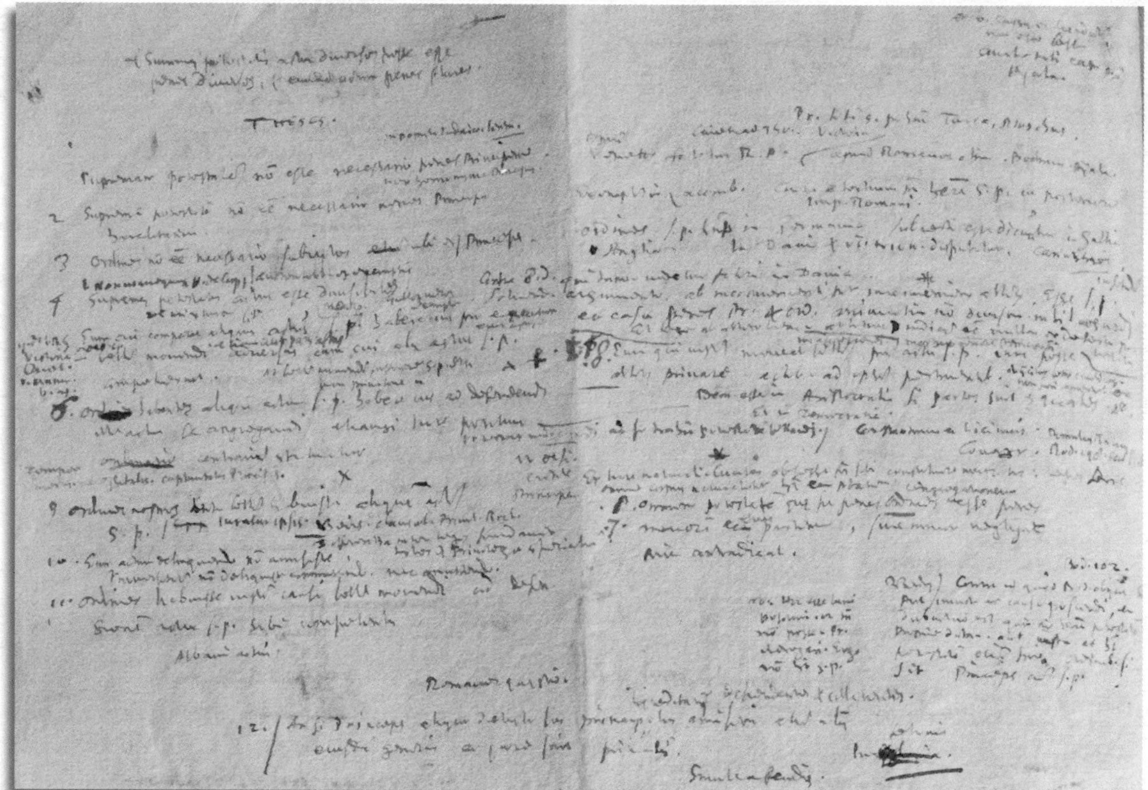

Illus. 43 Draft in the hand of Grotius belonging to the *Commentarius in Theses XI* (Commentary to Eleven Theses). (Leiden University Library, B.P.L. 922, fol. 286 verso)

the manuscripts found in the bundle at Leiden University Library, ms. B.P.L. 922. This contains the early autograph treatises, fragments and outlines titled *Commentarius in Theses XI* (Commentary to Eleven Theses), *De Societate Publica cum Infidelibus* (Of Public Society with Non-Christians), *De Pace* (Of Peace), *De Bello ob Libertatem Eligendo* (On Choosing War for Freedom) and the *Theses LVI* (Fifty-Six Theses) together with the reading notes prepared for each of these manuscripts. The originals of *De Iure Praedae* (Commentary on the Law of Prize and Booty), its spin-off publication *Mare Liberum* (The Free Sea) and especially also the manuscript bundle B.P.L. 922 yielded invaluable information about the working habits and thought processes of their author. They show how Grotius set out to structure his arguments, the sources which he actually consulted and also the manner in which he handled and worked with his materials. Additional information has been gleaned from his vast correspondence with leading politicians and intellectual luminaries from across the Netherlands, England, Germany, France and beyond.

What does all the evidence add up to? Apart from confirming that Grotius could be a sloppy researcher who sometimes only consulted the indices of the books he took in hand and often — if not usually — drafted his works in ferocious haste, the most intriguing conclusion is his reliance on a far narrower set of sources than has been hitherto assumed. It is still widely believed — tacitly or otherwise — that he was intimately familiar with all the sources that he mentions or cites.[1] With specific reference to the manuscript of *De Iure Praedae, Mare Liberum* and other related materials, there is no evidence to support such a conclusion. Established scholars, including Robert Feenstra, are now more willing to openly concede to Grotius' shortcomings and pecadillos.[2] This leads us back to the assertion of Robert Fruin that he had conducted independent research in the VOC's company archives. As I have stated earlier, there is not a shred of support for such a claim. The same holds for the postulation of Charles Alexandrowicz, who became convinced that Grotius had immersed himself with Asian maritime laws and custom at the time of drafting *De Iure Praedae* and *Mare Liberum*. It is evidenced by period correspondence that he found it difficult to source for materials about the Portuguese in the East Indies. His deference to Spanish authors such as Vitoria, Covarruvias y Leyva and also Vázquez de Menchaca should be viewed not as a tactical move to subvert the ideological justifications of the Iberian powers, but rather as a (tacit) concession that he lacked sources of Portuguese provenance. This inadequacy, therefore, becomes a compelling indication of Grotius' failure to grasp and appreciate the deeper legal, moral and commercial foundations upon which the Estado da Índia was founded.

While it is true that at the beginning of the 17th-century geographic knowledge of Asia — and especially the use of toponyms — was still evolving in Europe, *De Iure Praedae* displays only a sketchy command of Southeast Asian geography. The VOC cartographer Pieter Plancius certainly forwarded to him a map (or possibly two maps) of a basic type, but the treatise also shows a propensity to rely on the toponyms of largely unverifiable cartographies from European antiquity, such as Ptolemy and Strabo. This, in turn, also evidence a preference of classical Greco-Roman sources over more recent updates provided by either Iberian navigators or even VOC traders whose interests Grotius represented.

If access to sources and crude understanding of some of the major issues was one problem, falsification of evidence is a different matter altogether. *Mare Liberum*'s critics, including the two professors, William Welwood and Seraphim de Freitas, accused this Dutchman of quoting bogus references, citing passages out of context, or changing the wording of a quotation to fit the circumstances described. What is the present-day reader to make of these? Was Grotius quoting from memory? Or was he trying to deceive his readers with eloquence and lucid style? Was this simply the expected and foreseeable outcome of sloppy reading and working habits, as well as the wholesale lifting of (inaccurate) quotations or references from the works of other authors? The final verdict remains open, but after working extensively with his early letters, manuscripts, fragments and reading notes for the past two decades, I personally veer toward the latter.

At the time of writing and completing *De Iure Praedae*, Jan ten Grootenhuys (on behalf of the Amsterdam chamber of the VOC) and later Adriaen ten Haeff, Cornelis Matelieff de Jonge and possibly others supplied Grotius with a range of letters, memorials, affidavits, proclamations, reports, a court verdict and cartographic materials. It was also ten Grootenhuys who forwarded a 1557 edition of Francisco de Vitoria's *Relectiones Theologicae XII* (Twelve Theological Relections) which proved so invaluable for formulating early ideas on the just war, the defence of liberty against tyranny and of course the *ius communicationis* (right of [free and unimpeded] communication), the latter of which Grotius expanded to include persons, ideas and especially also goods (trade). These are the first and most easily verifiable sources that can be reconstructed chiefly on the basis of his correspondence. Although he intended to write to Plancius and ask about materials available in the Netherlands that touch on Portuguese Asia, it is astonishing that throughout the entire manuscript of *De Iure Praedae* (and even in *Mare Liberum*), Grotius does not once mention or quote a single Portuguese source proper. He gleaned concepts and insights from Vitoria (and other Spanish authors) and projected these from the Americas into the Southeast Asian theatre. In the process he revealed his sparse knowledge of Portuguese politics, commerce and diplomacy in Asia. Yet he was manifestly aware that the European presence in Asia had to be justified on a very different set of moral, religious, political and commercial grounds from the Spanish presence in the Americas.

It is not my intention to belittle the legacy of this early modern luminary or even cast him down from the pantheon of great thinkers, but simply to ask a set of very basic questions about what he verifiably knew, at which point in time, how he acquired his knowledge, as well as how the ideas he expounded — reflecting early modern European, largely pre-Westphalian concepts of politics, alliance-making and commerce — may have impacted the world of Southeast Asian politics and commerce. The question naturally also arises to what extent he may have been verifiably influenced by Southeast Asian ideas, customs or conventions.

At the time of drafting *De Iure Praedae* and even revising *Mare Liberum* for the press, Grotius' knowledge of Southeast Asia, its unique political and economic cultures, and the role of the Portuguese within that region was not extensive or well grounded. His familiarity with the region and its idiosyncrasies, however, would improve markedly in the years leading up to the Anglo-Dutch maritime and colonial conferences of 1613 and 1615. Despite this improved understanding, it is clear that his perceptions of Southeast Asian economics, political cultures and institutions proved historically influential, not least because he ascribed to Southeast Asian rulers full sovereignty and equal membership in the global family of polities. A close reading of *De Iure Praedae, Mare Liberum,* as well as related early treatises, fragments and reading notes featured in this book point to four basic facets that are of interest to historians, researchers of public law and international relations specialists today. These four facets, which are by all means inter-related can help unlock and appreciate the relatively rapid projection of Dutch power into

Southeast Asia through the VOC. The evidence presented in this book highlights that these four areas can all be traced directly and immediately to Vitoria's *Relectiones Theologicae XII.* Although confined to the chambers and boardrooms in Europe, Grotius worked out theoretical aspects of wider commercial, political, diplomatic and military engagement that would find a resounding echo in evolving VOC strategies well into the 18th century and arguably even beyond the lifespan of the company in 19th-century Dutch high imperialism. The four key areas can be briefly described as sovereignty, the just war, free trade and alliance-making. The findings on each of these can be summarised as follows.

Sovereignty

Sovereignty is the foundation for understanding the theoretical construct of Grotius. It clearly marks a significant point of departure in at least two of his works, namely *Commentarius in Theses XI* as well as his epoch-making *De Iure Belli ac Pacis.* Although he appears to have assumed the idea of sovereignty from the French historian and jurisconsult Jean Bodin (see the image on p. 160), Grotius also significantly departed from Bodin in one very crucial aspect: the rights of sovereignty in practice do not — and must not necessarily — come as a single, indivisible package.[3] The concept of divisible sovereignty is very important for unlocking the dynamics of international relations and diplomacy, particularly in a Southeast Asian context. For the French historian and jurisconsult Bodin, sovereignty in theory and as an ideal represented a single, well-defined package of entailed rights that was preferably vested in the person of the monarch, and in only very exceptional cases with a collective body comprising multiple members, such as the triumvirate in ancient Rome. But we should not be misled into believing that Bodin's recommendations were common practice in his own day, not even in Europe. Issues surrounding the rights of sovereignty in the early modern period were indeed complex and intellectually messy, as Grotius and some of his contemporaries certainly recognised.[4] The Holy Roman Empire, the Dutch Republic and, indeed, its plenipotentiary proxy in the East Indies, the VOC, are classic examples of a fluid division of sovereign rights among different parties. With reference to the latter, I point to the recent study of Kerry Ward titled *Networks of Empire* which seeks to understand the Dutch company through its historic "creation and management of … multiple and intersecting fields of partial sovereignty".[5]

The division of sovereign rights among different parties within (and technically even outside) a given polity assist Grotius in an early modern European context, especially in his *Commentarius in Theses XI*, to legitimise the existence of a mixed, oligarchic constitution for the Dutch Republic. On closer reading of *De Iure Praedae* and other early writings, his understanding of sovereignty was also to have significantly impacted the way he envisaged, and indeed justified, the projection of Dutch power into the East Indies. In developing his ideas of divisible sovereignty, and in turn applying these to the Southeast Asian context, Grotius (and the VOC) first attributed a range of sovereign rights to these rulers that were largely alien to their own political culture. In a second step, divisible sovereignty provided not only a possible mechanism, but importantly also yielded a convenient tool for gradually eroding sovereign rights. As time would pass, the Dutch company, and later the Dutch colonial government of the 19th and early 20th centuries, had effectively acquired and exercised many, if not all, the rights of sovereignty, leaving Asian rulers with little more than an empty titular shell. The "sovereign ruler" of high imperialism (and also of some post-colonial governments) was recognised as a hereditary monarch, but he held or exercised few, if any, residual rights of sovereignty proper.

There are four aspects of the early modern European concept of sovereignty advocated by Grotius and some of his contemporaries that created lines of friction with prevailing political cultures in Southeast Asia during the late 16th and early 17th centuries, especially with reference to the Malay world. This was at a time when the VOC began to establish a web of alliances across Asia. The first concerns the idea of sovereignty and the set of rights which this term implied in the minds of Europeans. In the context of early modern Europe, sovereignty encompassed rights tightly associated with a stratified feudal regime that emphasised territoriality. It is also tied to the mutual obligations of vassal and prince, and in turn their relationship with the emperor, the papacy and the church at large. Sovereign is he who does not hold his land in fief, and as a result does not recognise any higher worldly authority (*non agnoscens superiorem*). Here territoriality is closely tied to Medieval feudal arrangements of granting land in return for armed support and loyalty of the vassal. By contrast, kingship in the Malay world paid scant attention to ideas of territoriality, but instead placed emphasis on people and their loyalty to a given ruler. This loyalty could — and historically did — change, and some rulers even actively solicited or wooed new

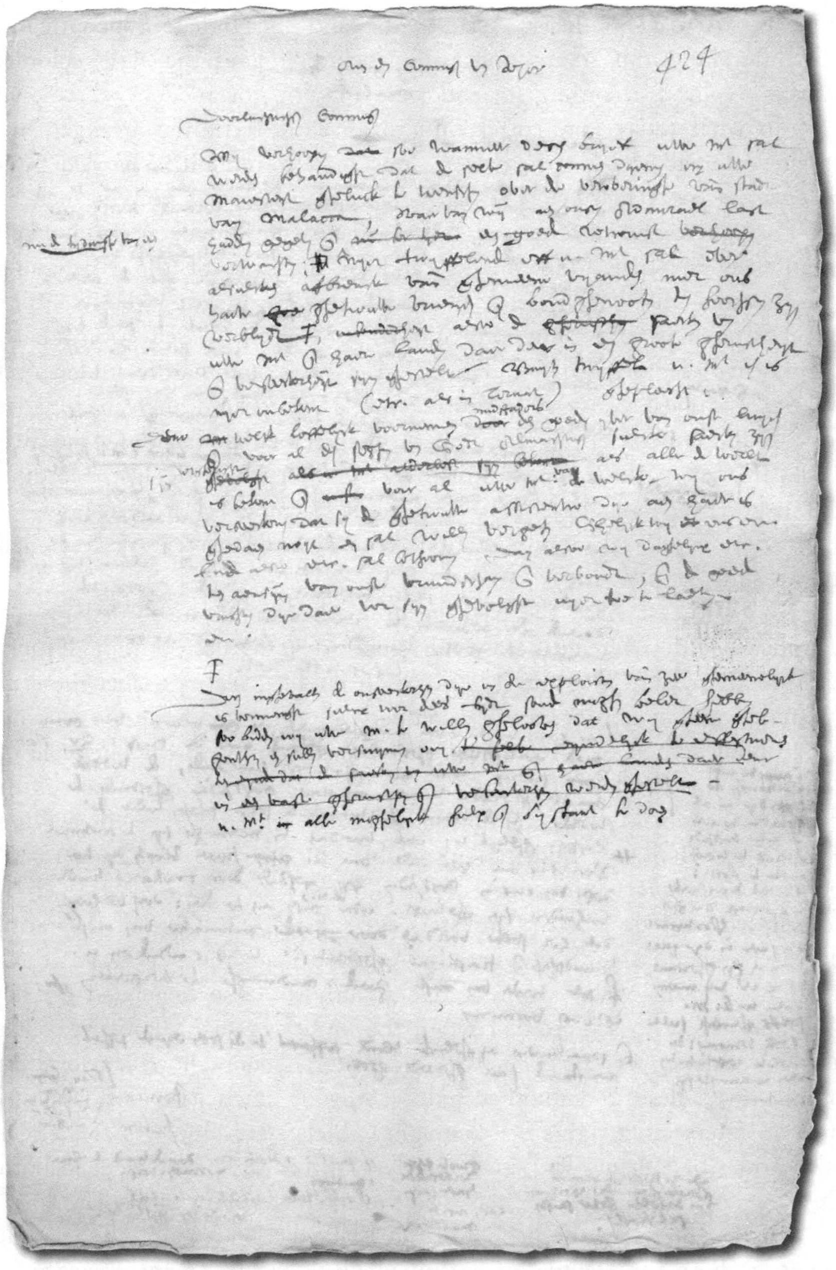

Illus. 44 Draft of a Dutch letter in the hand of Grotius to the King of Johor. It probably dates from the first decade of the 17th century. (The Hague, Nationaal Archief, *Collectie Hugo de Groot, Supplement I* [1.10.35.02, no. 40, fol. 424 recto])

subjects.[6] Across Southeast Asia, China and the Indian Subcontinent, the different trading communities — including later the early colonial powers — lived according to, and were in turn governed by, their own laws in what today may correspond to an extra-territorial arrangement. In pre-colonial Melaka, there were four such communities headed by a *shahbandar* (port master). The early European colonial powers such as the Portuguese and the Spanish, but also later the Dutch, accommodated themselves to such arrangements, and in the case of the Portuguese also became the beneficiaries of such self-government. Macao offers one of the most intriguing pre-colonial arrangements, self-governed by the Portuguese, originally undefined in its size and hardly understood by the Europeans in the period before 1800. The Dutch negotiated for self-administration in a number of agreements, including the two 1606 treaties with Johor. From the scant surviving details recording the negotiations of these two treaties, it becomes clear just how far apart notions of self-administration, control and sovereignty remained at the time.

In Southeast Asia, the package of implied rights associated by the Europeans with sovereignty was understood to be divisible. Although most early modern European analyses of Asian political regimes label these as "despotic" and sometimes also "absolutist" (in contrast to Europeans who often imbued their own republican political discourses in the language of "liberty"), the division of powers in Malay polities was far more subtle, fluid and complex than European observers were able — or willing — to grasp. For one, high-ranking nobles such as the *bendahara* (chief police), *laksamana* (commander of naval forces), or *temenggong* (chief of security) cannot be labeled "ministers" in a European sense of the term, but exercised their functions broadly removed from the purview of their overlord. In the Malay world a ruler's authority also depended on his skill and ability to acquire *and* retain the loyalty of such dignitaries such as the *bendahara* or *laksamana.* As the histories show, however, loyalties often proved fluid and multifaceted, leading in practice to "overlapping" or even intersecting rights of sovereignty. A classic example to this effect is the ruler of Pahang who, in the early 17th century acknowledged both the kings of Johor and separately also the ruler of Patani as his "overlord" or "patron". Similarly, the people of the Ryukyu islands paid homage and tribute to both the Daimyo of Satsuma as well as the Emperor of China. During the 17th and well into the 18th centuries, many of the sultans of the Malay Peninsula continued to pay tribute to the King of Siam.

This formal submission to the Siamese monarch is visible from a ritual ceremony whereby the *bunga mas* (tributary gifts) was presented to at the Siamese court in Ayutthaya. In turn, the King of Siam also dispatched tributary missions to the Emperor of China. The tributary system is the most visible and tangible manifestation of the hierarchy of rulers in East and Southeast Asia.

This hierarchy contrasts with the European idea of the nominal equality of all sovereign rulers, and implicitly, of sovereign, independent polities. (In practice the situation may have been different.) As is evidenced by considerations on overlapping sovereignty mentioned above, relations between Asian rulers were not governed by equality of status, but by a relatively fluid hierarchy of authority and reputation. As has been explained, the hierarchy of Asian rulers was most significantly reflected in patterns of tribute and ceremonial submission. In the Malay world — and even beyond — dignity (in some places called *nama*) of a given ruler, that is to say on his reputation among peoples and other rulers, assumed the centre stage.[7] Rulers jockeyed to improve their relative standing within the hierarchy of rulers and in the process enhanced their dignity or *nama* as well. When rulers first entered into alliances with the VOC, they do not regard themselves entering into an irreversible, perpetually binding contract along the lines envisioned by Grotius or Governor-General Jan Pieterszoon Coen, but sought to improve their relative standing among other rulers. Generally, they (willingly) abided by an agreement or contract for as long as it continued to enhance their relative standing. Needless to say, the unwilling were often coerced into obedience by their European treaty partners, especially by the Dutch, who upheld the maxim of *pacta sunt servanda* (treaties *must* be honoured). The principal beneficiaries of a European understanding of sovereignty that envisioned the "equality" of all sovereign rulers were of course the "petty princes" (as Grotius notably called them), in other words those rulers who assumed a low status in the hierarchy. In upgrading these "petty princes" to the status of full and equal sovereigns, one can easily understand different vantage points offered different perspectives on what was happening. From the vantage point of a "petty prince", an alliance with a European power or trading company could serve to boost both his recognition and reputation (*nama*) and therefore also enhance his relative standing within the hierarchy of Asian rulers.

The fourth line of friction caused by the European understanding of sovereignty touches on the meaning of terms such as "state" or "polity".

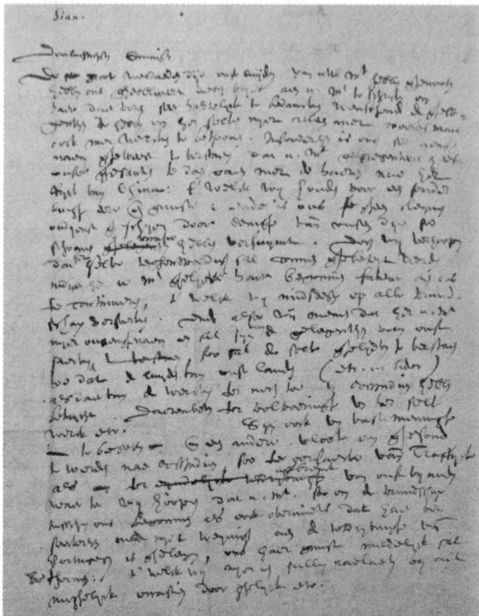

Illus. 45 Draft letter in the hand of Grotius addressed to the King of Siam of uncertain dating, but most probably from the period 1608 to 1615. (The Hague, Nationaal Archief, *Collectie Hugo de Groot, Supplement I* [1.10.35.02, no. 40, fol 364 verso])

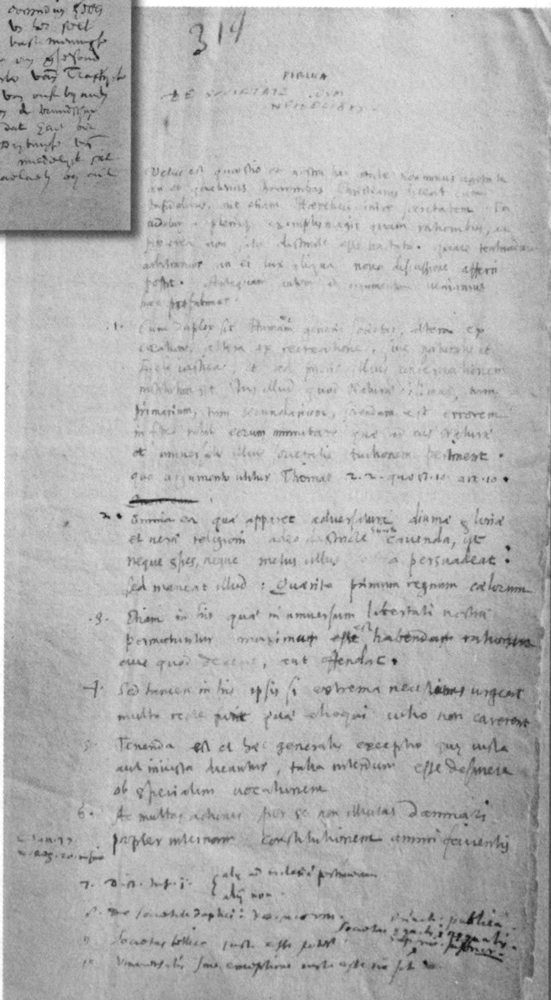

Illus. 46 First page of the skeletal treatise *De Societate Publica cum Infidelibus* (On Public Society with Non-Christians) written in the hand of Grotius. (Leiden University Library, B.P.L. 922, fol. 314 recto)

European feudalism placed a significant emphasis on territory as well as the definition and differentiation of vassal and overlord. After the Peace of Westphalia (1648) the concept of the state in western Europe became irreversibly fused with ideas of territoriality, constitutional government, and after the French Revolution also implicitly the sovereignty of the people. When Grotius, the VOC and indeed the officers of the Estado da Índia speak of forging treaties and alliances across the Malay Archipelago — and beyond — whom are they actually concluding such treaties with? A "state" or "polity"? Its ruler? Or both? A scrutiny of the actual texts capturing the very first treaties forged between the Dutch and Southeast Asian polities evidences that the vast majority of the agreements were signed with individual monarchs. Only in rare instances do we find contracts, treaties or alliances concluded with what the Dutch call *negrijen*, or *negeri*.[8] This is a Malay term that in many 17th-century European sources is translated in line with the word's Sanskrit origin, namely "settlement", "city" or sometimes also "polity".[9] The European commentators of the early modern period generally observe that a Malay "kingdom" can comprise one or several *negeri*, which in *their* understanding and *their* cultural-specific context is as much as to say a given "kingdom" comprises one or several "settlements", "cities" or perhaps loosely translated "civic polities".[10]

When Grotius and the VOC officers on the ground in Asia speak of, say, the "king of Johor", they see him possessing things and rights that "belong to a king", such as land, vassals and also subjects. Most important of all, they treat the Southeast Asian monarchs as full sovereigns according to a European understanding of the term. Knowingly — or inadvertently — they had ascribed to the rulers a set of rights they actually did not really possess within the context of their own politico-cultural traditions, practices and institutions. The longer-term consequences appear almost inevitable: VOC treaty and alliance-making (not unlike its Portuguese counterpart) often changed, altered or interfered with the politico-cultural institutions and practices within a given Asian polity. Johor in the early 17th century offers a well-documented case of how Dutch alliance policies interfered with the balance of power at the court and ultimately served to deepen existing divisions within the ruling elite.[11]

Among the materials touching on Admiral Matelieff's attack on Melaka, his conclusion of two treaties with Raja Bongsu and King 'Ala'uddin of Johor, as well as the time he spent at the Batu Sawar court — all in 1606 — we can find several supposed quotations from

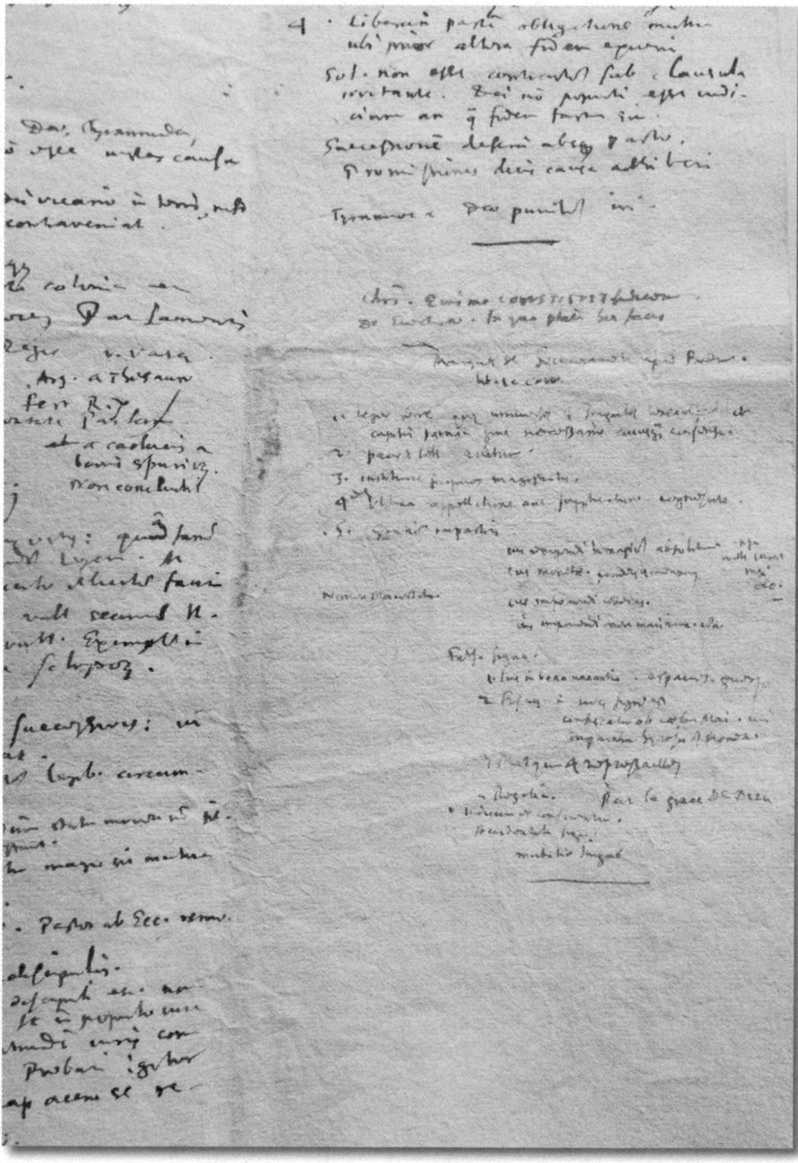

Illus. 47 Notes taken in the hand of Grotius relating to Jean Bodin's theory of sovereignty and specifically to the "marques de la souveraineté" (marks of sovereignty). It is evident that Grotius was working with French language edition of Bodin's *Six Livres de la République.* (Leiden University Library, B.P.L. 922, fol. 286 recto)

Raja Bongsu speaking of "his lands of Melaka" and other references of land "belonging to the king".[12] It would be fallacious, however, to take these and related statements as incontrovertible evidence that the pre-colonial Malay rulers worked with clear concepts of a territorial polity.[13] In the absence of the precise wording used in Malay, it is advisable not to jump to any unwarranted conclusions. Besides, Admiral Matelieff may have heard or understood the Raja having said what they *wanted* to hear. We do not — and cannot — really know for sure. What we do know is that the Europeans — doubtlessly for their own political convenience and advantage — treated the Johor ruler, 'Ala'uddin Ri'ayat Shah III, as an overlord in whom *all* rights of sovereignty were vested. But if Grotius would have only ventured to carefully scrutinise the two 1606 treaties signed by Admiral Matelieff, and especially the oath taken by the Johor side, it is clear that Raja Bongsu and King 'Ala'uddin, the "joint rulers of Johor", in practice did not conform and are over-simplistic outlook of sovereignty being concentrated in the person of the monarch.[14] Political authority at the Johor court seems to have been divided between the four royal brothers and the high functionaries of Johor, especially the *bendahara,* but always within the ramifications of the *daulat,* that is the religious, mystical and moral authority to rule (or lead) entailed by this concept of Arab origin.[15] The king represents political order, procedure, custom and tradition. The opposite, according to Malay sources, is confusion and disorder.[16] In establishing and maintaining order, the *daulat* is of course an important prerequisite,[17] and the ruler has the control of the population (and implicitly the labour) of at least one *negeri.*

Matelieff was well aware of the divisions and factions at the Johor court. He even commented that the four brothers ruled or controlled different regions or towns (speak: *negeri*) among the upstream settlements of the Johor River and in also in Siak on Sumatra (see appendix 13). Grotius, who was close to Matelieff, either failed to understand these and related complexities, or simply ignored them for the sake of convenience. The case of Johor in the early 17th century is of course not an isolated one.

By treating Southeast Asian monarchs as full sovereign lords of equal standing to their European counterparts, Grotius and the VOC effectively attributed to them a set of implied rights of sovereignty that were in fact alien to the Southeast Asian world of politics during the pre-colonial period. This would not only upset the hierarchy and its established patterns of interaction with other Asian overlords, but in fact gradually transformed the system to conform to recognisably European patterns. It should be immediately adjoined that, in the Malay world, laws were widely customary (*adat*) and only in exceptional cases codified.[18] Importantly also, Malay laws were variegated and hybrid, linking together different strands of pre-Islamic, Islamic and customary laws. Before high imperialism they certainly never enjoyed the rigidity widely associated with the Roman legal tradition of statutory law.[19] This impacted the manner and direction in which constitutional government evolved in Southeast Asia over the next three or even four centuries.

The Just War

The second cornerstone in the theoretical edifice of Grotius is his concept of the "just war" which in *De Iure Praedae* he divided into just wars that can be public or private. In staking out the theoretical parameters for a just war, he broadly followed the three well-known conditions set down by Thomas Aquinas and his commentators of the 16th century: authorisation by a prince (interpreted to mean a sovereign overlord proper), a sufficient cause and upright intentions. Private parties may wage war justly for and on behalf of a sovereign. The idea of a private war was technically not a new phenomenon in early modern warfare as merchants often turned into warriors and private vessels were frequently incorporated into fleets when the situation arose. Importantly, the practice of privateering — plundering the enemy under the laws of war and authorised by a letter of marque — was already well established by the early 17th century. Grotius' older contemporaries Walter Raleigh and Francis Drake immediately spring to mind here, but there were of course others as well. The text fragment titled *De Pace* contained in ms. B.P.L. 922, like other major works such as *De Iure Praedae* and later of course *De Iure Belli ac Pacis*, the morally and legally acceptable causes and plot the objectives of war. They are self-defence, the restitution of rights and the recovery of property stolen or robbed, a recompensation for damages and costs incurred during the course of warfare and punishment of the enemy for injuries suffered.[20]

In defending van Heemskerk's seizure of the *Santa Catarina*, the treatise *De Iure Praedae* embarked on a twin line of argument to underscore the legitimacy of this historic event. If this act fell under the category of a private war, then the Dutch acted in a capacity as allies of the Johor monarch who was an acknowledged sovereign and ostensibly at war with the Portuguese. So in this instance, van Heemskerk would have fought on the side of the independent and sovereign King of Johor as his ally in the latter's just war against the Portuguese. Certainly, the Dutch held their own grudges against the Iberian powers who violently impeded the former from sailing the high seas to reach the East Indies, attempted to bar them (through undue interference with local rulers) from accessing crucial emporia, and also brutally mistreated any Dutch citizen they could get their hands on. All these added up to sufficient grounds for a government-chartered organisation like the VOC to wage a just public war in self-defence. As a plenipotentiary representative of the Dutch Republic, the VOC was vested with quasi-sovereign powers, it could administer oaths of loyalty to its employees, wage wars, conclude peace agreements and sign international treaties. The most important cause for a just war was the effort on part of the two Iberian powers to deny or impede the exercise of a fundamental natural right. For Grotius, the Portuguese and Spanish denied the Dutch their natural right of free trade.

Free Trade

The third cornerstone in the theoretical edifice of Grotius is the right of free trade. It is important that one does not take this expression in a contemporary sense of free trade, but strictly against the backdrop of the arguments laid down in *Mare Liberum.* Many of the existing discourses touching on that treatise have taken as the work's central tenet the right of all nations to navigate the high seas. Whilst the freedom of maritime navigation does feature prominently in *Mare Liberum*, it remains only a single aspect in an overarching argument on free trade and access to emporia or marketplaces in the East Indies. To fully unpack this term, it is necessary to take into consideration several concepts, including of course sovereignty and the idea of the just war, but especially also the *ius communicationis* (right of [free and unimpeded] communication) mentioned above. The *ius communicationis* is really the core concept that underpins the whole agenda of *Mare Liberum* and arguably *De Iure Praedae* as a whole. It is in the light of free trade that we can appreciate the discourses on why commerce is necessary; why trade is anchored in Creation and foreseen by the Creator (although Grotius quotes mainly from the Greek and Roman classics to make his case) and why trade must therefore be good and beneficial for societies, as it is indeed, for the Low Countries.

Cicero and the authors of the classical era would have surely been pleased by *De Iure Praedae*'s line of rhetoric and reasoning. Enter the concept of the just war: any person (and especially also sovereign) who attempts to deny such a natural right must face the consequences in war. It almost goes without saying that, according to *De Iure Praedae*, this was precisely what the Portuguese and Spanish were doing in harassing Dutch shipping, mistreating Dutch mariners and inciting Asian rulers to bar Dutch access to their ports and emporia.

But what about the high seas? How does the argument about the freedom of navigation fit into this wider, overarching argument in favour of free trade? The key term here is "access". The oceans offer the maritime highways to reach these Asian emporia from Europe. Kings and princes can control overland routes; they can control who uses their roads, they levy tolls and issue passes of safe conduct. This endorses the importance of links between notions of sovereignty and territoriality or "space" generally speaking. Arguably the Portuguese sought to claim sovereignty over the maritime highways and pelagic spaces by issuing *cartazes* (free conduct passes) or by restricting licenses to trade in the East Indies to European-born Portuguese subjects. For Grotius the Dutch could only exercise their right of free trade if they were also given unimpeded access to the marketplaces in the East. The maritime highways across the high seas had to be navigable to all without hindrance, conditions or restrictions. For this reason Grotius sought to remove these maritime routes from the types of political control exercised by sovereigns on land. Any attempts to lodge exclusive claims to the vast expanse of the high seas, either by individuals or sovereigns, should be deemed little more than tyranny.

On close reading of *Mare Liberum*, one suspects that Grotius really wanted to address that vital issue of access to marketplaces by criticising Portuguese and Spanish policies of exclusion and obstruction. In fact, he was treading on proverbial thin ice, and he was evidently aware of that. Grotius knew that his arguments would raise the eyebrows of court lawyers across Europe, as they indeed did, judging not least from the responses of Welwood and de Freitas. Actual state practice went against the ideals of Grotius, who in the course of *Mare Liberum* made concessions to the control of coastal waters and bays. He restricted his case to those vast open maritime spaces used for the increasingly lucrative transoceanic long-distance trade. He may have been deliberately coy about mentioning names — Genoa and Venice are mentioned by name and *Mare Liberum* acknowledges their effective control of the Adriatic and Ligurian Seas — but he remained conspicuously silent on England, Scotland and Denmark. These three kingdoms advanced claims to waters of the North Sea and the open Atlantic.[21]

The focus of *Mare Liberum* is to take on the Portuguese and the Spanish, their violent efforts to shut out competitors and impede the right of free trade. Grotius hoped to secure Dutch access to marketplaces and emporia in the east by removing maritime highways from all facets of Iberian political control, real or alleged. Consequently, he did not see the high seas as spaces entirely devoid of law, but specifically as zones remaining in their natural state. Rulers could, however, project their authority onto their ships and subjects plying these pelagic spaces.

As is shown by these findings, free trade in *Mare Liberum* is closely connected with ideas of sovereignty and the just war. The treatise renders the high seas into spaces that represent highly competitive, but not lawless environments, over which an indivisible trinity of commerce, war and plunder reigns.

Alliance-Making

As one of his principal arguments justifying the seizure of the *Santa Catarina* as an act in a just (public) war, Grotius claimed that van Heemskerk acted as an ally-in-arms of the Johor monarch against Portuguese aggression. It is clear from the manuscript of *De Iure Praedae* as a whole, as well as from the treatises, fragments and notes contained in B.P.L. 922, that Grotius carefully considered the question of forging alliances with Asian rulers both at a theoretical, as well as at a practical level. On paper he reiterated the argument of Vitoria that it is just and right to defend the innocent against tyranny. But the contexts in which these two men advanced this point could not have been more different. Vitoria sought to legitimise Spanish intervention in the New World and justified pacts and alliances with friendly Amerindian tribes and rulers against aggression and violence of their neighbours. This was ultimately a very pragmatic consideration that sanctioned Spain's defence of tribes and peoples who were friendly to its political cause — and important for the theologian Vitoria — also its religious agenda. Grotius, by contrast, sought to justify van Heemskerk's alliance with a Muslim overlord against the Roman Catholic Portuguese. Seraphim de Freitas cried foul over this Dutch

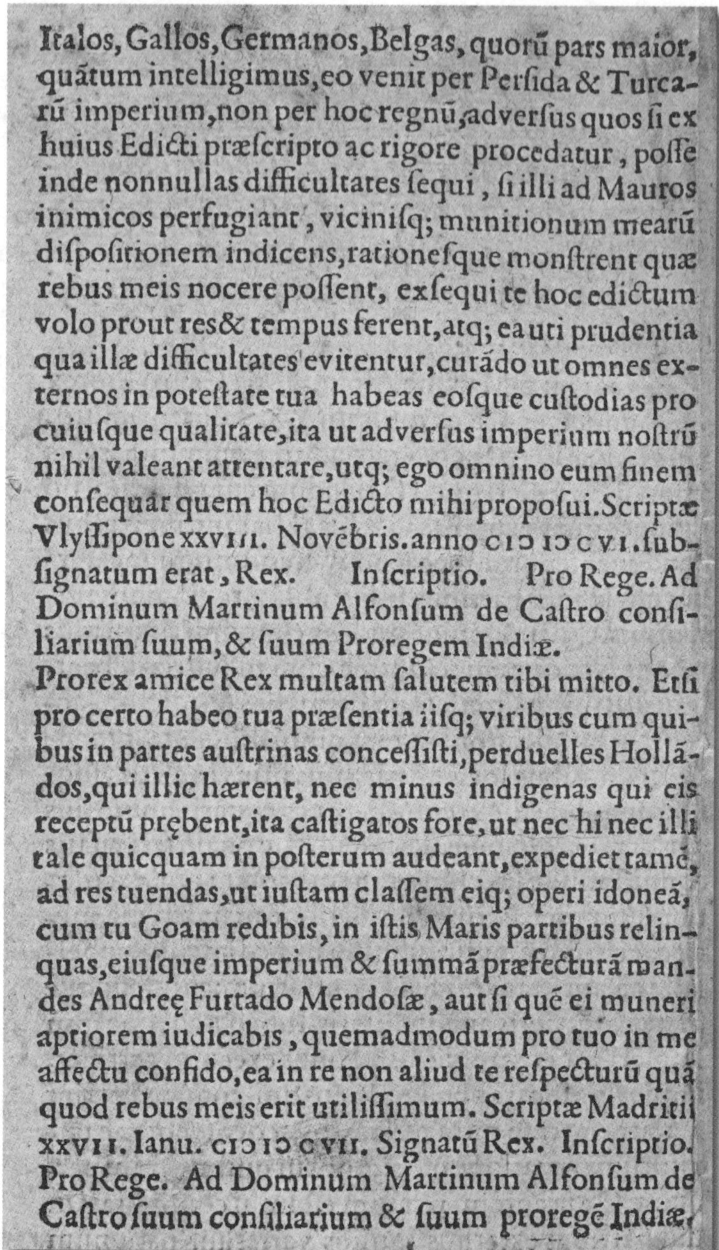

Italos, Gallos, Germanos, Belgas, quorũ pars maior, quãtum intelligimus, eo venit per Perſida & Turcarũ imperium, non per hoc regnũ, adverſus quos ſi ex huius Edicti præſcripto ac rigore procedatur, poſſe inde nonnullas difficultates ſequi, ſi illi ad Mauros inimicos perfugiant, viciniſq; munitionum mearũ diſpoſitionem indicens, rationeſque monſtrent quæ rebus meis nocere poſſent, exſequi te hoc edictum volo prout res & tempus ferent, atq; ea uti prudentia qua illæ difficultates evitentur, curãdo ut omnes externos in poteſtate tua habeas eoſque cuſtodias pro cuiuſque qualitate, ita ut adverſus imperium noſtrũ nihil valeant attentare, utq; ego omnino eum finem conſequar quem hoc Edicto mihi propoſui. Scriptæ Vlyſſipone XXVIII. Novẽbris. anno CIↃ IↃ C VI. ſubſignatum erat, Rex. Inſcriptio. Pro Rege. Ad Dominum Martinum Alfonſum de Caſtro conſiliarium ſuum, & ſuum Proregem Indiæ.

Prorex amice Rex multam ſalutem tibi mitto. Etſi pro certo habeo tua præſentia iiſq; viribus cum quibus in partes auſtrinas conceſſiſti, perduelles Hollãdos, qui illic hærent, nec minus indigenas qui eis receptũ prębent, ita caſtigatos fore, ut nec hi nec illi tale quicquam in poſterum audeant, expediet tamẽ, ad res tuendas, ut iuſtam claſſem eiq; operi idoneã, cum tu Goam redibis, in iſtis Maris partibus relinquas, eiuſque imperium & ſummã præfecturã mandes Andreę Furtado Mendoſæ, aut ſi quẽ ei muneri aptiorem iudicabis, quemadmodum pro tuo in me affectu confido, ea in re non aliud te reſpecturũ quã quod rebus meis erit utiliſſimum. Scriptæ Madritii XXVII. Ianu. CIↃ IↃ C VII. Signatũ Rex. Inſcriptio. Pro Rege. Ad Dominum Martinum Alfonſum de Caſtro ſuum conſiliarium & ſuum proregẽ Indiæ.

Illus. 48 Printed Latin translation of two letters by Philip III/II to Dom Martim Affonso de Castro, the Portuguese viceroy of India, dated 28 November 1606 and 27 January 1607. These had been forwarded to Grotius by Adriaen ten Haeff in 1608 and added on unfoliated pages at the end of the 1609 edition of *Mare Liberum*. (The Hague, Koninklijke Bibliotheek, 893 G 6) practice of allying with Muslims against Christians. His open disgust was symptomatic of widespread caution and deep reservations that lingered for centuries in Christian Europe. Although European scholars had warned of forging alliances and treaties with non-Christians for religious and moral reasons, realities on the ground called for a different attitudes. By the 16th century, the religious dogma and theological reservations of the Portuguese in Asia generally took a back seat to the profits generated by the wheels of commerce. It was simply poor business sense to let God get in the way of making money.

In *De Societate Publica cum Infidelibus,* Grotius set out to explore a range of issues on forging and maintaining open relations with non-Christians, both at a deeply personal level, as well as in the public domain. As shown in chapter 2, he also repeated in this skeletal outline many of the principles developed here in his *De Iure Praedae,* though in the latter the purpose was to superimpose them onto van Heemskerk's real or supposed alliance with Johor. Apart from justifying the *Santa Catarina* incident via arguments linking van Heemskerk to Johor and acting as its ally-in-arms, Grotius also found it necessary to carefully work out a general framework for Dutch interaction with Asian rulers. After all the VOC was actively scouting for Asian support in its ongoing war against the Iberian powers, forged pacts with willing rulers and also concluded exclusive delivery contracts for spices supposedly in return for protection against Portuguese and Spanish aggression. Indeed, Grotius himself had a hand in some of these agreements, as draft treaties addressed to, or destined for, Southeast Asian rulers can testify.

The conclusion of pacts and agreements of international standing between the VOC and the monarchs of insular and mainland Southeast Asia, however, came at a price hardly foreseen by the signatories. On the one hand these treaties were justified on the grounds that "petty princes" such as the rulers of Johor, Ternate and Tidor who were situated at the frontlines of Iberian expansion and presence in Southeast Asia, required Dutch help in protecting them against aggression or encroachment by the Portuguese and the Spanish.[22] This created one facet in their early dependency on the VOC which Grotius refers to as *coophandel met force* (trade supported by the force of arms). On the other hand the price exacted for such protection meant that the signatories were bound to honour exclusive contracts to supply spices such as nutmeg, mace, cloves and pepper. Grotius explained this process at the colonial conferences of 1613 and 1615 in terms of voluntarily curtailment or limitation of a sovereign prince's liberty via contractual obligations. But he understood this curtailment to be irreversible and irrevocable — an argument that was certainly based on Western attitudes toward, and traditions pertaining to, the rigidity of law. These assumptions stood in sharp contrast to the pre-modern, pre-colonial world of Southeast Asian commerce and political culture where laws and customs were always seen as something very fluid, inherently flexible and clearly adaptable. This is evidenced by uncodified *adat* (customary laws) in the Malay world as well as by its dynamic interaction with Islamic and other legal systems. *Pacta sunt servanda* (contracts *must* be honoured), he ominously reminded the English delegates at the London conference: A breach of contract was grounds for a just war. Through a just war it was possible to acquire some, or indeed all, rights of sovereignty (supposedly) vested in the Asian monarchs. The VOC's well-known spice monopoly, its practice of eroding at the political authority of monarchs under treaty, the gradual acquisition of territory through periodic aggression and warfare, as well as the Dutch company's notorious ill-treatment of their indigenous subjects was thus well in the making.

In the late 19th and for much of the 20th century, published research and public commemorations organised in Grotius' honour, upheld the Dutch humanist as a prince of peace whose love and concern for mankind survives in the published letter of his works and especially in his *De Iure Belli ac Pacis.*[23] Such misguided optimism, while still widespread today, cannot be sustained on a close reading of his letters, treatises, fragments, and reading notes that are found scattered across archives in the Netherlands and elsewhere. During the first decade of the 17th century the young Grotius was certainly far more aggressive and willing to go to war than the mature and seasoned author known from *De Iure Belli ac Pacis.* There is a growing awareness among researchers that he ranks not only one of the great forbearers of the post-Westphalian international state system, but also as one of the early architects of European colonial rule in Asia and beyond.[24] He helped lay the theoretical foundations for the VOC's web of alliances that was originally targeted against the interests of the Portuguese and the Spanish, but later also against the English. His ideas provided the theoretical and legal foundations that helped forge procurement of commodities and spices under contract to the exclusion of all other European nations, a wholesale barring that was soon also extended to Asian traders. His core belief in the inviolability of (international) contracts (*pacta sunt servanda*), the divisibility of sovereign rights, the attribution of full sovereignty to Asian rulers, the concept of the just war, together with his ideas on the freedom, necessity and utility of long-distance trade coalesced into a formidable intellectual enterprise that sanctioned the VOC's trading monopoly and helped sanction Dutch colonial rule across much of insular Southeast Asia.

Document Appendices

Appendix 1

Letter by Adriaen ten Haeff to Hugo Grotius dated 17 November 1607. Excerpt from the postscript summarising the packet of letters forwarded to Grotius titled "Letters from the King of Spain".[1]

[The following presents an abridged list of letters which Grotius received from Adriaen ten Haeff in 1607, a few months before the former began revising chapter 12 of *De Iure Praedae* for publication as *Mare Liberum*. On the basis of the short summary of their contents (see the images on pp. 128, 132), it is possible to reconstruct the thrust of their argument. The dates, author, addressee and short content descriptions have helped retrieve surviving originals in Lisbon and other archives in Europe. It is widely believed that some — if not all — of the letters forwarded to Grotius in late 1608 were originally seized by Admiral Paul van Caerden from a vessel that he captured off the coast of India. Two come in question. One is the Goa-bound carrack *Nossa Senhora do Loretto* which was taken near its destination on 10 October 1607, and a second smaller vessel near Cananor on 31 October 1607.[2] Van Caerden later passed the letters to Admiral Cornelis Matelieff de Jonge when they met in Banten in January 1608,[3] as is reported in his letter to the Heren XVII of 9 January 1608: "I passed on to Admiral Matelieff all the letters wich the King of Spain had written to the viceroy and the Estado da Índia,[4] keeping with me copies thereof, which I had made."[5] The different travelogues and letters report that Matelieff and van Caerden discussed the failed attacks on Melaka in 1606 as well as some opportunities for Dutch trade in China, Patani, Gresik and Aceh.[6] Matelieff passed to Paul van Caerden a set of secret instructions, which the latter subsequently discussed with members of his *breede raad* (officers council) and *krijgsraad* (war council). The councils resolved to proceed to Johor where they hoped to arrive in time to waylay Portuguese carracks inbound from China.[7] The strong winds of the northeast monsoon, however, prevented van Caerden's ships from reaching the Singapore Straits and the Johor River estuary. They eventually changed course and headed for Makassar.[8] Matelieff returned to the Netherlands in late 1608. Grotius probably worked with Dutch and French translations of the royal letters that had been prepared for him by the VOC. These copies were found among the Dutch humanist's working papers sold in 1864.[9]

Excerpt from the Original Dutch Text

No. 2, "Een brieff van 28 November anno 1606 wt Lisbona aen don Martin voorzegd, daerin hem gesonden wordt een placcaet, daerbij geordonneert wordt dat men alle vremdelingen als Franchoisen, Italiaenen, Hooghduytsen ende Nederlanders die in Indiën woonen ende wel over Persiën ende Turquijen daer gecomen sijn, sal doen vertrecken." Ibid., no. 3, "Een brieff van 27 January 1607 in Madril aen don Andrea Furtado Mendoza, daerbij hem geordonneert wordt aen den vice-roy wel te informeren van 't fortificeren van de stadt van Malacca, het maken van eenige forten in Sincapura en elders." Ibid., no. 4, "Een brieff van 27 January 1607 in Madril aen don Martin de Castro, daerin hij ernstigh vermaent wordt om tot Achem ende in de enghten van Sabaon ende Sincapura fortressen te maecken." Ibid., no. 5, "Een brieff van 24 November 1606 wt Lisbona aen den capiteyn van de fortresse van Megapatan, daermede incompt van de vremdelingen daer overall te doen vertrecken." Ibid, no. 6, "Een brieff van 23 December anno 1606 wt Lisbona aen den coninck van Cananor, daerin hij bedanckt wordt van de rebellen in sijn landt niet geadmitteert te hebben ende daerin voort te willen continueren, enz." ... ibid. no. 10, "Een brieff van 13 February 1607 wt Lisbona aen don Martin Alfonso de Castro, daerin getracteert wordt van Machau te fortificeren."

English Translation[10]

Number 2, "A letter dated 28 November 1606, from Lisbon to the aforementioned Dom Martin [de Castro] by which he is sent a placard by which all foreigners such as the French, Italians, Germans and the Dutch who live in the East Indies and may have come there via Persia and Turkey, are to be expelled."[11] Ibid., no. 3, "A letter of 27 January 1607, from Madrid and address to Dom André Furtado de Mendonça, by which he is instructed to promptly report to the viceroy on the fortifications undertaken in the city of Melaka and the construction of forts along the Singapore Straits and elsewhere."[12] Ibid., no. 4, "A letter of 27 January 1607, from Madrid and addressed to Dom Martin de Castro, in which he is earnestly admonished to construct fortresses around Aceh and in the Straits of Sabam and Singapore."[13] Ibid., no. 5, "A letter of 24 November 1606, from Lisbon and addressed to the captain of Nagapattinam, in which he is instructed to expel all foreigners from there."[14] Ibid., no. 6, "A letter dated 23 December 1606, from Lisbon and addressed to the King of Cananor, in which he is being thanked for not having admitted the [Dutch] rebels into his lands and in which he is encouraged to continue in this vein." Ibid., no. 10, "A letter dated 13 February 1607, from Lisbon and addressed to Dom Martim Alfonso de Castro, in which he is exhorted to strengthen the fortifications in Macao."[15]

Appendix 2

Letter by King Philip III of Spain/II of Portugal, addressed to Dom Martim Affonso de Castro, the Portuguese Viceroy of India, dated 28 November 1606.[16]

[Information provided in appendix 1 has enabled the retrieval of the following royal letter which formed part of a packet forwarded to Grotius in November 1607. It is featured in the list prepared by Adriaen ten Haeff as item number 2.]

Original Portuguese Text

Dom Martim Affonso de Castro, viso-rey amigo, eu el-rey vos envio muito saudar. Com esta vos será a copia impressa de hũa ley que mandei fazer, pela qual e rasões que por ella vereis e outras de meu serviço, prohibo o commercio dos estrangeiros e viverem n'essas partes da India e nas mais ultramarinas; e por isto ser materia de grande importancia e serviço meu, e convir que se execute com toda a brevidade, vos encommendo que, tanto que esta com a dita ley vos for dada, logo com muita diligencia em todos os logares e partes d'esse Estado a façaes publicar e dar á execução, sem excepção de pessoa de qualquer qualidade, idade e condição que seja, e sem duvida nem replica algũa, procedendose na execução e cumprimento d'ella por via meramente executiva, sem se admitterem embargos, appellações nem aggravos em contrario, de qualquer materia, sorte e qualidade que sejam; e assi o mando e hei por meu serviço que se faça, e o cumpram os ministros a que a dita execução tocar, significando-lhes que de mais de me haver por muito desservido dos que o contrario fizerem, e de mandar proceder contra elles com o rigor que houver por meu serviço, os hei de logo mandar privar dos officios em que me servirem. E porem, por quanto me foi feita relação que n'essas partes vivem como moradores muitos estrangeiros de diversas nações, italianos, francezes, allemães, flamengos, dos quaes a maior parte se entende haverem lá passado por terras da Persia e de Turquia, e poucos pola via d'este reino, e que querendo ora por vigor d'esta ley usar com elles de rigor, se poderão seguir alguns inconvenientes, passando-se aos mouros [en]imigos, dando-lhe avisos de minhas fortalezas a que estão visinhos, ensinando-lhe ardis e meios com que possam prejudicar, procedereis na execução da dita ley conforme ao que o tempo vos mostrar, havendo-vos n'ella de maneira que se não sigam os ditos inconvenientes, assegurando-vos pessoas conforme a qualidade de cada hũa, de modo que não possam commetter cousa que redunde emp prejuizo d'esse Estado, nem se deixe de alcançar o intento principal que tive na dita ley. Escripta em Lisboa a 28 de novembro de 1606. — Rey: — Pedro de Mendonça Furtado — Dom Francisco d'Almeida.

Latin Translation Reproduced by Grotius[17]

Domine Martine Alphonse de Castro Prorex amice, ego Rex multam tibi salutem mitto. Cum hisce literis perveniet ad te exemplum typis impressum Edicti quod faciendum curavi, quo ob rationes quas expressas videbis, aliasque meis rebus conducentes prohibeo commercium omne externorum in ipsis partibus Indiae aliisque regionibus tramarinis. Quandoquidem res haec est momenti atque usus maximi, et quae effici summa cum industria debeat, impero tibi, ut simulatque literas has et edictum acceperis, publicationem eius omni diligentia procures in omnibus locis ac partibus istius imperii, idque ipsum quod edicto continetur

Illus. 49 Printed portrait of Philip III/II of Spain and Portugal. Biblioteca Nacional de España, Madrid.

exequaris sine ullius personae exceptione, cuiuscunque qualitatis aetatis conditionisve sit, citra omnem moram atque excusationem, procedasque ad impletionem mandati via merae executionis, nullo admisso impedimento, appellatione, aut gravamine in contrarium: cuiuscunque materiae generis aut qualitatis. Iubeo itaque hoc ipsum impleri per eos ministros ad quos executio pertinet, iisque significari non modo eos qui contra fecerint malam operam mihi navaturos, sed eosdem me puniturum privatione officiorum in quibus mihi serviunt. Quia autem relatum est mihi commorari in istis partibus externos multos variatum nationum /[18] Italos, Gallos, Germanos, Belgas, quorum pars maior, quantum intelligimus, eo venit per Persida et Turcarum imperium, non per hoc regnum, adversus quos si ex huius Edicti praescripto ac rigore procedatur, posse inde nonnullas difficultates sequi, si illi ad Mauros inimicos perfugiant, vicinisque munitionum mearum dispositionem indicens, rationesque monstrent quae rebus meis nocere possent, exsequi te hoc edictum volo prout res et tempus ferent, atque ea uti prudentia qua illae difficultates evitentur, curando ut omnes externos in potestate tua habeas eosque custodias pro cuiusque qualitate, ita ut adversus imperium nostrum nihil valeant attentare, utque, ego omnino eum finem consequar quem hoc Edicto mihi proposui. Scriptae Ulyssipone XXVIII. Novembris. anno [MDCVI]. Subsignatum erat, Rex. Insciptio. Pro Rege. Ad Dominum Martinum Alfonsum de Castro consiliarium suum, et suum Proregem Indiae.

English Translation[19]

Dom Martim Affonso de Castro, viceroy, friend, I, the King, send you my best wishes. I am sending herewith a printed copy of a law[20] that I ordered be proclaimed, whereby and [for] the reasons that you will see in it and for other reasons of my service, I forbid trade by foreigners resident in those lands of India and in the other overseas territories. Since this is a very important matter, greatly in the interests of my service, and since it is advisable that it be implemented with all haste, I order that, as soon as you receive this letter with the said law, you will immediately publish it with a great deal of diligence in all the places and lands of that Estado [da Índia] and implement it. There are to be no exceptions for anyone, irrespective of the type of person, their age or condition, and without doubts or any contestations. You will proceed to implement and fulfil this law merely through executive channels, without entertaining impediments, appeals or pleas to the contrary, irrespective of their type, quality and matters. Thus I order, and think it fit for my service, that this be duly done. All the

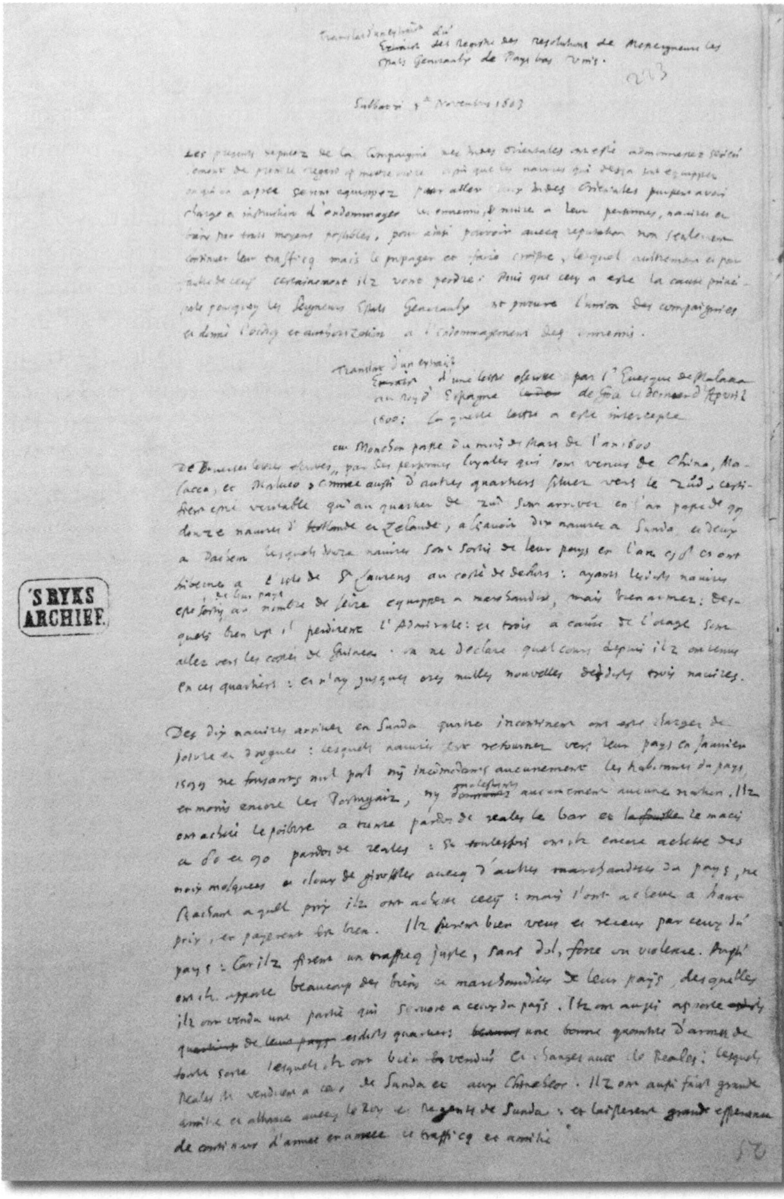

Illus. 50 French language excerpts in the hand of Grotius relating to the resolution of the States General dated 1 November 1603 (top third of the page). The VOC is instructed to attack Iberian targets and property in Asia wherever and whenever possible. The bottom two-thirds of the page represent excerpts in French translation from the letter of Dom João Ribeiro Gaio, Bishop of Melaka, to Philip III/II dated April 1600 (lower two-thirds of the page). (The Hague, Nationaal Archief, *Collectie Hugo de Groot, Supplement I* [1.10.35.02, no. 40, fol. 223 recto])

ministers who are affected by this said implementation [of the order] are to fulfil this, making it clear to them that those who do not do so will have done me a great disservice, and [you must] order that actions be taken against them with the rigour that is necessary for my service [and] I will later order that they be removed from the offices in which they are serving me. However, I have been told that many foreigners from diverse nations live in those lands, Italians, French, Germans [and] Flemish, most of whom I understand have gone there overland through Persia and Turkey and few through Portugal. Now, since I want this law applying to them to prevail rigorously, some inconveniences could subsequently arise. They could go to the enemy Moors, giving them information about my fortresses that are near them, teaching them tricks and means by which they could jeopardise [these fortresses]. You will proceed to implement the said law according to how you see the situation is evolving over the course of time, implementing it in such a way that the said inconveniences do not ensue. You will verify people according to the quality of each one, so that they cannot commit anything that results in harm to that Estado, and nor must you fail to achieve the main objective of the said law. Written in Lisbon on 28 November 1606. — The King: — Pedro de Mendonça Furtado, Dom Francisco d'Almeida.

Appendix 3

Letter by King Philip III/II, addressed to the King of Cananor, dated 23 December 1606.

[Information provided in appendix 1 has enabled the retrieval of the following letter of Philip III/II to the King of Cananor which formed part of a packet forwarded to Grotius in November 1607. It is featured in the list prepared by ten Haeff as item number 6. The original copy of this letter is preserved in Goa, India, and the present transcription has been prepared from a microfilm found in the *Filmoteca Ultramarina* in Lisbon, Portugal.][21]

Original Portuguese Text

Muito nobre Rei de Cananor eu Dom Felippe etc. vos faço saber que por carta do meu Viso Rey fui jnformado que nessas partes andauão roubando alguns leuantados dos estados de Flandes que sam sogeitos a minha coroa e indo ter ao porto de uossas terras offerecendo uos sua amisade e procurando uosso fauor e ajuda para poderem carregar suas naos não soo as não consentistes mas acodistes com gente a socorrer a minha fortalesa que tudo he comforme a uossa no[b]resa e lealdade nem fora comuenyente a ella dar entrada a piratas e aleuantados da obediencia de seu Rey e Senhor natural, e nesta boa comrespondeçia espero proçedaes sempre porque terey disso contentamento e vos encomendo que mãodeis aduirtir em todos os portos de uossas terras os não consintão nelles nem lhe dem carga para suas naos e delles não hajão paros a roubar de maneira que por falta de aduirtençia uossa não suçeda o contrario porque reçeberia disso muito dispraser e ao meu Viso Rey escreuo ordene que minhas armadas se emcontrem com os ditos rebeldes para lhe darem castigo que merecem, e o mesmo lhe mando faça aos que nessas partes lhe derem fauor e recolherem em seus portos e ho auiso que en tudo o que uos cumprir desse estado procure dar uos satisfação comforme ha muita que de uos tenho muito nobre Rei de Cananor Nosso Senhor uos alumie em sua graça e com ella uos aja senpre em sua guarda.

Escrita em Lixboa a 23 de Dezembro de 1606.

English Translation[22]

Very noble King of Cananore, I, Philip, etc. hereby inform you that I was informed by means of a letter from my viceroy that some rebels from the states of Flanders, who are subjects of my Crown, have been going about robbing in those lands, and when they went to the port in your lands, offering you their friendship and seeking your favour and help in order to be able to load their carracks, not only did you not consent but you also helped my fortress with additional men, which is all in keeping with your noble nature and loyalty; nor would it be convenient for pirates and rebels who do not obey their King and natural Lord to enter [that is take over] this fortress. And I hope you will always continue with this good correspondence because it would make me happy and I recommend that you order that a warning be sent to all the ports of your lands that [the rebels] not be allowed [to anchor] in them nor should they be given cargoes for their carracks and that there should be no *prahus* [left unguarded] for them to steal so that the contrary does not happen owing to a lack of warning from you, because that would displease me greatly. And I am writing to my viceroy to order that my armadas should go and pursue the said rebels to give them the punishment they deserve and I am ordering him to do the same to those who, in those lands, give them a favourable reception and allow them to anchor in their ports, and I am informing him that the Estado [da Índia] shall seek to satisfy you in all relevant aspects in conformance with the great satisfaction that I have [had] from you, very noble King of Cananore, may Our Lord always illuminate and guard over you with His grace.

Written in Lisbon on the 23rd of December 1606.

Appendix 4

Letter by King Philip III/II, addressed to Dom Martim Affonso de Castro, the Portuguese Viceroy of India, dated 27 January 1607.[23]

[Information provided in appendix 1 has enabled the retrieval of a second royal letter which formed part of a packet forwarded to Grotius by Adriaen ten Haeff in November 1607 and is featured as item number 4. Although the brief summary of the letter provided by ten Haeff reflects the actual contents of the letter, the supposed excerpt from this letter provided by Grotius as an addendum to his *Mare Liberum* does not. The present appendix reproduces the full original Portuguese text of the letter with English translation, together with Grotius' Latin excerpt from *Mare Liberum* together with a new English translation.]

Original Portuguese Text

Vice-rey amigo, eu el-rey vos envio muito saudar. Das cinco naus, que o anno passado vieram d'essas partes, chegaram ao reino as tres que saíram de Cochim, postoque as duas d'ellas tiveram na barra de Lisboa, com força de tempo, ruim successo, porque a nau Salvação deu em secco na praia de Cascaes e d'esta se salvou toda a fazenda, e a nau Martyres se perdeu entrando os cachopos, de que tive o sentimento que he rasão. Das duas que partiram de Goa não ha novas; permittirá Deos que invernariam em Moçambique; e de muita importancia será, para se segurar a viagem das naus que vem por aquella via, partirem mais cedo do que estas o fizeram, e assi procurareis que se tenha particular conta com isso.

De vossa chegada a esse Estado, e de como me ficaveis já servindo no governo d'elle, soube pela caravela que enviastes, porque das cartas, que dizeis me escrevestes por terra, se não recebeu nenhũa. A armada que o anno passado houvera de partir para essas partes o não pôde fazer, porque estando prestes e em ordem de sair, se poz o tempo de tal maneira contrario que não deu a isso logar, até ser passada a monção; nem depois se pôde effectuar, por algũas occasiões que succederam, a partida dos tres galeões, que tinha mandado se enviassem em setembro, como se vos tem avisado por terra com hum armenio morador n'essa cidade de Goa, que veiu despachado por Ayres de Saldanha, e tambem da causa por que as naus deixaram de partir.

Conforme ao que pola caravela e naus me escrevestes, da determinação com que ficaveis de passer ao Sul em execução do que vos tenho mandado, estou certo que esta minha carta vos achalará n'aquellas partes, e que me tereis feito n'ellas tantos e taes serviços, que correspondam bem á confiança com que vos encarreguei esta empreza, e por cujo respeito vos deva eu fazer toda a honra e mercê que houver logar.

E porque, assi polo que se tem entendido de muito tempo a esta parte de quam importante será fazer-se fortaleza no Dachem, como porque, achando-vos n'aquellas partes, entendereis melhor a necessidade que d'isso ha, e conforme a isto tenho por certo que o executareis, todavia he a materia de calidade que não posso deixar de vos encommendar e encarregar de novo, como faço, que por nenhum caso deixeis de fazer a dita fortaleza, como tambem tenho por mui necessario fazerem-se dous fortes nos estreitos de Sabão e Sincapura, para se assegurar a navegação de meus vassalos, e se atalhar aos damnos que dos inimigos os fazerem se lhes poderão seguir, polo que vos encommendo muito que procureis que em todo caso se façam os ditos fortes. Escripta em Madrid a 27 de janeiro 1607. — Rey: — Anrique de Sousa.

English Translation[24]

Viceroy, friend, I, the King, send you my best wishes. Of the five carracks that set out from those lands last year, the three that set sail from Cochin have reached Portugal, although two of them met a bad fate while reaching the harbour of Lisbon, owing to the weather. The carrack *Salvação* ran aground on the beach of Cascais and all the cargoes were saved from it, and the carrack *Mártires* was lost while entering the shoals, for which I was duly sorrowful. There is no news of the two [carracks] that set sail from Goa. God willing they will have wintered in Mozambique. To ensure the [safe] voyage of the carracks that use that route, it is very important that the ships leave earlier than these vessels did, and thus you will seek to ensure that particular care is taken in this regard.

I learnt about your arrival in that Estado and about how you have already begun serving me in its government from the caravel that you sent, because none of the letters that you said you had written to me [and sent] overland were received. The armada that should have left last year for those lands was unable to do so, because just when it was ready and about to set sail, the weather took such a turn for the worse that it was not possible, until the stormy weather had passed.[25] Nor was it possible for the three galleons that I had ordered be sent in September to leave subsequently, owing to some events that happened, as you have been informed overland through an Armenian, a resident of that city of Goa, who was sent by Aires de Saldanha, and [you were] also [informed] about the reason why the ships did not leave.

According to what you wrote to me via the caravel and the carracks, about how you were determined to go to the South to implement the orders I had given you, I am certain that this letter of mine will find you in those lands, and that you will have done many and great services for me in those parts, living up to the confidence I reposed in you when I entrusted you with this undertaking, owing to which I must confer upon you all due honour and grace and favour.

And because, according to what has been clear for a long time here about how important it is to build a fortress in Aceh, as well as because, since you are in those lands, you will better understand the need for this, I am certain that you will execute this accordingly. However, I must once again order and entrust you [to take care] about the quality of the materials, as I am doing [now]. You must build the said fortress no matter what, and I also feel it is very necessary to build two forts in the Straits of Sabam (Kundur) and Singapore, in order to ensure the navigation of my vassals and prevent the damage that enemies could do to them if they are able to follow them, owing to which I strongly urge you to ensure that the said forts are built in any circumstances. Written in Madrid on 27 January 1607. — The King: — Anrique de Sousa.

Appendix 5

Grotius' Text Fragment of a letter by King Philip III/II to Viceroy Dom Martim Affonso de Castro, dated 27 January 1607.[26]

[According to the brief summary provided by Adriaen ten Haeff to Grotius in 1608, the letter of Philip III/II to Dom Martim Alfonso de

Castro addressed the construction of fortifications in the region of Aceh as well as the Singapore and Kundur (Sabam) Straits (see appendices 1 and 4). Grotius, however, reproduces a Latin "excerpt" of a letter bearing the same date, 27 January 1607, but this is clearly not taken from the letter and summarised by ten Haeff. It is difficult to ascertain whether Grotius, as a result of his sloppy working habits, confused the dates of different letters, or whether the "excerpt" in question here is a forgery. The following Latin text is featured on the verso of an unnumbered double page that follows p. 66 (erroneously numbered as p. 42) in the first edition of *Mare Liberum*.]

Latin Translation Reproduced by Grotius

Prorex amice Rex multam salutem tibi mitto. Etsi pro certo habeo tua praesentia iisque viribus cum quibus in partes austrinas concessisti, perduelles Hollandos, qui illic haerent, nec minus indigenas qui eis receptum praebent, ita castigatos fore, ut nec hi nec illi tale quicquam in posterum audeant, expediet tamen, ad res tuendas, ut iustam classem, eique operi idoneam, cum tu Goam redibis, in istis Maris partibus relinquas, eiusque imperium et summam praefecturam mandes Andreae Furtado Mendosae, aut si quem ei muneri aptiorem iudicabis, quemadmodum pro tuo in me affectu confido, ea in re non aliud te respecturum quam quod rebus meis erit utilissimum. Scriptae Madritii XXVII Ianu. [MDCVII]. Signatum Rex. Inscriptio. Pro Rege. Ad Dominum Martinum Alfonsum de Castro suum consiliarium, et suum proregem Indiae.

English Translation of the Latin Text

Viceroy, friend, I, the king send you my best wishes:

I am quite certain that by your presence and by the forces with which you have gone to the southern regions, our enemies the Dutch who remain there, as well as the locals who welcome them, will be chastised in such a way that neither will dare do anything like that again. Nonetheless, in order to protect our interests, it will be useful if you leave a proper fleet that is up to the task in those parts of the sea when you return to Goa. Give command and supreme authority over the region to André Furtado de Mendonça, or to someone else if you think that [other person] is more qualified for the task. Given your

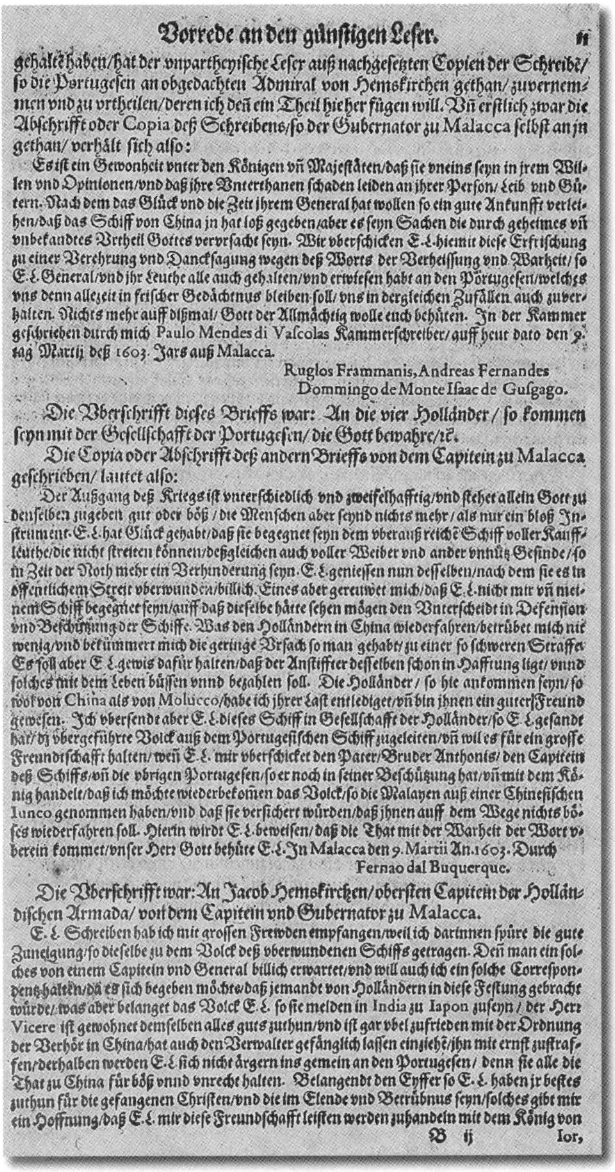

Vorrede an den günstigen Leser. 11

gehalte haben/hat der vnpartheyische Leser auß nachgesetzten Copien der Schreibẽ/ so die Portugesen an obgedachten Admiral von Hemskirchen gethan/ zuvernem-men vnd zu vrtheilen/deren ich deñ ein Theil hieher fügen will. Vñ erstlich zwar die Abschrifft oder Copia deß Schreibens/so der Gubernator zu Malacca selbst an jn gethan/ verhält sich also:

Es ist ein Gewonheit vnter den Königen vñ Majestäten/daß sie vneins seyn in jrem Willen vnd Opinionen/vnd daß jhre Vnterthanen schaden leiden an jhrer Person/ Leib vnd Gütern. Nach dem das Glück vnd die Zeit jhrem General hat wollen so ein gute Ankunfft verleihen/daß das Schiff von China jn hat loß gegeben/aber es seyn Sachen die durch geheimes vñ vnbekandtes Vrtheil Gottes vervrsacht seyn. Wir vberschicken E.L. hiemit diese Erfrischung zu einer Verehrung vnd Dancksagung wegen deß Worts der Verheissung vnd Warheit/ so E.L. General/vnd jhr Leuthe alle auch gehalten/vnd erwiesen habt an den Portugesen/welches vns denn allezeit in frischer Gedächtnus bleiben soll/ vns in dergleichen Zufällen auch zuverhalten. Nichts mehr auff dißmal/ Gott der Allmächtig wolle euch behüten. In der Kammer geschrieben durch mich Paulo Mendes di Vascolas Kammerschreiber/ auff heut dato den 9. tag Martij deß 1603. Jars auß Malacca.

Ruglos Frammanis, Andreas Fernandes
Dommingo de Monte Isaac de Gusgago.

Die Vberschrifft dieses Brieffs war: An die vier Holländer / so kommen seyn mit der Gesellschafft der Portugesen/ die Gott bewahre/rc.

Die Copia oder Abschrifft deß andern Brieffs von dem Capitein zu Malacca geschrieben/ lautet also:

Der Außgang deß Kriegs ist vnterschiedlich vnd zweifelhafftig/vnd stehet allein Gott zu denselben zugeben gut oder böß / die Menschen aber seynd nichts mehr / als nur ein bloß Instrument. E.L. hat Glück gehabt/daß sie begegnet seyn dem vberauß reichẽ Schiff voller Kauffleuthe/die nicht streiten können/deßgleichen auch voller Weiber vnd ander vnnütz Gesinde/so in Zeit der Noth mehr ein Verhinderung seyn. E.L. geniessen nun desselben/nach dem sie es in offentlichem Streit vberwunden/billich. Eines aber gereuwet mich/daß E.L. nicht mit vñ meinem Schiff begegnet seyn/auff daß dieselbe hätte sehen mögen den Vnterscheidt in Defension vnd Beschützung der Schiffe. Was den Holländern in China wiederfahren/betrübet mich nit wenig/vnd bekümmert mich die geringe Vrsach so man gehabt/ zu einer so schweren Straffe. Es soll aber E.L. gewis dafür halten/daß der Anstiffter desselben schon in Hafftung ligt/ vnnd solches mit dem Leben büssen vnnd bezahlen soll. Die Holländer / so hie ankommen seyn/ so wol von China als von Molucco/habe ich jhrer Last entlediget/vñ bin jhnen ein guter Freund gewesen. Ich vbersende aber E.L. dieses Schiff in Gesellschafft der Holländer/so E.L. gesandt hat/ dz vbergeführte Volck auß dem Portugesischen Schiff zugeleiten/vñ wil es für ein grosse Freundtschafft halten/ weñ E.L. mir vberschicket den Pater/Bruder Anthonis/ den Capitein deß Schiffs/vñ die vbrigen Portugesen/so er noch in seiner Beschützung hat/vñ mit dem König handelt/daß ich möchte wiederbekomẽ das Volck/so die Malayen auß einer Chinesischen Iunco genommen haben/vnd daß sie versichert würden/daß jhnen auff dem Wege nichts böses wiederfahren soll. Hierin wirdt E.L. beweisen/ daß die That mit der Warheit der Wort vberein kommet/vnser Herr Gott behüte E.L. In Malacca den 9. Martii An. 1603. Durch

Fernao dal Buquerque.

Die Vberschrifft war: An Jacob Hemskirchen/ obersten Capitein der Holländischen Armada/ von dem Capitein vnd Gubernator zu Malacca.

E.L. Schreiben hab ich mit grossen Frewden empfangen/weil ich darinnen spüre die gute Zuneigung/so dieselbe zu dem Volck deß vberwundenen Schiffs getragen. Deñ man ein solches von einem Capitein vnd General billich erwartet/vnd will auch ich ein solche Correspondentz halten/da es sich begeben möchte/daß jemandt von Holländern in diese Festung gebracht würde/ was aber belanget das Volck E.L. so sie melden in India zu Iapon zuseyn / der Herr Vicere ist gewohnet demselben alles guts zuthun/vnd ist gar vbel zufrieden mit der Ordnung der Verhör in China/hat auch den Verwalter gefänglich lassen einziehẽ/jhn mit ernst zustraffen/derhalben werden E.L. sich nicht ärgern ins gemein an den Portugesen/ denn sie alle die That zu China für böß vnnd vnrecht halten. Belangendt den Eyffer so E.L. haben jr bestes zuthun für die gefangenen Christen/vnd die im Elende vnd Betrübnus seyn/solches gibt mir ein Hoffnung/daß E.L. mir diese Freundschafft leisten werden zuhandeln mit dem König von

B ij Ior,

Illus. 51 German translations of a letter written by the *câmara* (city council) of Melaka (top third of page), together with two letters by Melaka's governor, Fernão d'Albuquerque addressed to Jacob van Heemskerk dated March 1603. These letters, which have also been transcribed and translated in appendices 7, 8 and 10, touch on developments and arrangements immediately after the seizure of the Portuguese carrack *Santa Catarina* off Changi on 25 February 1603. From M. Gotthard Arthus, *Achter Theil der Orientalischen Indien* (The Eighth Voyage of the Dutch to the East Indies), *Vorrede and den günstigen Leser* (Introduction to the benevolent reader), pp. 11–2. (Amsterdam University Library, OTM OF 82–5–7) affection for me, I trust that you will consider only my best interests in this matter.

Given at Madrid, 27 January 1607. Signed 'The King'. Addressed for the King. To Dom Martim Alfonso de Castro, his Councilor and Viceroy of the Indies.

Appendix 6

Portion of a letter by Dom João Ribeiro Gaio, the Bishop of Melaka, to Philip III/II, King of Spain and Portugal, dated 30 April 1600.[27]

[The present excerpt of a letter by Dom João Ribeiro Gaio, the Bishop of Melaka dates from the year 1600. Grotius refers to the letter in the main text of *Mare Liberum*, highlighting that the Dutch inflicted no harm either on the Portuguese or on the peoples of the East Indies, but engaged in peaceful, honest trade. The Dutch text represents a copy prepared in the 19th century by Frederik Muller for the historian Robert Fruin of Leiden University. The transcript was made from a now lost Dutch original which was found among the working papers of Grotius and sold at a public auction arranged by Martinus Nijhoff in 1864.]

Dutch Translation Sent to Grotius

Translaet uyt een auctentieq missive geschreven by den Busshop van Malucca aen den Co. Maj.t van Sp.a.

Heere!

Alle de voorleeden Jaren [1600] hebbe ick geschreven aen U Maj.t, ende gedachtich gemaeckt tgeene ic vernomen hadde, streckende ten dienste Godts, Ue Maj.t ende des gemeenen welvaerts: soo ic nu oock doen by desen.

In dese Monchaon ofte generale winden van April 600 ben ick wederom gecomen nae Malacca, omme van Malacca te schriven aen den Capiteyn, aen de Stadt en aent huys van de Il Barmerticheyt en aent Cabido; myne tegenwoordicheyt importeerde veele te Malacca, al waar ic myn Residentie doen sal, soo ick U Maj.t int breede geschreven hebben in December vant voorleden jaer 99. T' zal Godt believen dattet hem dienstich mach zyn en aen zyne kercke, soo oock U Maj.t en alle tvolck en aen alle die van den Zuyden. Mette schepen van de Landen van Indien, die verreyst zyn naer t' Rycke (te weten Portugael) in de maent van Janvier van dit tegenwoordich jaer, hebbe ick U Maj.t int breede geschreven; daer by verhaelt ende vermaent de dingen, die my goet gedocht hebben noodich te wesen, ten diense Godts en duwe, ende tot tgemeene welvaeren van desen State. Alle tselve hebbe ick oock gedaen int breede de voorleeden Jaeren ende hebbe daer by gevoucht de Coursen van Dachem ende van Sunda ende van de andere quartieren: tot welcke brieven ende Coursen ic my refereren, die daer berusten onder den Secretarissen. Derhalven en sal ick desen niet te lanck maecken: dan alleenelyck sal maecken eenige vermaeningen van de voors. zuyder quartieren ende van den staet daer inne zy nu tegenwoordich zyn.

Uyt veel brieven ende van geloffweerdige persoonen, die gecomen zyn van China, Malacca en Maluco, als oock van andre quartieren gelegen ten zuyden, geschreven in Indien, voorleeden Moncho ofte vaste winden van Martius anno 1600, die certificeren waer te zijn, dat int zuyder quartier gearriveert syn int voorleden jaer 99 twelff schepen uyt Hollant ende Zeelandt, te weten 10 schepen tot Sunda ende twee tot Dachem, welcke zyn 12 schepen, die uyt hun landt vertrocken zyn int jaer van 98 ende sy hebben overwintert int eylandt van St. Laureins, op de buyten zyde: welcke schepen wet hun landt gereyst zyn tot 16 coopvaarders toe, zynde wel gewapent. Van dewelcke sy straxs verlooren hun admirael, ende drie schepen trocken nae de Costen van Guinea ter causen vant weer. Daer en wort niet verclaert wat Cours dat sy gehouden hebben in deze quartieren ende tot noch toe en hebbe ick tydinge van voors. drie schepen.

Van de thien schepen, die tot Sunda arriveerden, van deselve sijn terstont viere gelaeden met peper ende drogerie, dewelcke schepen syn vertrocken nae hun landt ende dat in Janvier 99 geen leet oft quaet doende aan de Inwonders vanden Lande, min aan de Poortugysers, noch aen eenige andere natie hebben zy moeite oft verstoringe gedaen. Sy hebben die peper gecocht tot dertich pardos de reales de baer, ende de foille tot 80 ende 90 pardos de reales: ende evenwel hebben sy gecocht nooten ende naegelen t' sampt andere waren van dese landen; nyet weetende tot noch toe tot wat pryse sy die gecocht hebben, maer sy hebben die gecocht ten hoochsten pryse ende sy betaelden seer wel, zy waren wel gesien ende begeert by die vanden lande, want sy deden rechtvaerdige handelingen, sonder arch, verstoringe, oft gewelt te bedriven. Sy hebben oock veel goets, coopmanschappen ende waren wt hun landen gebrocht, waeraff de sommige vercocht hebben, die die vanden Lande dienstich waren. Deselve hebben oock daer gebrocht veel wapenen van alle sorten die sy wel vercocht hebben ende vermangelt tegens Reaelen, welcke

Reaelen sy vercochten aen die van Sunda ende aende Chincheos. Hebben oock groote vruntschap ende Aliantie gemaeckt mitten Conninck ende Regenten van Sunda ende sy maeckten ende lieten groote hope van alle jaren te continueren dese handelinge ende Vrientschap. Twelck Godt niet en wil toe laeten.

Twee andere schepe vande thiene zyn getrocken lancx de costen van Jaoa ende dat binnen deur nae tfort van Amboino, nae teylandt genaemt Hitto, alwaer sy gelaeden hebben naegelen ende syn alsoo vandaer vertocken, sonder dat men weet wat Cours, wat Bocquero ofte mont sy uyt getrocken zyn.

Twee andere schepen vande voors. 10e zyn van Sunda vertrocken nae de Costen van Jaoa binnens deure totte eylanden van Banda ende hebben daer gelaeden foille ende nooten: dese twee schepen zyn gelaeden nae hun geliefte ende syn alsoo gekeert nae Sunda ende van daer vertrocken inde maent van Augusti, 99, nae hun landt, ende sy seggen dat in die zee tot alle tyden bequame winden syn. Dese hebben tot Banda gelaeten 10 oft 12 mannen in Ostaigo, tot een teecken van vrientschap omme weederomme te commen; so sy oock sulcx gelaeten hebben inde voors. eylanden Hito ende int Rycke van Bali ende Sunda.

De twee andere shepen tot voldoeninge vande thiene die te Sunda arriveerden, syn tot Sunda gebleven verwachtende nieuwe peper, omme alsoo te vertrecken in Janvier 600; daeraff en es als noch geen seckere tydinge, oft die vertrocken syn oft niet, ende wat Cours deselve aengegaen syn.

De twee andere schepen tot voldoeninge van de 12e, die oock overwintert hebben int eylandt van St. Lorenzo waren aengecommen tot Dachem in Julyo, 99. In hun aencommen ende int eerste waren sy wel ontfangen ende onthaelt by den Coninck tot Dachem, alwaer hun vercocht wiert eenige peper: maer alsoo by eenige Portugysen, die tot dien tyden waren tot Dachem, totten Coninck geseyt wiert, by soo veere hy toeliet te handelen in zyn Rycke alsulcke volcken (denoterende Hollanders ende Zeelanders) dat hy geen vrient en soude syn vande Portugysers: ende hebben sooveere gehandelt mitten Coninck tot Dachem, dat men verbranden soude dese twee voors. schepen: waeraff die van de schepen gewaerschouwet wierden by sommige van des Conincks gouverneurs ende sy syn alsoo vertrocken van Dachem als fugitiven, ende sommige van des voors. schepes volcke waren opt landt gebleven, van dewelcke den Coninck tot Dachem twee gesonden heeft aende Capitain tot Malacca, die de spaensge spraecke wel verstonden ende spraecken: d'eene van hun was een pilot naturael Portuges van Zuricaia, die zy genomen hebben in een schip dat quaem van Brazil ende hebben hem met gewelt ende tegen synen wille medegenomen. Dese voorschreven twee personen heeft den voors. Capiteyn van Malacca gesonden aende Viseroy, opdat hy t'oogenmerck daerover soude hebben, omdat se in dese stadt gevangen waren. Deze twee voors. schepen, die daer vertrocken van Dachem, soo geseyt is, sy hebben hun keer genoomen nae Dachem, ic segge nae Cilao, waeraff tgrotste schip verlooren is op de coste van Cilao in Bathicator: van tander en weet men niet wat Cours dattet aengegaen es: men seght dattet verlooren is.

Alsoo ic boven geseyt hebbe, van dese zuyder quartieren, waeraff ic int breede geschreven hebben in den voorleden jaere, ende dit jaar 1600, hebbe ick aen U Maj.t veele ende int breede geschreven ende vermaent; daer by mede gesonden alle de Coursen van Sunda, Dachem, Patane, Gaidela, Siao ende van Combaja, mede adviserende deur wat orden men daerinne voorsien mach: twelck ic eerst hebbe geinventeert ende dat gecommuniceert mit persoonen van groote experientie ende hun verstaende inde voors. quartieren. Welcke brieven ende Coursen moeten berusten onder de Secretarissen, tot dewelcke U Maj.t zynde ten dienste Godes en d'uwe, mocht die doen besien ende doen voorsien deser zuyder quartieren, twelck is de Remedie van alle dese Standt en Staet: ende als inde voors. brieven ende Coursen doen nootelycke vermaninge, tot dewelcke ic my refereren. Tzal Godt believen U Maj.t te geven een lanck leven ende gesontheyt omme daerinne te moegen voorsien opt spoedichste. Boven alle dese zwaricheyden ende nieuwe vianden inde voorschreven zuyder quartieren, soo is daer vergaen een junco oft vrachtschip op de Reyse van Jappao, twelck quam van Jappam nae Macho, in welck schip verlooren is een million goudts ende meer dan vyff honderyt duysent Cruysaden, zynde alle de middelen vande Portugijsers Innewoonders van Macoa, die tegenwoordech bliven inde groote armoede ende in noot.

Int Rycke van Camboja syn doot geslaegen de Portugysers tsampt die Religieusen, ende syn alsoo gerebelleert tegen ons ende dat ter oirsaeke van eenige overlast oft agravien, die de onse hun aengedaen hebben.

In onse rycke van Siao hebben oock doot geslaegen alle de Portugesen ende de sommige hebben sy gebraden ende dat om de agravien die de onse hun aengedaen hebben.

In de Eylanden van Solor syn de Zwarte gerebelleert, die tegen ons waren ende sy hebben inne genomen onse sterckte ende syn daerover heerschap geweest omtrent een halven dach, want het wiert hun wederom affgenomen, ende is gebleven voor ons ende onse rycken van Balambuan, dewelcke waren grootelycs onse vrienden, alwaer kercken ende Religieusen waren, omdat sy heydenen syn, oock den Coninck van Passaruam, die een Javaen oft Mamotist is, heeft met een groot leger op die voors. Coninck gevallen ende is nu heer en Coninck van Balambuam, heeft de heydenen gedwongen Mooren te wesen, ende van alle die kercken hebben sy Musquiten gemaeckt ende hebben alle die Christenen gedoot.

Inde Rycken van Peguu hebben sy alle de Portugysers doot geslaegen. In Malucco, de sterckte oft fort van Thidore heeft krych met die van Ternate. Int landt van Amboino verwacht men krych: dit spruyt al omdatter geen goet Regardt genomen en wordt op deser zuyder gewesten, ende soo Ue Maj.t opt spoedichste daer inne voorsiet ende dat in corten tyt, soo alst moegelyck is, tot voordeele van deser zuyder quartieren, welcke syn de Remedien van desen gantsche staet ende van Portugael; dat U Maj.t 't Regardt ende die ogen daerop houdt, want tsyn seer excellente ende Costelycke landen: Tzal Godt believen dat hy daer inne geven ende verleenen zal veel Victorien mit groot aenwassen vande Christenheyt ende van U staet ende tproffyt van U goederen ende die van Uwe ondersaten.

Alle de stant van Indien brengt jaarlics te Rente tot Uwe goederen meer dan een million goudts ende vierhondert duysent Cruysaden, soo het my voor seker verclaert is van veel Officieren van de Rekeninge der behulpmiddelen, conquesten, ende armaden van de deelen int Zuyden. Soo veel aengaet dat de Renten niet meer bedragen danse tegenwoordech inne brengen, waert datter waere een conquesteerder ende een gedurige armada, de renten van de gewesten vant zuyden, souden voortaen wel seer aenwassen. Men soude nu tegenwoordelyck connen neemen wet de renten van desen staet totte voorschreven conquesten, die vier hondert duysent Cruysaden vant selve million goudts, die dese staet heeft boven de voors. vier hondert duysent cruysaden: zyn suffisant genouch voor die armaden van dese noorder quartieren ende die conquesten ende Conservatien van dien. Onsen Heere willet al voorsien gelyck zynen dienst dat vereyscht. Nopende de dingen van den stant in deser Noorder quartieren, soo ick inde brieven van den voorleeden Jaere int breede geschreven hebben, tot de welcke ick my refereren. In desen sal ick alleenlyck vermanen van dit jaer 1600. Onsen Heer heeft ons gedaen groote genaede deur 't omme brengen vande Cunhale, doer den Viseroy. Don Francisco de Cama tralhou [sic!], die gedaen heeft al dat hy doen mochte, ende nae hem Andre Furtado de Mendoza, die vooropperste Capiteyn, die hem oock ten volle heeft gequeten nae zijn plecht, soo oock gedaen hebben alle de Eedeluyden ende soldaten, die in dese victorie eere behaelt hebben, sonder yet anders voor te wenden. Onsen Heere gelieve U Coninclykcke [sic!] Maj.t te bewaren veel ende lange Jaren tot beschermінge van zynder kercken. Wet Goa desen lasten van April 1600. Onder stont geschreven ende geteyckent by een andere hant ende letter, Capellaen van U Maj.t. Ontert. [El Obispo][28] de Malacca; het opschrift luyde aldus: Aen den Coninck onsen Heere. Ende leger stont, Ut Eylandt van Malacca. Z.e via. Overgesett ende getranslateert dese voorschreven ar.len[29] uyten Auctentique Copie geschreven uyten Originalen brieff, by my Jan de Zwart, Openbaar Notaris, by den Hove en Raeden in Hollant geadmitteert, te Amstelredam residerende, de spansche taele sprekende ende verstaende, overgesett ende naer collatie, soo is dit extract mitte voors. copie accorderende. Actum desen 23e Octobre, anno 1604 in Amsterdam.

Ita attestor ego
(was geteekend)
Jo. de Zwarte. Not. Publ.
1604

English Translation[30]

Translation from an authentic despatch written by the Bishop of Melaka [and] addressed to His Majesty, the King of Spain.

[My] Lord!

Throughout the years preceding [1600][31] I have written to Your Majesty and informed You of the things that I have learnt pertaining to the service of God, Your Majesty, and [also] of the general welfare. This I shall now also perform in the following.

During the monsoon season or the {general} winds of April 1600 I returned to Melaka, so that I could write from Melaka to the captain, the city and the house of the *misericórdia* and the *cabildo;* my presence means a lot in Melaka, where I shall take up my residence, as I have extensively written to Your Majesty during the month of December in the preceding year 1599. May it please God that this may be of service to Him and to His church, as well as to Your Majesty and all the people and also the peoples of the southern [regions]. I have written extensively to Your Majesty [in a letter sent with] the ships from the lands of the [East] Indies that departed for the Empire (that is Portugal) in the month of January of the current year, [and] in these told and admonished about the things, that I thought to be necessary for the service of God and [for] You as well as for the general welfare of this state. All of this I also have extensively undertaken in the preceding years and appended to these the rutters of Aceh, Sunda and of other regions [in the East Indies]; to which letters and rutters I refer, [and] which are with the secretaries. For this reason I shall not dwell on these matters at length and shall limit myself to making some observations concerning the aforementioned southern regions and their present state.

From many letters as well as from credible persons who have arrived during the preceding monsoon or steady winds of March 1600 from China, Melaka and the Malukus, as well as from other southern regions of the Indies [and] who endorse the veracity of this information, 12 ships arrived in the southern regions from Holland and Zeeland during the preceding year 1599. Ten ships arrived at Sunda and two at Aceh, which [together] make 12 ships. These set sail from their country in the year 1598 and wintered on the eastern coast of Madagascar. Sixteen merchantmen had departed from their country and were well armed. These promptly lost their admiral, and three ships sailed to the coast of Guinea on account of the [bad] weather. There is no information concerning the course that they took in these regions and I have up until now not heard of any news pertaining to [the fate of] these three ships.

Of the ten ships that arrived at Sunda, four immediately received a cargo of pepper and spices, and these ships departed for their homeland in January 1599, they had not inflicted any evil on the locals, let alone on the Portuguese, nor had they caused problems or difficulties with any other nation. They purchased this pepper at 30 pardaos[32] per bahar,[33] and the mace at between 80 and 90 pardaos. They also purchased nutmeg and cloves together with other goods of these lands. I do not know until now what price they paid. But they bought these at the highest price and they paid very well. They were well respected and desired [clients] among the peoples of these lands, for they made honest purchases, without resorting to evil, disturbances, or force. They also brought many goods, merchandise and wares from their lands and they sold what was useful to the locals. The Dutch also brought there many weapons of all kinds and sold these or bartered them for ryals-of-eight, and in turn sold these ryals to the Sundanese and also to the Fujian traders.[34] They also forged great friendship and an alliance with the king and regents of Sunda, and they roused great hope to continue these dealings and friendship annually. God forbid that this may happen.

Two other ships of the ten sailed along the coast of Java, taking the inside route toward the fortress of Ambon, [and] to the island named Hitu, where they took on a cargo of cloves. They set sail from that [island], but it is not known what course they had set, or which *boquero,* or river estuary, they have sailed out toward.

Two other ships of the aforementioned [fleet of] ten departed from the Sunda [Strait] along the coast of Java [and headed] on the inside route to the Banda islands. There they took on a cargo of mace and nutmeg. These two ships loaded as much as they wanted and returned to Sunda and from there returned to their homeland in the month of August 1599. They claim that in that sea at any time [of the year] the wind blows a comfortable, steady wind.[35] The [Dutch] left behind in Ostaigo on Banda 10 or 12 men as a token of their friendship and [as a sign] of their [intention to] return. They also left behind some men on the islands of Hitu and in the empire of Bali and in Sunda.

The two other ships of the ten that arrived in [the] Sunda [Strait] remained there and waited for [a] new [cargo of] pepper, [and] waited for their departure from there in January 1600. We have not received any confirmed news about them, whether or not they have [already] departed, or what course they have set.

The two remaining ships of the twelve that also spent the winter on the island of Madagascar arrived at Aceh in July 1599. On their arrival they were initially well received and entertained by the King of Aceh, where they were sold some pepper. But there were some Portuguese, who at the time were at Aceh, [and] informed the king that if he continued to permit such peoples (meaning the Hollanders and Zeelanders) to trade in his empire he would not remain a friend of the Portuguese. They then negotiated with the King of Aceh to set fire to the two aforementioned vessels. Whereupon some of the king's officials warned the crews of the two vessels and they fled from Aceh. Some members of the crew of the aforementioned ships remained on land, two of which (who spoke and understood the Spanish language well) the King of Aceh [then] sent to the captain of Melaka. One of them was a pilot, a natural-born Portuguese [subject] of Zuricaia, who [the Dutch] had taken from a ship that was coming from Brazil and whom they had brought along with them by force and against his will. The said captain of Melaka sent these two aforementioned persons to the viceroy so that he may keep a close eye on them for they had been kept as prisoners in that city [Goa].[36] It is said that the two aforementioned ships, that departed from Aceh, returned there; I however claim that they headed for Ceylon where the larger of the two was lost along the coast of Ceylon at Batticaloa. One does not know which course the second ship took, but it is claimed that it was lost [at sea].

As I have said earlier about these southern regions (about which I have extensively written in last year and also in the present year 1600) I have written to, and informed, Your Majesty exhaustively and in depth. I appended thereunto all the rutters of Sunda, Aceh, Patani, Gaidela, Siam and Cambodia [and] also reported by what order one has communicated with persons of great experience and understanding in matters concerning the aforementioned regions. These letters and rutters should be with the secretaries who are employed in the services of God and of Your Majesty.[38] They should review these and consider possible remedies for these southern regions, for the [present] situation and of the entire Estado da Índia. The aforementioned letters and rutters make the necessary recommendations to which I refer. May it please God to grant Your Majesty a long life and health so that you may attend to these matters as soon as possible. Apart from all these difficulties and [the appearance of] new enemies in the aforementioned southern regions, a junk or freight ship sank on the trip from Japan, which was on its way from Japan to Macao, and more than 1.5 million[39] were lost with this ship which is all the funds belonging to the Portuguese residents of Macao, who are now reduced to great poverty and need.

In the empire of Cambodia all the Portuguese together with the clergy have been slain, and there the people have rebelled against us on account of some burden or injury that we have inflicted upon them.

In our empire of Siam all the Portuguese have also been slain and some of them burnt on account of the grievances caused to [the Siamese].

On the islands of Solor the blacks (who had been inclined against us) rebelled, seized our fortress and became masters thereof for about a half a day. This was later taken back from them, and the fort remains in our possession. Our empire of Balambangan — [the population of which] were generally well disposed toward us — had churches and missionaries, for they are pagans. The King of Pasaruan who is a Javanese and a Muslim, also attacked the said kingdom with a large army. He has now become the master and the King of Balambangan and has forced the pagan population to become Muslims. He had all the Christians killed and converted the churches into mosques.

In the empire of Pegu they have massacred all of the Portuguese. In the Malukus, the castle or fortress of Tidor is waging a war against the people of Ternate. In the lands of Ambon war is anticipated. This is happening because these southern regions have been neglected. And so Your Majesty should look into this quickly — in the near future — for the benefit of these southern regions, [because] these are the key to the entire Estado and of Portugal. Your Majesty should appreciate and keep a close eye on these, for they are very excellent and rich lands. May it please God to grant and bestow in this endeavour many victories, considerably enhancing the growth in the number of Christians, of Your Estado and of profits from Your [trading] goods and of those of Your subjects.

The entire Éstado da Índia generates annually more than 1.4 million cruzados in taxes for Your Majesty's benefit. This has been assured to me by many officers responsible for the accounts of supplies, conquests and the armadas in the southern regions. The costs are currently no greater than the revenues, and if there were a *conquistador* (commander) and a permanent armada, the tax revenues levied from these parts of the southern regions would grow considerably thereafter. It would now be possible to earmark for these conquests from the revenues of the Estado 400,000 [from a total of 1.4 million] cruzados.[40] This [sum is] by all means sufficient to equip the armada of the northern regions, fund [additional] conquests and safeguard [these regions]. May Our Lord provide as his service demands. Concerning matters pertaining to the status of the northern regions, I have written about this extensively in [my] letters during the preceding year [1599] and to which I refer. In this [letter] I shall limit myself only to the present year 1600. Our Lord has bestowed great mercy upon us through the execution of Cunhale[41] at the hands of Viceroy Dom Francisco da Gama Teralho,[42] who accomplished all he could, and after him André Furtado de Mendonça, the supreme captain, in fulfillment of his duty which he also fully discharged. Much the same can be said of all of the other noblemen and soldiers, who have gained honour through this victory, without any pretenses for more. May it please Our Lord to preserve Your Royal Majesty for many long years to safeguard His church. From Goa, this last day of April 1600. Below this was written and signed in a different hand and writing, Chaplain of Your Majesty. Signed: Bishop of Melaka. The address reads thus: To the King our Lord. And below: From the isle of Melaka. Transcribed and translated from an authentic copy made from the original letter by me, Jan de Zwarte, public notary, admitted by the Court and Council in Holland, residing in Amsterdam. I speak and understand the Spanish language, prepared the translation and upon comparing the text confirm that this corresponds to the aforementioned copy. This deed is dated 23 October 1604 in Amsterdam.

This I confirm
(signature)
J. de Zwarte, Notary Public
1604

Appendix 7

Letter of gratitude by the *câmara* (city council) of Melaka to Jacob van Heemskerk, dated 9 March 1603.[43]

[The four letter excerpts featured in appendices 5–8 represent fragments of correspondence exchanged between Admiral Jacob van Heemskerk with the Portuguese authorities on shore as well as with the ill-fated captain Sebastião Serrão in the days after the seizure of the *Santa Catarina* in the Singapore Strait on February 25 1603. Grotius added these as appendices to his treatise *Mare Liberum,* Dutch translations of which had been furnished to him by the VOC directors in the *Boek Tracteerende van de Wreede, Verradische ende Hostile procedure der Portugesen In Oost-Indien* (Book Concerning the Cruel, Treacherous and Hostile Proceedings of the Portuguese in the East Indies) sometime around or after October 1604. Almost concurrently, M. Gotthard Arthus published German translations of these letters in the *Achter Theil der Orientalischen Indien* (1606). A close comparison of the two different versions indicates that the German translation was probably not based on the Dutch, but represents a second independent translation from the original Portuguese text. In the absence of the Portuguese originals, the German translations have been added for comparison. Appendices 7–11 transcribe the Dutch translations prepared for and on behalf of the VOC, the printed German translation found in the *Achter Theil der Orientalischen Indien,* together with a translation of the letters into contemporary English. Excluded is a letter fragment that is featured both in the Dutch and in German materials but in terms of content is of almost no relevance to understanding the aftermath of the *Santa Catarina* incident.]

Dutch Translation Prepared on Behalf of the VOC

Het is gebruickelyck onder Coninghen ende potentaten, dat zij verscheijden zijn in haer wille ende meijnighen ende dat haere ondersaten schade lyden in haere persoonen ende ghoederen, sulx dat de fortuin ende den tyt hunnen generael zoo ghoeden voorspoet heeft willen gheven, dat sich dat Chineese Schip heeft opghegheven, maer het zyn saecken, die dor Godts secreete oordeelen veroorsaeckt syn. Wij senden dese ververschinghe aen ul. opdat se eene vereeringhe moghen hebben tot danckbaerheyt van hooghe woort ende waerheyt, die haeren generael ende ul. ghebruijct hebben tegen die portugijsen. Hetwelcke ons in vaster ghedachtenisse sal blyven om in dierghelycken onghelucken ons te bepalen ende daer en valt niet voor Godt almachtich, etc. Inde kamer gheschreven door mij Paulo Mendes de Vascola, schryver in derselver, huijden den 9 dach der maent Marty 1603, onderteeckent Ruijs Lestaomante, André frz. Pero de Carvalhaets, Domingos Domonte, Jhane de Gusgae.

Superscriptum:

Aen de vier hollanders, ghekomen in Comp.e. der portugijsen, dien Godt bewaere, vande Stadt Mallacca.

German Translation

Es ist ein Gewonheit unter den Königen un[d] Majestäten, dass sie uneins seyn in irem Willen und Opinionen, und dass ihre Unterthanen schaden leiden an jhrer Person, Leib und Gütern. Nach dem das Glück und die Zeit jhrem General hat wollen so ein gute Ankunfft verleihen, dass das Schiff von China jn hat loss gegeben, aber es seyn Sachen die durch geheimes un[d] unbekandtes Urtheil Gottes verursacht seyn. Wir uberschicken E.L. hiemet diese Erfrischung zu einer Verehrung und Dancksagung wegen dess Worts der Verheissung und Warheit, so E.L.[44] General, und jhr Leuthe alle auch gehalten, und erwiesen habt an den Portugesen, welches uns denn allezeit in frischer Gedächtnus bleiben soll, uns in dergleichen Zufällen auch zuverhalten. Nichts mehr auff dissmal, Gott der Allmächtig wolle

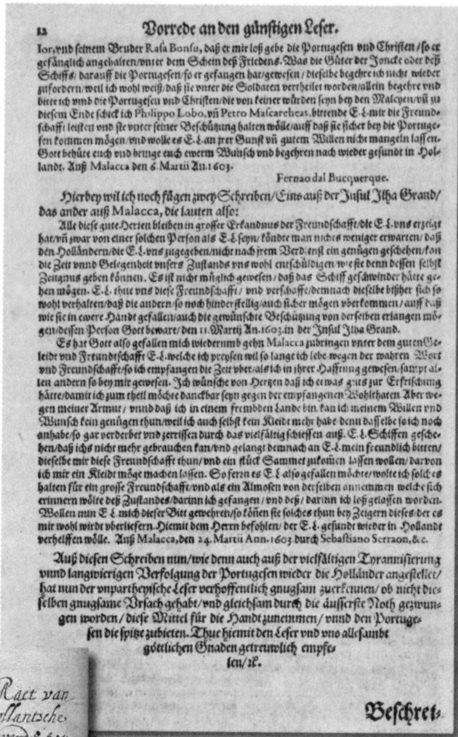

12 **Vorrede an den günstigen Leser.**

lor, vnd seinem Bruder Rasa Bonsu, daß er mir loß gebe die Portugesen vnd Christen/so er gefänglich angehalten/vnter dem Schein deß Friedens. Was die Güter der Joncke oder deß Schiffs/ darauff die Portugesen/so er gefangen hat/gewesen/dieselbe begehre ich nicht wieder zufordern/weil ich wohl weiß/daß sie vnter die Soldaten vertheilet worden/allein begehre vnd bitte ich vmb die Portugesen vnd Christen/die von keiner würden seyn bey den Maleyen/vñ zu diesem Ende schick ich Philippo Lobo, vñ Petro Mascarcheas, bittende E. L. mir die Freundschafft leisten vnd sie vnter seiner Beschützung halten wölle/auff daß sie sicher bey die Portugesen kommen mögen/vnd wolle es E. L. an jrer Gunst vñ gutem Willen nicht mangeln lassen. Gott behüte euch vnd bringe euch ewerm Wunsch vnd begehren nach wieder gesundt in Hollandt. Auß Malacca den 6. Martii An. 1603.

Fernao dal Bucquerque.

Hierbey wil ich noch fügen zwey Schreiben/Eins auß der Insul Ilha Grand/ das ander auß Malacca, die lauten also:

Alle diese gute Herren bleiben in grosser Erkandnus der Freundschafft/die E. L. vns erzeigt hat/vñ zwar von einer solchen Person als E. L. seyn/ köndte man nichts weniger erwarten/ daß den Holländern/die E. L. vns zugegeben/nicht nach jrem Verdienst ein genügen geschehen/kan die Zeit vnnd Gelegenheit vnsers Zustands vns wohl entschüldigen/wie sie denn dessen selbst Zeugnus geben können. Es ist nicht müglich gewesen/daß das Schiff geschwinder hätte gehen mögen. E. L. thue vns diese Freundschafft/ vnd verschaffe/demnach dieselbe bißher sich so wohl verhalten/daß die andern/so noch hinderstellig/auch sicher mögen vberkommen/auff daß wie sie in ewere Händt gefallen/auch die gewünschte Beschützung von derselben erlangen mögen/dessen Person Gott beware/den 11. Martij An. 1603. in der Insul Ilha Grand.

Es hat Gott also gefallen mich wiederumb gehn Malacca zubringen vnter dem guten Geleide vnd Freundtschafft E. L. welche ich preysen wil so lange ich lebe wegen der wahren Wort vnd Freundschafft/so ich empfangen die Zeit vber/als ich in jhrer Hafftung gewesen/sampt allen andern so bey mir gewesen. Ich wünsche von Hertzen daß ich etwas guts zur Erfrischung hätte/damit ich zum theil möchte danckbar seyn gegen der empfangenen Wohlthaten. Aber wegen meiner Armut/ vnnd daß ich in einem frembden Lande bin/kan ich meinem Willen vnd Wunsch kein genügen thun/weil ich auch selbst kein Kleidt mehr habe/denn dasselbe so ich noch anhabe/so gar verderbet vnd zerrissen durch das vielfältig schiessen auß E. L. Schiffen geschehen/daß ichs nicht mehr gebrauchen kan/vnd gelangt demnach an E. L. mein freundlich bitten/ dieselbe mir diese Freundschafft thun/vnd ein stück Sammet zukom̃en lassen wollen/ darvon ich mir ein Kleidt möge machen lassen. So fern es E. L. also gefallen möchte/wolte ich solches halten für ein grosse Freundschafft/vnd als ein Almosen von derselben annemmen/welche sich erinnern wölte deß Zustandes/darinn ich gefangen/vnd deß/ darinn ich loß gelassen worden. Wollen nun E. L. mich dieser Bitt gewehren/so köñen sie solches thun bey Zeigern dieses/der es mir wohl wirdt vberliefern. Hiemit dem Herrn befohlen/ der E. L. gesundt wieder in Hollandt verhelffen wölle. Auß Malacca, den 24. Martii Ann. 1603. durch Sebastiano Serraon, &c.

Auß diesen Schreiben nun/wie denn auch auß der vielfältigen Tyrannisierung vnnd langwierigen Verfolgung der Portugesen wieder die Holländer angestellet/ hat nun der vnpartheyische Leser verhoffentlich gnugsam zuerkennen/ ob nicht dieselben gnugsame Vrsach gehabt/vnd gleichsam durch die äusserste Noth gezwungen worden/ diese Mittel für die Handt zunemmen/ vnnd den Portugesen die spitze zubieten. Thue hiemit den Leser vnd vns allesambt göttlichen Gnaden getreuwlich empfehlen/ꝛc.

Beschret.

Illus. 52 See Illustration 51 on p. 183.

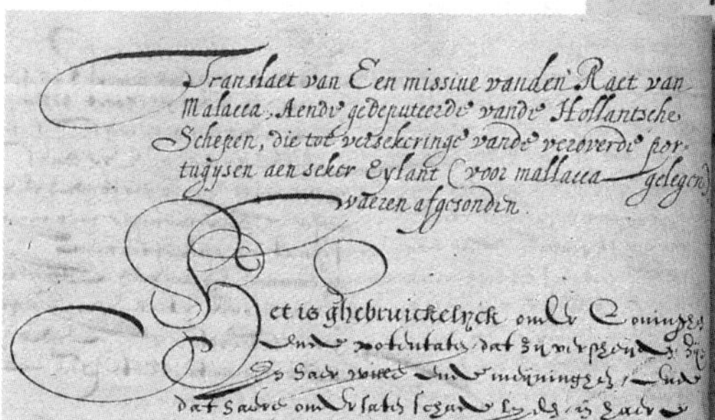

Translaet van Een missive vanden Raet van Malacca, Aendr gedeputeerde vande Hollantsche Schepen, die tot versekeringe vande veroverde portugysen aen seker Eylant (voor mallacca gelegen) waeren afgesonden.

Het is ghebruickelyck ...

Illus. 53 Dutch translation of the letter written by the *câmara* (city council) of Melaka to Jacob van Heemskerk on 9 March 1603. This forms part of a bound volume titled *Boeck Tracterende vande Wreede, Verradische ende Hostile Proceduren der Portugesen in Oost-Indien* (Book Concerning the Cruel, Treacherous and Hostile Proceedings of the Portuguese in the East Indies) (The Hague, Nationaal Archief, Collectie Baron H. van Zuylen van Nyevelt, suppl. 2, no. 13 [2.21.179.01 no. 13]). See also illustration 51, p. 183.

Achter Theil der Orientalischen Indien/
begreiffend erstlich
Ein Historische Beschreibung der
Schiffart/ so der Admiral Jacob von Neck
auß Hollandt in die Orientalische Indien
von Ann.1600. biß An.1603. gethan.
Darnach
Ein Historia/ so von Johan Herman von
Bree, Obersten Handelsmann auff dem Schiff
der Holländische Zaun genannt/ in gleichmessiger
Reyse von An. 1602. biß in An.1604.
auffgezeichnet worden.
Alles auß Niderländischer Verzeichnus in Hoch-
teutscher Sprache beschrieben/ Durch
M. Gotthardt Artus von Dantzig.
Auch mit schönen Kupfferstücken gezieret und
an Tag geben durch Johan Theodor. und Jo-
han Israel de Bry Gebrüder.

Franckfurt am Mayn/ Anno M. DCVI.

Illus. 54 Title page of M. Gotthard Arthus, *Achter Theil der Orientalischen Indien* (The Eighth Voyage [of the Dutch] to the East Indies) (Amsterdam University Library, OTM OF 82–5–7) euch behüten. In der Kammer geschrieben durch mich, Paulo Mendes di Vascolas Kammerschreiber, auff heut dato den 9. tag Martij dess 1603 Jars auss Malacca.

Ruglos Frammanis, Andreas Fernandes,
Domingo de Monte Isaac de Gusgago.

Die Uberschrift dieses Brieffs war: An die vier Holländer, so kommen seyn mit der Gesellschaft der Portugesen, die Gott bewahre, etc.

English Translation[45]

It is common among kings and majesties that they do not concur in their will and opinions, and that [as a result], their subjects suffer damage to their person, body and property. Good fortune and timing willed that Your Admiral be granted a safe arrival and that it delivered the ship from China to You, but these are matters caused by a secret and unknown judgment of God. We herewith send to Your Honour this refreshment as a [gesture of] respect and gratitude for your word of promise and truth that Your Honour, the Admiral, and your crew have kept and shown to the Portuguese. This shall remain for all times fresh in our memories and encourage us in like circumstances. Nothing more for now. May God the Almighty protect you. Written in chambers by me, Paulo Mendes di Vascolas, scribe, on this day the 9th of March in the year 1603 at Melaka. [Signed] Ruglos Frammanis, Andreas Fernandes, Domingo de Monte Isaac de Gusgago.

The address of the letter was: To the four Hollanders, who came in the company of the Portuguese, may God preserve them, etc.

Appendix 8

Letter by Fernão d'Albuquerque, Captain and Governor of Melaka, to Jacob van Heemskerk, dated 9 March 1603.[46]

[This is one of four letters featured as appendices to Grotius' *Mare Liberum.* For a more detailed explanation of the background and significance of this letter in Dutch, German and English translation, see the full entry under appendix 7.]

Dutch Translation Prepared on Behalf of the VOC

Die uytcoomsten der oorloghen sijn divers ende gode alleen staet het toe dezelve oft goede oft quade te gheven, want vanden menschen en is niet met allen.

Ul. heeft het gheluck ghehadt te ontmoeten een seer ryck Schip vol coopluijden, die niet en vechten ende vol vrouwen ende ander onnut volck, die inden weghe syn in tyt van moeyte. U.E. gheniete tselve, nademael hij tselve genomen heeft in rechter oorloghe. Tghene mij moeyt, is, dat gij niet en zyt ontmoetet myne Schip, want dan soudt ghij sien donderscheyt, datter ware tusschen deene ende tusschen dandere. Belangende tghene wedervaren is den hollanderen in China, dat heeft mij seer ghemoeyt om de kleijne oorsaecken, die men hadde tot soo groote straffinghe ende Ick verseckere ul. dat den Auditeur, die tselve ghedaen heeft, ghevanghen sit in de ysers om hem te straffen ende daervorens te sterven. Die hollanders, die hier ghearriveert syn soo van China als van Mallucco, hebbe Ick hen swarigheyt affghenomen, die sy hadden ende ben haer goet vriendt gheweest. Daeromme en ist gheen ghenoechsaeme redene, die ul. /[47] gheeft om oorsaecke te wesen van quaet te doen.

Ick sende daer dit Schip in comp.ie vande Hollanders, die ul. ghesonden heeft tot bewaringe ende gheleijde vant overwonnen volck van dat Schip. Ick sal ul. die handen kussen, soo ul. mij daerinne belieft te senden den pater Broer Anthonio ende den Cappiteyn vant Schip ende alle dandere portugijsen, die daer ghebleven sijn onder ul. bescherminghe. Ende oock mij de vrientschappe te doen, dat Ick mochte weder cryghen het volck vande Junck van China, die de Mallayen ghenomen hebben, ende datse moghen commen inde versekeringhe, dat het niet en ghebeure, dat men hun yets quaets doe, overwege ende daerinne sal u.E. bewijsen, dat zijne wercken overeencomen met de vromicheyt syns persoons.

Onse heere bewaere ul. etc. Vuijt Malacca den 9 marty 1603. Ferna. dalbuquerque.

Dopschrift: aen Jacob Heemskerck, opperCapiteyn [sic!] van de hollantsche vlote vanden Cappiteyn ende Governeur tot Mallacca.

German Translation

Der Aussgang dess Kriegs ist unterschiedlich und zweifelhafftig, und stehet allein Gott zu denselben zugeben gut oder böss, die Menschen aber seynd nichts mehr, als nur ein bloss Instrument. E.L. hat Glück gehabt, dass sie begegnet seyn dem uberauss reichen Schiff voller Kauffleuthe, die nicht streiten können, dessgleichen auch voller Weiber und ander unnütz Gesinde, so in Zeit der Noth mehr ein Verhinderung seyn. E.L. geniessen nun desselben, nach dem sie es in offentlichem Streit uberwunden, billich. Eines aber gereuwet mich, dass E.L. nicht mir un[d] meinem Schiff begegnet seyn, auff dass dieselbe hätte sehen mögen den Unterscheidt in Defension und Beschützung der Schiffe. Was den Holländern in China wiederfahren, betrübet mich nit wenig, und bekummert mich die geringe Ursach so man gehabt, zu einer so schweren Straffe. Es soll aber E.L. gewis dafür halten, dass der Anstiffter desselben schon in Hafftung ligt, unnd solches mit dem Leben büssen unnd bezahlen soll. Die Holländer, so hie ankommen seyn, so wol von China als von Molucco, habe ich jhrer Last entlediget, un[d] bin jhnen ein guter Freund gewesen. Ich ubersende aber E.L. dieses Schiff in Gesellschafft der Holländer, so E.L. gesandt hat, das ubergefuhrte Volck aus dem Portugesischen Schiff zugeleiten, un[d] will es für ein grosse Freundtschafft halten, wenn E.L. mir uberschicket den Pater, Bruder Anthonis, den Capitein des Schiffs un[d] die ubrigen Portugesen, so er noch in seiner Beschützung hat, un[d] mit dem König handelt, dass ich möchte wiederbekom[m]en das Volck so die Malayen auss einer Chinesischen Iunco genommen haben, und dass sie versichert würden, dass jhnen auff dem Wege nichts böses wiederfahren soll. Hierin wirdt E.L. beweisen, dass die That mit der Warheit der Wort uberein kommet, unser Herr Gott behüte E.L. In Malacca den 9 Martii An. 1603. Durch

Fernao dal Buquerque

Die Uberschrifft war: An Iacob Hemskirchen, obersten Capitein der Holländischen Armada, von dem Capitein und Gubernator zu Malacca.

English Translation[48]

The outcome of the battle is uneven and uncertain, and God alone has the power to effect good or evil. Man, however, is nothing more than [His] instrument. Your Honour was fortunate to have encountered this exceptionally rich carrack full of merchants, who could not fight [back. The ship] was full of women[49] and other useless hands, that, in an hour of need prove to be an impediment. Your Honour should now enjoy this carrack after it was taken in a public battle. One regret I have is that Your Honour did not encounter my [war] ship by which he could have seen for himself the difference in defence and protection of the [merchant] ships. What happened to the Hollanders in China aggrieves me greatly,[50] and I am concerned by the trifling grounds on which such a heavy punishment was meted out. Your Honour should know that the culprit has already been arrested and shall repent and pay for his misdeed with his life. I have dropped the charges against the Hollanders who came here both from China as well as from the Malukus and have demonstrated friendship toward them. {For this reason there is insufficient grounds upon which Your Honour may inflict harm [on the Portuguese]}.[51]

I place this ship in trust in the company of the Hollanders whom Your Honour has sent here to accompany the crew and passengers from the Portuguese carrack, and would take it as a great gesture of friendship, if Your Honour would also return the priest, Brother Anthony, [and] the captain of the [seized] carrack as well as the remaining Portuguese who remain under Your Honour's protection. [I also ask to] negotiate with the King [of Johor], so that he may return the crew and passengers that the Malays had taken from a Chinese junk and to ensure that nothing evil befall them on their way [to Melaka]. In fulfilling this, Your Honour will [also] prove that You act on Your word. May our Lord God protect Your Honour. In Melaka, 9 March, in the year 1603, by

Fernao dal Buquerque

The address was: To Jacob Heemskerk, supreme Captain of the Dutch armada, from the Captain and Governor of Melaka.

Appendix 9

Letter by Sebastião Serrão, Captain of the Captured Carrack *Santa Catarina* taken in the Singapore Strait, to Jacob van Heemskerk, dated 24 March 1603.[52]

[This is one of four letters featured as an appendix to Grotius' *Mare Liberum.* For an explanation of the background and significance of this letter in Dutch, German and English translation, see the entry under appendix 7.]

Dutch Translation Prepared on Behalf of the VOC

Het heeft Godt belieft mij hier tot Mallacca behouden laeten overkommen onder de goede bewaernisse ende faveur van uwer E., dewelcke ik roemen sal alle myn leefdaghe als mede tpunct van u woordt ende waerheyt ende de vrientschappen, die ick ontfanghen hebbe, als Ick syn ghevanghen was alsmede alle dander, die met my waren. Ick hebbe verlanckt om een cleyn goet beetken ververschinghe te hebben omme in eenighen deele dancbaer te syn aen u.E. over de ontfangene weldaden. Maer alsoo de armoede my is nu verselschappende in een vreemt landt, en hebbe ick mynen wille niet connen ten effecte brengen, want ick oock niet een cleedt hebbe om my mede te cleeden, wandt tgene ick aen hadde, vont ick soo doorhackelt door de vreeselycke scheuten van u.E., dat het niet en is om mij mede te cleeden. Derhalven bidde u.E. mij de vrientschap te willen doen ende te vereeren met een stuck flueel om my een cleed te doen maecken, want ick sal het alles houden voor groote weldaet ende als een almoesse van uwe E., sich ersinnende des staets, in welcken hy my /[53] nam ende my liete ende daer ick in syn mach ende Uwe E. mach brenger deses wel metgeven, tgene hem believen sal mij te gheven, hij sal het mij wel Brengen. Ende Ick sal het erkennen, alsoo uwer E. dinghen weerdich syn, Die onsen Heere bewaere ende behouden in Hollandt brenghe. Wt Mallacca den 24 marty 1603 ende was onderteeckent Sebastiaen Serram.

German Translation

Es hat Gott also gefallen mich wiederumb gehn Malacca zubringen unter dem guten Geleidt und Freundtschafft E.L. welche ich preysen wil so lange ich lebe wegen der wahren Wort und Freundschafft, so ich empfangen die Zeit uber, als ich in jhrer Hafftung gewesen, sampt allen andern so bey mir gewesen. Ich wünsche von Hertzen dass ich etwas guts zur Erfrischung hätte, damit ich zum theil möchte danckbar seyn gegen der empfangenen Wohlthaten. Aber wegen meiner Armut, unnd dass ich in einem frembden Lande bin, kan ich meinem Willen und Wunsch kein genügen thun, weil ich auch selbst kein Kleidt mehr habe, denn dasselbe so ich noch anhabe, so gar verderbet und zerissen durch das vielfältig schiessen auss E.L. Schiffen geschehen, dass ichs nicht mehr gebrauchen kan, und gelangt demnach an E.L. mein freundlich bitten, dieselbe mir diese Freundschafft thun, und ein stück Sammet zukommen lassen wollen, darvon ich mir ein Kleidt möge machen lassen. So fern es E.L. also gefallen möchte, wolte ich solches halten für eine grosse Freundschafft, und als ein Almosen von derselben annemmen, welche sich erinnern wölte dess Zustandes, darinne ich gefangen, und dess, darinn ich loss gelassen worden. Wollen nun E.L. mich dieser Bitt gewehren, so können sie solches thun bey Zeigern dieses, der es mir wol wirdt uberliefern. Hiemit dem Herrn befohlen der E.L. gesundt wieder in Hollandt verhelffen wölle. Auss Malacca den 24 Martii anno 1603 durch Sebastiano Serraon, etc.

English Translation[54]

It has pleased God to let me proceed to Melaka under the safe conduct and in the friendship of Your Honour which I will praise for as long as I live because You kept Your word, and on account of the friendship that I and all those who were with me, experienced during the time we were held as Your prisoners. I wish with all my heart that I had some refreshment that I could share as thanks for the good deeds received. But since I am now impoverished and also find myself in a foreign country, I cannot satisfy my will and my wish. I no longer have any clothes, except for those I am wearing, and these are so soiled and torn from all the gun fire from Your Honour's ships that I no longer can use them. I therefore humbly beseech that You send to me, as a gesture of friendship, a piece of velvet from which I can have new clothes sewn. If this pleases Your Honour I shall accept this as a great gesture of friendship and as an alms of Your Honour that may remind you of the condition in which I had been taken prisoner and later also set free. Should it please Your Honour to grant me this request, You can do so by indicating this to [the person] who will deliver [the piece of cloth] to me. May the Lord bring Your Honour safely back to Holland. From Melaka, the 24th of March, in the year 1603.

Appendix 10

Second letter by Fernão d'Albuquerque, Captain and Governor of Melaka, to Jacob van Heemskerk, dated 26 March 1603.[55]

[This is one of four letters featured as appendices to Grotius' *Mare Liberum*. For an explanation of the background and significance of this letter in Dutch, German and English translation, see the entry under appendix 7.]

Dutch Translation Prepared on Behalf of the VOC

Uwer E. brieff hebbe met grooter vreuchde ontfanghen, omdat ick daer inne ghesien hebbe tgenoegen, dat u.E. hadde te vernemen, dat behouden overghekomen waren al het volck vant overwonnen schip, want sulx verwacht men van oppercappiteyns als u.E. ende /[56] gelycke Corospondentie sal ick houden, bijaldien teenigen tijde in deze forteresse quaeme eenich hollants volck. Ende belanghende tvolck, welck u.E. segt te wesen in Indien ende in Japan, de heere Viceroey is ghewoone alle goet tractement te doen ende heeft seer verfoeyt die ordere vanden Auditor van China ende heeft hem ghedaen vanghen om met al rigueur hem te straffen. Derhalven en behoort sich u.E. niet te argeren int generael aen alle de portugijsen, want allen dunckt, hetghene in China gebeurt is, quaet te syne.

Ende overmidts den yver die u.E. heeft in sorghe te draghen voor alle ghevanghenen ende bedructe Christenen, soo hebbe ick op t'vertrouwen van dien u.E. willen bidden mij die faveur te doen ende handelen metten Coninck van Jor ende met synen broeder.

Dat hy mij loslate die Portugysen ende Christenen, die hij ghevanghen hout ende dat onder ende met bedroch van vrede ende belangende die goederen vande Juncke, daer handele ick niet van, noch eijsche die niet, want die sal al gherepartisseert syn ende verdeelt onder de soldaten van syne armade, alleenelyck versoeck ick de portugijsen ende Christenen, die van cleijnder importantien syn voor de Malayen ende tot dien effecte sende ick Philippe Lobo ende Pero Mascarenhas, welcke ul. sal believen onder zyne bescherminge aen te nemen, omdat sy versekert /[57] met de portugysen moghen comen ende dat henluyden niet en moge failleren u.E. faveur ende hulpe. Onse Heere Godt bewaere u.E. ende brenge deselve in hollant naer syn wensche. Vuijt Mallacca den 26 Martij ao. XVIdry ende was onderteykent Fernao Dalbuquerque.

German Translation

E.L. Schreiben hab ich mit grossen Frewden empfangen, weil ich darinnen spüre die gute Zuneigung, so dieselbe zu dem Volck des uberwundenen Schiffs getragen. Denn man ein solches von einem Capitein und General billich erwartet, und will auch ich ein solche Correspondentz halten, da es sich begeben möchte, dass jemandt von Holländern in diese Festung gebracht würde, was aber belanget das Volck E.L. so sie melden in India zu Iapon zuseyn, der Herr Vicere is gewohnet demselben alles guts zuthun,

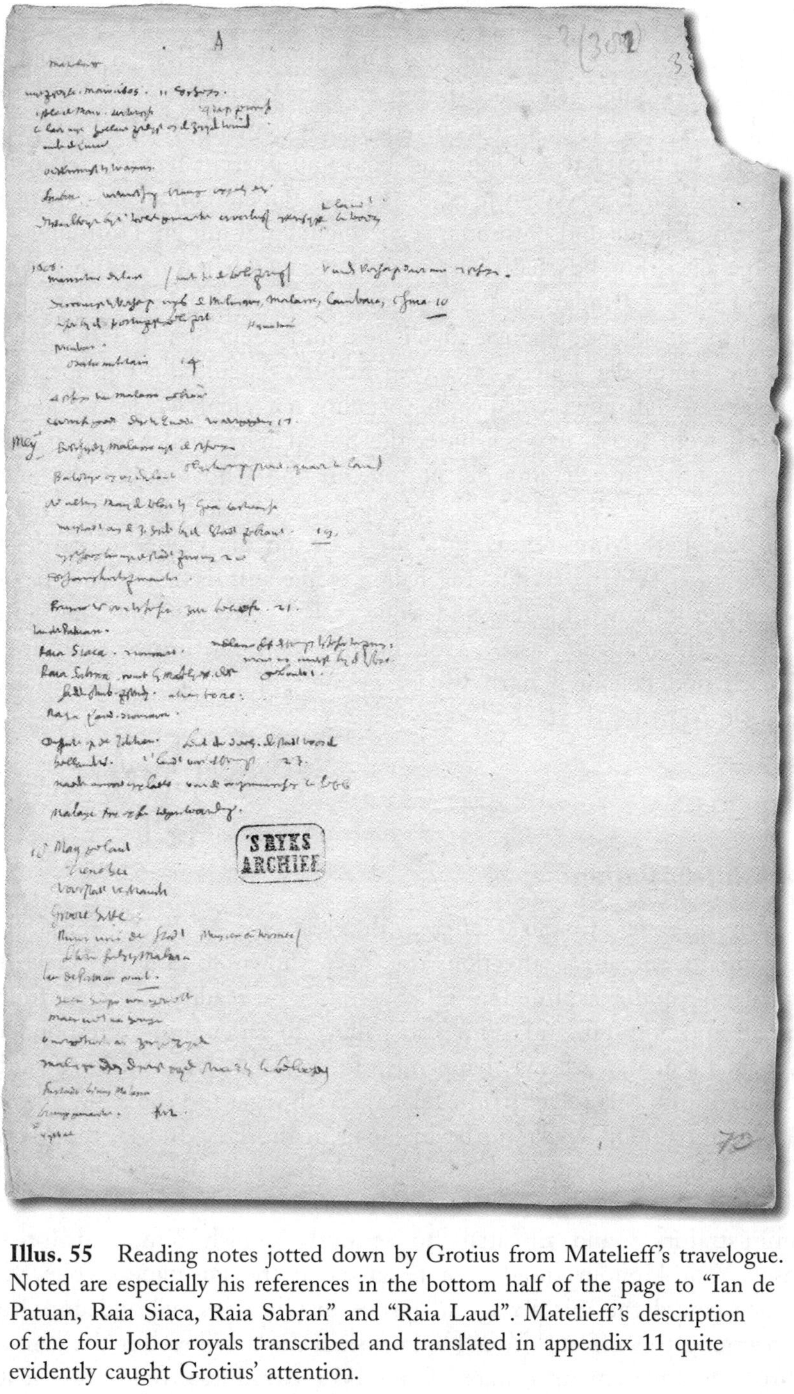

Illus. 55 Reading notes jotted down by Grotius from Matelieff's travelogue. Noted are especially his references in the bottom half of the page to "Ian de Patuan, Raia Siaca, Raia Sabran" and "Raia Laud". Matelieff's description of the four Johor royals transcribed and translated in appendix 11 quite evidently caught Grotius' attention.

und ist gar ubel zufrieden mit der Ordnung der Verhör in China, hat auch den Verwalter gefänglich lassen einziehen, jhn mit ernst zustraffen, derhalben werden E.L. sich nicht ärgern ins gemein an den Portugesen, denn sie alle die That zu China für böss und unrecht halten. Belangendt den Eyffer[58] so E.L. haben jr bestes zuthun für die gefangenen Christen, und die im Elende und Betrübnus seyn, solches gibt mir ein Hoffnung, dass E.L. mir diese Freundschafft leisten werden zuhandeln mit dem König von Ior und seinem Bruder Rasa Bonsu, dass er mir loss gebe die Portugesen und Christen, so er gefänglich angehalten, unter dem Schein dess Friedens. Was die Güter der Ioncke oder dess Schiffs, darauff die Portugesen, so er gefangen hat, gewesen, dieselbe begehre ich nicht wieder zu fordern, weil ich wohl weiss, dass sie unter die Soldaten vertheilet worden, allein begehre und bitte ich umb die Portugesen und Christen, die von keiner würden seyn bey den Maleyen, und zu diesem Ende schick ich Philippo Lobo und Pero Mascareheas, bittende E.L. mir die Freundschafft leisten und sie unter seiner Beschützung halten wölle, auff dass sie sicher bey die Portugesen kommen mögen, und wolle es E.L. an jrer Gunst und gutem Willen nicht mangeln lassen. Gott behüte euch und bringe euch ewerm Wunsch und begehren nach wieder gesundt in Holland. Auss Malacca den [2]6 Martii An. 1603.

Fernao dal Bucquerque

English Translation[59]

I received Your Honour's letter with great joy, as I can sense from its contents the great affection You have shown toward the crew and passengers of the captured vessel. Such can be readily expected from a captain and admiral, and I am also willing to enter into correspondence with such a man, for it may happen [in future], that one of the Hollanders is brought into this fortress [of Melaka]. With regard to the crew, however, that Your Honour reports to be in Japan in the East Indies, the Viceroy is accustomed to treating them well and is not at all satisfied with the course of the hearings in China. He has also imprisoned one of the administrators,[60] and threatens to seriously punish him, and for this reason Your Honour should not be angry at the Portuguese collectively, as they regard the miscarriage of justice in China as evil and unrightful. Concerning this effort,[61] Your Honour shall do Your best for the captured Christians who are in a state of misery and sadness, [and] this instills me with hope, that Your Honour will render this favour of friendship and negotiate with the King of Johor and his brother, Raja Bongsu for the release of the Portuguese and the Christians who he is holding captive on the pretext of peace. What concerns the goods from the junk or the ship, on which he had taken the [said] Portuguese captives, I do not demand to have these returned, because I know well that they have been distributed among the [said king's] warriors. I only desire and request that they release the Portuguese and the Christians who enjoy no dignity among the Malays. For this purpose I despatch Philip Lobo and Peter Mascarenhas and ask Your Honour to render this act of friendship and take them under Your protection, so that they may arrive safely with the Portuguese [hostages] and hope this meets Your Honour's approval and good will. May God protect You and may He fulfill your wish and desire to bring you back to Holland in good health. From Melaka, 26 March, in the year 1603.[62]

Fernao dal Buquerque

Appendix 11

Description of Batu Sawar, Kota Seberang and the surrounding region, by Cornelis Matelieff de Jonge, 24 August 1606.[63]

[Admiral Cornelis Matelieff de Jonge set sail with his fleet from the Netherlands in 1605 and arrived in the waters of the Melaka Strait the following year. He signed a treaty with the Johor monarchs in May 1606 and unsuccessfully attacked the Portuguese-held fort and city and engaged the Portuguese armada off Cape Rachado in the course of May through August 1606. Matelieff proceeded to the Johorese capital Batu Sawar to discuss a range of security and co-operation matters with 'Ala'uddin Ri'ayat Shah III and his sibling Raja Bongsu. This is a rare period eyewitness description of the capital and royal residence Batu Sawar. Its smaller sister settlement, Kota Seberang, was situated on the opposite bank of the river. This testimony is important for understanding how the VOC officers on the ground, such as notably Admiral Matelieff, assessed the security situation of the Johorese capital. This was subject to periodic attacks by the Portuguese during the first decade of the 17th century and after 1613 also by the Acehnese.]

Original Dutch Text

De Stadt Batusauwer leydt op de Revier van Iohor, ontrent vijf oft ses mijlen van der Zee. De Revier is seer schoon, breet ende diep, vloeyende tot voor de Stad toe op ende neder, doch voor de Stadt is sy versch. Het isser meest al laech lant. Het volck woont meest langs de Revier. De huysen staender op staken. Dat men de Fortresse heet, is tweederley, het een Batusauwer, het ander, leggende op d'ander zijd' van de Revier, heet Cotta Zabrang. Batusauwer is ontrent 1300. treden in't ront, een vierkante plaetse, met hooge Palissaden van 40. voet langh dicht by den anderen gevoecht, hebbende eenige flanckeringen, doch niet wel gemaeckt. Leyt op een effen velt, dicht by de Revier. De naeste bergen leggender een quartier mijls van daen. Men konde de Revier daer lichtelijck rondom brengen. Binnen is sy heel dicht bewoont met stroo huysen, behalven dat van den Coningh ende die van eenige Edelluyden, welcke van hout zijn. Daer zijn by gissinge soo in Batusauwer als Cotta Zabrang wel tusschen de drie ende vier duysend weerbare mannen, doch buyten de sterckte woont het meeste volck, dewelcke, alsser noot is, hare huysen altemael afbranden, ende loopen na de sterckte, want connen haest weder een huys maken elk met sijn Slaven. Het lant hoort alle den Coningh toe, ende is weynich of niet geacht, so dat wie 't maer van hem eyscht, Landts genoech kan krijgen. Nochtans schijnt het heel vruchtbaer te wesen, want staet vol gheboomte ende men gaeter tot den buyck toe in 't gras, doch wort niet bearbeyt, want indiense haer tot landtbouwinge begaven, souden van alles overvloedich hebben, daer sy nu veler dingen gebreck lijden.... Cotta Zabrang mach ontrent vier of vijf honderdt treden in't rondt hebben, ende is mede vierkant. Daer en woont niet veel volcxs in, ende aen de zijde van de Revier daer sy woonen, ist oock met Palissaden beset. Het lant is laech, ende loopt met alle springh-vloeden onder, soo dat men der geen geschut voor kan brengen. Den Admirael ordineerde haer in 't eerste drie bolwercken, om also langs de mueren te flancqueren, het welck haer wel behaeghde, maer ontsaghen den arbeydt.

English Translation[64]

The town of Batu Sawar is situated up the Johor River, approximately five or six [Dutch nautical] miles [that is about 30–35 kilometres] from the sea.[65] The river [there] is very beautiful, wide and deep,[66] [and depending on the tide] flows either up or down along the banks before the city,[67] but here the water is fresh. The land is mostly flat. The population generally lives along the river. The houses stand on stilts. What is meant by the term "fortress" consists of two things: one is Batu Sawar and the other situated on the opposite bank of the river is called Kota Seberang. Batu Sawar measures about 1,300 paces in circumference, is square in its layout and features high palisades that are closely lined up against one another and are 40 feet high [that is about 11 to 12 metres]. There are some fortifications which cover the flank,[68] but these are not well constructed. It is situated on a level plain close by the river. The closest hills are situated about a quarter of a [Dutch sea] mile [or about 1–1.5 kilometres] from there. It is easily possible to divert the river around the city. Inside, the city is densely populated featuring *atap* (thatched) houses, except for the residence of the king and of some other noblemen, which are constructed of wood. There are an estimated three to four thousand fighting men in Batu Sawar and Kota Seberang together, but most of the population lives outside the walled city. In times of danger, these people completely burn down their houses and head into the walled city, because they are able to quickly rebuild a house, each man with his slaves. All the land belongs to the king,[69] and is held in little or no esteem [at all]. So anyone who wants to have some from him can obtain enough land. It still appears to be very fertile, for it is full of trees and the grass reaches up to the waistline. But this land is not worked, for if the residents would engage in farming, they would have an abundance of all those many things that they now lack.... Kota Seberang may measure about four or five hundred paces in circumference and is also square in its layout. Not many people live here and where they live there are also palisades along the river bank. The land is flat and is submerged during all spring tides, so that it is not possible to station any artillery in front. Initially, Admiral [Matelieff de Jonge] ordered the residents to construct three bulwarks that would also run parallel to the walls. The residents liked the idea, but refused to work.

Appendix 12

Letter by Raja Bongsu, alias Raja Seberang to Admiral Cornelis Matelieff de Jonge, received 14 May 1606.[70]

[On his arrival in the waters of the Melaka Strait in May 1606, Admiral Matelieff de Jonge returned with the surviving members of the Johorese diplomatic mission to the Dutch Republic.[71] He sent members of his crew to the capital Batu Sawar to inform the Johor rulers, King 'Ala'uddin and Raja Bongsu, that the Dutch had arrived and were ready for a joint attack on Portuguese Melaka, as had been proposed earlier and evidently also discussed at length with the Johorese envoys. This is a Dutch text version with an English translation of the reply Matelieff received from Raja Bongsu of Johor.]

Original Dutch Text

De Coning van Iohor ghenaemt Radja Sabrang, (dat is Coning van de Over-syde) wenscht den Admirael geluc ende voorspoet in 't gene hy voorgenomen heeft. Ghy te weten de heer Admirael, die hier van den Coning van Hollant gesonden zijt, om onse ende uwer E. aller vyanden te bestryden, onghetwijffelt u.E. naem ende faem sal meriteren over de gantsche werelt verbreyt te worden, om reden dat U. E. hem niet en ontsiet hier te lande, als mede in U.E. landt, hem te stellen teghen de Tyranie van de Portugesen. Ick achte my geluckich gesien te hebben den genen die U.E. ghesonden heeft, naemelijck Lodewijck Isacksen, ende Hans van Hagen, die my van U.E. komste voor Malacca, veradverteert hebben, ja die ghekomen zijn om ons arme volck uyt de slavernye der Portugesen te redimeren. Den dienst die uwen Coning my onweerdich gedaen heeft sal dese bode recompenseren, naer myn kleyn vermoghen, aen den ghenen die uwe Coningh hier gesonden heeft. Geen Coningh op der aerden soude my sodanigen dienst connen doen, als ghereede uwen Coning al ghedaen heeft. Ick sende u.E. Yntse Amar met Yntse Camar, om u.E. mijn komste te adviseren, soo't God belieft. Ick verwachte myne roeyers, soo wanneer die sullen gekomen wesen, sal niet tarderen te komen, ja indien ick 2. Galeyen ghereet hadde, soude terstont selfs komen. Ick verwachte noch vele Bantins, sal deselve met den aldereersten senden. U.E. Amassadeurs Lodewijck Isacksen, ende Hans van Hagen, houde ick by my, sullen met my in myne Galeye treden, ende so gelijckelijck komen, om de intreprinse so te helpen effectueren. Syne Exelentie heeft my soo veel eere bewesen, dat ick de selve niet can recompenseren. Voorts so ben ick aen U.E. en aen alle die gesonden sijn om ons te verlossen so verobligeert, dat ick het tot geenen tyde kan verschuldigen, aengesien wy een arm volck zijn.

English Translation[72]

The King of Johor, named Raja Seberang (that is to say the King of the Other Side [of the River]) wishes the Admiral luck and success in his endeavors. You, to wit, Lord Admiral, have been sent by the King of Holland to fight against all our and Your enemies. Without doubt, Your Honour's name and fame are worthy to be spread over the whole world, because Your Honour is not afraid to stand up against the tyranny of the Portuguese irrespective of whether here or in Your country.[73] I am pleased to have seen the men that Your Honour has sent hither, namely Lodewijk Isacksen and Hans van Hagen, who notified me of Your Honour's arrival at Melaka; yes, who verily came to redeem our poor people from the slavery of the Portuguese. The service Your King has rendered unto my unworthy self this messenger shall recompense, according to my humble means, for the benefit of the people whom Your King has sent here. No King in this world could render unto me such a service as Your King has. I despatch to Your Honour Inceh Amar and Inceh Kamar to inform Your Honour of my arrival, as God wills. I am [still] expecting my rowers, and when they shall have arrived I shall not delay my arrival, nay, as soon as I have prepared two galleys, I shall immediately arrive myself.[74] I am still expecting many bantins and will despatch these to You at the first possible occasion. Your Honour's ambassadors, Lodewijk Isacksen and Hans van Hagen I retain in my company, and they shall step with me into my galley and shall come as soon as possible in order to help undertake the enterprise [of attacking Melaka]. Your Honour has rendered many honours to me that I cannot possibly think of repaying. Further, I am so much obliged to Your Honour and all those who have been sent here to redeem us that I cannot ever repay this debt, because we are a poor people.

Appendix 13

Description by Admiral Cornelis Matelieff de Jonge of the four Johor Rulers: 'Ala'uddin Ri'ayat Shah III, Raja Bongsu, Raja Siak and Raja Laut, 1606.[75]

[During his visit to the Batu Sawar court in August 1606, VOC Admiral Cornelis Matelieff de Jonge met many of the nobles, and especially the four sons of the late Johor ruler, Raja Ali Jalla Abdul Jalil.[76] The following excerpt taken from his travelogue, provides a frank and candid assessment of the late Ali Jalla's four surviving sons. This document evidences that the Admiral, like many other senior VOC officers who visited the court of

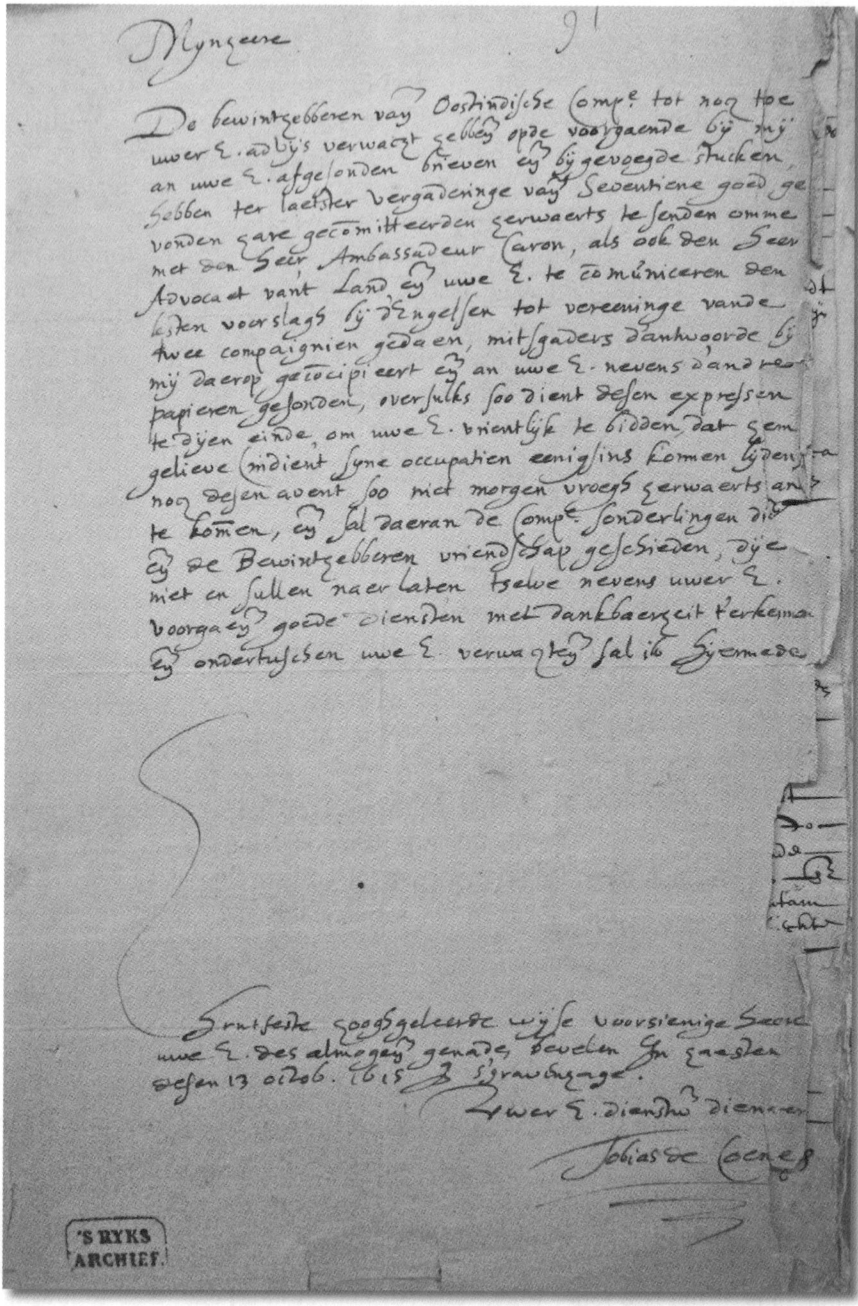

Myngeere

De bewinthebberen van Oostindische Comp.e tot noch toe uwer E. adbijs verwacht hebben opde voorgaende bij mij an uwe E. afgesonden brieven en bijgevoegde stucken, hebben ter laetster vergaderinge van Seventiene goed gevonden hare gecommitteerden herwaerts te senden omme met den Heer Ambassadeur Caron, als ook den Heer Advocaet vant Land en uwe E. te communiceren den lesten voorslags bij d'Engelsen tot vereeninge vande twee compaignien gedaen, mitsgaders d'antwoorde bij mij daerop geconcipieert en an uwe E. nevens d'andere papieren gesonden, oversulks soo dient desen expressen te dyen einde, om uwe E. vrientlijk te bidden, dat hem gelieve (indient syne occupatien eenigsins komen lyden) noch desen avent soo niet morgen vroegh herwaerts an te komen, en sal daeran de Comp.e sonderlingen dienst en de Bewinthebberen vrienschap geschieden, dye niet en sullen naerlaten tselve nevens uwer E. voorgaende goede diensten met dankbaerheit t'erkennen en ondertusschen uwe E. verwachten sal ik hiermede

Erntfeste hooghgeleerde wijse voorsienige Heere uwe E. des almogen genade bevelen. In haesten desen 13 octob. 1615 in s'Gravenhage.

Uwer E. dienstw. dienaer

Tobias de Coene

'S RYKS ARCHIEF

Illus. 56 Letter of Tobias de Coene to Grotius, dated 13 October 1615. The letter addresses among other issues the possible union of the English and Dutch East India Companies. (The Hague, Nationaal Archief, *Collectie Hugo de Groot, Supplement I* [1.10.35.02.40, fol. 91 recto])

Batu Sawar during the first decade of the 17th century, greatly respected Raja Bongsu, who was also known as Raja Seberang or Raja di Ilir.]

Original Dutch Text

Den 17. May kreeg den Admirael tijdinge, dat de Coning van Iohor alreede by de Schepen was met sijn Galeyen ende Fusten, waer op hy in alles mocht hebben ontrent 300. man, meest slaven. Het was Raya Bonsu, oft Raya Zabran, de selfde die de Gesanten in Hollandt gheschickt hadde met het present aen sijn Ex.tie.om wiens gelegentheyt te beter te verstaen, men weten moet, dat den ouden Coningh van Iohor, die een goet krijghsman was, ende oock dickwils tegen de Portugesen gheoorlocht heeft, 4. soonen heeft nagelaten, waer van den outsten nu tegenwoordich regerende van de Malayen ghenoemt wort Ian de Patuan, het welck nochtans niet sijn naem maer sijn tijtel schijnt te wesen. Van een ander vrouwe heeft hy gehadt Raia Siacai t' welc te seggen is Coning van Siaca, dat een leen is van de Croon van Iohor. Dese heeft getrout de dochter van Patane, zijnde een man van kleynen bedrijve, ende niet met eenige Coninglicke deugden verciert, maer een slecht bloet, die hem altijt hout binnen Siaca, en weynich komt tot Iohor. De Coning Ian de Patuan is oock een persoon van weynich bedrijfs, gewoon tot by den middag te slapen, dan te eten en te wasschen, ende voorts droncken te drincken, so dat na den middagh met hem niet en is te handelen, want men moet al mede met hem drincken, en droncke-mans dingen doen. Hy bemoeyt hem geen dingen, maer laet het al op de Edelen ende Raya Zabrang staen, mach van geen swaricheyt hooren, ende als men hem aenspreeckt van yet te doen, als volc op te brengen oft diergelijcke, so swijght hy al, en al vraegtmen hem 2. oft 3. mael, het is al 't selfde. In somma is nergens min bequaem toe, als tot Coning te wesen, denckt noch op Rijck noch op onderdanen, als hy slechts wijn heeft en vrouwen. Noch heeft de Coningh van Iohor by sijn tweede vrouwe gehadt Raya Bonsu, die nu wert ghenoemt Raya Zabrang, dat is Coning van d'ander zijde, door dien dat hy over d'ander zijde van de Rivier woont tegen over de Stadt Battusabar, daer hy oock een sterckte heeft ende een deel Ondersaten, doch is leen-man van Ian de Patuan, een man van ontrent 35. jaer, by nae wit, de grootste niet, maer discreet, langhmoedich, niet colerijck, ende verre siende, een vyandt van de Portugesen, neerstich in sijn saken, die hy ooc wel hart drijven soude, indien hy macht hadde, in somma weerdich Coning van Iohor en Malacca te wesen, by wien oock de hulpe die men aen hem besteden soude, wel erkent soude worden, ende die soo veel men aen hem vermercken konde den onsen heel was toe gedaen: sijnen broeder Ian de Patuan altijt respecterende, die ooc veel van desen hout, doch heymelijck en laetter niet al wat jalousie by Ian de Patuan te wesen. Bij sijn derde vrouwe heeft den ouden Coning van Iohor een sone genaemt Raya Laud, dat is Coning van der zee, een man nergens bequaem toe, als om Tabac en Arack te drincken, en Betele daer op te eten, ja waerdig handen en voeten gebonden in in Zee gesoncken te worden, een grooten dronckaert, dootslager, en hoereerder, die alles wat an die 3 puncten dependeert van buyten geleert heeft. Alle de broeders drincken wijn, uytgenomen Raya Zabrang, die noyt wijn noch stercken dranc geproeft heeft, en gelijck de Heer is, so sijn oock de Edel-luyden van alle dese Coningen.

English Translation[77]

On 17 May the Admiral received news that the King of Johor had already arrived at the ships with his galleys and foists, on which he might have about 300 men, mostly slaves. It was Raja Bongsu, also known as Raja Seberang, the same one who had dispatched the envoys to Holland with a present for His Excellency.[78] In order to better understand the situation of Raja Bongsu, one should note that the old King of Johor, who was a great warrior and also often went into battle against the Portuguese, left behind four sons, of which the oldest is currently ruling over the Malays and is called Yang di Pertuan. This does not appear to be his name, but his title. From another wife he had the Raja Siak, that is to say the "King of Siak", which is a fief belonging to the crown of Johor. This raja is married to a daughter of [the queen of] Patani. He is a man of little ambition and is not endowed with any royal virtues, but is an evil person. [The Yang di Pertuan] holds him back in Siak and he rarely comes to Johor. The King or Yang di Pertuan of Johor is also a person of little ambition, who is accustomed to sleeping until midday, then eats and washes himself and proceeds to drink himself drunk. As a result, after noon it is not possible to negotiate with him [anymore], for one has to drink along with him and do the things drunken men do. He does not care about anything, but places responsibility entirely on the nobles and on Raja Seberang. He does not like to hear of any difficulties, and when you approach him to do something, such as to muster people, he just remains silent. And even if you ask him two or three times, it is all the same. In sum, there is nothing less he is qualified to be than king, [for] he thinks neither about his empire nor about his subjects, as he only wants wine and women. Furthermore, the [old] King of Johor had from his second wife, Raja Bongsu, who is now called Raja Seberang, that is King of "the other side", because he lives on the other side of the [Johor] river across from the city of Batu Sawar.[79] He also has a fortress and group of subjects there.[80] Still, [Raja Seberang] is a vassal of the Yang di Pertuan and is about 35 years old, almost white,[81] not the tallest, but wise,[82] forgiving, not choleric, far-sighted, an enemy of the Portuguese, [and] assiduous in his affairs, which he would vigorously pursue, if he held [supremel] authority. In sum, he is worthy to be King of Johor and Melaka.[83] He will also recognise the help offered to him, and — as far as can be ascertained — is well disposed toward us. He always respects his brother, the Yang di Pertuan, who also thinks highly of him, but he secretly arouses a certain degree of jealousy with the Yang di Pertuan.[84] From his third wife the old King of Johor had another son named Raja Laut, that is "King of the Sea", a man qualified for nothing[85] but to consume tobacco, to drink *arak* [alcoholic beverage] and down betel over that; verily, he is only worthy to be thrust with bound hands and feet into the sea; a great drunkard, manslayer and womaniser who knows all that there is to know about these three things. All the brothers drink wine, except for Raja Seberang, who never consumes wine or strong drinks; and like the Lord, so are his nobles.

Appendix 14

Two Treaties signed between Admiral Cornelis Matelieff de Jonge and 'Ala'uddin Ri'ayat Shah III together with Raja Bongsu, the rulers of Johor, 17 May and 23 September 1606.[86]

[This appendix features the full treaty in Dutch with a new English translation of the treaty signed between Admiral Matelieff de Jonge, King 'Ala'uddin and Raja Bongsu (here called Raja Seberang). The latter two are jointly titled "the Kings of Johor". The treaty was ratified before launching the land and sea-borne attacks on Portuguese positions in and around Melaka. At the request of Raja Bongsu and the *bendahara* of Johor, the treaty was confirmed and appended in September 1606 after the unsuccessful attempt to pluck Melaka from the Portuguese.[87] The treaty of May together with the supplementary agreement of September 1606 are important for understanding the dynamics of relations and trade between the VOC and Johor in the first two decades of the 17th century.[88] The alliance with Johor was one of the reasons why the VOC directors at one stage considered Johor as a possible location for a rendezvous and as a permanent base for their operations in Asia.]

Original Dutch Text

Accoordt ghemaeckt tusschen den Admirael Cornelis Matelief de Ionge, uyt den name ende van wegen de Ed. Mog. Heeren Staten Generael der Vereenighde Nederlanden ter eenre, ende den Doorluchtighen ende Machtigen Coningh van Iohor ter ander zijde, desen 17. May 1606, in't Schip *Orangie*, leggende op de reede van Malacca.

1. Indien eersten belooft denselven Admirael,[89] {uyt den name als boven, ten versoecke van den selven Coningh},[90] hem te helpen innemen ende overweldighen de Stadt van Malacca uyt handen van de Portugesen haer beyder vyanden, waer toe elck sijn uyterste vermogen sal employeren, om de selve daer uyt te verdrijven. Welck exploit met Godes hulpe volbracht zijnde, sal de selve bemuyrde[91] Stadt, {gelijckse tegenwoordigh is binnen haer wallen ende muren blijven in vrijen eygendomme eeuwelijck, sonder eenige belastinge nochte Overheyt te erkennen},[92] aen de Heeren Staten voorsz.,[93] het welcke den voorsz. Coninck {midts desen tot eenen loon van den krijgh is gevende}.[94] Ende sal voorts het geheele Landt onder subjectie van sijne Majesteyt blijven, {wel verstaende, dat de Heeren Staaten voorsz. oft haeren Capiteyn[95] geoorloft sal wesen},[96] alsoose de Stadt meenen te verstercken,[97] soo veel landts tot de selve te nemen als haer geraden sal duncken.
2. Sullen de voorsz. Heeren Staten oock vermogen in alle des Conincx lant[98] hout te halen en te houwen tot bouwinge van Schepen en nootdruftigheyt vande Stadt.
3. Sullen {oock}[99] alle Vasallen van de Heeren Staten voorsz. hare Schepen ende goederen, {'t zy van wat plaetse datse comen, oock gehuerde Schepen, Joncken ende Prauwen}[100] in de voorsz. Stadt mogen lossen, sonder {dat de Coningh daer yet op te seggen sal hebben, noch}[101] eenigen tol daer af genieten in noch uyt.
4. Sal de Coningh oock niet toelaten, datter eenige Hollanders, Europische volckeren {oft hare nakomelingen},[102] in eenige van sijne landen sullen mogen handelen, of sullen moeten bescheyt

hebben van den Gouverneur[103] van Malacca, ende 't selve niet hebbende, sullen als vyanden vervolght ende gehouden worden.[104]

5. Hier teghen sal sijne Majesteyt de Voor-stadt Campo Clin, die nu afghebrandt is, peupleren ende regieren, sonder datter de Heeren Staten yet op te seggen sullen hebben, {ende}[105] soo 't moghelijck is sijne residentie[106] aldaer nemen, ende de selve doen[107] verstercken, waer toe hem de Heeren Staten voorsz. met raedt behulpelijck sullen wesen.
6. Sal sijne Majesteyt naer [de][108] veroveringhe vande Stadt ghenieten alle het geschut datter in ghevonden wort, waer af sy[109] vermoghen sal d'eene helft datelijck wegh te nemen, ende d'ander helft sal gehouden wesen in de Stadt tot defensie van deselve te laten, soo langhe tot datse by de Heeren Staten geprovideert wort.[110]
7. 't Gene in de Stad sal gevonden worden van koopmanschap, gelt, waren en andersins, sal komen in eene helft tot profijt vande Vasallen van de voorsz. Heeren Staten deser Vlote, ende d'ander helft aen sijne[111] Majest. voorsz.
8. Alle koopmanschappen niet toebehoorende de Vasallen van de Heeren Staten voorsz. sullen ghehouden wesen te[112] lossen onder des Conincx ghebiet in de Voorstadt, alwaer de Vasallen van de Heeren Staten vry sal staen de selve te komen koopen neffens andere, ende de selve in de Stadt te brengen.
9. Sullen voorts[113] malkanderen by staen en helpen met alle macht en na uyterste vermogen, om de Portugesen en Spaenjaerden harer beyder vyanden alle mogelijcke afbreucke te doen. En so yemant van de partijen oorloge aennam tegen yemant anders als Portugesen en Spanjaerden, sal d'ander partije niet gehouden wesen den selven te assisteren, dan alleenlijck in defensie.[114]
10. Sal oock geen van beyde de partijen pays mogen maken met den Coning van Spanjen, sonder beyder consent.
11. So wie eenig schandael in religions saken geeft, sal aengeklaegt en gestraft worden by sijn Overheyt daer hy onder sorteert, so wel van d'eene als van d'ander sijde.
12. Soo eenige persoonen van d'een of d'ander partije yet om den anderen hadden te seggen, van schult oft andersins, sal de verweerder voor sijne Overheyt gheroepen worden.

13. So der yemant van de Hollanders overliep by den Coninck van Iohor, om eenighe {quade delicten}[115] oft andersins,[116] oft van des Coninckx volck by de Nederlanders, sullen de partijen gehouden zijn den wech-gheloopenen aen sijne Overheyt in handen te leveren.

Forme van den Eedt daer mede de voorgaende Artijckelen aen weder zijde besworen zijn.

Wy, Ian di Patuan ende Raya Sabrang Coningen[117] tot Iohor, beloven midts desen t'onderhouden dit boven gheschreven Accoordt in alle sijne poincten ende articulen sonder daer in eenigher manieren teghen te doen, Soo waerlijck moet ons God helpen.

Ick Cornelis Matelief de Ionge, uyt den naem van de Ed. Mog. Heeren Staten Generael der Vereenigde Nederlanden, belove mids desen alle de bovengheschreven Artijckelen in alle hare deelen naer te komen, sonder daer in eeniger manieren tegen te doen, So waerlijck moet my God [almachtigh][118] helpen.

Tweede Accoort tusschen de voorgenoemde twee Partijen gemaect op den 23. Septembris 1606. inde Stadt van Bathasauwer.[119]

Inden eersten worden geconfirmeert alle Artijckelen begrepen in 't accoort tusschen Partijen ghemaeckt in date den 17 May deses jaers in 't schip Orange op de reede voor Malacca:

Doch dewijl dat het God [de Heer][120] Almachtig niet en heeft belieft, dat wy de Stad en Fortresse van Malacca tot noch toe hebben konnen veroveren, waer deur eenige Artijckelen van weersijden niet en konnen worden onderhouden,[121] als namelijck het besitten van de Stadt voor de Heeren Staten, ende van de Voor-stadt, mitsgaders het geheele Lant voor de Coningh van Ihor, willen sulcx tot naerder gelegentheyt uytstellen, dat Godt {de Heere}[122] de gratie sal believen te geven tot veroveringe der selver, door neerstigheyt vande Heeren Staten en den Coning van Ihor.

En alsoo 't noodig is, dat de Heeren Staten voor haer Ondersaten tot bevorderinge van de negotiatie van de selve in Oost-Indien een versekerde ende vaste plaets hebben, om hare goederen, koopmanschappen, ammunitien, toerustingen ende andersins te versamelen ende bewaren,[123] oock, des noot zijnde, ambachtsluyden ende huys-gesinnen te mogen brengen uyt haer Lant, Sal sijne Majesteyt de Coninck van Iohor aen de Heeren Staten oft haeren Capiteyn geven sulcken plaets als sy sullen begeeren, 't zy hier aen het vaste lant, oft in eenige Eylanden onder 't gebiet van sijne Majesteyt, wesende soo groot ofte kleyn als de Heeren Staten ofte haren Capiteyn sal goetduncken, om aldaer hare huysingen ende wooningen te mogen bouwen, ende die besitten als Malacca.

Des soo sullen wederom de Heeren Staten ende hare Ondersaten gehouden wesen te volbrengen de Artijckelen in 't accoort voor Malacca gemaeckt begrepen.

Aldus gedaen in Bathasauwer, ten dage ende jare als boven.

English Translation[124]

Agreement concluded between Admiral Cornelis Matelieff de Jonge, in the name and on behalf of the High Mighty Gentlemen States General of the United Provinces on the one hand and the great and mighty King of Johor on the other, this day, 17 May 1606, on the ship *Orange*, laying at anchor at Melaka roadstead.

1. First, the said Admiral in the name of the aforementioned Gentlemen and at the request of the said King, shall lend assistance to the latter in taking possession of and delivering the city of Melaka from the hands of the Portuguese, their mutual enemies. To this end each party shall undertake all efforts to drive out the Portuguese from [the city]. When this objective be achieved with God's assistance, the said walled city as it presently stands inside its earthen ramparts and stone walls shall perpetually remain the free possession of said the States [General] without the need to pay taxes or recognise an overlord. This the said King grants as a reward for the [successful conclusion of] the war. Further, all of the land shall remain under the subjection of His Majesty in the understanding that the said States [General], or their captain, shall be defended. The States [General] shall have permission to take as much land as they deem proper [to fulfill this end].
2. The said States [General] shall also be entitled to fell and harvest wood on all of the King's lands for the construction of ships and to satisfy the needs of the city.[125]
3. All the vassals of the said States [General] shall be entitled to unload their ships and cargoes, including hired ships, junks and prahus, no matter where they may arrive from, in the said city.

The King shall not be able to interfere in this matter, nor shall he be able to enjoy the revenue from any tolls levied on these ships, in- or outward bound.[126]

4. The King shall not permit any Dutchmen,[127] persons of European origin or their descendents to trade in any of his lands, unless they have permission from the Governor of Melaka, and should they not have this, they shall be deemed and prosecuted as enemies.[128]
5. His Majesty, however, shall repopulate and rule in the suburb Kampung Kling, which has been burnt down,[129] without any interference from the States [General]. If possible, he shall assume his residence here and fortify the settlement, to which end the States [General] shall lend him useful advice.
6. After the conquest of the city, His Majesty shall enjoy all the artillery found therein. The [Johorese] shall be able to take one half away immediately, and the other half shall be retained for defence for as long as the States [General] will maintain the city [as their stronghold].
7. Half of all the trade, merchandise, money and other goods that are found in the city shall be attributed to the vassals of the said States [General] belonging to this fleet, and the other [half] to His Majesty aforementioned.
8. All the trade that does not belong to the vassals of the said States [General] has to be unloaded in the suburb placed under the authority of the King. The vassals of the States [General], however, shall be free to come and purchase these along with others and to take [purchased] wares into the city.
9. Both parties shall assist each other to the best of their ability so as to inflict as much damage as possible on the Portuguese and the Spanish who are their mutual enemies. Should either party enter into war with a party other than the Portuguese and the Spanish, then the other party shall not be bound to lend assistance to the other, except for defence.[130]
10. Neither party shall enter into peace with the King of Spain without the consent of the other.[131]
11. Should there be any scandal committed in matters of religion, then the culprit shall be accused and punished by his own respective overlord, this being applicable to the one as well as the other side.[132]

12. If some persons from the one or the other party have something to report about the counterparty, be this about debt[133] or another matter, [then] the defendant shall be called [to appear] before his respective authority.[134]
13. Should one of the Hollanders defect to the King of Johor, on the grounds of some serious crime or otherwise, or should one of the King's subjects [defect to] the Dutch, then either party shall be bound to repatriate the defector to his respective overlord.

The wording of the oath by which the aforementioned articles were confirmed by the two respective parties

We, the Yang di Pertuan and Raja Seberang, the kings of Johor, swear herewith to sustain the above written agreement in all of its points and articles and not to undertake anything to infringe it, so help us God.

I, Cornelis Matelieff de Jonge, in the name of the aforementioned High Mighty Gentlemen States General of the United Provinces, herewith swear to fulfill all the above written articles in all their parts and not to undertake anything to infringe them, so verily help me God.

Second agreement Between the Two Aforementioned Parties, Concluded on 23 September 1606 in the City of Batu Sawar.[135]

First, herewith are confirmed all articles included in the agreement concluded between the parties made on 17 May of this year aboard the ship *Orange* anchored at Melaka roads.

As it has not pleased God the Lord Almighty until now that we have been in a position to conquer the city and fortress of Melaka and as a result of which certain articles concluded by the two parties cannot be sustained, such as notably the possession of the ,city for the States [General] and the suburb together with all the land for the King of Johor, we shall postpone these until another moment in the future when God may grant us the grace to conquer the aforementioned with the effort of the States [General] and the King of Johor.

And as it is necessary that the States [General] establish a safe and permanent base for the benefit of their subjects and for the promotion of trade in the said East Indies, where they may collect and store their goods, merchandise, ammunition, equipment and other such things and, if need be, also bring craftsmen and families from their homeland, His Majesty, the King of Johor shall concede to the States [General] such a

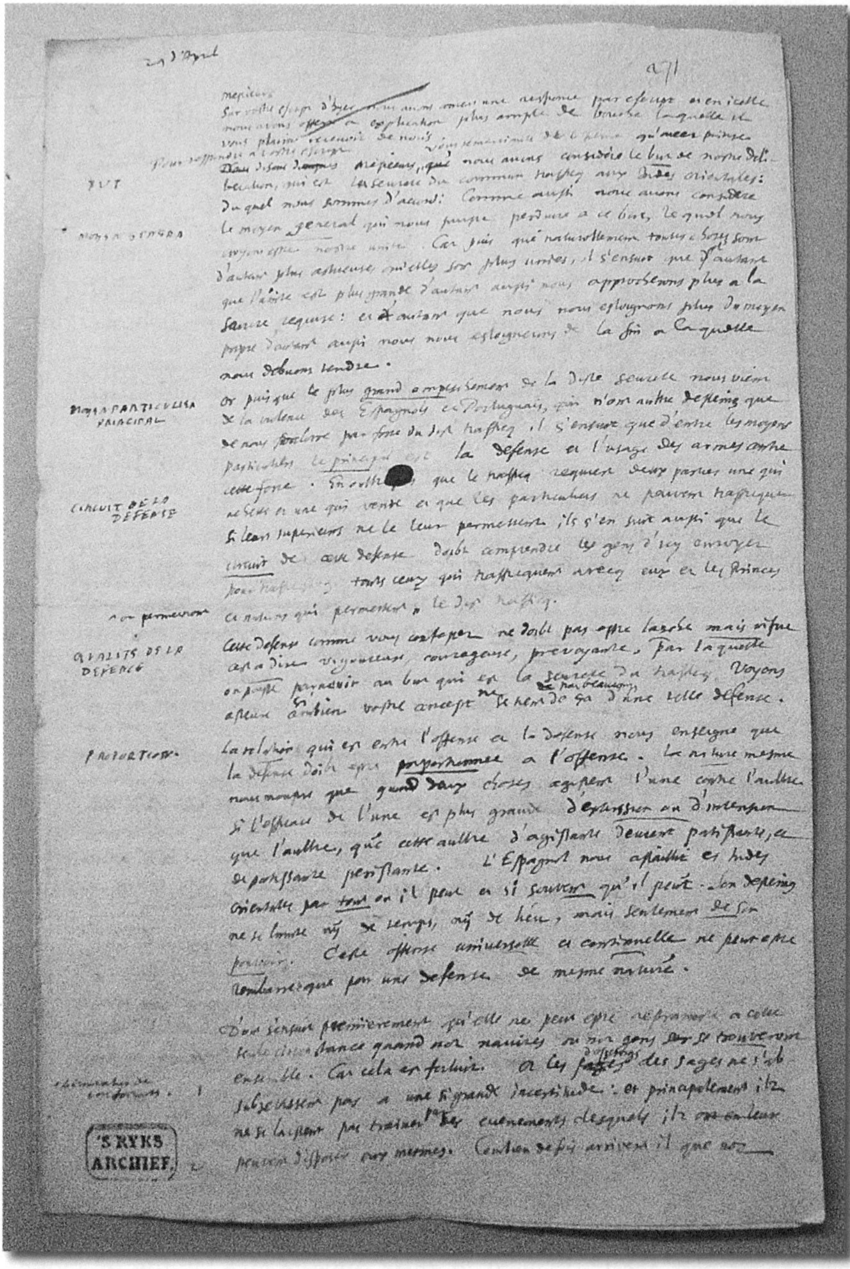

Illus. 57 Dutch reply of 29 April 1615, presented at the Anglo-Dutch colonial conference in The Hague in 1615. The document is written in French and is in the (neat) hand of Grotius. (The Hague, Nationaal Archief, *Collectie Hugo de Groot, Supplement I* [1.10.35.02, no. 40, fol. 271 recto])

place as [the States General] may desire. [This may] be located here on the mainland, or on one of the islands falling under the authority of His Majesty,[136] be it as large or as small as the States [General] or their captain may deem fit, to construct houses and living quarters, and to own these as they [would] in Melaka.

The States [General] and their subjects shall also be bound to fulfill the articles added to the agreement concluded at Melaka.

[This agreement] signed in Batu Sawar on the day and in the year mentioned above.

Appendix 15

Epistolary Memorial by Cornelis Matelieff de Jonge, addressed to Hugo Grotius, dated Rotterdam, 12 November 1608.[137]

[The memorial titled "Discourse on the State of the East Indies" by Cornelis Matelieff de Jonge was written on the Admiral's return to the Netherlands in 1608. It provides a sweeping synopsis of the security situation in the East Indies and stakes out a number of priorities for the VOC. Its contents overlap with another similarly titled piece which has been incorporated into Admiral Matelieff's *Journael* or travelogue.[138] The present copy of the memorial is found among the papers acquired by the Nationaal Archief in the Hague at the 1864 auction of Grotius' working papers. It has been previously transcribed and published in the *Rotterdamsche Historiebladen* (as appendix H) in 1871.[139] Matelieff's report is one of the most comprehensive documents touching on the state and affairs of the East Indies to pass through the hands of Grotius at the time of revising *Mare Liberum* for the press.]

Original Dutch Text[140]

Discours van den Oost-Indischen Staet hoe die jegenwoordigh staet ende int toecomende mogen onderhouden werden soo opt stuck van de oorloghe tegen de Portuguesen, Spanjaerden ende Ingeboorne, also op't gene den Coophandel aengaet daer de meeste proffyten souden mogen gedaen werden.

De Heeren Bewindh. van de Oost-Indische compagnie hier in dese Vereenichde Nederlanden hebben, door octoy van de E.M. Heeren Staten, voor desen diversche vloten, bestaende in menichte van schepen, die oock wel versien syn geweest van alle de nootsaeckelyckheden, gesonden nae Oost-India, om aldaer handelinghe tot haeren proffyt te dryven en den vyandt, de Portugesen, alsoo tegen te staen dat haeren handel in toecomende soude vast ende verseeckert mogen blyven.

Met welck tot noch toe sulcke vrucht is geschaft, dat den vyandt, hoe seer hy alle zyn vlyt heeft aengewent om ons daer vuyt te houden, nyet en heeft gevordert maer der treffeclycke schaede geleden, ende hoewel wy den vyandt tot noch toe daer nyet vuyt hebben connen dryven, 't selve moet men de grootheyt van de saecke toereeckenen, want den vyandt, die daer nu over de hondert jaeren heeft gedomineert, is daer te vast geseten dat wy hem op een corte sprongh soude mogen vuytdryven, te meer wy soo verre gelegen syn ende met soo groote costen onse forces daer moeten brengen, soo is myn meeningh tegenwoordigh te verclaren, wat middel daer is om aldaer gevoegelykst ende minste costen den vyandt aldaer in sulcker manieren te /[141] beiegenen, dat hy soo wel tegen alle ongemacken ende ongelegentheyt des tyts sal hebben te vechten, als wy tot noch toe gedaen hebben.

Men moet voor eerst weten, dat wy in India hebben drye tegenpartyen ofte vyanden, als namelyck de Portugesen ende Spanjaerden die ons met wapenen willen krencken, de Engelsche ende Fransoisen ende andere, de welcke, de wyle wy met den coninck van Spangien malcander smyten, vredelyck varen ende haren handel dryven met weynich ongelden ende laten ons, als hare beschermers, den vyandt tot onse costen schutten, die ons hyer naer, geen groote costen doende, met het brengen van haere speceryen in Europa de marct bederven, sonder ons convoy gelt te betaelen; ten derden de Indianen, de welcke door onze beschermінghe haer voelen verlost van de Portugesen, ende tweederhande coopluyden als Hollanders ende Engelsche op haere marckt, soecken het meeste proffyt sonder erkentenisse dat wij oorsaeck van haere verlossinghe syn, maer soecken, naer aert sulcker wilder natien, 't meeste gelt voor haere waeren te becomen, het welcke, soo elinge daer geen remedie in wert gestelt, sullen de ongelden op ons ende de vruchten op haer vallen, hier naer hebben wy ons desorderen in onse comptoiren, soo dat, alwaert wy ons geluckelyck ons mit de wapenen beschermden, soo soude het ons met den coophandel mogen in confusie loopen, soo wy anders geene ordre in onsen handel ende op ons comptoiren setten, ick sall eerst het stuck van beschermінghe aenroeren ende daernae van den handel.

Vooreerst ende all moeten wy in India een *rende vous* ofte gemeene plaetse verkiesen, alwaer alle de schepen vuyt dese landen recht op aen mochten comen, ende haer /[142] aldaer ververschen, daer oock alle proviande, lyftocht ende amunitie van oorloghe mocht werden gebracht ende langhsamerhandt bij een vergadert. Want in India is nyet metter haest te becomen, tot noch toe is daer gans niet na getracht, hoewel sulcx het nodichst van[143] den gantschen Oost-Indischen staet is, alwaer oock alle waren van alle quartieren soude mogen werden gebracht ende in goede verseeckerheyt aldaer bewaert, want altyd mette groote schepen binnen 's lants te seylen brengt oock veel costen ende ongemack, men mosten de grootste schepen meest tegen den vyandt gebruycken ende die daer toe meest ende naest by der handt hebben van alle de gene die in noot in Oost-Indien souden mogen wesen; de stadt van Bantam is wel een gelegen plaets, doch boven dat sy seer ongesont is, zoo is den tegenwoordigen koninck soo heel jonck, van 14 ofte 15 jaren, met wien oock nyet te handelen is, oock is synen raedt in sulcken partyschap gedeelt dat men niet en can te wege brengen; de stad Malaca, boven de swaericheyt dieder is van die te winnen, soo leyt de selve vry wat ongelegen, want men op alle tyden vant jaer daer nyet wel en can comen ofte ten minste met moeyte, principaal als men groote sware schepen heeft, die door de lange reyse vuyl ende nyet wel besylt syn, men moet een plaets hebben daer men van de Cabo de bona Esperanca comende geen mouson subiect en is om die aen te doen; oock de eerste plaets de beste Acheen is oock onbequaem, want heeft geen goede haven, oock cunnen van daer op alle plaetsen soo gevoechgelyk niet comen als uyt de straet van Bantam, daerom soude ick van twee plaetsen een kiesen ofte de stadt Jacatra ofte de versche rivier 3 ofte 4 mylen bewesten na Bantam toe /[144] ofte de stad Palumban in Sumatra, dan Palumban is oock all beswaerlyck te krygen als het tegen de mouson is ende men van buyten de straet van Bantam incomt, gelyck nu laetst is gebleken anno 1608 in January, dat Pauwels van Caerden, willende van Bantam nae Johor, en conde boven de eylanden van Jacatra niet seylen, daerom soude myn advys voort beste wesen, dat men met den koninck van Jacatra sage te handelen, 't sy in syn stadt ofte versche rivier voorsz. te mogen een fortressen bouwen; in de straet van Bantam voor de stadt ofte voor Jacatra can men op alle tyden van 't jaer comen, als men de Cabo de bona Esperanca is gepasseert ende men is geen mouson subiect.

Dan hier staen weder eenighe inconvenienten te verwachten van die van Bantam, want soo haest als men aldaar verneemt dat wy onse residentie aldaer willen houden, mochten zy wel mette Portugesen aen spannen ende ons met die van Jacatra vyandt werden, daarom dient hyer met voorsichticheyt gehandelt, opdat men de barbaren haer onverstand nyet te kennen en geeft voor ende all eer dat sy geen quaet en connen doen, want, soo veel ick noch aen haer hebbe connen vermercken, souden sij dat nyet voor quaet nemen, al begonden wy huys tot Jacatra te houden, als wy haer somtyts met wat kleetges versochten ende oock wat peper affcoften, wy mosten in alder manieren ons huys ende factorye voort eerste noch te Bantam houden om haer gantsch nyet te vervreemden, ondertusschen met die van Jacatra handelen.

Eerstelyck most aldaer een goet comandeur gesonden werden, die de saecken van 't landt en de Comp.ie wel behartichde, om op alles rypelyck te letten met synen /[145] raet, welcke plaetse 't sy by de versche rivier ofte de stadt Jacatra ons best gelegen waere, want dat vuyterlyck te beschryven is swaer om te doen; men moste oock de humeuren van den coninck weten, voor de rivier is wel de beste reede voor de schepen, doch een geheele stad te timmeren dat heeft oock syn swaricheyt ende wy en mogen de geheele stadt nyet bewonen met ons volck, de inwoonders moeten ons helpen, daer is van beyde syden swaricheyt, want in de versche rivier daer geen huysen en staen souden wy meerder vryheyt bedingen, doch de landouwe is daer geheel woest, daer vry wat arbeyt insteeckt, ick en weet nyet ofte door de nabijheid van eylanden, die daer de goede reede maken, de Portugesen geen occase soude werden gegeven om een van de selve met een casteel te besetten, na myn duncken, soude men van de selve eylanden, te weten van 't naeste, de reede wel mogen beschieten, doch is niet vast, dan nae myn voorstaet isser geen versch water op de eylanden, dat den vyandt soude desaccommederen; voor de stadt Jacatra leggen geen eylanden, men soude moeten twee hoffden slaen om gemackelyck wt ende in te comen met schuyten ende boots volck; met schepen die 12 en 13 voet diep gingen, doch dit alles soude men beter metter ooch als vuyt de pen verstaen.

Men soude met den selven coninck een seecker contract mogen maeken, want hy moste soo wel als wy by dit contract proffiteren, want sonder sulcx most men hem nyet te vooren leggen, 't welck men alder best in syn tegenwoordich soude connen doen, ende dan het eene verswaren ende het ander verlichten nae dat men hem genegen soude vinden, na myn opinie, soude dese wel noodigh syn, by nae op /[146] voet als de Portugesen met die van Cochyn hebben, indyen het tot Jacatra geschiede, soude ons sulcken plaetse soo groot ofte cleyn geven dicht aent water ende ryvier van Jacatra, daer wy ons plaetse ende fortresse soude mogen bouwen, om bewaert te wesen tegen [den aenloop][147] der Portugesen, want wy en mogen soo te landtwaert niet vlieden, als de Portugesen comen, ende ons goederen mede nemen, als de swarte doen, want ons dingen hebben meer moeiten en daerom moeten wy vast wesen, des ons nyet op de vluchten vertrouwen maer op ons defentie, deselve plaetse most soo groot wesen, dat alle de Hollanders, die wy metter tydt in India souden mogen brengen, daer gemackelyck souden mogen wonen, soude soo veel lants te lande waert ende ontrent de stadt geven, als sy bouwen ofte met beesten beweyden mochten, oock deselve laten onder de regeringhe van de Hollanders die daer begeren onder te staen, doch dit punt dient met discretie gehandelt, dat alle waren, die daer gebracht werden, nyet meer souden betalen als 4 ten hondert ofte ten utersten 5, ende dat alle 'tgene by de Hollanders ofte voor haer rekening gebracht werdt soude betalen aen de heeren Staten, hier inne oock begrepen die onder de heeren Staten gebiet stonden, ende ter contrarie alle Indianen, Chinesen ende vreemelinghen souden betalen aen den koninck de decisie hiervan mocht men aldaer in bester forma sien te accommoderen, dat den koningh d'eensyde van de hoffden van de have becosten ende de Hollanders d'andere syde.

Datter gants geene Europysche volcken en souden in syne stadt toegelaten worden, dan alleen vassalen van de heeren Staten, welcke erkentenis soude staen tot ordeel van den commandeur aldaer wonende, doch indien de /[148] stadt aen de versche rivyer geleyt werde, 't twelck alles soude staen naer humeuren van den koninck, most men bedingen, dat hy een deel van syn volck sont om ontrent ons te wonen, want van ons selven, alwaert mit syn consent, een plaets te peupleren heeft swaricheyt in, nademael de Portugesen ons soo nae op de hacken aldaer syn, doch indien men sulcx niet wilde insien, men soude tot de versche rivier wel beter contract connen bedingen als tott Jacatra, doch men most sien die van Bantam altydt in goede devotie te houden, ende als sy dan begonnen te syen dat haer Jacatra schadelyck was, souden te spade voor die van Bantam wesen, want souden alsdan een goet deel van hare handelinghe ende inwoonderen verloren hebben ende geen quaet connen doen, dat te beduyden soude wesen, daer syn noch eenighe articulen die den tyt ons dan wel naerder soude onderwysen.

Ende opdat de plaetse met inwoonderen mochte gepeupleert werden, souden men moeten soo veel volcx vuyt dese landen voeren als men soude connen, die altijt ten dienste van patria souden staen ende in plaets van soldaten wesen, want met dese groote costen van de maendtgelden, die de compagnie moet geven, valt het haer lastig, maer men moste de luyden, die aldaer gingen wonen, middel geven om aldaer wat te verdienen, 't welck aldaer wel te doen is, ende genoech dat de compagnie nyet can waer nemen, sulcke dingen, segge ick, die voor de compagnie nyet practicabel syn ende voor particuliere door yders industrie wel met goet proufyt can gehandelt werden, want die in dienste is, laet hem aen syn maent gelden genoegen sonder verder te practiseeren, want de mensche is vuyter natuyren soo, dat die practiseeren wil salt voor hem selve doen ende /[149] voor geen vreemden, het exempel van de Portugesen is wel aen te mercken, die in alle hare conquesten volck hebben gebannen, daar nae met premie verwillicht, hier conde voort eerste wel een goet expedient in gevonden werden, want ons hyer te lande aen geen leechgangers en gebreeckt, die men derwaerts wel conde seynden, gelyck dat de heeren wel connen verstaen.

Ons hooftplaets genomen hebbende, mosten verder sien te bevaren Amboina, Banda, de Molucas, Borneo, Chyna, Japan, het geheele eylant Sumatra, Johor, Patane, Queda, Tanassorim, Bengala, Siam, de custe van Choromandel, Aracam ende oock Cambaye met oock watter aen dependeert.

Doch eer wy vorder van India spreecken moeten eerst van Europa beginnen, onse vloten mosten hyer in Maert vuytvaeren, hoe vroeger, hoe beter, ende hoewel Texel daer nyet wel toegelegen is, want de heeren van Amsterdam connen hare schepen primo ofte ten langsten half Maert nyet vuyt seynden, sy mosten daer sulcke remedie in vinden datse 't selve conden doen, want als men spader vuyt dese landen 't seyl gaet, heeft men over al wint ende stroom tegen, gelyck aen diversche vloten wel is gebleecken, die alle in de bocht van St. Thome syn vervallen, alwaer sy soo veel tyt 't soecken maecken, dat sy eerst in November ofte December om de caep comen, 't welck dan een onbequame tyt geeft om op eenighe plaetsen in India te mogen varen, maer sall u op sommighe vaerten een jaer schelen ende op sommighe ses maenden, daerom de heeren gelieven dit poinct[150] wel te behartighen, want wat swaricheyt datter vuyt onstaet, soo spade vuyt dese landen te vertrecken, can men lichtelyck mercken, als men maer bedenckt, dat den vyandt overal met syn huysen voor ons is ende wy /[151] daerentegen ons volck mette lange reyse matteren, ende boven de oncosten die soo groot syn, connen geen versch volck met couragie in India brengen, maer comen met moedeloos volck tegen den vyandt, die al ses maenden, 't sy in wat plaetse wy comen, geadviseert vinden, want de twee maenden, die wy hyer vuyt dese landens spader tseyl gaen als wy behooren, verschillen ons een jaer op de reys ende wat verschil het is, een jaer vroeger ofte spader 't huys te comen, leert de ervarentheyt, datter dus veel volck door de langheyt van de reys ende heel oude spyse eten, hier tegent lant comende gelyck snee verdwynen ende wech sterven, twelck een saecke is die men voor al behoort te remedieren, want het is een verdrietighe saecke, dat men de schepen dus miserabel siet thuys comen met duysent peryckelen, dat ick het principael achte dat de luyden, soo lange te scheep syn ende broot ende vleys van vier jaer out eten, ende het arack drincken doet er geen deucht in, men most hem in India alles nieus versien, daer wel middel toe is, als men daer een vaste plaets souden hebben ende die victaille van langhsamer hant versamelen.

Een vaste plaets aldaer hebbende, ist voor al van noode, dat men aldaer een commandeur als voren most houden, geassisteert met synen raedt, oock geprovideert met ordre om een successeur te mogen hebben by afflyvicheyt van den selven, de welcke oock most met behoorlycke auctoriteyt becleet wesen, om alles te mogen vuytvoeren, ende geen tegenspreeckers aldaer te hebben, want syn te verre van huys gelegen om hare differenten te decideren, welcken commandeur aldaer most syn residentie houden, om in alle saecken te provideren, na den noodt soude vereysschen, want myn heeren sullen hyer op verdacht wesen, dat het tot groot /[152] schandael van onse saecke is, datter geen autoriteyt in India en is, want de desordre die hier mede soude geweert werden, soude de costen wel thyen dubbel betaelen, want nu doet elck wat hy wil ende niemant is straffe ofte correctie onderworpen, sulcx dat metter tyt hyer wel een confusie vuyt worden sall, soo in 't stuck van den oorloghe als in de coophandel, de autoriteyt van admiraels die in India syn, is niet genoech, want hebben geen blyvende plaetse, oock door dyversheyt van de voyage en connen op alles niet provideren, want eerse yet verstaen van de gelegentheyt soo moetense te lande vuyt, alwaert saecke datse de saeck ten besten wilden remedieren, terwylen datter altydt een nyeu admiraal verwacht wordt laet het den eenen op den anderem staen, als altyt genoech met syn reyse becommert wesende, veel van de Indianen bekennen rondt vuyt, seggende, de Hollanders is wel goet volck, geven ons meer voor onse waren als de Portugesen, trakteren ons oock beter, maer gelyckeren ons by een vogel, die op een boom komt ende hem sat etende vliecht weder wech, latende de resten tot een proye van de gene die na volgen, dat syn de Portugesen, die dan, de arme inwoonders vinden ontbloot van de Hollanders, daer wreedelyck mede omgaen ende die bederven, daerom hebben liever met de Portugesen wat armoede te lyden als weynich weelde mette Hollanders ende daer nae van de Portugesen bedorven, daerom most men geen plaets aendoen ofte wel verseeckeren tegen den vyant, daer syn veel plaetsen die men, so men seyt, haest met haer eygen smeer souden connen droopen.

Amboino.

Eerst most men syen Amboino te verstercken, daer ick den gouverneur Frederick de Houtman seer toe hebbe /[153] aengeporret, want Amboino ende Bande most men alsoo met malcander vercnoopen, dat het eene het ander mocht helpen, ende op dat men die van Banda te beter onder de heeren Staten soude mogen brengen diendemen 't selve soo behendich te doen, dat alle de omleggende coningen nyet jeloers en werden, want het eylant Banda is soo veel gout waert alst groot is ende wort by forme van een Republycque geregeert, ende 't syn een deel schelmse hovaerdighe moedwillighe arme bedelaers, ende hoeveel incomen dat se hebben soo synse noch altydt ten achteren, sy verlaten haer daer op, dat alleman haer van doen heeft, ende geven oock niemant een goet woort, hebben oock geen middel om haer te beschermen, doch de oneenicheyt van de omleggende coninghen geeft haer sterckte, daer hebben veel vryers nae geweest, ende noch syn die van Ternata in synen tydt, die van Tuban, die van Macasser ende oock die van Forbay, de Portugeesen meenden, ten tyden van Andre Furtado, die die van Hitto verdreeff, de Bandanesen, 't onder te brengen, doch door ander toevallen belett, soo dat ick hebbe verstaen, dat die van Tuban soude hebben geseyt, dat die van Banda moeten 't onder moeten gebracht syn, indient de Portugesen ofte Hollanders niet en doen, soude hy 't selve sien te doen, daerom soude men moeten een van dese voorsz. koningen in den arm nemen ende hem 't selve eylandt met onse hulp winnen, ende gelett hebbende wie ons proffytelycxt souden mogen wesen, hebben yemant connen bedencken als den coninck van Makassar, om dese reden, dat hy een coninck is, die corts over de 5 ofte 6 jaeren aen de mahometische religie is gebracht, ende beter hope hem tot het kristendom te brengen als andere die der in opgevoet syn, ende d'onderdanen noch /[154] veel heyden syn, dat syn lant het vruchtbaerste is van dat quartier van eetwaeren, het welcke Banda meest gebreeckt, dat syn lant oock soo gelegen leyt, dat indien hy vyandt van de Portugesen werdt, ick niet en weet waer dat sy een verversch soude mogen hebben om voortaen van Malacca na de Moluccas te mogen varen ende die te secoreren, 't soude alleen van de Manilhas moeten geschieden, dat all beswaerlyk valt, souden 't selve te Tuban ofte Grece moeten doen, daer all metter tydt remedie in soude connen gestelt werden, doch dese saecke dient soo sekreet gedaen, dat het noch Portugesen, Engelse, Fransoise Nochte Indianen vernemen voor dat het volbracht soude syn, want 't soude onse saecke seer mogen verachteren, soo wel haer autoriteyt als oock haer macht, 't welck sy haest souden te werck leggen, siende datt onse saecken alsulcken voortganck aldaer kregen, men soude mogen met den coninck dese ofte dier gelycke articulen maecken, ick en twyffel nyet ofte soude gants daer toe genegen syn, ick hebbe van langhsamerhant syn gemoet doen sonderen, daer ick noch geen antwoort op en hebbe, alsoo 't selve door Abram Mathysz. is belast te doen, die mit laetste van 't jaer 1607 van Bantam met 't schip de Groote Sonne derwaert gingh, dat wy hem souden leveren 't eylant van Banda, mits dat de heele conqueste onder synen naem geschiede ende hy nyet meer als met 7 ofte 800 mannen gereet maeckte, ende wy souden met 4 ofte 600 Hollanders ende 800 Amboinesen hem helpen, 't welck nae myn opinie volck genoech soude wesen, ende hem te meer 't onswaert soude obligeeren, naedemael hy totte conqueste gants nyet en dede, de beuyt most men all met discretie deelen, want hoewel die van Makassar, het geheele lant hebbende, genoech hadden, soo syn de /[155] swarten allegader alsoo, dat se liever een tegenwoordigh hebben dan tien toecomende, dat hy soude disponeren van alle de inwoonders, nae syn gelieffte, dat de heeren Staten geen proffyt nochte tollen daer vuyt wilden trecken, dan hem die alles laten houden, op datt hy haer vrundt bleve, ende dat hy alle de vruchten vant eylandt vry eygen soude genieten. Hiertegen, dat hy voortaen vrundt van den Koninck van Hollant (want dit is den tytel die men de heeren Staten daer geeft), wesen soude, als oock van syn vrunden ende vyandt van syn vyanden, ende malcander met alder macht tegen de Portugesen souden helpen, soo wel in offentie als in defentie, nochte geen pays d'een sonder d'ander maecken.

Dat hy alle den adel ende machtighe luyden soude doen op een plaets [i]nt eyland, te verkiesen by den Koninck van Hollandt, soude doen comen wonen, om 't selve sterck te maecken tegen den inval van de Portugesen ende andere.

Dat in de selve plaetse een sterck huys soude gebouwt werden, alwaer de Hollanders haer factorye souden hebben ende haer goederen alle versamelen, om voor brant ende overvall van de vyanden bewaert te wesen.

Dat den Koninck een vendel Hollanders soude houden, welcke hem ende den Koninck van Hollant soude sweren tot defentie van 't landt, welcke soldaten vuyt het incomen vant lant souden betaelt werden.

Datter geen vreemde natie int eylandt soude comen handelen als Hollanders ende Makassers.

Dat alle eetwaeren ende kleeden souden in Amboine gebracht werden ende van daer na Banda, door borgers van Amboina ende Banda. /[156]

Datter geen waren vuyt Banda souden mogen gevoert werden, als na Hollant ofte Amboina.

Men soude voorts eenighe articulen stellen, die hem metter tyt voorts souden openbaren oock daer den Koninck toescheen te inclineren, als vant halen van de Sagu vuyt Ceyram, Amboina ende anders.

Tot wat pryse men hem de noten ende folie soude affnemen most men oock besien, men most, by maniere van spreecken, een overvaert ofte veer maecken tusschen Amboina ende Banda, dat aldaer in die plaetse een duysent Hollanders ofte witten mochten den cost ryckelyck hebben met haer huysgesin ende slaven, hiertoe most men de noten ende folie in Amboina watt hooger stellen als in Banda, ende niemant die laeten vuytbrengen als witte inwoonders van Banda ende Amboina, gevende elcx[157] jaarlyex een seeckeren tax te mogen brengen, men soude die van Makassar oock hope geven van geheel Celebes onder haer te brengen, hyer mede achte ick Amboina ende Banda wel souden connen beschermt werden, asser goede ordre werdt gehouden, men most oock niet vergeten 70 ofte 80 van den principaelsten adel van Banda van daer te doen gaen, daer mede soude alle mutinatie op houden, 't selve dient beter gedaen als wel daervan geseyt.

Voorts Amboyna, na dat het casteel versterckt was, soude ick een forma van een stadt daer rontom begrypen, ende alle de inwoonders, te weten de principaelste, daer doen comen wonen, doch alsoo hyer in wat moeyte soude vallen, most men dit soo nae comen als men conde, dat ten minsten haer kinderen ofte een deel daervan quamen wonen, ende alst tydt ware de nagelen te plucken dat men dan na gelegentheyt soude handelen. /[158]

Soo veel de kristenen belanght, soude men daer terstont wel toe konnen brengen, doch die van Hitto mosten met inductie daer toe gebracht werden, daer se metter tydt toe soude verstaen, als men haer dede verstaen, dat mense anders qualyck soude connen defenderen, ende als men dit hiertoe conde brengen, ende dat de witte daer wonen mitte swaert ende anders haer conden bedroopen ende de cost winnen, soude men geen cost van soldaten houen te doen, want men soude een grooten hoop volck in die stadt connen hebben, als die wel in goede ordre werden gehouden most den vyandt al sterck comen eer hy die machtich soude werden, want heden ten dage synder wel tyen duysent mannen ondert gebiet van de heeren Staten van 18 jaeren ende daer over, daer van die meeste syn mahometisen ende heydenen ende omtrent een derde part kristen, diet metter tydt ons oock toegedaen sullen werden, als sy maer verseeckert waeren, dat wy onse saecke met ernst meenden om haer te beschermen, want, soe lange als wy onse saecke met geen meerder ernst en belyden, sien de luyden altydt te rugge. Hier mede, niet al het volck omtrent het casteel brengende, soude men alle de negotien aldaer in de handen hebben, want daer 't casteel leyt is een seer goede ende groote, haven daer menichte van schepen haer connen bergen.

Hier opt eylant is veel sagu, ook rys ende boontjes wert er veel gesayt, vis isser oock tamelyck, daer syn eenige koyen ontrent 60, die van de Portugesen tyden daer syn gebleven ende den Gouverneur toe behooren, daer synde wel soo veel die int wilde syn gevloden, die metter tydt haer seer sullen vermeerderen, oock synder veel wilde verckens, men soude oock mogen belasten alle schepen, /[159] die vroech genoech quamen om in Grece aen te loopen, ende aldaer soo veel koyen in te nemen als sy mochten, oock bocken ende geyten ende die in Amboino brengen, want daer is weyde genoech, sulcx dat Amboino van spyse wel can versien werden.

Aengaende 't groote eylandt van Ceyram, dat meest onder Ternata gestaen heeft, doch soo noch ten deele staet, soude metter tydt onder de heeren Staten gebracht werden ofte onder Ternata, dat altydt de vruchten daer van bij ons genoten werden, spreecke daer niet meer van, als nyet soo nodich voort eerste.

Nu volgen de Molucas, daer wat meerder swaricheyt soude vallen die te conquesteren, doch is nyet ondoenelyck nae myn oordeel, doen ick in Ternata quam, anno 1607 in mayo, vondt ick alle de Ternatanen verlopen ende gevloden, den meeste deel opt het eylandt Gilolo, hadden daer een sterckte gemaeckt, den Spaniaert hadde 'd oude stadt van Ternata wat cleynder gemaeckt ende gesterckt ende daer lagen op vyff vendelen, elck mocht 70 man sterck wesen, voorts het geheele eylandt ledich, ick hadde gaerne een prove opte stadt gedaen, doch hadde geen middel daertoe, want ick en conde boven de 240 man vuyt myn vloot nyet aen lant setten, ende de Ternatanen te vergaderen wilde langh aenloopen, daer ick nyet nae mochte wachten, want myn tydt nae Chyna te gaen was al opt hoochste, daeromme hebbe een fortresse op t' Noord eynde van teylandt gemaeckt, daer een dorp plach te staen genaemt Malaya, ende daer op gelaten eenigh geschutt met 50 man ende drye schepen met een jacht om de see te bevryden, soo datter mochten styff 200 man blyven van myn volck, de Ternatanen quaemen te met over van Gilolo om haer onder 't casteel te begeven, /[160] daer se metter tydt alle comen sullen, ten is niet doenlyck de swarten op een stel ende sprongh te vergaren, want behalven dat se vuyter naturen verlangsem syn, de eylanden ende plaetsen daer se van daen moeten comen leggen soo verre ende verstroyt dat tot alles tyt van nooden is.

De autoriteyt van den coninck van Ternata placht seer groot te wesen, want hadde veel eylanden ende volcken onder hem ende op zyn eylandt was hy alderswackste, soodat hij bij faulte van goede ordre is tonder gegaen, want de swarten syn vuyter natuyren onachtsaem, ende hy werdt door ons met het winnen van Tydore noch onachtsamer gemaeckt.

De saecke staet alsoo gelegen, van vijff Moluckse eylanden dat Ternate heeft, den vyant een fortresse opt suydeynde ende wy opt noorteynde, den vyant heeft nyet een Ternataen tot zyn devotie ende wy mogender 2 ofte 300 opt eylant hebben, alle nagelbomen staen aen ons syde, soodat nae mijn opinie den vyant geen nagelen can becomen, die van Tidore hebben genoech met het haere te doen.

Tydore heeft den vyandt int geheel, daer den coninck op woont. Makian placht onder Ternata te staen, behaleen dorpgen, doch is nu alles onder Tydore, doch de overheyt hebben by nacht twee van de haren aen myn schepen gesonden, die my presenteerden dat sy tegen de Spanjaerden wilden rebelleren, want er boven 30 ofte 40 Spanjaerden nyet op en waren, by sooverre ick haer wilde beschermen, ende dat sy gesint waren, alle voor haren koninck te sterven, daar op ik haar tot antwoordt gaff, haar seer bedanckende, datt het nog geen tyt en was haer te openbaren, want ick en wilde haer niet bedriegen, ende en conde haer nu nyet beschermen, want door het /[161] slaen tegen de Portugesen hadde ick oock wat volck verloren ende dat ick vuyt Hollant daer niet op versien en ware om soo veel te doen, dan dat sy haer gereet souden houden om met de eerste vlote die vuyt Hollant soude comen te samen gelyck de Spanjaarden aan te vallen, ende dat ick haer dit rade om haer nyet op den vleysbanck te brengen, doch dat ick nu alleen quam om een fortresse op Ternata te maeken, opdatt de gevloden Ternatanen mochten onderhouden werden tot de naeste vloot, daer over sy my bedanckten, ende belooffden soo haest daer een ander vloot quaeme haer gereet te houden, ende nae dat ick haer eenighe geschenken hadde gegeven syn na de hare vertrocken, altyt protesterende dat soo haest sy sagen dat den Stant van Ternata eenigen voet soude grypen, sy haer terstont souden openbaren. Dit alles geschiede in de presentie van Ternatanen die 't zelve oock alsoo verstonden ende voor goet achten.

Het eylant Pulo Cabaly geeft nyet veel nagelen, is onbewoont met dese Garbonilhe, die van Motir daer wel de schoonste nagelen vallen ende oock onder Ternata stonden synt verloopen ende wonen by de Ternatanen, soo dat 't selve oock woest leyt. Om nu de zelve eylanden weder tot onse vruntschap ende devotie te brengen en can men nyet voorslaen voor ende all eer men weet wat den admiraal van Kaerden sal uitgerecht hebben, met welcken ick alles hebbe overleyt ende mijnen raedt gegeven, oock hem van alles geinformeert, hoope dat Godt de Heere zijnen zegen sal geven, want hy heeft middel om wat goets daer te doen, als hebbende op syn vloot noch 850 gesonde mannen ende 200 van myne vlote op't lant, het schip de Groote Sonne ende Gelderlant, die aldaer oock sullen ge-/[162] comen syn oock met ontrent 200 man, soo dat hy byna 900 mannen aen lant sal mogen setten, behalven de Ternatanen, die metter tyt by het casteel sullen comen wonen syn; hyer bestaet het alles in, indien hy voor die van de Manilhas in Ternata is gecomen isser nyet te twyffelen ofte sall innemen waerover wy ons oock gespoet hebben, om op geen plaetze het ooch te nemen, als alleen syn beste te doen om langs Celebes na de Molucas sien te comen, want indien hy over Amboina, 't welck den ordinaris wech is, syn cours name soude niet eer als int begin van Mayo 1608 in Ternata mogen wesen, ende vuyt de Manilhas sullen int begin van April daer al wesen, ende hy is den 10 Januarij van Bantam 't seyl gegaen na Ternata, hem gebreekt een galeye om in stilte, die daer veel syn, dienstich te wesen, ende den vyandt heefter twee, d'een tamelyck d'ander wat cleynder, dan ick gisse datt de Spanjaerts die op Ternata syn, all vry watt sullen gemindert wesen, want de sieckte daer vry wat onder was, ende in die landen is nyet te eeten ofte moet er van buyten gebracht werden, hoe welt een zeer bequaem lant is om vee te houden, soo wel groot als cleyn, soo besluyte datter van Ternata noch de Molucas nyet te discoureren en is voor ende all eer men hoore wat succes den admirael van Caerden daer gehadt heeft.

Aengaende Bachia, dat een groot stuk van daer leyt, wel 60 meijlen, nae myn onthout, daer d'ander malcander all mogen sien, hoewel hij geen vrundt van den koninck van Ternaten was, nochtans behaechde het hem nijet wel dat men den Coninck van Ternata na de Manilhas voerde, hy heeft oock geen nagelen dat te beduyden heeft. Daer is noch een ander saeck, dat, indien den Admirael van /[163] Kaerden in Ternate niet en hadde bedreven, ofte hadde wat gedaen, dat men de ondersaten van Ternata alle sach te saemen te verbinden ende een armada van deselve te maeken, ende all en dede men 't fort van Ternata niet, men soude die van Tydore destrueren, ende dit most van langsamer hant gedaen werden, te weten, de eylanden van Xula die wel 22 corcorren elck met 70 ofte 80 mannen connen opbrengen, als ook die van Mindanas die veel machtiger is mede op te brengen ende indien Tydore 't onder gebracht soude mogen syn, een tocht nae de Manilhas te doen, daer die van Mindanas wel bedreven toe syn, doch dit alles soude niet te doen wesen ofte daer mosten hollantsche schepen ende autoriteyt by wesen, want anders is al swarten werck, ick en spreecke oock van macht van de selve niet als van hooren seggen van de Ternatanen.

Ick ben gants nyet van opinie datter eenich accoort met die van Tydore te maecken is, want het schynt dat alle mahometisten oversoenlyck syn, met den genen daer ze eens vijantschap mede hebben daerom sall hy nimmermeer mette Ternatanen versoent werden d'een ofte ander moet vuytgeroyt werden, want sy en houden malcander niet langer woort dan tot dat het haer te passe comt ende veel min houden syt den kristenen, daarom als men in India eenich accoort maeckt moeter een casteel terstont bij gemaeckt werden ende dan haer geen ocuasie van quaedtwillicheyt geven, dan sal men wel goede vrunden blyven alse[164] vreesen ende beminnen, want het beminnen alleen is na myn duncken nyet genoech, hyer dyent wel op gelett, dat de autoriteyt van den koninck van Ternata, voor syn gevanckenisse, seer groot was, sulcx dat, indien men hem /[165] met onse industrie ende raedt hadde gesecondeert, men zoude synen staet zeer vast hebben gestelt, jae soo, datter de Spanjaerts nyet en souden hebben aangecomen, en 't soude haest nyet alleen sonder onse schade maer met ons profyt syn geweest, dat nu verby is, ende 't schijnt dat men alle dingen beter bestraffen dan verbeteren can, doch men soude nu soowel den selven voet sien te volgen als mogelyck is, alles particulier hier int schrift te verhalen soude te langh vallen.

Nu laet ons weder te rugge comen nae Johor ende besien de Portugesen aldaer werck te snyden opdat haer de lust vergae op Moluccos ende Banda de dencken, ende ondertusschen met haer kijven om den chyneschen, choromandelsen ende bengaelsen handel, oock dye van Cambaya mede in 't spell brengen, men soude eerst en voor alle dingen moeten soecken de stadt van Johor vast te maecken, daer ick voor desen wel nae getracht hebbe, doch met mijn vertreck na de Moluccos ist weder al te rugge geloopen, ende de wyle hy zyn stadt nyet sterck hadde gemaackt, is den Portugees gecomen, ende vuyt vreese heeft hy syn stad verlaten ende te landewaart inne gevlucht, ende heeft zelff syn stadt in brandt gesteecken, doch de Portugees en quam noyt soo verre de rivier op, dat hy voor de stadt soude comen, ondertusschen heeft hy pays met den Portugees gemaeckt welcke articulen ick gesien hebbe, daer oock nyet te achten en is, want soo haest ick het schip Erasmus nae Johor hadde gesonden, hielt hy van den pays nyet, daarom most men aldaer eerst trachten om [de] stadt sterck te maecken, 't welck nyet toegaen en soude sonder een spetie van harde woorden te gebruycken, ende anders in sulcker forma dye men eer int werk most /[166] stellen als mette penne daar van discoureren, den jongen koningh Raha Zabran soude daer wel toegesint wesen, den ouden is een mensch meer tot drinken als tot regeren bequaem, 't soude oock een duysent realen vier ofte vyff moeten costen van onse syde, waert dat men die daer eens aen te coste leyde, men soude die metter tydt mogen innen, ofte soot qualyck wilde, men soude den vyandt so seer daarmede te rugge houden dat het ons wel veel meer soude importeeren, men moste oock besien ofte het nu soo gelegen ware als tertyt als ick daer was, van veel garnjsoen daer te houden, dat soude op groote costen loopen, dan de stad sterck gemaeckt hebbende, soude 't gemoet van de Malayen wat versekert wesen, als de Stadt gemaeckt ware, soude men met 50 ofte 60 witte Soldaten de Malayen wel soo verseekeren dat se by malcander souden blyven ende dan geen noot hebben, ofte daer most meerder macht comen als ick my zelven inbeelde dat vuyt India can te samen gebracht werden.

Men soude moeten 2 ofte 3 schepen ofte Jachten omtrent Malaca houden, dewelcke de navigatie van Malaca wel soo souden quellen met behulp van de Malayen, die met haer prauwen ende galeyen daer oock nyet quaelyck toe souden dienen, deselve souden den coninck van Johor oock courageren dat hij altijt schepen omtrent sijn stadt hadde ende sage.

Ende dat men nyet meenen soude datt ditt ondoenlyck ware voor de Oost-Indische comp.ie als anders nyet als cost sonder proffyt, ick en twyffel nyet of men soude wel particuliere, als mensse wel onderrechte, vinden die op prinsen ende beuyten haer tot sulcx wel souden willen laten gebruycken, de selve mosten soo wel by noorden als /[167] by suyden Malacca houden, 't welck de selve stadt dapper zoude desaccommodeeren, want alsoo ze anders geen victuaille heeft als haar van buyten werdt gebracht, soude het haer swaer vallen, principalyck als men wat straffelijk met die gene handelde, die haer victualje brengen, dat meest Javanan syn die vant suyden comen, doch de Portugesen brengen 't vuyt het noorden, als van Bengala ende van de custe van Coromandel, deselve vrybuyters mosten op haar tyden passen 't sy by noorden ofte by suyden Malaca houdende, elck op syn tydt.

Mochten oock op haer tydt gaen onder Ceylon in Februarij ende besien wat daer te haelen waer van 't gene dat van Bengalen ende Negapatan na Cochyn ende Goa gebracht werdt, twyffel nyet ofte als sulcx met goede ordre werdt gedaen ofte soude goede buyten geven, daer de armeerders haer wel souden van bedancken, ende alsoo ditt niet en soude geschien ofte de Portugesen souden terstont daer tegen armeren, most men de selve jachten ende schepen opt seylen maeken ende altyt wel schoon houden, daer goede middel toe is, men most oock handelen nae gelegentheyt van den tyt, ende alser een goede vlote by de hant waer de rede van Malaca besoecken ende de schepen aldaer vernielen, ende principalyck daer op passen dat men gereet ware tegen dat de schepen van Chyna na Malaca comen, omme de selve aen te vallen, want dat ist gene dat de Portugesen meest beschadicht, zoo wel de particuliere als des conincks tollen, alsoot de ryckste schepen syn, ende by de speceryen nyet en hebben te gelycken, het staet in Chyna tot Macao alsoo, dat met het verlies van 't nemen van eenighe schepen, oock de gene die ick in myn aencomste voor Malaca verbrande, die na Macao wilden, die /[168] van Macao alsoo gestelt waren, dat, indien de schepen die ik in Chyna vondt, daer nyet waeren met groot capitaal aengecomen, om twee jaren ladingh mede te nemen, dat sy het qualyck langer conden gaende houden, want, zoo haest de Chynesen geen proffyt van de Portuguesen voelen, beginnen haer met dwerse oogen aen te sien, ja, was soo verre, dat den mandoryn van Canton all verboden hadde geen victualje tot Macao te brengen, soodat ick mij gantselyck inbeelde dat, by sooverre ick met myn vloot na de Molucas nyet genootsaeckt ware te loopen ende alleen getracht hadde om Malaca te krencken, soo datter geen schepen ditt jaer na Macao hadde mogen gaen, ofte de stadt Macao soude vergaen hebben, ende de inwoonders verloopen; daer is wel een beginsel geweest om door den coninck van Siam vruntschap in Chyna te verwerven doch, met datter vant selve jaer geen gesanten na Chyna vuyt Siam gingen, is sulcx naegebleven, doch 't selve achte ick niet noodich, want ick en twyffel niet aan den handel van Chyna, na alle apparentie die ick in Chyna hebbe vernomen, ende indien de Chynesen nyet en wilden, isser wel middel om tussen Chyna ende de Manilhas sulcke prinsen op de Chynesen te doen, die een goet stuck gelt jaerlyck waerdich souden wesen, want er alle jaer 24 ofte 30 schepen vuyt Chencheo na de Manilhas loopen met allerhande costelycke waeren, dewelcke eensdeels voor rysico van de Spanjaerts doch meest van de Chynesen loopen.

Om Malaca 't onder te brengen soude men oock den koninck van Syam mogen gebruycken, de welcken wel veel volck te lande voor Malaca soude brengen, die oock seer tot ons gesint is ende gaarne van onsen voorspoet hoort, doch hyer van te spreken is maer van hooren seggen, /[169] gelijck nu Cornelis Specs, die aldaar eenen tijdt heeft gelegen, verclaert heeft, daer mede de tegenwoordighe ambassadeurs haer seggen over een comt, soo dat ick hier van nyet seekerlycx en can verclaren, men soude wel een groote macht van Indianan by malcander krygen, dan 't selve bestaat in soo veel hooffden dat het niet wel practicabel en is, die van Achem, Queda ende Jacatra, doch ick en sie geen remedie om die alle hij malcander te brengen, om Malaca te gaan beleggen, 't soude beter wesen met roovinghe te benauwen, 't welcke de stadt opt laetste soude consumeren, ten ware die van Siam soo groten secours dede als men wel van hem is vertellende.

Die van Bantam is in syne brieven aen den koninck van Hollant versoeckende twee Jachten om twee maenden tot synen dienst te staen om de stadt Palumbam 't onder te brengen, ende by so verre alsmen vrede met hem houden will, men sall hem metten eersten moeten doen, ofte sullen altijt tott Bantam met hem over hoop leggen, ende 't mocht opt 't laatste aldaer met ons volck wel qualyck afloopen, indien de Heeren Staten ofte Compagnie syn begeeren metten eersten nyet en consenteeren.

Dit ist gene ick wel hebbe willen vermanen van de saecke van Java, Amboino, Banda, Molucas, Johor ende Chyna, wat nu belanght de custe van Choromandell en can ick nyet besien wat wapenen daer te gebruycken syn, want de Portugesen hebben daer geen regeringe dat te beduyden heeft, alleen in Negapatan, nyet besonders, ende my dunckt voor die cust, soude men, met rooveryen genoech connen onrustich maeken, alsoo der op ander plaetsen genoeck is te doen, de handelingh voor ons in Masilipatan ende Petapoly can ick niet toe bedencken om die vasticheyt /[170] te geven, want alsoo die gants hanght aan den wille van den Coningh van Goleconda, is daer nyet te doen als hem te vrunden te houden ende hem metten eersten een geschenck doen van wegen de Heeren Staten om hem in devotie te houden.

Den koninck van Arracam, die ons wel noodicht om syn haven te besoecken, wete syn gelegentheyt nyet, dan datt hy een machtich Coninck is, de gesteenten als robynen syn daer in abondantie.

Aengaende de custe van Malabar, daer syn nu twee vloten geweest; als den Admirael Steven van der Hagen ende Pauwels van Kaerden, dan soo veel ick vuyt van Kaerden montt conde verstaen ist met Calecutt alles geveynstheyt, hyer te lange te verhalen, doch als ick wel aenmercke eenighe bryeven, die ick mette veroverde schepen hebbe gekregen, soo schynt dat den Coninck van Cochyn nyet wel mette Portugesen staat ende wel mochte syn lange vruntshap in vyantschap verkeeren, het welcke die van Calecutt schynt waer te willen nemen om door de Portugesen in syn vorigen standt gestelt te werden, ofte nu de vruntschap van Cochyn mette Portugesen soude wel te turberen wesen en can ick nyet wel onderkennen, men soude ditt alles mettertyt wel leeren ende beter cundich werden op de kuste, daer wy tot noch toe geen van die princen aldaer haer humeuren weten ofte kennen sooveel ick can bevroeden, dan dit wil ick hier wel byvoegen dat, als onse vloten alhyer vuyt dese landen in Maert gingen, zouden op de custe van Malabar wel comen om de Portugese schepen te vernielen ende dan noch tyt genoech hebben om 'tsy verby Malaca ofte in de straet van Bantam te comen, vroech genoech om nae de Molucas ende Banda te gaen, ende /[171] mochten dan alle hostiliteyt aen de Portugese schepen gebruiken, ende ondertussen met reputatie alle de koningen van die kuste leeren kennen, ick en soude nyet prysen op die custe te comen ofte wel geresolveert wesen den vyant aen te tasten alsser yet cans ware ende daertoe op de schepen ende ladinghe van hier aff ordre te stellen, op dat wy contrary doende de Portugesen in geene meerder reputatie en brengen onder de koningen, hier is wel op te letten.

Ditt hebbe van den staat van Indie wel willen verhalen, dat hyer alles inne beslooten is.

Op behoorlijcke tijdt vuyt dese landen te vertrecken, op dat men op alle plaetsen in India op syn behoorlycke tyde mach comen, ende door de lanckheyt van de vuytreys het volck nyet vuyt en tere ende onbequaem totte wederreys maecken, want het en is nyet mogelyck soo langh op een schip te wesen ofte aen malcandere in see te houden als wy gedaen hebben sonder 't volck te consumeren, oock dat men de comp.ie op soo grooten maentgelden niet en brenge sonder vrucht te schaffen, want anders werden de luyden mismoedich, siende datter jaerlyck soo grooten hoop volck werdt geconsumeerdt, 't welck voor een man met eeren die de reys selff doet een groot verdriet is, principaal als hij hem inbeelt datter middel is om de reys corter te doen.

Dat men menichte van volck derwaert seynde om aldaer onse plaets te peupleeren, daer men middel genoech toe sal vinden, om aldaer buyten des compag.ie maentgelden de cost ryckelyck te geven ende doch ter noot evenwel tot des comp.ie dienst verbonden te blyven, want daer voor particuliere vaert genoech is met goede proffyten die voor de comp.ie nyet practicabel en is.

Dat men hem aldaer stelle om alle hantwercken te heb-/[172] ben totte seevaert dienstich, principael timmerluyden, smits ende andere opdat men metter tyt aldaer oock schepen, galeyen ende schuyten mach bouwen, want men het hout aldaer om nyet heeft.

Maer principael dat men meerder autoriteyt in India hebbe als tot noch toe is geschiet, ende datter alles watter is onder een regeringh stae, sonder de ambitie van admiraelen voortaen subiect te syn alser twee int lant souden mogen wesen.

Datter belooningh totte deucht ende vromicheyt werdt getoont ende oock straffe tot schande ende datter gants niet meer mach gehoort werden als men eenich exploict zal doen, "wy en syn daer niet op aengenomen", waer door, alsser maer een waenperyckel voor handen is, een eenich man, die een weynich autoriteyt heeft, een geheele resolutie van importantie can tegen houden.

Men soude voorts eenighe dingen breeder mogen stellen, dan om moeyelyckheyt te schouwen soude sulcx mondelingh connen geschieden alser pro aut contra werde by gebracht.

Men soude moeten de humeuren, conditien ende macht van alle coningen in Oost-India aensien ende elck na syn qualiteyt tracteren, want den eenen is ons dienstich met syn havenen ende landen, den anderen met syn waren, weder eenighe met hare macht ende auctoriteyt, 'twelck wy elck ons mosten toeeygenen nae dat wy souden connen ende raedsam vinden.

English Translation[173]

Report on our interests in the East Indies: what the current situation is and how it can be maintained in the future — with regard to the war against the Portuguese, Spanish and natives, as well as trade interests and how the most profit can be made.

Based on the charter issued by the High Mighty Gentlemen States General, the directors of the East India Company here in these United Netherlands have despatched various fleets to the East Indies on their behalf. These fleets comprised a large number of ships that were well provisioned with all the necessities; their mission was to pursue profitable trade and to fight the Portuguese enemy in such a way that the Company's trade would remain safe and secure in the future.

This has been so successful that the enemy, despite all his efforts to keep us away, has not made any progress but has suffered serious damage. And although until now we have not been able to drive out the enemy, this should be considered a consequence of the magnitude of our undertaking; for the enemy, having dominated that region for more than a hundred years, is too well settled there for us to dislodge him in the short term — all the more since we have to come from so far away and bring our forces at such great cost. Thus, it is my intention to explain here what means are at hand to counter the enemy in the most convenient manner and at the lowest possible cost, in such a way that he will have to deal with all the inconveniences of circumstances and time which we had to deal with until now.

First, one should know that we have three opponents or enemies in the Indies, viz. the Portuguese and the Spanish, who seek to harm us by armed violence; the English and the French and others who, while we and the King of Spain are fighting each other, conduct their business in peace and at little cost while letting us ward off the enemy at our expense as their protectors, and who then spoil the European market by importing their spices at a low cost without paying us convoy fees. Thirdly the Indians, who thanks to our protection feel liberated from the Portuguese and two kinds of merchants such as Dutchmen and Englishmen on their market,[174] look for the biggest profit without acknowledging that we are the ones who liberated them; no, they strive after the best price for their goods, as is the nature of such wild tribes. As long as this is not remedied, the expenses will fall to us and the benefits to them. Accordingly, we have disorder in our coffers, which is such that even if we succeeded in protecting ourselves by force of arms, our commerce could still come to chaos if we do not bring order to our trade and our coffers. I shall deal first with the subject of protection and then with trade.

First of all, we must choose a rendezvous or meeting place in the Indies, where all ships from these lands can easily call and take in fresh supplies.[175] All provisions, foodstuffs and ammunition of war should also be brought there and amassed gradually, for in the Indies it is impossible to obtain these quickly. This has not been attempted at all thus far, although it is what we need most in the East Indies. All goods from all regions could also be brought and kept safely there, for inland navigation with large ships involves a lot of expenses and inconvenience. One ought to use the large ships mostly against the enemy and have them closest at hand to help all those who might be in distress in the East Indies. The city of Banten, albeit well-situated, is not only very unwholesome, but also has a very young king — fourteen or fifteen years old — who is impossible to negotiate with; moreover, his council is so divided by factionalism that one cannot accomplish anything. The city of Melaka, apart from the difficulty we would have to take it, is rather ill-situated: it is difficult to reach regardless of the season, especially if one has large and heavy ships which are filthy and have damaged sails from the long voyage.

We need a place where we can call coming from the Cape of Good Hope without being subjected to the monsoon. The first location along the route, Aceh, is not suitable either, since it has no good port and all destinations cannot be reached as easily from there as from the Sunda Strait.[176] Therefore, I would choose one out of two places: either the city of Jayakerta (Jacatra) (or the freshwater river there, three or four miles west in the direction of Banten), or the city of Palembang on Sumatra. Then again, Palembang is equally hard to reach when the monsoon approaches and one sails into the Sunda Strait from the outside. This has recently become evident, in January 1608, as Paul van Caerden tried to reach Banten from Johor, but was unable to sail very far.[177] My best advice would therefore be that we negotiate with the King of Jayakerta (Jacatra), so that we can build a fortress either in his city or at the aforementioned freshwater river; the Sunda Strait can be sailed in every season, either to Banten or to Jayakerta (Jacatra), if one has rounded the Cape of Good Hope and one does not have to endure the monsoon.

But then we can expect some inconveniences here from the people of Banten, for as soon as they learn that we want to establish our residence at Jayakerta (Jacatra), they may well make common cause with the Portuguese and become our and Jayakerta (Jacatra)'s enemies. We therefore have to proceed with caution here, so that we do not make the barbarians any wiser until they cannot do harm any more. For insofar as I have noticed in my dealings with them, they would not consider it bad if we set up our quarters at Jayakerta (Jacatra), if we visit them with some pieces of cloth from time to time and buy some of their pepper. In any case, we would have to keep our quarters and factory at Banten at first, so that we do not estrange them in any way, and negotiate with Jayakerta (Jacatra) in the meantime.

First, an able commander ought to be sent there, who would take good care of the country's and the Company's interests, to take everything into account carefully with his council, to decide which place would be the best situated for us, either the freshwater river or the city of Jayakerta (Jacatra), for it is difficult to give a clear description. One ought to know the king's inclinations as well. The best harbour for the ships is at the mouth of the river, but to construct a whole city also has its difficulties and we cannot populate the entire city with our people, the locals have to help us. There are problems on both sides: at the freshwater river, where there are no houses, we would have more freedom, but the grounds are completely uncultivated there and a lot of work would have to be done. I do not know if the vicinity of the islands — which makes it a good harbour — would not give the Portuguese occasion to occupy one of them by building a stronghold. In my opinion it would be possible to fire upon the harbour from these islands (from the closest one, that is), but that is not certain. Then again, to my knowledge there is no fresh water on these islands, which would be a disadvantage to the enemy. There are no islands before the city of Jayakerta (Jacatra); we would have to build two breakwaters to facilitate entering and leaving the harbour with boats and crews and ships with a draught of 12 or 13 feet. But all this can be understood better by sight than from paper.

We should forge a secure contract with this king, for he should profit from such a contract as much as we will, and without profit it should not be submitted to him. This would be best done in his presence, and then one thing given more weight and another less, depending on how one would find the king to be inclined. In my opinion such a contract would be necessary, rather similar to the one the Portuguese have with Cochin. If we choose Jayakerta (Jacatra), they should give us a suitable location, be it big or small, close to Jayakerta (Jacatra)'s river, where we could build our fortified quarters to protect ourselves from Portuguese attacks. For we cannot flee inland if Portuguese come and take our belongings with us as the blacks do, as our goods are more cumbersome. Therefore we have to be strong, placing our trust not in flight but in defence.

This location should be large enough that all the Dutch we could bring to the Indies over time could easily live there. There should be as much land, both inland and around the city, as they could cultivate or use as pasture. Those who wish to be under Dutch rule should be allowed this, but this point needs to be negotiated with discretion. All goods brought there should not be taxed over four per cent, or at most five, and taxes should be paid to the States General on everything brought there by the Dutch or on their account, including those who are under the States' authority. All the Indians, Chinese and foreigners, on the other hand, should pay their taxes to the king — the decision in this matter would be best optimised on the spot. The king should bear the cost for one side of the breakwaters and the Dutch for the other.

No Europeans should be allowed to enter the king's city except vassals of the States General; judgement of this matter should be left to the residing commander. But if the city were to be built at the freshwater river (this would all depend on the king's inclinations), it should be stipulated that he send some of his people to live around us; for populating a place just by ourselves, even with his consent, has its problems because the

Portuguese are so hot on our heels there. But if one does not want to see this, one could obtain a better contract for a location at the freshwater river than at Jayakerta (Jacatra), but it would be necessary to secure the permanent devotion of the Bantenese. And once they would begin to see that Jayakerta (Jacatra) harmed their interests, it would be too late for the Bantenese — they would already have lost a large part of their trade and population and be unable to inflict any significant harm. There are some more provisions to be made which time will tell.

In order to populate the place, one would have to send as many people as possible from these regions [the Republic], people who would always be at the fatherland's service and take the place of soldiers. For [hiring more soldiers] is not feasible for the Company because of the high cost of the monthly wages it has to pay them; instead, one should provide the people who would go and live there with means to make some money. That should be realized easily enough there, and there is enough that the Company cannot take on; the kind of things, I mean, which are impracticable for the Company but for private individuals can be quite profitable by their own diligence. If someone is in the Company's service, let him be content with his monthly pay without thinking further; for it is man's nature that if someone wants to think further, he will do it for himself and not for strangers. One should pay attention to the example set by the Portuguese, who in all their conquests have exiled people and then persuaded them with bonuses. It should be possible to arrange this well for the time being, because there is no lack of loafers in this country and one could well send them there, as the gentlemen can easily understand.

After occupying our main location, we should also sail to Ambon, Banda, the Malukus, Borneo, China, Japan, the whole island of Sumatra, Johor, Patani, Kedah, Tenasserim, Bengal, Siam, the Coromandel Coast, Arakan and also Cambay, together with their dependencies.

But before we say more about the Indies, we have to begin with Europe. Our fleets should depart from here in March, the earlier the better. Although Texel is not well suited for this purpose, since the directors of the Amsterdam chamber of the VOC cannot despatch their ships on the first or at the latest mid-March, they need to find a solution to accomplish this. For if one sets sail from these lands at a later date, one faces contrary winds and currents everywhere. Several fleets have experienced this when they had to wait for a fair wind in the bay of São Tomé for so long that they could not round the Cape until November or December, which in turn results in an unfavourable time to sail to some destinations in the

Indies. In some cases, this will make for a delay of one year, in some cases of six months. Therefore, the gentlemen[178] would be well advised to pay close attention to this point. For the problems caused by leaving this country at such a late date are plain to see if one only thinks of the fact that the enemy settles everywhere before we do, while we wear out our people with the long voyage.

Apart from the costs which are so high, we are unable to bring fresh people with a good morale to the Indies — we come with disheartened men against an enemy who is six months ahead of us, no matter where we come. For the two months we start later than we ought to from this country, make for a year's difference in the journey. And experience has taught us what difference it makes to come home a year earlier or later: many men who come ashore here [in the Republic] fade away and wither, due to the length of the voyage and the very old food they have eaten. This is a matter that should be remedied with priority, for it is a sad thing to see the ships coming home so miserably with a thousand difficulties. I think the most important cause is the fact that the men are aboard for so long and eat bread and meat which are four years old, nor does drinking *arak* do them any good. One ought to provide them with everything afresh in the Indies; and we have the means to do that, if we had a secure location where we would gradually gather all the necessary victuals.

Once we have a stronghold there, it is necessary first of all to keep a commander there as discussed above, assisted by his council and provided with orders to appoint a substitute when he himself is absent. He should be invested with sufficient authority to be able to bring everything about without having dissenters there, for they are too far from home to settle their differences. This commander should have his residence there in order to provide in all matters as necessity would dictate; for the gentlemen will be aware that the absence of an authority in the Indies is a great shame on our cause. The disorder such an authority would prevent, would compensate the costs ten times, for at present everyone does as he pleases and nobody is subject to punishment or correction. In this way, chaos will arise in the course of time, both in war and in commerce. The authority of the admirals who are in the Indies is insufficient because they have no fixed residence, they have to travel to various places and cannot see to everything: before they have an understanding of the matter, they have to leave again, even if they wanted to take care of the matter as best they could. Because a new admiral is always expected, one admiral leaves things to the next, as they are always occupied enough with their travels.

Many Indians openly state that the Dutch are good people who give them more for their goods than the Portuguese do and treat them better as well, but they compare us to a bird which alights on a tree, sates itself and flies away, leaving the rest at the mercy of those who come after it: the Portuguese, who find the poor locals without the protection of the Dutch, treat them cruelly and ruin them. For this reason, the Indians prefer suffering some poverty with the Portuguese over a little luxury with the Dutch which is then ruined by the Portuguese. Therefore, we should not call on places without securing them well against the enemy; there are a lot of places which can practically be greased with their own fat, as they say.

Ambon

First, one ought to see to it that Ambon is fortified. I have strongly encouraged Governor Frederik de Houtman[179] to do this, for we should link Ambon and Banda in such a way that they may help one another. And the better to bring the people of Banda under the States' authority, this should be done so craftily that none of the neighbouring kings become jealous, for the isle of Banda is worth as much gold as it is large. Its form of government is a republic; they are a bunch of villainous, haughty, malevolent poor beggars who are always in arrears, no matter what their income. They rely on the fact that everyone needs them and they can never spare a friendly word. Nor do they have the means to protect themselves, but the dissension among the neighbouring kings lends them strength. There have been, and still are, a lot of interested parties; Ternate in its time, Tuban, Makassar and Forbay; the Portuguese in the time of André Furtado [de Mendonça] (who drove away the people of Hitu) intended to subdue Banda,[180] but they were prevented by the circumstances. As a result, I have been informed that the King of Tuban has said that Banda must be subdued, and if the Portuguese or the Dutch did not do it, he would see to it himself. For this reason, we should consult one of the aforementioned kings and let him win the island with our help.

After considering which kings would be most useful to us, I could think of none but the King of Makassar, the reason being that this king was converted to the Muhammadan religion[181] a little more than five or six years ago. There is more hope of making him a Christian than those who were raised Muhammadan. Furthermore, many of his subjects are still pagan, his land is the most fertile in that region when it comes to foodstuffs (which Banda largely lacks), and his country's position is such that were he to become the enemy of the Portuguese, I do not know where they would henceforth go to take in fresh supplies in order to sail from Melaka to the Malukus and give support there. They could sail from the Philippines only, which alone would be difficult, and they would have to do it at Tuban or Gresik. All of this could be remedied in time. But the matter would have to be arranged so secretly that neither Portuguese, English, French nor Indians would hear of it before it was done. For what they would hasten to effect if they saw that our interests were prospering so greatly there would mean a serious set-back to our cause, both in its authority and in its effectivity.

One could make a treaty with these or similar provisions with the king; I do not doubt that he would be quite willing. I have sent someone to gradually sound him out, but I have no answer yet, for I have given this assignment to Abraham Mathysz., who aboard the *Groote Sonne*[182] set sail for Makassar from Banten at the end of 1607.[183] He was to tell the king that we would deliver the island of Banda into his hands, on the condition that the entire conquest would be in his name and that he would prepare no more than 700 or 800 men. We would help him with 400 to 600 Dutch and 800 Ambonese; in my opinion, this number of troops would be sufficient and would oblige him to us all the more, since he did not have to contribute anything to the conquest. The spoils would have to be divided with discretion; for although possessing the whole island should be enough for the people of Makassar, all the blacks[184] are such that they prefer one present boon to ten future ones.

[Further conditions would be] that he could do with all the inhabitants as he pleased, and that the States General would not make a profit or levy tolls on that, but would let him keep everything so that he might remain their friend; and that he could freely enjoy all the island's produce. In return, he would be the King of Holland's (for that is the title the States General are given there) friend as well as his friends' friend and the enemy of his enemies, and they would help each other with all their might against the Portuguese, both in the offensive and the defensive, and one would not make peace without the other.

That he would move all the noblemen and people of influence to one place on the island, to be chosen by the King of Holland, and make them live there, in order to reinforce it against incursions by the Portuguese and others.

That a fort should be built in that place, where the Dutch would have their factory and collect all their wares to protect them from fire and attacks by enemies.

That the king would keep a company of Dutch soldiers, sworn to him and the King of Holland, to defend the land, and paid from the income of the land.

That no foreign nation would come and conduct trade on the island, except the Dutch and people from Makassar.

That all foodstuffs and textiles should be brought to Ambon and from there to Banda, by citizens of Ambon and Banda.

That no goods be exported from Banda but to Holland or Ambon.

Some more provisions could be made which will become clear in due course — depending also on how the king would seem to be inclined — concerning the import of sago[185] from Seram, Ambon and other things.

We would also have to see at what price we would buy nutmeg[186] and mace from him. One should create a ferry, so to speak, between Ambon and Banda, so that a thousand Dutch or whites could live very well there with their families and slaves. In order to achieve this, one should price the nutmeg and mace a little higher on Ambon than on Banda and let nobody export them but white inhabitants of Banda and Ambon, which would yield a certain tax every year. We would also give the people of Makassar hope of subduing the whole of Celebes, which I think would protect Ambon and Banda if we keep good order. One should not forget to make seventy or eighty members of the highest nobility of Banda leave the island, which would stop all mutiny. This should just be done rather than discussed.

Regarding Ambon: after the fortress had been reinforced, I would conceive of a kind of city around it, where all the most important inhabitants should be made to live. But since this would be somewhat of an effort, one should come as close as possible — at least their children, or some of those, should live there. And when the time comes to harvest the cloves, we would act according to circumstances.

As for the Christians, they would be readily persuaded, although those from Hitu would take some inducing to bring them there, but they would agree in time if they were given to understand that we could hardly defend them otherwise. If we could arrange this, and if the whites live there fending for themselves and making a living with the sword and otherwise, then we need to spend money on soldiers, for we would have a multitude of people in the city. If the order was well kept, the enemy would have to come with a mighty force to overpower them. For at present there are no less than ten thousand men of eighteen years or more, under the States' command; most of them Muhammadans and pagans and about a third Christian. Given time, they will side with us, if only they were assured that we are serious about protecting them; for as long as we do not commit ourselves more earnestly, people will always look back. Thus, without bringing all the people to the fortress, we would control all trade there, for near the fortress is a good, large harbour where many ships can moor.

The island is rich in sago, while rice and beans are often sown as well. Fish catches are reasonable and there are about 60 cows which have remained from the time of the Portuguese and belong to the governor, and again as many who have fled into the wild, a herd that will multiply in time. There are many wild pigs, too. One could also use the ships which arrive early enough to call at Gresik and take in as many cows as they could and goats as well, and bring them to Ambon. It is rich enough in pasture and could well be provided with food in this way.

Concerning the large island of Seram, which mostly was, and partly still is, in Ternate's power: in due course it would fall to the States General, or to Ternate, so that it would benefit us anyway. I shall not speak of it now, since the matter is not urgent.

Now to the Malukus, which would be a little more difficult to conquer, but in my opinion it is not impossible. When I arrived at Ternate in May 1607, I found that all its inhabitants had fled, most of them to the island of Jilolo.[187] They had made a fortress there. The Spaniard had made the old city of Ternate a bit smaller and had fortified it; five companies were stationed there, let us say of 70 men each, and the rest of the island was depopulated. I would have liked to have attempted an attack on the city, but had no means: I was unable to disembark more than 240 men from my fleet, and gathering the Ternatans was going to take a long time. I was unwilling to wait for that, because it was high time for me to leave for China. Therefore I made a fort at the north end of the island, where there used to be a village called Malaya.[188] I left some artillery with fifty men and three ships with a cutter to protect them; in all, I left a good two hundred of my men behind, while the Ternatans were gradually coming over from Jilolo in order to live under the fort's protection. In time they will all come over. It is impossible to gather the blacks quickly, for apart from the fact that they are slow by nature, the islands and places from which they have to come are so far apart that everything needs time.

The King of Ternate used to have great authority because he commanded many islands and peoples, while he was very weak on his own island, so that he went down because there was no order. For the blacks are careless by nature, and we made him more careless by winning Tidor.

The situation is as follows. There are five Maluku isles which belong to Ternate; the enemy has a fortress at the south end, and we have one at the north end.[189] Not a single Ternatan is loyal to the enemy, while we have two or three hundred on the island. All the clove trees are on our side, so that in my opinion the enemy cannot obtain any cloves. The people of Tidor are occupied with their own business.

The enemy holds all of Tidor,[190] where the king lives. Bacan used to be in Ternate's power, but is now entirely in Tidor's.[191] Its authorities, however, sent two of their people to my ships at night, who told me that they wanted to rebel against the Spanish (for there were no more than 30 or 40 Spaniards on the island), inasfar as I wanted to protect them, and that they were all willing to die for their king. I answered them, thanking them warmly, that it was not yet time to reveal themselves; for I did not want to deceive them and was unable to protect them at that moment, since by doing battle with the Portuguese I had also lost some men. I told them that I had not come from Holland equipped to do that much, but that they should keep ready to attack the Spanish together with the first fleet that would arrive from Holland. That I advised them not to let themselves be slaughtered, but that I had come only to make a fortress on Ternate, so that the Ternatan fugitives could be supported until the next fleet [arrives]. They thanked me and promised to keep themselves ready as soon as another fleet came; and after I had given them some gifts, they went back to their people, protesting all the time that they would reveal themselves immediately when they saw that Ternatan nobility was gaining a foothold. All this took place in the presence of Ternatans who understood what was being said and concurred.

The isle of Pulau Kabali has a low clove yield and is uninhabited, like Garbonilhe; the people of Motir (which does yield beautiful cloves), who were also under Ternate's authority, have left it and live with the Ternatans, so that Motir is lying fallow as well. We cannot make plans to win back these islands' friendship and loyalty before we know what Admiral van Caerden will have accomplished. I have conferred with him on everything, given him my advice and informed him on all matters. I hope the Lord God will bless him, for he has the means to accomplish some good things there: he still has 850 healthy men on his fleet and 200 from my fleet on land. The *Groote Sonne* and the *Gelderland* will also have arrived there with around 200 men, so that he can bring ashore almost 900, apart from the Ternatans who will have settled near the fort in the meantime. It all depends on whether he arrives at Ternate before the people from the Philippines; if he does, there is no doubt that he will take it. We have made haste to achieve this, not to explore any place but only to do his best to reach the Malukus by way of Celebes;[192] for if he took a course over Ambon, which is the ordinary route, he would not arrive at Ternate before the beginning of May 1608, while those from the Philippines will already be there in the beginning of April. He has left port from Banten for Ternate on 10 January. He lacks a galley to serve during calms,[193] which often occur there, while the enemy has two, one reasonably big and the other a bit smaller. Then again, I would guess that the number of Spanish on Ternate will have dwindled, since many were taken ill, and there is no food in those regions unless it is imported, although it is a very suitable land to keep cattle, both big and small. To conclude: we cannot discuss Ternate nor the Malukus until we have heard how things have gone there for Admiral van Caerden.[194]

Regarding Makian, which lies a long distance from there, 60 miles if memory serves, where the others can all see each other: although the king was no friend of the King of Ternate, he was not pleased that the latter was brought to the Philippines and he has no cloves to speak of. There is another matter: regardless whether Admiral van Caerden accomplishes something or not in Ternate, we should bring together all Ternate's subjects and form them into an armada. Even if we could not attack the Ternatan fort, we would annihilate the forces of Tidor. This should be done gradually: calling up the Sula islands, which can muster no less than 22 kora-koras, each with 70 or 80 men, as well as Mindanao, which is much more powerful; and once Tidor has been brought down, by making an expedition to Manila, something the people of Mindanao are well capable of. But none of this would be feasible without the presence of Dutch ships and authority, for otherwise it would be all blacks' work; and what I have said of the strength of their troops I know only from hearsay by the Ternatans.

I definitely do not think that any agreement could be reached with the King of Tidor. It appears that all Muhammadans are irreconcilable to anyone who once has become their enemy; therefore he will never be reconciled to the Ternatans, one or the other has to be destroyed. They keep word to one another only as long as it suits them and much less to Christians. This is why, whenever one concludes a treaty in the Indies, one should straightaway build a fort to go with it and then be careful not to give them occasion for malevolence. Then one will be good friends with them, as long as they fear and love you, for in my opinion love alone is not enough. One should pay attention to the fact that the King of Ternate's authority used to be very great, so that if we had supported him with our diligence and counsel, we would have much fortified his position, even to such a degree that the Spanish would not have arrived. Not only would this not have cost us anything, but it would most likely have benefited us. But that is over now, and it seems that all things are better punished. However, we should now try to do things that way as much as possible. Writing down all the particulars here would take too long.

Now let us go back to Johor and see that we keep the Portuguese busy there (so that they will lose their appetite for thinking about the Malukus and Banda), while we quarrel with them over the Chinese, Coromandel and Bengal trade, bringing Cambay into it as well. We should first of all seek to fortify the city of Johor;[195] I have attempted that earlier,[196] but after I had left for the Malukus everything has declined. And because he [the King of Johor] had not strengthened his city, the Portuguese have come, and out of fear he has left his city and fled inland, setting fire to his city himself.[197] But the Portuguese never came upstream far enough to reach the city. Meanwhile, he has made a peace treaty with the Portuguese (I have seen the treaty) which one should not take seriously, for as soon as I had sent the *Erasmus* to Johor, he no longer cared for it.[198]

Therefore we ought to try fortifying the city first; this would not work without using some harsh words, or else in such a way as would be best put into practice, not discussed in writing. The young king, Raja Seberang,[199] would be favourably inclined to this; the old one is more capable of drinking than of ruling.[200] It would cost us four or five thousand reales,[201] but if we made the investment we could collect it in due course; or if that went badly, we would still set the enemy back with it to such a degree that it would be of much greater importance to us. We should see if the situation is still as it was when I was there. Keeping a big garrison there would bring high costs with it; but after fortifying the city, the Malays would be somewhat reassured. Once the city had been reconstructed, we could reassure the Malays with fifty or sixty white soldiers, so that they would stay together and be all right; unless there came an army larger than I imagine can be called up from the Indies.

One ought to keep two or three ships or cutters around Melaka, which would harass navigation from Melaka with help from the Malays, who would well serve this purpose with their prahus and galleys.[202] They would also encourage the King of Johor to keep ships in sight around his city at all times.

One should not think that this is not feasible for the East Indian Company, being only cost without profit. I do not doubt that we could find private individuals who, if we instruct them well, for the sake of prize and booty would let themselves be used for this. They should guard Melaka both to the north and to the south, which would hinder the city greatly. Because it has no food other than that which is imported, Melaka would find this hard to deal with, especially if we were a little rough with those who bring the city food. Those importing food from the south are mostly Javanese, but the Portuguese bring it from the north, both from Bengal and from Coromandel. These privateers should take care at which times they would have to guard Melaka in the south and at which times in the north.

In good time they could also go near Ceylon in February, to see what they could get from the goods which are brought to Cochin and Goa from Bengal and Nagapattinam. If this is done with good discipline, I do not doubt that it would yield good spoils, for which the armourers would be grateful to them. And since this could not happen without the Portuguese instantly arming themselves against it, we should keep these cutters and ships clean and ready to sail, for which there are ample means available. For the rest, one should act according to circumstances and if we have a good fleet at our disposal, visit the harbour of Melaka and destroy the ships moored there. Most of all, we should see to it that we are ready by the time that the ships from China come to Melaka, to attack them — for that is what damages the Portuguese the most, both the private and the royal tolls, since these are the richest ships and are incomparable to the spices.

In China, the situation at Macao is as follows: after the loss of some ships that had been taken, and those which I had burnt when I arrived before Melaka, and which had been destined for Macao, the situation of the people at Macao was such that if the ships I found in China had not arrived there with a large sum of money to take aboard two years' cargo, they could hardly keep things going any longer. For as soon as the Chinese are not aware of any profit from the Portuguese, they start looking askance at them — this had even gone so far that the mandarin of Guangzhou had already prohibited transporting foodstuffs to Macao — so that I definitely imagine that if I had not been forced to take my fleet to the Malukus and had attempted to damage only Melaka, so that no ships could have gone to Macao this year, the city of Macao would have disintegrated and its inhabitants gone elsewhere.

There has been an initiative to make friends in China through the King of Siam's intervention, but as no envoys were sent to China from Siam that year, this has remained undone.[203] I do not think it is necessary either, for I have no doubts about Chinese trade, based on the impressions I got in China. And if the Chinese were unwilling, we would have ways to seize such ships from the Chinese between China and the Philippines, as would be worth quite some money every year; for 24 to 30 ships annually sail from Zhangzhou[204] to the Philippines with all sorts of costly goods, part of them at the risk of the Spanish, but most of them at the Chinese.[205]

In order to ruin Melaka we could also use the King of Siam, who would bring a lot of men ashore before Melaka and who moreover is quite favourably inclined towards us and likes to hear that we prosper. But all this is just hearsay — Cornelis Specx, who was stationed there for a while,[206] has told me so, and the present ambassadors' reports concur[207] — so that I cannot state anything for certain in the matter. We could gather a large army of Indians, but it would consist of so many men that it becomes impracticable; the people of Aceh, Kedah and Jayakerta (Jacatra), but I see no means to bring them all together to besiege Melaka. It would be better to drive the city into a corner by robbery, which in the end would consume it; unless the King of Siam came to our help with such forces as is said of him.

The King of Banten in his letters to the King of Holland is requesting two cutters to be at his disposal for two months in order to subdue the city of Palembang. Inasfar as we want to keep the peace with him, we will have to do this for him as soon as possible, or we will always quarrel with him at Banten, and things could go badly for our people there in the end, if the States General or the Company do not fulfil his wish as soon as possible.

This is what I wanted to advise concerning Java, Ambon, Banda, the Malukus, Johor and China. Now as regards the coast of Coromandel, I cannot judge what weapons should be used there, for the Portuguese have no administration to speak of there, only at Nagapattinam, nothing special, and in my opinion one could create enough trouble for that coast by robberies, since there is enough to do in other places. As to our trade in Masulipatnam and Nizampatnam:[208] I cannot think of anything to secure it, because it depends completely on the wishes of the King of Golconda. We can only make sure that he remains our friend and send him a gift from the States General as soon as possible, to keep him on our side.

The King of Arakan does invite us to visit his port, but I do not know his situation except that he is a powerful king; precious stones such as rubies abound there.

As to the coast of Malabar, two fleets have been there now, that of Admiral Steven van der Hagen and that of Paul van Caerden.[209] From what I was told by van Caerden, with Calicut it is all pretence. The story is too long to tell here, but I note that from a few letters which came into my hands with the ships that were taken,[210] it appears that the King of Cochin is not on good terms with the Portuguese and their long-standing friendship might turn to enmity. The King of Calicut apparently wants to grasp the opportunity to have the Portuguese restore him to his former position. I cannot judge well if Cochin's friendship for the Portuguese would be disturbed easily; one would learn all this in time and gather information on the coast itself, because so far we know the inclinations of none of the princes there, as far as I know.

Then I would like to add that if our fleets were to sail from here in March, they would reach the coast of Malabar to destroy the Portuguese ships and still have time enough to go either past Melaka or to the Sunda Strait, early enough to go to the Malukus and Banda. Then they could treat the Portuguese ships with all kinds of hostility and meanwhile, after earning themselves a reputation, gather information about all the kings of that coast. I would not advise going to the Malabar Coast unless one were resolved to damage the enemy if any opportunity presented itself; one should keep that goal in mind when equipping the ships and cargo here, so that we do not enhance the Portuguese reputation among the kings if we act otherwise. Close attention should be paid to this.

This is what I wanted to say about the situation in the Indies. To give a summary:

Leaving from this country at the right time, in order to arrive at all the destinations in the East Indies at their right times, and to prevent our people from wasting away by the length of the voyage out, so that they become unfit for the journey home. For it is impossible to keep them on a ship or at sea for such a long and uninterrupted time as we have done, without using up our people, and we should not burden the Company with such high monthly pays if they bear no fruit. For otherwise, the people will lose heart when they see that such a great number of people is used up every year — which for a man who makes the voyage himself is a great sorrow, especially if he imagines that there is a way to shorten the journey.

We should send a lot of people there in order to populate our place. One will find sufficient means to provide them with a generous livelihood outside of the Company's monthly wages, while they nonetheless remain bound to the Company's service in emergencies, for there is enough trade there that is impracticable for the Company, but will yield private trade good profits.

We should also move them there in order to have all the crafts at our disposal which are of use in navigation at sea, especially carpenters, blacksmiths and others. In that way, we could build ships, galleys and boats over there in the course of time, for timber is free there.[211]

But most of all, we should have more authority in the Indies than we have had thus far; everything there is, should be under a government without being subject to the admirals' ambitions anymore, should there be two admirals in the country.

Virtue and devotion should be shown to be rewarded and shameful behaviour punished. When preparing for an exploit, one should never at all hear again: "We were not hired for this." With that, a single man with a little authority can impede an entire resolution of importance, if some imaginary danger is at hand.

Some things could be discussed more at large, but in order to prevent difficulties this could be done orally, with a discussion of the pros and cons.

We should assess the inclinations, conditions and power of all the kings in the East Indies and treat each one according to his quality. For one is of use to us with his harbours and lands, the other with his goods, some others again with their power and authority, each of which we should appropriate as we can and find expedient.

Appendix 16

Description of Raja Bongsu of Johor by Johann Verken, 1609.[212]

[Johann Verken, a native of Meissen in Saxony, was a member of Admiral Verhoeff's crew who visited the region around the Singapore Straits, the Johor River estuary and the upstream towns of Batu Sawar and Pasir Raja, the latter which was still under construction at the time. The larger ships belonging to Verhoeff's fleet remained anchored around Johor Lama, while smaller craft brought the admiral and some of his officers to the capital Batu Sawar for discussions with King 'Ala'uddin and Raja Bongsu. Verken was a member of the crew that remained on the ships at Johor Lama. His diary or log was first published in German as part of de Bry's illustrated travel series where it is printed in full within the German language *Neundter Theil der Orientalischen Indien* or liberally translated "Ninth Voyage [of the Dutch] to the East Indies", published in Frankfurt am Main in 1612. It is among the oldest travel accounts generated from among German-born servants of the VOC and is widely acknowledged as an important eyewitness report recounting Verhoeff's voyage to the East Indies as well as the Admiral's assassination on the Bandas.]

Original German Text

Was aber den regierenden König von Goer, genannt Ratispontus, belanget, derselbe is noch ein junger Herr, ungefehr etlich unnd driessig Jahr alt. Als er an die Schiff kam, hatte er ein weiss Baumwollen Hembd an, so jm biss auff die Knie reichet, unnd umb den Leib hatte er ein schön farbig gestreiffet Baumwollen Tuch gewickelt, welches jhm dann biss halb auf die Füsse reichet, sonst war er am Leibe und Beinen gantz bloss, aber an seinen Füssen hatte er ein schwartz par sammete Pantoffeln an, umb seinen Kopff hatte er ein schwartzen seydenen Schleyer gewickelt, an seinem Halse hatte er drey güldene Ketten hangen, welche voller Edelgesteine versetztet waren, um seinen lincken Arm hatte er zween dicke güldene Ringe, und umb den rechten Arm einen. Noch hatte er sechs sehr köstliche Ringe an den Fingern stecken, dessgleichen hatte er einen Dolchen an seiner Seyten stecken, auff ein fast seltzame Art gemacht, welche sie den Cris nennen, dessen Häfft sampt der Scheyden war von klarem geschlagenen Golt gemacht, mit vielen Diamanten und Rubinen und Saphieren versetzet, also daß derselbe Dolch von den

Holländern, auff die etlich und funfftzig tausend Gülden geschetzt worden. An Gestalt und Farben war er ein fast wol geproportionierte Person, einer ziemlichen Länge, und sitsamer Rede, fast gantz weisslecht am Leib und Angesicht …

English Translation[213]

As for the King of Johor, however, who is also known as Raja Bongsu, he is still a young man in his 30s. When he came aboard our ship, he was wearing a white cotton shirt that reached down to knee level. Around his body he wore a beautifully coloured, striped cotton cloth, which reached halfway down to his feet. Otherwise, he was bare on his body and legs. But he wore on his feet a pair of black velvet slippers and around his head he had wrapped a black head piece of silk. Around his neck he wore three golden chains, which were completely inlaid with gem stones. Around his left arm he wore two thick golden rings and around his right arm [another] one. On his fingers he wore six precious rings. He also had a dagger at his side which was made in a very extraordinary manner and which they [the Malays] call a "kris". The handle and the blade were made of pure, clear wrought gold and were studded with diamonds, rubies and sapphires in such a way that the same dagger was estimated by the Dutch to have a value of more than 50,000 guilders. [Raja Bongsu] was in his appearance and body a well-proportioned person, rather tall, articulate and fair-skinned both on his body and on his face.

Appendix 17

Opening address of Hugo Grotius held before King James I/VI at the Maritime and Colonial Conference in London on 6 April 1613.[214]

[At the opening of the Anglo-Dutch maritime and colonial conferences in London in April 1613, Grotius held an address in Latin before King James I/VI as well as the members of the English and Dutch delegations. According to the permanent Dutch envoy to the court in London, Noël Caron, the opening address was attentively followed by the king, but "lasted a bit too long". Translated into English for the first time, Grotius' address provides a summary of the state of Anglo-Dutch relations in the East Indies.]

Latin Text Transcribed by Clark and Eysinga[215]

Serenissime Princeps.

Post foelicissimi matrimonii solemnia, qua S.T.M. non Britannas tantum germanasque,[216] sed omnes nationes, quae divini cultus normam a Deo, non ab hominibus petunt, aeterno inter se foedere devinxit, auspicatissimo tempore venimus supplices novasque et longinquas afferimus [preces],[217] quae M.T. et sapientiam et bonitatem sollicitant. Maior est et haec et illa quam ut uni se hemisphaerio includi patiatur: coelestis est utraque; coelum suum ut imitetur ab uno mundi cardine ad alterum se debet extendere.

Nec tenuis est precum nostrarum fiducia. Scimus enim nos {unde}[218] quo veniamus, scit M.T. unde veniamus. Ordinum Foederatorum iussu adsumus, a Societate Indicana, quae est in Batavis, missi, eius reipublicae cives, quam T.M. multos inter socios atque amicos praecipuam extare voluit clementiae suae materiam. Hic est ille generosus ardor vere regiarum mentium, constanter diligunt quos diligere coeperunt, nec ob aliud magis quam quia coeperunt, et nobilissimam benefaciendi causam habent benefecisse. Primum igitur hoc spei nostrae praesidium est quod regem accedimus qui non minus bene nobis vult quam nosmet ipsi, et eam a Deo accepit potestatem ut quae vult, effecta posset reddere. Accedit quod nec diuturna (ut debent) esse possint T.M. beneficia, nisi novo hoc beneficio muniantur.

Nostra enim patria (et quis melius haec scit quam T.M.) arctissimis inclusa finibus immensam hominum vim coercet. Nec tamen aut metalla promittit aut in vitem terra nostra luxuriat; ne segetum quidem aut lanitii apud nos copia est. Negavit nobis quae aliis tribuit Natura, et ne tamen nos exhaeredaret communis omnium parens, in vicem tot dotium, quas caeteris liberaliter indulsit, concessit nobis maria et ventos et mercandi periculosam et difficilem industriam. Haec apud alios ne praecipua quidem, apud nos sola sunt queis tantam multitudinem sustentamus, per quae nec hostibus ludibrio nec amicis inutiles sumus; itaque et veteres omnes et recentes nostrae gentis rectores his in rebus summam semper rempublicam posuerunt.

Orto inter nos Hispanosque bello, per nos non stetit quominus consisterent arma ubi coeperant neque de Belgio extra Belgium quaereretur. Sed aliter illis visum, qui per Cantabriae, Castellae et Lusitaniae portus pro hostibus comprehenderunt quos ut mercatores admiserant; homines, non innocentes minus quam inermes, spoliati, addicti remis aut exquisitissimis suppliciis trucidati; nec semel id ab Hispanis, sed saepius factitatum, interposita dissimulatione, quo lucrosius fallerent. /[219] Ita domi multorum res afflictae. Hoc tempore nostrorum non paucos optima magistra Necessitas adegit indociles carere commerciis, propinquis exclusos, longinqua quaerere. Fuere inter caeteros, anni iam sunt prope viginti, qui contractis societatibus diversis, et magno pretio petitis ab ipsa Lusitania itineris monstratoribus, ea loca adiere, quae a Bonae Spei Promontorio in solem orientalem patent.

Sed iidem homines, qui ex Belgio in Hispaniam hostilia facta traduxerant, ex Europa quoque in Asiam ultimam bellum transtulerunt. Nam Lusitani calumniis, dolis, vi aperta obstitere quominus liberi cum liberis, volentes cum volentibus negotiaremur; nec eo nomine nostros dumtaxat oppugnabant, sed Indos quoque, nec imperiis ipsorum obnoxios, nec ullis legibus ipsis adstrictos, quod nostros mercatu iuvassent ferro ac flamma persequebantur. Ita Bantamum ab ipsis obsessum a nostris servatum. Jorae regulus saepe subtractus imminenti exitio, Ternatam, Bandam, Ambonam aliasque oras vastare agressus hostis, nostri defendere; crematae utriusque aut captae naves, patrataque alia, sumptu praegravi, exitu ancipiti.

Crescente in dies rerum mole facile animadverterunt Ordines Foederati non posse diu sustineri ruentes in Indiam imperii potentissimi[220] vires, ni diversae nostrorum societates unum in corpus coalescerent, ut et mercatus et bellum iuncta vi unisque consiliis administraretur. Perfectum id non sine multo labore circa annum exacti saeculi ultimum: collecta ex multis una Societas in annos viginti et unum firmatur, addita lege ne quis interea nostratium hanc extra Societatem in Orientalem Indiam navigaret.

Exinde Societatis huius rectores, edocti unicam se suaque tutandi rationem esse si hostis quae fecerat timere cogeretur, auctoribus Foederatis Ordinibus validas classes misere, quae Lusitanis, pacem nolentibus, bellum longe lateque inferrent et saeva ac superba ipsorum consilia in ipsos verterent. Tum vero conspectis nostrorum animis viribusque Indorum principes ac nationes, acerbissimis vexati Hispanorum iniuriis, nostram opem ac societatem imploravere extremisque suis rebus salutem a nostris auxiliis habuerunt; nam ipsorum in copiis nihil praesidii. Sed cum nec quies gentium sine armis, nec arma sine stipendiis, nec stipendia sine tributis haberi possunt, illi, vice tributi socialis, id solum polliciti sunt, quod minime ipsis onerosum erat, ne, paratis nobis iusto pretio ipsorum aromata mercari, aliis et potius quam servatoribus suis venderent; facta in hoc et iurata foedera; quidam etiam domesticarum dissensionum pertaesi nostrum regimen praeoptavere. Imprimis vero Deo gratias agimus quod, uti Ipsi visum, /[221] nostra opera[222] ut plurimi Indorum, a Mahumetica aut pagana superstitione ad Christianam religionem traducti, baptismi signaculum ministrorum nostrorum manibus acciperent. Arces aliquot ereptae Lusitanis, structae aliae sociis defensandis.

Interea Lusitani quo acrius petebantur, hoc pertinacius obniti: augere vires suas accitis ex America Castellanorum auxiliis; emere quorundam Indorum perfidiam; nihil denique intentatum pati. Secutae sunt ex tam animoso certamine res magnae, ut ingentis periculi, ita sumtus incredibilis. Tarnatam irruptam ab hostibus, abducto regulo, a nostris recuperatam; obsessas Lusitanorum colonias Malaccam et Mosambicam; ad ipsam Malaccam XXXIII navium classe bis cruentissimo proelio certatum aliaque id genus narrare nos nihil necesse est; satis fama loquitur.

Fatiscentes sub tanto onere nostros spes ex induciis refovit, quae Hispanos inter et nos initae a Tuae quoque Maiestatis nomine sanctimoniam acceperunt, praesertim cum pacta eius foederis Indicani commercii securitatem satis clare continerent. Sed post exactum ab induciis annum et serius, significatis ipsi induciis, rogatus ut pactis staret, Iohannes Silva, Hispanorum ductor illis in partibus, captis nostrorum ad Manilias navibus aliaque ausus hostilia, satis ostendit ita se arbitrari ius, fas et fidem huius esse coeli vocabula, nec ad antipodum orbem quicquam pertinere.

Facilis hinc coniectura quantum oneri accesserit ex quo Hispani potentia, Europae bello liberata, illuc tota incubuit. Arces nunc eo in orbe obtinemus decem queis custodiendis maximo stipendio miles conducitur. Naves aut in India aut iam paratae Indicano itineri quadraginta sunt et tres, pleraeque magnae amplitudinis et machinis omnique belli apparatu instructae.

Summa haec est quod totum hoc tempus, quo in Indiam nostri navigarunt, tuendis magis quam fruendis commerciis est insumtum factaeque impensae in bellum extra mercaturam multa millena millia florenorum conficiunt. Estque evidens eius rei argumentum quod novae Societatis participes per annos tredecim sortis suae vix partem dimidiam perceperunt, nec minus est percepto aes alienum, quod facere interea Societas coacta est.

Quae cuncta fortiter tolerata spe futuri, cum nova ecce difficultas et cunctis maior exoritur. Nam Angli, M.T. subditi, eas insulas adeuntes quarum et custodia et foedera tanti nobis constiterunt constantque adhuc, messem quaerunt in nostra semente, sumtus refugiunt, de fructu postulant partem; et tamen negare ne ipsi quidem audebunt /[223] ni illos sumtus nostri fecissent iamdudum Lusitanos voti compotes ea in populos Indorum statuturos fuisse exempla, atque iis se munituros praesidiis, ut non magis aliis illuc pateret accessus quam nunc in potissima America patet.

Hic nos quid faceremus, Rex optime ac sapientissime? Contenderemus cum Anglis, subditis T.M., nostris amicis, sociis foederatis? Non possumus, non volumus, non debemus. Permitteremus ipsis quod volunt, ut nostrarum impensarum fructum ferant? Primum iudicet T.M. aequane sit an leonina societas, ubi alterum damna urgent, alter sine damno lucrum capit. Deinde quae consecutura sint videamus: si nobis quaestus eripitur cuius spe sola tantos sumptus tam diu fecimus, sumptus omitti plusquam necesse est; omissis sumptibus restat ut praesidia deserantur; desertis praesidiis ut relinquantur[224] Indi praeda saevitiae Hispanicae. Quid deinde porro? nisi ut Hispanus de nostro certamine victoriam ferat, nostrisque simul et vestris ex India exclusis aromatum omnis generis usum Europae tanti aestimet, quanti velit, atque ita accessione immensa firmet potentiam non nobis tantum sed saepe et regibus formidatam.

His de causis S.T.M. iussi sumus accedere ut aut iustitia ipsius quod aequum est statuat, aut sapientia id quod in commune est utile inveniat. Abraham olim orta inter suos cognatique sui pastores controversia maluit ipse in Occasum abire relictis Lotho quae in Ortum patebant, quam ut possessionibus coniuncti animis dissiderent. Non decet nos (inquiebat) iurgare, fratres enim sumus. Non deseret defensorem fidei sapiens consilium quod in re simili non deseruit fidelium patrem. Quo in voto desinemus, testati prius rectores ac participes Indicanae apud nos Societatis, devotissimos T.M. clientes, prius omnia aequa facturos, imo quaedam potius iniqua passuros quam ullum impedimentum intercedat ei amicitiae, quae T.M. subditis ac nobis est et esse debet perpetua.

English Translation[225]

Your Majesty!

After the celebration of the most happy marriage[226] by which Your Majesty has tied together in an eternal covenant not only the British nation and her sisters, but all nations which look to God, not to men, to set the rules of Divine worship, we have come as supplicants at this most auspicious of times to convey new pleas from afar, which appeal to Your Majesty's wisdom and goodness alike. Both are too great to allow themselves to be confined to one hemisphere, since both are celestial in nature: in order to imitate the heavens from which they come, they must extend from pole to pole.

Nor is our trust in these pleas feeble. For we know whither we come, and Your Majesty knows whence we come. We are here at the instructions of the States General,[227] sent by the Dutch East India Company; and we are here as citizens of that republic which Your Majesty has chosen to stand out amongst his many allies and friends as the foremost object of his clemency. This is the noble ardour of truly royal minds: whom they have begun to love, they love constantly — not for any other reason than the fact that they have begun, and their noblest reason to do good is that they have already done so. Therefore this is the first stronghold of our hope: that we come to a king who wishes us well, not less than we do him,[228] and who has received such power from God that he may effect what he wants. We may add that Your Majesty's favours cannot last long (as they must), unless they are fortified by a new favour.

For our fatherland (and who would know this better than Your Majesty?), enclosed within extremely narrow confines, holds a huge number of people. Yet our land does not promise metals or produce luscious vines; we do not even have an abundance of crops and wool. Nature has denied us what she has granted others; but since the mother of all did not wish to disinherit us, instead of the many gifts she showered on others she left us the seas and the winds and the perilous and difficult business of trading. For others, these are not even the most important, but for us they are the only means by which we can support such a numerous people and prevent being mocked by our enemies and useless to our friends. For this reason, both the ancient and the recent leaders of our people have always regarded these things as most important to the common good.

After the beginning of our war with the Spaniards, it was not our fault that the hostilities did not stop where they had begun, and that the Netherlands were looked for outside the Netherlands. It was the Spaniards' idea to arrest as enemies whom they had admitted as merchants, throughout the ports of northern Spain and Portugal. Men who were both innocent and unarmed were robbed and sent to the galleys or killed in the cruellest ways. The Spaniards did not do this once, but quite often, putting up a pretence to make their deceit more lucrative. In this way, the interests of many in our country were harmed. At this time, necessity, who is an excellent teacher, forced many of our people who would not do without trade but had been excluded from nearby destinations, to seek farther ones. Nearly twenty years ago, there were, among others, those who formed several consortia,[229] at a high price hired men from Portugal itself to show the way and sailed the route that leads to the Orient from the Cape of Good Hope.

But the same men who had exported hostilities from the Netherlands to Spain, transferred the war from Europe to East Asia as well. For the Portuguese by slander, deceit and outright violence kept us from dealings between free and consenting people. Nor was it only our people whom they attacked for this reason, but the Indians as well, who were neither subjects to to their empire nor bound to them by any law, but whom they nonetheless persecuted by fire and sword because of their friendly trade relations with our countrymen. Thus, Banten was besieged by them and saved by our men.[230] The King of Johor was often rescued from imminent destruction.[231] The enemy came to plunder Ternate, Banda, Ambon and other shores; our men defended them. Ships from both sides were burnt or captured and other things achieved — at exorbitant cost, while the outcome remained uncertain.

As the burden grew heavier with each day, it was quite clear to the States General that it could not be borne for long that the empire's best forces rushed to the Indies, unless the various Dutch companies were to coalesce into one body, so that both trade and war could be managed with united force and coherent counsel.[232] This was achieved, not without much trouble, around the last year of the past century: a single Company was forged from many for the duration of 21 years,[233] and a law made that none of ours were to sail to East India outside this Company in the meantime.

Immediately the directors of this Company, understanding that the only way to protect themselves and their possessions was to frighten the enemy, at the instigation of the States General sent a powerful fleet to make war on the Portuguese — who did not want peace — from all sides, turning their cruel and haughty plans against them. When the East Indian princes and nations, suffering under the Spaniards' harsh injustice, saw the courage and strength of the Dutch, they implored our aid and alliance and were saved from extreme danger by our troops; for their own offered no protection. But there can be no peace among nations without armies, no armies without pay and no pay without tributes. Therefore, by way of alliance tribute, they just promised something that was no trouble to them at all, namely that if we were prepared to buy their spices for a reasonable price, they would not sell them to others rather than their rescuers. To this end, a solemn treaty was made;[234] some of them even preferred our rule, since they were weary of domestic quarrels.[235] But most of all we thank God that He saw fit to use us, so that a great many Indians were converted from the Muhammadan or pagan to the Christian religion and received the sacrament of baptism at the hands of our ministers. Some fortifications were seized from the Portuguese,[236] others were built to defend our allies.

In the meantime, the more the Portuguese were under attack, the more persistently they fought back. They increased their forces by summoning auxiliary troops from Spanish America, bribed several treacherous Indians and generally left nothing untried. Great things have followed from such a bitter fight, things which were hugely dangerous as well as incredibly expensive. Ternate was invaded by the enemy and its king abducted, but it was recaptured by our men;[237] we besieged the Portuguese colonies of Melaka and Mozambique;[238] we need not talk of the two bloody naval battles that were fought at Melaka with a fleet of 33 ships,[239] nor of other such things: they are well known.

As the Dutch grew weary under this heavy burden, their hope was rekindled by the truce[240] that was agreed upon between the Spaniards and ourselves — a truce which was also made sacred by Your Majesty's name — especially since the arrangements of that truce contained the security of the Indian trade sufficiently clearly. More than a year after the conclusion of the truce,[241] Juan de Silva, the Spanish leader in that region,[242] was reminded of the truce and asked to uphold its arrangements. However, by capturing Dutch ships at Manila[243] and daring to undertake other hostilities, he made clear his opinion that law, justice and faith are words of this part of the world and do not belong to the Antipodes in any way.

At this point, it is easy to conjecture how much our burden was enlarged when the Spaniard's power, freed from the war in Europe, concentrated entirely on that part of the world. We now have ten forts in that region; to guard them, we hire soldiers for extremely high wages. We have forty-three ships either in the Indies or ready to sail there, most of them very large and equipped with all the machinery of war.

To sum up: the entire time since we first sailed to the Indies has been spent protecting rather than enjoying our commerce, and the expenses that we have made for the war, apart from trade, amount to many millions of florins. This is proven clearly by the fact that the stakeholders in the new Company have barely received back half of their deposit in thirteen years' time; and the debts which the Company had to make in the meantime are no less than the dividend.

All this was bravely borne in the hope of what was to come, when a new difficulty arose, one that loomed larger than all the others. For when the English, Your Majesty's subjects, came to those islands whose safeguarding and treaties have cost and still cost us so much, they wanted to harvest from what we had sown, fled from making expenses and demanded a share in the yield. And yet not even they would dare deny that if our countrymen had not made those expenses, the Portuguese would long since have gained what they wanted; that they would have punished the Indians in such a way and would have made such fortifications for themselves that access to these islands would not be open to others any more than it is now in the mainland of America.[244]

What were we to do then, good and wise King? Were we to contend with the English, Your Majesty's subjects, our friends, our sworn allies? We cannot, we will not, we must not. Were we to grant them what they want and let them enjoy the yield of our expenses? Your Majesty should first judge whether it is a fair partnership in which one is burdened with losses and the other makes a profit without any loss. And secondly, let us consider the consequences: if we are robbed of the profit in the hope of which alone we have made such big investments for such a long time, it is more than necessary to discontinue the investments; once the investments have been discontinued, the fortifications will be deserted; once the fortifications have been deserted, the Indians will be left prey to the Spaniards' cruelty. And what will happen next? The Spaniard will reap the victory of *our* battle, and having excluded both your people and ours from the Indies, will charge any price he likes for any kind of spice in Europe. Thus he will reinforce his power with this huge increase in wealth — a power feared not only by us, but often by kings as well.

Because of these matters, we have been ordered to appear before Your Majesty, so that either his sense of justice may state what is equitable, or his wisdom find what is useful to the common good. Abraham, when there was a strife between his own and his kinsman's herdsmen, preferred going west himself, leaving to Lot the lands in the east, to being united in possessions but divided in minds. "Let there be no strife between me and thee", he said, "for we be brethren".[245] The wise counsel which in a similar case did not deceive the father of the faithful, will not deceive the Defender of the Faith.[246] With this wish we shall cease, after having testified that the directors and stakeholders of our East India Company, Your Majesty's most devoted clients, will first do all that is right and even suffer some wrongs, before letting any obstacle hinder the friendship which is, and should be, eternal between Your Majesty's subjects and us.

Appendix 18

Farewell address of Hugo Grotius held before King James I/VI at the close of the Maritime and Colonial Conference in London, 21 May 1613.[247]

[At the close of the Anglo-Dutch maritime and colonial conference in London in May 1613, Grotius held an address before King James I/VI and the members of both delegations. Translated into English for the first time, this address summarises the state of Anglo-Dutch relations in the East Indies and focuses on some of the principal points of agreement and contention that arose in the course of the London conference.]

Latin Text Transcribed by Clark and Eysinga[248]

Serenissime ac Potentissime Rex.

Hactenus de re ardua atque difficili et maximi tum privatim tum publice momenti scriptis, colloquiis egimus cum viris nobilissimis ac amplissimis, quos visum est Maiestati Tuae isti negotio praeficere. Sunt quae nobis conveniant, sunt quae discrepent. Convenit inter nos Hispanum, utcunque callidis interdum consiliis utitur, quo aut nos inter nos committat aut vires nostras dissociet, id tamen agere ut utrosque nostrum tam per Orientalem quam per Occidentalem Indiam regionesque alias, quae mundi /[249] partem longe maiorem efficiunt, aditu et commerciis prohibeat. Convenit quoque debere nos in medium consulere ne quantum Hispano libet tantum et liceat. Sed quibus modis obviam sit eundum isti iniuriae, hic nostrae sententiae videntur dissidere: nos experiundo didicimus ex quo Hispanus illo in orbe lacessitus vim et prudentiam auxit, aliter commercium cum Indis haberi servarique non posse, nisi maritimis viribus quam maximis adiungantur etiam terrestres, et earum gentium, quae nos ad mercaturam admittunt, suscipiatur defensio. Neque enim dubium habemus quin per contraria evertatur et firmetur commercium. Hispanus per annos iam aliquam multos classes, exercitus admovit insulis, ut quarundam poena caeteras ab externis commerciis deterreret. Nobis quid restabat nisi ut oppugnatos ab ipso tueremur aut excideremus mercaturae?[250] Hoc ne eveniret illud fecimus; auctores nobis eius rei fuerunt Ordines Foederati iam ante inducias. Induciae cum fierent legati Galliae ac Tuae Serenissimae Maiestatis ore ac scripto declararunt hanc esse regum sententiam: Si Hispanus vim inferret Indis amicis sociisque nostris, nobis eos tuendi ius fore. Post inducias vim illis novam nec clam nec semel intulit Hispanus. Hic nostri in India quid facerent? Sumenda arma armorum ultricia iudicarunt, probarunt idem Ordines Foederati. Haec ratio tutandae mercaturae Tuae Ma.tis subditis videtur non placere. At nos a consilio post longissimas deliberationes auctoritate publica suscepto recedere non possumus; haec controversia aliam trahit: nam nos impendia facta in defensionem Indorum ad servandam mercaturam existimamus necessaria, ideoque aequum non esse ut, quibus locis castella aut[251] erepta Lusitanis aut a nobis structa obtinemus, particeps sit fructuum nisi qui factorum quoque sumtuum velit esse particeps. Oneramur menstruis centenis florenorum millibus, naves non mercaturae tantum, set et bello structae tres et quadraginta cum omni apparatu non minus quater millenis florenorum millibus constiterunt; neque nos in amicorum iniuriam foedus cum Indis fecimus — quibus nos ipsorum tutelam suscepimus, illi nobis vicissim messes suas addixerunt — sed coacti inevitabili necessitate, quia nulla alia est ratio sumtus tolerandi aut sine sumtibus servandi commercium. Tuae autem Maiestatis subditi ita verba instituunt, quasi privati et mercatores tantas impensas, tot labores ac pericula suscepissent citra ullam necessitatem; quod si verum est sumus sine dubio accusandi magnae imprudentiae. De his cum inter nos non conveniat, satisfecimus iam mandatis nostris, quae /[252] hoc nobis imperabant, ut statum Indiae rationemque tutandi commercii nostra ex sententia exponeremus.

Superest ut Societati Indicanae atque ipsis Ordinibus Foederatis renuntiemus quae hic acta sunt, quod faciemus non tantum fide optima sed summa quoque in subditos Tuae Ma.tis benevolentia, suasoresque erimus omnibus eorum, quae ad concordiam pertinebunt. Tuae autem Ma.tis subditos rogatos volumus ut de toto negotio (quando plurimis implicatur difficultatibus) amplius deliberent, quod illis iam facere est promptius cognitis nostri consilii rationibus. Hoc autem vellemus imprimis ipsos expendere de belli sumtibus nihil nos dixisse, quod non sit verissimum; tantos fuisse ut belli et mercaturae quaestus omnes absumti sint. Itaque quae ante annos tredecim institui coepit Societatis participes ex proventu sortis dimidium non ultra percepisse; aes autem alienum (quod facere Societas coacta est) itidem efficere sortis dimidium; unde facile colligi potest verum esse quod diximus; et, si adhuc dubitatur, rationum codices fidem facere possunt. Et nunc ad tempus sane aliquod continuari aut augeri onera necesse est, quae nisi ex fructibus tolerari nequeunt. Horum si pars nobis decedit longe certissimum est imminutis nostrorum impendiis Hispanum occupaturum insulas, quas nos praesidiis nunc tenemus, ut iam partes quasdam occupavit, dum nos sumtibus nimium parcimus; illis insulis occupatis caeteras quoque gentes, quibuscum utrique commercia habemus, invasurum. Cogitent Tuae Ma.tis subditi an id ipsis utile sit futurum, et, si damnosum iudicant, rogamus quaerant diligenter rationes, quibus id impediri possit easque tum nostris indicent: sentient nostros nec iniquos nec pertinaces; nos sane operam dabimus ut omnia pacifica, aequa atque salubria consilia locum apud nostros inveniant.

Interea, dum de re tota mature deliberatur, cautio adhibenda est ne medio tempore vulnus aliquod accipiatur postea insanabile; quod ne fiat rogamus obnixe Tuam Augustissimam Maiestatem, ut sine detrimento iuris cuiusquam haec interea Tuae Ma.tis auctoritate statuantur: Primum ne altera natio alterius sociis et foederatis occasionem det aliquid faciendi contra foedera; nam aliter si fit, pares non sumus illis sumtibus, qui ad Hispanum ab insulis arcendum sint necessarii. Petimus autem dumtaxat dum deliberatur; postea expenso omni negotio id statuetur in posterum, quod Tuae Ma.ti et Ordinibus Foederatis aequissimum et in commune utilissimum videbitur. Secundum ut omnibus aliis Indiae in locis utraque natio omnia amicitiae signa atque officia altera alteri exhibeant, et libere pro suo quaeque arbitrio exerceant mercaturam.[253] Tertium ne Lusitanis, Hispanis eorum-/[254] que sociis ac subditis arma aut belli instrumenta aliaque necessaria in communem perniciem subministrentur. Nos interim omnem adhibebimus diligentiam ut ad componendum perpetua aliqua lege negotium nostrorum animos praeparemus.

Gratias vero agimus summas Sacratissimae Tuae Ma.ti, quod nos benigne audierit et nos ipsius regiae benevolentiae quam devotissime commendamus, ipsam autem Deo Op. Max., quem rogamus ut bono publico totius orbis Christiani T.M. largiatur vitam longam, firmam valetudinem, foelix regnum.

English Translation[255]

Your Most Powerful Majesty!

Thus far we have dealt of an arduous and difficult matter of great private and public importance, in writing and speech, with the great and noble men which Your Majesty has seen fit to appoint to this matter. There are things on which we agree and things on which we disagree.

We agree that whenever the Spaniard uses (sometimes cunning) counsel to either pit us against one another or divide our forces, his intention in any case is to bar both of us from access to, and trade with, the East as well as the West Indies, and other regions which together form the largest part of the world by far. We also agree that we have to take counsel together to prevent the Spaniard from getting as much as he wants. But how we should ward off this injustice is where our opinions appear to differ. We have learnt from experience since the Spaniard[256] was aroused in that part of the world and increased his power and sagacity, that commerce with the Indians cannot be secured unless a naval force, as big as possible, is augmented with land troops, and we take on the defence of those peoples who will trade with us.[257] For there is no doubt in our minds that in adversity, commerce is destroyed and fortified. For several years already, the Spaniard has moved fleets and armies to the islands in order to punish some of them and thereby deter the others from overseas trade. What options did we have left except to protect from him those who were under attack, or to lose the business? To prevent the latter we did the first; we were under orders from the States General to do this, already before the truce.[258] When the truce was agreed upon, the French legate and Your Majesty's legate declared in speech and writing that the kings' opinion was this: if the Spaniard was to harm our Indian friends and allies, we would have the right to protect them.[259] After the conclusion of the truce, the Spaniard did harm them again, openly and repeatedly. Then what were our men in the Indies to do? They judged that they had to take up arms to avenge, and their judgment was approved by the States General. To protect our trade this way seems to displease Your Majesty's subjects. But we cannot withdraw from a counsel taken by public authority after very lengthy deliberation. This controversy brings another in its wake: for we consider the expenses made for the Indians' defence, in order to save our trade, a necessity; and therefore consider it inequitable that in the places where we have fortifications that were either taken from the Portuguese[260] or built by us, anyone should participate in the yield who would not participate in the cost. We have to spend hundreds of thousands of florins every month; 43 vessels built not just for commerce but for warfare as well,[261] with all the equipment, have cost no less than four million florins;[262] nor did we make a treaty with the Indians (by which we have taken their protection upon ourselves and they have promised us their harvest in return) to harm our friends, but because we were forced by inexorable necessity, while there is no other way to bear the cost or to save our commerce without cost. Your Majesty's subjects, however, arrange their words in such a way as if civilians and merchants had undertaken such investments and so many troubles and dangers without any need whatsoever — if that is true, we are certainly to be accused of great imprudence. Since we do not agree on these matters, we have now fulfilled our mandate, which ordered us to expound the state of the Indies and our way or protecting our trade from our point of view.

All that remains for us to do is to report to the East India Company and the States General themselves what has been done here, which we will not only do very faithfully, but also with the utmost benevolence toward Your Majesty's subjects. We will plead with all for the way of concord.[263] We would like to ask Your Majesty's subjects to consider the entire matter (seeing that it is complicated by many difficulties) at greater length, which they can do more easily now that they know the reasons for our policy. But this is what we would want first of all: that they weigh the fact that we have said nothing concerning the costs of war which was not very true; that they were so great that the entire gain from war and commerce has been consumed. Because of this, the stakeholders in the Company which was instituted thirteen years ago,[264] have received no more than half their deposits from the yield, whereas the debts (which the Company was forced to make) also take up half of the deposit. From this, it is easily concluded that what we have said is true — and if there remain doubts, the account books will provide proof. At this moment as well it will be unavoidable, for some time in any case, to continue or increase our investments, which can only be borne if we also make a profit. If we lose part of that profit, it is perfectly certain that after we have cut back our expenses, the Spaniard will occupy the islands which we now hold with our forts, as he has already occupied some parts now that we whittle down our investments.[265] Having occupied those islands, he will also attack the other peoples with whom we both trade. Let Your Majesty's subjects consider whether this would be useful to them, and if they judge it harmful, we bid them to carefully seek out ways to prevent this and then indicate them to our countrymen: they will find them neither unjust nor stubborn. We, of course, will do our best to ensure that all peaceable, equitable and wholesome counsels find a place with our countrymen.

Meanwhile, as the whole matter is amply deliberated upon, we must exercise caution that in the meantime no wound is sustained that cannot be healed afterwards. To prevent that, we firmly ask Your August Majesty that, for the time being, these statements be confirmed by Your Majesty's authority, without damage to anybody's rights. First, that neither nation should give the other's associates and allies an occasion to act against that alliance; for if it happens otherwise, we are unable to bear the costs necessary to keep the Spaniard away from the islands. But we ask this only for as long as the matter is under deliberation; after that, when all matters have been duly considered, such agreements will be made for the future as Your Majesty and the States General will deem most equitable and useful to both parties. Secondly, that in all other parts of the Indies, both nations extend to each other every possible token of friendship, both freely conducting business according to their wishes. Thirdly, that no weapons or instruments and other things necessary for war be supplied — to our common detriment — to the Portuguese, the Spanish and their allies and subjects. Meanwhile, we will make every effort to prepare the minds of our countrymen to settle the matter with some permanent agreement.

To Your Most Sacred Majesty we are deeply grateful that he has benignly heard us and we devotedly commend ourselves to his royal benevolence, as we commend him to God, whom we ask to grant Your Majesty long life, a robust health and a happy reign, for the public benefit of the entire Christian world.

Appendix 19

Excerpt from the Political Memoirs of Hugo Grotius (1619) concerning his contributions toward the cause of the VOC, his attitudes toward Spain, the Twelve Years Truce and Johan van Oldenbarnevelt.[266]

[On his release from months of detention in custody in the Hague and the beginning of what was to be a life sentence served in the fortress of Loevesteyn, Grotius wrote a lengthy apology and political memoir at the age of 36. In this Grotius reports that he was very sick and he probably believed that he would not live much longer. The *Memoriën* (political memoires) spell out his position on many of the issues that had arisen during his detention, charges and trial. In the present excerpt, Grotius spells out his contributions to the VOC's case in the war against the Spanish Empire, as well as matters relating to Dutch trade in the East and West Indies.]

Original Dutch Text

Jegens Spaignie enn haere adherenten ben ick altijdt ten uyterste geresolveert geweest, en hoezeer ick mij selve daermede heb gemaeckt irreconciliabel, can mijn boeck *de Antiquitate Reipublicae Batavae* en mijne *Poëmata* doorgaens als oock mijn *Historie* getuygen. Welcke *Historie* bij mij meest tot dien eynde is aengeleyt, opdat de posteriteyt niet en soude vergeten de Bararische wreedtheden, die dese Landen door de Spaingiaerden sijn overgecomen. Hierom heb ick alles helpen vorderen, dat de Spaigniaerden conde tegen zijn, alles helpen omstooten, daeruyt zij bij eenige consequentie conden zijn gebaet. De vlijdt, bij mij aengewent tot conservatie van den handel van Oost Indië is velen bekent; ende omdat ick vreesde, dat de faveur de Austraelsche Compagnie bij eenige van de Vergadering van Hollant toegedrangen, niet sonder schijn van recht, de Compaignie van Oost Indië hinderlijck soude connen zijn, soo hebbe ick de saecke gebracht aen de Vergadering van de Staten Generael, enn aldaer alles nae mijn beste vermogen tot conservatie van de voors. Oost Indische Compaignie gedirigeert. Alles nu met oordel inzyende, inclineer ick om te geloven, dat de Advocaet, Sal. Ged., ende anderen de Compaignie van Oost Indië met de woorden van het Octroy wat hebben willen intimideren, om daerdoor deselve te bewegen tot een goede uytcoop van de gerechticheyt van de Austraelsche Compaignie, welcke voet van uytcoop buyten twijfel de beste was.

In 't stuck van de West Indische Compaignie was d'Advocaet deurgaens wat difficijl, vresende off de intentie van de aenleggers (waeronder Husseling, die sijn credit verloren hadde, de yverighste was) soude sijn, haer te begeven tot roverije, jegens het tractaet van de Trefves. Ick evenwel zyende dat de Coning van Spaignie daerdoor con werden gecrenckt menende oock dat de saecke wel soo soude werden beleyt, dat de rupture van de Trefves in West Indië, soo wel als in Oost Indië, niet bij ons schuldt soude toecomen, maer bij de schuldt van den Spaigniaert, ons weygerende, dat rechtmatig was, te weten: vrijen handel in de plaetsen, daer hij geen castelen en heeft, heb de saecken in alle getrouwicheyt gefacilliteert, met vaste intentie van daer niet uyt te scheyden, eer dat ick 't voorgenomen werck soude hebben geëffectueert.

English Translation

Against Spain and her supporters I have always shown great resolve. The extent of my irreconcilable determination is evidenced by my book *De*

Antiquitate Reipublicae Batavae (On the Antiquity of the Batavian Republic), across my *Poëmata* (Poetry) as well as my *History* [*of the Low Countries*]. This History is largely written to the end that future generations should not forget the barbaric cruelties that these [Low] Countries suffered at the hands of the Spaniards. For this reason I helped promote everything against the interests of the Spanish and also helped remove everything from which they might gain some benefit as a consequence. The efforts undertaken by myself to preserve [our] trade with the East Indies is well known. Since I feared that the favourable disposition shown by some in the States of Holland to the *Austraelsche Compagnie* (Company of Australia),[267] not without the appearance of legality, would prove disadvantageous to the [interests of the] East India Company, I raised the matter with the assembly of the States General and there directed everything to the best of my abilities [and] the preservation of the aforementioned East India Company. Seeing everything now judiciously, I incline to believe that the late *advocaat* [Johan van Oldenbarnevelt] and others sought to coerce the East India Company with the wording of the [company] charter so that they would buy up the interests of the *Austraelsche Compagnie* on favourable terms. The proposed buyout was, beyond doubt, the best solution.

In the matters concerning the West India Company,[268] the *advocaat* [van Oldenbarnevelt] proved to be rather difficult throughout, fearing whether the actual intention of the investors (among them Usselincx,[269] who had lost his investment, being doubtlessly the most active) would be to engage in plunder against the principles of the Twelve Years Truce. I realised that the King of Spain could be offended by this and was also of the opinion that it would be best if the breach of the Twelve Years Truce, both in the West as well as in the East Indies, should not be blamed on us, but on the Spaniards, who refuse what is rightfully ours, namely: free trade in those places, where they have no fortresses.[270] I have faithfully facilitated these matters, with the firm intention not to desist therefrom until I had achieved the intended result. A few days before my incarceration, I handed over to the States General the documents that were in my possession and I informed them of my concerns.

Notes

General Introduction

1. Anon., *Mare Liberum, sive de iure quod Batavis competit ad indicana commercia dissertatio* (Leiden: Ex officina Ludovici Elzevirij, 1609), TMD, p. 211, no. 541.
2. *Huygh de Groots Vrye zeevaert, ofte Bewiis Van 't recht dat de Inghesetenen deser geunieerde Landen toecomt over de Indische coop-handel. Ten tweedemael overseen ende verbetert door den Autheur selfs. Uten Latijne vertaelt door P[ieter] B[ertius]. Tot vorderinghe des Vaderlandts* (Leiden: Ian Huybertsz. .., 1614), TMD, p. 218, no. 554.
3. Hugo Grotius, *De Iure belli ac pacis Libri Tres, In quibus ius naturae et gentium: item iuris publici praecipua explicantur* (Paris: Apud Nicolaum Buon, 1625), TMD, p. 222, no. 565.
4. On this, see also CiT, introduction, pp. 32–3; Peter Borschberg, "Grotius, the Social Contract and Political Resistance", *IILJ Working Paper,* History and Theory of International Law Series 6 (2006): 4–5. [This working paper can be downloaded directly from the website of the Social Science Research Network (SSRN) at <papers.ssrn.com> and from the website of the Institute for International Law and Justice of New York University at <www.iilj.org>.] Martine J. van Ittersum, "Dating the Manuscript of *De Jure Praedae*", *History of European Ideas* 35 (2009): 128–30. The Martinus Nijhoff auction catalogue was annotated, and manuscripts known to remain in the Netherlands are featured in L.J. Noordhoff, *Beschrijving van het zich in Nederland bevindende en nog onbeschreven gedeelte der papieren afkomstig van Huig de Groot welke in 1864 te 's-Gravenhage zijn geveilt* (Groningen-Djakarta: Noordhoff, 1953).
5. At Leiden University Library, the manuscript currently bears the shelfmark ms. B.P.L. 917.
6. M.J. van Ittersum, "Preparing *Mare Liberum* for the Press: Hugo Grotius' Rewriting of Chapter 12 of *De Jure Praedae* in November–December 1608", *GNS* 27–8 (2005–7): 246–80.

7. Hugo Grotius, *De Iure Praedae Commentarius*, ed. H.G. Hamaker (The Hague: Martinus Nijhoff, 1868), TMD, p. 303, no. 684. For a modern, scholarly assessment of this edition, see Jan Waszink, "Using the Work. Remarks on the Text of *De iure praedae*", *GNS* 27–8 (2005–7): 215–45.
8. A new critical edition of the Latin text is being prepared. An editorial committee was formed in 2004–5 and met at the Netherlands' Institute for Advanced Studies (NIAS) in Wassenaar, and an international colloquium discussing facets of *De Iure Praedae* took place at NIAS in May 2005. A selection of papers presented at this conference was published as *Property, Piracy and Punishment,* ed. Hans Blom (Leiden: Brill, 2009).
9. On the commercial and legal significance of this merger, and especially also its implications for the evolution of Dutch relations with the East Indies, see Niels Steensgaard, *The Asian Trade Revolution of the Seventeenth Century. The East India Companies and the Decline of the Caravan Trade* (Chicago and London: University of Chicago Press, 1974), pp. 126–31; concerning the formation of the VOC in 1602 generally, see esp. Femme S. Gaastra, *De geschiedenis van de VOC,* 4th ed. (Zutphen: Walburg Pers, 2002).
10. Peter Haggenmacher, *Grotius et la doctrine de la guerre juste* (Paris: Presses Universitaires de France, 1983).
11. CC, pp. 1–270; CE, pp. 1–155.
12. Concerning the broader historical reception of Grotius as the father of the "science" of modern international law, its link to the emergence of the Westphalian state system and the rise of European imperialism, see the excellent contributions of Edward Keene, *Beyond the Anarchical Society: Grotius, Colonialism and Order in World Politics* (Cambridge: CUP, 2002) and his chapter "Images of Grotius" in *Classical Theories of International Relations,* ed. Beate Jahn (Cambridge: CUP, 2006), pp. 233–52.
13. W.Ph. Coolhaas, "Een bron van het historische gedeelte van Hugo de Groot's De Jure Praedae", *BMH* 79 (1965): 415–537. The historical section spans chapters 11 through 15 and includes chapter 12, which was published separately as *Mare Liberum.*
14. M.J. van Ittersum, *Profit and Principle: Hugo Grotius, Natural Rights Theories and the Rise of Dutch Power in the East Indies, 1595–1615* (Leiden: Brill, 2006). In this study van Ittersum has so generously acknowledged her indebtedness to my earlier research on Grotius as well as early colonial politics and trade in Asia. See especially her recent article "Dating the Manuscript of *De Jure Praedae*", *History of European Ideas* 35 (2009): 125–93.
15. CiT, introduction, pp. 31–101, 193–9; also Borschberg, "Commentarius in Theses XI. Ein unveröffentlichtes Kurzwerk von Hugo Grotius", *ZRG*, RA 109 (1992): 450–74; "De Societate Publica cum Infidelibus. Una obra juvenil de Grocio", *Revista de Estudios Políticos* 83: 113–36; "De Pace. Ein

unveröffentlichtes Fragment von Grotius über Krieg und Frieden", *ZRG*, RA 113 (1996): 268–92; "'De Societate Publica cum Infidelibus': Ein Frühwerk von Hugo Grotius", *ZRG*, RA 115 (1998): 355–93.

16. CiT, pp. 36–7; concerning the *Theses LVI,* see Borschberg, "Grotius, the Social Contract and Political Resistance", *IILJ Working Paper* 6 (2006): 1–64.
17. Charles H. Alexandrowicz, *An Introduction to the History of the Law of Nations in the East Indies* (Oxford: Clarendon Press, 1967).
18. Alexandrowicz, *An Introduction,* esp. pp. 14–97.
19. Concerning the latter, see the preface to Grotius, *Mare Liberum, The Freedom of the Seas, or, The Right which Belongs to the Dutch to Take Part in the East Indian Trade,* tr. Ralph van Deman Magoffin, ed. and intr. James Brown Scott (New York: OUP, 1916), TMD, p. 216, no. 551. The introduction of Scott is best read against the background of reactions to Grotius emanating at the time from legal circles in the German Reich. See, for example, Josef Kohler, *Grundlagen des Völkerrechts. Vergangenheit, Gegenwart, Zukunft* (Stuttgart: Ferdinand Enke, 1918), pp. 90–3, for the latter's position on submarine warfare of the Reich; pp. 105–8 concerning sovereignty of states over coastal waters; and pp. 218–26 on the right to attack and plunder merchant vessels of neutral parties.
20. I refer here more specifically to the publications of David Armitage, Mark Goldie, Anthony Pagden, Quentin Skinner, Richard Tuck, James Tully and others who have examined many of the great classics of political thought in context. They seek to tease out what the author "was up to" and explore what authors "may have meant by writing as they did".
21. BW (Supplement), 107A, p. 37. The letters are also mentioned in the appendices of the published text of *Mare Liberum,* see CML, p. 77.
22. The two letters are found in *Documentos Remettidos da Índia ou Livros das Monções*, ed. Raymundo de Bulhão Pato and António de Silva Rego, 10 vols. (Lisbon: Typographia da Academia Real das Sciencias and Academia das Sciencias de Lisboa, 1880–1978), I, pp. 47–8, 130–1.
23. See esp. also Leiden University Library, Loket 1555–39, "Catalogue des Manuscrits Autographes de Hugo Grotius", p. 6, "Translaet vuyt een Auctenticq missive geschr. by den Bisschop van MALACCA aen Co. May.t van Espagne. (wt Goa, 30 Apr. 1600). Copie authent. de 1604. 7 pag. Avec extrait en français. 4 pag.". Note also the manual commentary in the left-hand margin by Robert Fruin: "Fred. Muller copy by Dr. Hamaker."
24. Leiden University Library, Loket 1555–39, Robert Fruin, *Aantekeningen op zijn werken,* incip. "Translaet uyt een auctenticq missive…". See also CIPC, pp. 380–4, esp. the editorial note on p. 384, and van Ittersum in IPC, p. 517, note 34.
25. CIPC, pp. 380–4; IPC, pp. 517–22.

26. The Hague, Nationaal Archief, Collectie 102, Baron H. van Zuylen van Nyevelt, suppl. 2, no. 13 (2.21.179.01, no. 13).
27. Coolhaas, "Een bron van het historische gedeelte van Hugo de Groot's De Jure Praedae", *BMH* 79 (1965): 415–540.
28. See Leiden University Library, Loket 1555–39, Fruin, *Aantekeningen op zijn werken*, "Discours ende advertisement van de navolgende schepen", fol. 8 recto, "Van gelycken heeft den Coninck gelieft zynen Ambassadeur, zyende een jonck Edelman van staet naest den Coninck, met zyn volck in onse schepen herwaerts te zenden." (Likewise it has pleased the king [of Johor] to send us hither on our ships his ambassador together with a young nobleman of status close to the king and an entourage.) See also Borschberg, *The Singapore and Melaka Straits: Violence, Security and Diplomacy in the 17th Century* (Singapore: NUS Press and KITLV Press, 2010), pp. 122, 158; Borschberg, "The Johor-VOC Alliance and the Twelve Years Truce: Factionalism, Intrigue and International Diplomacy, c.1606–1613", *IILJ Working Paper*, History and Theory of International Law Series 8 (2009): 14. This article can be downloaded directly from the website of the Social Science Research Network (SSRN) at <papers.ssrn.com> and from the website of the Institute for International Law and Justice of New York University at <www.iilj.org>.
29. See also Borschberg, *The Singapore and Melaka Straits*, pp. 157–62.
30. Concerning the internal Dutch obstacles to, and international considerations against, forming the Dutch West India Company (WIC) between 1606 and the expiry of the Twelve Years Truce, see esp. Henk den Heijer, *De geschiedenis van de WIC* (Zutphen: Walburg Pers, 2002), pp. 21–30; Heijer, "The Dutch West India Company, 1621–1791", in *Riches from Atlantic Commerce: Dutch Transatlantic Trade and Shipping, 1585–1817*, ed. Johannes Postma and Victor Enthoven (Leiden: Brill, 2003), esp. pp. 77–80.
31. Jean Bodin, *The Six Bookes of a Commonweale. A Facsimile Reprint of the English Edition of 1606, Corrected and Supplemented*, ed. K.D. McRae (Cambridge, Mass.: Harvard University Press, 1962), pp. 152 *et seq.*, esp. pp. 155, 159–60, 163, 166, 168, 175, 177.
32. An explanation of these Malay titles is warranted here. Raja Seberang derives from the fact that the king's brother, Raja Bongsu, had established his base on the opposite side of the river from the Johor royal residence and court at Batu Sawar. This fortified settlement is described by Admiral Cornelis Matelieff de Jonge in appendix 11. After the court was moved upstream from Batu Sawar, Raja Bongsu was sometimes also referred to as "Raja di Ilir", that is, downstream from the vantage point of the new royal residence.

Chapter 1

1. See especially the two works Henk J.M. Nellen, *Hugo de Groot (1583–1645). De loopbaan van een geleerd staatsman* (Weesp: Uitgeverij Heureka, 1985); Nellen, *Hugo de Groot: Een leven in strijd om de vrede, 1583–1648* (Amsterdam: Uitgeverij Balans, 2007), p. 612, as well as Jan and Annie Romein, *Erflaters van onze beschaving. Nederlandse gestalten uit zees eeuwen,* reprint (Amsterdam: Querido, 1973). This latter collection of 12 portraits of famous Dutch personalities was first published in 1938–40. For a brief account of the historical and historiographical backdrop of this collection, see for example Jurrien van Goor, *Prelude to Colonialism. The Dutch in Asia* (Hilversum: Uitgeverij Verloren, 2004), pp. 71–2.
2. Concerning the origins of the "myth" of Grotius as the "Father of International Law" during the Enlightenment, see the useful exposé by Michael Kempe, "Der Anfang eines Mythos. Zum grotianischen Natur- und Völkerrecht in der europäischen Aufklärung", in *Staat bei Hugo Grotius,* ed. Norbert Konegen and Peter Nitschke (Baden-Baden: Nomos Verlag, 2005), pp. 139–57.
3. *Bronnen tot de geschiedenis der Leidsche universiteit,* vol. I, 1575–Feb. 1610, ed. Philipp C. Molhuysen (The Hague: Martinus Nijhoff, 1913), p. 469.
4. BW 402, pp. 384–7. This letter is featured in English translation in Jesse S. Reeves, "Grotius on the Training of an Ambassador", *The American Journal of International Law* 23, 3 (1929): 621–25.
5. W.S.M. Knight, "Grotius' earliest Years as Lawyers", *TGS* 8 (1922): 5. In fact, Knight reckons Grotius could not have formally studied law for a year before commencing his legal practice.
6. See for example Laurens Winkel, "Problems of Legal Systematization from De iure praedae to De iure belli ac pacis. De iure praedae Chapter II and the Prolegomena of De iure belli ac pacis Compared", *GNS* 26–8 (2005–7): 63, 69–70. Concerning the influence of Bronckhorst, see also Annabel Brett, "Natural Right and Civil Community: The Civil Philosophy of Hugo Grotius", *Historical Journal* 45, 1 (2002): 38.
7. See the letters by Grotius to his brother Willem de Groot dated 18 May 1615, BW 405, pp. 389–91, and BW 450 dated 28 February 1616, pp. 499–503.
8. Grotius' most recent biographer, Henk Nellen, concedes that the degree from Orléans was probably purchased. See Nellen, *Hugo de Groot. Een leven in strijd om de vrede*, p. 51. See also Knight, "Grotius' earliest Years as Lawyer", *TGS* 8 (1922): 3, citing the 18th- century biography of the Dutch humanist by Caspaer Brandt and Adriaan van Cattenburgh, observed that the doctorate was awarded "because of his [that is Grotius'] honest behaviour, pious life, literature and famous name". On the following p. 4, Knight intimated that recipients of degrees often dished out hefty bribes to university officials and professors. There was nothing unusual about this at the time.
9. On the life and career of this great Dutch statesman, see Jan den Tex, *Oldenbarnevelt*, 5 vols. (Haarlem-Groningen: H.D. Tjeenk Willink & Zoon,

1960–72), as well as its abridged English translation in 2 vols. published by CUP in 1973.

10. Leiden University Library, Ms. Papenbroeckii Cod. 13A, Hugo Grotius, "Annotata de vita sua", fol. 3. This *curriculum vitae* features a list of key works written by Grotius before 1613.
11. Concerning the understanding and uses of history in the age of Renaissance and Humanism with a focus on the Low Countries, see the synopsis in Nicholas Wickenden, *G.J. Vossius and the Humanist Concept of History* (Assen: Van Gorcum, 1993), esp. pp. 75–80, and the moral lessons of "history" understood in terms of a humanistic discipline. Blom's introduction to *Property, Piracy and Punishment. Hugo Grotius on War and Booty in De Iure Praedae — Concepts and Contexts* (Leiden: Brill, 2009), p. 6, completely dismisses the "spin doctor" label as a little more than a facet of the post-colonial critique of Grotius: "The post-colonial critic looks at Grotius as a spin doctor of the V.O.C., as the Karl Rove of Oldenbarnevelt, but spin doctors don't normally go so far as to develop a brand new theory of natural law ... or introduce a concept of divided sovereignty.... It is here that the post-colonial critic joins forces with the Scholastic interpretation, with a difference though: in the new vision, Grotius is no longer interested in Scholastic doctrine per se, but only 'pinched' whatsoever suited him and the case of his patrons. The theoretical argument of *De iure praedae,* on the post-colonial critic's reading is just the necessary support for colonial aggression in Asia. It is bad conscience turned into abstract talk." Blom's edited volume published by Brill in 2009, corresponds in content and page breaks to the special edition of the journal *Grotiana New Series* (abbreviated in the present book as *GNS*), vols. 26–28, covering the years 2005–7.
12. Grotius, *Liber de Antiquitate Reipublicae Batavicae* (Leiden: Ex officina Plantiniana Raphelingij, 1610), TMD, p. 309, no. 691; Grotius, *On the Antiquity of the Batavian Republic*, with the notes of Petrus Scriverius, ed. and tr. Jan Waszink (Assen: Van Gorcum, 2000); Grotius, *Annales et Historiae de Rebus Belgicis* (Amsterdam: Ioannis Blaeu, 1657), TMD, p. 337, no. 741. On the writing of *De Antiquitate* after April 1609, see specifically also Nellen, *Hugo de Groot. Een leven in strijd om de vrede*, p. 97. The *Annales et Historiae,* were completed around 1612 but published posthumously through the efforts of Grotius' son Pieter de Groot. See also Borschberg, "Zur Entstehung von Grotius' De Imperio Potestatum circa Sacra", *ZRG,* KA 79 (1993): 348, esp. note 31.
13. The text of *De Republica Emendanda* first appeared as an appendix to Fiorella de Michelis, *Le origini storiche e culturali del pensiero di Ugo Grozio* (Florence: La Nuova Italia, 1967), pp. 169–89, and "De Republica Emendanda: A Juvenile Tract by Hugo Grotius on the Emendation of the Dutch Polity", ed. Arthur Eyffinger and P.A.H. de Boer, *GNS* 5 (1984): 2–79. Grotius, *Parallelon rerumpublicarum liber tertius: De moribus ingenioque populorum Atheniensium, Romanorum, Batavorum*, 4 vols. (Haarlem: A. Losjes, 1801–3).

14. The most comprehensive and up-to-date reconstruction of this seminal event and the writing of *De Iure Praedae* can be found in van Ittersum, "Hugo Grotius in Context", *AJSS* 31, 3 (2003): 511–48, and van Ittersum, *Profit and Principle,* pp. 1–52, esp. 30–43. For the broader Asian context of this event, see Borschberg, "The Seizure of the *Santa Catarina* off Singapore: Dutch Freebooting, the Portuguese Empire and Intra-Asian trade at the Dawn of the Seventeenth Century", *RC,* International Edition, 11 (2004): 11–25.
15. Leiden, University Library, B.P.L. 917. The manuscript was originally sold in two parts at the 1864 auction, see Noordhoff, *Beschrijving van ... papieren afkomstig van Huig de Groot,* part I, lot 11, p. 13 and part IX, lot 72, p. 25. The transcript of the reconstructed Latin text was published as, *De Iure Praedae Commentarius*, ed. H.G. Hamaker (The Hague: Martinus Nijhoff, 1868). The first translation into English was prepared almost a century later: *De Jure Praedae Commentarius. Commentary on the Law of Prize and Booty. A Translation of the Original Manuscript of 1604*, tr. Glwadys L. Williams and Walter H. Zeydel (Oxford: Clarendon Press, 1950).
16. The text was first printed in *De Gids* in 1868. The full article in the Dutch original can be found in *Fruin's Verspreide Geschriften*. An English translation was prepared and published in 1925 in the Leiden-based law series *Bibliotheca Visseriana*. See Fruin, *Verspreide geschriften met aantekeningen, toevoegsels en verbetering uit des schrijvers nalatenschap*, ed. P.J. Blok and P.L. Muller (The Hague: Martinus Nijhoff, 1900–5), III, pp. 367–412; also "An Unpublished Work of Hugo Grotius", *Bibliotheca Visseriana* 5 (1925): 3–71.
17. Coolhaas, "Een bron van het historische gedeelte van Hugo de Groot's De Jure Praedae", *BMH* 79 (1965): 415–540.
18. Van Ittersum, *Profit and Principle,* esp. pp. 105–88. This has since been supplemented by a learned article redating the autograph manuscript of based on the "material evidence" at hand. See van Ittersum, "Dating the Manuscript of *De Jure Praedae*", *History of European Ideas* 35 (2009): 125–93.
19. See esp. van Ittersum, "Hugo Grotius in Context", *AJSS* 31, 3 (2003): 512–3, *Profit and Principle,* p. 119, together with her references to Fruin and Grotius correspondence. The dating has not been questioned by Grotius scholars until recently. See esp. Fruin, "An Unpublished Work by Hugo Grotius", *Bibliotheca Visseriana* (1925): 39–40; CML, pp. 11–2; and CIPC, introduction, p. xiii.
20. This manuscript is filed at Leiden University Library as Ms. B.P.L. 917.
21. These are among the findings presented by van Ittersum and the author to the Grotius Research Group in 2005 at the Netherlands Institute for Advanced Studies in Wassenaar. See also van Ittersum, "Preparing *Mare liberum* for the Press: Hugo Grotius' Rewriting of Chapter 12 of *De iure praedae* in November–December 1608", *GNS* 26–8 (2005–7): 246–80 and van Ittersum, "Mare Liberum in the West Indies? Hugo Grotius and the Case

of the Swimming Lion, a Dutch Pirate in the Caribbean at the Turn of the Seventeenth Century", *Itinerario* 31, 3 (2007): esp. 76–80; van Ittersum, *Profit and Principle,* esp. pp. 321–31.

22. R. Huijbrecht, "Hugo de Groot als Advocaat-Fiscaal van het Hof van Holland, Zeeland en West-Friesland, 1607–1614", *De Hollandse jaren van Hugo de Groot (1582–1621). Lezingen van het colloquium ter gelegenheid van de 350-ste sterfdag van Hugo de Groot ('s-Gravenhage: 31 augustus –1 september 1995),* ed. H.J.M. Nellen and Jan Trapman (Hilversum: Verloren, 1996), pp. 45–56.
23. Period materials and some contemporary secondary literature refer to the Dutch Republic as the United Provinces. In this book, these two terms will be employed synonymously. Grotius confessed (admittedly after his arrest and incarceration) that he had nothing to do with the negotiations for a truce with Spain. He reminded that the negotiations predated his appointment as *advocaat fiscaal,* and in his declaration of 24 January 1619, confirmed that the matters surrounding the truce negotiations happened "before my time [in politics]". Grotius averred that the continuation of the war against Spain is visible, significantly, from his petitions lodged with the Dutch States General on behalf of the VOC. See "Verhooren en andere bescheiden betreffende het rechtsgeding van Hugo de Groot", ed. Fruin, *WHGU* 14 (1871): 30, 226; also Nellen, *Hugo de Groot. Een leven in strijd om de vrede,* pp. 90–1. Concerning Grotius' pamphleteering during the period of the truce negotiations, see esp. van Ittersum, *Profit and Principle,* pp. 283–358, esp. pp. 331–55.
24. Nellen, *Hugo de Groot. Een leven in strijd om de vrede,* p. 87.
25. This treatise was purchased by the Leiden University in part IX, lot 78, of the 1864 auction. It is listed there as "Dissert[atio] de Principum jure ac potestate" (Dissertation on the right and power of princes). See Noordhoff, *Beschrijving van … papieren afkomstig van Huig de Groot,* p. 27.
26. Leiden, University Library, B.P.L. 922–I; Noordhoff, *Beschrijving van … papieren afkomstig van Huig de Groot,* part IX, lot 78, p. 27; Willem J.M. van Eysinga, "Eene onuitgegeven nota van de Groot", *MKNAW,* NR 10, 10 (1955): 235–52; Borschberg, "Commentarius in Theses XI. Ein unveröffentlichtes Kurzwerk von Hugo Grotius", *ZRG,* RA 110 (1992): 452–5; and more extensively in CiT; Borschberg, "De Pace. Ein unveröffentlichtes Fragment von Hugo Grotius über Krieg und Frieden", *ZRG,* RA 113 (1996): 268–92; "De Societate Publica cum Infidelibus. Ein Frühwerk von Hugo Grotius", *ZRG,* RA 115 (1998): 355–93. "Grotius, the Social Contract and Political Resistance", *IILJ Working Paper* 6 (2006): 5–9. A transcript and discussion of the fragment *De Pace* can also be found in the unpublished thesis by Marco Zaglio, *Jus Pacis e Concezione della Pace in Ugo Grozio,* unpublished Laureate thesis (Milan: Università degli Studi di Milano, 2008). Concerning the fragment *De Bello ob Libertatem Eligendo,* see Borschberg, "De Pace", *ZRG,* RA 113 (1996): 269, note 6; "Grotius, the Social Contract and Political

Resistance", p. 7. The unpublished manuscript was placed on exhibit on the occasion of the Grotius exhibit in 1925 commemorating the third centenary of the publication of *De Iure Belli ac Pacis*. See the exhibit catalogue *Grotius-Tentoonstelling te 's-Gravenhage, 13–28 Juni 1925* (Leiden: A.W. Sijthoff, 1925), exhibit number 222.

27. Grotius, *Mare Liberum, sive de iure quod Batavis competit ad Indicana commercia dissertatio,* TMD, p. 210, no. 541. For a period translation into English, see Grotius, *The Free Sea*, tr. Richard Hakluyt, ed. and int. David Armitage (Indianapolis: Liberty Fund, 2004).
28. The Zeeland Chamber of the VOC commissioned the work from Grotius after negotiations between the Spanish and the Dutch broke down in early August 1608. There were serious differences in matters of religion and trade in the Indies.
29. These objections were voiced in February 1609. See Nellen, *Hugo de Groot. Een leven in strijd om de vrede*, p. 96; on the delays in the production of the book, see ibid., pp. 95–6. See also van Ittersum, "Mare Liberum in the West Indies?", *Itinerario* 31, 3 (2007): 77–80.
30. John C. Grayson, *From Protectorate to Partnership, Anglo-Dutch Relations, 1598–1625*, unpublished doctoral dissertation (London: University of London, 1978).
31. Letter of the Dutch States General to Dutch ambassador Noël Caron, dated 23 March 1613, in CC, pp. 82–3, and letter of the Dutch States General to King James I/VI dated 23 March 1613, CC, pp. 83–4; and the letter of English ambassador Ralph Winwood to King James I/VI dated 6 April 1613, CC, p. 85, "Now here are readye to depart for England three Commissioners, to treate w.th the Governor and companye of yo.r east Indian Marchants, they are two BourgheM.rs, Pavius [Reynier Pauw] of Amsterdam and Bourrell [Jacob Boreel] of Middelborough, and Meirman [Dirk Meerman], one of th'eschevins of Delfe, [and] by order from the states of Holland, to assist in this negociation, one Mons.r Grotius is required to accompanye them, who lately was Advocate-fiscall of Holland, and now is chosen Pensionary of Rotterdam, in place of Mons.r Barnevelts [Johan van Oldenarnevelt's] brother [Elias], lately deceased. They come onely authorised to treate, from the companye of the east Indian-marchants of these Provinces, yet bring w.th them, letters of recommendation, issued from the states generall to yo.r Mat.ye ..." Text in square brackets has been inserted for clarification and for the benefit of the reader.
32. For the full text of this opening address, see appendix 13.
33. David K. Bassett, "The 'Amboyna Massacre' of 1623", *JSEAH* 1, 2 (1960): 4, ".... [T]he English directors had reluctantly agreed to an alliance with the 'Hollanders' in 1619, by which they were allowed to establish factories alongside the Dutch ones in the Moluccas, the Bandas and Amboyna, in return for bearing one third of the maintenance costs of the Dutch garrisons."

34. This text has been published as Grotius, *The Free Sea*, tr. Hakluyt, ed. and int. Armitage, esp. pp. xxi–xxiii.
35. On this, see for example Borschberg, "Zur Entstehung von De Imperio", *ZRG*, KA 79 (1993): 345 *et seq*.
36. Some of the more important contributions on this subject include: Carl Bangs, *Arminius, a Study in the Dutch Reformation* (Nashville: Abingdon Press, 1971); Enno Conring, *Kirche und Staat nach der Lehre der niederländischen Calvinisten in der ersten Hälfte des 17. Jahrhunderts* (Neukirchen-Vluyn: Neukirchner Verlag des Erziehungsvereins, 1965); Douglas Nobbs, *Theocracy and Toleration: A Study of the Disputes in Dutch Calvinism from 1600 to 1650* (Cambridge: CUP, 1938). For additional literature, see Borschberg, "Zur Entstehung von De Imperio", *ZRG*, KA 79 (1993): 347, note 27.
37. See esp. the letter by Antonious Walaeus to Grotius dated 1 November 1611, BW 214, and Grotius' reply dated 11 November 1611, BW 215, pp. 185–7.
38. Grotius, *Meletius, sive de iis quae inter Christianos conveniunt epistola*, ed. Guillaume H.M. Posthumus-Mejyes (Leiden: Brill, 1988).
39. In fact, Grotius was convinced that he left a stellar impression during his visit in London, especially with the King. He later claimed in his political memoirs that James I/VI was favorably disposed toward Grotius succeeding Noël Caron as Dutch ambassador to England in the event that the latter should retire or pass away in office. See "Memorië van Mijne Intentiën", ed. Fruin, *WHGU* 14 (1871): 30.
40. See also Borschberg, "Zur Entstehung von De Imperio", *ZRG*, KA 79 (1993): 350–1.
41. Grotius, *Ordinum Hollandiae ac Westfrisiae pietas ab Improbissimis multorum calumniis, praesertim vero a nupera Sibrandi Lubberti epistola quam ad reveren dissimum Archiepiscopum Cantuariensem scripsit vindicata* (Leiden: Iohannes Patius, 1613), TMD, pp. 390–2, no. 817. For a modern edition and translation of this work, see Grotius, *Ordinum Hollandiae ac Westfrisiae Pietas (1613)*, ed. and tr. Edwin Rabbie (Leiden: Brill, 1995).
42. This treatise was published posthumously in 1648, TMD, pp. 436–7, no. 894. For the most up-to-date and comprehensive study of this work, see Grotius, *De imperio summarum potestatum circa sacra*, ed. and intr. Harm-Jan van Dam, 2 vols. (Leiden: Brill, 2001). A neat secretarial copy containing notes in the hand of Grotius is found in the Hague, Koninklijke Bibliotheek, Ms. 131. C.21, Hugo Grotius, *De Imperio Summarum Potestatum circa Sacra*.
43. Concerning this appointment, see Nellen, *Hugo de Groot. Een leven in strijd om de vrede*, p. 174.
44. Fruin, *Geschiedenis der Staatsinstellingen in Nederland tot den val der Republiek*, ed. H.T. Colenbrander and I. Schöffer (The Hague: Martinus Nijhoff, 1980), pp. 224–5, 239.

45. The autograph text of the *Decretum* can be found among the Grotius papers of the Remonstrant Church, presently lodged in the University of Amsterdam, III.C.5, fol. 139. See also Borschberg, "Zur Entstehung von De Imperio", *ZRG*, KA 79 (1993): 354, note 60.
46. Grotius, *Decretum … Ordinum Hollandiae et Westfrisiae pro pace ecclesiarum, munitum Sacrae scripturae auctoritate,et Conciliorum, Antiquorum Patrum, Confessionum publicarum et recentiorum Doctorum testimoniis* (Leiden: J. Patius, 1614), TMD, p. 397, no. 826. The *Defensio Decreti Ordinum Hollandiae ac Westfrisiae Pro pace Ecclesiarum* was first published posthumously in his *Opera Omnia Theologica* (Amsterdam: J. Blaeu, 1679), IV, pp. 195–200, TMD p. 444, no. 910 and 910a.
47. On this issue, see Grotius, *Verklaeringe vande E.E. Heeren magistraten ende regeerders der Stadt Haerlem, door haren ghedeputeerden ghedaen inde Vergaderinghe der Ed. Mo. Heeren Staten van Hollandt ende West-Vrieslandt, ende by de Heeren Edelen ende meeste Leden vande zelve Vergaderinghe gheapprobeert* (Publisher unknown, 1618), pp. 4–9, TMD, pp. 412–3, no. 855. On the Scherpe Resolutie and the *waardgelders*, see also Grotius, "Memorië van mijne Intentiën", in "Verhooren en andere bescheiden betreffende het rechtsgeding van Hugo de Groot", ed. Fruin, *WHGU* 14 (1871): 19 *et seq.*, TMD, p. 448, no. 918. These valuable but doubtlessly self-serving political memoirs written by Grotius while serving his prison sentence in the fortress of Loevesteyn are found in Amsterdam University Library, Ms. Z 104, were used by Caspar Brandt and Adriaan van Cattenburgh, the latter who also deposited the manuscript with the Remonstrant Library in Amsterdam on 14 October 1737. The biographers transcribed the text and interspersed it with other documents and letters in their *Historie van het leven des heeren Huig de Groot, Beschreven tot den aanvang van zyn Gezantschap wegens de Koninginne en Kroone van Zweden aan't Hof van Vrankryk,* 2 vols. (Amsterdam and Dordrecht: Joannes van Braam and Geerard onder den Linden, 1727), I, pp. 135–217.
48. See for example Geeraerd Brandt, *The History of the Reformation and other Ecclesiastical Transactions in and about the Low-Countries,* 4 vols. (London: printed by T. Wood for Timothy Childe, 1720–3), II, pp. 407–8.
49. See esp. Grotius, *Verklaringhe vande E.E. Heeren Magistraten ende Regeerders der Stadt Haerlem*, TMD 864, pp. 4–9. This position, incidentally, marks a sharp about-face in Grotius' understanding of the Dutch Republican constitution when compared to his early treatise *De Republica Emendanda.* In this latter work, sovereignty is said to be vested collectively with the Dutch States General.
50. Grotius, "Memorië van mijne Intentiën", ed. Fruin, *WHGU* 14 (1871): 36–7. Borschberg, "Hugo Grotius", in *The Oxford Encyclopedia of Maritime History,* ed. John B. Hattendorf, 4 vols. (Oxford: OUP, 2007), II, p. 115. Concerning Grotius' appointment as Pensionary of Rotterdam between 1613–8, see J.G.

Smit, "De Rotterdamse jaren van Hugo de Groot", in *De Hollandse jaren van Hugo de Groot,* ed. Nellen and Trapman, pp. 125–43; and for the deteriorating relationship between Oldenbarnevelt and Prince Maurice up to 1618, see A.Th. van Deursen, "Oldenbarnevelt en Maurits", in *De Hollandse jaren van Hugo de Groot,* pp. 155–60.

51. Grotius, "Memorië van mijne Intentiën", ed. Fruin, *WHGU* 14 (1871): 37 *et seq.*; "Verhooren en andere bescheiden betreffende het rechtsgeding van Hugo de Groot", ed. Fruin, *WHGU* 14 (1871): 71. See also the text in Brandt and Cattenburgh, *Historie van het leven des Heeren Huig de Groot*, I, pp. 197–206, which reproduces the sentence against Grotius. Significantly, his library was confiscated. The list of titles taken from his private library is important to researchers today (even if it is believed to be incomplete), as a clearer picture emerges of the various titles (but not necessarily the editions) to which Grotius had ready access. See the older discourses by G. Moll, "De confiscatie der goederen van Hugo de Groot", *Oud-Holland, Niuewe Bijdragen voor de Geschiedenis der Landerlandsche Kunst, Letterkunde, Nijverheid, enz.*, 20 (1902): 83–112, and P.C. Molhuysen, "De bibliotheek van Hugo de Groot in 1618", *MKNAW*, afd. letterkunde, NR 6.3 (1918): 50–63; and E. Rabbie, "The History and Reconstruction of Hugo Grotius' Library. A Survey of the Results of Former Studies with an Indication of New Lines of Approach", in *Bibliothecae selectee da Cusano a Leopardi,* ed. E. Canone (Florence: Casa Editrice Leo S. Olschki, 1993), pp. 119–37, esp. pp. 124–5 concerning the incompleteness of the list. See also the useful discussions by E.J.J. van der, Heijden, "Der boekerij van Grotius", *Grotiana* 3 (1930): 18–38; C.S.M. Rademaker, "Books and Grotius at Loevestein", *Quaerendo* 2 (1972): 2–29; and P.P. Witkam, "A short book list compiled by Hugo Grotius", *Quaerendo* 12 (1982): 221–36.
52. Grotius, "Memorië van mijne Intentiën", ed. Fruin, *WHGU* 14 (1871): 76.
53. See among other sources R.W. Lee, "The Family Life of Grotius", *TGS* 20 (1934): esp. 13–4.
54. The date of completion given for his political memoirs is 17 July 1619; see Grotius, "Memorië van mijne Intentiën", ed. Fruin, *WHGU* 14 (1871): 80.
55. TMD, pp. 421–4, no. 872. See also H.C. Rogge, "De 'Verantwoordingh' van Hugo de Groot", *Bijdragen voor Vaderlandsche Geschiedenis* 7 (1893): 89–134.
56. TMD, pp. 349–51, no. 757. See also Grotius, "Memorië van mijne Intentiën", ed. Fruin, *WHGU* 14 (1871): 79, refers to this work as *Onderwijs in de Hollantsche Rechten* (Instructions on the Laws of Holland). Grotius also lamented that he did not have access to all the sources he needed. Concerning the genesis of this work in general, see Fruin, "Hugo de Groots Inleidinge tot de Hollandsche Rechts-geleerdheid", in *Fruin's Verspreide Geschriften,* VIII, pp. 10–31.

57. These Biblical annotations, which were published in 1641 (New Testament, TMD, pp. 555–7, no. 1135) and 1644 (Old Testament, TMD, pp. 557–9, no. 1137) respectively, are featured in the *Opera Omnia Theologica* (1679). With reference to the academic value of these Biblical annotations, Henk J. de Jonge opines: "…[d]eze kunnen zonder risico als de beste bijbelse comentaar worden beschowd die in Europa in de 17de eeuw is geproduceert" (… these [annotations] can be regarded without risk as the best Bible commentary produced in the 17th century). See H.J. de Jonge, *De bestudering van het Nieuwe Testament aan de Noordnederlandse universiteiten en het Remonstrants Seminarie van 1575 tot 1700* (Amsterdam and New York: Noord Hollandse Uitgevers, 1980), p. 54. For a brief historical account of their genesis at Loevesteyn, see also "Hugo Grotius: exégète du Nouveau Testament", *The World of Hugo Grotius (1583–1645). Proceedings of the International Colloquium Organized by the Grotius Committee of the Royal Netherlands Academy of Arts and Sciences, Rotterdam, 6–9 April, 1983,* ed. Robert Feenstra (Amsterdam and Maarssen: APA-Holland University Press, 1984), pp. 98–9. Concerning the relevance of the theological works of Grotius in general within the body of his writings on the law of nations, see the important exposé by Willian P. George, "Grotius, Theology and International Law: Overcoming Textbook Bias", *Journal of Law and Religion* 14, 2 (1999–2000): 605–31.
58. Grotius, *Bewys Van den waren godsdienst In ses Boecken gestelt* (Publisher unknown, 1622), TMD 143. A manuscript copy of the *Bewys* titled *Gheloofs Voorberecht,* (but containing slightly different readings with autograph corrections) is deposited with the Bibliothèque Nationale in Paris. See the entry in *Catalogue des manuscrits néerlandais de la Bibliothèque Nationale,* ed. by Gideon Busken Huet (Paris: Publisher unknown, 1886), p. 39, no. 34, "Rédaction en vers néerlandais de la 'Défense de la Religion Chrétienne'" de H. de Groot. Texte avec des nombreuses corrections, et des notes marginales qui contiennent le résumé des paragraphes.... Ce ms. n'est pas une copie du texte imprimé.... Dernier vers (raturé): "En denckt, och Heer, het is te Loevestein gemaect, Einde." (Version in Dutch verse of the "Defence of the Christian Religion" by H. de Groot. Text with numerous corrections and marginalia that summarise the paragraphs.… This manuscript is not a copy of the printed text. The last verse (deleted): "And think, O Lord, this is written at Loevesteyn, End.").
59. Other activities in Loevesteyn are mentioned in Grotius, "Memorië van mijne Intentiën", ed. Fruin, *WHG* 14 (1871): 78–9, and include the translation (from Greek into Latin) of Johannes Stobaeus' *Florilegium* as well as the *Sentences* of Publius Primus (from Latin into Dutch).
60. R.W. Lee, "The Family Life of Grotius", *TGS* 20 (1934): esp. 14–5; Rogge, "Hugo de Groot te Parijs van 1621 tot 1625", *De Gids* 3 (1893): 249–73, 450–77.

61. BW 727, annex 2, dated 26 February 1622.
62. See also H.C. Rogge, "Hugo de Groot te Parijs van 1621 tot 1625", I, *De Gids,* 4 serie, 57 (1893): 261–2. Louis Aubery du Maurier, *Mémoires pour servir à l'Histoire de Hollande et des autres Provinces Unis. Où l'on verra les veritable causes des divisions qui sont depuis soixante ans dans cette Republique, et qui la menacent de ruine* (Paris: Jean Villette, 1680), p. 340, appraises the stipend at 1,000 écus. In any case, according to Grotius' own account, payment was irregular and frequently in arrear. See also H.J.M. Nellen, *Grotius: Geschichte seines Lebens basierend auf seiner Korrespondenz,* Nachbarn, 28 (Bonn: Niederländische Botschaft, 1983), p. 24; Nellen, *Hugo de Groot (1583–1645). De loopbaan van een geleerd staatsman,* pp. 40–1.
63. For the Hamburg years of Grotius, see esp. M. Grimm, "Hugo Grotius' Aufenthalt in Hamburg in den Jahren 1632–1634", *Zeitschrift des Vereins für Hamburgische Geschichte* 27 (1926): 130–40. Nellen, *Hugo de Groot. Een leven in strijd om de vrede,* pp. 380–8.
64. Concerning the appointment in Mainz or Worms, see Nellen, *Hugo de Groot. Een leven in strijd om de vrede,* p. 388.
65. Grotius, *Dissertatio de origine gentium Americanarum* (Publisher unknown) 1642, TMD, pp. 326–7, no. 725; and *Dissertatio altera de origine gentium Americanarum* (Publisher unknown) 1643, TMD pp. 329–30, no. 731. On the background of the debate that evidently took place against the backdrop of the 150th anniversary of the discovery of the New World by Columbus, see also Nellen, *Hugo de Groot. Een leven in strijd om de vrede,* pp. 551–5, and Joan-Pau Rubiés, "Hugo Grotius's Dissertation on the Origin of the American Peoples and the Use of Comparative Methods", in *Grotius,* ed. John Dunn and Ian Harris, 2 vols. (Cheltenham: Edward Elgar Publishing, 1997), II, pp. 575–98.
66. John Selden, *Mare Clausum seu De Dominio Maris Libri Duo* (London: Will Stanesbeius for Richard Meighen, 1635). On the use of Selden's text against Dutch whalers in Norway, see BW 2416, letter by Grotius to Nicolaas van Reigersberch, 28 December 1635, p. 440; also BW 2430, p. 460, BW 2432, p. 463; BW 2475, p. 524. In a letter to Ludwig Camerarius dated 14 February 1636, however, Grotius noted with evident relief that Sweden's interests were not affected by the publication of Selden's work (see BW 2475, p. 524). Similar observations were expressed in a letter by Grotius to Sweden's Axel Oxenstierna (BW 2478, p. 529). See also Borschberg, "Hugo Grotius", in *The Oxford Encyclopedia of Maritime History,* ed. Hattendorf, II, p. 115.
67. R. Warden Lee, "Grotius — the Last Phase, 1635–45", *TGS* 31 (1945): 207.
68. BW, 2227, letter by Grotius to P. du May, dated 10 August 1635, pp. 148–9, esp. p. 149. Also cited in Nellen, *Hugo de Groot. Een leven in strijd om de vrede,* p. 403.
69. BW 2178, letter by Grotius to Axel Oxenstierna dated 10 July 1635, p. 80; BW 2179, letter by Grotius to his brother-in-law Nicolaas van Reigersberch

dated 10 July 1635, p. 81, Grotius speculates that the States of Holland would commission Pieter Cunaeus to pen a reply to Selden (which indeed happened by January 1636), see BW 2427, p. 455; BW 2439, p. 474; BW 2449, p. 489; BW 2450, p. 490). In a letter to Ludwig Camerarius dated 16 July 1635, BW 2181, p. 86, Grotius rightly anticipated new hostilities with the English on the question of fisheries. The printed edition does not appear to have been ready until the final weeks of 1635, and a copy of which was rushed by the Dutch ambassador in London, Albert Joachimi, to the Dutch States General (BW 2410, p. 431). See also Nellen, *Hugo de Groot. Een leven in strijd om de vrede,* pp. 403–4.

70. The thesis is advanced by P.H. Winkelman, *Remonstranten en katholieken in de eeuw van Hugo de Groot* (Nijmegen: Centrale Drukkerij, 1945) among other authors.
71. BW 5808, pp. 339–40. The postscript on p. 340 reads "Neque tamen praefestino". (Still, I am not in a hurry). On this letter and the prospect of Grotius' conversion to Catholicism, see the comprehensive list of references in Nellen, *Hugo de Groot: De loopbaan van een geleerd staatsman*, note 244, pp. 124–5. See also Borschberg, "Hugo Grotius", in *The Oxford Encyclopedia of Maritime History,* ed. Hattendorf, II, p. 115.
72. BW 7242, appendix 3, letter by Queen Christina of Sweden to Marc Duncan de Cerisantes dated 21 January 1645, p. 330.
73. BW 7460A, dated 28 August/7 September 1645, p. 523.
74. BW 7460A, p. 523. See also Nellen, *Hugo de Groot. Een leven in strijd om de vrede,* p. 585. A different sum amounting to 12,000 *Rijksdaalder* is cited by Aubery du Maurier in his *Mémoires pour servir à l'Histoire de Hollande et des autres Provinces unis,* p. 358.
75. BW 7460A dated September 1645, letters concerning the death of Grotius, p. 523. A close reading of the published correspondence reveals that Grotius had kept a close eye on the Duc de Longueville's movements between France and Münster; see BW 7248 dated 4 February 1645, p. 418; BW 7309 dated 11 February 1645, p. 451; BW 7330 dated 24 February 1645, p. 486; BW 7333 dated 24 February 1645, p. 490; BW 7396 dated 1 April 1645, p. 605; BW 7398 dated 1 April 1645, p. 609; and BW 7399 dated 11 April 1645, p. 612.
76. BW 7460A, p. 523. Nellen, *Hugo de Groot. Een leven in strijd om de vrede,* p. 588.
77. Gerhard Reintanz and Friedrich Elchlepp, "Grotius stirbt in Rostock", in Hugo Grotius, 1583–1645. *Beiträge zum nationalen und internationelen Seerecht,* Heft 7 (Rostock: Gesellschaft für Seerecht der Deutschen Demokratischen Republik, 1983), p. 33; Nellen, *Hugo de Groot. Een leven in strijd om de vrede,* p. 589.
78. Nellen, *Hugo de Groot,* pp. 589–91.

Chapter 2

1. These are described in P.A. Tiele, *Catalogue de manuscrits autographes de Hugo Grotius dont le vente a eu lieu à la Haye le 15. novembre 1864 sous la direction et au domicile de Martinus Nijhoff,* 2nd ed. with annotations by W.J.M. van Eysinga and L.J. Noordhoff (The Hague: Martinus Nijhoff, 1952), part I, "Receuil concernant les voyages des Hollandais aux Indes Orientales, la Compagnie des Indes, etc. 1600–6"; W.E. Smelt, "Beschrijving eener verzameling papieren afkomstig van Hugo de Groot", in *Inventarisse van Rijks- en andere archieven van rijkwege uitgegeven,* 4 vols. (The Hague: Algemeene Landsdrukkerij, 1928–32), I (1928), pp. 73–105. See esp. no. 3.
2. For a study of this fragment, see Borschberg, "'De Societate Publica cum Infidelibus': Ein Frühwerk von Hugo Grotius", *ZRG*, RA 115 (1998): 355–93.
3. The Flemish merchant Jacques de Coutre, who was based in Portuguese Melaka at the time, specifically places the *Santa Cataraina* incident "enfrente el río de Jor" (before the Johor River), meaning around the Johor River estuary. This location is correct. See Jacques de Coutre, *Andanzas asiáticas*, ed. Eddy Stols, Benjamin Teensma and Johan [V]erbeckmoes (Madrid: História 16, 1991), p. 169.
4. Borschberg, *The Singapore and Melaka Straits,* p. 68; also Charles Ralph Boxer, *Fidalgos in the Far East, 1550–1770: Fact and Fancy in the History of Macao* (The Hague: Martinus Nijhoff, 1948), p. 50.
5. The *Santa Catarina* incident and its aftermath have moved in recent years to the forefront of scholarly attention, specifically in the context of *De Iure Praedae* and its commission, the evolution of early VOC policy in Asia, as well as the historic origins of the Dutch-Johor alliance. See esp. Borschberg, "The Seizure of the *Santa Catarina* off Singapore", *RC*, International Edition, 11 (2004): 11–25; "The Seizure of the *Santa Catarina* Revisited", *JSEAS* 33, 1 (2002): 31–62, esp. pp. 48–50; "A Portuguese-Dutch Naval Battle in the Johor River Delta", *Zeitschrift der Deutschen Morgenländischen Gesellschaft* 153, 1 (2003): 157–75; "Luso-Johor-Dutch Relations in the Straits of Malacca and Singapore", *Itinerario* 28, 2 (2004): 15–33, *The Singapore and Melaka Straits*, pp. 60–99, as well as van Ittersum, "Hugo Grotius in Context", *AJSS* 31, 3 (2003): 511–48 and more extensively in her book *Profit and Principle.*
6. Around the time the *Santa Catarina* was seized, the Archbishop of Goa wrote on 6 April 1603 to the King of Portugal: "As naus holandesas e inglesas são tantas este ano, que todos estes mares estão salpicados delas". (There are so many Dutch and English ships this year that all these seas are dotted with them.) See Paulo J. de Sousa Pinto, *Portugueses e Malaios: Malaca e os Sultanatos de Johor e Achém, 1575–1619* (Lisbon: Comissão Nacional para as Comemorações dos Descobrimentos Portugueses, 1997), document 13, p. 285.

7. An entrenched but erroneous view holds that *De Iure Praedae* was written with the objective, among others, of addressing the concerns of Mennonite stakeholders of the V.O.C. who objected to the use of violence. On this point see, for example Richard Tuck, "Grotius and Selden", *The Cambridge History of Political Thought, 1450–1700*, ed. J.H. Burns and Mark A. Goldie (Cambridge: CUP, 1991), p. 504. This interpretation has been convincingly rebuffed in van Ittersum, *Profit and Principle*, pp. 113–9, pp. 167 *et seq*. See also chapter 4.
8. An English translation of the verdict can be found in IPC, pp. 510–4; the early modern German translation of Levinus Hulsius is found in CIPC, appendix B.II, pp. 375–9.
9. IPC, p. 514; CIPC, p. 378.
10. Borschberg, "The Johor-VOC Alliance and the Twelve Years Truce", *IILJ Working Paper* 8 (2009): 7. See also *Johan van Oldenbarnevelt. Bescheiden betreffende zijn staatkundig beleid en zijn familie,* ed. Sikko P. Haak and Augustus J. Veenendaal, 3 vols. (The Hague: Martinus Nijhoff, 1934–67), II, pp. 174 *et seq*., where Oldenbarnevelt recorded his discussions with the Spanish delegates over the East Indies trade. See also Jonathan I. Israel, *Dutch Primacy in World Trade, 1585–1740* (Oxford: Clarendon Press, 1989), p. 81.
11. For an in-depth study of the historical background to the Anglo-Dutch conferences, especially from an English perspective, see the unpublished doctoral thesis of Grayson, *From Protectorate to Partnership.*
12. Letter of the Dutch States General to Dutch ambassador Noël Caron, dated 23 March 1613 in CC, p. 83; letter of the States General to King James I/VI dated 23 March 1613, in CC, p. 84; resolution of the States General of 25 March 1613, in CC, p. 86.
13. Grotius was originally not supposed to participate at this conference, but he was suggested as a deputy shortly before the Dutch delegation set off for London; BW 256, pp. 229–30; W. Noël Sainsbury, *Calendar of State Papers, Colonial Series, East Indies, China and Japan, 1513–1616, Preserved in Her Majesty's Public Record Office and Elsewhere* (London: Longman, Green, Longman & Roberts, 1862), no. 641, p. 251 (23 March 1613). — Various aspects of Grotius deputation to London, including the religious aspects of his mission, have been discussed in Borschberg, "Zur Entstehung von Grotius' De Imperio Summarum Potestatum circa Sacra", *ZRG,* KA 79 (1993): 342–79; the older contribution by W.S.M. Knight, "Grotius in England: His Opposition There to the Principles of *Mare Liberum*", *TGS* 5 (1920): 5–15, as well as in the latest critical edition of Grotius, *De imperio summarum potestatum circa sacra,* ed. and int. van Dam.
14. Winwood conveyed an unfavourable impression of Grotius, not least during the latter's visit to London in 1613. See Ralph Winwood, *Memorials of Affairs*

of State in the Reign of Queen Elizabeth and James I, ... ed. Edmund Sawyer, 3 vols. (London: W.B. for T. Ward, 1725), III, p. 459, "You must take heed how you trust Doctor Grotius too far.... At his first coming to the King, by reason of this good Latine Tongue, [Grotius] was so tedious and full of tittle tattle, that the King's Judgment of him was that he was some Pedant, full of Words and of no great Judgment...." This was particularly the case, Winwood explains, at a supper hosted by Lancelot Andrewes, the Lord Bishop of Ely.

15. Letter of English ambassador Ralph Winwood to King James I/VI dated 23 March 1613, in CC, p. 85.
16. Den Tex, *Oldenbarnevelt*, III, pp. 311–2. Jan A. Somers and Cornelis G. Roelofsen opine that Grotius was the "logical choice" as he was "Oldenbarnevelt's Indian and legal expert" and was "well informed on Indian affairs". This verdict is problematic in the light of additional evidence presented in chapter 4 of this book. See Somers and Roelofsen, "*Mare Liberum* and the Dutch East India Company. The Freedom of the Seas and Feedom of Trade as the Legal Bases of the Dutch Colonial State in the Indonesian Archipelago", *GNS* 24–5 (2004–5): 74.
17. Cornelis Roelofsen, "Hugo de Groot en de VOC", in *De Hollandse jaren van Hugo de Groot,* ed. Nellen and Trapman, p. 59, as well as his acknowledged historical sources in n. 9.
18. Jan Somers and Cornelis Roelofsen, "*Mare Liberum* and the Dutch East India Company", *GNS* 24–5 (2004–5): 74; Roelofsen, "Hugo de Groot en de VOC", *De Hollandse Jaren van Hugo de Groot,* ed. Nellen and Trapman, pp. 63–4.
19. Letter by Caron to the Dutch States General dated 6 April 1613, in CC, p. 89.
20. See, for example, London, Public Records Office, State Papers, 105/95, letter by Archbishop George Abbot to Dudley Carleton (then serving as the ambassador of England to the Dutch Republic) dated 27 December 1616, fol. 1 verso, "He [Grotius] is a person much prejudged amongst us for a busy and factious fellow, and the higher opinion he hath of himselfe, the more unworthily wee esteeme of him. And this is not onely the conceite of our merchants who have had to do with him, but of some learned men and that of the highest ranke, for an olde and skirvy pranke parte which he played with my Lord of Ely at his last being in England. Wee hold him no true man of his worde, but apt to faine and lye which is a pranke very unfitt for civill societie."
21. Sainsbury, *Calendar of State Papers, Colonial Series, East Indies, China and Japan, 1513–1616,* no. 642, p. 252. The English delegates are mentioned in Grotius' *Verbael* written at the end of his mission dated 24 May 1613 and transcribed in BW, pp. 628–9.

22. Letter by Ralph Winwood to Robert Cecil, the Earl of Salisbury and Lord High Treasurer of England, dated 30 March 1612, in CC, p. 58. See also the resolution of the Dutch States General dated 1 February 1612, in CC, p. 49, and the letter of English ambassador Ralph Winwood to Robert Cecil, the Earl of Salisbury, dated 10 February 1612, in CC, pp. 51–2.
23. See esp. BW 424, letter of Tobias de Coene to Grotius, dated 13 October 1615, pp. 412–3 (see image on p. 212); CE, pp. 130 *et seq*. The English delegates decided to pursue a "communion of commerce in the East Indies", see Sainsbury, *Calendar of State Papers, Colonial Series, East Indies, China and Japan, 1513–1616*, no. 955, p. 400. The Dutch-language text of the cooperation accord concluded some years later in 1619 is reprinted in Lieuwe van Aitzema's *Saken van staet en oorlogh in ende omtrent de Vereenigde Nederlanden*, I, pp. 206 *et seq*. For a summary of these negotiations and their outcome, see K.N. Chaudhuri, *The English East India Company: The Study of an Early Joint-Stock Company 1600–1640* (New York, 1965), pp. 49–50 and more extensively in Grayson, *From Protectorate to Partnership*. During the functioning period of this Anglo-Dutch cooperation agreement, treaties and delivery contracts with Asian rulers were sometimes signed by, and in the name of, the two East India companies, as is evidenced by the treaty dated 24 July 1620, with Jambi. See "Corpus Diplomaticum Neerlando-Indicum", ed. Jan Ernst Heeres, eerste deel (1596–1650), *BKI* 57 (1907): 156–8, "A consulltacion off agreement maghe in Jambie the 24th Julio 1620 on the behallffe off the two Companyes: orn hon.ble jmployers off England and the Netherlands tradinge the East Indias, etc.a." as well as the contract with Jambi dated 25 October 1621, "Corpus Diplomaticum", pp. 174–5, "Articulen gereaemt ende geaccordeert tusschen de gedeputeerde van de Engellsche ende Nederlandersche Comp.e in Jambi ..." (Articles framed and agreed between the deputies of the English and Dutch Companies in Jambi ...). The existence and wording of these two separate agreements also reveal the strained working relationship of the English and Dutch East India Companies on the ground.
24. See also appendix 14 — Addressing the merger of the two East India companies, Dutch Admiral Steven van der Hagen in a letter to the Heren XVII dated 20 August 1618, saw the objective of the proposed merger as follows: "... with our combined powers [Dutch and the English] we can impede the Portuguese from trading in Surat and along the Coromandel Coast, make us masters of the Singapore Straits, and ensure that no junks call at Melaka to trade. [We can also leave the task] to the subjects of the King of Johor so that we do not have to bear the wrath of these East Indian nations." See *Bouwstoffen voor de Geschiedenis der Nederlanders in den Maleischen Archipel*, ed. Pieter Anton Tiele and Jan Ernst Heeres, 3 vols. (The Hague: Martinus Nijhoff, 1886–95), I, p. 233.

25. The Hague, Nationaal Archíef, *Collectie Hugo de Groot, Supplement I* (ms. 1.10.35.02 no. 40, fols. 137–41, 142, 143–4, 145–52). These four documents dating from the negotiations of 1615 spell out the advantages and disadvantages of the proposed merger. The objections of the London merchants to this scheme are found on fol. 142.
26. The Hague, Nationaal Archíef, *Collectie Hugo de Groot, Supplement I* (ms. 1.10.35.02 no. 40, fols. 203–4, 219–20), featuring notes and draft replies to the English delegates by Grotius made during the 1613 conference. These stress the costs of maintaining an armed Dutch presence in the East Indies. The objections and replies of the English are found on fols. 204a–9. Additional materials are found on fols. 566–87 and also appear to date from the 1613 conference, as the cut-off date is 1612. See also *Verbael* of the Dutch delegation dated early June 1613, in CC, p. 143. Concerning the so-called "internationalization of protection costs", see generally Niels Steensgaard, *The Asian Trade Revolution of the Seventeenth Century: The East India Companies and the Decline of the Caravan Trade* (Chicago and London: University of Chicago Press, 1974), pp. 151–2, and Gaastra, *De geschiedenis van de VOC,* p. 109. Simply put, military costs were deemed legitimate business expenses.
27. The emphasis on covering costs is evident from Grotius' *Verbael* of 1613 (BW, pp. 627, 632, 634). However, it is also clear from this document that the English counterparts, especially Daniel Donne, had their doubts about the veracity not only of the alleged costs, but also of the virtue of "defending the natives" (BW, I, appendix, p. 632). See also *Verbael* of the Dutch delegation dated early June 1613, in CC, p. 143, and generally also Gaastra, *De geschiedenis van de VOC,* p. 24.
28. Sainsbury, *Calendar of State Papers, Colonial Series, East Indies, China and Japan, 1513–1616,* no. 860, p. 364, 2 January 1615.
29. Final report of the English delegation dated 16 February 1615 in CC, p. 175.
30. See the individual items of correspondence between the two men that survive, especially Matelieff's memorial of 12 November 1608, reproduced in transcript in P.J.A.N. van Rietbergen, *De eerste Landvoogd Pieter Both (1568–1615). Governeur-Generaal van Nederlandsch Indië (1609–1614),* 2 vols. (Zutphen: Walburg Pers, 1987), II, pp. 237–64; the letter dated 14 December 1613, BW, 309, pp. 285–7; and the letter of 3 March 1616, BW 451, pp. 503–6. Concerning the claim Grotius had immersed himself in Asian law and customs, see especially Alexandrowicz, *An Introduction to the Law of Nations in the East Indies,* pp. 61–5; Ram Prakash Anand, *Origin and Development of the Law of the Sea. History of International Law Revisited* (The Hague: Martinus Nijhoff, 1983), p. 5; K.S. Mathew, "Trade in the Indian Ocean and the Portuguese System of Cartazes", in *The First Portuguese Colonial Empire,* ed. Malyn D.D. Newitt (Exeter: University of Exeter, 1986), p. 73; as well as chapter 4.

31. Letter by Matelieff de Jonge to Grotius dated 12 September 1615, BW 420, p. 409 and letter of 3 March 1616, BW, 451, p. 505. See also Nellen, *Hugo de Groot. Een leven in strijd om de vrede*, p. 175.
32. Several treaties with South and Southeast Asian rulers were hastily concluded by the Dutch between 1607 and 1610 in anticipation of a truce between the Dutch Republic and the Spanish Empire. See Borschberg, "The Johor-VOC Alliance and the Twelve Years Truce", *IILJ Working Paper* 8 (2009): 5–6, 8.
33. This hitherto unpublished fragment is contained in Leiden, University Library, B.P.L. 922, fols. 314–5, 317. A description of B.P.L. 922 and other manuscripts of Grotius purchased at the 1864 auction can be found in Borschberg, "Commentarius in Theses XI. Ein unveröffentlichtes Kurzwerk von Hugo Grotius", *ZRG,* RA 109 (1992): 450–5. A discussion of the fragment is found in Borschberg, "'De Societate Publica cum Infidelibus': Ein Frühwerk von Hugo Grotius", *ZRG,* RA 115 (1998): 355–93; "De Societate Publica cum Infidelibus. Una obra juvenil de Grocio", *Revista de Estudios Políticos* 83 (1993): 113–36.
34. See the parallel account in Grotius, *Annales et Historiae de Rebus Belgicis* (Amsterdam: Ioannis Blaeu, 1658), p. 468. The section relevant to the Heemskerk expedition is found in Coolhaas, "Een bron van het historische gedeelte van Hugo de Groot's De Jure Praedae", *BMH* 79 (1965): 521–31, Verclaringe van Jacob van Heemskerck van de hostile Proceduren der portugysen mitsgaders translaet van eenige portugyse brieven (Declaration of Jacob van Heemskerk concerning the hostile proceedings of the Portuguese together with translations of some Portuguese letters) and its translation in IPC, appendix II.4, letter by Heemskerk to the directors of the United Amsterdam Company (one of the voorcompagniën merged into the VOC) dated 27 August 1603, pp. 533–45. Another source underlying Grotius' account of the seizure of the *Santa Catarina* in *De Iure Praedae* is the "Discours ende advertisement van de navolgende Schepen uyt de Geunieerde Provincien" (Discourse and Announcement concerning the following Ships from the United Provinces) dated 17 March 1604. The latter manuscript was sold as part I, lot 23, at the 1864 auction of Grotius' working papers and is presently preserved in the Nationaal Archief, the Hague. A full transcript is found in P.A. Tiele, "Documenten voor de Geschiedenis der Nederlanders in het Oosten", *BMH* 6 (1883), III, "Discours ende advertisement van de navolgende schepen", pp. 243–58. The passages relating to the diplomatic prelude and seizure of the *Santa Catarina* can be found on pp. 244–9.
35. Coolhaas, "Een bron van het historische gedeelte van Hugo de Groot's De Jure Praedae", *BMH* 79 (1965): 526–7; van Ittersum, "Hugo Grotius in Context", *AJSS* 31, 3 (2003): 518. According to Heemskerk's testimony, Raja Bongsu had proceeded to Patani with the Raja Siak to attend the

latter's wedding ceremony there. The Raja Siak's exact relation to the Johor monarch remains uncertain. The travelogue of Admiral Cornelis Matelieff de Jonge, reproduced in Isaac Commelin's *Begin ende Voortgang Vande Vereenigde Neerlandsche Geoctroyeerde Oost-Indische Compagnie* (Beginning and Continuation of the United Netherlands Chartered East India Company), claims that he is a sibling from a different mother. Netscher, who probably used Commelin or another printed edition of Matelieff's voyage as his source, interprets Matelieff's testimony to mean an "illegitimate brother" of the monarch 'Ala'uddin Ri'ayat Shah III. The Standish-Croft Journal recounting Thomas Best's voyage to the East Indies treats him as a brother-in-law. See "Historische Verhael Vande treffelijkcke Reyse, gedaen naer de Oost-Indien ende China … door … Cornelis Matelief de Ionge", *BV* III: 11; E. Netscher, *De Nederlanders in Djohor en Siak* (Batavia: Bruining & Wijt, 1870), p. 29, and *The Voyage of Thomas Best to the East Indies 1612–1614,* ed. William Foster (London: Hakluyt Society, 1934), p. 169.

36. IPC, appendix II.4, letter by Heemskerk to the directors of the United Amsterdam Company, dated 27 August 1603, p. 535. See also Leiden, University Library, Loket 1555–39, Fruin, *Aantekeningen op zijn werken*, in "Discours ende advertisement van de navolgende schepen", fol. 7 recto. Heemskerk left Amsterdam on behalf of the United Amsterdam Company and was unaware of the creation of the VOC in 1602 that had taken place during his voyage. On the creation of the United Amsterdam Company, see briefly Gaastra, *De geschiedenis van de VOC,* p. 19.
37. These sources have been transcribed at large by Coolhaas, "Een bron van het historische gedeelte van Hugo de Groot's De Jure Praedae", *BMH* 79 (1965): 415–537; IPC, appendix sections I and II, pp. 504–56, especially the letter by Heemskerk to the directors of the United Amsterdam Company, 27 August 1603, pp. 522–45; and Leiden, University Library, Loket 1555–39, Fruin, *Aantekeningen op zijn werken* in "Discours ende advertisement van de navolgende schepen", fols. 7 verso–8 recto. See also the critical source discussion in chapter 4.
38. IPC, appendix II.4, letter by Heemskerk to the directors of the United Amsterdam Company, 27 August 1603, p. 536. See also van Ittersum, "Hugo Grotius in Context", *AJSS* 31, 3 (2003): 528.
39. IPC, p. 297; CIPC, p. 213; Coolhaas, "Een bron van het historische gedeelte van Hugo de Groot's De Jure Praedae", *BMH* 79 (1965): 528.
40. IPC, appendix II.4, letter by Heemskerk to the directors of the United Amsterdam Company, 27 August 1603, p. 536, and Leiden, University Library, Loket 1555–39, Fruin, *Aantekeningen op zijn werken,* in "Discours ende advertisement van de navolgende schepen", fol. 7 verso; Tiele, "Documenten voor de Geschiedenis der Nederlanders in het Oosten", *BMH* 6 (1883), III, Discours ende Advertisement van de Navolgende Schepen,

p. 246. See also Borschberg, "The Seizure of the Santa Catarina Revisited", *JSEAS* 33, 1 (2002): 45; van Ittersum, "Hugo Grotius in Context", *AJSS* 31, 3 (2003): 528.

41. IPC, p. 297; CIPC, p. 213; Coolhaas, "Een bron van het historische gedeelte van Hugo de Groot's De Jure Praedae", *BMH* 79 (1965): 527–8.
42. This information does not quite square with the report provided by Heemskerk in his letter to the directors of the United Amsterdam Company. In this epistolary testimony emphasis is not placed on the "help" accorded by Heemskerk to Johor in their fresh tensions with Portuguese Melaka, but on the invitation extended by the Johor royals, Raja Bongsu in particular, to prey on Portuguese shipping in the Singapore Straits. See IPC, appendix II.4, letter by Heemskerk, pp. 535–8; also Leiden, University Library, Loket 1555–39, Fruin, *Aantekeningen op zijn werken,* in "Discours ende advertisement van de navolgende schepen", fols. 7 verso–8 recto, and van Ittersum, "Hugo Grotius in Context", *AJSS* 31, 3 (2003): 518, 527–8.
43. See Borschberg, *The Singapore and Melaka Straits,* pp. 71–5; "The Johor-VOC Alliance and the Twelve Years Truce", *IILJ Working Paper* 8 (2009): 14. According to Heemskerk's testimony, he was specifically invited by Raja Bongsu and the king to prey on the *Santa Catarina* near the Johor River estuary; see IPC, appendix I, letter by Heemskerk, pp. 535–6 and Coolhaas, "Een bron van het historische gedeelte van Hugo de Groot's De Jure Praedae", *BMH* 79 (1965): 528–9, III, Discours ende Advertisement van de Navolgende Schepen, pp. 247–9.
44. IPC, appendix II.4, letter by Heemskerk, pp. 538–9. A more detailed description of the naval confrontation between Heemskerk's three ships and the *Santa Catarina* can be found in Borschberg, "The Seizure of the *Santa Catarina* Revisited", *JSEAS* 33, 1 (2002): 31–62; "The Seizure of the *Santa Catarina* off Singapore", *RC,* International Edition, 11 (2004): 11–25; *The Singapore and Melaka Straits,* pp. 68–75; van Ittersum, "Hugo Grotius in Context", *AJSS* 31, 3 (2003): 530–1; *Profit and Principle,* pp. 35–6.
45. IPC, p. 298; CIPC, p. 214.
46. IPC, appendix I, letter by Heemskerk, pp. 538–9.
47. Leiden, University Library, Loket 1555–39, Fruin, *Aantekeningen op zijn werken,* in "Discours ende advertisement van de navolgende schepen", fol. 8 recto, mentions nothing about the presence of any Johor "royals" aboard Dutch ships during the attack on the *Santa Catarina.* See also van Ittersum, "Hugo Grotius in Context", *AJSS* 31, 3 (2003): 533; van Ittersum, *Profit and Principle,* p. 40; also Borschberg, "The Seizure of the Santa Catarina Revisited", *JSEAS* 33, 1 (2002): 47–8.
48. D.F.A. Hervey, "François Valentyn's Account of Malacca", *JSBRAS* 16 (1885): 128, "[The supercargo Jacob] Buyzen added, besides, that Radja Bongsoe, the brother of the King), intended to come very soon on board … and remain there till their joint efforts should have vanquished the Portuguese; it was this

very Radja Bongsoe who was with Admiral Hemskerk when he had captured the carrack [the *Santa Catarina*] already mentioned." See also Borschberg, "The Seizure of the Santa Catarina Revisited", *JSEAS* 33, 1 (2002): 47. Concerning the stationing of Jacob Buys (who was Raja Bongsu's choice) as factor in Batu Sawar in lieu of the factor designate, Pieter Opmeer, see also IPC, appendix I, letter by Heemskerk, pp. 539, 543.

49. Concerning the geo-strategic, commercial and political context of this broader policy for Southeast Asia between the founding of the VOC in 1602 and the ratification of the Twelve Years Truce in April 1609, see Borschberg, "The Johor VOC Alliance and the Twelve Years Truce", *IILJ Working Paper* 8 (2009): 1–12.
50. See classicly the letter of Ternate's ruler Haydan to James I/VI, dated 18 July 1605, a copy of which is found among the working papers of Grotius. In this letter the ruler of Ternate explains that he is unable to admit the English to trade in Ternate on the grounds that he has already promised all produce of trade (speak cloves) to the Dutch in return, amongst others, for protection against the Spanish and Portuguese. The Hague, Nationaal Archief, *Collectie Hugo de Groot, Supplement I* (ms. 1.10.35.02, no. 40, fols. 302–3).
51. IPC, p. 432; CIPC, p. 314. See also van Ittersum, "Hugo Grotius in Context", *AJSS* 31, 3 (2003): 538; van Ittersum, *Profit and Principle,* p. 48.
52. IPC, pp. 434–5; CIPC, p. 315.
53. According to Johannes Thumfart, Vitoria foresaw the possibility of the pope legitimately denying the exercise of the *ius communicationis* as a facet of his spiritual supremacy. See Thumfart "On Grotius's *Mare Liberum* and Vitoria's *De Indis*, Following Agamben and Schmitt", *GNS* 30 (2009): 83–4. Concerning the wider significance of Vitoria, see also Antony Anghie, "Francisco de Vitoria and the colonial origins of international law", in *Imperialism, Sovereignty and the Making of International Law,* ed. A. Anghie (Cambridge: CUP, 2004), pp. 13–31; "Vitoria and the Colonial Origins of International Law", in Eve Darian-Smith and Peter Fitzpatrick, *Laws of the Postcolonial* (Ann Arbor: University of Michigan Press, 1999), pp. 89–107.
54. See the principles expounded in Dig. 49.15.24 (Ulpian); 50.16.118 (Pomponius). On the specific preconditions of Grotius' just public war, see Borschberg, "'De Pace', Ein unveröffentlichtes Fragment von Hugo Grotius über Krieg und Frieden", *ZRG*, RA 113 (1996): 268–92.
55. IPC, pp. 433–4; CIPC, pp. 314–5.
56. Van Ittersum, "Hugo Grotius in Context", *AJSS* 31, 3 (2003): 540.
57. IPC, p. 435; CIPC, pp. 315–6.
58. Leiden, University Library, Loket 1555–39, Fruin, *Aantekeningen op zijn werken*, in "Discours ende advertisement van de navolgende schepen", fol. 7 recto. Concerning the identity of the two brothers, see appendix 11.

59. Coolhaas, "Een bron van het historische gedeelte van Hugo de Groot's De Jure Praedae", *BMH* 79 (1965): 528–9.
60. John Villiers, "Doing Business with the Infidel: Merchants, Missionaries and Monarchs in Sixteenth Century Southeast Asia", in *Maritime Asia: Profit Maximisation, Ethics and Trade Structure, c. 1300–1800*, ed. Karl Anton Sprengard and Roderich Ptak (Wiesbaden: Otto Harrassowitz Verlag, 1994), pp. 162, 168.
61. Ernest Nys, *Les origines du droit international* (Brussels: Castaigne, 1894), p. 162.
62. The English subsequently signed a commercial treaty with the Ottoman sultan in 1579.
63. Mat. 4:43; Luc. 10:29 *et seq.*; Augustine of Hippo, *De Doctrina Christiana,* ed. and tr. R.P.H. Green (Oxford: OUP, 1995), 1.30.32; Francisco de Vitoria, *Relectiones Theologicae XII* (Lyon: Iacobus Boyerius, 1557), III.5, 7, sections 15, 17, pp. 368–9, 370–1 (Latin text) and Vitoria, *Political Writings*, ed. Anthony Pagden and Jeremy Lawrence (Cambridge: CUP, 1991), pp. 287–8, 288–9 (English translation); a parallel reference is found in IBP 2.20.10.2.
64. In another work, Grotius himself stipulated that Christians, even if they belong to different denominations, are obliged to enter into leagues and alliances to fend off known enemies of the Christian religion; see IBP 2.15.8–12.
65. IPC, p. 434; CIPC, p. 315.
66. Van Ittersum, "Hugo Grotius in Context", *AJSS* 31, 3 (2003): 539; *Profit and Principle,* pp. 49–50.
67. For Grotius' specific references and parallel discussions, see Gen. 14:13, 21:27, 26:29; 1 Sam. 22:3; 27:1–4; 2 Sam. 5:11; 1 Kng. 3:1; 5:1; 5:11–12; 9:12; 1. Mac. 8:18; Mat. 5:45; Luk. 10:33 *et seq.*; Augustine of Hippo, *De Doctrina Christiana,* 1.30.32; IPC, pp. 412–3; CIPC, p. 298; *Verbael* of the Anglo-Dutch conference filed early May 1615, BW (Supplement) 399A, p. 128; IBP, 2.15.9.2; 2.15.9.4; 2.15.9.6; 2.20.10.2. See also van Ittersum, "Hugo Grotius in Context", *AJSS* 31, 3 (2003): 539 and *Profit and Principle,* p. 50. — One needs to be wary about Grotius' use of Biblical references in support of his arguments, as is critically discussed in Mark Somos, "Secularization in *De Iure Praedae*: from Bible Criticism to International Law", *GNS* 26–8 (2005–7): 147–91, esp. p. 153, "… I fully appreciate that Grotius was happy to wrench and cite any passage out of context, as long as it helped him make a case. However, the Bible references in *[De Iure Praedae]* oftentimes do not help, but contradict his arguments, whether about prize-taking, collective responsibility, or the treatment of non-combatants. The Bible passages are not only taken out of their context, but are carefully placed in new contexts and consistly put to uses that flagrantly discredit them."
68. Grotius' contemporary and one of the forerunners of the modern science of politics, Johannes Althusius, in his *Politica Methodice Digesta* (3rd ed. of 1614)

against forging alliances with peoples and rulers of different religious beliefs as such agreements were "dubious and extremely dangerous". See Althusius, *Politica Methodice Digesta*, ed. and intr. Carl J. Friedrichs (Cambridge, Mass: Harvard University Press, 1932), chapter 25, section 22, p. 233, "An alliance concluded with infidels is doubtful and very dangerous." Pacts should be concluded on the basis of shared customs and values (*similitudo morum*); see also chapter 17, sections 25 *et seq*., pp. 127 *et seq*. Seraphim de Freitas, an avowed adversary of Grotius', *Mare Liberum* lamented in his *De Justo Imperio Lusitanorum Asiatico* (cited in Alexandrowicz, *An Introduction to the Law of Nations in the East Indies*, p. 57), "[I]t is deplorable … that the Dutch conclude alliances with the Turks and infidels for mutual assistance by supply of weapons, troops and armies … the prohibition of such alliances is based on divine law.…"

69. IPC, p. 433; CIPC, p. 314.
70. IPC, p. 436; CIPC, p. 316.
71. IPC, p. 436; CIPC, p. 316. Italics in the English translation are mine.
72. See van Ittersum, "Hugo Grotius in Context", *AJSS* 31, 3 (2003): 541, "Following the carrack's capture, it was van Heemskerck who rewarded the Sultan, not the other way around. Grotius was clearly ignorant of the 10,000 guilders worth of presents given to the Sultan, and denied the existence of a 'formal agreement as to compensation' between the ruler and van Heemskerck." See also van Ittersum, *Profit and Principle,* pp. 43–4, 51–2.
73. IPC, p. 436; CIPC, p. 316.
74. The italics are mine. The same rule applies in the event of a public war, whereby in the absence of a formal arrangement, the booty automatically becomes the possession of the captors, see IPC, pp. 241–2; CIPC, p. 167.
75. IPC, p. 296; CIPC, pp. 212–3.
76. Leonard Andaya, *The Kingdom of Johor 1641–1728: Economic and Political Developments* (Kuala Lumpur: OUP, 1975), p. 26.
77. See appendix 15.
78. See esp. Borschberg, *The Singapore and Melaka Straits,* esp. chapters 1–3, pp. 1–136; "Jacques de Coutre as a Source for the 17th Century History of Singapore, the Johor River and the Straits", *JMBRAS* 81, 2 (2008): 71–97; "The Johor-VOC Alliance and the Twelve Years Truce", *IILJ Working Paper* 8 (2009): esp. 1–6; Derek S.T. Heng, Kwa Chong Guan and Tan Tai Yong, *Singapore: A 700-Year History. From Emporium to World City* (Singapore: National Archives of Singapore, 2009), pp. 63–82.
79. The selection of Johor as a possible site is raised, among other documents, in IPC, appendix II.4, letter by Heemskerk to the directors of the United Amsterdam Company of 27 August 1603, p. 242. See also Gaastra, *Geschiedenis van de VOC,* p. 40; Borschberg, "The Seizure of the *Santa Catarina* Revisited", *JSEAS* 33, 1 (2002): 31–62; memorial of Admiral Cornelis Matelieff de Jonge in appendix 15. In a letter to Grotius of 31 August 1610 in BW (Supplement) 198A, p. 72, and RH, pp. 329–30,

the merits of Johor as a rendezvous location are weighed in further detail. Matelieff came to reject the Johor location on the grounds that, unlike the Sunda Strait, it was not possible to access and depart from the Singapore and Melaka Straits, or reach Johor from other locations around Southeast Asia, all year round.

80. Several documents and log entries from the early Dutch voyages touch on restoring the lands of Melaka to the Johor monarch. This is evident from Admiral Cornelis Matelieff's two treaties with Johor of 1606 reproduced in appendix 14, as well as from the recorded discussions between Pieter Willemsz. Verhoeff and Raja Bongsu of January 1609. For additional background information on the forging of the two Johor-Dutch treaties of 1606 and the discussions with Admiral Verhoeff, see Borschberg, *The Singapore and Melaka Straits,* pp. 158–9; "The Johor-VOC Alliance and the Twelve Years Truce", *IILJ Working Paper* 8 (2009): 14–5.
81. Richard O. Winstedt, "A History of Johore", *JMBRAS* 10, 3 (1932): 27–8.
82. Different angles of these tensions between Johor, Aceh and Portuguese Melaka have been discussed generally in Borschberg, *The Singapore and Melaka Straits* and Pinto, *Portugueses e Malaios.*
83. Borschberg, *The Singapore and Melaka Straits,* esp. pp. 71–5; "The Johor-VOC Alliance and the Twelve Years Truce", *IILJ Working Paper* 8 (2009): esp. 16–25.
84. This was evidently not unique to the Dutch, but in fact also practised by the Portuguese since the end of the 15th and beginning of the 16th centuries. See Villiers, "The Estado da Índia in South East Asia", in *South East Asia: Colonial History,* ed. Paul H. Kratoska and Peter Borschberg, 6 vols. (London: Routledge, 2001), I, p. 156, "The numerous treaties of peace and commerce concluded between the Estado da Índia and different Asian rulers proved by their existence that the Portuguese fully recognised the legitimacy of those rulers and their right to rule, and show that they did not seek to overthrow them and incorporate their sovereign territories into the Estado da Índia."
85. Borschberg, "De Societate Publica cum Infidelibus. Ein Frühwerk von Hugo Grotius", *ZRG,* RA 115 (1998): 392–3.
86. Borschberg, "De Societate Publica", pp. 365–7, 371 *et seq.*
87. Borschberg, "Grotius, the Social Contract and Political Resistance", *IILJ Working Paper* 6 (2006): 8 *et seq.*
88. For the sources and passages identified, see Borschberg, "'De Societate Publica cum Infidelibus': Ein Frühwerk von Hugo Grotius", *ZRG,* RA 115 (1998): 356–8. The same observation is valid for other contemporary writings, including the *Commentarius in Theses XI* and the *Theses LVI.* See CiT, pp. 48–9 and Borschberg, "Grotius, the Social Contract and Political Resistance", *IILJ Working Paper* 6 (2006): 14. Other contemporary researchers

have made similar observations with regard to Grotius' use of Vitoria. See van Ittersum, *Profit and Principle,* pp. 327–8, 329 note 38; Thieme, "Natürliches Privatrecht in der Spätscholastik", *ZRG,* GA 70 (1953): 235–6, 262–6; António Truyol y Serra, "Francisco de Vitoria y Hugo Grocio", *Ciencia Tomista,* 111 (1984): 23. Similar observations — including the authors of the School of Salamanca as sources in Grotius generally — are made by Robert Feenstra in several of his earlier publications including "L'influence de la scolastique Espagnole sur Grotius en droit privé: quelques experiences dans des questions de fond et de forme, concernant notamment les doctrines de l'erreur et de l'enrichissement sans cause", in *Fata Iuris Romani: Études d'Histoire du Droit,* ed. Robert Feenstra (Leiden: Leiden University Press, 1974), pp. 338–63; "Quelques remarques sur les sources utilisées par Grotius dans ses travaux de droit naturel", in *The World of Hugo Grotius,* ed. Feenstra, pp. 65–81.

89. Leiden, University Library, ms. B.P.L. 922, H. Grotius, "De Societate Publica cum Infidelibus", fol. 314 recto.
90. IPC, p. 303; CIPC, p. 218; HML, p. 11.
91. The "School of Salamanca" which is often used interchangeably with the "Second Scholastic", refers to a group of professors in the 16th and early 17th century who were active at universities on the Iberian Peninsula, and chiefly (but not exclusively) Salamanca. See G. Cavallar, *The Rights of Strangers. Theories of International Hospitality, the Global Community and Political Justice since Vitoria* (Aldershot: Ashgate, 2002), p. 81, esp. his list of more recent publications touching on the achievements of the "School of Salamanca" in note 17.
92. Leiden, University Library, ms. B.P.L. 922, H. Grotius, "De Societate Publica cum Infidelibus", fol. 315 recto, "Deus Optimus Maximus solem suum oriri facit et pluat super bonos et malos: ubi per solem et pluviam cuncta naturae bonae intelligi voluit." This particular passage from the Sermon on the Mount is also a favourite among the authors of the School of Salamanca. See for example Vitoria, *Relectiones XII,* p. 293; Domingo de Soto, *De Iustitia et Iure – De la Justicia y del Derecho,* bi-lingual edition in Latin-Spanish, the Latin text being a facsimile of the 1556 edition printed in Salamanca, tr. M. Gonzales Ordoñez, 5 vols. (Madrid: Instituto de los Estudios Políticos, 1967), book 4, qu. 2, p. 287B; Seneca, *De Beneficiis,* 4.23.1 [contained in vol. III of *Moral Essays, Seneca,* ed. and tr. John William Basore, 3 vols. (Cambridge, Mass., and London: Harvard University Press and Heinemann, 1928–35)], advances a similar point, and Grotius employed the citation again in IBP 2.15.10.1 in an almost identical context. See also Borschberg, "De Societate Publica cum Infidelibus. Ein Frühwerk von Hugo Grotius", *ZRG,* RA 115 (1998): 374.
93. Leiden, University Library, ms. B.P.L. 922, H. Grotius, "De Societate Publica cum Infidelibus", fol. 314 verso, "Secunda propositio sit: Beneficia, officia commercia charitatis, civilitatis et utilitatis ergo inter fideles et infideles aut

haer. ultro citroque recte colantur. Sunt enim et haec ex natura prodeuntia, atque ideo cunctis hominibus communia...." See also Borschberg, "De Societate Publica cum Infidelibus. Ein Frühwerk von Hugo Grotius", *ZRG*, RA 115 (1998): 373.

94. See Alexandrowicz, *An Introduction to the Law of Nations in the East Indies*, pp. 54 *et seq*.
95. Leiden, University Library, ms. B.P.L. 922, H. Grotius, "De Societate Publica cum Infidelibus", fol. 314 recto. See Thomas Aquinas, *Summa Theologiae Cura Fratrorum eiusdem Ordinis*, vol. III, *Secunda Secundae*, 3rd ed. (Madrid: Biblioteca de Autores Cristianos, 1963), qu. 10, art., 10, *respondeo*, and Grotius' related thoughts in IPC, p. 308; CIPC, p. 221, HML, p. 14. In the margin, Grotius credits as his immediate source Diego de Covarruvias y Leyva's *Relectio in Regula Peccatum*. This work is also contained in his *Opera Omnia quae hactenus extant*, 2 vols. (Frankfurt/M.: Ex Officina Nicolai Bassaei, Impensis Sigismundi Feierabend, 1573), II, sec. 10, no. 2, p. 509, and nos. 4–5, p. 510.
96. Alexandrowicz, *An Introduction to the Law of Nations in the East Indies*, p. 55, note 2.
97. Concerning the denial of dominium to non-Christians, notably in the context of Spain's earlier colonisation of the Canary Islands, see for example Thumfart, "On Grotius's *Mare Liberum* and Vitoria's *De Indis*, Following Agamben and Schmitt", *GNS* 30 (2009): 73, esp. the quotation from Pope Clement VI, "Forte enim infideles ratione infidelitatis merentur perdere omnem dominium" (Perhaps then the infidels by reason of their infidelity deserve to lose all dominium).
98. For a useful summary of the position developed by the School of Salamanca and the Spanish thinkers of the 16th and 17th centuries, see Anthony Pagden, "Dispossessing the barbarian: the language of Spanish Thomism and the debate over property rights of the American Indians", in *The Languages of Political Theory in Early-Modern Europe*, ed. Anthony Pagden (Cambridge: CUP, 1987), pp. 79–98.
99. IPC, pp. 308–9; CIPC, pp. 221–2, HML, pp. 14–5.
100. An indication that he contended with this and similar issues is found in chapter 2 of *De Iure Praedae*. In the context of disputing Portugal's claims to the East Indies by historic precedence, Grotius wrote: "Alia enim India, alia Americana ratio est" (The case of India and America is different). He subsequently deleted these words in the manuscript.
101. See also van Goor, *Prelude to Colonialism*, pp. 28–9. Concerning the equality of all rulers, Christian and non-Christian, in Grotius' *De Iure Praedae* see also Thumfart, "On Grotius's *Mare Liberum* and Vitoria's *De Indis*, Following Agamben and Schmitt", *GNS* 30 (2009): 74.
102. CiT, pp. 140–4; Borschberg, "Commentarius in Theses XI. Ein unveröffentlichtes Kurzwerk von Hugo Grotius", *ZRG*, RA 109 (1992): 466; "De Pace.

Ein unveröffentlichtes Fragment von Hugo Grotius über Krieg und Frieden", *ZRG,* RA 113 (1996): 279–80.

103. For a connection of this view to the works of the Thomists in general and specifically to the authors of the School of Salamanca, see Annabel Brett, "The development of the idea of citizens' rights", in *States and Citizens. History, Theory, Prospects,* ed. Quentin Skinner and Bo Stråth (Cambridge: CUP, 2003), pp. 97–112, esp. pp. 101–2.
104. Richard Tuck, *Hobbes* (Oxford: Oxford Universtity Press, 1989), pp. 20 *et seq.*
105. Leiden, University Library, ms. B.P.L. 922, H. Grotius, "De Societate Publica cum Infidelibus", fol. 314 verso. Dig. 1.1.10.1 (Ulpian); Inst. 1.1.3. See also Borschberg, "De Societate Publica cum Infidelibus. Ein Frühwerk von Hugo Grotius", *ZRG,* RA 115 (1998): 372–3; van Ittersum, "Hugo Grotius in Context", *AJSS* 31, 3 (2003): 540.
106. Leiden, University Library, ms. B.P.L. 922, H. Grotius, "De Societate Publica cum Infidelibus", fol. 314 verso.
107. Gal. 6:10; Leiden, University Library, ms. B.P.L. 922, H. Grotius, "De Societate Publica cum Infidelibus", fol. 315 recto. See also fol. 314 recto; Borschberg, "De Societate Publica cum Infidelibus. Ein Frühwerk von Hugo Grotius", *ZRG,* RA 115 (1998): 373.
108. Borschberg, "De Societate Publica cum Infidelibus. Ein Frühwerk von Hugo Grotius", *ZRG,* RA 115 (1998): 368.
109. Leiden, University Library, ms. B.P.L. 922, H. Grotius, "De Societate Publica cum Infidelibus", fol. 315 verso, citing Juvenal, *Satyres,* 14.103–4 (on being Jewish); the reference is also repeated in IBP 2.15.9.3. See also Borschberg, "De Societate Publica cum Infidelibus. Ein Frühwerk von Hugo Grotius", *ZRG,* RA 115 (1998): 374.
110. Tim. 6:1, Aquinas, *Summa Theologiae,* 2a–2ae, qu. 10, art 9; and *The Theodosian Code and Novels, and the Sirmondian Constitutions,* tr. and ed. C. Pharr with T.S. Davidson and M.B. Pharr (Princeton: Princeton University Press, 1952), 16.9.4. From these passages it is evident that Christians are permitted to enter into the services of non-Christians and are even permitted to employ non-Christian servants. However, in the event that such domestic relationships should affect one's faith, the service should be terminated, that is, the servant should be dismissed.
111. Leiden, University Library, ms. B.P.L. 922, H. Grotius, "De Societate Publica cum Infidelibus", fol. 313 recto. See also IPC, p. 100; CIPC, p. 65; and Grotius' elaborations on offensive and defensive alliances in IBP 2.15.6.3.
112. Leiden, University Library, ms. B.P.L. 922, H. Grotius, "De Societate Publica cum Infidelibus", notes, fol. 316 verso, featuring references to pp. 368 and 370 of the first edition of Vitoria's *Relectiones XII.* See also Borschberg, "De

Societate Publica cum Infidelibus. Ein Frühwerk von Hugo Grotius", *ZRG,* RA 115 (1998): 364.

113. Vitoria, *Relectiones XII,* section 15, pp. 368–9. Concerning Grotius' ideas on a similar proposition see Leiden, University Library, ms. B.P.L. 922, H. Grotius, "De Societate Publica cum Infidelibus", fol. 317 recto, "Concl. 3: In bello autem iusto infideles recte fidelibus defenduntur, etiamsi ii, qui infideles opprimunt, fideles habere velint. Imo hoc opus non modo licitum, sed et summa laudabile, et ex circumstantiis saepe necessarium est" (Conclusion 3: In a just war, however, the unbelievers are righly defended by the believers, even if those, who oppress the unbelievers, want to make converts. Thus this deed is not only permitted, but also most praiseworthy and, depending on circumstances, often also necessary). Also Borschberg, "De Societate Publica cum Infidelibus. Ein Frühwerk von Hugo Grotius", *ZRG,* RA 115 (1998): 379.

114. Vitoria, *Relectiones XII,* III.7, section 17, pp. 370–1; Vitoria, *Political Writings,* pp. 289–90.

115. Gen. 14:13 *et seq.*

116. Leiden, University Library, ms. B.P.L. 922, H. Grotius, "De Societate Publica cum Infidelibus", fol. 314 verso. See also Borschberg, "De Societate Publica cum Infidelibus. Ein Frühwerk von Hugo Grotius", *ZRG,* RA 115 (1998): 372. Similar arguments were advanced again during the colonial conference at the Hague, as is evident from the *Verbael* of the Dutch delegation of May 1615 in CC, pp. 253–4. Another copy of the text is published as BW (Supplement) 399A, pp. 122–37, esp. p. 28.

117. My observations on Vitoria and the Spanish Late Scholastics should not be understood as celebrating the superiority of the Spanish authors in the vein of James Brown Scott. Scott's pro-Hispanic, pro-Catholic bias, together with the avid reception of his works during the decades of Spain's Franco regime, have only served to seriously taint a what is a valid and interesting question concerning the importance of Vitoria and other Salmantino authors as sources for Grotius. For Scott's controversial exaltation of Spanish authors, see especially his *The Spanish Origins of International Law: Francisco de Vitoria and His Law of Nations* (Oxford and London: Clarendon Press and Humphrey Milford, 1934). For an excellent and incisive criticism of Scott's questionable agenda and scholarship, see Arthur Nussbaum, *A Concise History of the Law of Nations,* revised ed. (New York: Macmillan, 1954), appendix II, "James Brown Scott on the Superiority of the Spanish Scholastics over Hugo Grotius", pp. 296–306.

118. Borschberg, "The Johor-VOC Alliance and the Twelve Years Truce", *IILJ Working Paper* 8 (2009): esp. 5–6. See also appendix 15.

119. The admixture of armed intervention and money politics was already raised among other concerns in a petition of the VOC's Heren XVII to the Dutch

States General of August 1612, where the directors blamed the Twelve Years Truce for creating a situation where the King of Spain diverted substantial sums and military forces to the East Indies. They used this an excuse to petition the States General for financial support or a subsidy. See CC, p. 72. See also the draft 1609 petition in the hand of Grotius addressed to the States General, in which he requested on behalf of the VOC directors a raise in the annual subsidy for the company with the aim of purchasing more weapons and ammunition. The Hague, Nationaal Archief, *Collectie Hugo de Groot, Supplement I* (ms. 1.10.35.02, no. 40, fol. 337–40).

120. First and second Dutch memorial dated 18 and 27 February 1615, respectively in CC, pp. 182, 191. Concerning these vulnerable but important regions at the frontline in the VOC's conflict with the Iberian powers, see Borschberg, "The Johor-VOC Alliance and the Twelve Years Truce", *IILJ Working Paper* 8 (2009): 5–7.
121. Second Dutch memorial dated 27 February 1615 in CC, p. 191; also CE, p. 105.
122. See the petition of the Heren XVII to the Dutch States General of 1612 in CC, p. 63 *et seq.* and another petition of 28 August 1612, in CC, p. 72.
123. See also appendices 15 and 16 which touch on the main differences between the English and the Dutch in 1613.
124. Petition of Ambassador Ralph Winwood to the Dutch States General dated 1 February 1612, in CC, p. 49; Reply of the English delegates dated 27 April 1613, in CC, pp. 103, 106. Even the Iberian jurists had concluded that despite asserting claims of sovereignty over pelagic spaces, obstruction of trade was in practice highly problematic. See T.W. Fulton, *The Sovereignty of the Sea: An Historical Account of the Claims of England to the Dominion of the British Seas, and of the Evolution of the Territorial Waters; with special reference to the Rights of Fishing and the Naval Salute* (Edinburgh: William Blackwood & Sons, 1911), p. 107, "… the Spanish lawyers had come to the conclusion that the Venetians could not legally inhibit others from trading in the Adriatic, and therefore, by the same reasoning, neither could the Spaniards or Portuguese prohibit orderly and lawful traffic to their Indies."
125. For this reason Dutch documents speak of "coophandel met force", meaning there can be no trade without the support of armed intervention. See the petition of the Heren XVII to the Dutch States General dated July 1612, in CC, p. 61; Record of the discussions between Hugo Grotius and Christopher Perkins in London dated 16 April 1613 in CC, p. 97; see also appendix 15 and note 127. The origins of this policy are explained in terms of Portugal's desire to expel the Dutch from the East Indies. See the counter-memorial of the Dutch delegates dated 20 April 1613, in CC, pp. 99–100. In chapter 12 of the *Commentary on the Law of Prize and Booty*, Grotius claims that the Dutch were initially interested only in pursuing purely commercial objectives,

but were forced by the behavior of the Portuguese into a state of armed conflict. See IPC, pp. 384–5; CIPC, p. 278. The section in question was not taken into print in *The Free Sea.*

126. For this reason it was argued that the treaties of alliance with Asian rulers needed to be honoured by recourse to violence against Spain and Portugal. See the counter-memorial of the Dutch delegation of 20 April 1613 in CC, p. 101, "... foedera sine sumptu bellico conservari non posse ..." ([T]reaties cannot be preserved without recourse to war.) See also the memorial of the Dutch delegates to Dutch ambassador Noël Caron in London, 14 May 1613, in CC, p. 128.

127. See the summary in Dutch of the discussions held between Grotius and Sir Christopher Perkins dated 16 April 1616, in London, CC, p. 97, where the term "coophandel met force" was employed by Grotius to differentiate VOC policy in Asia from the practices of the English East India Company. See also Borscherg, "The Seizure of the *Santa Catarina* Revisited", *JSEAS* 33, 1 (2002): 33. For the wider contextualisation of the "coophandel met force" consult also Thumfart, "On Grotius's *Mare Liberum* and Vitoria's *De Indis*, Following Agamben and Schmitt", *GNS* 30 (2009): 76, and note 125 above.

128. See the Dutch counter-memorial dated 20 April 1613, in CC, p. 100. The English evidently could not be persuaded such arguments, as becomes clear, for example, from the memorial of the English delegation dated 18 April 1613, in CC, p. 98. — Note the sharply contrasting position assumed by Grotius in chapter 12 of his *Commentary to the Law of Prize and Booty* or *Mare Liberum*, IPC, p. 260; CIPC, p. 260, "... what could be more unjust than the complaint of the Portuguese that their own profits are drained away by the multitude of persons bidding against them?" Richard Hakluyt translated this slightly differently, see HML, pp. 54–5, "But what is more unjust than that complaint that the Portugals say their gains are consumed and spent through the multitude of those who are licensed to the contrary?"

129. On the specifically negative impact of the English competition, see the petition of the Heren XVII of the VOC of 28 July 1612, to the Dutch States General in CC, pp. 63–4. See also Grotius' two Latin addresses of 1613 in appendices 15 and 16. Concerning the evolution of the VOC monopoly and the early competition from other seafaring peoples of northern Europe, see among others the useful exposés of David K. Bassett, "European Influence in the Malay Peninsula, 1511–1786", *JMBRAS* 33, 3 (1960): 9–35; Bassett, "European Influence in Southeast Asia, c.1500–1630", *Journal of Southeast Asian History* 4, 2 (1963): 134–65; Stefan Diller, *Die Dänen in Indien, Südostasien und China (1620–1845)* (Wiesbaden: Otto Harrassowitz Verlag, 1999); Peter Kirsch, "VOC — Trade Without Ethics?" in *Maritime Asia. Profit Maximisation, Ethics and Trade Structure,* ed. Sprengard and Ptak, pp. 189–202; Steensgaard, *The Asian Trade Revolution of the Seventeenth Century.*

130. Petition of the Heren XVII to the Dutch States General dated July 1612, in CC, p. 63. See also their petition dated August 1612, in CC, p. 72.
131. See appendix 17. This suspicion was not far from actual events on the ground in Southeast Asia. Since about 1610, the Spanish governor in Manila, Juan de Silva, had a large fleet constructed with which he sought to unite with the Portuguese armada from Goa and eventually expel the VOC from the spice producing islands of the Malukus. The expedition set sail in 1615 and hoped to unite forces with the Portuguese in the waters around the Singapore Straits. By the time de Silva arrived in Melaka, the Portuguese ships had been destroyed and the Spanish governor himself died of a sudden, high fever. The fleet returned to Manila without ever having fired a single shot against the Dutch. See Borschberg, *The Singapore and Melaka Straits,* pp. 137–56. However, in a memorandum drafted after the conclusion of the 1615 conference in the Hague, the English also mention Spanish concerns about the weakness of the Portuguese in the East Indies. See Sainsbury, *Calendar of State Papers, Colonial Series, East Indies, China and Japan, 1513–1616,* no. 986, p. 412.
132. Petition of the Heren XVII to the Dutch States General dated August 1612, in CC, p. 72.
133. Instructions of the Heren XVII to the Dutch delegation dated 28 February 1613, CC, p. 74.
134. CE, p. 114, esp. note 4, "War grounded on a just fear of invasion was called preventive and recognised as just."
135. CC, pp. 267–8, annexe 94, "Rapport de la délégation anglaise à partir du 7 avril 1615. Extraits du British Museum, mss. Harleian 147", fol. 80 verso.
136. That is of the members of the Dutch delegation.
137. See additionally Sainsbury, *Calendar of State Papers, Colonial Series, East Indies, China and Japan, 1513–1616,* esp. no. 943, p. 395; no. 957, p. 401; no. 961, pp. 403–4, "On taking leave of the States, Mr. Barnevelt [i.e. van Oldenbarnevelt] spoke of the reasons which moved the deputies to insist upon some course to break the power and the violence of the Spaniards in the Indies, 'assuring us [the English] that if this question had happened in any part of Europe, we would, without further delay, have accepted the Union'."; see also no. 970, p. 407; and no. 975, pp. 408–9.
138. This is a reference to the *landsadvocaat* Johan van Oldenbarnevelt.
139. The Twelve Years Truce was concluded in Antwerp on 10 April 1609.
140. The word marked in brackets is an editorial clarification originally added by Clark and van Eysinga.
141. Concerning the historical background to the explanation of article 4, see also Nellen, *Hugo de Groot. Een leven in strijd om de vrede*, p. 92, and Borschberg, "The Johor-VOC Alliance and the Twelve Years Truce", *IILJ Working Paper* 8 (2009): 9. For additional information, see Peter Brightwell, "The Spanish System and the Twelve Years Truce", *The English Historical Review* 89, 351

(1974): 279–81. — The working papers of Grotius sold at the 1864 auction in the Hague contain an excerpt of the treaty of guarantee between France, England and the Dutch Republic concluded on 17 June 1609, in other words just weeks after the ratification of the Twelve Years Truce on 10 April 1609. A description found in Nordhoff's annotated edition of the auction catalogue, states that Grotius' excerpt represents an "Uittreksel uit het garantie-verdrag ... weergevende het artikel, dat bepaalt, dat Frankrijk en Engeland zich tijdens het bestand ook tot hulpverlening verplichten, indien de Spanjaarden de Nederlanders in Oost-Indië of hun vrienden en bondgenoten aldaar overlast zullen aandoen." (Extract from the Treaty of Guarantee, reproducing the article, which states that France and England also oblige themselves to render assistance during the validity of the [Twelve Years] Truce in the event that the Spaniards should harass the Dutch in the East Indies or their friends and allies in that region.) See Noordhoff, *Beschrijving van ... papieren afkomstig van Huig de Groot,* pp. 20–1 under fol. 86. Additional materials pertaining to the explanation of articles 4 and 5 of the 1609 Truce are found (Noordhoff, pp. 22–3) under "Afschrift van de akte d.d. 1609 Maart 31" (Copy of the act dated 31 March 1609), together with Noordhoff's editorial notes thereunto. Materials relating to the explanation of articles 4 and 5 and the Anglo-French guarantee of June 1609 were found among the working papers of Grotius. They are currently filed as Rotterdam, Gemeentearchief, portef. Buitenlandse Handel, no. 803, fol. 86.

142. Van Oldenbarnevelt and the Dutch States General sought to include the VOC's Asian treaty partners in the Twelve Years Truce. The inclusion of Asian allies was endorsed and ratified by the States General both before and after the conclusion of the treaty of 10 April 1609. See Archief Oldenbarnevelt (3.01.14, no. 3153), "Extract wt het register der resolutiën vande Ho. ende Mo. Heeren Staten Generael der Vereenichde Nederlanden. Mercurij 18 Meert 1609 post prandium" (Extract from the register of the High and Mighty Gentlemen States General of the United Netherlands, Wednesday, 18 March 1609, after lunch ".... [I]n dese onderhandelinge van Trefves soude mogen werden gestipuleert, dat deselve Coningen, Princen ende volckeren daerinne begrepen worden, als namentlijck den Coninck van Chiam, die tegenwoordich sijnen Ambassadeur alhier heeft, die Coningen van Calicut, Bantam, Johor, Achin, Paham, Queda, Macassar, Banda, Tarranata, ende andere daer Alliantie mede gemaect is." (It shall be stipulated during these negotiations for a truce that the said [East Indian] kings, princes and peoples be included, such as the King of Siam, who currently has his ambassador here, the Kings of Calicut, Banten, Johor, Aceh, Pahang, Kedah, Makassar, Banda, Ternate and others, with whom an alliance has been concluded.) See also *Resolutiën der Staten-Generaal van 1576 tot* 1609, vertiende deel, 1607–1609, ed. H.P. Rijperman (The Hague: Martinus

Nijhoff, 1970), p. 658. The Truce was to take effect east of the Cape of Good Hope in April 1610, one full calendar year after its implementation in Europe. The silence of arms in the Asian theatre, however, was not to last, and the Truce was pretty much a dead letter by 1613. Several developments are worth mentioning in this context. In Europe, the directors of the VOC submitted a petition to the Dutch States General requesting that commanders in India be charged to inflict as much damage on the enemy as possible, resume the armed conflict and seize control of all forts of the enemy in Asia. Noordhoff, *Beschrijving van ... papieren afkomstig van Huig de Groot,* p. 12, together with the manuscript filed in the Nationaal Archief, *Collectie Hugo de Groot, Supplement I* (ms. 1.10.35.02, no. 40, fols. 116–9). Evidently the pressure exerted by the VOC directors on the States General bore fruit, for in that very year the Dutch overwhelmed Portuguese positions on the island of Solor and gained control of the fort. Concerning the latter development, see Borschberg, "The Johor-VOC Alliance and the Twelve Years Truce", *IILJ Working Paper* 8 (2009): 7–9. By this time at the very latest, the Twelve Years Truce had become a dead letter in the Asian and Indian Ocean theatre.

143. The English were evidently concerned that the Dutch wanted to pursue an offensive war under the pretext of defending trade and the liberty of Asian kings and peoples. See the report of the English delegation in the Hague on the course of negotiations to 16 February 1615, in CC, p. 177; second memorial of the English delegation of 27 February 1615, in CC, p. 187; *Verbael* of the Dutch delegation of May 1615, in CC, pp. 260, 262 *et seq.*; report of the English delegation on their departure from the Hague, dated 7 April 1615, in CC, p. 268; and letter by the advocate of the VOC, Tobias de Coene, to Grotius dated 30 May 1615, in CC, p. 269. These explain King James I/VI's reluctance to engage the Spanish and his fears about the consequences such armed conflict may have on England's peace with Spain. The report by the Dutch delegation in the Hague to Dutch ambassador Noël Caron in London, dated 6 May 1615, CC, p. 243, states that the English delegates were favourably disposed toward vigorous action against the Iberian powers in the East Indies, but were not negatively disposed to taking offensive action as well. The English were concerned how various aspects of defensive or offensive military action could be cleanly separated.

144. Instructions of the Heren XVII to the Dutch delegation dated 28 August 1612, in CC, pp. 74; letter of Dutch ambassador Noël Caron to the Dutch States General dated 3 April 1613, in CC, p. 88; address of Grotius presented before King James I/VI dated 6 April 1613 (see appendix 17); reply of the Dutch delegation dated 30 April 1613, in CC, p. 107; report of the English delegation to the Privy Council, dated 10 May 1613, in CC, p. 118.

145. Instructions of the Heren XVII to the Dutch delegation dated 28 August 1612, in CC, pp. 74–5.
146. Reply of the Dutch delegation dated 30 April 1613, in CC, p. 107.
147. Undated Dutch memorial on the benefits and disadvantages of a proposed merger of the VOC and EIC, in CC, pp. 238–45; CE, pp. 118, 126. See also Sainsbury, *Calendar of State Papers, Colonial Series, East Indies, China and Japan, 1513–1616*, no. 978, p. 410.
148. See for example "Corpus Diplomaticum Neerlando-Indicum", ed. Heeres, eerste deel (1596–1650), *BKI* 57 (1907): 32, treaty with Ambon dated February 1605, art. 2, "Van gelycken zweeren wij voorschreven, dat wij niemandt eenige nagelen zullen verkoopen als aen de Hollanders, ten zij met voorwetten van den Gouvern[eu]r." (We above mentioned also swear that we will not sell cloves to anyone other than the Dutch, except with prior knowledge of the Governor.) Also the treaty signed between Admiral Cornelis Matelieff de Jonge with the King of Ternate dated 26 May 1607, pp. 50–3, see art. 10, p. 52, "Sullen geene nagelen moogen verkoopen, 't zy aen wadt natie offte volck hetselve soude mogen wesen dan alleen aen den factoor die van wegen de Heeren Staten in Ternate sall woonen ende dat tot sulcken prijs als de Heeren Staten sullen ordineeren ende met den Koningh accordeeren." (The [Ternatans] shall not be allowed to sell cloves, regardless to which community or people, except to the factor of the Gentlemen States [General] who shall live on Ternate and at such a price as the Gentlemen States [General] shall determine and agree with the king.) For the historical backdrop to this treaty, see also Gaastra, *De geschiedenis van de VOC*, p. 45.
149. See esp. English ambassador Winwood's memorial added to the resolution of the States General of 1 February 1612, CC, p. 49; memorial of the English delegation dated 18 April 1613 in CC, p. 98; counter-memorial of the English delegation dated 27 April 1613, in CC, pp. 103–4, 106; third English counter-reply dated 9 May 1613, pp. 115–6; final report of the English delegates to the Privy Council of 10 May 1613, in CC, p. 118; the first English memorial dated 16 February 1615, in CC, p. 180; second English memorial dated 23 February 1615, in CC, p. 184; third English memorial dated 6 March 1615, in CC, p. 201; letter of the Dutch delegation to Dutch ambassador Noël Caron dated 6 May 1615, in CC, p. 231.
150. Sainsbury, *Calendar of State Papers, Colonial Series, East Indies, China and Japan, 1513–1616*, no. 900, pp. 379–80 and no. 901, p. 380; CC, pp. 104, 119–20, 179, 180, 185, 198. CC, pp. 191 and 208 mention the activities of Francis Drake and Thomas Cavendish. A reference to Drake's treaty with the "King of Teronata for the trade of cloves on that Island and the rest of the Islands under his dominion" is also found in the original petition of

the merchants of London in the East Indies trade to Robert Cecil dated 15 October 1611, in CC, p. 41. Grotius concerned himself with the voyage of Drake and of other Englishmen, such as Cavendish and Walter Raleigh, but the date of Grotius' reading notes is admittedly uncertain. These can be found in the Hague, Nationaal Archief, *Collectie Hugo de Groot, Supplement I* (ms. 1.10.35.02, no. 40, fol. 403; see the image on p. 73).

151. The text has been slightly modified for the contemporary reader. This excerpt is taken form the final report of the English delegates to the Privy Council dated 10 May 1613, in CC, p. 118. See also Ambassador Winwood's memorial added to the Resolution of the States General dated 1 February 1612, CC, p. 49, "La liberté de commerce tire sa source du droict des gens la quelle n'est bornée ny des limites de lieu, ny de temps, ains passe librement par tout l'univers, et est communicable à tout le monde." (The freedom of trade springs from the law of nations which is limited neither by place or time, thus passes freely across the whole universe, and is open to everyone.) Further, the letter of Robert Cecil to Ambassador Winwood dated 14 January 1612, in CC, p. 47; the memorial of the English delegates of 18 April 1613, p. 98.
152. See the excerpt of the English memorial cited in the *Verbael* dated May 1615, CC, p. 261, point 3.
153. Third English reply to the Dutch delegation dated 9 May 1613, CC, p. 116, "...scripserit assertor Maris liberi: 'Commerciandi (inquit) libertas, quae ex iure est primario gentium et quae naturalem et perpetuam causam habet, tolli non potest et, si posset, non tamen nisi omnium gentium consensu'." (The defender of *Mare Liberum* had written: "The freedom of trade (he said) which derives from the primary law of nations and which has a natural and perpetual cause, cannot be abrogated, and if it can, then only with the consent of all peoples." The final report of the English delegates to the Privy Council of 10 May 1613, in CC, p. 120, "And do not the Hollanders deny this argument propounded by the Spaniard, and declare themselves in the behalf of free Trade, and to all nations, with as much liberty and freedom as *mare liberum*?"
154. English memorial dated 18 April 1613, CC, p. 98.
155. The mood is also reflected in a comment added to the English translation of Grotius' final speech at the conference of 1613, CE, p. 73, "Their inviolable contracts, if there be any, were forced from them [the peoples of Asia] by violence and therefore no iniustice if they breake them." See also the letter of George Cockayne dated 16 July 1615 in CE, p. 126, "Their [the Hollanders'] proceedings is in blood and so they must continue. They have not enough to do with the Spaniardes and Portigales, but they will make wars with all the inhabitants where they come, which ere long they will not find profit but much sorrow and grief.... The trade that comes by

compulsion is not profitable.... They have many castles with much trouble and little profit."

156. Report of the English delegation to the Privy Council dated 10 May 1613, in CC, p. 120.
157. Second reply of the Dutch delegation dated 30 April 1613, in CC, p. 113.
158. Report of the English delegation to the Privy Council dated 10 May 1613, CC, pp. 119–20.
159. Second reply of the Dutch delegation dated 30 April 1613, in CC, p. 109.
160. Dig., 2.14.1.pr.; Aristotle, *The Art of Rhetoric,* with tr. by J.H. Freese, reprint of 1926, Loeb Classical Library, 193 (Cambridge, Mass.: Harvard University Press and London: Heinemann, 1975), 1.15; Marcus Tullius Cicero, *De Officiis,* with tr. by W. Miller, reprint of 1913, Loeb Classical Library, 30 (Cambridge, Mass.: Harvard University Press and London: Heinemann, 1975), 3.24 (92); counter-memorial of the Dutch delegation dated 20 April 1613, in CC, p. 101; Report of the English delegation to the Privy Council dated 10 May 1613, in CC, p. 119; CE, p. 105. See also the principle of canon law laid down by Pope Innocent III in his *Liber Extra,* 1.35.1, contained in the Corpus of Canon Law or *Corpus Juris Canonici, editio lipsiensis secunda,* ed. A.E. Richter, 2 vols., facsimile edition of 1879 (Graz: Akademische Druck- und Verlagsanstalt, 1995), "Universi dixerunt: pax servetur, pacta cusdodiantur". (Universally it is said: peace is to be guarded, contracts are to be honoured.) For the wider significance of this premise against the backdrop of early Dutch expansion in Asia, see also van Goor, *Prelude to Colonialism,* pp. 29–30.
161. Final memorial of the Dutch delegation presented before King James I/VI dated 13 May 1613, in appendix 15; see also the report of the English delegation to the Privy Council dated 10 May 1613, p. 120; *Verbael* of the Dutch delegation dated May 1615, p. 254.
162. CE, p. 105.
163. CE, p. 73.
164. These two qualities were commonly attributed by European authors to Asian peoples at the time. See Althusius, *Politica Methodice Digesta,* chapter 23, section 6, p. 201. See also what Althusius has to say in section 3, p. 200 about East Asians, whom he describes in such flattering terms as *urbanior et humanior* (more urbane and humane).
165. CE, p. 108.
166. Undated Dutch memorial on the benefits and disadvantages of a proposed merger of the VOC and the English East India Company in CC, p. 241, point 9, "Par ceste union pourra estre empesché le trafficq des Chinois, Maleyens, Javanois et aultres trafiquants aux Moluques.... Au contraire durant

la diversité des dictes compaignies les Maleyens, Chinois, Javanois et aultres nous guasteront de plus en plus de tout le trafficq des Indes et sur tout celuy de la coste de Chormandel des Molucques et aultres." My translation from French. The original document is found in the Hague, Nationaal Archief, *Collectie Hugo de Groot, Supplement I* (ms. 1.10.35.02, no. 40, fols. 137–41).

167. See more extensively the medium-term consequences of the *Santa Catarina* incident in Borschberg, *The Singapore and Melaka Straits,* pp. 88–136; "The Seizure of the *Santa Catarina* Revisited", *JSEAS* 33, 1 (2002): 31–62.
168. Leonard Blussé, "Brief Encounter at Macao", *Modern Asian Studies* 22, 3 (1988): 663.
169. See generally Borschberg, *The Singapore and Melaka Straits,* chapters 2–4, pp. 60–156. With specific reference to Johor, see also Borschberg, "The Johor-VOC Alliance and the Twelve Years Truce", *IILJ Working Paper* 8 (2009): 1–32.
170. Concerning Grotius' role as an architect of colonial rule, see also Martin van Gelderen, "The Challenge of Colonialism: Grotius and Vitoria on Natural Law and International Relations", *GNS* 14–5 (1993–4): 3–37. Such conclusions are reached in sharp contrast to Roelofsen, who opines that ascribing to Grotius a role in early Dutch expansion in Asia poses a "paradox". See Roelofsen, "Hugo de Groot en de VOC", *De Hollandse Jaren van Hugo de Groot,* ed. Nellen and Trapman, p. 66.

Chapter 3

1. Van Heemskerk's operation against the Portuguese carrack is described in considerable detail and a sense of drama in the German language edition of the *Achter Theil der Orientalischen Indien,* pp. 38–40. See also Borschberg, *The Singapore and Melaka Straits,* pp. 72–5; Borscherg, "The Seizure of the *Santa Catarina* Revisited", *JSEAS* 33, 1 (2002): 34 *et seq.*
2. Early appraisals of the *Santa Catarina's* cargo were clearly inflated and exaggerated, but are indicative of how this particular prize fired the imagination of its contemporaries. See the rare 1604 pamphlet *Corte ende sekere Beschryvinghe vant veroveren der rijcke ende gheweldighe krake, comende uytet gheweste van China, door den Admirael Jacobus Heemskerke* ... (Ghedruckt na de copy van Middelborch by Richard Schilders, 1604) (A short and accurate description of the seizure of a large and rich[ly laden] carrack sailing from the region of China by Admiral van Heemskerk) as well as the testimony of Joris van Spilbergen of 20 June 1603 in *De Reis van Joris van Spilbergen naar Ceylon, Atjeh en Bantam, 1601–1604*, ed. F.C. Wieder (The Hague: Martinus Nijhoff, 1933), pp. 83–2, where the value cargo is appraised at "tseventich hondert duysend Gulden" (7,000,000 guilders or florins). Other Portuguese sources speak of a cost value of one "conto de oro"

(1,000,000 cruzados), see Borscherg, "The Seizure of the Santa Catarina Revisited", *JSEAS* 33, 1 (2002): 32, 50, 57. De Coutre speaks of a cost value of "dos millones de oro" (two million in gold), see de Coutre, *Andanzas Asiáticas,* p. 169. See further Pontanus, *Rerum et Urbis Amstelodamensium Historia,* p. 206.

3. Actual proceeds from the auction of the *Santa Catarina*'s cargo amounted to about 3.5 million guilders, or approximately half the paid-in capital of the VOC at the time. See Borschberg, "The Seizure of the *Santa Catarina* Revisited", *JSEAS* 33, 1 (2002): 35, 57.
4. This policy and instruction of the Dutch States General is significantly expressed in a resolution of 1 November 1603, several copies of which are found among the working papers of Grotius. One written in the hand of Grotius, is found in the Hague, Nationaal Archief, *Collectie Hugo de Groot, Supplement I* (ms. 1.10.35.02, no. 40, folio 223; see the image on p. 176, top third of the page), and a Dutch excerpt of the same on fol. 83 in the same manuscript collection. Another copy not mentioned by Noordhoff is a secretarial copy sold as part of lot 32 at the 1864 auction: "Pièces diverses conç. le commerce e la navigation aux Indes en holland. e franc., 1603–1613, 10 pièces." (Diverse items concerning commerce and navigation to the Indies in Dutch and in French, 1603–1610, 10 items.) This lot is currently owned by the Gemeentearchief Rotterdam and is filed as Handschriftenverzameling Rotterdam, 33.01, inv. 3366. See esp. the document "Translaet d'un extract du Registre des resolutions de Messeigneurs les Estats Generaulx des païs bas unies" (Translation of an excerpt from the Register of the Resolution of the Gentlemen States General of the United Netherlands), dated 1 November 1603. The excerpt on fol. 233 reads as follows: "Les presents deputéz de la Compaignie des Indes Orientales ont esté admonestér serieusement de prendre regard et mettre ordre, afin que les navires qui dejia sont equipez ou qui en apres seront equipez pour allér aux Indes Orientales, puissent avoir charge et instruction d'endommager les ennemys, et nuire à leur personnes, navires et bien par touts moyens possibles, pour aussi pouvoir avecq reputation non seulement continuer leur trafficq, mais le propager et faire croistre, lequel aultrement et par faulte de cecy certainement ils vont perdre: Puis que cecy a esté la cause principale pourquoy les Seigneurs Estats Generaulx ont procuré l'union des Compaignies et donné l'octroy et authorisation á l'endommagement des ennemis." (The present deputies of the East India Company are seriously admonished to look into and give orders to the effect that the ships, which are already equipped or afterwards shall be equipped to sail to the East Indies, can have charge and instruction to damage the enemies and inflict harm on their persons, ships and goods by all means possible, so that they may with reputation not only continue their trade, but also expand it and make it grow, otherwise by neglecting this they will certainly lose it. For this was the principal reason why the

Gentlemen States General have undertaken the union of the Companies and awarded them a charter and authorisation to inflict damage on the enemies.) While admirals and commanding officers of the voorcompagniën were instructed to avoid armed conflict and only engage enemies in self-defence, the formation of the VOC marked a formal shift in policy by the Dutch States General toward the offensive. Article 37 of the VOC charter lists Portugal as well as Spain as state enemies, "rendering their interest liable to attack and seizure as booty of war". The year 1603 (specifically the instructions issued by the VOC to Steven van der Hagen) is also noted by Steensgaard, *The Asian Trade Revolution,* p. 132 (together with his sources). For a useful background study, see Geoffrey Parker, "Power and Profit in the Policy of the United East India Company", in his *Spain and the Netherlands, 1559–1659. Ten Studies* (London: Collins, 1979), pp. 131–41, as well as M.-A.P. Meilink-Roelofsz', "Aspects of Dutch Colonial Development in Asia in the Seventeenth Century", in *Britain and the Netherlands in Europe and Asia. Papers delivered to the Third Anglo-Dutch History Conference,* ed. John Selwyn Bromley and Ernst H. Kossmann (London: Macmillan, 1968), pp. 56–79, esp. pp. 60–3 on the evolution of early VOC policy.

5. See also Borschberg, *The Singapore and Melaka Straits,* passim.
6. According to the Dutch historian Victor Enthoven a total of about 200 sailing craft of various sizes and capacities were seized by the VOC in Asian waters during the opening two decades of the 17th century. See Enthoven, *Zeeland en de opkomst van de Republiek: Handel en Strijd in de Scheldedelta, ca. 1550–1621* (Leiden: Proefschrift, 1996), pp. 210–1.
7. Nellen, *Hugo de Groot. Een leven in strijd om de vrede,* p. 83; van Ittersum, "Dating the Manuscript of *De Iure Praedae*", *History of European Ideas* 35 (2009): 125–93 and van Ittersum, "Hugo Grotius in Context", *AJSS* 31, 3 (2003): 512. Concerning the revision, completion and publication of this portion of *De Iure Praedae* against the backdrop of Dutch–Spanish negotiations for a truce, see van Ittersum, "Preparing *Mare Liberum* for the Press", *GNS* 27–8 (2005–7): 246–80.
8. Van Ittersum, *Profit and Principle,* esp. chapters 3 and 5, pp. 105–88, 283–358. Van Ittersum, "*Mare Liberum* in the West Indies? Hugo Grotius and the Case of the Swimming Lion, a Dutch Pirate in the Caribbean at the Turn of the Seventeenth Century", *Itinerario* 31, 3 (2007): 59–94; van Ittersum, "Preparing *Mare Liberum* for the Press: Hugo Grotius' Rewriting of Chapter 12 of *De iure praedae* in November–December 1608", *GNS* 27–8 (2005–7): 246–80.
9. Alexandrowicz, *An Introduction to the Law of Nations in the East Indies,* p. 44.
10. Recourse to the legal terminology shall be very circumspect, as the present chapter does not engage in an interpretation of the text based on law.

11. The Latin text was first reproduced as an appendix in Samuel Muller, *Mare Clausum. Bijdrage tot de geschiedenis der rivaliteit van Engeland en Nederland in de zeventiende eeuw*, pp. 331–61. The first English translation was published in Herbert F. Wright, *Some Less Known Works of Hugo Grotius, Consisting of: A Translation of his Works on the Fisheries in his Controversy with William Welwood; A Translation of Extracts from his Letters Concerning International Natural Law and Fisheries; An Account of his Controversy with Johan de Laet on the Origin of the American Aborigines; and a Translation of Peerlkamp's Appreciation of his Ability as a Poet* (Leiden: Brill, 1928), pp. 154–205. A more recent translation into English can be found in Grotius, *The Free Sea*, pp. 77–130. See also van Ittersum, "'Mare Liberum' versus the Propriety of the Seas? The Debate between Hugo Grotius and William Welwood and Its Impact on Anglo-Scotto-Dutch Fishery Disputes in the Second Decade of the Seventeenth Century", *Edinburgh Law Review* 10 (2006): 239–75.
12. Scholarship on the Iberian Peninsula has established that the work was written around 1616 and subsequently revised in the 1620s. De Freitas' work does not represent a commissioned reply by the Iberian monarch, but a study in its own right. The delay in its publication was more than just an aspect of a "policy of peace and good will" by the Spanish monarchy [according to Mónica Brito Vieira, "Mare Liberum vs. Mare Clausum: Grotius, Freitas and Selden's Debate on Dominion of the Seas", *Journal of the History of Ideas* 63, 3 (2003): 362]; it appears that the Inquisition had a leading hand in the delay as well. See Marcelo Caetano's introduction in Seraphim de Freitas, tr. Pinto de Menezes, 2 vols. (Lisbon: Instituto de Alto Cultura, 1959–61) and its reprint *Do Justo Império Asiático dos Portugueses*. Latin-Portuguese bilingual edition, 2 vols. (Lisbon: Instituto Nacional de Investigação Científica, 1983), I, pp. 40–1; 44–6, concerning a royal committee appointed to ascertain the nature and viability of de Freitas' arguments. Caetano opines that some changes to the text were required before the *imprimatur* was issued on 24 October 1624.
13. Concerning the influence of Vázquez de Menchaca on Grotius in general, see also Annabel Brett, *Liberty, Right and Nature: Individual Rights in Later Scholastic Thought* (Cambridge: CUP, 1997), esp. pp. 204–5.
14. The original Latin title reads *Mare Liberum, sive de iure quod Batavis competit in rebus Indicanis.*
15. LML, p. 1; CML, p. 7, "Every nation is free to travel to every other nation and … trade with it." See also HML, p. 1; IPC, p. 302; CIPC, p. 218.
16. LML, pp. 52, 53–4; CML, pp. 61, 63; HML, pp. 49, 50–1; IPC, p. 356; CIPC, pp. 256–7.
17. LML, pp. 65–6; CML, p. 75; HML, pp. 59–60.
18. The intra-Asian market was to grow only in later years of the 17th century and became an important source of income for the VOC during its corporate lifetime.

19. There is evidence to suggest that Grotius became aware of the significance, dynamics and profitability of the intra-Asian trade by the time he attended the Anglo-Dutch Conferences of 1613 and 1615.
20. In the past, scholarship on *Mare Liberum* has focused on the "freedom on the seas" and legal aspects of the treatise. Comtemporary scholars are beginning to unravel a more complex set of arguments. See, for example, Helen Thornton, "Hugo Grotius and the Freedom of the Seas", *International Journal of Maritime History* 16, 2 (2004): 20–1, where the issues of trade and access to marketplaces assume a more prominent position than in the past for the overall interpretation of *Mare Liberum*.
21. This was, of course, under the strict proviso that the Portuguese were not actually sovereign overlords of the territories to which the Dutch sailed, and Grotius was well aware that the Lusitanian crown did indeed legitimately possess sovereignty over certain territories in the East Indies, including Goa and Melaka. See LML, p. 4; CML, p. 11, "The Portuguese are not sovereigns of those parts of the East Indies to which the Dutch sail, that is to say, Java, Taprobana [Sumatra] and many of the Moluccas." See also HML, p. 13; IPC, p. 306; CIPC, p. 220. Taprobana, a geographic name known from the ancient world (specifically Megasthenes and Ptolemy), was variously applied to the islands Ceylon or Sumatra by geographers and humanist scholars during the early modern period. Van Deman Magoffin, the editor of CML (p. 11) translates this name as "Ceylon" which is almost certainly incorrect in this context.
22. On the wider historic context of this passage and its biblical origins in Numbers 21:21–5, see Dieter Janssen, "Bellum iustum und Völkerrecht im Werk des Hugo Grotius", in *Krieg und Kultur. Die Rezeption von Krieg und Frieden in der Niederländischen Republik und im Deutschen Reich, 1568–1648*, ed. Horst Lademacher and Simon Groenvelt (Münster: Waxmann, 1998), pp. 138–9. See also the useful summary and discussion in Anthony Pagden, "Human Rights, Natural Rights and Europe's Imperial Legacy", *Political Theory* 31 (2003): esp. 185–6; Karl-Heinz Ziegler, "Völkerrechtliche Aspekte der Eroberung Lateinamerikas", *Zeitschrift für Neuere Rechtsgeschichte* 23 (2001): 9, 20 *et seq.*, and more extensively in Isabel Trujillo Pérez, *Francisco de Vitoria: il diritto alla comunicazione e i confini della socialità umana* (Turin: G. Giappichelli, 1997).
23. Borschberg, "De Societate Publica cum Infidelibus: Ein Frühwerk von Hugo Grotius", *ZRG*, RA 115 (1998): 355–93.
24. Borschberg, "De Pace. Ein unveröffentlichtes Fragment von Grotius über Krieg und Frieden", *ZRG*, RA 113 (1996): 268–92. A transcript of the Latin text of *De Pace* can be found in Zaglio, *Jus Pacis e Concezione della Pace in Ugo Grozio*, pp. 246–8.
25. CiT; also "Commentarius in Theses XI. Ein unveröffentlichtes Kurzwerk von Hugo Grotius", *ZRG*, RA 109 (1992): 450–74. Concerning the possible

dating of the *Commentarius in Theses XI* and its genesis in relation to *De Iure Praedae Commentarius,* see also van Ittersum, "Hugo Grotius in Context", *AJSS* 31, 3 (2003): 542–4, appendix I.

26. The original is preserved in Leiden University Library as ms. B.P.L. 918. It was found among the working papers of Grotius and acquired at the 1864 auction. See Noordhoff, *Beschrijving van ... papieren afkomstig van Huig de Groot,* part IX, lot 77, p. 27.
27. This treatise was first published in 1625, and its text was revised several times by Grotius until his death in 1645.
28. This line of reasoning, whereby Grotius establishes or identifies a right and at the same time establishes prohibitions, not only transpires here in *Mare Liberum*, but is also manifest from the fragment *De Societate Publica cum Infidelibus*. See Borschberg, "De Societate Publica cum Infidelibus", *ZRG,* RA 115 (1998): 372–3, esp. note 80. Concerning *ius communicationis* in general, see also chapter 2.
29. LML, p. 52; CML, p. 61: "Nature had given all things to all men." Also HML, p. 49; IPC, p. 354; CIPC, p. 255.
30. LML, pp. 59, 60, 61; CML, pp. 69, 70, 71; HML, pp. 54, 55, 56.
31. LML, p. 52; CML, p. 61; HML, p. 49; IPC, p. 354; CIPC, p. 255.
32. LML, p. 52; CML, p. 61, "By the law of nations the principle was introduced that the opportunity to engage in trade, of which no one can be deprived, should be free to all men." HML, p. 49; IPC, p. 354; CIPC, p. 255, with the corresponding reference to Dig. 1.1.5. See also Inst., II.2.
33. LML, pp. 63–6 [last page erroneously numbered 42]; CML, pp. 73–6 *passim*; HML, pp. 50–2; IPC, pp. 355–8; CIPC, pp. 256–8. See also Borschberg, "De Pace. Ein unveröffentlichtes Fragment von Hugo Grotius über Krieg und Frieden", *ZRG,* RA 113 (1996): 281. For its roots in Vitoria and the Spanish Late Scholastics in general, see also Diego Panizza, "Political Theory and Jurisprudence in Gentili's De Iure Belli: The Great Debate Between 'Theological' and 'Humanist' Perspectives from Vitoria to Grotius", *Institute for International Law and Justice (IILJ) Working Paper,* History and Theory of International Law Series, New York University School of Law, 15 (2005): 29–30.
34. LML, p. 1; CML, p. 7; HML, p. 11; IPC, pp. 303–4; CIPC, p. 218.
35. Knight, "Grotius in England: His Opposition There to the Principles of *Mare Liberum*", *TGS* 5 (1919): 9; W.S.M. Knight, *The Life and Works of Hugo Grotius* (London: Sweet & Maxwell, 1925), p. 94; Jonathan Ziskind, "International Law and Ancient Sources: Grotius and Selden", *Review of Politics* 35, 4 (1973): 540, "At the beginning of his first chapter, [Grotius] states the premise 'Every nation is free to travel to every other nation, and to trade with it.' But as Knight has already shown, the rest of the chapter, including most of the ancient and modern references, that support Grotius' claim, is probably scribbled from the first chapter of Alberico Gentili's *De Iure Belli,* and, in fact, Grotius distorts Gentili's ideas since nowhere did

Gentili mention that a ruler could not prevent foreigners from access to his subjects and from trading with them. Furthermore, in the seventh chapter, Grotius openly states his dependence upon Vázquez de Menchaca, quoting long extracts from his work." As will be seen, even this claimed reliance on Vázquez de Menchaca is highly questionable. See also Ziskind, "International Law", p. 548. Concerning Grotius' indebtedness to Gentili, see also Theodor Meron, "Rights of Mankind in Gentili, Grotius and Suarez", *The American Journal of International Law* 85, 1 (1991): 110–6, esp. pp. 113–4.

36. LML, p. 1; CML, p. 7; HML, p. 10; IPC, pp. 302–3; CIPC, p. 218, and the additional references LML, p. 53; CML, pp. 62–3; HML, p. 50; IPC, pp. 255–6; CIPC, pp. 355–6. On the specifically Ciceronian aspects of Grotian Stoicism which supposedly derive from Vázquez de Menchaca, see Annabel Brett, "Natural Right and Civil Community: The Civil Philosophy of Hugo Grotius", *Historical Journal* 45, 1 (2002): 38. Compare this with Thumfart, "On Grotius's *Mare Liberum* and Vitoria's *De Indis*, Following Agamben and Schmitt", *GNS* 30 (2009): 78, "With this argument [that is the citation in the main text] Grotius invoked a pre-Christian tradition of economic theology that reaches from Philo of Alexandria and Libanius to the early fathers of the Church such as Chrysostomus and Origen.... However, Grotius's principle of Free Trade cannot be fully understood when thought of as being derived solely from Stoic or other pre-Christian concepts."
37. LML, p. 61; CML, p. 53; HML, p. 49; IPC, p. 354; CIPC, p. 255, citing Aristotle, *Politics,* tr. H. Rackham, reprint of 1932, Loeb Classical Library, 264 (Cambridge, Mass.: Harvard University Press and London: Heinemann, 1972), 1.3, "For the art of exchange extends to all possessions, and it arises at first in a natural manner from the circumstance that some have too little, others too much."
38. LML, p. 52; CML, p. 62; HML, p. 50; IPC, pp. 354–5; CIPC, pp. 255–6.
39. LML, p. 53; CML, p. 62, "Hence commerce was born out of necessity for the commodities of life, as Pliny shows by a citation from Homer. But after immovables also began to be recognized as private property, the consequent annihilation of universal community of use made commerce a necessity not only between men whose habitations were far apart, but even between men who were neighbours...." Also HML, p. 50; IPC, p. 256; CIPC, pp. 354–5. See also the account of how trade supposedly began among the Chinese, CML, p. 62, "They say that trade arose among the Chinese in about this way. Things were deposited at places out in the desert and left to the good faith and conscience of those who exchanged things of their own for what they took." See also HML, p. 49; IPC, p. 354; CIPC, p. 255. It is noteworthy in this context to highlight that the source of Grotius' claim about the Chinese (Latin: *Ceres*) is one of the Latin ancients (Pomponius), and not a period or Asian source!

40. LML, pp. 14–5; CML, pp. 23–4; HML, pp. 21–2; IPC, pp. 314–5; CIPC, pp. 226–7. See also LML, pp. 16–7; CML, p. 25; HML, pp. 22–3; IPC, pp. 318–9; CIPC, pp. 229–30 and *Mare Liberum*, chapter 2. Grotius of course assumes the same position in his later works, see IBP, 1.1.10.4 and Grotius, *Inleidinge tot de Hollandsche Rechts-Geleerdheid*, ed. F. Dovring, H.F.W.D. Fischer and E.M. Meijers, 2nd ed. (Leiden: Universitaire Pers, 1965), I, 2.3, pp. 50–5.
41. LML, p. 17; CML, pp. 28–9; HML, p. 26; IPC, p. 322; CIPC, p. 232 . See also Inst. II.1.1 and Dig. 1.8.2.
42. Inst. II.i.1, "Et quidem naturali iure communia sunt omnium haec: aer et aqua profluens et mare et per hoc litora maris." (By natural law the following things belong to all, namely: air, running water, the sea, and for this reason the seashore). — See the useful summary of Grotius' position in Ziskind, "International Law and Ancient Sources: Grotius and Selden", *Review of Politics* 35, 4 (1973): 542–3, especially his verdict: "… any attempt to coalesce public ownership, as Grotius does, with commonness is mistaken". See also the issues surrounding *Mare Liberum* and the appropriation of private property in John Salter, "Hugo Grotius: Property and Consent", *Political Theory* 29, 4 (2001): 537–55, esp. pp. 539, 544–5.
43. This is a core argument brought forward by John Locke in his *Second Treatise on Government*. See John Locke, *Two Treatises of Government*, ed. and intr. Peter Laslett (Cambridge: CUP, 1988), pp. 285 *et seq*., but esp. no. 31, p. 290.
44. LML, pp. 60–1; CML, pp. 70–1; HML, p. 56; IPC, p. 362; CIPC, p. 261.
45. LML, p. 20; CML pp. 29–30; HML, pp. 26–7; IPC, pp. 322–3; CIPC, p. 232.
46. Borschberg, "De Societate Publica cum Infidelibus", *ZRG*, RA 115 (1998): 367; see also chapter 2.
47. On the ruler's right to publish, see specifically also the recent contribution by Guus van Nifterik, "Grotius and the Origin of the Ruler's Right to Punish", *GNS* 27–8 (2005–7): 396–415; Benjamin Straumann, "Natural Rights and Roman Law in Hugo Grotius's *Theses LVI, De iure praedae* and *Defensio capitis quinti maris liberi*", *GNS* 27–8 (2005–7): 341–65. Concerning the historic reception of this doctrine of the "just war", see also António Vasconcelos de Saldanha, *Iustum Imperium, dos tratados como fundamento do império dos portugueses no Oriente: estudo de história do direito internacional e do direito português* (Lisbon: Fundação Oriente, 1997), pp. 202 *et seq.*
48. Inst. II.ii.1–2; compare this with Borschberg, "Commentarius in Theses XI", *ZRG*, RA 109 (1992): 468.
49. LML, pp. 63–6 [last page erroneously numbered 42]; CML, pp. 73–6; HML, pp. 58–60; generally also Borschberg, "Commentarius in Theses XI", *ZRG*, RA 109 (1992): 467; Borschberg, "De Pace", *ZRG*, RA 113 (1996): 280–1.

50. LML, p. 63; CML, p. 73; HML, p. 59; Borschberg, "De Pace", *ZRG*, RA 113 (1996): 279–80.
51. CiT, pp. 258–61.
52. For a critical account of Grotius' use and handling of his sources, see esp. Waszink, "Using the Work. Remarks on the Text of De iure praedae", *GNS* 27–8 (2005–7): 224. See also Borschberg, "Grotius, the Social Contract and Political Resistance. A Study of the Unpublished Theses LVI", *IILJ Working Paper* 6 (2006): 9–23.
53. The most relevant being *Commentarius in Theses XI, De Societate Publica cum Infidelibus, De Pace* and the *Theses LVI.*
54. Van Nifterik, "Grotius and the Origin of the Ruler's Right to Punish", *GNS* 27–8 (2005–7): 396–415; Straumann, "Natural Rights and Roman Law in Hugo Grotius's *Theses LVI, De iure praedae* and *Defensio capitis quinti maris liberi*", *GNS* 27–8 (2005–7): 341–65; Straumann, *Hugo Grotius und die Antike. Römisches Recht und römische Ethik im frühneuzeitlichen Naturrecht* (Baden-Baden: Nomos Verlag, 2007), esp. pp. 191–5; van Ittersum, *Profit and Principle.*
55. IBP, 2.20.40.4. On the question of how individuals (and implicitly sovereigns) acquire rights over others, see Borschberg, "Grotius, the Social Contract and Political Resistance. A Study of the Unpublished Theses LVI", *IILJ Working Paper* 6 (2006): 31, and for the right to punish also Straumann, *Hugo Grotius und die Antike,* p. 194.
56. LML, p. 26; CML, p. 34; HML, p. 30; IPC, p. 328; CIPC, p. 236.
57. IBP, 2.20.9.2; Straumann, *Hugo Grotius und die Antike,* p. 193.
58. Borschberg, "Grotius, the Social Contract and Political Resistance. A Study of the Unpublished Theses LVI", *IILJ Working Paper* 6 (2006): 31 *et seq*., esp. also pp. 43 *et seq.*
59. LML, unpaginated introduction, fols. ix, xi; CML, pp. 4, 6; HML, pp. 7, 9.
60. LML, unpaginated introduction, fol. ix; CML, p. 4; HML, pp. 7–8.
61. LML, unpaginated introduction, fol. ix; CML, p. 5; HML, p. 8.
62. LML, unpaginated introduction, fol. xi; CML, p. 6; HML, p. 9, on the supposed antiquity of this practice.
63. LML, p. 65; CML, p. 75, "Following these principles a good judge would award to the Dutch the freedom of trade, and would forbid the Portuguese and others from using force to hinder that freedom, and would order the payment of just damages." See also HML, p. 59.
64. Note the observation of Knight, "Grotius in England: His Opposition There to the Principles of *Mare Liberum*", *TGS* 5 (1920): 6, "... it should be noted that at this time Spain, of which power Portugal was then a constituent, was at war with Holland as also with England. Her prohibition of enemy trading with lands, or navigation in waters, over which she claimed dominion

was therefore in perfect accord with principles which, today certainly, are generally recognized. But this aspect of the case is entirely ignored by Grotius."

65. LML, pp. 62–3; CML, pp. 72–3; HML, pp. 57–8. Borschberg, "De Pace. Ein unveröffentlichtes Fragment von Hugo Grotius über Krieg und Frieden", *ZRG*, RA 113 (1996): 281.
66. LML, p. 65; CML, p. 75, "... would forbid the Portuguese and others from using force to hinder that freedom [of trade], and would order the payment of just damages". See also HML, p. 59.
67. Vitoria, *Relectiones Theologicae*. Two different editions of Lyon 1557 and Salamanca 1564 feature starkly different page breaks and page numbering. Both have been reproduced in facsimile in *Relecciones Teológicas. Edición crítica y versión castellana*, ed. and tr. Luís G. Alonso Getino, 3 vols. (Madrid: Imprenta la Rafa-Abtao, 1933), I, pp. 212–452. The present author's own careful study of Grotius' reading notes, including those specifically taken from Vitoria and featured in Ms. B.P.L. 922 at Leiden University Library, reveal that the young humanist worked with the first edition of the *Relectiones*, a copy of which had been passed on to him through VOC channels (see the image on p. 63).
68. Grotius briefly touches on this point in his treatise. See LML, p. 7; CML, pp. 13–4, "Nor are the East Indians stupid and unthinking; on the contrary, they are intelligent and shrewd, so that a pretext for subduing them on the grounds of their character could not be sustained.... And now that well-known pretext of forcing nations into a higher state of civilization against their will, the pretext once monopolized by the Greeks and by Alexander the Great, is considered by all theologians, especially those of Spain, to be unjust and unholy." Also HML, pp. 14–5; IPC, pp. 308–9; CIPC, p. 222. Also note Grotius' reference to Vázquez de Menchaca here. — See also LML, p. 11; CML, pp. 19–20; HML, pp. 18–9; IPC, pp. 312–3; CIPC, p. 225 (quotation from Cajetanus' Commentary to Thomas Aquinas, *Summa Theologiae*, 2a–2ae, qu. 4, art. 66, n. 8). The problem is also discussed by Diego de Covarruvias y Leyva, *Opera Omnia quae hactenus extant*, I, *Regula Peccatum*, section 10.2, pp. 508–9; some of his acknowledged references are repeated by Grotius. Compare this with the observations in Brito Vieira, "Mare Liberum vs. Mare Clausum. Grotius, Freitas and Selden's Debate on Dominion of the Seas", *Journal of the History of Ideas* 63, 3 (2003): 366.
69. LML, p. 7; CML, p. 14; HML, p. 15; IPC, p. 309; CIPC, p. 222.
70. Vitoria, *De Indis Recenter Inventis et De Jure Belli Hispanorum in Barbaros; Vorlesungen über die kürzlich entdeckten Inder und das Recht der Spanier zum Kriege gegen die Barbaren, 1539*, ed. Walter Schätzel and intr. Paul Hadrossek (Tübingen: J.C.B. Mohr, 1952), II, sections 1 *et seq.*, pp. 48 *et seq.* (Latin text); Vitoria, *Political Writings*, pp. 252 *et seq.* (English

translation); Covarruvias y Leyva, *Opera Omnia*, I, *Regula Peccatum*, section 9.5, pp. 501–4. Concerning the historical background to these arguments on universal monarchy of the Holy Roman Emperor, see the very useful chapter in Anthony Pagden, *Lords of All the World: Ideologies of Empire in Spain, Britain and France, c. 1500–c. 1800* (New Haven and London: Yale University Press, 1995), pp. 29–62 in general, its express rejection later by Grotius on p. 39, as well as the Dutch humanist's evidently heavy reliance on the writings of Vázquez de Menchaca in formulating his own conclusions on p. 56.

71. Julius Pacius à Beriga, *I.C. Regii Consiliarii et Iuris ex prima sede in illustri Valentina Academia Professoris De Dominio Maris Hadriatici disceptatio* (Lyon: Bartholomaeus Vicentus, 1619), pp. 15 *et seq*.
72. Vitoria's *ius communicationis* has been the subject of several discussions in recent years, including Trujillo Pérez, *Francisco de Vitoria: il diritto alla comunicazione e i confini della socialità umana*; Anthony Anghie, *Imperialism, Sovereignty and the Making of International Law* (Cambridge: CUP, 2004), pp. 21–2, and more recently also in Johannes Thumfart, *Die Begründung der global-politischen Philosophie. Zu Francisco de Vitorias de indis recenter inventis von 1539* (Berlin: Kulturverlag Kadmos, 2009) and also his article Thumfart, "On Grotius's *Mare Liberum* and Vitoria's *De Indis*, Following Agamben and Schmitt", *GNS* 30 (2009): 65–87. For a recent bibliography touching upon the works of Vitoria, see Ramón Hernández Martín, *Francisco de Vitoria y su "Relección sobre los Indios". Los derechos de los hombres y de los pueblos. Homenaje al Fundador del Derecho Internacional de Gentes en el 50 Aniversario de la Declaración Universal de los Derechos Humanos, 1948–1998* (Madrid: Edibesa, 1998).
73. Vitoria, *De Indis Recenter Inventis*, ed. Schätzel, III.1, sections 4 *et seq*., pp. 96 *et seq*. (Latin text); Vitoria, *Political Writings*, pp. 280–1 (English translation). For Grotius' application of this, see also LML, p. 64; CML, p. 74, "If many writers, Augustine himself (City of God, 5.1) among them, believed it was right to take up arms because innocent passage was refused across foreign territory, how much more justly will arms be taken up against those from whom the demand is made of the common and innocent use of the sea, which by the law of nature is common to all?" See also HML, pp. 58–9.
74. This point is also raised in LML, p. 12; CML, pp. 20–1; HML, p. 19; IPC, p. 314; CIPC, pp. 225–6.
75. According to Vitoria in his *Relectio de Indis*, II, esp. section 36, pp. 78, 80 (Latin text) and Vitoria, *Political Writings*, pp. 270–1 (English translation), the natives may be compelled to listen to the word of God, but they cannot be compelled to embrace the Christian religion. The Latin text makes this very clear: "Item necessarium est eis ad salutem credere in Christum et baptizari (Marc. ult: 2) … Sed non possunt credere, nisi audient (Rom. 10:3). Ergo

tenentur audire alias essent extra statum salutis sine culpa sua, si non tenentur audire." (Therefore, in order to secure their salvation [that is the salvation of the Amerindians] they need to believe in Christ and be baptized {Mark, last chapter: 2} … But they cannot believe, unless they listen {Rom. 10:3}. Therefore, they can be compelled to listen, for if they are not compelled to listen, they would otherwise remain outside a state of salvation on account of no guilt of their own.) It appears however, that for practical reasons, Vitoria moderates this basic position in the following sections, notably by appeal to the canonists and canon law, and in section 38, p. 80 (Latin text) and p. 271 (English translation), also on the grounds of "insufficiently pious exposure" to Christian teachings. Further curtailment follows in section 39, pp. 80, 82 (Latin text) and p. 272 (English translation), where Vitoria states that war may not be waged to force people to accept the Christian religion, nor may victory in war be taken as proof of Christianity's veracity. However, should the Spaniards be impeded in exercising any of their rights, including the preaching of the Gospel and sharing in things held in common, force may be applied in order to establish a secure operating environment. On the latter see esp. Vitoria, *Political Writings*, III.2, section 12, p. 285.

76. De Soto's little-known *Relection de Dominio* (Relection or Re-reading on Dominium) was held at the end of the academic year 1535. For the full text, see Domingo de Soto, *Relección de Dominio*, ed., intr. and tr. Jaime Brufau Prats (Granada: Universidad de Granada, 1964).
77. Reference to de Soto's book I, question 6, article 4 is found in Grotius' autograph manuscript B.P.L. 917 on fol. 34 verso.
78. References are made by Grotius to his exposé *In Regula Peccatum*. This is contained in Covarruvias' *Practicarum quaestiones liber unus*. See also LML, p. 52; CML, p. 61; HML, p. 49; IPC, p. 354; CIPC, p. 255.
79. Rodrigo Juárez (Latinised: Zuaresius), *Consilia duo de usu maris et navibus transvehendis*, bound together with Benvenuto Straccha, *De Mercatura seu Mercatore tractatus* … secunda editio.… (Lyon: Publisher unknown, 1558). See also CML, pp. 44, 50; HML, pp. 37, 41; IPC, pp. 338, 443; CIPC, pp. 244, 248. The editors of HML and CIPC render the name Zuaresius as "Suárez".
80. LML, unpaginated introduction, fol. ix, pp. 4, 35–6; CML, pp. 4, 44; HML, pp. 7–8, 37; IPC, p. 338; CIPC, p. 244.
81. De Freitas, *De Iusto Imperio Asiatico*. According to his published letters, Grotius was well aware that a reply to *Mare Liberum* had been written in Spain. He later admitted to having read de Freitas' printed work. Despite the customary Baroque pose of flattery, it does appear that Grotius was somewhat impressed by de Freitas' work, commenting that it was a piece worthy of a reply. There is presently no English translation of this important work of de Freitas, but there are English translations into Portuguese, Spanish, French and German. One of the most accessible editions is the Latin-

Portuguese text *De Iusto Imperio Lusitanorum Asiatico*. The present article, however, will work with the Latin text as well as the German translation prepared and critically annotated by Jörg P. Hardegen. See Seraphim de Freitas, *Über die Rechtmässige Herrschaft der Portugiesen in Asien. Freitas gegen Grotius im Kampf um die Freiheit der Meere*, tr. J.P. Hardegen, doctoral dissertation (Kiel: Christian-Albrechts-Universität Kiel, 1976).

82. De Freitas, *Über die Rechtmässige Herrschaft der Portugiesen in Asien*, pp. 88, 91, 92, 195, 283. It should be stated that de Freitas does not believe the law of nations to be the outcome of a consensus of all peoples, but only the product of "natural reason". See de Freitas, *Über die Rechtmässige*, p. 300.
83. LML, pp. 3–4; CML, p. 9; HML, p. 12; IPC, p. 304; CIPC, p. 219. De Freitas bitterly disagreed with Vitoria's position; see de Freitas, *Über die Rechtmässige Herrschaft der Portugiesen in Asien*, p. 92.
84. See chapter 2 above; also Richard Tuck, *The Rights of War and Peace: Political Thought and the International Order from Grotius to Kant* (Oxford: OUP, 1999), pp. 92–4.
85. Allying with non-Christians against other non-Christians seems perfectly acceptable to the Salmantinos and, indeed, the Iberian jurists.
86. De Freitas, *Über die Rechtmässige Herrschaft der Portugiesen in Asien*, pp. 289–90.
87. On the general issue of forging alliances with infidel overlords at the time, see esp. de Saldanha, *Iustum Imperium, dos tratados como fundamento do Império dos Portugueses no Oriente*, pp. 212 *et seq*.
88. The classic example of this can be found in the autograph manuscript of *De Iure Praedae*, Ms. B.P.L. 917, in Leiden University Library. On fol. 69 verso there is a cluster of quotations referring to the Glossators, Aquinas, Adrian, Florus, John Mair, Alfonso de Castro, Tiraqueau, etc. The whole list is evidently extracted in that very sequence from Covarruvias, *In Regula Peccatum*, part II, section 11. For similar observations on the text of *De Iure Praedae* as a whole, see also Waszink, "Using the Work. Remarks on the Text of De iure praedae", *GNS* 27–8 (2005–7): esp. 224.
89. Knight, "Seraphim de Freitas: Critic of Mare Liberum", *TGS* 11 (1925): 8. Several instances are also identified and discussed in some depth by Ziskind, "International Law and Ancient Sources: Grotius and Selden", *Review of Politics* 35, 4 (1973): 537–59.
90. LML, p. 21; CML, p. 30; HML, pp. 26–7; IPC, p. 323; CIPC, p. 232; de Freitas, *Über die Rechtmässige Herrschaft der Portugiesen in Asien*, p. 238. Hugo Donellus, *Commentariorum de iure civili Libri viginti octo: in quibus jus civile universum singulari artificio atque doctrina explicatum continetur Scip. Gentilis posteriors libros supplevit, expolivit* (Frankfurt/M.: apud Andreae Wecheli heredes, Claudium Marnium et Ioan. Aubrium, 1596), *Commentariorum de iure civili Libri viginti octo*, p. 230.

91. Knight, "Seraphim de Freitas", *TGS* 11 (1925): 7.
92. LML, p. 44; CML, p. 52; HML, p. 43; IPC, p. 346; CIPC, p. 250.
93. LML, p. 43; CML, p. 52; HML, p. 43; IPC, p. 346; CIPC, p. 249; also IBP, Proleg. no. 55.
94. Ferdinando Vázquez de Menchaca, *Conversiarum illustrium aliarumque usu frequentium libri tres/ Controversias fundamentales y otras de mas frecuente uso: remprese por acuerdo de la Universidad de Valladolid*, tr. Fidel Rodríguez Alcalde (Valladolid: Cuesta, 1931–4), 2.20.11 *et seq.* that are not favourable to navigation on the high seas; and 2.89.16 *et seq.* and 2.89.30 *et seq.* Vázquez de Menchaca states in 2.89.30 that arguments in favour of the Venetians and Genoese prohibiting navigation on "their seas" are "suspect" (apparet supecta sit sententia), not least because they run "counter to natural law or primary law of nations which, as said, cannot be changed" (… est contra ipsum jus naturae, aut gentium primaevum, quod mutari non posse diximus).
95. Vázquez de Menchaca, *Conversiarum illustrium*, 2.20. no. 13 navigare contra naturam est (to navigate is against nature); no. 14: Navigare periculosissimum est (to navigate is extremely dangerous); no. 19: Navigare est ire contra leges naturae (to navigate is to infringe the laws of nature).
96. In fact several modern authors including Jonathan Ziskind and Mark Somos have commented on the comparative dearth of references to the Holy Scriptures in *Mare Liberum.* See Ziskind, "International Law and Ancient Sources: Grotius and Selden", *Review of Politics* 35, 4 (1973): 554–5 and generally also Somos, "Secularization in *De Iure Praedae*: from Bible Criticism to International Law", *GNS* 26–28: 147–91.
97. LML, p. 54; CML, p. 63; HML, p. 50; IPC, p. 356, CIPC, pp. 256–7. Concerning this passage see also Ziskind, "International Law and Ancient Sources: Grotius and Selden", *Review of Politics* 35, 4 (1973): 551–2.
98. LML, p. 26; CML, p. 34; HML, p. 30; IPC, p. 328; CIPC, p. 236.
99. Grotius refers only to the bulls of donation dating from 1494 and issued by Pope Alexander VI. He is evidently not aware that within the context of the Portuguese Estado da Índia, the donation of Nicholas V, dating from 1455, is of much greater historical significance. In my opinion, this in itself can be taken as yet another proof that Grotius was not familiar with the legal literature from the Portuguese side, and that he had at best carefully studied some Spanish sources, for example, Vitoria and Covarruvias y Leyva, who both discuss the Alexandrine bulls. It is indeed questionable as to how close Grotius actually read the writings of Ferdinando Vázquez de Menchaca at the time of writing *De Iure Praedae*, or even at the time of revising one of its chapters as *Mare Liberum*. Further research on Grotius' reading notes and on the autograph manuscript owned by Leiden University will hopefully shed new light on this question.

100. LML, pp. 38 *et seq.*, 57–9; CML, pp. 47 *et seq.*, 67–8; HML, pp. 39 *et seq.*, 53–4; IPC, pp. 340 *et seq.*, 258–60; CIPC, pp. 246 *et seq.*, 358–60. Concerning Grotius' refutation of all these aspects, see also Ziskind, "International Law and Ancient Sources: Grotius and Selden", *Review of Politics,* 35, 4 (1973): 539–41, 544, for a useful summary of Grotius' counter-arguments.
101. John Villiers, "The Estado da India in South East Asia", in *South East Asia: Colonial History*, ed. Kratoska and Borschberg, I, p. 156, "The whole of the maritime area of the Estado da India was declared to be *mare clausum* [closed sea, un-free sea] by right of *quasi possessio* [quasi-possession] of the Portuguese crown. This provided the sole legal justification for the *cartaz* system, whereby every Asian trading vessel had to purchase a pass or *cartaz* from the Portuguese authorities, in return for which it qualified for Portuguese protection. Each *cartaz* stated the size of the ship, listed her crew and gave particulars of her captain. It also described the cargo and stated for which port the vessel was bound. Every ship had to pay dues on her cargo at the *forteleza* [fortress] or *feitoria* [factory] where the cartaz was issued and had to leave a sum as security for the payment of similar dues on her return. Certain goods, notably spices and pepper, iron, copper and naval stores, were prohibited, as was giving passage to Turks and other Muslims. Any ship that was found to be sailing without a *cartaz* or that violated the terms of the *cartaz* was automatically confiscated and her crew either killed or sent to slavery in the galleys."
102. A law passed in 1601 prohibited the issuance of *cartazes* to non-Portuguese persons. Dutch aggression and privateering in the Atlantic appears to have been one of the immediate reasons behind this law.
103. Inst., II.i.3, "Est autem litus maris, quatenus hibernus fluctus maximus excurrit" (The shore of the sea extends to the point attained by the highest tide in winter).
104. LML, pp. 30–1; CML, pp. 38–9; HML, pp. 33–4; IPC, pp. 332–3; CIPC, pp. 239–40.
105. On Genoese claims to sovereignty in the Mediterranean, see Pietro Baptista Burgus, *De Dominio Serenissimae Genuensis Reipublicae in Mari Ligustico* (Rome: Dominicus Marcianus, 1641), esp. p. 141. Sovereignty over the Ligurian Sea is claimed chiefly on the basis of prescription, rather than title or (papal) donation (Burgus, *De Dominio*, esp. pp. 228, 237). Appeal is made in this context to the mediaeval Italian jurisconsults Baldus de Ubaldis and Jason, who claim that the Genoese (Burgus, *De Dominio*, p. 232), "suum mare habent distinctum ex inveteratissima consuetudine" (have their own sea by most ancient custom), and "Genuenses licite perscripserunt sinum maris" (The Genoese have legally prescribed the maritime gulf). Other

authorities invoked include Johannes Gryphiander and Pacius. Claims that the Genoese historically also exercised *dominium* over oceanic spaces other than the Ligurian and Aegean Seas are found in Burgus, *De Dominio*, pp. 234–6.

106. The edition consulted was printed in Venice in 1685 and consists of two parts featuring separate page numbering: *Dominio del Mar Adriatico* and *Dominio del Mar Adriatico per il Ius Belli*. On a dating of the treatise, see the introduction in Paulo Sarpi, *Il Dominio del Mare Adriatico*, ed. and intr. Roberto Cessi (Padua: Giampolo Tolomei Editore, 1945), p. xxxiii, and also the sources and information provided in note 2. For the historic context of the treatise, see also Gaetano Cozzi, *Paolo Sarpi Tra Venezia e l'Europa* (Turin: Einaudi, 1979), pp. 268 *et seq*.
107. Cessi's introduction in Sarpi, *Il Dominio* (1945), p. xxxiv, "... possessione per antichità di tempo elonghissima e consuetudine immemorabile" (possession across the longue durée and custom since time immemorial).
108. Paulo Sarpi, *Dominio del Mar Adriatico della Serenissima Republica di Venetia* (Venice: Roberto Meietti, 1685), II, p. 12. A similar point is also made by Gasparo Contarini, *De Magistratibus et Republica Venetorum Libri Quinque* (Venice: Apud Io. Bapt. Ciottum Senensem sub Signo Minervae, 1592), fol., 65 verso. See also Vázquez de Menchaca, *Conversiarum illustrium*, 2.89.16 *et seq*. on the prescription of the seas with his many references to mediaeval juridical sources.
109. Sarpi, *Dominio del Mar Adriatico*, I, p. 6; also Contarini, *De Magistratibus*, pp. 64 recto–65 verso, passim. For Botero, see John Robertson, *A Union for Empire. Political Thought and the British Union of 1707* (Cambridge: CUP, 1995), pp. 12–3; Romain Descendre, *L'état du monde. Giovanni Botero entre raison d'État et géopolitique* (Geneva: Droz, 2009), p. 236. Grotius would not speak of *dominium*, but of *imperium* of the Adriatic. The former term is closely associated with the property (*proprietas*) of the head of household (*paterfamilias*), the latter with public jurisdiction (*iurisdictio*) and protection.
110. Pacius, *De Dominio*, p. 9.
111. See, for example, ibid., pp. 26, 30, 31, and especially the five grounds listed and annotated with quotational evidence on pp. 35–8.
112. On this, see also Cessi's introduction in Sarpi, *Il Dominio*, p. xxxiv.
113. Also, Grotius does not write a single word about Denmark's historic claims to the Sound (the narrow channel linking the North Sea to the Baltic) and, indeed, to the whole of the North Sea between the European mainland and Iceland. At the open of the 17th century, this claim was of considerable concern not only to the Dutch, but also to the English. Extensive Dutch commercial interests in the Baltic may help explain the Dutch humanist's silence. See the "Instructions given by Queen Elizabeth to the British envoys for the Bremen negotiations with Denmark on fishing licenses and sound tolls" (1602), in *Fontes Historiae Iuris Gentium. Sources Relating to the History of the Law of Nations*, ed. Wilhelm G. Grewe, 3 vols. (Berlin-New York: Walter de Gruyter, 1988–92), II, p. 157.

114. CML, p. 58; also LML, pp. 49–50; HML, p. 47; IPC, p. 352; CIPC, p. 253.
115. Tuck, *Rights of War*, p. 91; also Cavallar, *The Rights of Strangers*, pp. 149–50, concerning the occupation of "parts of the sea" such as bays and straits in Grotius.
116. See, for example, the occupation of gulfs and bays in IBP 2.3.8 and of coastal waters in IBP 2.3.102 and 2.3.13.2. These concessions are clearly made on the grounds of expediency and established custom. In defence of his earlier, theoretical interpretation in *Mare Liberum*, Grotius argued that one can also conceive of maritime space that cannot be occupied. See IBP 2.2.3 and 2.3.10.3.
117. Welwood's attack on Grotius first appeared in chapter 26 of his *Abridgement of All Sea-Lawes, Gathered Forth of all Writings and Monuments which are to be Found among any People or Nation, upon the Coasts of the Great Ocean and Mediterranean Sea*; see especially the discussion on pp. 61 *et seq.* or the reproduction of the text found in HML, pp. 65–74. On the Welwood-Grotius debate, see also van Ittersum, "'Mare Liberum' versus the Propriety of the Seas? The Debate between Hugo Grotius and William Welwood and Its Impact on Anglo-Scotto-Dutch Fishery Disputes in the Second Decade of the Seventeenth Century", *Edinburgh Law Review* 10 (2006): 243–9.
118. Selden, *Mare Clausum seu De Dominio Maris Libri Duo*. See also the article by Ziskind, "International Law and Ancient Sources: Grotius and Selden", *Review of Politics* 35, 4 (1973): 537–59.
119. See the translation of the *Defensio Capitis Quinti Maris Liberi* (Defence of Chapter Five of Mare Liberum) in Wright, *Some Less Known Works of Hugo Grotius*, p. 202; the identical translation is also found in HML, p. 127.
120. See for example LML, pp. 22–3; CML, p. 31; HML, pp. 27–8; IPC, pp. 323–4; CIPC, pp. 232–3. Some provisions of Roman law, as Grotius acknowledged, permitted the occupation of the shore. This was permitted not because the shores were public property, but because Rome sought to ensure that the principles of natural law were not violated; see also Inst., II.i.1.
121. LML, pp. 22–3, 34–6; CML, pp. 31, 43; HML, p. 26; IPC, pp. 324–5, 337–8; CIPC, pp. 233, 243–4, where Grotius already produced arguments to counter this particular position. See also the useful observations in this vein advanced by Ziskind, "International Law and Ancient Sources: Grotius and Selden", *Review of Politics* 35, 4 (1973): 541–2, in the process of which he also delineates the difference between Grotius and Selden.
122. As is, for example, found in Inst., II.i.6.
123. See Inst., II.i.1.
124. It should be underscored here that the wording in the Institutes of Justinian treats the seas and shores as freely usable to according to the *ius gentium*. Influenced by the explanation of paragraph 11 (See Inst. II.i.11), Grotius

equates the *ius gentium* or law of nations with the *ius naturale* or law of nature. He sees the same relation in IBP, 1.2.4, "De jure naturali ergo, quod et gentium dici potest. …" (By the law of nature, which can also be called the law of nations). Technically, however, the dictates of nature and the standing consensus of men may not be the same, the latter resembling a positive law that is also subject to change or alteration.

125. Wright, *Some Less Known Works of Hugo Grotius,* p. 158; HML, p. 80.
126. Wright, *Some Less Known Works of Hugo Grotius,* p. 165; also HML, pp. 88–9.
127. Text refers here to Dig. 43.8.3.1.
128. Text refers to Dig. 41.1.14.
129. This point is very similar to the one advanced in the *Verbael* filed at the end of the Anglo-Dutch Conference at the Hague by the Dutch faction in early May 1615. In addressing their problems with the Portuguese in Asia, the Dutch reportedly explained to the English, BW (Supplement) 399A, p. 128, "… dat wij oock mette Portuguesen gheensins en hadden gecontesteert om den vrijen handel te hebben in Goa, Cochin, Malacca ende andere plaetsen daer sij hadden recht van gouvernement ofte particuliere verbintenisse, maer om denselven handel te hebben met andere natiën, hemluyden niet onderworpen nochte eenichsins verbonden sijnde." (… that we also did not contest the Portuguese in any way regarding free trade in Goa, Cochin, Melaka and other places where they possessed a right of government or had a particular contract, but rather to establish such [free] trade with other nations, who were not subject to them nor allied [to them] in any way.) See also Knight, "Grotius in England: His Opposition There to the Principles of *Mare Liberum*", *TGS* 5 (1919): esp. 7, 10–1.
130. Wright, *Some Less Known Works of Hugo Grotius,* p. 158, and HML, p. 81 (attacking Welwood), "Far different is the opinion of my little book, as is clear even from that Chapter V itself. For there it is shown that by nature neither land nor sea is the property of anyone, but that land through nature can become property, while the sea can not. A great difference, therefore is established in this part between land and sea."
131. See also LML, pp. 22–3; CML, p. 31, "The nature of the sea, however, differs from that of the shore, because the sea, except for a very restricted space, can neither easily be built upon, nor inclosed; if the contrary were true yet this could hardly happen without hindrance to the general use. Nevertheless, if any small portion of the sea can thus be occupied, the occupation is recognized." HML, pp. 27–8; IPC, p. 325; CIPC, pp. 233–4.
132. My translation from the original German.
133. Heinrich von Treitschke, *Vorlesungen gehalten an der Universität zu Berlin*, ed. Max Cornecesius, 2 vols. (Leipzig: S. Hirzel, 1898), II, p. 572.
134. See also Thumfart, "On Grotius's *Mare Liberum* and Vitoria's *De Indis*, Following Agamben and Schmitt", *GNS* 30 (2009): 76, "While Grotius's

formulation of the freedom of the seas seems, on the surface, to be a recipe for mere anarchy, on closer examination the Grotian principle of the Freedom of the Seas appears to represent a monist, universalist line of legal thought."

135. Vitoria also speaks of unappropirated goods that the Amerindians and visitors to their lands hold in common. As they have remained in their original state of nature, such goods can be freely acquired in accordance with the principles set out in Inst. II.1. as *res nullius* (a thing that does not yet belong to anyone). If the Amerindians were to bar or impede the Spaniards from appropriating such shared but still unappropriated goods, such action would be deemed sufficient for commencing and waging a just war. See Vitoria, *De Indis*, ed. Schätzel, III, sections 4 *et seq.*, pp. 96 *et seq.* (Latin text) and Vitoria, *Political Writings*, pp. 280–1 (English translation). For Grotius, there are "common things" that remain unappropriated in their natural state and cannot ever be appropriated by an individual or sovereign. Any attempt to impede the enjoyment of such common things (that also must include common rights), including the right of trade and navigation on the high seas, offers sufficient grounds for a just war.
136. LML, p. 4; CML, p. 10; HML, p. 12; IPC, p. 305; CIPC, pp. 219–20.
137. LML, p. 56; CML, p. 66; HML, p. 52; IPC, p. 258; CIPC, p. 357.
138. LML, p. 58; CML, p. 68 HML, p. 54; IPC, pp. 359–60; CIPC, p. 259. The emphases are mine.
139. Knight, "Grotius in England: : His Opposition There to the Principles of *Mare Liberum*", *TGS* 5 (1919): 14.
140. Several of these are contained in the monumental publication by Julio Firminio Judice Biker, *Collecção de tratados e concertos de pazes que o Estado da Índia Portugeza fez com os reis e senhores com quem teve relações nas partes da Ásia e Africa Oriente, desde o princípio da conquista até ao fin do século XVIII*, 10 vols. (Lisbon: Imprensa Nacional, 1881–7), I, pp. 189–92, treaty concluded with the Mughal Emperor Jahangir dated 7 June 1615; treaty with the King of Kandy dated 30 June 1617, pp. 205–6, para. 5 (where it is expressly stated that the Indian monarch should not trade with the Dutch, English or French); and the treaty with the King of Arakan, 1620, pp. 229–33.
141. CE, pp. 73, 126.
142. CML, p. 72; LML, p. 62; HML, p. 57.
143. LML, p. 61; CML, p. 71; HML, p. 56; Concerning the issue of monopolies, see also Ziskind, "International Law and Ancient Sources: Grotius and Selden", *Review of Politics* 35, 4 (1973): 557, "In objecting to what amounts to monopolistic practices, Grotius cites Ambrose on the matter of interfering with the freedom of the sea, Augustine on blocking trade routes and Gregory of Nazianzus on immoral profiteering." IPC, p. 367; CIPC, p. 265.
144. Third Dutch memorial of 13 March 1615, in CC, p. 207; CE, p. 118. Costs remained a sticky issue, and during the negotiations Grotius was supplied

with sets of "actual" figures. The English also mention the "huge subsidies" in their memoranda to London, see Sainsbury, *Calendar of State Papers, Colonial Series, East Indies, China and Japan, 1513–1616,* no. 957, p. 402. In a letter to Grotius dated 3 May 1615 (BW 400, p. 383), Matelieff de Jonge explained that total costs incurred by the company amounted to 4.35 million guilders. He also underscored that "... de onderhoudinge van de soldaten in India verre excedeert de winninge die op den Inlantsen handel gedaen wert jaerlijx" (... the maintenance of soldiers in the [East] Indies far exceeds the profits reaped annually in the local trade).

145. As Martin van Gelderen underscores, Grotius engaged in a subtle play, arguing that sovereignty can be divided between different agencies or officeholders of a given polity. This is achieved by distinguishing between *maiestas personalis* (personal rights of majesty or sovereignty) and *maiestas realis* (sovereign rights of the polity or of the people). See van Gelderen, "The State and its Rivals in Early Modern Europe", in *States and Citizens,* ed. Skinner and Stråth, pp. 79–96, esp. p. 86.

146. The recently completed studies of Martine van Ittersum, Edward Keene and Eric Wilson exemplify particularly well this shift in thinking about Grotius and his role in establishing the foundations of colonial rule. On the growing interest in the Grotian concept of divisible sovereignty, see CiT, pp. 117 et seq; IBP, 1.3.17; Borschberg, "Grotius, the Social Contract and Political Resistance. A Study of the Unpublished Theses LVI", *IILJ Working Paper* 6 (2006): 19–21, 49–57; Edward Keene, *Beyond the Anarchical Society*; Frank Grunert, *Normbegründung und politische Legitimität. Zur Rechts- und Staatsphilosophie der deutschen Frühaufklärung* (Tübingen: Max Niemeyer Verlag, 2000), pp. 137–40; Norbert Konegen, "Hugo Grotius und die modern Politikwissenschaft", in *Staat bei Hugo Grotius,* ed. Norbert Konegen and Peter Nitschke, pp. 173–4; Thomas Berns, "La souverainté saisi par ses marques", *Bibliothèque d'Humanisme et Renaissance* 62, 3 (2000), esp. p. 615; Martin van Gelderen, "From Domingo de Soto to Hugo Grotius: Theories of Monarchy and Civil Power in Spanish and Dutch Political Thought, 1555–1609", *Il Pensiero Politico: Revista di Storia delle Idee Politiche e Sociali* 32, 2 (1999): 202. The article by van Gelderen is also found in *The Origins and Development of the Dutch Revolt,* ed. by Graham Darby (London and New York: Routledge, 2001), pp. 151–70. Concerning the divisibility of sovereignty and particularly the idea of "multiple intersecting fields of partial sovereignty" as a paradigm for the study of the VOC, see esp. Kerry Ward, *Networks of Empire. Forced Migration in the Dutch East India Company* (Cambridge: CUP, 2009), esp. pp. 6, 7, 12, 14–7, 55–7, 302.

147. This is an issue Grotius struggled with in some of his other writings, including significantly the early fragment *Theses LVI,* where the ability to sign away one's liberty, and the acquisition of rights over other persons,

assume an important position in laying the foundations for civil society and the social contract. See Borschberg, "Grotius, the Social Contract and Political Resistance. A Study of the Unpublished Theses LVI", *IILJ Working Paper* 6 (2006): 28–32.

148. Cornelis van Vollenhoven, *Mr. C. van Vollenhoven's Verspreide Geschriften*, ed. F.M. van Asbeck, 3 vols. (Haarlem and The Hague: Tjeenk Willink and Martinus Nijhoff, 1934–5), I, p. 391, particularly on the humanity, "love" and "confidence" that is "radiated" by Grotius' classic work *De Iure Belli ac Pacis*. See also ibid., p. 388, where the 17th-century Dutchman is credited for "practically [knowing] everything written by sacred or classical authors and … practically every event in ancient or biblical history". Grotius did harvest the occasional unflattering comment from 20th-century luminaries, such as the German professor of law Josef Kohler. With his inimitable bluntness, the Berlin-based jurisconsult opined that *De Iure Belli ac Pacis* was intellectually messy, unsystematic and utterly confused — in short, a "total mess". In Kohler's own indicting words: "[M]it Gentilis teilt er [i.e. Grotius] das anekdotenhafte, unmethodische, tumultuarische Erzählen geschichtlicher und fabelhafter Kleinigkeiten und das Durcheinanderwerfen privat–und öffentlicher Erörterungen" (Grotius shares with Gentili a [habit] of narrating details from history and legend in an anectotal, unmethodical, confused manner, as well as jumbling together considerations on private and public law). With Grotius, so Kohler claims, the theory of natural law was rendered inflexible (*erstarrt*) and made unbearable through a unbearable jungle of quotations (*durch einen unerträglichen Zitatenwust*). Kohler's views on Grotius' freedom of the seas are in line with this candid assessment. See Josef Kohler, *Grundlagen des Völkerrechts. Vergangenheit, Gegenwart, Zukunft* (Stuttgart: Ferdinand Enke, 1918), pp. 4, 5, 41. On the scholarly significance of Kohler's views to more contemporary scholarship, see Hans Thieme, "Natürliches Privatrecht in der Spätscholastik", *ZRG*, GA 70 (1953): 230 *et seq*.

149. Ram Prakash Anand, "Maritime Practice in Southeast Asia until 1600 A.D. and the Modern Law of the Sea", *The International and Comparative Law Quarterly* 30, 2 (1981): 440.

150. On this, see generally J. Alan Beesley, "Grotius and the New Law", *Ocean Yearbook* 18 (2004): esp. 100 *et seq*.

151. Beesley, "Grotius and the New Law", p. 105, where it is made clear that Grotius did not foresee that overfishing could ever become a problem.

152. Many of the issues raised by Grotius, de Freitas and Welwood are also pressing issues today, demanding swift resolution. See Shigeru Oda, "Some Reflections on Recent Developments in the Law of the Sea", *Yale Journal of International Law* 27 (2002): 218–21. On the possibility of occupying the ocean bed (together with air, water and other "spaces"), see esp. de Freitas, *Über die Rechtmässige Herrschaft der Portugiesen in Asien*, pp. 229–30.

153. De Freitas argues for a similar "possession" of airspace. *Über die Rechtmässige Herrschaft der Portugiesen in Asien*, p. 230.
154. Oda, "Some Reflections", pp. 219, 221.

Chapter 4

1. Exactly who commissioned the work from Grotius remains uncertain. Based on Grotius' correspondence, some authors claim it was the VOC directors, while others opine that it was Oldenbarnevelt who earlier "defended a similar case". On the latter position, see den Tex, *Oldenbarnevelt*, IV, p. 172. Fruin recognises a link between the writing of *De Iure Praedae* and Grotius' earlier output as a legal counsel while the *Santa Catarina* incident was pending before the Admiralty Court. See "Een onuitgegeven werk", *Fruin's Verspreide Geschriften*, III, pp. 443–5; its English translation is "An Unpublished Work of Hugo Grotius: Translated from an Essay in Dutch (1868)", contained in *Bibliotheca Visseriana* 5 (1925): 3 *et seq*. See also "Een onuitgegeven werk", III, p. 391. Grotius does not appear to have been personally involved with the *Santa Catarina* case as it was pending before the admiralty court. See van Ittersum, "Dating the Manuscript of *De Jure Praedae*", *History of European Ideas* 35 (2009): 130, esp. note 18.
2. Fruin, "Een onuitgegeven werk", in *Fruin's Verspreide Geschriften*, III, p. 372. The exact nature, purpose, form and intention of the text is still a puzzle to many contemporary scholars. See Waszink, "Using the Work. Remarks on the Text of De iure praedae", *GNS* 27–8 (2005–7): 236.
3. Grotius, *Annales et Historiae de Rebus Belgicis* (completed around 1612 and published posthumously in 1657) and *De Antiquitate Reipublicae Batavicae* (1610). For the modern critical edition of the text with English translation, see *The Antiquity of the Batavian Republic*, ed. Jan H. Waszink.
4. Similar, but by no means identical positions are taken by van Ittersum, *Profit and Principle*, esp. pp. 486 *et seq*., where the VOC is placed at the centre of attention in unlocking the authorial meaning and intention of *De Iure Pradae*. By contrast, Eric Wilson, significantly expands the authorial intention of the work to encompass a hybridity of global commercial hegemony and political discourses of the early Dutch Republic, or, as he also bluntly explains, the VOC was "simultaneously a "'corporation'" and a 'republic'" whose historical activities in Asia expanded into "an amalgamation of Colonialism and Republicanism". See Eric Wilson, *Savage Republic. De Indis of Hugo Grotius, Republicanism and Dutch Hegemony within the Early Modern World-System (c. 1600–1619)* (Leiden-Boston: Martinus Nijhoff Publishers, 2008), esp. pp. 8–10, 513–4, and in greater depth, pp. 137–260. Concerning the propagandistic qualities of some of Grotius' early writings, see also Henk J.M. Nellen, "Hugo Grotius's Political and Scholarly Activities in the Light of his Correspondence", *GNS* 27–8 (2005–7): 20–4.

5. Concerning Tiele's role in preparing Grotius' working papers for the 1864 auction at Martinus Nijhoff in the Hague, see U.J. Jinkes de Jong and A.P.W.M. Kosten, *Dr. Pieter Anton Tiele. Documentaire Bijdrage tot een Biografie* (The Hague: P.A. Tiele Academie, 1981), esp. p. 25. For a contemporary critical assessment of the title *De Iure Praedae Commentarius,* see the article by Eric Wilson, "On Heterogeneity and the Naming of De Indis of Grotius", *Journal of the Philosophy of International Law* 1, 1 (2006): 72–115, esp. pp. 76–85.
6. Fruin, "Een onuitgegeven werk", in *Fruin's Verspreide Geschriften*, III, p. 367, "No. 72 werd aldus beschreven: *H. Grotii opus de jure Praedae in XVI capita divisum*, 280 pag. Mscr. autographe inédit. Seulement une partie du chapitre XII a été publié en 1609, sous le titre *Mare Liberum*" (Lot number 72 is described as follows: H. Grotius, work *On the Law of Prize*, divided into 16 chapters, 280 pages. Unpublished autograph manuscript. Only one part, chapter 12, was published in 1609 under the title *The Free Sea*). See also Noordhoff, *Beschrijving van ... papieren afkomstig van Huig de Groot,* p. 55.
7. See esp. the editorial comment in BW 148, p. 129, note 6, "... zoals Grotius indertijd 'de Jure Praedae' 'de Rebus Indicanis noemde'" (... just as Grotius at the time called his "De Iure Praedae" "De Rebus Indicanis").
8. The question of the proper title for *De Iure Praedae* has been raised by Tuck, especially in his widely read work *Rights of War and Peace: Political Thought and the International Order from Grotius to Kant* (1999) as well as in his earlier *Philosophy and Government, 1572–1651* (Cambridge: CUP, 1993). See specifically also Tuck, "Grotius and Selden", in *The Cambridge History of Political Thought 1450–1700*, ed. Burns and Goldie, p. 504.
9. The most commonly used English translation is *De Jure Praedae Commentarius. Commentary on the Law of Prize and Booty. A Translation of the Original Manuscript of 1604*, tr. Williams and Zeydel. This edition contains several errors that have been duly corrected in the 2006 revised edition by van Ittersum.
10. On the dating of *De Iure Praedae Commentarius,* see the most recent contribution by van Ittersum, "Dating the Manuscript of *De Jure Praedae*", *History of European Ideas* 35 (2009): 125–93, esp. her history of the dating on pp. 129–32. See also TMD, p. 304; CiT, pp. 16–7; van Ittersum, "Hugo Grotius in Context", *AJSS* 31, 3 (2003): 544–5, appendix II, and the older article by van Eysinga, "Quelques observations au sujet du Mare Liberum et du De Iure Praedae de Grotius", *Grotiana* 9 (1941–2): 72–5.
11. *Mare Liberum, sive de iure quod Batavis competit in rebus Indicanis.* This first edition, printed in Leiden in 1609, was published anonymously and thus did not bear the name of Grotius, the work's author (see the image on p. 2). See *The Free Sea*, tr. Richard Hakluyt, ed. and intr. David Armitage, is superior

to the edition prepared by Ralph van Deman Magoffin and James Brown Scott. The initial dating of *De Iure Praedae* was set by Fruin between October 1604 and 1605. Molhuysen subsequently revised it to the autumn of 1606. In a letter to the Heidelberg-based councillor Georg Michael Lingelsheim, Grotius announced that he had completed his "little treatise" on the affairs of the (East) Indies, but wondered aloud whether he should publish the whole book or only the parts pertaining to the law of prize and booty. See esp. BW 86, p. 72, letter by Grotius to Lingelsheim, dated 1 November 1606, p. 72 and its translation into English in IPC, appendix II.8, p. 552, "The little treatise on Indian affairs (*opusculum de Rebus Indicanis*) is complete: but I do not know whether it should be published as it was written or only those parts which pertain to the universal law of war and booty. Many indeed have dealt with this subject both old and new. But I believe that new light can be thrown on the matter with a fixed order of teaching, the right proportion of divine and human law mixed together with the dictates of philosophy."

12. The *pars historica*, or the historical part of *De Iure Praedae*, derives its title from the words *sequuntur historica* scribbled at the top of the page marking the beginning of chapter 11. The first part of the work, widely known as the *pars dogmatica* or theoretical section, spans chapters 1 through 10.
13. Fruin, "Een onuitgegeven werk", in *Fruin's Verspreide Geschriften*, III, pp. 443–5; see also van Ittersum, *Profit and Principle*, p. 4.
14. Borschberg, *The Singapore and Melaka Straits*, pp. 60–77; "The Seizure of the *Santa Catarina* off Singapore: Dutch Freebooting, the Portuguese Empire and Intra-Asian Trade at the Dawn of the Seventeenth Century", *Revista de Cultura,* International Edition, 11, 1 (2004): 11–25; "The Seizure of the *Santa Catarina* Revisited: The Portuguese Empire in Asia, VOC Politics and the Origins of the Dutch-Johor Alliance (c. 1602–1616)", *JSEAS* 33, 1 (2002): 31–62; van Ittersum, "Hugo Grotius in Context", *AJSS* 31, 3 (2003): 511–48; van Ittersum, *Profit and Principle*, pp. xix, 35.
15. The claim is found both in *De Iure Praedae* as well as in the *Annales et Historiae de Rebus Belgicis*. See esp. also Nellen, *Hugo de Groot. Een leven in strijd om de vrede*, p. 82.
16. Boxer, *Fidalgos in the Far East*, p. 50; Dirk van der Cruysse, *Louis XIV et le Siam* (Paris: Fayard, 1991), pp. 57–60. An English translation of this work is now available as D. van der Cruysse, *Siam and the West, 1500–1700,* tr. Michael Smithies (Seattle: University of Washington Press, 2002); IPC, p. xiii; de Coutre, *Andanzas Asiáticas,* p. 169. Like some period publications, including significantly the pamphlet by Richard Schilders, Grotius himself wrongly placed the *Santa Catarina* incident in the Strait of Melaka. For this geographical error. See the *Corte ende sekere Beschryvinghe vant veroveren der rijcke ende gheweldighe krake, comende uytet gheweste van China, door den Admirael Jacobus Heemskercke.*

17. On these objections, see Nellen, *Hugo de Groot. Een leven in strijd om de vrede*, p. 83.
18. See, for example, Tuck, "Grotius and Selden", in *The Cambridge History of Political Thought 1450–1700*, ed. J.H. Burns and M.A. Goldie, p. 504.
19. Van Ittersum, *Profit and Principle*, pp. 3, 113–9, 167 *et seq*. See also Waszink, "Using the Work. Remarks on the Text of De iure praedae", *GNS* 27–8 (2005–7): 238.
20. Fruin, "Een onuitgegeven werk", in *Fruin's Verspreide Geschriften*, III, p. 403, "Het schrijven van zulk een betoog nam Hugo de Groot op zich. Ik kan niet verzekeren dat hij er door de bewindhebbers daartoe angezocht is; geen bewijs daarvan heb ik kunnen ontdekken. Maar dat hij tot de Companie in nauwe betrekking heeft gestaan, zegt hij zelf in een brief an zijn broeder van latere dagteekening. En dat hij de archieven der Vereenigde Companie en van haar voorganster bij het schrijven van zijn verhandeling heeft gebruik, lijdt geen twijfel."
21. Reference is here to the six voorcompagniën of the VOC.
22. Alexandrowicz, *Introduction to the Law of Nations in the East Indies*, p. 65.
23. See BW 53, pp. 44–5, letter by Grotius to Jan ten Grootenhuys dated 15 October 1604, and BW 54, p. 45, letter by ten Grootenhuys to Grotius dated c. 20 October 1604. See also van Ittersum, "Hugo Grotius in Context", *AJSS* 31, 3 (2003): 523–4.
24. Jan ten Grootenhuys was the younger brother of VOC Director Arendt ten Grootenhuys who like Grotius had studied at Leiden. See also van Ittersum, *Profit and Principle*, pp. 24–5; IPC, p. xv. Grotius is reported by van Ittersum to have been on close or "intimate" terms with Jan ten Grootenhuys during the first decade of the 17th century. See van Ittersum, *Profit and Principle*, p. 295, note 6. Arendt ten Grootenhuys served on the board of directors of the "Old East India Company" (Oude O.I.C.) together with Petrus Plancius. See Jan Parmentier, Karel Davids and John G. Everaert, *Peper, Plancius en Porselein. De reis van het schip Swarte Leeuw naar Atjeh en Bantam* (Zutphen: Walburg Pers, 2003), p. 80, note 9.
25. See BW 53 and 54, pp. 44–5; IPC, appendix II.5, pp. 545–7.
26. IPC, appendix II.5, pp. 545–6; BW 53, pp. 44–5. See also van Ittersum, *Profit and Principle*, p. 26.
27. IPC, appendix II.6, p. 547.
28. IPC, appendix I.1, "Edict of the Estates General of the United Provinces", 2 April 1599, pp. 503–10. A German translation of the edict is found in CIPC, pp. 375–9. A transcript of the verdict in German survives in Leiden, University Library, Loket 1555–39, Fruin, *Aantekeningen op zijn werken*, envelope titled "Documenta, behoorende bij het boeck van De Groot, de Iure praedae", fols. 7 recto–10 recto.
29. IPC, appendix I.3, Decree of the Estates of Holland, September 1, 1604, pp. 515–6.

30. See also Noordhoff, *Beschrijving van … papieren afkomstig van Huig de Groot,* p. 22, "Afschrift van de resolutie der Staten van Holland, dd. 1604 September 1" and the editor's note thereunto.
31. These observations coincide with the claims of van Ittersum, *Profit and Principle*, p. 27.
32. The Hague, Nationaal Archief, Collectie 102, Baron H. van Zuylen van Nyevelt, suppl. 2, no. 13 (2.21.179.01, no. 13), *Boeck Tracterende vande Wreede, Verradische ende Hostile Proceduren der Portugesen In Oost-Indien.* Additional materials not found in the bound volume are retrieved among Grotius' working papers presently preserved at the Nationaal Archief. See the *Collectie Hugo de Groot, Supplement I* (ms. 1.10.35.02, no. 40, fols. 434–56).
33. Published in *BMH* 79 (1965): 415–540. See also van Ittersum, "Dating the Manuscript of *De Jure Praedae*", *History of European Ideas* 35 (2009): 130.
34. At the auction of 1864, chapter 11 of *De Iure Praedae* was identified as a distinct and separate piece in its own right. It was also sold separately from the main text (lot 72) as lot 11, titled "*H. Grotius, De bello Batavorum cum Lusitanis, imprimis de rebus per Indiam gestis dissertatio*, 48 pag. – Mscr. autographe inédit. Il parait que ce traité a été destiné primitivement pour faire partie de l'ouvrage décrit sous le no. 72". See also Noordhoff, *Beschrijving van … papieren afkomstig van Huig de Groot,* p. 55, and van Ittersum, *Profit and Principle*, p. 27.
35. IPC, appendix II.6, p. 547. For the original Latin text of the letters, see BW 54, p. 45.
36. See *Catalogue des Manuscrits Autographes de Hugo Grotius,* part, I, lot 22, p. 6, "Attestatie van Mar. Apius (ten verzoeke van Bewindhebb. der O.-Ind. Comp.), ontrent het gebeurde met de Portugezen te Macao in 1602 (onder Jacob van Neck). 12 pag. Pièce authentique". (Affidavit of Mar[tin] Apius, at the request of the Directors of the East India Company, concerning the events with the Portuguese at Macao in 1602 under Jacob van Neck. 12 pages. Authentic piece.) A Dutch transcript of this document is found in Loket 1555–39, Fruin, "Aantekeningen op zijn werken", fols. 1 recto–4 verso, as well as in Tiele, "Documenten voor de Geschiedenis der Nederlanders in het Oosten", *BMH* 6 (1883), II, "Verklaring van Martinus Apius…" (Declaration of Martin Apius), pp. 228–42. This affidavit bears the date 18 October 1604 (Tiele, "Documenten", p. 242). The affidavit is also mentioned in Coolhaas, "Een bron van het historische gedeelte van Hugo de Groot's De Jure Praedae", *BMH* 79 (1965): 416.
37. For an English translation of this document, see IPC, appendix I.2, pp. 510–4. The affidavit bears the date [Thursday] 9 September 1604. For a summary of resolutions passed by the Admiralty Court that year, see the useful compilation in Leiden, University Library, Loket 1555–39, Fruin,

Aantekeningen op zijn werken in "Admiraliteit van Amsterdam", fols. 13 recto–16 verso. The case of the *Santa Catarina* is featured on fol. 16 recto.

38. IPC, appendix II.6, p. 547, and BW 54, p. 45.
39. The words "Map of the East Indies" appears twice on the letter. It is not clear whether Grotius had forgotten that he had already jotted down this point, or whether he might have possibly received two maps of the East Indies. I place both scenarios within the realm of possibilities.
40. The original was found among the working papers of Grotius. See Noordhoff, *Beschrijving van ... papieren afkomstig van Huig de Groot,* p. 22.
41. English translations of all these documents can be found in IPC, appendices I.1–3, pp. 503–16.
42. Borschberg, "The Seizure of the Santa Catarina Revisited", *JSEAS* 33, 1 (2002): 45; van Ittersum, *Profit and Principle*, pp. 19–20; van Ittersum, "Hugo Grotius in Context", *AJSS* 31, 3 (2003): 520.
43. IPC, pp. 279 *et seq.*; Parmentier, Davids and Everaert, *Peper, Plancius en Porselein*, pp. 58–9.
44. See *Catalogue des Manuscrits Autographes de Hugo Grotius,* part I, "Recueil concernant les voyages des Hollandais aux Indes Orientales, la Compagnie des Indes, etc. 1600–1616", p. 6, lot nos. 23, "Discours ende Advertentie ontr. het wedervaren van Jac. van Neck in Cochinchina in 1602, van Jac. v. Heemskerck in Patana, Tiaman, enz. in 1602–3, en van Wybr. van Warwyck en Seb. de Weert op Ceylon in 1602–3. 7 pag." (Discussion and Announcement concerning the experiences of Jacob van Neck in Cochin China in 1602, of Jacob van Heemskerk in Patani, Tioman, etc., in 1602-3, and of Wybrand van Warwyck and Sebald de Weert on Ceylon in 1602–3. 7 pages.) A Dutch transcript of this document is found in Loket 1555–39, Fruin, "Aantekeningen op zijn werken", fols. 7 recto–8 recto.
45. Borschberg, *The Singapore and Melaka Straits,* pp. 73–5; Coolhaas, "Een bron van het historische gedeelte van Hugo de Groots De Jure Praedae", *BMH* 79 (1965): 528–9; van Ittersum, "Hugo Grotius in Context", *AJSS* 31, 3 (2003): 523–4. For further details see also chapter 4.
46. BW 53, p. 44, note 2. See also Sjoerd de Meer, "Het kaartenmakersbedrijf van de Verenigde Oostindische Compagnie", in *Het Zeekartenboek. Vroege zeekarten uit de collectie van het Maritiem Museum Rotterdam,* ed. S. de Meer (Zutphen: Walburg Pers, 2007), esp. pp. 50–2.
47. For a comprehensive account of Plancius' life and works, see J. Keuning, *Petrus Plancius: theoloog en geograaf 1552–1622* (Amsterdam: Van Kampen, 1946).
48. Gaastra, *De geschiedenis van de VOC,* pp. 19, 30.
49. Gaastra, *De geschiedenis van de VOC,* pp. 15, 20.
50. On the significance of Plancius during the early Dutch voyages to the East Indies, see Parmentier, Davids and Everaert, *Peper, Plancius en Porselein,* pp. 43 *et seq.*

51. Late 16th-Century Portuguese cartographical materials of the Malay Peninsula and the Indonesian Archipelago feature many Malay and other local Asian toponyms. See Luís-Filipe R. Thomaz, "The Image of the Archipelago in Portuguese Cartography of the 16th and Early 17th Century", in *South East Asia: Colonial History,* ed. Kratoska and Borschberg, I, pp. 42–88.
52. The list of books confiscated from Grotius' library in 1618 can be found in P.C. Molhuysen, "De bibliotheek van Hugo de Groot in 1618", *MKNAW*, afd. letterkunde, *NR* 6, 3 (1918): 50–63. — For the modern critical text version, see van Linschoten, *Itinerario. Voyage ofte Schipvaert van Jan Huygen van Linschoten naer Oost ofte Portugaels Indien*, and *Reys-geschrift vande navigatiën der Portugaloysers*, ed. Hans Kern and Johan C.M. Warnsinck, 2nd ed., 5 vols. (The Hague: Martinus Nijhoff, 1939).
53. The Hague, Nationaaal Archief, *Collectie Hugo de Groot, Supplement I* (ms. 1.10.35.02 no. 40, fol. 429).
54. This is possibly a reference to Tomás López Medel, a 16th-century member of the Audiencia of Guatemala and author on the Mayans of Central America.
55. One of the most commonly used English translations of this important Portuguese travel account remains *The Book of Duarte Barbosa, An Account of the Countries bordering on the Indian Ocean and their Inhabitants ... completed about the year 1518,* tr. Mansel Longworth Dames (London: Hakluyt Society, 2 vols., 1918–21).
56. It appears under the heading "Sommario di Tutti li Regni, Città, e Popoli Orientali", in Giovanni Battista Ramusio, *Delle navigationi et viaggi in molti luoghi corretta, et ampliata nelle quale si contengono da descrittione dell'Africa, & del paese del Prete Ianni, con varij viaggi, dalla Città di Lisbona, et dal Mar Rosso à Calicut, & infin'all'isole Molucche, dove nascono le Spetierie, Et la Navigatione attorno il Mondo* (Venice: Stamperia de Giunti, 1554), I, fols. 349–63. On Ramusio's addition of the *Suma Oriental* to his *Viaggi*, see especially also Rui Manuel Loureiro, "O Manuscrito de Lisboa da 'Soma Horiemtall' de Tomé Pires", p. 31; see also Loureiro, "O Sudeste Asiático na Suma Oriental de Tomé Pires", *Revista de Cultura*, International Edition, 4 (2002): 109–10, together with Ramusio's testimony on how difficult it was to obtain even an imperfect or corrupted copy of the manuscript while he was in Lisbon.
57. Noordhoff, *Beschrijving van ... papieren afkomstig van Huig de Groot,* p. 20, under "fol. 87". The original is presently found in the Gemeentebibliotheek Rotterdam, Handschriftenverzameling Rotterdam, 33.01, inv. 3366, fol. 87, "Copie d'un extract d'un livre intitulé Conqueste des isles de Molucques pour le Roy Philippe troisieme, escript en Espaignol au neufiesme livre." (Copy of an excerpt of a book titled Conquest of the Maluku Islands by King Philip III, written in Spanish, in Book IX.) The passage that caught the attention of Grotius concerns the arrival of English ships at

Ambon and their attempts to purchase cloves from the locals there, and English dealings with the Portuguese captain of Tidor, Pedro Alvares Abreu.

58. *The Suma Oriental of Tome Pires. An Account of the East from the Red Sea to Japan. Written in Malacca and India in 1512–1515*, ed. and tr. Armando Cortesão, 2 vols. (London: Hakluyt Society, 1944). Newer fascsimile editions of this important work are also available. For modern text-critical aspects of Pires' *Suma*, see Loureiro, *O Manuscrito de Lisboa da 'Suma Oriental' de Tomé Pires (Contribuição para uma Edição Crítica)* (Macao: Instituto Português do Oriente, 1996), especially the introduction. The printed edition of the text is almost identical to his doctoral dissertation, Loureiro, *O Manuscrito de Lisboa da "Soma Horiemtall" de Tomé Pires,* unpublished doctoral dissertation (Lisbon: Universidade de Lisboa, 1994), a copy of which is deposited in the Biblioteca Nacional de Portugal in Lisbon. See also Loureiro, "A malograda embaixada de Tomé Pires a Pequim", *Portugal e a China — Conferências no II Curso Livre de História das Relações entre Portugal e a China (Séculos XVI–XIX)* (Lisbon: Fundação Oriente, 1999), pp. 39–55; Loureiro, "O Sudeste Asiático na *Suma Oriental* de Tomé Pires", *RC,* International Edition, 4 (2003): 107–23. Concerning the problems surrounding the extant manuscripts of the *Suma Oriental*, see also Borschberg, *The Singapore and Melaka Straits,* appendix I, pp. 203–4.
59. On the significance of Pires as a source on the nature of trade in the pre-colonial period and the early Luso-Asian trading regime, see Meilink-Roelofsz, *Asian Trade and European Influence in the Indonesian Archipelago between 1500 and about 1630*, p. 1; Loureiro, "Sixteenth Century Iberian Accounts of Indonesia: A Preliminary Survey", *Indonesia-Portugal: Five Hundred Years of Historical Relationship*, ed. Ivo Carneiro de Sousa and R.Z. Leirissa (Lagos: CEPESA, 2001), p. 23.
60. See Loureiro, *O Manuscrito de Lisboa da "Suma Oriental" de Tome Pires (Contribuição a uma edição crítica)*, pp. 33–43.
61. See the *Seer cort verhael vande destructie van d'Indien vergadert deurden Bischop Don Fray Bartholome de las Casas* (Publisher unknown, 1578).
62. See *Den Spieghel Vande Spaensche Tyrannie beeldelijken afgemaelt, leest breederen in-hout door het schrijven van den E. Bisschop van Chiapa in Nieu Spaengien, ghenaemt Don Fray Bartolome de las Casas, van S. Dominicus Orden, aen den grootmaechtigen Coninck van Spaengien Philips de tweede* (Amsterdam: Cornelis Claesz, 1609).
63. Van Ittersum, *Profit and Principle*, pp. 328–9, note 38.
64. For a comprehensive selection of his works, see Covarruvias y Leyva, *Opera Omnia quae hactenus extant.*
65. Francisco de Vitoria, *Relectiones Theologicae XII.*
66. Interestingly, the copy of Vitoria's *Relectiones* is not featured in the list of books confiscated from Grotius' library in 1618. See Molhuysen, "De

bibliotheek van Hugo de Groot in 1618", *MKNAW,* afd. letterkunde, *NR* 6, 3 (1943): 50–63.

67. See BW 6205, p. 252, letter by Grotius to Petter Spiring Silvercrona of 9 May 1643; and BW 6282, p. 360, letter by Grotius to his brother Willem de Groot of 27 June 1643.
68. On Grotius' use of Vitoria, see also van Ittersum, *Profit and Principle,* pp. 327–8, 329, note 38; Thieme, "Natürliches Privatrecht Spätscholastik", *ZRG,* GA, 70 (1953): 235–6, 262–6.
69. On the de facto reciprocity of this arrangement, see also Somers and Roelofsen, "*Mare Liberum* and the Dutch East India Company", *GNS* 24–5 (2003–4): 71.
70. IPC, appendix II.9, pp. 553–5.
71. See the Hague, Nationaal Archief, *Collectie Hugo de Groot, Supplement I* (ms. 1.10.35.02, no. 40, fols. 359–60, 361–2, 364, 430). Grotius evidently had access to sets of treaties signed with Southeast Asian rulers. He gained access to definitive as well as draft treaties through his VOC contacts and in some instances may have even had a hand in drafting some of the treaties contained here in the *Collectie Hugo de Groot, Supplement I,* thought to date from around 1606. Siau is an island to the north-northeast of Celebes, in the border area between modern Indonesia and the Philippines. For an image of the draft letter to the "King of Johor", see p. 155.
72. IPC, p. 432, "There is in India a kingdom called Johore, which has long been considered a sovereign principality...."
73. Alexandrowicz, *Introduction to the History of the Law of Nations in the East Indies*, p. 47, note 1.
74. Unlike the Spaniards, the Portuguese generally dropped their religious biases in order to maximise trading profits and preserve peace with neighbouring Asian overlords. For a synopsis of the Southeast Asian context, see the article by John Villiers, "Doing Business with the Infidel", in *Maritime Asia: Profit Maximisation, Ethics and Trade Structure*, ed. Sprengard and Ptak, pp. 151–70.
75. On this, see also van Ittersum, "Mare Liberum in the West Indies?", *Itinerario* 31, 3 (2007): 59–94, esp. also p. 80.
76. On this problem, see also Borschberg, "De Societate Publica cum Infidelibus. Ein Frühwerk von Hugo Grotius", *ZRG*, RA 115 (1998): 369–70.
77. On this point, see also chapter 2. On Vitoria's *ius communicationis* in general, see Ziegler, "Völkerrechtliche Aspekte der Eroberung Lateinamerikas", *Zeitschrift für Neuere Rechtsgeschichte* 23 (2001): 9, 20 *et seq*., and more extensively Trujillo Pérez, *Francisco de Vitoria: il diritto alla comunicazione e i confini della socialità umana.*
78. See also chapter 2. For a short general background and overview of the papal donations in favour of Portugal during the 15th century, see also

J.M. Hobson, *The Eastern Origins of Western Civilisation* (Cambridge: CUP, 2004), pp. 135–7.

79. For English translations of these key documents, see Emma H. Blair and James A. Robertson, *The Philippine Islands, 1493–1898*, 55 vols. (Cleveland: A.H. Clark Co., 1903–9), I, pp. 105–11 for the bull *Inter Caetera* of 4 May 1493, and pp. 111–4, for the extension of the apostolic concession (revision of the original line of demarcation contained in the bull *Inter Caetera* of May 1493), dated 25 September 1493.
80. See also Jan A. Somers, *De VOC als volkenrechtelijke actor* (Deventer: Gouda Quint, 2001), pp. 30–4, for a useful synopsis of Portugal's claims to the East Indies.
81. See Blair and Robertson, *The Philippine Islands*, I, pp. 136–8 for the bull of Leo X dated 3 November 1504, which confirms and also extends the apostolic concessions of the 15th century.
82. See Blair and Robertson, *The Philippine Islands*, I, pp. 115–29 for the Treaty of Tordesillas and pp. 222–39 for the Treaty of Zaragoza. Concerning the broader significance of this treaty and its implications for the Spanish and Portuguese Empires in Asia, see also Borschberg, "The Johor-VOC Alliance and the Twelve Years Truce", *IILJ Working Paper* 8 (2009): 3–4.
83. BW 567, p. 611; The question could arise as to whether the Roman Inquisitor Sylvester Mazzolini de Prierias, whose *Summa Sylvestrinae* is cited in *De Iure Praedae*, should also be included among the "Domenicans" generally speaking. A closer scrutiny of the dictionary-like *Summa* and of Grotius' references thereunto shows that he looked up only select terms and expressions important to the overall argument of *De Iure Praedae*. See Sylvester Mazzolini de Prierias, *Summa Sylvestrinae qua Summa Summarum merito nuncupatur*, ed. Pietro Vendramini, 2 vols. (Venice: Ad Candentis Salamandrae insigne, 1593).
84. IPC, p. 497.
85. English translations of these documents can be found in IPC, appendices I.1-3, pp. 503–16.
86. For their incorporation into the text of chapter 12 of *De Iure Praedae (Mare Liberum)*, see, for example IPC, p. 383.
87. See also Borschberg, *The Singapore and Melaka Straits*, pp. 75–7; Borschberg, "The Seizure of the *Santa Catarina* Revisited", *JSEAS* 33, 1 (2002): 34, "At least one junk, said to belong to André Furtado de Mendonça, apparently sailed as part of the convoy, and this vessel was captured by Heemskerk's Johorean allies. It is known that, apart from supplies, this junk also carried on board a Portuguese pilot, a Catholic priest and 'many Christians'". See also, Borschberg, "The Seizure of the *Santa Catarina* Revisited", p. 49. According to the autobiography of de Coutre, about 50 Christian hostages had been taken around the time of the attack on the *Santa Catarina.* De Coutre claims that on his return to Melaka from Batu Sawar he delivered to Fernão

d'Albuquerque a reply from the Johor monarch as well as despatches from the (presumably Portuguese) *embaxador* (envoy, ambassador) to Johor. See de Coutre, *Andanzas Asiáticas,* pp. 168–9.

88. *Achter Theil der Orientalischen Indien…,* tr. by M. Gotthard Arthus with illustrations by Johann Theodor and Johann Israel de Bry, in the section titled "Vorrede an den günstigen Leser" (Foreword to the benevolent reader), pp. 11–2. Transcripts of German translations of the letters excerpted from de Bry are also found among the working papers of Robert Fruin. See Leiden, University Library, Fruin, *Aantekeningen op zijn werken,* Loket 1555–39, envelope titled "Documenta, heboorende bij het boeck van De Groots de Iure Praedae", fols. 3 recto–5 verso.
89. The Hague, Nationaal Archief, *Collectie Hugo de Groot, Supplement* (1.10.35.02, no. 40, fol. 223 recto–verso). Additional notes in French and Dutch are mentioned by Noordhoff, *Beschrijving van … papieren afkomstig van Huig de Groot,* p. 11, under fol. 83 (French), and p. 22, under fol. 180 (Dutch).
90. CIPC, p. 384, unnumbered editorial note.
91. IPC, p. 517, note 34. For the full text of the letter, see IPC, appendix I.4, pp. 517–22.
92. See appendix 6.
93. For the full text and English translation, see appendix 6. This passage cited also exists in a French translation written in the hand of Grotius. See The Hague, Nationaal Archief, *Collectie Hugo de Groot, Supplement I* (1.10.35.02, no. 40, fol. 223 recto; an image is found on p. 176).
94. On this claim, see Grotius, *Commentary on the Law of Prize and Booty,* p. 286.
95. E.N. van Kleffens, "Over zes briefen uit het bezit van Hugo de Groot", *MKNAW,* afd. letterkunde, NR 23 (1960): 447–91.
96. BW 107A (Suppl.), pp. 37–8.
97. BW 107A (Suppl.), p. 37; also on the recto of an unnumbered sheet that follows p. 66 [erroneously printed as p. 42] incip. *Cum sub hoc tempus*; CML, p. 77. However, when comparing Grotius' text to the Portuguese originals, it becomes clear that the second excerpt dated 27 January 1607, is bogus. See the texts set out in appendix 3. Given Grotius' generally sloppy working habits, he possibly confused this letter with another document. — Concerning ten Haeff's letter in general, see also van Ittersum, *Profit and Principle* (2006), pp. 224–5. Van Ittersum recognised a direct link between ten Haeff's letter, the list of documents and the commission by the VOC's Zeeland Chamber (at Middelburg) to prepare *Mare Liberum* for publication. See van Ittersum, p. 226.
98. BW (Supplement) 107A, p. 37. The originals and their translations into Dutch and French had survived among the working papers of Grotius. They were sold at a public auction in 1864 and are listed in the original auction

catalogue under vol. I, "Recueil concernant les voyages des Hollandais aux Indes Orientales, la Compagnie des Indes, etc., 1600–1616" (Collection Concerning the Voyages of the Dutch to the East Indies, the East India Company, etc. 1600–1616) as lots number 1–10. See also Noordhoff, *Beschrijving van ... papieren afkomstig van Huig de Groot,* pp. 11–3.

99. With specific reference to the Singapore and Melaka Straits, the Estado da Índia's security issues during the late 16th and early 17th century have been discussed more extensively in Borschberg, *The Singapore and Melaka Straits,* pp. 117–21, and "The Seizure of the *Santa Catarina* Revisited", *JSEAS* 33, 1 (2002): 31–62.

100. The *Estreito de Sabam* or *Sabão* runs along a north-south axis between the eastern seaboard of the great island of Sumatra and the present-day islands of Karimun Besar and Kundur in Indonesia's Kepulauan Riau province.

101. BW (Supplement) 107A, p. 38, no. 2.

102. See Borschberg, *The Singapore and Melaka Straits,* chapters 2 and 3, pp. 60–136.

103. Patani, a port and polity by the same name, is located on the Gulf of Siam in present-day Thailand near the border with Malaysia. For more on this second incident, see Borschberg, *The Singapore and Melaka Straits,* pp. 93–9; "The Seizure of the *Santa Catarina* Revisited", *JSEAS* 33, 1 (2002): 31–62.

104. See also Borschberg, *The Singapore and Melaka Straits,* pp. 157–65.

105. Van Ittersum, *Profit and Principle,* p. 225, note 34.

106. BW (Supplement) 107A, p. 37, note 1, "In zijn brief verwijst hij naar bijgevoegde documenten, die Grotius van nut konden zijn bij zijn verdediging van de belangen van de compagnie; deze belangen waren als gevolg van de onderhandelingen met Spanje over vrede of bestand onder druk komen te staan. Grotius kan de documenten van ten Haeff verwerkt hebben in een nota die hij in deze tijd in voorbereiding had en die in verscheidene redacties in zijn papieren bewaard is gebleven." See also van Ittersum, *Profit and Principle,* pp. 226–7.

107. A copy was found among the working papers of Grotius and sold at the 1864 auction. See Noordhoff, *Beschrijving van ... papieren afkomstig van Huig de Groot,* no. 24, p. 15. It currently forms part of the the bundle *Collectie Hugo de Groot, Supplement I* (ms. 1.10.35.02, no. 40) at the Nationaal Archief in the Hague. The document has been transcribed and published in RH, pp. 237–65, and has been reproduced and translated in this book as appendix 15.

108. See also the undated Portuguese brief titled "Relação do sucesso que teve a armada do viso-rei Dom Martim Afonso" which is featured as appendix 16 in Pinto, *Portugueses e malaios,* pp. 293–7. According to this document on p. 294, the Dutch siege of Portuguese Melaka was supported by the eleven Dutch ships, 1,400 Dutch troops, seven (Malay) rulers [and presumably

their soldiers] as well as an estimated 16 thousand Javanese troops. See also Borschberg, *The Singapore and Melaka Straits,* pp. 159–62.

109. J.J.L. Duyvendak, "The First Siamese Embassy to Holland", *T'Oung Pao* 32 (1936): 289, "In the instructions given by the Committee of XVII [the Heren XVII] to Admiral Matelief ... it had also been recommended to make use of the King of Siam's intermediary for the Chinese trade."
110. Van der Cruysse, *Louis XIV et le Siam,* pp. 63–9; Paul Pelliot, "Les relations du Siam et de la Hollande en 1608", *T'Oung Pao* 32 (1936): 223–9; Duyvendak, "The First Siamese Embassy to Holland", *T'Oung Pao* 32 (1936): 285–92.
111. Several copies of this important document are preserved in the Nationaal Archief in the Hague, including Archief Oldenbarnevelt, ms. 3104 fols. 53 recto–60 recto. Concerning its historic significance as a blueprint for shaping early VOC policy, see also Borschberg, *The Singapore and Melaka Straits,* pp. 162–4.
112. See also Somers and Roelofsen, "*Mare Liberum* and the Dutch East India Company", *GNS* 24–5 (2003–4): 73.
113. BW 451, p. 503, letter by Matelieff to Grotius, dated 3 March 1616; another copy in RH, pp. 345–9. See also Noordhoff, *Beschrijving van ... papieren afkomstig van Huig de Groot,* p. 22.
114. BW (Supplement) 198A, pp. 71–5; another copy RH, pp. 328–36; also R. Bijlsma, "De discoursen van Cornelis Matelieff de Jonge over den staat van Oost-Indië", *Nederlandsch Archievenblad* 35 (1927–8), I: 49–53.
115. BW 309, pp. 285–7. See also Noordhoff, *Beschrijving van ... papieren afkomstig van Huig de Groot,* p. 22.
116. According to Gaastra, *De geschiedenis van de VOC,* pp. 30–40, Matelieff's memorials were taken seriously in the nascent Dutch republic, especially also by the VOC directors, the Heren XVII. He recognised the substantial advantages and benefits that derived form a centralised system that the Portuguese had already successfully established in Goa. Matelieff's proposal for a rendezvous in the East Indies should be seen against the backdrop of seeking to secure the same financial, commercial and administrative benefits for the VOC in Asia.
117. See appendix 15.
118. See for example BW (Supplement) 198A, p. 72.
119. BW (Supplement) 198A, p. 72, especially also the note in the left-hand margin "Den houc van Johor tot een rende[z]-vous onbequaem, P[iete]r de Bot." (The Hook of Johor is not suitable for a rendezvous. Pieter de Both.) This testimony partially penned in the hand of Grotius is important historically, for it gives contemporary researchers the more precise location in Johor that the VOC and Dutch politicians were contemplating for the rendezvous. The "houc van Johor" mentioned in the marginalia is without doubt what other period Dutch sources call the the "Hook of Berbukit".

It is situated across the Johor River estuary from present-day Changi in Singapore and approximately marks the location where the *Santa Catarina* was taken under fire in February 1603. See also the image on p. 71.

120. See appendix 15.
121. This term, in the Dutch original "swarten", is often a pejorative reference to the peoples of South and Southeast Asia. In modern usage it could be translated throughout as "Asians", or simply as "locals".
122. BW (Supplement) 198A, p. 73. See also Noordhoff, *Beschrijving van … papieren afkomstig van Huig de Groot,* p. 23, "Afschrift van een geschrift van Cornelis Matelieff de Jonge d.d. 1609 Mei 18, waarin hij o.a. nogmaals het nut betoogt van de stichting van eener vaste hoofdplaats in de buurt van Jacatra…. en aandringt op het zenden van een hooft of president naar Indië." (Copy of a memorial by Cornelis Matelieff de Jonge, dated 18 May 1609, in which he, among other points, again stresses the benefit of establishing a permanent base in the vicinity of Jacatra … and exhorts the despatch a head or president to the East Indies.) A memorial by Claes Puyck written on behalf of Matelieff dated 20 August 1614, warns of the difficulties of sailing from Jayakerta (Jacatra) toward the Strait of Sunda against the monsoon winds. It is reported that one vessel needed six weeks to reach Banten from Jayakerta (Jacatra) against the wind, and for this reason, the rendezvous should be established at the entrance of the strait. See RH, p. 337. See also the Hague, Nationaal Archief, *Archief Johan van Oldenbarnevelt* (3.01.14, no. 3117).
123. BW 400, p. 382, "Die van Banten wil nyet toelaten dat wy ons huys hooger timmeren als 2 vadem…" [The (authorities) in Banten refuse to permit that we build our lodge higher than two fathoms (that is about 3.4 metres).]
124. See esp. Borschberg, "The Johor-VOC Alliance and the Twelve Years Truce", *IILJ Working Paper* 8 (2009): 3–6.
125. BW (Supplement) 198A, p. 73.
126. BW (Supplement) 198A, p. 72, "Het innenemen van Banda maekt ons hatich"; and p. 73, "Dat de Nederlanden hoe langer hoe meer in haet comen van Indiën". Also RH, pp. 330, 331.
127. BW (Supplement) 198A, p. 72, "… de onervarenheyt van onse natie om de mahometisten te gouverneuren…."
128. BW (Supplement) 198A, p. 73, "Want gaen wij op de Portuguesche manier te werck, gelijck wij begonnen hebben, met innemen van landen en steden, soo werden wij gehaet ende gaen wij op de Engelsche manier te werck, soo werden wij cleyn geacht."
129. See also Borschberg, "The Johor-VOC Alliance and the Twelve Years Truce", *IILJ Working Paper* 8 (2009): 7–8. The Twelve Years Truce was to take effect in the East Indies after the lapse of one calender year from the date of its ratification in Europe, that is 10 April 1610. With the benefit of hindsight, however, the truce was unsustainable in the Asian theatre,

and by 1613 at the very latest (that is about the time the Dutch attack Portuguese positions on the island of Solor near Timor), the Twelve Years Truce had definitively broken down in the regions covered by the VOC charter. Against the backdrop of this breakdown, Grotius copied a set of instructions issued by the Dutch States General to the VOC governor-general, the Council of India (*Raad van Indië*) and all company servants dated 4 March 1614. See Noordhoff, *Beschrijving van ... papieren afkomstig van Huig de Groot,* p. 20.

130. See the "Oost-Indische Voyagie onder den Admirael Pieter W. Verhoeven", *BV* III: 207–8. The paraphrased reply of 'Ala'uddin and Raja Bongsu to the proposals of Verhoeff and his *breede raad* (officers council) is printed on p. 208. See also Netscher, *De Nederlanders in Djohor en Siak,* p. 21.
131. Borschberg, "The Johor-VOC Alliance and the Twelve Years Truce", *IILJ Working Paper* 8 (2009): 22–4. Raja Bongsu's letter to Stadholder Prince Maurice of Orange bears the date 8 December 1609.
132. BW (Supplement), 198A, p. 72, "Con[inck] van Johor onwillich om een fort in sijn lant te gedoogen". See also the full text in the letter here as well as another copy in RH, pp. 328–35, esp. p. 329.
133. See Jan Karel K. de Jonge, *Opkomst van het Nederlandsch gezag in Oost-Indië. Verzameling van onuitgegeven stukken uit het oud-coloniaal archief,* 16 vols. (The Hague: Martinus Nijhoff, 1866–1909), III, pp. 304–5, letter by Jacques Obelaer to the Heren XVII; also Netscher, *De Nederlanders in Djohor en Siak,* pp. 17–20, 27; *De reis van de vloot van Pieter Willemszoon Verhoeff naar Azië, 1607–1612*, ed. Margot E. van Opstall, 2 vols. (The Hague: Martinus Nijhoff, 1972), II, p. 255; Borschberg, "The Johor-VOC Alliance and the Twelve Years Truce", *IILJ Working Paper* 8 (2009): 23.
134. BW (Supplement), 198A, p. 73, "Die van Johor, dat onse vrudt is, werdt om onse vruntschap in ellende gebracht, ja dat meer is, den peper dye in sijn lant valt wert nae Patane gebracht ende bij ons aldaer dierder ingecoft als tot Johor, soodat wij hem ontblooten van negotie daer wij ter contrarye behooren te doen ende die van Patane, dye nyet vuyt haerselven hebben, jagen wij de negotie toe ende sij nemen ons sooveel toll aff als sij willen." The same passage is also found in RH, p. 332.
135. See also Borschberg, "The Johor-VOC Alliance and the Twelve Years Truce", *IILJ Working Paper* 8 (2009): 22–4.
136. See appendix 15.
137. BW (Supplement), 198A, p. 74, "Het is oock een groote faute van de heeren bewinthebberen dat men alle jaeren nyeuwe commandeurs nae India heeft gesonden, want altijdt wilden nyeuwen 't gedaen werck beschelden ofte verbeteren, die dickwils door de onervarenheyt dat weynigh verstaet 'tgene den voorgaende gedaen heeft dye langer als hij in India is geweest ende de humeuren van de Indianen best bekent, gelijck geschiet is met den coninck van Johor, met denwelcken den admirael Pyeter Willemsz. een ander accoort

wilde maecken als hetgene, dat ick met hem gemaeckt hadde, waerover den coninck qualijck tevreden wesende seyde dat hij alledaghe geen nyeu accord en wilde maecken ende dat denghene dye nae hem, Pieter Willemsz., soude comen weder een ander accoort, soude willen maecken, soodatter dyent een goeden voet geraemt ende daer dan vorder opgevolcht ende nyet alledaechs wat nyeus." The same passage can be found in RH, p. 334.

138. Ignorance of Asian customs and languages proved to be a significant obstacle in the early decades of the Dutch company and was a serious problem not just among the senior officers, but especially also with the servants at more junior levels. As Peter Kirsch succinctly notes in his chapter "VOC — Trade without Ethics?" in *Maritime Asia: Profit Maximisation, Ethics and Trade Structure,* ed. Sprengard and Ptak, p. 198, "The average man going to the Indies had no training and no knowledge of foreign languages. What he knew of Asia before leaving Amsterdam was very little, usually based on hearsay — or he knew nothing at all. His contract with the VOC obliged him to serve in the East for some years only. After that, he hoped to return to Europe as a wealthy man. In other words, his expectations were limited to the issue of money-making during a temporary sojourn abroad."

139. Lund, University Library, Bibl. Grotiana 13, Emmanuel van Meteren, *Memoriën der Belgische Ofte Nederlantsche Historie van onsen tijden* (Delft: Jacob Cornilisz Veenecool, 1599). See also Folke Dovring, "Une partie de l'héritage littéraire de Grotius retrouvée en Suède", *MKNAW*, afd. letterkunde, nieuwe reeks, 12 (1949): 237–50. The copy in Lund University Library is a restored copy of the book that spans up until the year 1598. Grotius' notes are clustered in areas dealing with key topics of historical interest, such as the creation of the union under Holy Roman Emperor Charles V in 1528 and the years of the Dutch Revolt. On the early Dutch voyages to the East Indies, see esp. van Meteren, *Memoriën*, fol. 406 verso and 407 recto. On the latter page, the names of van Heemskerk, van Neck and van Warwijk are all underlined by Grotius. There are also underlinings or marginalia of interest on fol. 414 recto and in the book's register. Concerning the history of this first edition of van Meteren and the controversy that erupted over it, together with the notes found in Grotius' copy preserved at Lund University, see C.M. Ridderikoff, "Een aristocratische geschiedenis van de Opstand: Grotius' Annales et Historiae de rebus Belgicis", *De Zeventiende Eeuw* 10, 2 (1994): 278–9.

140. See also Villiers, "The Estado da India in South East Asia", in *South East Asia: Colonial History,* ed. Kratoska and Borschberg, I, p. 158, "The majority of the *fortalezas* and *feitorias* of the Estado da Índia, however, were in places where the Portuguese exercised neither sovereignty in theory nor hegemony in practice."

141. The strongest statement to this effect is made in a memorial issued by the

VOC to all its admirals, vice-admirals and leading servants in Asia and bears the date 11 April 1608. According to this memorial, negotiations with the Spanish (and implicitly also Portuguese) were well on the way and it was foreseen that a truce would come into effect for a period of nine years. It then stipulates (de Jonge, *Opkomst van het Nederlandsch gezag in Oost-Indië*, III, p. 308), "… geduyrende welcken tyt van 9 jaren de geoctroyeerde Comp. in allen plaetse van Europa, Africa ende Asia niet weesende onder tgebiet van den Coninck van Spaengien sal mogen handelen ende traffiqueren, maer in plaetsen daer den Coninck van Spaignien ofte de synen tgebiet hebben, daer en sal men niet mogen handelen ofte traffiqueeren…." (For a period of nine years the chartered [Dutch East India] Company shall be entitled to visit and trade in all places in Europe, Africa and Asia that are not under the sovereignty of the King of Spain; but in places which the King of Spain and his dependents hold sovereignty, there it shall not be possible to visit or trade.) The instructions of 11 April 1608 are believed to have given the impetus for the conclusion of many contracts by the VOC in the course of 1609 and 1610. See Borschberg, "The Johor-VOC Alliance and the Twelve Years Truce", *IILJ Working Paper* 8 (2009): 8.

142. Van Ittersum, *Profit and Principle*, p. 119. In addition to this bound bundle of affidavits (that is the Book Concerning the Cruel, Treacherous and Hostile Proceedings of the Portuguese in the East Indies) preserved in the Nationaal Archief in the Hague, there are also a number of (notarised) documents found among the working papers of Grotius preserved as *Collectie Hugo de Groot, Supplement I* (ms. 1.10.35.02, no. 40, fols. 434–60).
143. How the Estado da India functioned can be reconstructed on the basis of treaties signed with Asian princes. See the exposé of de Saldanha, *Iustum Imperium. Dos tratados como fundamento do império dos Portugueses no Oriente*. For a collection of Luso-Asian treaties, see Biker, *Collecção de tratados e concertos de pazes que o Estado da Índia Portugeza fez com os reis e senhores com quem teve relações nas partes da Ásia e Africa Oriente*.
144. Grotius cited, from the works of Ptolemy as well as Pliny and Strabo. He applied the geographic term "Taprobana" to Sumatra and the "Golden Chersonese" to either the Malay Peninsula or Japan. See IPC, pp. 264–5, 355.
145. Fruin, "Een onuitgegeven werk", in *Fruin's Verspreide Geschriften*, III, p. 372.
146. Very similar conclusions have been reached by Michael Kempe and Cornelis G. Roelofsen. See Michael Kempe, "Beyond the Law: The Image of Piracy in the Legal Writings of Hugo Grotius", *GNS* 27–8 (2005–7): 385; Roelofsen, "The Sources of Mare Liberum; the contested origins of the Doctrine of the Freedom of the Sea", in *International Law and its Sources,* ed. W.P. Heere (Deventer: Kluwer, 1988), pp. 93–124.

147. On this question, see van Ittersum, *Profit and Principle*, p. 27, "It cannot be emphasized enough that the manuscript's *dogmatica de Iure Praedae* were written last, not first. The evidence is admittedly circumstantial, but nonetheless convincing." Very similarly, van Ittersum, "Dating the Manuscript of *De Jure Praedae*", *History of European Ideas* 35 (2009): esp. 125–93, and "Hugo Grotius in Context", *AJSS* 31, 3 (2003): 525. See also Wilson, *Savage Republic,* p. 13, and Wilson, "On Heterogeneity and the Naming of De Indis of Grotius", *Journal of the Philosophy of International Law* 1, 1 (2006): 86.

General Conclusion

1. Similarly, see Robert Feenstra, "Ius commune et droit comparé chez Grotius. Nouvelles remarques sur les sources citées dans ses ouvrages juridiques, à propos d'une réimpression du De iure belli ac pacis", *Revista internazionale di diritto commune* 3 (1992): 7–36; "Quelques remarques sur le soures utilisées par Grotius dans ses traveaux de droit naturel", in *The World of Hugo Grotius*, ed. Feenstra, pp. 65–81.
2. This is most recently evident from the introduction to the 2009 edition of *Mare Liberum.* See *Hugo Grotius Mare Liberum, 1609–2009,* ed. Robert Feenstra and intr. Jeroen Vervliet (Leiden: Brill, 2009).
3. See esp. CiT, introduction, pp. 53–5, 117–35; Borschberg,"Commentarius in Theses XI, ein unveröffentlichtes Werk von Hugo Grotius", *ZRG*, RA 109 (1992): 463–4; Borschberg, "Grotius, the Social Contract and Political Resistance", *IILJ Working Paper* 6 (2006): 19–21, 49–57 and 65–6.
4. Among them the syndic of Emden, Johannes Althusius, who critiqued the idea that the rights of sovereignty are vested in the person of the prince or ruler and specifically the theory of Jean Bodin. Althusius staked out his basic differences with the French jurisconsult Bodin in the foreword to the 1603 Latin edition of his *Politica Methodice Digesta* (Politics Methodologically Set Forth). See Johannes Althusius, *Politica Methodice Digesta*, p. 5.
5. Ward, *Networks of Empire,* p. 6.
6. See for example A. Milner, *The Malays* (Oxford: Wiley-Blackwell, 2008), pp. 55–6.
7. Hierarchy among the rulers was evidently a reflection of the microcosm prevailing at the individual royal courts. On the latter, see Anthony Milner, *Kerajaan. Malay Political Culture on the Eve of Colonial Rule* (Tucson: University of Arizona Press, 1982), pp. 104–6, and Milner, *The Malays,* pp. 66–7.

8. For the list and contents of these treaties, see Heeres, "Corpus Diplomaticum Neërlando-Indicum", *BKI* 57 (1907). Treaties with the aforementioned *negrijen* on the island of Ambon were concluded, for example in March, April and August 1609. However, in Malay language versions of the treaties, such as notably Jan Pietersz. Coen's treaty with Banda dated 9 May 1621, the Dutch party calls itself "negri Hollande" and the Gentlemen States General are referred to as *orang kaya*. See Heeres, p. 166, The Malay language preamble thus reads "Jan Pietersz Coen, Gouvernador Generael deri pada prince Orange, dengan orang caya caya sacalien deri negri Hollande…." (Jan Pieterszoon Coen, Governor-General from the Prince of Orange, along with all the most powerful men together from the negeri of Holland.) I assume that the term "the most powerful men together from the negeri of Holland" is to be taken as a translation into Malay of the Dutch expression "Hoogmogende Heeren Staten Generaal der Vereenigde Nederlanden" (The High Mighty Gentlemen States General of the United Netherlands).
9. See Milner, *The Malays,* p. 59, "The way in which *negeri* is used in royal letters is worth noting here: a ruler was usually described as being (literally) 'on the throne of a *kerajaan* located in a specific *negeri*'. Thus, in 1787 we see a letter from Sultan Alauddin who is 'on the throne of the *kerajaan* that is in the *negeri* Perak'…. He is not described as the 'ruler of the *negeri* Perak'." Concerning the kerajaan, see also Milner, *Kerajaan. Malay Political Culture on the Eve of Colonial Rule,* pp. 7–8 and 112–6. A period 17th-century understanding of the term *negeri* also derives from de Coutre, *Andánzas Asiáticas*, book 1, chapter 4, pp. 97–8, "Es de saber que es un reyno pequeño; no tiene más de una ciudad del mismo nombre que es la corte y adonde redizen muchos mercaderes ricos alredador, y algunos lugares pequeños. — Podemos llamar propriamente ducado, pero se intitula rey. — … Enquanto la tierra, aunque pequeña era muy fértil y fresca, y tiene minas de oro." (It must be said that it [that is Pahang] is a very small kingdom. It has only one city and that bears the same name where the court is situated and where many rich merchants reside nearby. There are also some small settlements. — In truth, [Pahang] is only a duchy, but [its ruler] calls himself king. — … Although the kingdom is small, it is fertile and cool and has gold mines.) In this 17th century description, de Coutre employs the term city *(ciudad)* for *negeri.* Also Borschberg, "Jacques de Coutre as a Source for the 17th Century History of Singapore, the Johor River and the Straits", *JMBRAS* 81, 2 (2008): 94.
10. Milner, *The Malays,* p. 59, "The substance of the *negeri,* however, was neither the land nor the institutions — it was simply the people."
11. Borschberg, "The Johor-VOC Alliance and the Twelve Years Truce", *IILJ Working Paper* 8 (2009).
12. See appendix 11.

13. Milner, *The Malays*, pp. 57, 58–9 (with references to the situation as late as the 19th century). "Unlike the sensitivity 'Malay' rulers expressed with respect to subjects, they sometimes admitted to having almost no idea of the territorial dimensions of their realms.... Much territory seemed to be a type of no-man's land; what mattered was whether there were people working there, and if so, to whom these people owed allegiance.... What certainly would have concerned the Pahang ruler was whether he had subjects in the region, not the presence of any specific territorial markings. In Borneo the situation was similar.... We gain no sense of the state having an external periphery that might define it territorially." See also Milner, *Kerajaan. Malay Political Culture on the Eve of Colonial Rule*, pp. 7–8; Kratoska, "The Peripatetic Peasant and Land Tenure in British Malaya", *JSEAS* 16, 1 (1985): 19.
14. See appendix 12.
15. Leonard Andaya, "De VOC en de Maleise wereld in de 17de en 18de eeuw", in *De VOC in Azië*, ed. M.-A.P. Meilink-Roelofsz (Bossum: Fibula-Van Dieshoeck, 1976), p. 110. In the context of Malay polities, Andaya treats the *daulat* as a source from whence all political power, moral and institutional legitimacy proceeds and places it in relation to its opposite *derhaka,* which he understands as *verrad aan de staat of de heersers* (treason committed against the state or ruler). In a Javanese context, for example, *daulat* can also refer to a "dynasty", "fortuitous event" or simply "good fortune" and in same ways represents the equivalent in the Malay world to the Chinese Emperor's "Mandate of Heaven". In its modern usage *daulat* often means "sovereignty", such as for example in the expression *daulat rakyat* or "popular sovereignty", "sovereignty of the people". This latter understanding of the term is almost certainly influenced by European and colonial ideas of power and political authority.
16. Milner, *The Malays,* p. 68.
17. In simple terms, Milner defines *daulat* as a "supranatural power only possessed by royalty". See Milner, *Kerajaan. Malay Political Culture on the Eve of Colonial Rule*, p. 54.
18. A noteworthy exception are the *Undang-undang Melaka* (Laws of Melaka) and the *Undang-undang Laut Melaka* (Melaka Sea Code), both compilations or digests which have incorporated laws from the pre-colonial and colonial period. See *Undang-undang Melaka: A Critical Edition*, ed. Liaw Yock Fang (The Hague: Martinus Nijhoff, 1976); R.O. Winstedt and P.E. de Josselin de Jong, "The Maritime Laws of Malacca. Edited, with an outline translation", *JMBRAS* 29, 3 (1956): 51, "Article 1, These are the laws given by Sultan Mahmud Shah, ... Know these laws, in order that all matters be peacefully settled. Article 2: The sea-captains desiring a code of maritime law, the Dato Bendahara, Paduka Seri Maharaja Mangkubumi put their request to Sultan Muhammad [sic] Shah. The Sultan consented. This code, which was composed in the days when Malacca was still powerful, under the rule of

Mahmud Shah, is now set down in writing." — Concerning the nature and interrelation of the two legal codes of Melaka, see Liaw Yock Fang, "The Undang-undang Melaka", in *Melaka: The Transformation of a Malay Capital, c. 1400–1980,* ed. Kernial Singh Sandhu and Paul Wheatley (Kuala Lumpur: OUP, 1983), I, pp. 170, 181, 183.

19. See also Mona Abaza, "Ada/Custom in the Middle East and Southeast Asia", in Carol Gluck and Anna Lowenhaupt Tsing, *Words in Motion: Toward a Global Lexicon* (Durham and London: Duke University Press, 2009), pp. 67–82, esp. the section "How did Custom become Law in Indonesia?", pp. 72–5. A second chapter by A.L. Tsing found in the same volume titled "Adat/Indigenous. Indigeneity in Motion", pp. 40–64, casts yet more light on the fluidity of the term *adat* in the Southeast Asian and specifically Indonesian context.
20. Borschberg, "De Pace. Ein unveröffentlichtes Fragment von Grotius über Krieg und Frieden", *ZRG*, RA 113 (1996): 279–82.
21. See Fulton, *The Sovereignty of the Sea*, where the disputes of England and Scotland with Denmark (pp. 108–12) and the Dutch Republic (pp. 118–203) are discussed in more detail.
22. Concerning the idea of frontline polities, see esp. Borschberg, "The Johor-VOC Alliance and the Twelve Years Truce", *IILJ Working Paper* 8 (2009): 3–6.
23. See esp. Cornelis van Vollenhoven, "Grotius and the Study of Law" (1925), republished in his *Verspreide Geschriften*, I, p. 391, "No book on international law written since Grotius radiates so much love, inspires so much confidence and restfulness to the soul as his book [De Iure Belli ac pacis] does." Van Vollenhoven attributed near superhuman qualities to the Dutch humanist on p. 388, where Grotius is credited for "practically [knowing] everything written by sacred or classical authors and ... practically every event in ancient or biblical history". But in the article "Het Gesloten Boek" (The Closed Book) first published in 1927, van Vollenhoven conceded that *De Iure Belli ac Pacis* is "not book about peace, but a book about war, and this exposé is [actually] an exposé on war". See *Verspreide Geschriften*, I, p. 475.
24. See for example Martin van Gelderen, "The Challenge of Colonialism: Grotius and Vitoria on Natural Law and International Relations", *GNS* 14–5 (1993–4): 3–37; van Ittersum, *Profit and Principle.*

Document Appendices

1. The Hague, Nationaal Archief, *Collectie Hugo de Groot, Supplement I* (ms. 1.10.35.02, no. 40, fols. 331–2). A transcript is also found in BW (Supplement) 107A, p. 38. See also LML, on the recto of an unnumbered sheet that

follows p. 66 [erroneously printed as p. 42], incip. *Cum Sub Hoc Tempus*; CML, p. 77, "As several letters of the King of Spain have come of late into our hands, in which his design and that of the Portuguese is clearly disclosed, it seemed worth while to translate into Latin two of them which had particular bearing upon the controversy at issue, and to append them here." As is shown in appendix 5, one of these Latin excerpts, namely the royal letter 27 January 1607, cannot be reconciled with the Portuguese original.

2. *De derde reis van de V.O.C. naar Oost-Indië onder het beleid van Admiraal Paulus van Caerden,* ed. A. de Booy, 2 vols. (The Hague: Martinus Nijhoff, 1970), II, pp. 37–8, where it is reported that a Portuguese vessel captured contained "veel Portugijse briven" (many letters in Portuguese). The seizure of the Portuguese carrack *Nossa Senhora do Loretto* is described in *De derde reis,* ed. de Booy, II, pp. 132–3, letter of van Caerden to the Heren XVII, dated 9 January 1608. The crew was reportedly in a "desolate condition" and many had already died of scurvy en route from Lisbon.
3. The ships of Admiral Matelieff were anchored at Banten between 6 and 10 January 1608. See also *De derde reis,* ed. de Booy, I, p. 121.
4. Compare this with Matelieff's statement (see appendix 15): "From what I was told by van Caerden, with Calicut it is all pretence. The story is too long to tell here, but I note that from a few letters which came into my hands with the ships that were taken, it appears that the King of Cochin is not on good terms with the Portuguese and their long-standing friendship might turn to enmity."
5. *De derde reis,* ed. de Booy, II, pp. 136–7, letter of van Caerden to the Heren XVII dated 9 January 1608, "Ick hebbe aen den heer admirael Matelieff gelevert alle de brieven die den Coninck van Spanien aen den visorey ende Staet van Indien geschreven heeft, behoudende bij mij de copien daarvan, die ick hebbe doen maken."
6. *De derde reis,* ed. de Booy, II, p. 136, letter by van Caerden to the Heren XVII dated 9 January 1608; and also "Historische Verhael Vande treffelijkcke Reyse, gedaen naer de Oost-Indien ende China … door … Cornelis Matelief de Ionge", *BV* III: 129–30.
7. *De derde reis,* ed. de Booy, II, p. 45; and "Historische Verhael", *BV* III: 129.
8. *De derde reis,* ed. de Booy, II, pp. 44–6, but esp. pp. 44–5, "Soo quamen wij voor Bantam te reden, daer vonden wij den admierael Cornelis Matelieff met 2 schepen, het één genoempt Ooraengen ende [de] ander Mouverittius, dat in den nacht tseyl ginck, daer ick een brieff meden sont nae huys ende een aen der meysters tot Amsterdam. Daer verstont ick van den admierael Madelyeff, dat hij voor Malacken hadden van sijn vloot verlooren 2 schepen in den brant voor sijn vijant ende den vijant clein ende groot omtrent 20 samen. Men seyden den vijant seven duysent sylen gelaten te hebben ende d'onse geen hondert; den slacht was seer affgrieselycken voor d'onse door

de sterckten van den vijant." (We came to anchor at Banten roads where we encounterd Admiral Cornelis Matelieff de Jonge with two ships, one named *Orange* and the other *Mauritius*. The latter set sail that night [of our arrival] and carried on board a letter I had written home and another one I addressed to the superiors in Amsterdam. I understood from Admiral Matelieff that he lost two ships of his fleet to fire against his [Portuguese] enemy, and the enemy lost [both] large and small [vessels], about 20 in all. It is reported that the enemy lost [about] 7,000 souls and our side not even 100. The battle was very horrifying for our men on account of the enemy's strength.) See also *De derde reis,* ed. de Booy, II, pp. 135–6, letter of van Caerden to the Heren XVII dated 9 January 1608, and "Historische Verhael Vande treffelijkcke Reyse, gedaen naer de Oost-Indien ende China … door … Cornelis Matelief de Ionge", *BV* III: 129–30. The latter reports that, after the unsuccessful attempt to reach Johor, van Caerden set course for the Bandas. Similarly de Jonge, *Opkomst van het Nederlandsch gezag in Oost-Indië*, III, Jacques l'Hermite to the Heren XVII, dated 28 January 1608, pp. 247–8.

9. *Catalogue des Manuscrits Autographes de Hugo Grotius,* p. 5, under "Recueil concernant les voyages des Hollandais aux Indes Orientales, la Compagnie des Indes, etc. 1600–1616", p. 5, lot nos. 1–10. The auctioneers at Martinus Nijhoff wrongly surmised that it was Admiral Cornelis Matelieff de Jonge who had originally seized or captured these letters. See the commentary on p. 5, under lot no. 10, "Les letters no. 1–10 furent probablement interceptés par Corn. Matelieff de Jonge pendant son voyage aux Indes, et aportées par lui en Hollande." (The letters 1–10 were probably intercepted by Corn[elis] Matelieff de Jonge during his voyage to the Indies and brought to Holland by him.)
10. My translation and annotations from the Dutch original.
11. The original of this and some other letters were retrieved among the working papers of Grotius sold at the auction of 1864 and bought by Frederik Muller of Amsterdam. The letter was featured in the *Catalogue des Manuscrits Autographes de Hugo Grotius,* p. 5, lot no. 2, "Lettre orig. sig. du même à Don Mart. de Castro, Viceroi des Indes, 28 Nov. 1606, avec trad. franc. et holland." (Original letter signed by the same [King Philip III/II], 28 November 1606, with translations into French and Dutch.)
12. *Catalogue des Manuscrits Autographes de Hugo Grotius,* part I, p. 5, lot no. 7, "Lettre orig. sig. du même à André Furtado de Mendonça, 27 Janv. 1607, avec trad. holl." (Original letter signed by the same [King Philip III/II] to André Furtado de Mendonça, 27 January 1607, with Dutch translation.)
13. *Catalogue des Manuscrits Autographes de Hugo Grotius,* part I, p. 5, lot no. 8, "Lettre orig. sig. du même, à Don Mart. de Castro, 27 Janv. 1607, 2 pag., avec trad. holl." (Original letter signed by the same [King Philip III/II] to Dom Martin de Castro, 27 January 1607, 2 pages with Dutch translation.)

14. *Catalogue des Manuscrits Autographes de Hugo Grotius,* p. 5, lot no. 1, "Lettre originale signée, du Roi d'Espaigne, au Capitaine du fort de Negapatnam, 24 Nov. 1606. Avec tradition franc. et holland." (Original letter signed by the King of Spain [Philip III/II] to the captain of the fort of Nagapattinam, 24 November 1606. With translation into French and Dutch.) The original and translations have not been retrieved.
15. *Catalogue des Manuscrits Autographes de Hugo Grotius,* part I, p. 5, lot no. 10, "Lettre du même à Mart. a Fonco de Castro, 13 Févr. 1607. 2 pag. Traduction holl." (Letter of the same [Viceroy Jerónimo de Azevedo] to Martim Affonso de Castro, 13 February 1607. 2 pages. Dutch translation.)
16. Portuguese text as transcribed in document 14, *Documentos Remettidos da Índia ou Livros das Monções,* ed. R.A. de Bulhão Pato, I, pp. 47–8. A Latin translation prepared by Grotius is featured as an appendix in LML, on the recto of an unnumbered sheet that follows p. 66 [erroneously printed as p. 42]. As the Latin translation featured in the 1609 edition of *Mare Liberum* generally corresponds to the Portuguese original it has not been reproduced in this appendix. See also CML, pp. 77–8.
17. LML, pp. 67–8 (unfoliated).
18. LML p. 68 (unfoliated).
19. Translated from the Portuguese original by Roopanjali Roy, Lisbon. The annotations are mine.
20. This law is dated 18 March 1605.
21. Lisbon, *Filmoteca Ultramarina,* (banda 29, fotograma 1), ficheiro 2, gaveta 1, divisão 8–9, fol. 116. I would like to thank Pedro Pinto of the Centro de Estudos Históricos at the Universidade Nova de Lisboa for tracking down this letter and also preparing a transcript of the Portuguese original.
22. Translated from the Portuguese original by Roopanjali Roy, Lisbon. The annotations are mine.
23. Portuguese text as transcribed in document 14, *Livros das Monções,* ed. de Bulhão Pato, I, pp. 130–1. A supposed fragment of this letter which Grotius translated into Latin as an appendix to *Mare Liberum* (LML, p. 66, CML, pp. 78–9, appendix 3) does not correspond in any part to the full Portuguese original. It is likely that, in the haste of preparing *Mare Liberum* for the press, Grotius mixed up the various letters which had been forwarded to him by ten Haeff.
24. Translated from the Portuguese original by Roopanjali Roy, Lisbon. The annotations are mine.
25. The Portuguese literally reads "monsoon"; the expression "stormy weather" has been employed to describe the weather patterns prevailing in southwestern Europe.
26. LML, p. 68 (unfoliated). Translated from the original Latin by Dr. Corinna Vermeulen, Noctua Taal en Tekst, Leiden.

27. Leiden University Library, Loket 1555–39. See also the notes from this letter found among Grotius' working papers in the Hague, Nationaal Archief, *Collectie Hugo de Groot, Supplement I* (ms. 1.10.35.02, no. 40, fol. 222–6). Excerpts of a French translation of the letter written in the hand of Grotius appear on fol. 223 recto. See also the transcript in CIPC, pp. 380–4, titled "Pars epistolae episcopi Malacensis ad regem" (Part of a letter by the Bishop of Melaka to the king); another English translation in IPC, pp. 517–22.
28. Ms. reads the abbreviation "Jobp".
29. Ms. reads the abbreviation "ar.len".
30. My translation; Dutch original with annotations.
31. The text in CIPC erroneously reads 800 instead of 600.
32. The *pardao de reales,* or simply *pardao* in English, was a coin minted in Goa and was in terms of value and fine silver content equivalent to the *peso de a ocho*, ryal-of-eight, or piece of eight. The latter was widely used in Asia during the early modern period and was minted in the Spanish Americas (present-day Mexico and Bolivia). The fine silver content was about 27 grammes and therefore equivalent in value to about 2.5 Holland guilders.
33. As a rule of thumb, a *bahar* is a measurement of weight equivalent to 3 *picul* or 300 *kati*, but there are notable local variations. Generally, the *bahar* weighed between 181 and 185 kilogrammes, but in Goa it was equivalent to 225 and in Surat 408 kilogrammes.
34. The term *Chincheo* is generically employed to the "Chinese" but usually refers to traders from Fujian (Amoy) who called at ports around Southeast Asia.
35. A similar observation is made by Admiral Cornelis Matelieff de Jonge in appendix 15.
36. This represents a free translation of the original but in essence captures what the Bishop is trying to say.
37. This is most probably a corrupted name or a transcription error.
38. See Bishop Ribeiro Gaio's rutter published by Jorge M. dos Santos Alves and Pierre-Yves Manguin, *O Roteiro das Cousas do Achem de D. João Ribeiro Gaio: Um olhar português sobre o norte de Samatra em finais do século XVI* (Lisbon: Comissão Nacional para as Comemorações dos Descobrimentos Portugueses, 1997).
39. A "million in gold" is known in Portuguese as a *conto de oro.* It is equivalent to one million cruzados. A cruzado was roughly equivalent to one pardao or one ryal-of-eight. As a rule of thumb, the difference in value between the cruzado and ryal-of-eight was about ten per cent, but in practice they were often traded as equivalents.
40. The actual text translates "… 400,000 cruzados from the one *conto de oro* [one million cruzados] which it already has in excess of the aforementioned 400,000."

41. Cunhale an ally of the Samorin of Calicut was according to François Pyrard de Laval feared "from the Cape of Hope to China as cruel and brutal pirate". He attacked Portuguese shipping along the Malabar Coast. After major campaigns had been launched against him and his family's stronghold in 1599, he was finally defeated by André Furtado de Mendonça and executed in 1600.
42. Francisco da Gama, the Portuguese viceroy of India between 1597–1600.
43. The Dutch translation used by Grotius appears in the Hague, Nationaal Archief, Collectie 102, Baron H. van Zuylen van Nyevelt, suppl. 2, no. 13 (2.21.179.01, no. 13), *Boeck Tracterende vande Wreede, Verradische ende Hostile proceduren der Portugesen In Oost-Indien,* p. 134, titled "Translaet van Een missive vanden Raet van Malacca, Aende gedeputeerde vande Hollantsche Schepen, die tot versekeringe vande veroverde portugysen aen seker Eylant (voor Mallacca gelegen) waeren afgesonden". A transcript of this Dutch translation was published in Coolhaas, "Een bron van het historische gedeelte van Hugo de Groot's De Jure Praedae", *BMH* 79 (1965): 531–2. The German translation appears in Amsterdam University Library, OTM OF–82–7 (supplement), p. 11; a transcript in Leiden, University Library, Fruin, *Aantekeningen op zijn werken,* Loket 1555–39, envelope titled "Documenta, heboorende bij het boeck van De Groot de Iure Praedae", fol. 3 recto, and in CIPC, p. 385, titled "Epistola senatus Malaccensis, A[nno] 1603 Mart[is] 9" (Letter of Melaka City Council, dated 9 March in the year 1603); another English translation is available in IPC, p. 523.
44. The German expression "Euer Laucht", abbreviated in the original printed text as "E.L." has been translated as "Your Honour".
45. My translation of the text from the Dutch and German originals with annotations.
46. The Dutch original used by Grotius is found in the Hague, Nationaal Archief, Collectie 102, Baron H. van Zuylen van Nyevelt, suppl. 2, no. 13 (2.21.179.01, no. 13), *Boeck Tracterende vande Wreede, Verradische ende Hostile proceduren der Portugesen In Oost-Indien,* pp. 135–6, "Translaet vande missive vanden gouverneur van Mallacca geschreven aenden Admirael Jacob Heemskerck". A transcript of this Dutch translation was published in Coolhaas, "Een bron van het historische gedeelte van Hugo de Groot's De Jure Praedae", *BMH* 79 (1965): 532–3. The German translation is found in Amsterdam University Library, OTM OF–82–7 (Appendix), p. 11 and a transcript in Fruin, *Aantekeningen op zijn werken,* Loket 1555–39, envelope titled "Documenta, behoorende bij het boeck van De Groots de Iure Praedae" (Documents belonging to Grotius' book *De Iure Praedae),* fol. 3 recto–4 recto; another transcript in CIPC, pp. 385–6 as "Epistola praefecti Malaccensis ad Jacobum Hemserckium eod[em] d[ato]" (Letter by the governor of Melaka to Jacob van Heemskerck bearing the same date); another English translation in IPC, pp. 524–5.

47. The Hague, Nationaal Archief, Collectie 102, Baron H. van Zuylen van Nyevelt, suppl. 2, no. 13 (2.21.179.01, no. 13), *Boeck Tracterende vande Wreede, Verradische ende Hostile proceduren der Portugesen In Oost-Indien,* p. 136.
48. My translation of the text from the Dutch and German with annotations.
49. Leiden, University Library, Loket 1555–39, Fruin, *Aantekeningen op zijn werken* in "Discours ende advertisement van de navolgende schepen", fol. 8 recto, mentions the presence of about 100 women (from among 750 souls) aboard the *Santa Catarina* at the time of Heemskerk's attack.
50. This passage alludes to the fate of 17 members of Admiral Jacob van Neck's crew at Macao. The majority were executed by the Portuguese in what was evidently a miscarriage of justice. See chapter 4.
51. The sentence marked in brackets does not feature in the German translation. The Dutch reads: "Daeromme en is gheen ghenoechsaeme redene, die ul. gheeft om oorsaecke te wesen van quaet te doen."
52. The Dutch translation used by Grotius appears in the Hague, Nationaal Archief, Collectie 102, Baron H. van Zuylen van Nyevelt, suppl. 2, no. 13 (2.21.179.01, no. 13), *Boeck Tracterende vande Wreede, Verradische ende Hostile proceduren der Portugesen In Oost-Indien,* pp. 139–40, "Een Missive vanden Capitein van het veroverde galioen Aenden Admiral Jacob Heemskerck". A transcript of this Dutch letter has been published in Coolhaas, "Een bron van het historische gedeelte van Hugo de Groot's De Jure Praedae", *BMH* 79 (1965): 535. The German translation appears in Amsterdam University Library, OTM OF–82–7 (appendix), p. 12 and a transcript in Fruin, *Aantekeningen op zijn werken,* Loket 1555–39, envelope titled "Documenta, behoorende bij het boeck van De Groot de Iure Praedae", fol. 5 recto–verso; another transcript in CIPC, p. 387 titled "Epistola capitanei captae galeonis ad Jacobum Hemskerckium A[nno] 1603 Mart[is] 24" (A letter by the captain of the captured galleon to Jacob van Heemskerk, dated 24 March, in the year 1603); an English translation in IPC, pp. 526–7. The type of the vessel indicated by the Latin term is technically incorrect and should read "carrack", not "galleon".
53. The Hague, Nationaal Archief, Collectie 102, Baron H. van Zuylen van Nyevelt, suppl. 2, no. 13 (2.21.179.0,1 no. 13), *Boeck Tracterende vande Wreede, Verradische ende Hostile proceduren der Portugesen In Oost-Indien,* p. 140.
54. My translation of the text from the Dutch and German originals with annotations.
55. The Dutch translation used by Grotius is found in the Hague, Nationaal Archief, Collectie 102, Baron H. van Zuylen van Nyevelt, suppl. 2, no. 13 (2.21.179.01 no. 13), *Boeck Tracterende vande Wreede, Verradische ende Hostile proceduren der Portugesen In Oost-Indien,* pp. 136–8. A transcript of the Dutch translation has been published in Coolhaas, "Een bron van

het historische gedeelte van Hugo de Groot's De Jure Praedae", *BMH* 79 (1965): 533–4. The German translation is featured in Amsterdam University Library, OTM OF–82–7, pp. 11–2, and a transcript in Fruin, *Aantekeningen op zijn werken,* Loket 1555–39, envelope titled "Documenta, heboorende bij het boeck van De Groot de Iure Praedae", fol. 4 recto-verso; another transcript in CIPC, pp. 386–7 as "Epistola altera ejusdem ad eundem A[anno] 1603 Mart. 26" (Second letter by the same to the same, dated 26 March in the year 1603); another English translation in IPC, pp. 525–6.

56. The Hague, Nationaal Archief, Collectie 102, Baron H. van Zuylen van Nyevelt, suppl. 2, no. 13 (2.21.179.01, no. 13), *Boeck Tracterende vande Wreede, Verradische ende Hostile proceduren der Portugesen In Oost-Indien,* p. 137.
57. The Hague, Nationaal Archief, Collectie 102, Baron H. van Zuylen van Nyevelt, suppl. 2, no. 13 (2.21.179.01, no. 13), *Boek Tracterende,* p. 138.
58. CIPC erroneously transcribes this word as "Cyffer", which makes no sense in the present context. The letter is clearly a capital "E" and not a "C", even if the typecasts appear very similar.
59. My translation of the text from the Dutch and German with annotations.
60. According to Coolhaas, "Een bron van het historische gedeelte van Hugo de Groot's De Jure Praedae", *BMH* 79 (1965): 533, note 4, one João Rui do Couto was indeed tried for his role in killing the 17 Dutch sailors at Macao.
61. CIPC erroneously reads "Eyffer" (effort, zeal) instead of "Cyffer" (number).
62. The Dutch translation correctly dates the letter with March 26 on p. 138. The printed German translation of 1606 erroneously prints the date of this letter as March 6 1603.
63. "Historische Verhael Vande treffelijkcke Reyse, gedaen naer de Oost-Indien ende China … door … Cornelis Matelief de Ionge", *BV* III: 30–1. A paraphrase of this historically important description of the Johor capital and royal residence Batu Sawar found in the travelogue of Matelieff de Jonge is also reproduced in François Valentijn, *Oud en Nieuw Oost-Indiën, Vervattende Een Naauwkeurige en Uitvoerige Verhandelinge van Nederlands Mogentheyd in de Gewesten, etc.*, 5 parts in 8 vols. (Dordrecht and Amsterdam: Johannes van Braam and Gerard Onder de Linden, 1724–6), part V, p. 335.
64. My translation from the Dutch original.
65. A copy of this Dutch-language description of Batu Sawar and Kota Seberang with commentary is also found in Pieter Gerritsz Rouffaer, "Was Malaka Emporium vóór 1400 A.D. genaamd Malajoer? En waar lag Woerawari, Ma-Hasin, Langka, Batoesawar?", *BKI* 77 (1921): 482–3.
66. See Rouffaer, "Was Malaka Emporium", p. 483, where the depth of the water is given at 5–5.5 metres and the width of the river at about 90 metres.

67. This observation implies that the waters of the Johor River at Batu Sawar were affected by changes in the oceanic tides, but the location was too far removed from the sea for salt water to enter the river with the incoming tide. See also See Rouffaer, "Was Malaka Emporium", p. 483.
68. Reference is here most probably to supplementary fortifications which cover the flank of another fortification structure, similar to the ones found at the archaeological site in Johor Lama. These blocked blind spots at the fort Kota Seberang, probably because of a bend in the river or another natural feature. Concerning the bend in the Johor River near Batu Sawar, see Rouffaer, "Was Malaka Emporium vóór 1400 A.D. genaamd Malajoer? En waar lag Woerawari, Ma-Hasin, Langka, Batoesawar?", *BKI* 77 (1921): 438–9.
69. On this point see esp. the explanation in Milner, *Kerajaan: Malay Political Culture on the Eve of Colonial Rule*, p. 7, "Moreover, a restless, frontier spirit characterized Malay land tenure. Territories were not owned by villages, clans or familes. Rather, although the Raja of a state had 'absolute property in the soil', the proprietary right over land was created by the 'clearing of land followed by continuous occupation'. The absence of a concept of permanent ownership is expressed in the fact that the literal meaning in the Malay phrase for 'land sale' is simply 'return of expenses'. Land was used rather than possessed."
70. "Historische Verhael Vande treffelijkcke Reyse, gedaen naer de Oost-Indien ende China … door … Cornelis Matelief de Ionge", *BV* III: 10–1.
71. Johor's diplomatic mission was dispatched to the Netherlands, headed by one Megat Mansur, who in one period document is described as a "young nobleman" close to the King of Johor. Megat Mansur passed away during the long sea voyage to Europe, but other, arguably inferior members of the embassy survived and returned to Johor with the fleet of Admiral Cornelis Matelieff de Jonge in 1605–6. See Leiden, University Library, Loket 1555–39, Fruin, *Aantekeningen op zijn werken* in "Discours ende advertisement van de navolgende schepen", fol. 8 recto. See also Borschberg, *The Singapore and Melaka Straits,* chapters 2 and 5, pp. 60 *et seq.* and 157 *et seq.*; Borschberg, "The Johor-VOC Alliance and the Twelve Years Truce", *IILJ Working Paper* 8 (2009): 14.
72. My translation from the Dutch original.
73. This opening of the letter is almost certainly a preamble, written in the third person singular, and conforms to Malay custom and verbal forms of politeness. The preamble appears to be a response to an earlier letter or despatch sent to Raja Bongsu by Cornelis Matelieff de Jonge or possibly also Stadholder Prince Maurice of Orange, the latter whom he addresses as the "King of Holland".
74. According to the travelogue of Admiral Matelieff, Raja Bongsu arrived on 17 May 1606, with 300 men. See appendix 11 and "Historische Verhael

Vande treffelijkcke Reyse, gedaen naer de Oost-Indien ende China ... door ... Cornelis Matelief de Ionge", *BV* III: 11.

75. "Historische Verhael Vande treffelijkcke Reyse, gedaen naer de Oost-Indien ende China ... door ... Cornelis Matelief de Ionge", *BV* III: 11–2.
76. Borschberg, "The Johor-VOC Alliance and the Twelve Years Truce", *IILJ Working Paper* 8 (2009): 13–6; Winstedt, "A History of Johore", *JMBRAS* 10, 3 (1932): 52.
77. My translation from the Dutch original.
78. The following passage concerning king 'Ala'uddin is also featured in Rouffaer, "Was Malaka Emporium vóór 1400 A.D. genaamd Malajoer?", *BKI* 77 (1921): 445.
79. The following description of Raja Bongsu, alias Raja Seberang, is also reproduced in Rouffaer, "Was Malaka Emporium vóór 1400 A.D. genaamd Malajoer?", *BKI* 77 (1921): 445–6.
80. This fortified settlement is described in more detail in appendix 1.
81. This is a reference to his skin colour. A similar observation is made in the German-language description of Johann Verken. He belonged to the fleet of Pieter Willemsz Verhoeff and visited Johor in 1609. See appendix 16.
82. This understanding of the Dutch term "discreet" suggested by Rouffaer, "Was Malaka Emporium vóór 1400 A.D. genaamd Malajoer?", *BKI* 77 (1921): 446.
83. It is not certain what the name "Malacca" exactly refers to here. It could be taken as a reference to the town, the region around the town, or in line with formal and colloquial usage in the Netherlands during the early modern period, also the whole of the Malay Peninsula. It should also be noted that several documents from both the Portuguese and Dutch side echo the Johor monarchs' efforts to position themselves as the heirs of the Melaka Sultanate. This is implicit from Admiral Cornelis Matelieff's two treaties with Johor and later also from recorded discussions between Admiral Pieter Willemsz. Verhoeff and Raja Bongsu of January 1609. For a summary of these records that, among other issues, touch upon the legacy of Melaka, see esp. *De reis van de vloot van Pieter Willemszoon Verhoeff naar Azië*, ed. van Opstall, I, pp. 252–3, entry for 19 January 1609. See also Borschberg, "Jacques de Coutre as a Source for the Early Seventeenth-Century History of Singapore, the Johor River and the Straits", *JMBRAS* 81, 2 (2008): 90, translation from the Spanish *Vida de Jacques de Coutre*, written with reference to the situation in the 1590s, "The King [of Johor] is named *Raxale* [Raja Ali]. His grandfather was the King of Malacca, which was an ancient city [polity] spanning 12 *leguas* [along the coastline]. He gave himself the title 'Emperor of the Malays', which lapsed on his death and has not been revived." See also Borschberg, "Jacques de Coutre", p. 90, note 97, citing the letter by Dom Paulo Lima de Pereira to King Philip II/I dated 28 November 1587, "Raja

Ali, King of Johor, who among the kings of the south bears the title 'Emperor of the Malay Kings'." My translations from the original Dutch and Portuguese sources. See also Borschberg, *The Singapore and Melaka Straits,* pp. 209–28, esp. p. 226.

84. The interpretation of the Dutch wording "en laetter niet al" as "ontbreekt er niet geheel" is based on the interpretation suggested in Rouffaer, "Was Malaka Emporium vóór 1400 A.D. genaamd Malajoer?", *BKI* 77 (1921): 446.

85. This description of the Raja Laut is also found in Valentijn, *Oud en Nieuw Oost-Indiën*, part 5, p. 331; Netscher, *De Nederlanders in Djohor en Siak,* p. 11, and Rouffaer, "Was Malaka Emporium vóór 1400 A.D. genaamd Malajoer?", *BKI* 77 (1921): 446, note 2. Rouffaer concluded that the Raja Laut is almost certainly the same individual as the *laksamana* or admiral of Johor. See Rouffaer, "Was Malaka", p. 488, note 1.

86. "Historische Verhael Vande treffelijkcke Reyse, gedaen naer de Oost-Indien ende China ... door ... Cornelis Matelief de Ionge", *BV* III: 13–4. The two treaties are also found in Heeres, "Corpus Diplomaticum", *BKI* 57 (1907): 42–7 and in Netscher, *De Nederlanders in Djohor en Siak,* p. 2, and Valentijn, *Nieuw en Oud Oost-Indiën,* part 5, pp. 331–2. (This source only reproduces the treaty of 17 May and not the agreement of 23 September 1606.) For an earlier English translation of the treaty of 17 May, see Winstedt, "A History of Johore", *JMBRAS* 10, 3 (1932): 31–3. The following transcript represents the text version as found in BV. Only significant variations in wording have been provided to capture the differences between the extent copies of the treaties. The present transcript ignores the numerous differences in orthography, capitalisation and punctuation. The text of the treaty broadly follows an established format pledging to sustain hostilities against the Iberian powers, making specific provisions for the felling or harvesting of wood (to facilitate the repair of ships and the gathering of firewood), excluding foreign traders in the territory under contract, as well as the handling and extradition of criminals. For a very similar treaty in both wording and spirit, see the agreement signed between Olivier van Vivere and Aceh on 17 June 1607 found in Heeres, "Corpus Diplomaticum", *BKI* 57 (1907): 48–50. Concerning the wider diplomatic, strategic and commercial backdrop leading up to this first Dutch-Johor treaty, see also Borschberg, "The Seizure of the Santa Catarina Revisited", *JSEAS* 33, 1 (2002): 59–60. The current texts reads as printed in Commelin; H is the variant text in Heeres' *Corpus Diplomaticum.* Valentijn's *Nieuw en Oud Oost-Indië,* part V, pp. 331–2, does not actually reproduce the text of the treaty verbatim, but only loosely paraphrases the individual articles. Major variations and readings are provided under V. A summary of the articles of the Johor-VOC treaty of May 1606 is also found in the second letter of Jacques l'Hermite de Jonge to his father which is featured as an appendix

to the "Historische Verhael Vande treffelijkcke Reyse, gedaen naer de Oost-Indien ende China … door … Cornelis Matelief de Ionge", *BV* III: 152–3.

87. The negotiations between Matelieff, Raja Bongsu and the *bendahara* on or around 2 October 1606 are described in "Historische Verhael Vande treffelijkcke Reyse, gedaen naer de Oost-Indien ende China … door … Cornelis Matelief de Ionge", *BV* III: 31–3. According to Matelieff's travelogue, the initiative to sign the supplementary treaty clearly came from the Johorese side.
88. The articles signed by Matelieff with Johor in May 1606 are in parts almost identical to the treaty ratified by Vice-Admiral Olivier van Vivere with Aceh on 17 January 1607. See Heeres, "Corpus Diplomaticum", *BKI* 57 (1907): 48–50.
89. V: Zee-Voogd.
90. V: omits text in brackets.
91. V: omits word.
92. V: omits text in brackets.
93. V: Algemeine Staten.
94. V: omits text in brackets.
95. H: capiteijnen.
96. V: omits text in brackets. V only speaks generally of "wy", that is we, the Dutch, without mentioning any specific institution or officer.
97. H: verstrecken – evidently a typographical error.
98. H: landen.
99. H: omitted.
100. V: omits text in brackets.
101. V: omits text in brackets.
102. V: omits text in brackets.
103. V: Land-Voogd.
104. H: (reverses the wording) gehouden, ende vervolght worden.
105. H: omitted
106. V: verblyf.
107. H: daer.
108. H: word added
109. H: hij
110. H: wordt.
111. C: aensjine – evidently a typographical error.
112. H: de
113. H: voorschreven.
114. V: … dog geenzins zoo een van beide tegen andre quam te Oorlogen…
115. V: bedrevene misdaden.
116. V: (adds) zich daar wilden verbergen.
117. H: Coning. N: Coningen.

118. H: adds word.
119. H: (reads) "Tweede accoordt gemaeckt tusschen den heer admiraell Cornelis Matelieff de jonge uyt den name en van wegen d'Ed.en Mogende H.ren Staten generaell der Vereenighde Nederlanden ten eenre ende den doorlughtigen en manhaften Koningh van Johor ter andere zyde desen 23.e 7.ber jnt jaer onses Heeren Jesu Christij 1606 jn de stadt Batosauwer." (Second agreement concluded between Admiral Cornelis Matelieff de Jonge in the name and on behalf of the High Mighty Gentlemen States General of the United Provinces on the one side and the great and manly King of Johor on the other, [on] this day the 23 of September in the year of our Lord Jesus Christ, 1606, in the city of Batu Sawar.)
120. H: omits words in brackets.
121. H: onderhouden worden.
122. H: adds words in brackets.
123. H: bevaeren – obviously a copying error.
124. My translation from the Dutch original.
125. This provision is almost identical to article 5 of the VOC treaty with Aceh of 17 January 1607, Heeres, "Corpus Diplomaticum", *BKI* 57 (1907): 49, "Sullen de voorschreven Heeren Staten oock vermogen in alle des Coninghs landen hout te haelen ende te houwen tot bouwingh van de schepen ende noodrufftigheijt van haere woonplaets" (The said Gentlemen States [General] shall be permitted to harvest and fell wood in all of the kings lands for the construction of ships as well as for covering the needs of their residences).
126. Compare this with article 3 of the VOC treaty with Aceh of 17 January 1607, Heeres, "Corpus Diplomaticum", *BKI* 57 (1907): 49, "Sullen de vasalen van de Heeren Staten voorschreven haere schepen ende goederen, t zij van wadt plaetsen dat zij komen, ook wederom versonden worden, mogen disponeeren, sonder dat Sijne Maijesteijt daerijets op sall te seggen hebben nogh eenige toll daeraff te nemen, nogh uijt nogh in." (The vassals of the said Gentlemen States [General] shall be able to dispose of their ships and their goods, no matter from where they may come from, and shall be able to take them out again. His Majesty shall have no authority over these and shall not be able to levy any tolls on them, whether they be brought in or taken out.)
127. The original term "Hollander" is taken to mean any citizen of the Dutch Republic, not just a person from the province of Holland.
128. See article 4 of the VOC treaty with Aceh of 17 January 1607, Heeres, "Corpus Diplomaticum", *BKI* 57 (1907): 49, "Sall ook sijne Maij.t niet toelaeten, datter eenige Hollanders, Europische volckeren offte naekommelingen in eenige van zijne landen sullen mogen handelen, offte zullen bescheijdt van onse coningh moeten brengen ende het zelve niet hebbende, sullen als vijanden gehouden en vervolght worden." (His Majesty [of Aceh] shall also not permit that any Hollander, European peoples or their progeny trade in his lands,

lest they have permission from our "king", and should they not have this, they shall be deemed and persecuted as enemies.) As mentioned elsewhere the "King of Holland" is common a reference to the Dutch States General in treaties and correspondence with Asian overlords, and in rare instances it can be taken as a reference to the Stadholder.

129. In fact, according to the travelogue of Admiral Matelieff, most of the lands surrounding the town of Melaka had been devastated by fire deliberately set by the Portuguese of Melaka. See "Historische Verhael Vande treffelijkcke Reyse, gedaen naer de Oost-Indien ende China … door … Cornelis Matelief de Ionge", *BV* III: 9, 15.

130. This is almost identical to article 10 of the the VOC treaty with Aceh of 17 January 1607, Heeres, "Corpus Diplomaticum", *BKI* 57 (1907): 50, "Hier en tegen sullen de Heeren Staten sijne Mayesteijt helpen met alle maght naer uijtterste vermogen, om de Portugesen en Spanjiaerden, haerer beijder vijanden, alle mogelijcke affbreuck te doen; ende soo ijmandt van de partijen oorlogh aennam tegen ymandt anders als de Portugesen ende Spangiaerden zall de andere partije niet gehouden wesen deselve te assisteren, dan alleenlijck in defensie." (The Gentlemen States [General] shall assist His Majesty [of Aceh] with all their power and ability to inflict as much damage as possible on the Portuguese and the Spanish who are enemies of both. If one party should enter into war against an enemy other than the Portuguese and the Spanish the other party shall not be obliged to render assistance, except for defence.)

131. Compare this with article 6 of the the VOC treaty with Aceh of 17 January 1607, Heeres, "Corpus Diplomaticum", *BKI* 57 (1907): 49, "Sal oock geene van d'beijde partijen vermogen paijs te maeken met de koninghk van Spangien sonder breeder consent." (Neither party shall be able to make peace with the king of Spain without unanimous consent.) The actual Dutch text reads: "breeder consent" or literally translated "broader consent". In an editorial note, Heeres suggests that the text should perhaps read "beider" rather than "breeder", that is as much as to say: no peace may be concluded with the King of Spain without the agreement of both parties. My translation here is admittedly free, but certainly captures the spirit of this clause.

132. See similarly article 7 of the the VOC treaty with Aceh of 17 January 1607, Heeres, "Corpus Diplomaticum", *BKI* 57 (1907): 49, "Soo wie eenige schandale in eenige religions saeken geefft, die sall aengeklaeght ende gestrafft worden bij sijne overheijt, daer hij onder sorteert, zoo well van d'eene als van de andere zijde." (If someone commits a scandal in matters of religion, he shall be accused and punished by the overlord to whom he is subjected, no matter if this be the one or the other party.)

133. The Dutch term *schuld* is multi-faceted and could also be translated more generally as "guilt".

134. A similar provision is found in article 8 of the the VOC treaty with Aceh of 17 January 1607, Heeres, "Corpus Diplomaticum", *BKI* 57 (1907): 49.
135. Raja Bongsu and the *bendahara* of Johor are said to have pushed for the drafting and implementation of this second agreement. See "Historische Verhael Vande treffelijkcke Reyse, gedaen naer de Oost-Indien ende China … door … Cornelis Matelief de Ionge", *BV* III: 31.
136. "Historische Verhael Vande treffelijkcke Reyse, gedaen naer de Oost-Indien ende China … door … Cornelis Matelief de Ionge", *BV* III: 31. Discussions between Admiral Matelieff, Raja Bongsu and the Johor *bendahara* identified as possible locations the region around the Johor River, Bintan, Lingga and Karimun.
137. RH, pp. 237–65. This manuscript was originally found among the working papers of Grotius and was sold at the 1864 auction under part I, lot 25. (See Noordhoff, *Beschrijving van … papieren afkomstig van Huig de Groot,* p. 15.) A second transcript was published in *BMH* 6 (1883): 223–58. There are at least two (variant) copies of this memorial available in the Nationaal Archief van Nederland in the Hague. The text transcribed by Frederiks in 1871 derives from a copy filed in the *Collectie Hugo de Groot, Supplement I* (1.10.35.02, no. 40, fols. 486–510). In the context of the present study which focuses on the documents and materials Grotius had his disposal around the time of writing *De Iure Praedae* and revising *Mare Liberum* for the press, this is the more important text variant. For this reason it is reproduced here in the original Dutch together with its first translation into English. A second very similar but not identical copy is found among the working papers of the Archief Oldenbarnevelt (3.01.14, no. 3104, fols. 53 recto–60 recto). The latter has been transcribed in Rietbergen, *De eerste Landvoogd Pieter Both,* II, pp. 196–211.
138. "Historische Verhael Vande treffelijcke Reyse, gedaen naer de Oost-Indien ende China … door … Cornelis Matelief de Ionge", *BV* III: 72–6, "Discours ghestelt by den Admirael C. Matelief op den Staet ende handel van Indien" (Discourse written by Admiral C. Matelieff on the state and trade of India). This memorial is not featured among the transcripts prepared Frederiks and published in the *Rotterdamsche Historiebladen.*
139. RH, pp. 204–357.
140. RH, p. 237.
141. RH, p. 238.
142. RH, p. 239.
143. RH, p. 239, erroneously reads *nodichst evan.*
144. RH, p. 240.
145. RH, p. 241.
146. RH, p. 242.
147. RH, p. 242 reads: *de naenloop.*
148. RH, p. 243.

149. RH, p. 244.
150. Erroneously reads *poinet.*
151. RH, p. 245.
152. RH, p. 246.
153. RH, p. 247.
154. RH, p. 248.
155. RH, p. 249.
156. RH, p. 250.
157. RH, p. 250, reads "elex".
158. RH, p. 251.
159. RH, p. 252.
160. RH, p. 253.
161. RH, p. 254.
162. RH, p. 255.
163. RH, p. 256.
164. RH, p. 256, a lone letter "v" eliminated from the transcript here.
165. RH, p. 257.
166. RH, p. 258.
167. RH, p. 259.
168. RH, p. 260.
169. RH, p. 261.
170. RH, p. 262.
171. RH, p. 263.
172. RH, p. 264.
173. Translated from the original Dutch by Dr. Corinna Vermeulen, Noctua Taal en Tekst, Leiden. The annotations are mine.
174. The Dutch text is incomprehensible here. Perhaps the sense should be that the Indians, feeling liberated from the Portuguese, make use of the fact that there are two kinds of merchants on their market.
175. According to Gaastra, *De geschiedenis van de VOC,* pp. 30–40, Matelieff's epistolary memorials were taken seriously by the powers that be in the nascent Dutch Republic, especially also by the VOC directors, the Heren XVII. He clearly recognised the substantial advantages and benefits that derived from a centralised system that the Portuguese had already successfully established in Goa. Matelieff's proposal for a rendezvous in the East Indies should be seen against the backdrop of seeking to secure the same financial, commercial and administrative benefits for the VOC in Asia. Concerning the role of Portuguese Goa as a model for the Dutch, see also Roelofsen, "Hugo de Groot en de VOC", *De Hollandse Jaren van Hugo de Groot,* ed. Nellen and Trapman, p. 57.
176. The Sunda Strait is called the Strait of Banten throughout the original Dutch text. The present-day name has been used here in order not to confuse the reader.

177. *De derde reis,* ed. de Booy, II, pp. 44–6. In the travelogue of van Caerden (p. 46) it is reported that, due to contrary winds, the ship set sail for Celebes on 23 January 1608.
178. This almost certainly a reference to the Heren XVII or "Gentlemen Seventeen", the board of directors of the VOC.
179. Frederick was the older brother of Cornelis de Houtman, known from the second voyage of the Dutch to the East Indies. Frederick had been imprisoned in Aceh and as a result of his long exposure to the region came to speak Malay fluently. Following his brief return to the Netherlands in 1603 he published an influential dictionary and grammar of the Malay language. Frederick de Houtman served as the Dutch governor of Ambon after its takeover from the Portuguese in 1605 until 1611. Concerning Matelieff's contacts with Governor de Houtman in 1607, see also de Jonge, *Opkomst van het Nederlandsch gezag in Oost-Indië*, III, p. 126.
180. This is almost certainly a reference to one of the major naval campaigns of Furtado de Mendonça in the early 1600s. He launched a fresh campaign in 1603 to oust the Dutch from the Malukus and Sunda. In the same year he assumed the position of governor of Melaka, and launched several campaigns against Johor. For an overview of the events in Johor and the region at large between 1603–5, see Borschberg, *The Singapore and Melaka Straits,* pp. 67–94. Concerning the developments in the Malukus and Banda, see the "Historische Verhael Vande treffelijkcke Reyse, gedaen naer de Oost-Indien ende China … door … Cornelis Matelief de Ionge", *BV* III: 59.
181. That is he converted to Islam.
182. The ship's name in English is *The Great Sun.*
183. This is also written in Matelieff's travelogue for 4 and 14 December 1607, that the ship *Groote Sonne* was sent to Jayakerta (Jacatra) (setting sail from Banten on 3 December) to take on an unspecified amount of *arak.* It was to call at Gresik (Java) or Makassar to purchase rice. Thereafter, the crew was to set course for Ambon and ultimately Ternate where a cargo of cloves could be procured. See "Historische Verhael", *BV* III: 113, 126–7, 130; Borschberg, *The Singapore and Melaka Straits,* pp. 102, 286 note 185.
184. This is a derogatory reference to the local population.
185. Sago is a starchy substance extracted from the trunk of the sago palm. Like rice, it was — and still is — consumed in parts of Southeast Asia as a staple food.
186. The Dutch term *noten* (literally "nuts") is a reference to nutmeg.
187. This included the young King of Ternate, who just as his brother and also the King of Jilolo, was reportedly in his early teens. The king (and his people) returned to the island after Matelieff and his ships arrived. See "Historische Verhael Vande treffelijkcke Reyse, gedaen naer de Oost-Indien ende China … door … Cornelis Matelief de Ionge", *BV* III: 63–4.
188. See also "Historische Verhael", pp. 64, 66.

189. According to the testimony of Matelieff, the Dutch fortress at Malaya was situated on the northeastern coast of the island.
190. See also "Historische Verhael Vande treffelijkcke Reyse, gedaen naer de Oost-Indien ende China … door … Cornelis Matelief de Ionge", *BV* III: 63–4.
191. See "Historische Verhael", pp. 63, 65.
192. See also *De derde reis,* ed. de Booy, II, p. 46.
193. That is when there is little or no wind.
194. Van Caerden and his ships did reach the Malukus, but he was captured by the Spanish near Ternate, set free on payment of a ransom, but later recaptured and brought to Manila for trial. He was sentenced to hard labour.
195. That is Batu Sawar, variously known from Dutch and Portuguese sources as "New Johor".
196. See "Historische Verhael Vande treffelijkcke Reyse, gedaen naer de Oost-Indien ende China … door … Cornelis Matelief de Ionge", *BV* III: 29–30. The date indicated is 18 September 1606. The fortification of the royal residence Batu Sawar is mentioned as the first of four demands made by Matelieff. See similarly Jacques l'Hermite de Jonge's second letter to father which printed as an appendix to the travelogue of Matelieff, "Historische Verhael", *BV* III: 173. The date provided by Commelin has been erroneously given as 18 September 1607.
197. Earlier rumors reported in Matelieff's travelogue (entry of 30 December 1607) claim that the Portuguese had launched a naval campaign against Aceh with two galleys and 20 foists over a period of six weeks. They also are reported to have "burnt down Johor". See "Historische Verhael", *BV* III: 129.
198. Matelieff's travelogue reports that the fiscal Martin Aep (Apius) was dispatched on the *Erasmus* to Johor in November 1607. Apius expressed concern that the Johor monarch was about to make peace with the Portuguese and even managed to procure a copy of the draft clauses. One article reportedly stated that the Johor monarch was to hand over (*overleveren*) all Dutchman to the Portuguese authorities. As Apius was not of the opinion that the agreement would be implemented, Matelieff resolved that priority should be given to fortifying of the Malukus. See "Historische Verhael Vande treffelijkcke Reyse, gedaen naer de Oost-Indien ende China … door … Cornelis Matelief de Ionge", *BV* III: 131.
199. The "young king" is a litteral translation from the Malay "Raja Bongsu" who of course is also known as Raja Seberang and later also Raja di Ilir.
200. 'Ala'uddin Ri'ayat Shah of Johor, the elder brother of Raja Bongsu and titular monarch of Johor, is also described in Matelieff's travelogue as a drunkard. See appendix 13.
201. This is presumably a reference to the ryal-of-eight (piece of eight), a silver coin minted in the Spanish Americas and commonly used among European and Asian traders during the early modern period.

202. The prahu or *proa* is a type of vessel that can be either sailed or rowed. They were used as vessels of burden and also in naval warfare in many parts of Asia. The galley is a rowed vessel that was deployed in the Mediterranean and also around parts of Asia. Galleys mainly served as war ships and feature one or two masts with rows of oars on each side.
203. According to instructions issued by the Heren XVII to Matelieff, he was to ascertain the possibility of tapping into the China trade by piggybacking onto a Siamese tributary mission to the Chinese court. See also Duyvendak, "The First Siamese Embassy to Holland", *T'Oung Pao* 32 (1936): 289.
204. The original reads *Chincheo,* a name commonly used in sources of European provenance, especially Portuguese and Spanish documents, for the port of Zhangzhou, or the Amoy Coast of China in general. The term is also generically employed as a synonym for "Chinese".
205. The trade between China and Manila in the late 16th and the beginning of the 17th century is described in detail by Antonio de Morga, *The Philippine Islands, Moluccas, Siam, Cambodia, Japan and China at the Close of the Sixteenth Century*, ed. L.V. de Torres and H.E.J. Stanley (London: Hakluyt Society, 1868) and is also mentioned in the *Itinerario* of Jan Huyghen van Linschoten. See also Borschberg, "The Seizure of the *Santa Catarina* Revisited", *JSEAS* 33, 1 (2002): 38–9, esp. note 33.
206. Cornelis Specx had sailed with the fleet of Wybrandt van Warwijk to the East Indies and was charged with attending to the Company's business in Siam. He passed away on the return voyage to Europe on or around 11 June 1608. See "Historische Verhael", *BV* III: 137.
207. The "ambassadors" in question here are almost certainly the members of the first ever embassy sent by the King of Siam to the west. They are known to have travelled with Matelieff's return voyage to Europe, even if such diplomatic missions from Asia were greatly discouraged by the Dutch Company because of the high costs they entailed. See the classic articles by Pelliot, "Les Relations du Siam et de la Hollande en 1608", *T'Oung Pao* 32 (1936): 223–9, Duyvendak, "The First Siamese Embassy to Holland", *T'Oung Pao* 32 (1936): 285–92. For the account in the travelogue of Matelieff, see "Historische Verhael", *BV* III: 127, which reports that the ambassadors arrived in Banten in the company of Cornelis Specx "from Siam".
208. The original document reads *Petapoly* an older name commonly used in sources of European provenance for Nizampatnam.
209. Van Caerden reached Calicut on 13 October 1607 and learnt that Steven van der Hagen had visited the port only days before his arrival, offering gifts to the Great Samorin and holding discussions there. See *De derde reis,* ed. de Booy, II, pp. 133–5.
210. This is evidently a reference to the "letters by the King of Spain" which van Caerden had originally seized from a carrack outbound to Goa from

Lisbon. In January 1608 van Caerden passed these letters to Matelieff at their meeting in Banten. See also the explanation in appendix 1.

211. Matelieff secured supplies of free timber through the treaties signed with Johor (1606, see appendix 13) and Aceh (1607). The latter was signed by his deputy, Vice-Admiral Olivier van Vivere.
212. Johannes Verken, "Molukkenreise 1607–1612", in *Reisebeschreibungen von Deutschen Beamten und Kriegsleuten im Dienst der Niederländisch West- und Ost-Indischen Kompanien, 1602–1797*, ed. S.P. l'Honoré Naber, II, pp. 58–9.
213. My translation from the German original.
214. CC, pp. 89–93, annexe 30, "Discours de Grotius au Roi Jacques I du 6 avril 1613". According to the reference given by Clark and van Eysinga, the present text should be found in the State Papers, Colonial East Indies, 1513–1615, number 645, annexes C and D. Several e-mail communications with the archivists at the Public Records Office in London, however, have confirmed that the reference is evidently false and attempts to locate the originals have so far proven futile. In the course of preparing the English translation, some questions arose about the accuracy of the original, or the transcript prepared by Clark and van Eysinga. The Latin texts with some editorial comments and corrections by the translator, Dr. Corinna Vermeulen, feature in appendix 17, together with its translation into English.
215. CC, p. 90.
216. If this is the correct reading, there is a playful allusion to *Germanasque*, which alternatively may be the correct text. (Translator's note.)
217. This term, according to Clark and van Eysinga, was added later to the text.
218. According to an editorial comment by Clark and van Eysinga, this word should be omitted from the text.
219. CC, p. 91.
220. The lost manuscript seems to have read *potissimi* here; reading *potissimae* would make more sense, and I have translated accordingly. (Translator's note.)
221. CC, p. 92.
222. A different punctuation yields a better sense, especially in the light of *acciperent* (not *accepissent*). The translation is based on reading "quod uti ipsi visum nostra opera...", in which case *uti* is not the collateral form of *ut* but the present infinitive of the verb *utor*. (Translator's note.)
223. CC, p. 93.
224. Corrected from *reliquantur* in the edition. (Translator's note.)
225. Translated from the Latin original by Dr. Corinna Vermeulen, Noctua Taal en Tekst, Leiden. The annotations are mine.
226. Reference is made here to the wedding of Frederick V of the Palatinate (later the "Winter King" during the Bohemian phase of the Thirty Years

War) with the Stuart princess Mary on 7 April 1613. See Nellen, *Hugo de Groot. Een leven in strijd om de vrede*, p. 133.

227. See the letter to the Dutch States General to Dutch ambassador Caron, dated 23 March 1613, in CC, pp. 82–3, and letter of the Dutch States General to King James I/VI dated 23 March 1613, CC, pp. 83–4; and the letter of English ambassador Ralph Winwood to King James I/VI dated 6 April 1613, CC, pp. 84–5. Grotius was evidently selected by the Dutch States General as a deputy to this conference in the proverbial last minute.

228. The Latin can also mean: "not less than we do ourselves". (Translator's note.)

229. Grotius speaks here of the preparations for the earliest Dutch voyages under Cornelis de Houtman and and later Jacob van Neck at the close of the 16th century. Direct Dutch navigation to the East Indies was spurred by the publication of Jan Huyghen van Linschoten's *Reysgeschrift* and *Itinerario* that contained in translation detailed navigational instructions of Portuguese provenance.

230. Reference is made here to the attack on Banten by the Portuguese armada under the command of André Furtado de Mendonça in January 1602. The Dutch had been tipped off by Chinese merchants of the imminent approach of the Portuguese fleet, thus greatly enhancing the prospects of a successful Dutch repulse. See Borschberg, "The Seizure of the *Santa Catarina* Revisited", *JSEAS* 33, 1 (2002): 51.

231. According to Grotius' work *De Iure Praedae*, the Portuguese periodically attacked Johor, such as in the period immediately preceding the seizure of the *Santa Catarina* in February 1603, as well as in the following trading season (October 1603) when Vice-Admiral Pietersz van Enkhuysen engaged the ships of Estêvão Teixeira de Macedo in the Johor River estuary and the Singapore Strait. Other episodes followed in the period leading up to the implementation of the Twelve Years Truce in Asia. See Borschberg, *The Singapore and Melaka Straits*, pp. 79–90.

232. Reference is made here to the founding of the VOC in 1602 via the amalgamation of six trading firms known as the voorcompagniën.

233. The VOC's first *octrooi* or charter established the company as a standing partnership for a period of twenty-one years, granting a monopoly of trade East of the Cape of Good Hope. The charter area broadly covered the lands in and around Indian and Pacific Oceans.

234. See classicly the treaty concluded between Admiral Cornelis Matelieff de Jonge and the King of Ternate dated 26 May 1607, in "Corpus Diplomaticum Neërlando-Indicum", ed. Heeres, *BKI* 57 (1907): 50–3, esp. p. 52, article 10, "Sullen geene nagelen moogen verkoopen, 't zy aen wadt natie offte volck hetselve soude mogen wesen dat alleen aen den factoor die van wegen de Heeren Staten in Ternate sall woonen ende dat tot

sulcken prijs als de Heeren Staten sullen ordineeren ende met den Koningh accordeeren." (That the [the Ternatans] shall not be able to sell cloves, no matter from what nation or people the [purchasers] may be, except only to the factor (who shall live in Ternate) of the Gentlemen States [General] and at such a price as the Gentlemen States [General] shall agree with the [said] king.) My translation from the original Dutch. For the broader historical context of this treaty, see also Borschberg, "The Johor-VOC Alliance and the Twelve Years Truce", *IILJ Working Paper* 8 (2009); and Gaastra, *De geschiedenis van de VOC,* p. 45.

235. This appears to be a specifically a reference to the political situation in the Malukus or "Spice Islands".
236. Such as notably Ambon in 1605 or Solor in 1613.
237. Admiral Matelieff reported to Grotius in a letter dated 14 December 1613, BW 309, p. 286, that the Spaniards had returned the King of Ternate to his island. An earlier letter by Matelieff may very well have been the source of Grotius' information concerning this development.
238. This is a reference to Admiral Matelieff's seaborne assault on Portuguese Melaka in 1606, as well as Admiral van Caerden's attacks on Portuguese positions in Mozambique in 1607. See Borschberg, *The Singapore and Melaka Straits,* pp. 157–64.
239. Admiral Matelieff engaged the Portuguese armada in two major naval battles that took place in the Melaka Strait in 1606.
240. This is a reference to the Twelve Years Truce concluded in Antwerp on 9 April 1610. Concerning the validity and implementation of the agreement in Southeast Asia, see Borschberg, "The Johor-VOC Alliance and the Twelve Years Truce", *IILJ Working Paper* 8 (2009): 1–11.
241. The Twelve Years Truce was to come into effect in Asia one year after its ratification in Europe, that is on 10 April 1610.
242. Juan de Silva served as the governor of the Spanish Philippines. He scored a number of successes against the VOC in the Philippines and the Malukus. His armada was slated to join with Portuguese ships, rushed by the viceroy in Goa, with the objective of battling the Dutch in the Malukus. The joint operation failed, not least because Juan de Silva passed away mysteriously in Melaka in April 1616. For a background on the failed joint Luso-Spanish offensive, see Borschberg, *The Singapore and Melaka Straits,* pp. 137–56.
243. This is almost certainly a reference to the naval battle in the course of which Vice-Admiral François Wittert and ships under his command were defeated by Juan de Silva's forces on 25 April 1610, in other words two weeks after the Twelve Years Truce was slated to take effect in the Asian theatre. Wittert had attacked Spanish positions in the Philippines and the Malukus in a series of naval operations. See the older narrative by Norman MacLeod, *De Oost-Indische Compagnie als Zeemogendheid in Azië,* 2 vols. (Rijswijk: Blankwaardt

& Schoonhoven, 1927), I, pp. 73–84, esp. pp. 80–4; and also Borschberg, "The Johor-VOC Alliance and the Twelve Years Truce", *IILJ Working Paper* 8 (2009): 8–9.

244. The VOC memorial of 11 April 1608 and the Twelve Years Truce of 1609 generally aimed at opening up ports and emporia in Africa and Asia to the Dutch. The Americas, however, were to remain closed or off-limits because, unlike the situation in Africa and especially Asia, the Spanish and Portuguese claimed dominion over the whole continental landmass of the Americas.
245. Gen. 13:8.
246. Grotius is playing here with the title *Defensor Fidei* (Defender of the Faith) bestowed by Pope Leo X to King Henry VIII (before he embraced to the Reformation). It has been carried by successive English monarchs as a politico-religious title.
247. CC, pp. 123–8, annexe 42, "Dernier mémoire néerlandais adressé au Roi le 13 mai 1613" (Final Dutch memorandum addressed to the King, 13 May 1613). According to the reference given by Clark and van Eysinga, the present text should be found in the State Papers, Colonial East Indies, 1513–1615, number 645 (annexes Q and R). Several e-mail communications with the archivists at the Public Records Office in London, however, have confirmed that the reference is evidently false and attempts to locate the originals have so far proven futile. In the course of preparing the English translation, several questions arose about the accuracy of the original, or the transcript published by Clark and van Eysinga. Despite the apparent faults, their transcripts of the Latin text is reproduced in appendix 18, together with editorial notes and comments by the translator, Dr. Corinna Vermeulen, and a translation into English.
248. CC, p. 129.
249. CC, p. 130.
250. Corrected from *mercuturae* in the edition. (Translator's note.)
251. According to an editorial note of Clark and van Eysinga, the ms. reads *non* rather than *aut.*
252. CC, p. 131.
253. Corrected from *excerceant mercuturam* in the edition.
254. CC, p. 132.
255. Translated from the original Latin by Dr. Corinna Vermeulen, Noctua Taal en Tekst, Leiden. The annotations are mine.
256. As in some of Grotius' other writings, and indeed period VOC documentation at large, the term "Spaniard" should be taken generically to encompass all subjects loyal to the King of Spain, which of course includes the Portuguese. It can be understood as being synonymous with "Iberians". As a general rule, the Portuguese are mentioned when events or developments refer specifically to them.

257. This is clearly a reformulation of the idea of *coophandel met force*, that is trade supported by the force of arms, a concept used by Grotius at the Anglo-Dutch conferences and an idea most certainly — as well as infamously — shared by leading VOC officials such as Governor-General Jan Pieterszoon Coen.
258. Reference is here of course to the Twelve Years Truce (1609).
259. See also the minute books of the Dutch States General of 26 July 1609. In a session held just weeks after the ratification of the Twelve Years Truce in early April that year, the directors of the VOC petitioned the States General to include the company's Asian allies and treaty partners under the provisions and conditions of the truce. This was in line with the secret clauses ratified before the French and English ambassadors to the Dutch Republic. The secret articles were designed to thwart Spanish and Portuguese intervention in, or destabilisation of, these Asian polities. The Asian allies and treaty partners mentioned by name in the minute book of the States General are "… the King of Siam (who currently has his ambassador here [in the Dutch Republic], the kings of Calecut, Banten, Johor, Aceh, Pahang, Kedah, Makassar, Banda, Ternate and others". See *Resolutiën der Staten-Generaal van 1576 tot 1609*, ed. Rijperman, p. 658. — The Siamese ambassadors had arrived with the ships of Admiral Matelieff de Jonge in 1608. See the articles by Duyvendak, "The First Siamese Embassy to Holland", *T'Oung Pao* 32 (1936): 285–92, and Pelliot, "Les relations du Siam et de la Hollande en 1608", *T'Oung Pao* 32 (1936): 223–9. The embassy is also briefly mentioned in van der Cruysse, *Louis XIV et le Siam*, pp. 63–9.
260. Such as notably Ambon, taken by the VOC from the Portuguese in 1605.
261. This repeats a statement of a factual nature already made by Grotius in his opening address before the King. See appendix 17.
262. See also BW 400, p. 383, letter of Admiral Cornelis Matelieff to Grotius, dated 3 May 1615, where total costs to the VOC to November 1614 are calculated at 4.353 million florins or guilders.
263. See the final report (*Verbael*) of the Dutch delegation printed as an appendix to BW, I, pp. 626–35.
264. Technically the VOC was founded in 1602, that was eleven years before the first maritime and colonial conference was held in London (1613). The discrepancy in the number of years can be explained thus: The VOC simply amalgamated on paper six voorcompagniën whose ships had earlier sailed to the East Indies. Grotius is calculating the return based on the dates of the voorcompagniën voyages in 1600 and 1601, not of the formal creation of the VOC in 1602.
265. This is almost certainly a reference to the Malukus, especially Spanish activities on the island and kingdom of Tidor.
266. "Memorie van Mijne Intentiën en Notable Bejegeningen", ed. Fruin, *WHGU* 14 (1871): pp. 32–3.

267. Concerning this "favourable disposition" and generally the scheme of Willem Cornelisz. Schouten and Isaac le Maire (a former VOC stakeholder) to establish the *Austraelsche Compagnie* (Company of Terra Australis or Southern Company), see den Tex, *Oldenbarnevelt,* III, p. 690, as well as J.G. van Dillen, Geoffrey Poitras and Asha Majithia, "Isaac le Maire and the early trading in Dutch East India Company Shares", *Pioneers of Financial Economics,* ed. Geoffrey Poitras (Cheltenham: Edward Elgar Publishing, 2006), I, p. 60. The company was founded with the deliberate intention of circumventies the monopoly and charter of the VOC. Several documents surviving among the working papers of Johan van Oldenvarnevelt reveal that the controversy between the *Austraelsche Compagnie*, its petition for a charter from the Dutch States General and conflict with the VOC reached an apex in between March and August 1618, that is just weeks before Oldenbarnevelt and Grotius were arrested. The Hague, Archief Johan van Oldenbarnevelt (3.01.14, nos. 3127–34). The ships of the *Austraelsche Compagnie* were to access marketplaces in the East Indies via Cape Hoorn and the Pacific Ocean, regions in other words claimed directly by Spain. Instructions issued by father Isaac le Maire to his son Jacques of 24 March 1614, can be found in the Hague, Nationaal Archief, Archief Johan van Oldenbarnevelt (3.01.14, no. 3125). In this he recommended commerce with undiscovered lands and refrain from trading in marketplaces that are situated outside the charter area of the VOC. An expedition of two vessels to Tierra del Fuego (Cape Hoorn) set sail form the Netherlands in June 1615. See also R.C. Bakhuizen van den Brink, *Isaac Le Maire. Eene Voorlezing* (Amsterdam: P.N. van Kampen, 1865), esp. pp. 43–5.
268. Concerning the background to the founding of the Dutch West India Company (or WIC), see generally den Heijer, *De Geschiedenis van de WIC,* and den Tex, *Oldenbarnevelt,* II, pp. 575–6, and III, p. 690.
269. Willem Usselincx, was a religious refugee from Flanders, and a merchant in the West Indies' trade. He is known to have played a role in the 1617 Counter-Remonstrant or Gomarist uprisings directed against the Oldenbarnevelt administration. See also den Tex, *Oldenbarnevelt,* III, p. 437.
270. Grotius' wording here reflects the tone of the V.O.C. memorial dated 11 April 1608 addressed to all the admirals, vice-admirals and leading company servants in Asia. According to this memorial, the Dutch would gain trading access to all ports and emporia in the East Indies that were not under "Spanish" (speak here the Spanish and the Portuguese) sovereignty (*ghebiet*). See de Jonge, *Opkomst van het Nederlandsch gezag in Oost-Indië,* III, p. 309. For the context, see also den Tex, *Oldenbarnevelt,* II, pp. 607–8.

Bibliography

Manuscripts and Unpublished Materials by Grotius

Amsterdam University Library, Ms. III.C.5, fol. 139: "Decretum ... pro pace ecclesiarum", 1614 (in the hand of Grotius).

———, Ms. Z 104, "Memorië van Mijne Intentiën".

The Hague, Koninklijke Bibliotheek, Ms. 131.C.21, Hugo Grotius, *De Imperio Summarum Potestatum circa Sacra.*

The Hague, Nationaal Archief van Nederland, *Collectie Hugo de Groot, Supplement I* (ms. 1.10.35.02, no. 40).

———, Collectie 102, Baron H. van Zuylen van Nyevelt, suppl. 2, no. 13 (2.21.179.01, no. 13). *Boeck Traçterende vande Wreede, Verradische ende Hostile proceduren der Portugesen In Oost-Indien.*

———, Collectie Johan van Oldenbarnevelt (3.01.14, nos. 3125, 3127–34, 3153). These manuscripts comprise working papers of Oldenbarnevelt pertaining to negotiations for the Twelve Years Truce, Isaac and Jacques Le Maire, as well as the *Austraelsche Compagnie* and its competition with the VOC.

———, Inventaris van het archief van de Verenigde Oostindische Compagnie (VOC) 1602–1795/1811 (1.04.02, nos. 461–66, 476). Instructions issued by the Heren XVII to Admiral Cornelis Matelieff de Jonge 1605; letters drafted or received by Admiral Matelieff in 1608; advisory (*advies*) by Cornelis Matelieff to Admiral Paul van Caerden concerning secret instructions of the Heren XVII and the conditions in the East Indies in 1608.

Leiden, University Library, Loket 1555 part 39, Robert Fruin, "Aantekeningen op zijn werken, gebruikt bij de uitgave van de Verspreide Geschriften".

———, Ms. Cod. B.P.L. 917, Hugo Grotius, "De Iure Praedae" (in the hand of Grotius).

———, Ms. Cod. B.P.L. 918, Hugo Grotius, "Defensio capitis quinti 'Maris Liberi' oppugnati a Guilelmo Welwodo iuris civilis professore capite XXVII

eius libri cui titulum fecit 'Compendium legum maritimarum'" (in the hand of Grotius).
———, Ms. Cod. B.P.L. 919, Hugo Grotius, "Over de Rechten van de Vorsten van het Huis van Orange op het Princedom Orange" (in the hand of Grotius).
———, Ms. Cod. B.P.L. 920, Hugo Grotius, "Over de Rechten van de Vorsten van het Huis van Orange op het Princedom Orange" (copy in secretary's hand).
———, Ms. Cod. B.P.L. 922, Hugo Grotius, "Collectanea Autographa" containing: "Commentarius in Theses XI" (fols. 376–83), "De Bello ob Libertatem Eligendo" (fols. 293–301), De Pace (fols. 302–7), "De Societate Publica cum Infidelibus" (fols. 314–7) and the "Theses LVI" (fols. 287–90).
———, Ms. Papenbroeckii Cod. 9, Hugo Grotius, "Historiarum de Rebus Belgici Libri ab anno 1588 ad annum 1609" (copy).
———, Ms. Papenbroeckii Cod. 11A, Hugo Grotius, "Annales belli Belgici a digressu Philippi II Regis Hispaniarum, ad Indicas usque, annorum plus quadraginta tempus libris viginti tribus complexi" (in the hand of Grotius).
———, Ms. Papenbroeckii Cod. 13A, Hugo Grotius, "Annotata de vita sua" (in the hand of Grotius).
London, Public Record Office, State Papers, 105/95, Letter of George Abbot to Sir Dudley Carleton, 27 December 1616, fols. 1–2.
Lund University Library, Bibl. Grotiana 13, Emmanuel van Meteren, *Memoriën der Belgische Ofte Nederlantsche Historie van onsen tijden* (Delft: Jacob Cornilisz Veenecool, 1599). Printed source containing underlinings, marginalia and comments in the hand of Grotius.
———, Bibl. Grotiana 16, *Summae S. Thomae Aquinatis, Doctoris Angelici, ordinis Fratrum Praedicatorum, Universam Sacram Theologiam Complectens, in tres partes divisa ad Romanum examplar diligenter recognita: Cum Commentariis R. DD. Thomae de Vio Caietanis Cardinalis S. Xysti. Nunc vero eruditissima R.F. Chrysostomi Iavelli Commentari in primam partem primum in lucem prolata, hic adiecimus, etc.* bound in 4 vols. (Lyon: Publisher unknown, 1581). This set derives from the private library of Grotius. See the dedication featured in vol. I, fol. 1, revealing that Grotius received this set as a gift from Dom Emmanuel, son of Dom Antonio, King of Portugal. The volumes contain underlinings and annotations in the hand of Grotius.
Rotterdam, Gemeentearchief, Handschriftenverzameling Rotterdam, 33.01, no. 3366, Pièces diverses concernantes le commerce et la navigation aux Indes, 1603–13, working papers from the possession of Hugo Grotius acquired at the public auction at Martinus Nijhoff in the Hague in November 1864, representing part I, lot 32 of the auction.
———, portef. Buitenlandse Handel, no. 803, fol. 86. (Excerpt of the treaty of guarantee between the Dutch Republic, France and England of 17 June 1609, originally belonging to the working papers of Grotius sold in November 1864.)

Reference Works

Catalogue des Manuscrits Autographes de Hugo Grotius. Vente à La Haye, 15 Novembre 1864, sous la direction et au domicile de Martinus Nijhoff (The Hague: Martinus Nijhoff, 1864).

Grotius-Tentoonstelling te 's-Gravenhage, 13–28 Juni 1925 (Leiden: A.W. Sijthoff, 1925).

Inventarissen van Rijks- en andere archieven van rijkwege uitgegeven, voorzover zij niet zijn afzonderlijk afgedrukt, 4 vols. (The Hague: Algemeene Landsdrukkerij, 1928–32).

VOC-Glossarium. Verklaringen van termen, verzameld uit de Rijks Geschiedkundige Publicatiën die betrekking hebben op de Verenigde Oost-Indische Compagnie (The Hague: Instituut voor Nederlandsche Geschiedenis, 2001).

Bruin, J.R., F.S. Gaastra and I. Schöffer, *Dutch-Asiatic Shipping in the 17th and 18th Centuries,* 2 vols. (The Hague: Martinus Nijhoff, 1979–87).

Hooykaas, J.C., ed., *Repertorium op de Koloniale Literatuur of Systematische Inhoudsopgaaf van hetgeen voorkomt over de Koloniën (beoosten de Kaap) in Mengelwerken en Tijdschriften van 1595 tot 1865 uitgegeven in Nederland en zijne overzeesche bezittingen* (Amsterdam: P.N. van Kampen & Zoon, 1877–80).

Huet, G.B., ed., *Catalogue des manuscrits néerlandais de la Bibliothèque Nationale* (Paris: Publisher unknown, 1886).

Knuttel, W.P.C., *Catalogus van de Pamfletten-Verzameling berustende in de Koninklijke Bibliotheek,* 10 vols., reprint of the original edition, 1890–1920, with corrections (Utrecht: HES Publishers, 1978).

Meulen, J. ter and P.J.J. Diermanse, *Bibliographie des écrits imprimés de Hugo Grotius* (The Hague: Martinus Nijhoff, 1950).

Molhuysen, P.C., *Codices Bibliothecae Publicae Latini* (Leiden: Brill, 1912).

Molhuysen, P.C., ed., *Bronnen tot de geschiedenis der Leidsche universiteit,* 7 vols. (The Hague: Martinus Nijhoff, 1913–24).

Landwehr, J., *VOC. A bibliography of publications relating to the Dutch East India Company, 1602–1800,* ed. Peter van der Krogt (Utrecht: HES Publishers, 1991).

Noordhoff, L.J., *Beschrijving van het zich in Nederland bevindende en nog onbeschreven gedeelte der papieren afkomstig van Huig de Groot welke in 1864 te 's-Gravenhage zijn geveilt* (Groningen-Djakarta: Noordhoff, 1953).

Rogge, H.C. and P.A. Tiele, *Catalogus van Handschriften op de Bibliotheek der Remonstrantsch-Gereformeerde Gemeente te Rotterdam* (Rotterdam: I.J. Rogge, 1869).

Sainsbury, W.N., *Calendar of State Papers, Colonial Series, East Indies, China and Japan, 1513–1616, Preserved in Her Majesty's Public Record Office and Elsewhere* (London: Longman, Green, Longman & Roberts, 1862).

Schöffer, I. *et al.* ed., *Icones Leidenses. De portretverzameling van de Rijksuniversiteit te Leiden* (Leiden: Universitaire Pers, 1973).

Tideman, J., ed., *Catalogus der boeken en handschriften van de bibliotheek der Remonstrantsche gemeente te Amsterdam* (Amsterdam: Rogge, 1877).

Tiele, P.A., ed., *Mémoire bibliographique sur les journaux des navigateurs néerlandais réimprimés dans les collections de De Bry et de Hulsius, et dans les collections hollandaises du XVIIe siècle, et sur les anciennes éditions hollandaises des journaux de navigateurs étrangers; la plupart en la possession de Frederik Muller a Amsterdam* (Amsterdam: Frederik Muller, 1867).

Tiele, P.A., *Catalogue de manuscrits autographes de Hugo Grotius dont le vente a eu lieu à la Haye le 15. novembre 1864 sous la direction et au domicile de Martinus Nijhoff*, 2nd ed. with annotations by W.J.M. van Eysinga and L.J. Noordhoff (The Hague: Martinus Nijhoff, 1952).

Printed Works of Hugo Grotius

Annales et Historiae de Rebus Belgicis (Amsterdam: Ioannis Blaeu, 1657).

Bewys Van den waren godsdienst In ses Boecken gestelt (Publisher unknown, 1622).

Briefwisseling van Hugo Grotius, eerste deel, 1597–Augustus 1618, ed. P.C. Molhuysen (The Hague: Martinus Nijhoff, 1928).

Briefwisseling van Hugo Grotius, derde deel, 1626–8, ed. P.C. Molhuysen and B.L. Meulenbroek (The Hague: Martinus Nijhoff, 1961).

Briefwisseling van Hugo Grotius, vijfte deel, 1632 tot met mei 1635, ed. B.L. Meulenbroek (The Hague: Martinus Nijhoff, 1966).

Briefwisseling van Hugo Grotius, dertiende deel 1642, ed. H.J.M. Nellen and C.M. Ridderikhoff (The Hague: Instituut voor Nederlandse Geschiedenis, 1990).

Briefwisseling van Hugo Grotius, zeventiende deel, Supplement 1583–1645, ed. H.J.M. Nellen, with the addenda compiled by C.M. Ridderikhoff (The Hague: Instituut voor Nederlandse Geschiedenis, 2001).

Hugo Grotius Commentarius in Theses XI. An Early Treatise on Sovereignty, the Just War, and the Legitimacy of the Dutch Revolt (Berne: Peter Lang, 1994).

Commentary on the Law of Prize and Booty, ed. and intr. M.J. van Ittersum (Indianapolis: Liberty Fund, 2006).

Commentatio ad Loca quaedam Novi Testamenti quae de Antichristo agunt, aut agere putantur, expendenda eruditis (Amsterdam: J. Blaeu, 1640).

Decretum … Ordinum Hollandiae et Westfrisiae pro pace ecclesiarum, munitum Sacrae scripturae auctoritate, et Conciliorum, Antiquorum Patrum, Confessionum publicarum et recentiorum Doctorum testimoniis (Leiden: J. Patius, 1614).

De dichtwerken van Hugo Grotius, in opdracht van de Commissie voor de uitgave van de briefwisseling en de dichtwerken van Grotius van de Koninklijke Nederlandse Akademie van Wetenschappen, ed. B.L. Meulenbroek *et al.*, 10 vols. (Assen: Van Gorcum, 1970–92).

De imperio summarum potestatum circa sacra, ed. and intr. H.J. van Dam, 2 vols. (Leiden: Brill, 2001).

De jure belli ac pacis libri tres, ed. B.J.A. de Kanter-van Hettinga Tromp with notes by R. Feenstra and C.E. Persenaire (Aaalen: Scientia Verlag, 1993).

De Iure belli ac pacis Libri Tres, In quibus iius naturae et Gentium: item iuris publici praecipua explicantur (Paris: Apud Nicolaum Buon, 1625).

De Iure Belli ac pacis Libri tres, in quibus ius naturae et gentium, item iuris publici praecipua explicantur, ed. P.C. Molhuysen (Leiden: A.W. Sijthoff, 1919).

De Iure Praedae Commentarius, ed. H.G. Hamaker (The Hague: Martinus Nijhoff, 1868).

De Jure Belli ac Pacis, tr. F.W. Kelsey, ed. J.B. Scott, reprint of the original edition of 1925 (New York: Oceana Publications, 1964).

De Jure Praedae Commentarius. Commentary on the Law of Prize and Booty. A Translation of the Original Manuscript of 1604, tr. G.L. Williams and W.H. Zeydel (Oxford: Clarendon Press, 1950).

De Rebus Belgicis: Or, The Annals and History of the Low-Countrey Warrs, tr. T[homas] M[anley] (London: Printed for Henry Twyford … and Robert Paulet, 1665).

"De Republica Emendanda: A Juvenile Tract by Hugo Grotius on the Emendation of the Dutch Polity", ed. and tr. A. Eyffinger and P.A.H. de Boer, *Grotiana*, New Series, 5 (1984): 2–79.

Dissertatio de origine gentium Americanarum ([Paris]: Publisher unknown, 1642).

Dissertatio altera de origine gentium Americanarum adversus obtrectatorem Opaca quem bonum facit barba ([Paris?]: Publisher unknown, 1643).

Explicatio Decalogi ut Graece exstat, et quomodo ad Decalogi locos Evangelica praecepta referantur (Amsterdam: J. Blaeu, 1640).

Explicatio trium utilissimorum locorum Novi Testamenti: Capitis I. Pauli ad Ephesios. Posterioris partis capitis II Iacobi, commatis XIV, et sequentium. Capitis III. Epistolae I Ioannis. In quibus agitur de Fide et Operibus (Amsterdam: J. Blaeu, 1640).

Inleidinge tot de Hollandsche Rechts-Geleerdheid, ed. F. Dovring, H.F.W.D. Fischer and E.M. Meijers, 2nd ed. (Leiden: Universitaire Pers, 1965).

Liber de Antiquitate Reipublicae Batavicae (Leiden: Ex officina Plantiniana Raphelingij, 1610).

Liber de Antiquitate Reipublicae Batavicae (Arnhem: Gouda Quint, 1995).

Mare Liberum, sive de iure quod Batavis competit ad indicana commercia dissertatio (Leiden: Ex officina Ludovici Esevirii, 1609).

Mare Liberum, The Freedom of the Seas, or, The Right which Belongs to the Dutch to Take Part in the East Indian Trade, tr. R. van Deman Magoffin, ed. and intr. J.B. Scott (New York: OUP, 1916).

Hugo Grotius Mare Liberum, 1609–2009. Original Latin Text and English Translation, ed. R. Feenstra and intr. J. Vervliet (Leiden: Brill, 2009).

Meletius, sive de iis quae inter Christianos conveniunt epistola, ed. G.H.M. Posthumus-Mejyes (Leiden: Brill, 1988).

"Memorie van Mijne Intentiën en Notable Bejegeningen", in *Verhooren en andere bescheiden betreffende het rechtsgeding van Hugo de Groot*, ed. Robert Fruin, *WHGU* 14 (1871): 1–80.

Opera Omnia Theologica, 4 vols. (Amsterdam: J. Blaeu, 1679).

Ordinum Hollandiae ac Westfrisiae pietas ab Improbissimis multorum calumniis, praesertim vero a nupera Sibrandi Lubberti epistola quam ad reverendissimum Archiepiscopum Cantuariensem scripsit vindicata (Leiden: Iohannes Patius, 1613).

Ordinum Hollandiae acWestfrisiae Pietas (1613), ed. and tr. E. Rabbie (Leiden: Brill, 1995).

Parallelon rerumpublicarum liber tertius: De moribus ingenioque populorum Atheniensium, Romanorum, Batavorum, 4 vols. (Haarlem: A. Losjes, 1801–3).

The Antiquity of the Batavian Republic, with notes by Petrus Scriverius, ed. and intr. J.H. Waszink (Assen: Van Gorcum, 2000).

The Free Sea, tr. Richard Hakluyt, ed. and intr. D. Armitage (Indianapolis: Liberty Fund, 2004).

Verklaringhe vande E.E. heeren Magistraten ende Regeerders der Stadt Haerlem, door haren Ghedeputeerden ghedaen, inde Vergaderinghe der E. Mo. Heeren Staten van Hollandt ende West-Vrieslandt, ende by de Heeren Edelen ende meeste leden vande zelve Vergaderinghe gheapprobeert (Publisher unknown, 1618).

Verantwoording van de Wettelijcke Regieringh van Hollandt ende West-Vrieslandt, Midtsgaders Eenigher nabuyrighe Provincien, sulcks die was voor de veranderingh, ghevallen in den Jare [1618] (Publisher unknown, 1622).

Via ad pacem ecclesiasticam. In qua continentur Confessio Fidei, Secundum Conc. Trid. Confessio Fidei Augustana. Consultatio Cassandri. … (Amsterdam: J. Blaeu, 1642).

Vrye zeevaert, ofte Bewiis Van 't recht dat de Inghesetenen deser geunieerde Landen toecomt over de Indische coop-handel. Ten tweedemael overseen ende verbetert door den Autheur selfs. Uten Latijne vertaelt door P[ieter] B[ertius]. Tot vorderinghe des Vaderlandts (Leiden: Ian Huybertsz..., 1614).

Votum pro pace ecclesiastica, contra examen Andreae Riveti, et alios irreconciliabiles. Ecce quam bonum et quam jucundum habitare fratres in unum (Amsterdam: J. Blaeu, 1642).

Printed Sources and Secondary Sources

Ahsmann, M.J.A.M., R.E.O. Ekkert and R.A. Leeuw, ed., *Het Delfts orakel: Hugo de Groot* (Delft: Stedellijk Museum Het Prinsenhof, 1983).

Aitzema, L. van, *Saken van staet en oorlogh, in, ende omtrent de Vereenigde Nederlanden, beginnende in het jaer 1621*, 6 vols. (The Hague: Johan Veely, Johan Tongerloo and Jasper Doll, 1669–72).

Alexandrowicz, C.H., *An Introduction to the History of the Law of Nations in the East Indies* (Oxford: Clarendon Press, 1967).

Althusius, J., *Politica Methodice Digesta. Reprint of the Third Edition of 1614*, ed. and intr. C.J. Friedrichs (Cambridge, Mass: Harvard University Press, 1932).

Alves, J.M. dos Santos and P.-Y. Manguin, *O Roteiro das Cousas do Achem de D. João Ribeiro Gaio: Um olhar português sobre o norte de Samatra em finais do século XVI* (Lisbon: Comissão Nacional para as Comemorações dos Descobrimentos Portugueses, 1997).

Alves, J.M. dos Santos, *Portugal e a China — Conferências no II Curso Livre de História das Relações entre Portugal e a China, Séculos XVI–XIX* (Lisbon: Fundação Oriente, 1999).

Anand, R.P., *Origin and Development of the Law of the Sea: History of International Law Revisited* (The Hague: Martinus Nijhoff, 1983).

Andaya, L., *The Kingdom of Johor 1641–1728: Economic and Political Developments* (Kuala Lumpur: OUP, 1975).

Anghie, A., *Imperialism, Sovereignty and the Making of International Law* (Cambridge: CUP, 2004).

Anon., *Achter Theil der Orientalischen Indien, begreiffend erstlich Ein Historische Beschreibung der Schiffart, so der Admiral Jacob van Neck auss Hollandt in die Orientalische Indien von Ann. 1600 biss 1602 gethan, Darnach Ein Historia, soo von Johann Herman von Bree Obersten Handelsmann auff dem Schiff der Holländische Zaun genannt, in gleichmessiger Reyse von An. 1602 biss in An. 1604 auffgezeichnet worden. …* tr. M. Gotthard Arthus with illustrations by Johann Theodor and Johann Israel de Bry (Frankfurt/M.: Publisher unknown, 1606).

———, *Corte ende sekere Beschryvinghe vant veroveren der rijcke ende gheweldighe krake, comende uytet gheweste van China, door den Admirael Jacobus Heemskercke* ... (Ghedruckt na de copy van Middelborch by Richard Schilders, 1604).

———, *Seer cort verhael vande destructie van d'Indien vergadert deurden Bischop Don Fray Bartholome de las Casas* (Publisher unknown, 1578).

———, *Den Spieghel Vande Spaensche Tyrannie beeldelijken afgemaelt, leest breederen in-hout door het schrijven van den E. Bisschop van Chiapa in Nieuw Spaengien, ghenaemt Don Fray Bartolome de las Casas, van S. Dominicus Orden, aen den grootmaechtigen Coninck van Spaengien Philips de tweede* (Amsterdam: Cornelis Claesz, 1609).

———, *Hugo Grotius, 1583–1645. Beiträge zum nationalen und internationalen Seerecht*, Heft 7 (Rostock: Gesellschaft für Seerecht der Deutschen Demokratischen Republik, 1983).

Aristoteles, *Politics*, with tr. by H. Rackham, reprint of 1932, Loeb Classical Library, 264 (Cambridge, Mass.: Harvard University Press and London: Heinemann, 1972).

———, *The Art of Rhetoric,* with tr. by J.H. Freese, reprint of 1926, Loeb Classical Library, 193 (Cambridge, Mass.: Harvard University Press and London: Heinemann, 1975).

Armitage, D., *The Ideological Origins of the British Empire* (Cambridge: CUP, 2000).

Armitage, D. and M.J. Braddick, *The British Atlantic World, 1500–1800* (Basingstoke: Palgrave Macmillan, 2002).

Aubery du Maurier, L., *Mémoires pour servir à l'Histoire de Hollande et des autres Provinces Unis. Où l'on verra les veritable causes des divisions qui sont depuis soixante ans dans cette Republique, et qui la menacent de ruine* (Paris: Jean Villette, 1680).

Augustine of Hippo, *De Doctrina Christiana,* ed. and tr. R.P.H. Green (Oxford: OUP, 1995).

Bakhuizen van den Brink, R.C., *Isaac Le Maire. Eene Voorlezing* (Amsterdam: P.N. van Kampen, 1865).

Bangs, C., *Arminius, a Study in the Dutch Reformation* (Nashville: Abingdon Press, 1971).

Barbosa, D., *The Book of Duarte Barbosa, An Account of the Countries bordering on the Indian Ocean and their Inhabitants…completed about the year 1518,* tr. M.L. Dames, 2 vols. (London: Hakluyt Society, 1918–21).

Biker, J.F. Judice, *Collecção de tratados e concertos de pazes que o Estado da Índia Portugeza fez com os reis e senhores com quem teve relações nas partes da Ásia e Africa Oriente, desde o princípio da conquista até ao fin do século XVIII*, 10 vols. (Lisbon: Imprensa Nacional, 1881–7).

Blair, E.H. and J.A. Robertson, *The Philippine Islands, 1493–1898*, 55 vols. (Cleveland: A.H. Clark Co., 1903–9).

Blom, H. (ed.), *Property, Piracy and Punishment: Hugo Grotius on War and Booty in De Iure Praedae – Concepts and Contexts* (Leiden: Brill, 2009).

Bodin, J., *The Six Bookes of a Commonweale. A Facsimile reprint of the English edition of 1606, Corrected and supplemented,* ed. K.D. McRae (Cambridge, Mass.: Harvard University Press, 1962).

Booy, A. de, *De derde reis van de V.O.C. naar Oost-Indië onder het beleid van Admiraal Paulus van Caerden, uitgezeild in 1606,* 2 vols. (The Hague: Martinus Nijhoff, 1970).

Borschberg, P., *The Singapore and Melaka Straits: Violence, Security and Diplomacy in the 17th Century* (Singapore and Leiden: NUS Press and KITLV Press, 2010).

Boxer, C.R., *Fidalgos in the Far East, 1550–1770: Fact and Fancy in the History of Macao* (The Hague: Martinus Nijhoff, 1948).

Brandt, C. and A. van Cattenburgh, *Historie van het leven des heeren Huig de Groot, Beschreven tot den aanvang van zyn Gezantschap wegens de Koninginne en Kroone van Zweden aan't Hof van Vrankryk,* 2 vols. (Amsterdam and Dordrecht: Joannes van Braam and Geerard onder den Linden, 1727).

Brandt, G., *The History of the Reformation and other Ecclesiastical Transactions in and about the Low-Countries,* 4 vols. (London: printed by T. Wood for Timothy Childe, 1720–3).

Brett, A.S., *Liberty, Right and Nature: Individual Rights in Later Scholastic Thought* (Cambridge: CUP, 1997).

Bromley, J.S. and E.H. Kossmann, ed., *Britain and the Netherlands in Europe and Asia: Papers delivered to the Third Anglo-Dutch History Conference* (London: Macmillan, 1968).

Burgus, P.B., *De Dominio Serenissimae Genuensis Reipublicae in Mari Ligustico* (Rome: Dominicus Marcianus, 1641).

Burns, J.H. and M.A. Goldie, *The Cambridge History of Political Thought 1450–1700* (Cambridge: CUP, 1991).

Canone, E., ed., *Bibliothecae selecte da Cusano a Leopardi* (Florence: Leo S. Olschki, 1993).

Cavallar, G., *The Rights of Strangers. Theories of International Hospitality, the Global Community and Political Justice since Vitoria* (Aldershot: Ashgate, 2002).

Chaudhuri, K.N., *The English East India Company: The Study of an Early Joint-Stock Company 1600–1640* (New York, 1965).

Cicero, M.T., *De Officiis,* with tr. W. Miller, reprint of 1913, Loeb Classical Library, 30 (Cambridge, Mass.: Harvard University Press and London: Heinemann, 1975).

Clark, G.N. and W.J.M. van Eysinga, *The Colonial Conferences between England and the Netherlands in 1613 and 1615*, 2 vols. (Leiden: Brill, 1940–51).

Commelin, I., *Begin ende Voortgang vande Vereenigde Neerlandsche Geoctroyeerde Oost-Indische Compagnie*, 4 vols., facsimile edition of the original of 1646 in 2 vols. (Amsterdam: Facsimile Uitgaven Nederland, 1969).

Conring, E., *Kirche und Staat nach der Lehre der niederländischen Calvinisten in der ersten Hälfte des 17. Jahrhunderts* (Neukirchen-Vluyn: Neukirchner Verlag des Erziehungsvereins, 1965).

Contarini, G., *De Magistratibus et Republica Venetorum Libri Quinque* (Venice: Apud Io. Bapt. Ciottum Senensem sub Signo Minervae, 1592).

Corpus Juris Canonici, editio lipsiensis secunda, ed. A.E. Richter, 2 vols., facsimile edition of 1879 (Graz: Akademische Druck- und Verlagsanstalt, 1995).

Corpus Juris Civilis: The Civil Law, tr. S.P. Scott, 17 vols. (New York: AMS Publishers, 1973).

Coutre, J. de, *Andanzas asiáticas*, ed. E. Stols, B. Teensma, and J. [V]erbeckmoes (Madrid: História 16, 1991).

Covarruvias y Leyva, D. de, *Opera Omnia quae hactenus extant*, 2 vols. (Frankfurt/M.: Ex Officina Nicolai Bassaei, Impensis Sigismundi Feierabend, 1573).

Cozzi, G., *Paolo Sarpi tra Venezia e l'Europa* (Turin: Einaudi, 1979).

Cruysse, D. van der, *Louis XIV et le Siam* (Paris: Fayard, 1991).

———, *Siam and the West, 1500–1700,* tr. Michael Smithies (Seattle: University of Washington Press, 2002).

Daalder, R., *Rotterdam en de VOC. Tentoonstelling gehouden in het Schielandhuis van 6 maart tot 24 mei, 1988* (Rotterdam: Historisch Museum Rotterdam, 1988).

Dam, P. van, *Beschryvinge van de Oostindische Compagnie*, ed. F.W. Stapel, 8 vols. (The Hague: Martinus Nijhoff, 1931).

Darby, G., ed., *The Origins and Development of the Dutch Revolt* (London and New York: Routledge, 2001).

Darian-Smith, E. and P. Fitzpatrick, *Laws of the Postcolonial* (Ann Arbor : University of Michigan Press, 1999).

Descendre, R., *L'état du monde. Giovanni Botero entre raison d'État et géopolitique* (Geneva: Droz, 2009).

Diller, S., *Die Dänen in Indien, Südostasien und China (1620–1845)* (Wiesbaden: Otto Harrassowitz Verlag, 1999).

Donellus, H., *Commentariorum de iure civili Libri viginti octo: in quibus jus civile universum singulari artificio atque doctrina explicatum continetur Scip. Gentilis posteriors libros supplevit, expolivit* (Frankfurt/M.: apud Andreae Wecheli heredes, Claudium Marnium et Ioan. Aubrium, 1596).

Dunn, J. and I. Harris, ed., *Grotius,* 2 vols. (Cheltenham: Eward Elgar Publishing, 1997).

Enthoven, V., *Zeeland en de opkomst van de Republiek: Handel en Strijd in de Scheldedelta, ca. 1550–1621* (Leiden: Proefschrift, 1996).

Eysinga, W.J.M. van, *Sparsa Collecta, een aantal der verspreide geschriften van Jonkheer Mr. W.J.M. van Eysinga* (Leiden: A.W. Sijthoff, 1958).

Feenstra, R., ed., *The World of Hugo Grotius (1583–1645),* Proceedings of the International Colloquium Organised by the Grotius Committee of the Royal Netherlands Academy of Arts and Sciences, Rotterdam, 6–9 April 1983 (Amsterdam and Maarsen: APA-Holland University Press, 1984).

———, *Fata Iuris Romani: Études d'Histoire du Droit* (Leiden: Leiden University Press, 1974).

Feenstra, R., *Legal Scholarship and Doctrines of Private Law, 13th–18th Centuries* (Ashgate: Variorum, 1996).

Finkentscher, W., *De Fide et perfidia: Der Treuegedanke in den Staatsparallelen des Hugo Grotius aus heutiger Sicht* (Munich: Bayerische Akademie der Wissenschaften, 1979).

Foster, W., ed., *The Voyage of Thomas Best to the East Indies 1612–1614* (London: Hakluyt Society, 1934).

Freitas, S. de, *De Iusto Imperio Lusitanorum Asiatico*, tr. M. Pinto de Menezes, intr. M. Caetano, 2 vols. (Lisbon: Instituto de Alto Cultura, 1959–61).

———, *Über die Rechtmässige Herrschaft der Portugiesen in Asien. Freitas gegen Grotius im Kampf um die Freiheit der Meere*, tr. J.P. Hardegen, doctoral dissertation (Kiel: Christian-Albrechts-Universität Kiel, 1976).

———, *Do Justo Império Asiático dos Portugueses*, Latin-Portuguese bilingual ed., 2 vols. (Lisbon: Instituto Nacional de Investigação Científica, 1983).

Fruin, R., *Robert Fruin's verspreide geschriften: met aanteekeningen, toevoegsels en verbeteringen uit des schrijvers nalatenschap*, ed. P.J. Blok, P.L. Muller, and S. Muller, 10 vols. (The Hague: Martinus Nijhoff, 1900–5).

———, *Geschiedenis der Staatsinstellingen in Nederland tot den val der Republiek*, ed. H.T. Colenbrander and I. Schöffer (The Hague: Martinus Nijhoff, 1980).

Fulton, T.W., *The Sovereignty of the Sea: An Historical Account of the Claims of England to the Dominion of the British Seas, and of the Evolution of the Territorial Waters; with special reference to the Rights of Fishing and the Naval Salute* (Edinburgh: William Blackwood & Sons, 1911).

Gaastra, F.S., *De geschiedenis van de VOC*, 4th ed. (Zutphen: Walburg Pers, 2002).

García Villoslada, R., *La universidad de París durante los Estudios de Francisco de Vitoria* (Rome: Università Gregoriana, 1938).

Gluck, C. and A. L. Tsing, *Words in Motion. Toward a Global Lexicon* (Durham and London: Duke University Press, 2009).

Goor, J. van, *Prelude to Colonialism: The Dutch in Asia* (Hilversum: Uitgeverij Verloren, 2004).

Grewe, W.G., ed., *Fontes Historiae Iuris Gentium: Sources Relating to the History of the Law of Nations*, 3 vols. (Berlin-New York: Walter de Gruyter, 1988–92).

Grunert, F., *Normbegründung und politische Legitimität. Zur Rechts- und Staatsphilosophie der deutschen Frühaufklärung* (Tübingen: Max Niemeyer Verlag, 2000).

Haak, S.P. and A.J.Veenendaal, ed., *Johan van Oldenbarnevelt. Bescheiden betreffende zijn staatkundig beleid en zijn familie*, 3 vols. (The Hague: Martinus Nijhoff, 1934–67).

Haggenmacher, P., *Grotius et la doctrine de la guerre juste* (Paris: Presses Universitaires de France, 1983).

Hattendorf, J.B., ed., *The Oxford Encyclopedia of Maritime History*, 4 vols. (Oxford: OUP, 2007).

Heere, W.P., ed., *International Law and its Sources: Liber Amicorum Maarten Bos* (Deventer: Kluwer, 1988).

Heijer, H. den, *De Geschiedenis van de WIC* (Zutphen: Walburg Pers, 2002).

Heng, D.S.T., C.G. Kwa, and T.Y. Tan, *Singapore: A 700-Year History – From Emporium to World City* (Singapore: National Archives of Singapore, 2009).

Hernández Martín, R., *Francisco de Vitoria y su "Relección sobre los Indios". Los derechos de los hombres y de los pueblos. Homenaje al Fundador del Derecho Internacional de Gentes en el 50 Aniversario de la Declaración Universal de los Derechos Humanos, 1948–1998* (Madrid: Edibesa, 1998).

Hobson, J.M., *The Eastern Origins of Western Civilisation* (Cambridge: CUP, 2004).

Hulsius, L., ed., *Achte Schiffart. Kurtze Beschreibung, was sich mit den Holländern und Seeländern, in den Ost Indien, die nechst verlauffene vier oder fünff Jahre, als Anno 1599, 1600, 1601, 1602 und 1603 zugetragen, wie sie sich etlich mal mit den Portugesern und Hispaniern geschlagen, davon etliche Schiff An. 1604 in Holland ankommen, und was darauff erfolgt* (Frankfurt/M.: bey Wolfgang Richern in Verlegung, 1605).

———, *Zehende Schiffart oder Reyse der Holländer und Seeländer, beschehen unter dem Admiral Cornelis Matelief dem Jungen, so mit eylff grossen Schiffen Anno 1605 den 12 Maij auss Hollandt abgeloffen und im Mertzen diese 1608 wider mit zwei Schiffen wol ist angekommen. Zusammengebracht und beschrieben auss Niderländischer Verzeichnuss durch einen Liebhaber der Schiffahrten* (Frankfurt/M.: bey Erasmo Kempffern, 1613).

Israel, J.I., *Dutch Primacy in World Trade, 1585–1740* (Oxford: Clarendon Press, 1989).

Ittersum, M.J. van, *Profit and Principle: Hugo Grotius, Natural Rights Theories and the Rise of Dutch Power in the East Indies, 1595–1615* (Leiden: E.J. Brill, 2006).

Jahn, B. ed., *Classical Theories of International Relations* (Cambridge: CUP, 2006).

Jinkes de Jong, U.J. and A.P.W.M. Kosten, *Dr. Pieter Anton Tiele. Documentaire Bijdrage tot een Biografie* (The Hague: P.A. Tiele Academie, 1981).

Jonge, H.J. de, *De bestudering van het Nieuwe Testament aan de Noordnederlandse universiteiten en het Remonstrants Seminarie van 1575 tot 1700* (Amsterdam and New York: Noord Hollandse Uitgevers, 1980).

Jonge, J.K.J. de, *Opkomst van het Nederlandsch gezag in Oost-Indië. Verzameling van onuitgegeven stukken uit het oud-coloniaal archief*, 16 vols. (The Hague: Martinus Nijhoff, 1866–1909).

Juárez, R., *Consilia duo de usu maris et navibus transvehendis*, bound together with Benvenuto Straccha, *De Mercatura seu Mercatore tractatus* ... secunda editio .... (Lyon: Publisher unknown, 1558).

Justinian I, *Corpus Juris Civilis*, ed. T. Mommsen and P. Krüger, ed. stereotypica, 3 vols. (Berlin: Apud Weidmannos, 1928–9).

Keene, E., *Beyond the Anarchical Society: Grotius, Colonialism and Order in World Politics* (Cambridge: CUP, 2002).

Keuning, J., *Petrus Plancius: theoloog en geograaf 1552–1622* (Amsterdam: P.N. van Kampen & Zoon, 1946).

Klee, H., *Hugo Grotius und Johannes Selden: von den geistigen Ursprüngen des Kampfes um die Meeresfreiheit* (Bern: Paul Haupt, 1946).

Knight, W.S.M., *The Life and Works of Hugo Grotius* (London: Sweet & Maxwell, 1925).

Kohler, J., *Grundlagen des Völkerrechts. Vergangenheit, Gegenwart, Zukunft* (Stuttgart: Ferdinand Enke, 1918).

Konegen, N., and P. Nitschke, ed., *Staat bei Hugo Grotius* (Baden-Baden: Nomos Verlag, 2005).

Kratoska, P.H., ed., *South East Asia: Colonial History*, 6 vols. (London: Routledge, 2001).

Lademacher, H. and S. Groenvelt, *Krieg und Kultur: Die Rezeption von Krieg und Frieden in der Niederländischen Republik und im Deutschen Reich, 1568–1648* (Münster: Waxmann, 1998).

l'Hermite, J. (de Jonge), *Breeder verhael ende klare beschrijvinghe van tghene den Admiral Cornelis Matelief de Jonge inde Oost-Indien voor de stadt Malacca, ende int belegh der zelver wedervaren is: als ooc den vreesselijcke strijdt ter zee, tusschen den admirael voorsz. ende de Portugijsen, ende andere geschiedenissen meer. Overgeschreven bij eenen der commisen inde vlote* (Rotterdam: Jan Janssz., 1608).

Liaw Y.F., ed. and tr., *Undang-undang Melaka: A Critical Edition* (The Hague: Martinus Nijhoff, 1976).

Linschoten, J.H. van, *Itinerario. Voyage ofte Schipvaert van Jan Huygen van Linschoten naer Oost ofte Portugaels Indien, 1579–1592*, and *Reys-geschrift vande navigatiën der Portugaloysers*, ed. H. Kern and J.C.M. Warnsinck, 2nd ed. (The Hague: Martinus Nijhoff, 1939).

Locke, J., *Two Treatises of Government*, ed. and intr. P. Laslett (Cambridge: CUP, 1988).

Loureiro, R.M., ed. and intr., *O Manuscrito de Lisboa da 'Suma Oriental' de Tomé Pires (Contribuição para uma Edição Crítica)* (Macao: Instituto Português do Oriente, 1996).

MacKenna, C.H., H. Wright, and J.B. Scott, *Francisco de Vitoria: Addresses in Commemoration of the Fourth Centenary of His Lectures 'De Indis' and 'De iure belli', 1532–1932* (Washington, D.C.: Wright, 1932).

MacLeod, N., *De Oost-Indische Compagnie als Zeemogendheid in Azië*, 2 vols. (Rijswijk: Blankwaardt & Schoonhoven, 1927).

Matelieff de Jonge, C., *Historiale ende ware beschrijvinge vande reyse des admiraels Cornelis Matelief de Jonghe, near de Oost-Indien, wtghetrocken in Mayo 1605. Midsgaders de belegeringhe voor Malacca, also ooc den slach ter zee teghen de Portugijsche armade, ende andere discourssen* (Rotterdam: Jan Jansz, 1608).

Meer, S. de, ed., *Het Zeekartenboek. Vroege zeekarten uit de collectie van het Maritiem Museum Rotterdam* (Zutphen: Walburg Pers, 2007).

Meilink-Roelofsz, M.-A.P., *Asian Trade and European Influence in the Indonesian Archipelago between 1500 and about 1630* (The Hague: Martinus Nijhoff, 1962).

Meilink-Roelofsz, M.-A.P., ed., *De VOC in Azië* (Bossum: Fibula-Van Dieshoeck, 1976).

Meilink-Roelofsz, M.-A. P., M. E. van Opstall, and G. J. Schutte, *Dutch Authors on Asian History: A Selection of Dutch Historiography on the Verenigde Oostindische Compagnie* (Dordrecht: Foris Publications, 1988).

Meursius, J., *Illustris Academia Lugd-Batava: id est virorum Clarissimorum icones, elogia ac vitæ, qui eam scriptis suis illustrarunt* (Leiden: Apud Andreas Cloucquius, 1613).

———, *Athenae Batavae, sive de urbe Leidensi et academia, virisque claris, qui utramque ingenio suo, atque scriptis illustrarunt, libri duo* (Leiden: Apud Andream Cloquium et Elsevirios, 1625).

Michelis, F. de, *Le origini storiche e culturali del pensiero di Ugo Grozio* (Florence: La Nuova Italia, 1967).

Milner, A.C., *Kerajaan: Malay Political Culture on the Eve of Colonial Rule* (Tucson: The University of Arizona Press, 1982).

———, *The Malays* (Oxford: Wiley-Blackwell, 2008).

Morga, A. de, *The Philippine Islands, Moluccas, Siam, Cambodia, Japan and China at the Close of the Sixteenth Century*, ed. L.V. de Torres and H.E.J. Stanley (London: Hakluyt Society, 1868).

Muller, S., *Mare Clausum: Bijdrage tot de geschiedenis der rivaliteit van Engeland en Nederland in de zeventiende eeuw* (Amsterdam: Frederik Muller, 1872).

Nellen, H.J.M., *Grotius: Geschichte seines Lebens basierend auf seiner Korrespondenz*, Nachbarn, 28 (Bonn: Niederländische Botschaft, 1983).

———, *Hugo de Groot (1583–1645). De loopbaan van een geleerd staatsman* (Weesp: Uitgeverij Heureka, 1985).

———, *Hugo de Groot. Een leven in strijd om de vrede, 1583–1648* (Amsterdam: Uitgeverij Balans, 2007).

Nellen, H.J.M. and E. Rabbie, *Hugo Grotius — Theologian. Essays in Honour of G.H.M. Posthumus Meyjes* (Leiden: Brill, 1994).

Nellen, H.J.M. and J. Trapman, ed., *De Hollandse jaren van Hugo de Groot (1582–1621). Lezingen van het colloquium ter gelegenheid van de 350-ste sterfdag van Hugo de Groot ('s-Gravenhage: 31 augustus–1 september 1995)* (Hilversum: Verloren, 1996).

Netscher, E., *De Nederlanders in Djohor en Siak* (Batavia: Bruining & Wijt, 1870).

Newitt, M.D.D., ed., *The First Portuguese Colonial Empire* (Exeter: University of Exeter, 1986).

Nobbs, D., *Theocracy and Toleration: A Study of the Disputes in Dutch Calvinism from 1600 to 1650* (Cambridge: CUP, 1938).

Nussbaum, A., *A Concise History of the Law of Nations*, rev. ed. (New York: Macmillan, 1954).

Nys, E., *Études de droit international et de droit politique* (Brussels: A. Castaigne, 1896).

———, *Le droit des gens et les anciens jurisconsultes espagnols* (The Hague: Martinus Nijhoff, 1914).

———, *Les origines du droit international* (Brussels: A. Castaigne, 1894).

Opstall, M.E. van, ed., *De reis van de vloot van Pieter Willemszoon Verhoeff naar Azië, 1607–1612*, 2 vols. (The Hague: Martinus Nijhoff, 1972).

Pacius à Beriga, J., *Iulii Pacii a Beriga I.C. Regii Consiliarii et Iuris ex prima sede in illustri Valentina Academia Professoris De Dominio Maris Hadriatici disceptatio* (Lyon: Bartholomaeus Vicentus, 1619).

Pagden, A.R., ed., *The Languages of Political Theory in Early-Modern Europe* (Cambridge: CUP, 1987).

Pagden, A.R., *Lords of All the World: Ideologies of Empire in Spain, Britain and France, c. 1500–c. 1800* (New Haven and London: Yale University Press, 1995).

Parker, G., *Spain and the Netherlands, 1559–1659: Ten Studies* (London: Collins, 1979).

Parmentier, J., K. Davids, and J.G. Everaert, *Peper, Plancius en Porselein. De reis van het schip Swarte Leeuw naar Atjeh en Bantam* (Zutphen: Walburg Pers, 2003).

Pato, R.A. de Bulhão and A. de Silva Rego, ed., *Documentos Remettidos da Índia ou Livros das Monções*, 10 vols. (Lisbon: Typographia da Academia Real das Sciencias and Academia das Sciencias de Lisboa, 1880–1978).

Pauw, F. de, *Grotius and the Law of the Sea* (Brussels: Institut de Sociologie de l'Université Libre de Bruxelles, 1965).

Pearson, M.N., *Before Colonialism: Theories on Asian-European Relations, 1500–1700* (New Delhi: OUP, 1988).

Pinto, P.J. de Sousa, *Portugueses e Malaios: Malaca e os Sultanatos de Johor e Achém, 1575–1619* (Lisbon: Comissão Nacional para as Comemorações dos Descobrimentos Portugueses, 1997).

Pires, T., *The Suma Oriental of Tome Pires: An Account of the East from the Red Sea to Japan. Written in Malacca and India in 1512–1515*, ed. A. Cortesão, 2 vols. (London: Hakluyt Society, 1944).

Poitras, G., *Pioneers of Financial Economics*, vol. I (Cheltenham : Edward Elgar Publishing, 2006).

Pontanus, J. I., *Rerum et Urbis Amstelodamensium Historia, in qua Hollandiae primum atque inde Amstelandiae, oppidique, natales, exordia, progressus, privilegia, statuta eventaque mirabilia cum novis urbis incrementis commerciisque ac navigationibus longinquis, aliaque ad politiam spectantia* ... (Amsterdam: excudit Judocus Hondius, 1611).

Postma, J. and V. Enthoven, eds., *Riches from Atlantic Commerce: Dutch Transatlantic Trade and Shipping, 1585–1817* (Leiden: Brill, 2003).

Ramsay, G.G., tr., *Juvenal and Persius*, Loeb Classical Library, no. 91, reprint (Cambridge, Mass. and London: Harvard University Press and Heinemann, 1950).

Ramusio, G.B., *Delle navigationi et viaggi in molti luoghi corretta, et ampliata nelle quale si contengono da descrittione dell'Africa, & del paese del Prete Ianni, con varij viaggi, dalla Città di Lisbona, et dal Mar Rosso à Calicut, & infin'all'isole Molucche, dove nascono le Spetierie, Et la Navigatione attorno il Mondo* (Venice: Stamperia de Giunti, 1554).

———, *Navigazioni e Viaggi*, ed. Marica Milanesi, 6 vols. (Turin: Giulio Einaudi Editore, 1978–88).

Rietbergen, P.J.A.N. van, *De eerste Landvoogd Pieter Both (1568–1615). Governeur-Generaal van Nederlandsch Indië (1609–1614)*, 2 vols. (Zutphen: Walburg Pers, 1987).

Rijperman, H.P., ed., *Resolutiën der Staten-Generaal van 1576 tot 1609*, vol. XIV, 1607–9 (The Hague: Martinus Nijhoff, 1970).

Robertson, J., *A Union for Empire. Political Thought and the British Union of 1707* (Cambridge: CUP, 1995).

Romein, J. and A. Romein, *Erflaters van onze beschaving. Nederlandse gestalten uit zees eeuwen* (Amsterdam: Querido, 1973).

Saldanha, A. Vasconcelos de, *Iustum Imperium, dos tratados como fundamento do Império dos Portugueses no Oriente: estudo de história do direito internacional e do direito português* (Lisbon: Fundação Oriente, 1997).

Sarpi, P., *Dominio del Mar Adriatico della Serenissima Republica di Venetia* (Venice: Roberto Meietti, 1685).

———, *Il Dominio del Mare Adriatico*, ed. and intr. Roberto Cessi (Padua: Giampolo Tolomei Editore, 1945).

Scott, J.B., *Le progrès du droit des gens: conférences et études internationales* (Paris: Les éditions internationales, 1934).

———, *The Spanish Origins of International Law: Francisco de Vitoria and His Law of Nations* (Oxford and London: Clarendon Press and Humphrey Milford, 1934).

———, *Selections from three works of Francisco Suárez S.J., De legibus ac Deo legislatore, 1612. Defensio fidei catholicae et apostolicae adversus anglicane sectae errores, 1613. De triplici virtute theologica, fide spe et charitate, 1621* (Oxford and London: Clarendon Press and Humphrey Milford, 1944).

Selden, J., *Mare Clausum seu De Dominio Maris Libri Duo* (London: Will Stanesbeius for Richard Meighen, 1635).

Seneca, *Moral Essays*, ed. and tr. J.W. Basore, 3 vols. (Cambridge, Mass. and London: Harvard University Press and Heinemann, 1928–35).

Singh Sandu, K. and P. Wheatley, ed., *Melaka: The Transformation of a Malay Capital, c. 1400–1980*, 2 vols. (Kuala Lumpur: OUP, 1983).

Skinner, Q.R.D. and M. van Gelderen, *Republicanism: A Shared European Heritage* (Cambridge: CUP, 2002).

Somers, J., *De VOC als volkenrechtelijke actor* (Arnhem: Gouda Quint, 2001).

———, *Nederlandsch-Indië, Staatskundige ontwikkelingen binnen een koloniale relatie* (Zutphen: Walburg Pers, 2005).

Soto, D. de, *Relección de Dominio*, intr. and tr. J. Brufau Prats (Granada: Universidad de Granada, 1964).

———, *De Iustitia et Iure — De la Justicia y del Derecho*, bi-lingual edition Latin-Spanish, Latin text being a facsimile of the 1556 edition printed in Salamanca, tr. M. Gonzales Ordoñez, 5 vols. (Madrid: Instituto de Estudios Políticos, 1967).

Sousa, I. Carneiro de and R.Z. Leirissa, *Indonesia-Portugal: Five Hundred Years of Historical Relationship* (Lagos: CEPESA, 2001).

Sprengard, K.A. and R. Ptak, ed., *Maritime Asia: Profit Maximisation, Ethics and Trade Structure, c. 1300–1800* (Wiesbaden: Otto Harrassowitz Verlag, 1994).

Steensgaard, N., *The Asian Trade Revolution of the Seventeenth Century: The East India Companies and the Decline of the Caravan Trade* (Chicago and London: University of Chicago Press, 1974).

Straumann, B., *Hugo Grotius und die Antike. Römisches Recht und römische Ethik um frühneuzeitlichen Naturrecht* (Baden-Baden: Nomos Verlag, 2007).

Sylvester Mazzolini de Prierias, *Summa Sylvestrinae qua Summa Summarum merito nuncupatur,* ed. P. Vendramini, 2 vols. (Venice: Ad Candentis Salamandrae insigne, 1593).

Teeuw, A. and D.K. Wyatt, ed., *Hikayat Patani. The Story of Patani,* 2 vols. (The Hague: Martinus Nijhoff, 1970).

Terpstra, H., *De factorij der Oostindische Compagnie te Patani*, Verhandelingen van het Koninklijk Instituut voor de Taal-, Land- en Volkenkunde van Nederlandsch-Indië, vol. I (The Hague: Martinus Nijhoff, 1938).

Tex, J. den, *Oldenbarnevelt*, 5 vols. (Haarlem-Groningen: H.D. Tjeenk Willink & Zoon, 1960–72).

Theodosius, *The Theodosian Code and Novels, and the Sirmondian Constitutions*, tr. with commentary, glossary, and bibliography by C. Pharr with T.S. Davidson and M.B. Pharr. Intr. C.D. Williams (Princeton: Princeton University Press, 1952).

Thomas Aquinas, *Summa Theologiae Cura Fratrorum eiusdem Ordinis,* vol. III, *Secunda Secundae,* 3rd ed. (Madrid: Biblioteca de Autores Cristianos, 1963).

Thumfart, J., *Die Begründung der global-politischen Philosophie. Zu Francisco de Vitorias de indis recenter inventis von 1539* (Berlin: Kulturverlag Kadmos, 2009).

Tibbets, G.R., *Arab Navigation in the Indian Ocean before the Coming of the Portuguese, Being a Translation of Kitāb al-Fawā'id fī usūl al-bahr wa'l-qawā 'id of Ahmad b. Mājid al-Najdī, Together with an Introduction on the History of Arab Navigation, Notes on Navigational Techniques and on the Topography of the Indian Ocean, and a Glossary of Navigational Terms* (London: The Royal Asiatic Society of Great Britain and Ireland, 1971).

Tiele, P.A. and J.E. Heeres, *Bouwstoffen voor de Geschiedenis der Nederlanders in den Maleischen Archipel*, 3 vols. (The Hague: Martinus Nijhoff, 1886–95).

Treitschke, H. von, *Vorlesungen gehalten an der Universität zu Berlin*, ed. Max Cornecesius, 2 vols. (Leipzig: S. Hirzel, 1898).

Trujillo Pérez, I., *Francisco de Vitoria: il diritto alla comunicazione e i confini della socialità umana* (Turin: G. Giappichelli, 1997).

Tuck, R., *Natural Rights Theories* (Cambridge: CUP, 1979).

———, *Hobbes* (Oxford: OUP, 1989).

———, *Philosophy and Government, 1572–1651* (Cambridge: CUP, 1993).

———, *The Rights of War and Peace: Political Thought and the International Order from Grotius to Kant* (Oxford: OUP, 1999).

Tully, J., *A Discourse on Property: John Locke and His Adversaries* (Cambridge and New York: CUP, 1980).

Valentijn, F., *Oud en Nieuw Oost-Indiën, Vervattende Een Naauwkeurige en Uitvoerige Verhandelinge van Nederlands Mogentheyd in de Gewesten, etc.*, 5 parts in 8 vols. (Dordrecht and Amsterdam: Johannes van Braam and Gerard Onder de Linden, 1724–26).

Vázquez de Menchaca, F., *Conversiarum illustrium aliarumque usu frequentium libri tres. Controversias fundamentales y otras de mas frecuente uso:* remprese por acuerdo de la Universidad de Valladolid, ed. and tr. F. Rodríguez Alcalde, 4 vols. (Valladolid: Cuesta, 1931–4).

Veen, E. van, *Decay or Defeat: An Inquiry into the Portuguese Decline in Asia, 1580–1645* (Leiden: Research School of Asian, African and Amerindian Studies, 2000).

Veen, E. van and L. Blussé, *Rivalry and Conflict, European Traders and Asian Trading Networks, 16th and 17th Century* (Leiden: Centre for Non-Western Studies, 2005).

Vitoria, F. de, *Relectiones Theologicae XII* (Lyon: Iacobus Boyerius, 1557).

———, *Relecciones Teológicas. Edición crítica y versión castellana*, ed. and tr. L.G. Alonso Getino, 3 vols. (Madrid: Imprenta la Rafa-Abtao, 1933).

———, *De Indis Recenter Inventis et De Jure Belli Hispanorum in Barbaros; Vorlesungen über die kürzlich entdeckten Inder und das Recht der Spanier zum Kriege gegen die Barbaren, 1539*, ed. W. Schätzel, intr. P. Hadrossek (Tübingen: J.C.B. Mohr, 1952).

———, *Political Writings*, ed. A. Pagden and J. Lawrence (Cambridge: CUP, 1991).

Vollenhoven, C. van, *Mr. C. van Vollenhoven's Verspreide Geschriften*, ed. F.M. van Asbeck, 3 vols. (Haarlem and The Hague: Tjeenk Willink and Martinus Nijhoff, 1934–5).

Ward, K., *Networks of Empire. Forced Migration in the Dutch East India Company* (Cambridge: CUP, 2009).

Welwood, W., *Abridgement of All Sea-Lawes, Gathered Forth of All Writings and Monuments which Are to Be Found among Any People or Nation, upon the Coasts of the Great Ocean and Mediterranean Sea* (London: Humfrey Lownes for Thomas Man, 1613).

Wickenden, N., *G.J. Vossius and the Humanist Concept of History* (Assen: Van Gorcum, 1993).

Wieder, F.C., ed., *De Reis van Joris van Spilbergen naar Ceylon, Atjeh en Bantam, 1601–1604* (The Hague: Martinus Nijhoff, 1933).

Wilson, E., *Savage Republic. De Indis of Hugo Grotius, Republicanism and Dutch Hegemony within the Early Modern World-System (c. 1600–1619)* (Leiden-Boston: Martinus Nijhoff Publishers, 2008).

Winkelman, P.H., *Remonstranten en katholieken in de eeuw van Hugo de Groot* (Nijmegen: Centrale Drukkerij, 1945).

Winwood, R., *Memorials of Affairs of State in the Reign of Queen Elizabeth and James I, ...* ed. Edmund Sawyer, 3 vols. (London: W.B. for T. Ward, 1725).

Wright, H.F., *Some Less Known Works of Hugo Grotius, Consisting of: A Translation of his Works on the Fisheries in his Controversy with William Welwood; A Translation of Extracts from his Letters Concerning International Natural Law and Fisheries; An Account of his Controversy with Johan de Laet on the Origin of the American Aborigines; and a Translation of Peerlkamp's Appreciation of his Ability as a Poet* (Leiden: Brill, 1928).

Wyduckel, Dieter, *Princeps Legibus Solutus. Eine Untersuchung zur frühmodernen Rechts- und Staatslehre* (Berlin: Duncker & Humblot, 1979).

Zarka, Y.C., ed., *Politique, droit et théologie chez Bodin, Grotius et Hobbes* (Paris: Éditions Kimé, 1997).

Journal Articles

Anand, R.P., "Maritime Practice in Southeast Asia until 1600 A.D. and the Modern Law of the Sea", *The International and Comparative Law Quarterly* 30, 2 (1981): 440–54.

Armitage, D., "The Fifty Years' Rift: Intellectual History and International Relations", *Modern Intellectual History* 1, 1 (2004): 97–109.

Bassett, D.K., "European Influence in the Malay Peninsula, 1511–1786", *JMBRAS* 33, 3 (1960): 9–35.

———, "The 'Amboyna Massacre' of 1623", *JSAH* 1, 2 (1960): 1–19.

———, "European Influence in Southeast Asia, c.1500–1630", *JSAH* 4, 2 (1963): 134–65.

Beesley, J.A., "Grotius and the New Law", *Ocean Yearbook* 18 (2004): 98–116.

Benton, L. and B. Straumann, "Acquiring Empire by Law", *Law and History Review* 28 (2010): 1–38.

Berns, T., "La souveraintè saisi par ses marques", *BHR* 62, 3 (2000): 611–23.

Bijlsma, R., "De discoursen van Cornelis Matelieff de Jonge over den staat van Oost-Indië", *Nederlandsch Archievenblad* 35 (1927–8), I: 49–53.

Blom, H., and L. Winkel, "Grotius and the Stoa: Introduction", *GNS* 22–23 (2001–2): 3–20.

Blussé, L., "Brief Encounter at Macao", *Modern Asian Studies* 22, 3 (1988): 647–64.

Borschberg, P., "Commentarius in Theses XI. Ein unveröffentlichtes Kurzwerk von Hugo Grotius", *ZRG*, RA 109 (1992): 450–74.

———, "De Societate Publica cum Infidelibus. Una obra juvenil de Grocio", *Revista de Estudios Políticos* 83 (1993): 113–36.

———, "Zur Entsehung von Grotius' De Imperium Summarum Potestatum circa Sacra", *ZRG,* KA 79 (1993): 342–79.

———, "De Pace. Ein unveröffentlichtes Fragment von Grotius über Krieg und Frieden", *ZRG,* RA 113 (1996): 268–92.

———, "'De Societate Publica cum Infidelibus': Ein Frühwerk von Hugo Grotius", *ZRG,* RA 115 (1998): 355–93.

———, "The Seizure of the *Santa Catarina* Revisited: The Portuguese Empire in Asia, VOC Politics and the Origins of the Dutch-Johor Alliance (c. 1602–1616)", *JSEAS* 33, 1 (2002): 31–62.

———, "A Portuguese-Dutch Naval Battle in the Johor River Delta and the Liberation of Johor Lama, 1603", *Zeitschrift der Deutschen Morgenländischen Gesellschaft* 153, 1 (2003): 157–75.

———, "Luso-Johor-Dutch Relations in the Straits of Malacca and Singapore, ca. 1600–1623", *Itinerario* 28, 2 (2004): 15–33.

———, "The Seizure of the *Santa Catarina* off Singapore: Dutch Freebooting, the Portuguese Empire and Intra-Asian Trade at the Dawn of the Seventeenth Century", *RC,* International Edition, 11 (2004): 11–25.

———, "Grotius, the Social Contract and Political Resistance", *Institute for International Law and Justice (IILJ) Working Paper,* History and Theory of International Law Series, New York University School of Law, 6 (2006): 1–83.

———, "The Trade, Forgery and Medicinal Use of Porcupine Bezoars in the Early Modern Period (c.1500–1750)", *Revista Oriente* 14 (2006): 60–78.

———, "Jacques de Coutre as a Source for the Early 17th Century History of Singapore, the Johor River, and the Straits", *JMBRAS* 81, 2 (2008): 71–97.

———, "The Johor-VOC Alliance and the Twelve Years Truce. Factionalism, Intrigue and Diplomacy, c.1606–1613", *Institute for International Law and Justice (IILJ) Working Paper,* History and Theory of International Law Series, New York University School of Law, 8 (2009): 1–69.

Branquinho, I., "O Tratado de Tordesilhas e a questão das Molucas", *Mare Liberum: Revista de História dos Mares* 8 (1994): 9–17.

Brett, A.S., "Natural Right and Civil Community: The Civil Philosophy of Hugo Grotius", *Historical Journal* 45, 1 (2002): 31–51.

Brightwell, P., "The Spanish System and the Twelve Years Truce", *The English Historical Review* 89, 351 (1974): 270–92.

Clark, G.N., "Grotius's East India Mission to England", *TGS* 20 (1935): 45–84.

Coolhaas, W.P., "Een bron voor het historische gedeelte van Hugo de Groots de jure praedae", *BMH* 79 (1965): 415–537.

Daveau, S., "La géographie dans les 'roteiros' portugais des XVe et XVIe siècles", *Mare Liberum: Revista de História dos Mares* 3 (1991): 161–79.

Dovring, F., "Une partie de l'héritage littéraire de Grotius retrouvée en Suède", *MKNAW*, afd. letterkunde, NR 12 (1949): 237–50.

Duyvendak, J.J.L., "The First Siamese Embassy to Holland", *T'Oung Pao* 32 (1936): 285–92.

Eysinga, W.J.M. van, "Eene onuitgegeven nota van de Groot", *MKNAW*, afd. letterkunde, NR vol. no. 10, 10 (1955): 235–52.

———, "Huig de Groot als Nederlandsch Gezant", *MKNAW*, afd. letterkunde, NR 3 (1940): 359–78.

———, "Quelques observations au sujet du Mare Liberum et du De Iure Praedae de Grotius", *Grotiana* 9 (1941–2): 61–75.

Feenstra, R., "Ius commune et droit comparé chez Grotius. Nouvelles remarques sur les sources citées dans ses ouvrages juridiques, à propos d'une réimpression du De iure belli ac pacis", *Revista internazionale di diritto comune* 3 (1992): 7–36.

Frederiks, J.G., "Cornelis Cornelisz Matelieff de Jonge en zijn geslagt", *Rotterdamsche Historiebladen,* ed. J.H. Scheffer and Fr. D.O. Obreen, 3 afd., 1, 1 (1871): 204–357.

Gelderen, M. van, "The Challenge of Colonialism: Grotius and Vitoria on Natural Law and International Relations", *GNS* 14–5 (1993–4): 3–37.

———, "From Domingo de Soto to Hugo Grotius: Theories of Monarchy and Civil Power in Spanish and Dutch Political Thought, 1555–1609", *Il Pensiero Politico. Revista di Storia delle Idee Politiche e Sociali* 32, 2 (1999): 186–205.

George, W.P., "Grotius, Theology and International Law: Overcoming Textbook Bias", *Journal of Law and Religion* 14, 2 (1999–2000): 605–31.

Gomes, P.M., "L'Espagne et l'Orient au debut du XVIème siècle: Un autre droit que dans l'Amérique", *Mare Liberum: Revista de História dos Mares* 13 (1997): 83–93.

Grimm, M., "Hugo Grotius' Aufenthalt in Hamburg in den Jahren 1632–1634", *Zeitschrift des Vereins für Hamburgische Geschichte* 27 (1926): 130–40.

Heeres, J.E., ed., "Corpus Diplomaticum Neërlando-Indicum. Verzameling van politieke contracten en verdere verdragen door de Nederlanders in het Oosten gesloten, van privilegiebrieven, aan hen verleend, enz.", eerste deel (1596–1650), *BKI* 57 (1907): 1–586.

Heijden, E.J.J. van der, "Der boekerij van Grotius", *Grotiana* 3 (1930): 18–38.

Hervey, D.F.A., "François Valentyn's Account of Malacca", *JSBRAS* 16, 1 (1885): 289–301.

Irwin, D.A., "Mercantilism as Strategic Trade Policy: The Anglo-Dutch Rivalry for the East India Trade", *Journal of Political Economy* 99 (1991): 1296–1314.

Ittersum, M.J. van, "Hugo Grotius in Context: Van Heemskerk's Capture of the *Santa Catarina* and Its Justification in *De Jure Praedae* (1604–1606)", *AJSS* 31, 3 (2003): 511–48.

———, "'Mare Liberum' versus the Propriety of the Seas? The Debate between Hugo Grotius and William Welwood and Its Impact on Anglo-Scotto-Dutch Fishery Disputes in the Second Decade of the Seventeenth Century", *Edinburgh Law Review* 10 (2006): 239–75.

———, "Preparing *Mare Liberum* for the Press: Hugo Grotius' Rewriting of Chapter 12 of *De iure praedae* in November–December 1608", *GNS* 27–8 (2005–7): 246–80.

———, "*Mare Liberum* in the West Indies? Hugo Grotius and the Case of the Swimming Lion, a Dutch Pirate in the Caribbean at the Turn of the Seventeenth Century", *Itinerario* 31, 3 (2007): 59–94.

———, "Dating the Manuscript of *De Jure Praedae (1604–1608)*: what watermarks, foliation and quire divisions can tell us about Hugo Grotius' development as a natural rights and natural law theorist", *History of European Ideas* 35 (2009): 125–93.

Keene, E., "The Reception of Hugo Grotius in International Relations Theory", *GNS* 20–21 (1999–2000): 135–58.

Kempe, M., "Beyond the Law. The Image of Piracy in the Legal Writings of Hugo Grotius", *GNS* 27–8 (2005–7): 397–95.

Knight, W.S.M., "Grotius' Earliest Years as Lawyer", *TGS* 8 (1922): 1–19.

———, "Grotius in England: His Opposition There to the Principles of Mare Liberum", *TGS* 5 (1919): 1–38.

———, "Seraphim de Freitas: Critic of Mare Liberum", *TGS* 11 (1925): 1–9.

Kleffens, E.N. van, "Over zes briefen uit het bezit van Hugo de Groot", *MKNAW*, afd. letterkunde, NR 23, 16 (1960): 447–91.

Kratoska, P.H., "The Peripatetic Peasant and Land Tenure in British Malaya", *JSEAS* 16, 1 (1985): 16–45.

Lee, R.W., "The Family Life of Grotius", *TGS* 20 (1934): 11–24.

———, "Grotius – the Last Phase, 1635–45", *TGS* 31 (1945): 193–215.

Linehan, W., "History of Pahang", *JMBRAS* 14, 2 (1936): 1–256.

Loureiro, R.M., "O Sudeste Asiático na Suma Oriental de Tomé Pires", *RC*, International Edition, 4 (2002): 107–23.

MacGregor, I.A., "Notes on the Portuguese in Malaya", *JMBRAS* 28, 2 (1955): 5–47.

Matos, L.J.R. Semedo de, "As navegações Árabes e Portuguesas no Oceano Índico durante os séculos XV e XVI", *Mare Liberum: Revista de História dos Mares* 10 (1995): 565–80.

Mautner, T., "Not a Likely Story", *British Journal for the History of Philosophy* 11, 2 (2003): 303–7.

———, "Grotius and the Skeptics", *Journal of the History of Ideas* 66, 4 (2005): 577–601.

Meijers, E.M., "Boeken uit de bibliotheek van De Groot in de Universiteits-bibliotheek te Leiden", *MKNAW* 12, 3 (1949): 251–79.

Meron, T., "Rights of Mankind in Gentili, Grotius and Suarez", *The American Journal of International Law* 85, 1 (1991): 110–6.

Molhuysen, P.C., "De bibliotheek van Hugo de Groot in 1618", *MKNAW*, NR 6, 3 (1918): 50–63.

Moll, G., "De confiscatie der goederen van Hugo de Groot", *Oud-Holland, Nieuwe Bijdragen voor de Geschiedenis der Nederlandsche Kunst, Letterkunde, Nijverheid, enz.* 20 (1902): 83–112.

Nellen, H.J.M., "Hugo Grotius's Political and Scholarly Activities in the Light of His Correspondence", *GNS* 27–8 (2005–7): 16–30.

Nifterik, G. van, "Grotius and the Origin of the Ruler's Right to Punish", *GNS* 27–8 (2005–7): 396–415.

Oda, S., "Some Reflections on Recent Developments in the Law of the Sea", *Yale Journal of International Law* 27 (2002): 218–21.

Pagden, A.R.D., "Human Rights, Natural Rights, and Europe's Imperial Legacy", *Political Theory* 31 (2003): 171–99.

Panizza, D., "Political Theory and Jurisprudence in Gentili's De Iure Belli: The Great Debate Between 'Theological' and 'Humanist' Perspectives from Vitoria to Grotius", *Institute for International Law and Justice (IILJ) Working Paper*, History and Theory of International Law Series, New York University School of Law, 15 (2005): 1–51.

Pelliot, P., "Les Relations du Siam et de la Hollande en 1608", *T'Oung Pao* 32 (1936): 223–9.

Rademaker, C.S.M., "Books and Grotius at Loevestein", *Quaerendo* 2 (1972): 2–29.

Reeves, J.S., "Grotius on the Training of an Ambassador", *The American Journal of International Law* 23, 3 (1929): 619–25.

Ridderikoff, C.M., "Een aristocratische geschiedenis van de Opstand: Grotius' Annales et Historiae de rebus Belgicis", *De Zeventiende Eeuw* 10, 2 (1994): 277–91.

Roelofsen, C.G., "Het trieste slot van een reis om de wereld in het begin van de zeventiende eeuw: de affaire Carletti", *Mededelingen van de Nederlandse Vereeniging voor Zeegeschiedenis* 20 (1970): 13–30.

Rogge, H.C., "De 'Verantwoordingh' van Hugo de Groot", *Bijdragen voor Vaderlandsche Geschiedenis* 7 (1893): 89–134.

———, "Hugo de Groot te Parijs van 1621 tot 1625", part I, *De Gids* 3 (1893): 249–73.

———, "Hugo de Groot te Parijs van 1621 tot 1625", part II, *De Gids* 3 (1893): 450–77.

Rouffaer, G.P., "Was Malaka Emporium vóór 1400 A.D. genaamd Malajoer? En waar lag Woerawari, Ma-Hasin, Langka, Batoesawar?", *BKI* 77 (1921): 1–174 and 359–604.

Salter, J., "Hugo Grotius: Property and Consent", *Political Theory* 29, 4 (2001): 537–55.

Schwarz, R. and O. Jütersonke, "Divisible Sovereignty and the Reconstruction of Iraq", *Third World Quarterly* 26, 4–5 (2005): 649–65.

Somers, J.A. and C.G. Roelofsen, "*Mare Liberum* and the Dutch East India Company. The Freedom of the Seas and Freedom of Trade as the Legal Bases of the Dutch Colonial State in the Indonesian Archipelago", *GNS* 24–5 (2004–5): 67–76.

Somos, M., "Secularization in *De Iure Praedae:* From Bible Criticism to International Law", *GNS* 26–8 (2005–7): 147–91.

Straumann, B., "Natural Rights and Roman Law in Hugo Grotius's *Theses LVI, De iure praedae* and *Defensio capitis quinti maris liberi*", *GNS* 27–8 (2005–7): 341–65.

Thieme, H., "Natürliches Privatrecht Spätscholastik", *ZRG*, GA 70 (1953): 230–66.

Thornton, H., "Hugo Grotius and the Freedom of the Seas", *International Journal of Maritime History* 16, 2 (2004): 17–34.

Thumfart, J., "On Grotius's *Mare Liberum* and Vitoria's *De Indis,* Following Agamben and Schmitt", *GNS* 30 (2009): 65–87.

———, "John Selden's Response to Hugo Grotius", *International Journal of Maritime History* 18, 2 (2006): 105–27.

Tibbets, G.R., "The Malay Peninsula as Known to the Arab Geographers", *Malayan Journal of Tropical Geography* 9 (1956): 21–57.

Tiele, P.A., "Documenten voor de geschiedenis der Nederlanders in het Oosten", *BMH* 6 (1883): 222–376.

———, "De Europeërs in den Maleischen Archipel", *BKI*, part VI (1882): 141–242.

———, "De Europeërs in den Maleischen Archipel", *BKI*, part VII (1884): 49–118.

Truyol y Serra, A., "Francisco de Vitoria y Hugo Grocio", *Ciencia Tomista* 111 (1984): 17–27.

Vieira, M. Brito, "Mare Liberum vs. Mare Clausum. Grotius, Freitas and Selden's Debate on Dominion of the Seas", *Journal of the History of Ideas* 63, 3 (2003): 361–77.

Waszink, J., "New documents on the prohibition of Grotius' *Annales et Historiae* by the Roman Index", *GNS* 24–5 (2003–4): 77–138.

———, "Tacitisme in Holland: de 'Annales et Historiae de Rebus Belgicis' van Hugo de Groot", *De Zeventiende Eeuw* 20, 2 (2004): 240–63.

———, "Using the Work. Remarks on the Text of *De iure praedae*", *GNS* 27–8 (2005–7): 215–45.

Wilson, E., "On Heterogeneity and the Naming of De Indis of Grotius", *Journal of the Philosophy of International Law* 1, 1 (2006): 72–115.

———, "The VOC, Corporate Sovereignty and the Republican Sub-Text of *De iure praedae*", *GNS* 27–8 (2005–7): 310–40.

Winkel, L., "Les origines antiques de l'appetitus societatis de Grotius", *Tijdschrift voor Rechtsgeschiedenis* 68 (2000): 393–403.

Winstedt, R.O., "A History of Johore", *JMBRAS* 10, 3 (1932): 1–167.

Winstedt, R.O. and P.E. de Josselin de Jong, "The Maritime Laws of Malacca: Edited, with an Outline Translation", *JMBRAS* 29, 3 (1956): 22–59.
Witkam, P.P., "A short book list compiled by Hugo Grotius", *Quaerendo* 12 (1982): 221–36.
Wright, G., "Tuck's Grotius: De iure praedae in Context", *GNS* 27–8 (2005–7): 366–78.
Ziegler, K.-H., "Völkerrechtliche Aspekte der Eroberung Lateinamerikas", *Zeitschrift für Neuere Rechtsgeschichte* 23 (2001): 1–29.
Ziskind, J., "International Law and Ancient Sources: Grotius and Selden", *The Review of Politics* 35, 4 (1973): 537–59.

Unpublished Theses

Grayson, J.C., "From Protectorate to Partnership, Anglo-Dutch Relations, 1598–1625", Unpublished doctoral dissertation, University of London, 1978.
Loureiro, R.M., "O Manuscrito de Lisboa da 'Soma Horiemtall' de Tomé Pires", Unpublished doctoral dissertation, Universidade de Lisboa, 1994.
Murteira Martins, A., "A Carreira da Índia e o Corso Neerlandês, 1595–1625", Unpublished Master's thesis, Universidade Nova de Lisboa, 2006.
Zaglio, M., "Jus Pacis e Concezione della Pace in Ugo Grozio", Unpublished Laureate thesis, Università degli Studi di Milano, 2008.

Index

This index does not capture comprehensive and separate entries for terms and expressions used so frequently that it would be counter-productive to include them. Among the most important words, terms, names and expressions omitted include significantly in alphabetical order *Dutch* (with the exception of *Dutch Republic*), *Europe, European, Grotius, Lusitanian, Portugal, Portuguese* and *VOC.* Searching for an entry on relations between Portugal and England can thus be found in a subentry under "England" and the VOC treaty with Jambi can be retrieved under "Jambi". As a Dutch company, the VOC is generally indexed as "Dutch", so the VOC treaty with Jambi is indexed as "Jambi" and as a subentry "treaty with the Dutch". Texts featured in the Document Appendices have been indexed according to their English translation. Individual works of Grotius are captured under *Grotius' works* but this index does not capture the numerous references to the treatises *De Jure Praedae* (On the Law of Prize and Booty) and *Mare Liberum* (The Free Sea).